Lecture Notes in Computer Scie

Edited by G. Goos, J. Hartmanis and J. van

T0254047

Springer
Berlin
Heidelberg
New York
Barcelona
Hong Kong
London
Milan
Paris
Singapore
Tokyo

Kwangjo Kim (Ed.)

Public Key Cryptography

4th International Workshop on Practice and Theory
in Public Key Cryptosystems, PKC 2001
Cheju Island, Korea, February 13-15, 2001
Proceedings

 Springer

Series Editors

Gerhard Goos, Karlsruhe University, Germany
Juris Hartmanis, Cornell University, NY, USA
Jan van Leeuwen, Utrecht University, The Netherlands

Volume Editor

Kwangjo Kim
Information and Communications University, Information Security Group
58-4 Hwaam-dong, Yusong-gu, Taejon 305-732, Korea
E-mail: kkj@icu.ac.kr

Cataloging-in-Publication Data applied for

Die Deutsche Bibliothek - CIP-Einheitsaufnahme

Public key cryptography : proceedings / 4th International Workshop on
Practice and Theory in Public Key Cryptosystems, PKC 2001, Cheju
Island, Korea, February 13 - 15, 2001. Kwangjo Kim (ed.). - Berlin ;
Heidelberg ; New York ; Barcelona ; Hong Kong ; London ; Milan ;
Paris ; Singapore ; Tokyo : Springer, 2001
   (Lecture notes in computer science ; Vol. 1992)
   ISBN 3-540-41658-7

CR Subject Classification (1998): E.3, G.2.1, D.4.6, K.6.5, F.2.1-2, C.2, J.1

ISSN 0302-9743
ISBN 3-540-41658-7 Springer-Verlag Berlin Heidelberg New York

Springer-Verlag Berlin Heidelberg New York
a member of BertelsmannSpringer Science+Business Media GmbH
© Springer-Verlag Berlin Heidelberg 2001
Printed in Germany

Typesetting: Camera-ready by author, data conversion by Steingräber Satztechnik GmbH, Heidelberg
Printed on acid-free paper   SPIN: 10782094   06/3142   5 4 3 2 1 0

Preface

The PKC 2001 conference was held at Shilla Hotel, Cheju Island, Korea, 13–15 February 2001. Continuing the first conference PKC 1988 in Yokohama, Japan, PKC 1999 in Kamakura, Japan, and PKC 2000 in Melbourne, Australia, PKC 2001, the fourth conference in the international workshop series was dedicated to practice and theory in public key cryptography.

The program committee of the conference received 67 submissions from 14 countries and regions (Australia, Austria, China, Denmark, Esponia, France, Germany, Greece, Korea, Singapore, Spain, Taiwan, UK, and USA), of which 30 were selected for presentation. All submissions were anonymously reviewed by at least 3 experts in the relevant areas. Revisions were not checked, and the authors bear full responsibility for the contents of their papers. In addition, there were three invited talks by Jun-Cheol Yang of the Ministry of Information and Communication, Korea; Mihir Bellare of the University of California at San Diego, USA; and Ko Itoh of the Organization for Road System Enhancement, Japan.

The program committee consisted of 20 experts in cryptography and data security drawn from the international research community: Kwangjo Kim (Chair, Information and Communications University, Korea), Claude Crepeau (McGill University, Canada), Ed Dawson (Queensland University of Technology, Australia), Yvo Desmedt (Florida State University, USA), Chi Sung Laih (National Cheng Kung University, Taiwan), Pil Joong Lee (POSTECH, Korea), Arjen Lenstra (Citibank, USA), Tsutomu Matsumoto (Yokohama National University, Japan), David Naccache (Gemplus, France), Eiji Okamoto (University of Wisconsin-Milwaukee, USA), Tatsuaki Okamoto (NTT Labs, Japan), Choonsik Park (ETRI, Korea), Sung Jun Park (BCQRE, Korea), Josef Pieprzyk (University of Wollongong, Australia), Claus Schnorr (Frankfurt University, Germany), Nigel Smart (University of Bristol, UK), Jacques Stern (ENS, France), Susanne Wetzel (Bell Labs, USA), Moti Yung (CertCo, USA), and Yuliang Zheng (Monash University, Australia). Members of the committee spent numerous hours in reviewing the submissions and providing advice and comments on the selection of papers.

The program committee also asked the expert advice of many of their colleagues, including: Ingrid Biehl, Colin Boyd, Marco Bucci, Gary Carter, Seong Taek Chee, Jean-Sébastien Coron, Nora Dabbous, Jean-François Dhem, Marc Fischlin, Roger Fischlin, Pierre Girard, Jaeseung Go, Juanma Gonzalez-Nieto, Helena Handschuh, Marie Henderson, Markus Jakobsson, Marc Joye, Jinho Kim, Seungjoo Kim, Ju Seung Kang, Tri V. Le, Byoungcheon Lee, Hyejoo Lee, Phil MacKenzie, David M'Raïhi, Renato Menicocci, Bernd Meyer, Pascal Paillier, Sang Joon Park, Béatrice Peirani, Jason Reid, Hein Roehrig, Amin Shokrollahi, Igor Shparlinski, Jessica Staddon, Ron Steinfeld, Christophe Tymen, and Kapali Viswanathan. We apologize for any omission in this list.

We would like to take this opportunity to thank all the program committee members and external experts for their invaluable help in producing such a high quality program.

Our appreciation also goes to members of C&IS Lab. (Cryptology and Information Security Laboratory), including Gookwhan Ahn, Jaeseung Go, Jinho Kim, Heesun Kim, Myungsun Kim, Manho Lee, Byoungcheon Lee, Jaegwan Park, Hyuncheol Park, and Boyeon Song for their skillful and professional assistance in organizing this conference. Choyoung Kim deserves special thanks for her help with preparation of the various tasks of the conference. We are also grateful to all the organizing committee members for their volunteer work.

Last, but not least, we would like to thank all the authors who submitted their papers to the conference (including those whose submissions were not successful), as well as the conference participants from around the world, for their support, which made this conference possible.

February 2001   Kwangjo Kim

PKC 2001

2001 International Workshop
on Practice and Theory
in Public Key Cryptography

Shilla Hotel, Cheju Island, Korea
13–15 February 2001

Sponsored by

Cryptology and Information Security Laboratory (C&IS Lab.)
of Information and Communications University
(caislab.icu.ac.kr)

In cooperation with

Korea Institute of Information Security and Cryptology (KIISC)
(www.kiisc.or.kr)

Under the Patronage of

Ministry of Information and Communication (MIC), Korea

Financially Supported by

Electronic and Telecommunications Research Institute (ETRI),
SAMSUNG SECUi.COM, STI (SECURITY Technologies Inc.),
BCQRE, KSIGN, SECUVE, and SOFTFORUM

General Co-chair

Hideki Imai   (University of Tokyo, Japan)
Kil-Hyun Nam   (Korea National Defense University, Korea)

Program Committee

Kwangjo Kim, Chair   (Information and Communications University, Kore
Claude Crepeau   (McGill University, Canada)
Ed Dawson   (Queensland University of Technology, Australia)
Yvo Desmedt   (Florida State University, USA)
Chi Sung Laih   (National Cheng Kung University, Taiwan)
Pil Joong Lee   (POSTECH, Korea)
Arjen Lenstra   (Citibank, USA)
Tsutomu Matsumoto   (Yokohama National University, Japan)
David Naccache   (Gemplus, France)
Eiji Okamoto   (University of Wisconsin-Milwaukee, USA)
Tatsuaki Okamoto   (NTT Labs, Japan)
Choonsik Park   (ETRI, Korea)
Sung Jun Park   (BCQRE, Korea)
Josef Pieprzyk   (University of Wollongong, Australia)
Claus Schnorr   (Frankfurt University, Germany)
Nigel Smart   (University of Bristol, UK)
Jacques Stern   (ENS, France)
Susanne Wetzel   (Bell Labs, USA)
Moti Yung   (CertCo, USA)
Yuliang Zheng   (Monash University, Australia)

Organizing Committee

Kyung Hyune Rhee, Chair   (Pukyong National University, Korea)
Donnie Choi   (STI, Korea)
Hyon Cheol Chung   (SOFTFORUM, Korea)
Ki-Yoong Hong   (KSIGN, Korea)
Kwangjo Kim   (Information and Communications University, Kor
Kyong-Soo Oh   (SAMSUNG SECUi.COM, Korea)
Ji-Hwan Park   (Pukyong National University, Korea)
Dae Hyun Ryu   (Hansei University, Korea)

Table of Contents

On the Security of a Williams Based Public Key Encryption Scheme

Siguna Müller[*]

University of Klagenfurt, Dept. of Math., A-9020 Klagenfurt, Austria
`siguna.mueller@uni-klu.ac.at`

Abstract. In 1984, H.C. Williams introduced a public key cryptosystem whose security is as intractable as factorization. Motivated by some strong and interesting cryptographic properties of the intrinsic structure of this scheme, we present a practical modification thereof that has very strong security properties. We establish, and prove, a generalization of the "sole-samplability" paradigm of Zheng-Seberry (1993) which is reminiscent of the plaintext-awareness concept of Bellare et. al. The assumptions that we make are both well-defined and reasonable. In particular, we do not model the functions as random oracles. In essence, the proof of security is based on the factorization problem of any large integer $n = pq$ and Canetti's "oracle hashing" construction introduced in 1997. Another advantage of our system is that we do not rely on any special structure of the modulus $n = pq$, nor do we require any specific form of the primes p and q. As our main result we establish a model which implies security attributes even stronger than semantic security against chosen ciphertext attacks.

Keywords: Chosen Ciphertext Security, Plaintext Awareness, (Weak)-Sole-Samplability, Factorization Intractability, Oracle Hashing, Williams' Encryption Scheme

1 Introduction and Summary

1.1 Provable Security and Attack Models

A desirable property of any cryptosystem is a proof that breaking it is as difficult as solving a computational problem that is widely believed to be difficult. A cryptographic scheme is provably secure if an attack on the scheme implies an attack on the underlying primitives it employs. While RSA is undoubtedly the most well-known and widely used public-key cryptosystem, it is not known if breaking RSA is as difficult as factoring (cf. [6]). A variety of factorization equivalent RSA modifications have been proposed which are essentially based on the same idea of unambiguous decryption (cf. also [18]). The sender can manipulate the decoder to decrypt a 'wrong message' which then can be used to factorize the modulus. Because of this problem, all these systems are vulnerable

---

[*] Supported by the Austrian Science Fund (FWF), P 13088-MAT and P 14472-MAT

to a *chosen ciphertext attack* (CCA). Under such an attack the adversary selects the ciphertext and is then given the corresponding plaintext. The strongest such attack is known as the *adaptive* CCA [19], in which an attacker can access a decryption oracle on arbitrary ciphertexts (except for the target ciphertexts which he is challenged with).

It is known that plain RSA can broken under a CCA [21], which allows total recovery of a complete plaintext, resp. generation of a complete signature on an entire message. But RSA is also vulnerable to attacks that compromise the semantic security of the scheme. An adaptive CCA can successfully be mounted on some randomized versions of RSA (PKC # 1), when only partial information of the plaintext is leaked [5].

The underlying goal of any encryption scheme is to achieve *semantic security* (informally, 'whatever can be computed by an attacker about the plaintext given an object ciphertext, can also be computed without the object ciphertext') under strong attack models (such as CCA) under well-specified assumptions and primitives.

1.2   The General Goal of this Paper

The two most often applied cryptographic primitives are the Diffie-Hellman (DH) problem and the factorization problem. There are a number of systems secure against CCA which are based on the DH problems, e.g., on the decisional DH and the existence of a collision resistant hash function [10], on the decisional DH in the random oracle model (ROM) [22], and on the computational DH in the ROM [1,17]. Also, suggestions have been made which are based on various new primitives (cf. e.g. [17]), but no encryption scheme secure against CCA has been published yet which utilizes the factorization utility of arbitrary numbers in a model without random oracles. Very recently, proposals have been made [16,17] of encryption schemes whose security rely on the ROM, and additionally require the very specific structure of the modulus, $n = p^2 q$.

Most of the above methods require random oracles. Although the ROM is a convenient setting, we do not have a general mechanism for transforming protocols that are secure in the ROM into protocols that are secure in real life. Actually, it is proved [8] that there are schemes which are secure in the ROM, but have no secure implementation in the "real world". Moreover, we do not even know how to specify the properties for a transformation from the ROM into the real world. A natural goal thus is to design a chosen ciphertext secure system which is practical and *proven secure under well defined intractability assumptions*.

On the other hand, although it is not know to what extend there exist algorithms that can exploit a special structure of the modulus for more efficiently factoring n, it would be desirable to establish a scheme based *on the general factorization primitive* $n = pq$ with p and q arbitrarily. The only factorization equivalent RSA modification known that does not require a specific form of the modulus, nor any special structure of the primes, is the Williams scheme [23].

Our proposed suggestion will consist of enhancing this scheme in order to obtain very strong cryptographic properties.

Decrypting the Williams system is provably equivalent in difficulty to factoring $n = pq$. However, it is vulnerable to a CCA. The main result of the paper is to enhance this system. We will establish some new model which yields properties even stronger than security against CCA.

1.3   Previous Methods for Proving CCA Security

There are several methods for proving security against adaptive CCA [1].

Typically, in the ROM, semantic security against CCA is achieved by proving semantic security against chosen plaintext attacks (CPA) [2], and successively proving that the system is *plaintext aware* [2]. In the first definition given in [3] this basically meant that an adversary cannot produce a ciphertext without knowing ('being able to compute') the corresponding plaintext.

The original definition required some modification. This is due to the way as how a valid ciphertext [2] is created. If its creation involves some internal RO-hash queries, the adversary that produced the ciphertext would not be able to compute the underlying plaintext [2]. The refined definition given in [2] involves some *plaintext extractor* which serves as a *simulator* of the decryption oracle. The extractor is required to find the underlying plaintext to a ciphertext without making any queries to the decryption oracle. A necessary requirement for the plaintext extractor to be successful is that the generation of the ciphertext only involved direct RO-queries. In that case, decryption can be simulated by the extractor, otherwise, it cannot. The fact that there exist some valid ciphertexts that cannot be decrypted by the simulator immediately leads to a smaller success rate of any CCA-attacker and to some loss of 'advantage' [2].

For practical realisations [1,17] the problem firstly consists in showing that such a plaintext extractor exists. Secondly, several probability estimates are necessary to ensure that the *failure probability of the simulator* remains small enough.

Moreover, plaintext awareness (PA), as defined by Bellare et. al. has only been defined in the ROM. In [2] it is argued, why this concept would not make sense in the standard model.

A more direct approach for proving security against CCA was done in [10]. It is shown that if their scheme could be broken under a CCA then this would lead to some method for breaking the underlying primitive (the decisional DH problem).

In [20] it was recently shown that under certain settings security against adaptive CCA is not even enough. Schnorr-Jakobsson demonstrate new and reasonable attack models ('one-more attack') which cannot be covered by CCA

---

[1] We do not consider the multi user setting, as this would require additional features going beyond the scope of this paper

[2] a valid ciphertext is usually understood as one that passes the validity test and hence does not get rejected by the decryption oracle

security. Indeed, they show that the most important and general attack models can be captured by some sort of proof of knowledge, which is also called *plaintext awareness* in [20] but is different from the definition of PA given in [2]. The PA in [20] also requires that any party that creates a valid ciphertext, must 'know' the secret parameters involved in its creation (for details we refer to [20]). Although the arguments of [20] clearly demonstrate that security against CCA is not sufficient, their method requires the ROM as well and thus cannot be applied to our proposed scheme.

The idea of incorporating some proof of knowledge in proving security against CCA goes back to [11,15]. Although these suggestions do not require the ROM, they are quite impractical as they rely on general and expensive constructions which make these cryptosystems difficult to realize in practice.

The first practical approach for establishing security against adaptive CCA without the ROM was proposed by Zheng-Seberry already in 1993 [26]. They require their encoding functions f to be **sole-samplable**. Basically, this property means that there is no other way to generate any valid ciphertext than to first choose a plaintext x and evaluate f at x. Thus, an adversary cannot generate a new valid ciphertext without starting from a known plaintext.

The underlying idea is obvious. If the party that generates a valid ciphertext must know the corresponding plaintext then it cannot abuse the system as it must have known the result of any decryption-query to begin with. Sole-samplability is one of the strongest notions of security that exists. It would automatically imply security against non-malleability [11], against adaptive CCA, and also against the one more attack. Additionally, it does not require the ROM.

The problem with the Zheng-Seberry suggestion is that they were not able to prove that their functions are indeed sole-samplable. They merely base the proof of CCA security on this *assumption*. Although their concept seems to be the strongest the difficulty is to actually achieve it.

1.4   The New Method and Our Main Results

We suggest that the underlying primitive to be chosen in the standard model must be some form of sole-samplability. Obviously the most natural and important concept to be established is some 'proof of knowledge', as plaintext awareness in the ROM, or the Schnorr-Jakobsson plaintext awareness in the generic model. Our main results are the following.

– We introduce a comparable notion to the sole-samplability paradigm of Zheng-Seberry. Although the proposed concept is slightly weaker than theirs, it has the advantage that all the established claims can rigorously be proved. We call an encryption scheme **weak-sole-samplable** if the following conditions hold. *If C is a valid ciphertext then it either has to be the result of an encryption query, or it has to be the result of some specific function (algorithm) F. In the latter case, this F must be explicitly known, and additionally, it must be possible to efficiently generate the underlying plaintext with publicly available information only.*

- This means, that if there do exist ways to find a valid ciphertext other than running the encryption oracle, then *all these other ways must be explicitly known*. Also, whenever a valid ciphertext was generated by such an (explicitly known) alternative method, then it must be possible to *find the corresponding plaintext, without having to make any decryption-oracle queries*.
- The advantages of this concept are obvious. If all the ways of establishing valid ciphertexts are known, and if none of these cases is possible apart from knowing the underlying plaintext, then the behaviour of any adversary is the same as in the Zheng-Seberry model, which implies extremely strong security attributes. The adversary cannot obtain more information via any decryption-oracle queries, as he must have known the answers to begin with.
- Another advantage is that *this eliminates the need for a simulator and* additionally, the necessity for establishing *the failure probability* of any plaintext extractor (simulator). Any adversary that creates a valid ciphertext, is always successful in finding the corresponding plaintext. There are not any valid ciphertext that can be created without the plaintext.
- We establish the prove of 'weak-sole-samplability' on well-formulated and explicit properties. We *only* require *Canetti's oracle hash functions* and the *general factorization primitive*. To the best of our knowledge this is the first proposal that does not require any structure of the modulus, nor any special form of the primes. Additionally, the scheme remains quite practical and can efficiently be realized by means of very rapid methods for the evaluation of combined Lucas sequences [24,25].

From the RSA family, the only factorization equivalent scheme for arbitrary p, q in the modulus $n = pq$ is the Williams scheme. This system has a number of very interesting properties. Indeed, it was a better understanding of the intrinsic structure of this scheme that lead us to establish the new model and the enhanced security properties. Since 'weak-sole-samplability' is strongly based on underlying properties of the Williams system, we present it in terms of this particular system.

Outline: After a short description of the Williams scheme and some essential properties thereof (section 2), we present the proposed enhanced version (section 3). Semantic security against CPA will be derived in section 4.1. In section 4.2 we finally prove the property 'weak-sole-samplability'.

2 Some Preliminaries

2.1 The Underlying Williams Scheme

Let $\alpha, \overline{\alpha}$ be the distinct roots of $x^2 - Px + Q$ for $P, Q \in \mathbb{Z}$ with $Q \neq 0$ and discriminant $D = P^2 - 4Q$. Then the Lucas sequences of the first and second kind of degree k, are defined by $U_k(P,Q) = \frac{\alpha^k - \overline{\alpha}^k}{\alpha - \overline{\alpha}}$ and $V_k(P,Q) = \alpha^k + \overline{\alpha}^k$, respectively. It follows that these are sequences of integers that fulfill a number of interesting identities and arithmetical properties [25].

Williams [23] utilizes the Lucas sequences for the special case where $P = 2a$, and $Q = 1$. Then, if p is an odd prime, one obtains the fundamental congruence $\alpha^{p-(D/p)} \equiv \overline{\alpha}^{p-(D/p)} \equiv 1 \bmod p$. Analogously as in Rabin's case, the basis of the system is the congruence $\alpha^{(p-(D/p))/2} \equiv \overline{\alpha}^{(p-(D/p))/2} \equiv \pm 1 \bmod p$. Williams develops a method to specify the correct signs. When working modulo $n = pq$, and for e, d the public and private key, respectively, he obtains $\alpha^{2ed} \equiv \overline{\alpha}^{2ed} \equiv \pm \alpha \bmod n$. This then establishes the equivalence between decryption and factoring [23].

Let $n = pq$, where p and q are two large primes. Further, let $s, c \in \mathbf{Z}_n^*$ be chosen such such that $p \equiv -\left(\frac{c}{p}\right) \bmod 4$ and $q \equiv -\left(\frac{c}{q}\right) \bmod 4$, $\gcd(s^2 - c, n) = 1$ and $\left(\frac{s^2-c}{n}\right) = -1$. In the following $w \in \mathbf{Z}_n$ is assigned the role of the message to be encrypted.

Let the public encryption key e and the secret decryption key d with $\gcd(e, (p+1)(q+1)) = 1$ be determined according to $ed \equiv \frac{m+1}{2} \bmod m$, where $m = \frac{(p-(\frac{c}{p}))(q-(\frac{c}{q}))}{4}$. The numbers n, e, c, s constitute the *Public Key*, whereas the numbers p, q, m, d are kept *secret*. Throughout the paper, let $b_1 = 1$, if $\left(\frac{w^2-c}{n}\right) = 1$, and $b_1 = -1$, if $\left(\frac{w^2-c}{n}\right) = -1$.

Suppose $\gcd(w^2 - c, n) = 1$ and denote $a \equiv a(w), b \equiv b(w) \bmod n$, and $\alpha \equiv \alpha(w) \equiv a + b\sqrt{c} \bmod n$, where [3]

$$\begin{cases} \text{for } b_1 = 1: \quad a \equiv \frac{w^2+c}{w^2-c}, \quad b \equiv \frac{2w}{w^2-c} \bmod n, \\ \text{for } b_1 = -1: \quad a \equiv \frac{(w^2+c)(s^2+c)+4csw}{(w^2-c)(s^2-c)}, \quad b \equiv \frac{2s(w^2+c)+2w(s^2+c)}{(w^2-c)(s^2-c)} \bmod n. \end{cases} \quad (1)$$

Define the sequences $X_i(a) = \frac{\alpha^i + \overline{\alpha}^i}{2} = \frac{V_i(2a,1)}{2}$, and $Y_i(a,b) = b\frac{\alpha^i - \overline{\alpha}^i}{\alpha - \overline{\alpha}} = bU_i(2a,1)$.

In order to minimize problems concerning the existence of the above multiplicative inverses mod n (cf. [14]) it is preferable to work with a slightly modified version of the original scheme. In the following we will exclusively be applying this modification which essentially consists of reversing numerator and denominator of the original encryption function $X_e(a)/Y_e(a,b) \bmod n$ of [23] and adapting the decryption scheme.

Williams' Encryption: The first step of the encryption process consists of calculating $a(w), b(w)$ from the message w by means of (1). Then w is encoded as

$$E(w) \equiv \frac{Y_e(a(w), b(w))}{X_e(a(w))} \bmod n.$$

The cryptogram C to be transmitted is the triple $[E(w), b_1, b_2]$, where b_1 is defined via $\left(\frac{w^2-c}{n}\right)$ as above and $b_2 \equiv a(w) \bmod 2$, $b_2 \in \{0, 1\}$.

---

[3] It turns out that the quantities $a(w)$ and $b(w)$ for both cases $b_1 = 1$ and -1 can be comprised into a more comprehensive formula. It can easily be shown that for a and b as above, $a = a(w) \equiv \frac{\hat{w}^2+c}{\hat{w}^2-c} \bmod n$, $b = b(w) \equiv \frac{2\hat{w}}{\hat{w}^2-c} \bmod n$, where $\hat{w} \equiv w \bmod n$, if $b_1 = 1$, and $\hat{w} \equiv \frac{ws+c}{w+s} \bmod n$, if $b_1 = -1$.

Williams' Decryption. Upon receiving C the receiver firstly calculates the values $a_0 \equiv \frac{1+E(w)^2c}{1-E(w)^2c} \bmod n$, and $b_0 \equiv \frac{2E(w)}{1-E(w)^2c} \bmod n$.

The second step consists of determining $\sigma = (-1)^{b_2-X_d(a_0)}$ and $a(w)$ and $b(w)$ by means of $a(w) \equiv \sigma X_d(a_0) \bmod n$ and $b(w) \equiv \sigma Y_d(a_0, b_0) \bmod n$.

Finally, the message w can be retrieved from $a(w)$ and $b(w)$ via

$$w = \begin{cases} \frac{a(w)+1}{b(w)} \bmod n, & \text{if } b_1 = 1, \\ \frac{cb(w)-s(a(w)+1)}{a(w)+1-sb(w)} \bmod n, & \text{if } b_1 = -1, \end{cases} \tag{2}$$

provided [4] $\gcd(b(w), n) = 1$ for $b_1 = 1$, and $\gcd(a(w) + 1 - sb(w), n) = 1$ for $b_1 = -1$.

Remark 1. By utilizing efficient methods for the combined evaluation of the Lucas sequences [24,25], it can be shown that the Williams scheme requires about twice as many multiplications as RSA, with additionally two multiplicative inverses modulo n for both encryption and decryption.

2.2 The Williams Scheme Under a CCA

Definition 1. *Let $a'(w)$ and $b'(w)$ be chosen such that $a'(w)$, $b'(w)$ correspond to $a(w), b(w)$ for the (wrong) case $b'_1 = -b_1$.*

Further denote the 'false encryption of w' by $E'(w) \equiv \frac{Y_e(a'(w),b'(w))}{X_e(a'(w))} \bmod n$, that is defined by following the formulas of the above encryption routine with respect to $b'_1 = -b_1$ (rather than b_1).

As with the Rabin scheme, the equivalence of decryption and factorization gives rise to a CCA [23]. One can even show the following [14].

Proposition 1. – *If $\left(\frac{w^2-c}{n}\right) = 1$ or -1 then $E'(w) \equiv E(z) \bmod n$ and $b'_1(w)$ $= b_1(z)$. Then $z \equiv D(E(z)) \bmod n$ where the parameters for the decryption routine are $b'_1(w)$ and b_2. Then $\gcd(w - z, n)$ gives the factorization of n.*
  – *For $\left(\frac{w^2-c}{n}\right) = -1$ and $E'(w) \equiv E(z) \bmod n$, the problem of finding $a(z)$ for a known $a'(w)$ respectively w (and, similarly for $b(z)$) is computationally equivalent to the problem of factorizing n.*
  – *If there exists an algorithm for retrieving $\pm a(w) \bmod n$ from $E(w)$ (where both values correspond to the same b_1) then there exists an efficient algorithm for factorizing n.*

2.3 Some Interesting Properties

Proposition 2. *Let b_1 be fixed and $E(w)$ as well as $a(w)$ be given. Then there is an efficient algorithm for evaluating the underlying message w.*

---

[4] It was shown in [14] that the number of messages not fulfilling these gcd-conditions is negligible.

Proof. For establishing this result we adopt the ideas of the attack developed in [4,9,12]. Let $A = a(w) - 1 = \frac{2c}{\hat{w}^2 - c}$ and $B = 2A^{-1} + 1$. Then $\hat{w}^2 = cB$. We may assume that $A^{-1} \bmod n$ exists.

We now consider the extension $R = \mathbf{Z}[x]/(x^2 - cB, n)$, i.e. the elements of R are polynomials of degree 1 at most with coefficients modulo n. All arithmetic operations (addition, multiplication, division) over R can be done without the knowledge of the factorization of n (where we assume that practically division is always possible). We now define a mapping $\phi : R \mapsto \mathbf{Z}_n$ by $\phi(kx+l) \equiv k\hat{w} + l \bmod n$ for $k, l \in \mathbf{Z}_n$, where according to the value b_1, $\hat{w}$ equals w, respectively $\frac{ws+c}{w+s}$. Since $\hat{w}^2 \equiv cB \bmod n$ it can easily be verified that ϕ is a ring homomorphism.

We show the result for $b_1 = -1$, since $b_1 = 1$ can be proved analogously. In particular, we then have $\phi(x - s) = \hat{w} - s = \frac{c-s^2}{w+s}$, $\phi(-xs + c) = w\frac{c-s^2}{w+s}$ and consequently $\phi(\frac{-xs+c}{x-s}) = w$. In R the expression $\frac{-xs+c}{x-s}$ becomes $\frac{c-s^2}{cB-s^2}x + \frac{cs(1-B)}{cB-s^2} \bmod n$ which we will denote by $w_1 x + w_2$. Observe that, although we do not know the message w, we do know the polynomial that maps unto w, that is, w is now implicitly given by $w_1 x + w_2$.

The idea behind the attack in [4,9,12] is now to encrypt this polynomial in R which gives us a polynomial in x. The homomorphic image of this encrypted polynomial then equals $E(w)$ since ϕ is a homomorphism. The combined knowledge of $E(w)$ and this homomorphic image then can be used to derive w.

To encrypt the polynomial $w_1 x + w_2$ we follow the routines w.r.t. a fixed b_1. We firstly have to find the corresponding values to $a(w)$ and $b(w)$ in R. Since $\phi(x) = \hat{w}$ and $x^2 = cB$ in R, this can easily be shown to be accomplished. One obtains $a(w) \equiv \frac{B+1}{B-1}$, $b(w) \equiv \frac{2x}{c(B-1)} \bmod n$ in R.

Consequently, one evaluates the Lucas sequences w.r.t. the $a(w)$ in R modulo n and obtains the encryption in R. Let this result be denoted as $ux+v$. We stress that, since $a(w)$ and $b(w)$ in R merely consist of the public information, c, B, we know u and v. But then we know $\phi(ux + v)$ which equals $E(w)$ and therefore we have $u\hat{w} + v = E(w)$. Hence, we can solve for $\hat{w}$, if $(u, n) = 1$, which is very likely. Finally we now obtain w from $\hat{w}$ as desired.   □

Remark 2. It is essential that the homomorphic image of the encrypted polynomial, which is determined by $a = a(w)$, equals $E(w)$. If a were some $a(x)$, the results obtained would be different from w. In other words, to each $E(w) = E'(z)$ correspond exactly two possible a, namely $a(w)$ and $a(z)$. Observe that from a given pair $E(w), a$ only the output z can be obtained when the factorization of n is known (cf. Proposition 1).

Proposition 3. *If $b_1 = -1$ and $a(x) \equiv a(y) \bmod n$, then $\hat{x}^2 \equiv \hat{y}^2 \bmod n$, where $\hat{x} \equiv \frac{xs+c}{x+s} \bmod n$ and $\hat{y} \equiv \frac{ys+c}{y+s} \bmod n$.*

Proof. ¿From $a(x) \equiv \frac{\hat{x}^2 + c}{\hat{x}^2 - c} \bmod n$ we see that $\hat{x}^2 \equiv -c\frac{1+a(x)}{1-a(x)} \bmod n$, and, analogously, for $a(y)$, $\hat{y}^2 \equiv -c\frac{1+a(y)}{1-a(y)} \bmod n$. By hypothesis the right hand sides are equal, which gives the result.   □

Proposition 4. *For all $x \in \mathbb{Z}_n^*$ we have $-a(x) \equiv a(c/x) \bmod n$.*

Proof. Observe that $-a(x) \bmod n$ corresponds to the situation where during decryption the wrong $\sigma = \sigma(a(x))$ is obtained. By footnote 7 the decryption routine evaluates $x(-\sigma) \equiv \frac{c}{x} \bmod n$. Since also $\widehat{x}(-\sigma) \equiv \frac{c}{\widehat{x}} \bmod n$ the definition of a gives $a(x(-\sigma)) \equiv \frac{\left(\frac{c}{\widehat{x}}\right)^2 + c}{\left(\frac{c}{\widehat{x}}\right)^2 - c} \equiv \frac{\widehat{x}^2 + c}{-\widehat{x}^2 + c} \bmod n$. $\qquad\square$

Corollary 1. *If for the case $b_1 = -1$ one has $a(x) \equiv -a(y) \bmod n$ then $\widehat{x}^2 \equiv \widehat{(c/y)}^2 \bmod n$.*

3 The Proposed Scheme

3.1 Requirements on the Hash Function

Usually, semantic security is achieved via random oracles. Due to the ongoing controversy about the existence of such 'truly random' hash functions, we design our scheme in a way where we do not require the ROM. Instead, all our hash functions involved are special instances of Canetti's **oracle hash functions**. For the exact definitions we refer to [7] and only recall the fundamental concepts required for our scheme. The primitive, oracle hashing, informally describes a hash function h that, like random oracles, '*hides all partial information on its input*'.

A salient property of oracle hashing is that it cannot be deterministic, which traditionally is the case with any hash function, where two invocations on the same input yield the same answer. However, any deterministic function F is inadequate for oracle hashing, since it is bound to disclose some information on the input, as $F(x)$ itself is some information on x.

Thus, oracle hash functions need to be probabilistic in the sense that different invocations on the same input result in different outputs. The output of x is additionally determined by some *randomizer r* which is responsible for the different hash values of x. That is, the hash of x is the output of $h(x, r)$ for the random value r. Still, there needs to be some means as to verify whether a given hash value was generated from a given input x. There needs to exist a verification [5] algorithm, V, that correctly decides, given x and y, whether y is a hash of x. We use Canetti's suggestion of a **public randomness scheme**. The randomizer r appears directly in the output of $h(x, r)$. We write $h(x, r) = r, \widetilde{h}(x, r)$.

The fundamental property of our underlying hash functions is Canetti's **oracle indistinguishability**. Informally, the hashes of x and y with respect to the same randomizer r, $h(x, r)$ and $h(y, r)$, should be computationally indistinguishable to any polytime adversary.

---

[5] The verification property is somewhat reminiscent of signature schemes. Indeed, this is exactly what will be required in our decryption verification step below. It is stressed, however, that here no secret keys are involved and all the functions can be invoked by everyone [7].

Canetti also considers the case where some (partial) information on x is already known. E.g., if for some public function f, $f(x)$ leaks some partial information on x, [6] then $\big(f(x), h(x,r)\big)$ still should be computationally indistinguishable from $\big(f(x), h(y,r)\big)$ (for details see [7], p. 467).

3.2   The Proposed Encryption and Decryption Schemes

Let $|x|$ denote the length of the string x. The concatenation of two strings x and y is denoted by $x||y$ and the bit-wise exclusive-or of x and y is denoted by $x \oplus y$. We generally use the notation $a \equiv b \bmod n$ to denote the principal remainder a, that is the unique integer $a \in \{0, ..., n-1\}$ that is congruent to b modulo n. We will assume that all calculations are carried out modulo $n = pq$. If $\overline{w}$ is the message to be encrypted let $w = 0...0\overline{w}$ be the padded message of $\overline{w}$ such that $|w| = |n|$.

Throughout, g will denote a cryptographic hash function to $\{0,1\}^{|n|}$ that is both collision resistant and pre-image resistant, while h will denote a Canetti-oracle hash function (cf. section 3.1).

The Proposed Encryption Routine $\mathcal{E} = \mathcal{E}(w)$.

1. Choose randomly a session key S and a randomizer R from $\{0,1\}^{|n|}$ such that for
$$w_R = w \oplus h(S,R), \text{ and } S_R = S \oplus h(w_R, R),$$
one has $\left(\frac{w_R^2 - c}{n}\right) = \left(\frac{S_R^2 - c}{n}\right) = -1$.
2. Calculate $a(w_R), b(w_R), E(w_R)$ and $a(S_R), b(S_R), E(S_R)$ w.r.t. $b_1 = -1$ following the routines of section 2.1.
3. Put $H = g\big(\underbrace{0...0\, a(w_R)}_{\text{length.}=|n|} \; || \; \underbrace{0...0\, a(S_R)}_{\text{length.}=|n|} \; || \; S\big)$.
4. Send the cryptogram $\mathcal{C} = [c_1, c_2, c_3, c_4] = [E(w_R), E(S_R), R, H]$.

The Proposed Decryption Routine $\mathcal{D} = \mathcal{D}(c_1, ..., c_4)$.

1. Decrypt c_1 to obtain $\sigma(w_R)a(w_R) \bmod n$, $\sigma(w_R)b(w_R) \bmod n$ following the formulas of section 2.1 for $b_1 = -1$.
2. Decrypt c_2 to obtain $\sigma(S_R)a(S_R) \bmod n$, $\sigma(S_R)b(S_R) \bmod n$ following the formulas of section 2.1 for $b_1 = -1$.
3. Select the signs σ, $\sigma(w_R) \in \{-1,1\}$, $\sigma(S_R) \in \{-1,1\}$ and calculate the corresponding w_R and S_R.
4. Calculate $S = h(w_R, c_3) \oplus S_R$.
5. Check whether
$$c_4 = g\big(\underbrace{0...0\, \sigma(w_R)a(w_R)}_{\text{length.}=|n|} \; || \; \underbrace{0...0\, \sigma(S_R)a(S_R)}_{\text{length.}=|n|} \; || \; S\big). \tag{3}$$

---

[6]   It only makes sense to consider the case where f does not give full information on x. Thus, f should be one-way, or uninvertible (without the use of the secret key).

6.   - If step (5) returns 'true', output $w = h(S, c_3) \oplus w_R$.
      - Otherwise goto step (3), select another sign and repeat.
      - If step (5) returns 'false' for all $\sigma(w_R) \in \{-1, 1\}$, $\sigma(S_R) \in \{-1, 1\}$ then return "NULL".

Note that b_1 is fixed. The correct values b_2 follow directly from construction, since $a(x)$ is directly in the scope of h. It can easily be seen that the signs σ of $\pm a(w_R), \pm a(S_R) \bmod n$, respectively, that pass the test in the decryption routine, are exactly the signs of the input to the hash function in the encryption routine, respectively [7]. Hence, we have

Lemma 1. *For the above routines, the decryption of an encryption of any message always gives this message.*

Remark 3.   – The testing check during decryption captures Canetti's verification property. H takes the role of the signing algorithm (with respect to the underlying w and S), and the testing step (3) takes the role of the signature verification algorithm.
  – Due to the strong security properties which are achieved, some message expansion is to be expected. The entire cryptogram can be viewed as an encryption with combined signature. The hash value provides a proof of knowledge of the plaintext w and the secret parameter S. In such a setting message expansion is typical, e.g., [10,20]. More length efficient proposals have been made in [26] but the claims were not proved. This was recently done in [1] in the ROM.

4   Proof of Security

4.1   Semantic Security against Chosen Plaintext Attacks

An adversary $A = (A_1, A_2)$ defining security against CPA is usually described via the well-known game play [2]. At first, A_1 is run on input the public key, pk. At the end of $A_1's$ execution he outputs a triple (w_0, w_1, s), where w_0, w_1 are messages of the same length and s is some state information. A random one of w_0 and w_1 is selected, say w_b, and a 'challenge' y is determined by encrypting w_b under pk. A_2 is given y but not w_b. It is now $A_2's$ job to determine b, that is, to decide, if y is the encryption of w_0 or of w_1. In public key cryptography such an attack is always possible, since any adversary has access to the encryption oracle, as pk is always publicly known.

---

[7]   Clearly, the party evaluating the hash value H can replace (the correct) $a(x)$ by $-a(x) \bmod n$ and use this as a forged hash input. Then in the deciphering process the wrong σ will be determined. In that case, it can easily be seen [14] that the (Williams)-decryption of x obtained equals $x(-\sigma) = c\frac{1}{x} \bmod n$. Contrary to the forgery w.r.t. b_1 this however, does not expose the factorization of n.

Canetti showed how oracle hash functions can be used to build a crypto scheme that is semantically secure against chosen plaintext attacks [7], p. 466f. Typically, some information $f = f(x)$ is part of the cryptogram and hence establishes some public information on the secret parameter x. Canetti assumes that f is uninvertible so that this information leakage does not allow complete retrieval of x.

In our case this leads to the following technical requirement. We will assume that given $E(S_R)$, $g = g(0...0\,a(w_R) \parallel 0...0\,a(S_R) \parallel S)$, it is impossible to find the complete underlying secret parameter S.

Remark 4. This assumption actually is not very strong. Informally, we have the following. Due to the Canetti hash function h involved, by construction no information on w_R leaks from $E(S_R)$ even if E does leak some information on S_R, where E denotes the Williams encryption of section 2.1. Also, if $a(w_R)$ did leak from $E(S_R)$ and g, then, since retrieving w_R from $a(w_R)$ is equivalent to factoring n, w_R cannot completely be recovered, so that an adversary has no information on $h(w_R, R)$. A lack of complete knowledge of $h(w_R, R)$ implies a lack of complete knowledge of S, even if S_R could completely be recovered from $E(S_R)$ and g. Similarly, if some partial information on S_R and w_R can be obtained by the combined knowledge of $E(S_R)$ and g, again by the Canetti-hash function h, S cannot completely be recovered. Thus, S would need to leak in full from g to violate our assumption.

Analogously as in [7], we obtain the semantic security of the proposed scheme.

Theorem 1. *The proposed cryptosystem is semantically secure against adaptive chosen plaintext attacks, if the factorization of $n = pq$ is hard, h is a Canetti oracle hash function with the additional technical assumption above on the cryptographic function g.*

Proof. (Sketch) Assume an adversary $\mathcal{A}$ that does break the scheme under a CPA. Let the probability for his success be as defined in the proof to Theorem 10 in [7]. The tuple $E(S_R)$, $g = g(0...0\,a(w_R) \parallel 0...0\,a(S_R) \parallel S)$, yields some information f on S which by the assumption above corresponds to the uninvertible function f in Canetti's case.

Construct an algorithm $\mathcal{D}$ that distinguishes between $(f(S), h(S, R))$ and $(f(S), h(S', R))$, where S, S', R are randomly chosen and $f(S) = (E(S_R), g)$. Since R is public, $h(S, R) = R, \tilde{h}(S, R)$, and by the requirement that h is a Canetti hash function, it follows that for uniformly chosen S, R the value $h(S, R)$ is uniform in $\{0, 1\}^l$ for some l.

Given $f(S), R, \xi$ (where ξ is either $\tilde{h}(S, R)$ or $\tilde{h}(S', R)$), the distinguisher $\mathcal{D}$ will construct a ciphertext in the following way. $\mathcal{D}$ may choose either one of w_0 or w_1 as message in the game play defining security against CPA. Assume that he chooses w_1. Then he obtains $w_R = w_1 \oplus \xi$ and he can hand $\mathcal{A}$ the 'ciphertext' $C = [E(w_R), E(S_R), R, g]$. Now, if $\mathcal{A}$ outputs 'w_1' then $\mathcal{D}$ outputs '$\xi = \tilde{h}(S, R)$'. Otherwise $\mathcal{D}$ outputs '$\xi = \tilde{h}(S', R)$'.

As in Canetti's case this follows since in the former event the constructed w_R was the correct one, while in the latter, it must must have been equal to

$w_R = w_1 \oplus \tilde{h}(S', R) \neq w_1 \oplus \tilde{h}(S, R)$. In particular, then $\mathcal{A}$ is given an encryption of a uniformly chosen message. The decryption cannot be w_1, hence in that case, by the CPA game, it can only be w_0, which $\mathcal{A}$ outputs.

Analyzing $\mathcal{D}$ is straightforward with the exact success probability given in [7]. The existence of such a distinguisher yields a contradiction to the assumption.

$\square$

4.2 'Weak-Sole-Samplability'

Recall the notion of a valid ciphertext. This is such where the decryption oracle does not reject. We now completely characterize all possibilities how for the proposed scheme valid ciphertexts can be obtained.

The randomizer R, since it directly occurs in C, plays a unique role. Nonetheless, this information cannot be used for any attack. (Compare also Canetti's discussion on this public randomizer [7]).

Lemma 2. *Let* $C = [c_1, c_2, c_3, c_4]$ *be a valid ciphertext, h a Canetti oracle hash function, g a cryptographic hash function, and suppose that the factorization of n is infeasible. If in C the c_3 gets modified, then a necessary condition for obtaining another valid ciphertext is that all entries in C get modified.*

Proof. We analyze any adversary that tries to obtain another valid ciphertext. Let c_3' be the modified value and let C be the encryption of the message w relative to the session key S and the randomizer R. We can assume that the adversary knows w (e.g. by mounting a CCA). We can also assume that he knows S (e.g. by his own encryption) because otherwise any such attack would not be possible (this follows from the fact that c_4 remains unchanged, g is both collision resistant and pre-image resistant and since the given C is a valid ciphertext). By their definition he then also knows w_R and S_R.

Suppose firstly that $C' = [c_1, c_2, c_3', c_4]$ is also valid. Then the validity check (3) passes if $c_4 = g(...||S) = g(....||S')$, where $S' = S'(c_3')$ is in the fourth step of the deciphering oracle computed as $S' = h(\sigma(w_R)w_R, c_3') \oplus S_R$. By the choice of h necessarily $S' = S$ so that $h(\sigma(w_R)w_R, c_3')$ has to evaluate to $S \oplus S_R$. But that would imply that $h(w_R, c_3) = h(w_R, c_3')$ which is extremely unlikely [7].

Similarly, we see that $C' = [c_1, c_2', c_3', c_4]$ where c_2' is determined a priori, leads to a contradiction. Consequently, the adversary needs to evaluate a modified c_2 accordingly, i.e. such that the properties of the hash function are not being violated. This is only possible if at first the hash input, that is some c_3', is being selected. As above, we again need to have $S' = S$, where now $S' = h(w_R, c_3') \oplus D(c_2')$, and D is the Williams decryption of section 2.1. ¿From the hash output and $S' = S$ the adversary then obtains the decrypted value $x = D(c_2')$ (w.r.t. $b_1 = -1$) of the forged c_2', that is, $x = S_R'$ (respectively c/S_R').

However, this x has to be of a special form (this will lead to the contradiction below), because in the validity check it is required that

$$c_4 = g(...||0..0\,\sigma(S_R)a(S_R)||...) = g(...||0..0\,\sigma(x)a(x)||...)$$

(where we assume that the hash input is split up according to the appropriate lengths).

By Proposition 4 the above identity is only possible if either $a(S_R) \equiv a(x)$ mod n, or $a(S_R) \equiv a(c/x) \bmod n$, depending on whether the above σ's correspond or not. According to Proposition 3 and Corollary 1,

$$\text{either } \widehat{S_R}^2 \equiv \hat{x}^2 \bmod n \text{ or } \widehat{S_R}^2 \equiv \widehat{(c/x)}^2 \bmod n.$$

But we also have that $c_2 \not\equiv c_2' \bmod n$. Also, by assumption, both $\mathcal{C}$ and $\mathcal{C}'$ are valid which means that the test passes for exactly one $\sigma(S_R)$ and thus for exactly one $\sigma(x)$ which then yields the corresponding values, x or c/x, respectively.

Since the decryption of c_2', as well as that of c_2, is being conducted w.r.t. $b_1 = -1$, the preimages, x and S_R, respectively c/x and S_R, need to be distinct mod n. Then also $\hat{x}$ and $\widehat{S_R}$, respectively $\widehat{c/x}$ and $\widehat{S_R}$ need to be distinct since otherwise $s^2 \equiv c \bmod n$, contrary to the choice of s.

Further, we can show that $x \not\equiv -S_R$, respectively $c/x \not\equiv -S_R \bmod n$. These two cases can be dealt with the same way. Observe that x was defined according to the hash output of c_3', i.e. as $x = h(w_R, c_3') \oplus S$. If we assume that $x \equiv -S_R \bmod n$ then c_3' (which has been selected a priori) would hash to the specific output $S \oplus (-S_R) \bmod n$, a contradiction. Analogously, $\hat{x} \not\equiv -\widehat{S_R}$, respectively $\widehat{c/x} \not\equiv -\widehat{S_R} \bmod n$. But then $\gcd(\hat{x} - \widehat{S_R}, n)$, respectively $\gcd(\widehat{c/x} - \widehat{S_R}, n)$ is a proper factor of n. To find this factor the adversary only needs to know $\hat{x}$, respectively $\widehat{c/x}$ and $\widehat{S_R}$, which he does when he knows x.

Observe that the adversary already knows w, w_R and S_R. However, Proposition 2 asserts that the adversary can calculate x from $E(x) = c_2'$ and $a(x) \equiv a(S_R)$ respectively $-a(S_R) \bmod n$.

Thus, the adversary would find the factorization of n. The derived contradiction to the hypothesis of the lemma implies that the adversary cannot compute a valid ciphertext by just forging c_2 and c_3.

The adversary can also try to forge c_1. But, in order to pass the test, then he would need to know c_1' along with the corresponding $\sigma(y)a(y)$, where y (respectively c/y) is the decryption of c_1' (w.r.t. $b_1 = -1$).

As decrypting c_1' or determining this $a(y)$ is equivalent to factoring (Proposition 1), the adversary can only, conversely, define y as w_R' and encrypt y (w.r.t. $b_1 = -1$) to obtain his forged c_1'. Similarly as above, he needs to evaluate S_R' as $h(w_R', c_3') \oplus S$ in order to fulfill the requirement on the hash function in (3) with respect to the last block in the input. But this now constitutes a special form of the attack considered above. The adversary would have to forge c_2 which is impossible, independent of the choice of c_1.   □

Let us consider an adversary that has access to $g, h, \mathcal{E}$, and $\mathcal{D}$. He can play with his encryption oracle, and may also make t queries of the decryption oracle. He then produces a new valid ciphertext that he outputs. As in [2] we demand that the adversary never outputs a string that coincides with the value returned from some $\mathcal{E}$-query.

The basic idea in both Lemma 2 and Theorem 2 below is to analyze the different possibilities as how an attacker might be able to reuse existing valid ciphertexts. That is, we investigate all ways for obtaining valid ciphertexts (other than running the encryption oracle).

We will give a complete characterization of all possibilities to find a valid ciphertext. Depending on whether the adversary knows the secret parameter S corresponding to some known valid ciphertext, he may follow only one of the specific steps given in the proof below. In each of these particular cases the proof also shows that the adversary is not able to generate any new valid ciphertext whose plaintext he does not know.

For $1 \leq i \leq t$, let $C_i = [c_1^{(i)}, c_2^{(i)}, c_3^{(i)}, c_4^{(i)}]$ be the ith valid cryptogram that the adversary gets decrypted. Let C' be the new valid ciphertext that the adversary produces. By Lemma 2 we only need to distinguish between the following types of attacks.

- Type I: There is some $1 \leq j \leq t$ such that for $C_j = [c_1, c_2, c_3, c_4]$,
  (a) $C' = [c_1' \neq c_1, c_2, c_3, c_4]$,   (b) $C' = [c_1, c_2' \neq c_2, c_3, c_4]$,
  (c) $C' = [c_1' \neq c_1, c_2' \neq c_2, c_3, c_4]$,
- Type II: There is some $1 \leq j \leq t$ such that for $C_j = [c_1, c_2, c_3, c_4]$, (a) $C' = [c_1, c_2, c_3, c_4' \neq c_4]$,   (b) $C' = [c_1' \neq c_1, c_2, c_3, c_4' \neq c_4]$,
  (c) $C' = [c_1, c_2' \neq c_2, c_3, c_4' \neq c_4]$,   (d) $C' = [c_1' \neq c_1, c_2' \neq c_2, c_3, c_4']$,
- Type III: For all i, $C' = [c_1' \neq c_1^{(i)}, c_2' \neq c_2^{(i)}, c_3' \neq c_3^{(i)}, c_4' \neq c_4^{(i)}]$.

Theorem 2. *Assume that h is a Canetti oracle hash function, g is a cryptographic hash function, and that it is computationally infeasible to find the factorization of n. Then the above encryption scheme is weak-sole-samplable. Any valid cryptogram that is not an $\mathcal{E}$ output, has to be the result of some type II or III attack with the individual steps described below. In both cases, the adversary then knows the underlying w, S, as well as the underlying signs σ in the hash-input.*

Proof. **Type I attacker:**
Suppose we have a type I (a) attacker. Because c_4 is fixed we can as in the proof to Lemma 2 assume that the attacker knows the corresponding w and S. Observe that, since C is valid, the $S = h(w_R, c_3) \oplus S_R$ obtained in the fourth step of $\mathcal{D}$ passes the test (3) for the unique $\sigma(w_R)$ and thus for the unique w_R. If now $c_1 \neq c_1'$ then the S' obtained will be different from S. This follows, since for fixed $b_1 = -1$ the decryption of c_1' is either w_R' or c/w_R'. These values are different from w_R because otherwise $c_1 = c_1'$. Therefore the test will reject for this S'. In order to obtain the same S, also c_2 would have to be modified, which is not the case under the type of attack under inspection.

Similarly we see that a type I (b) attack will be rejected by the test because the S' obtained in step (4) will not match the valid S.

Now consider a type I (c) attacker. In order to guarantee that the S' obtained in step (4) equals the valid S, the adversary can only proceed analogously as in the proof to Lemma 2. He needs to define the (Williams) decryption of the modified c_2', that is S_R', as $S \oplus h(y, c_3)$, where $y = w_R'$ is the decryption of c_1'. But these w_R' and S_R' need to pass (3). Similarly as in Lemma 2, he would be able to factorize n, a contradiction. Hence, any type I attack will get rejected as well.

Type II attacker:
For a type II (a) attacker observe that by definition c_1, c_2, c_3 remain unchanged. Hence, in steps 2 and 3 during decryption, the quantities $\pm a(w_R)$, $\pm a(S_R)$ corresponding to the original w and S are obtained. Since $c_4 = g(\sigma(w_R)a(w_R) \| \sigma(S_R)a(S_R) \| S)$ for the specific $\sigma(w_R)$, $\sigma(S_R)$, one can only obtain a modified hash output w.r.t. different signs, $\sigma(w_R)$ and/or $\sigma(S_R)$. The requirement on g necessitates that the adversary knows the individual blocks in the hash input (he can only obtain the output from the input). As he also needs to know c_1 and c_2, by Lemma 2, he knows the modified message w as well as the modified S that result in the modified cryptogram due to the change of the σ's.

In a type II (b) attack the test only passes if the hash output, c_4' is calculated as the hash-output w.r.t. the modified c_1'. Then the adversary has to know the $\sigma(w_R')a(w_R')$ that is obtained by decrypting c_1'. As usual, by Lemma 2, we conclude that he can find w_R', respectively c/w_R'. To obtain the hash value c_4' he also needs to know the $\sigma(S_R)a(S_R)$. Again, since he knows c_2 he then knows S_R. Depending on the σ's selected he obtains two different (modified) S and four different (modified) w. He can easily verify which of those have the desired encryptions c_1' so that he knows the modified w and S that result in $\mathcal{C}'$.

Exactly the same way we can show that in a type II (c) attack the adversary needs to know the underlying quantities that result in $\mathcal{C}'$.

A type II (d) attack can be dealt with analogously, because knowledge of $a(x)$ and $E(x)$ is equivalent to knowing x, where x firstly is w_R' and then secondly S_R'.

Type III attacker:
The result follows exactly as for a type II (d) attacker because the value c_3 is not essential. The adversary would need to know the first two blocks of the input to the hash function. Along with c_1' and c_2' this is equivalent to knowing w_R' and S_R' where $c_3' = R'$. However, since c_3' is public one easily finds the underlying w' and S' from the randomized w_R' and S_R'.

We have shown that valid ciphertexts cannot be obtained apart from knowing their underlying parameters, which completes the proof of Theorem 2 in all cases.

$\square$

Acknowledgements

I am deeply grateful to the following people for their valuable comments and for their support: Dr. A. Desai, Professors A. Menezes, W.B. Müller, D. Pointcheval, P. Rogaway, C.P. Schnorr, and N. Smart. Also, I would like to thank the referees for their careful reading of the manuscript and for their insightful and helpful remarks.

References

1. J. Baek, B. Lee, K. Kim, Provably Secure Length-saving Public-Key Encryption Scheme under the Computational Diffie-Hellman Assumption. *ETRI J.*, Dec. 2000.
2. M. Bellare, A. Desai, D. Pointcheval and P. Rogaway, Relations among notions of security for public-key encryption schemes, Extended abstract in *Advances in Cryptology - Crypto 98, LNCS*, 1462, H. Krawczyk (ed.), Springer (1998); full version available at www-cse.ucsd.edu/users/mihir/papers/crypto-papers.html.
3. M. Bellare, P. Rogaway, Optimal asymmetric encryption – How to encrypt with RSA, *Advances in Cryptology - Eurocrypt 94, LNCS* 950, A. De Santis (ed.), Springer (1995) pp. 92–111.
4. D. Bleichenbacher, On the Security of the KMOV Public Key Cryptosystem, *Advances in Cryptology - Crypto'97, LNCS* 1294, Springer (1997) pp. 235 – 248.
5. D. Bleichenbacher: Chosen Ciphertext Attacks Against Protocols Based on the RSA Encryption Standard PKCS #1. *Adv. in Cryptology - Crypto'98, LNCS* 1462, H. Krawczyk (ed.), Springer (1998) pp. 1–12.
6. D. Boneh, R. Venkatesan, Breaking RSA May Not Be Equivalent to Factoring, *Advances of Cryptology - Eurocrypt '98, LNCS* 1403, K. Nyberg (ed.), Springer (1998) pp. 59–71.
7. R. Canetti, Towards Realizing Random Oracles: Hash Functions That Hide All Partial Information, *Advances in Cryptology - Crypto'97*, 455-469.
8. R. Canetti, O. Goldreich, S. Halevi, The random oracle model, revisited, In: *30 th Annual ACM Symp. on Theory of Computing* (1998).
9. D. Coppersmith, M. Franklin, J. Patarin, M. Reiter, Low-Exponent RSA with Related Messages, *Advances of Cryptology - Eurocrypt' 96, LNCS* 1070, U. Maurer (ed.), Springer (1996) pp. 1–9.
10. R. Cramer, V. Shoup, A Practical Public Key Cryptosystem Provable Secure against Adaptive Chosen Ciphertext Attack, *Advances of Cryptology - Crypto '98, LNCS* 1462, H. Krawczyk (ed.), Springer (1998) pp. 13–25.
11. D. Dolev, C. Dwork, M. Naor, Non-malleable cryptography, In *23rd Annual ACM Symp. on Theory of Computing,* (1991) pp. 542–552.
12. R. Gennaro, A. Shamir, Partial Cryptanalysis of Koyama's Eurocrypt'95 scheme, LCS Technical Memo 512, May 10 (1996) MIT.
13. S. Goldwasser, S. Micali, Probabilistic Encryption, *Journal of Computer and System Sciences* 28 (April 1984) pp. 270–299.
14. S. Müller, Some Observations on Williams General Encryption Scheme, Some Remarks on Williams' Public Key Crypto Functions, Manuscripts, submitted, University of Klagenfurt (2000).
15. M. Naor, M. Yung, Public-key cryptosystems provably secure against chosen ciphertext attacks, In *22nd Annual ACM Symp. on Theory of Computing,* (1990) pp. 427–437.
16. T. Okamoto, S. Uchiyama, E. Fujisaki: EPOC: Efficient Probabilistic Public-Key Encryption, submission to P1363a (1998).
17. D. Pointcheval, Chosen-Ciphertext Security for any One-Way Cryptosystem, *PKC'2000*, H. Imai, Y. Zheng (eds.), Springer (2000).
18. M. O. Rabin: Digitalized signatures and public-key functions as intractable as factorization. MIT/LCS/TR-212, MIT Laboratory for Computer Science, 1979.
19. C. Rackoff, D. Simon, Non-interactive zero-knowledge proofs of knowledge and chosen ciphertext attack, *Advances in Cryptology - Crypto'91, LNCS*, 576, Springer (1991).

20. C.P. Schnorr, M. Jakobsson, Security of Signed ElGamal Encryption, To appear, Asiacrypt'00.

21. V. Shoup, Using Hash Functions as a Hedge against Chosen Ciphertext Attack, `http://philby.ucsd.edu/cryptolib/1999.html` (1999).

22. Y. Tsiounis, M. Yung, On the security of ElGamal-based encryption, *PKC'98*, LNCS 1431, Springer (1998), pp. 117-134. `www.ccs.neu.edu/home/yiannis/pubs.html`.

23. H.C. Williams, Some Public-Key Crypto-Functions as Intractable as Factorization, *Cryptologia* 9 (1985) pp. 223-237.

24. H.C. Williams, A $p + 1$ method of factoring. *Math. Comp.* **39**, no. 159 (1982) pp. 225–234.

25. H.C. Williams, "Édouard Lucas and Primality Testing", Canadian Mathematical Society Series of Monographs and Advanced Texts, Vol. 22 (1998), John Wiley & Sons.

26. Y. Zheng, J. Seberry, Immunizing public key cryptosystems against chosen ciphertext attacks, *IEEE Journal on Selected Areas in Communications*, Vol. 11, No. 5 (1993) pp. 715–724.

Semantically Secure
McEliece Public-Key Cryptosystems
–Conversions for McEliece PKC–

Kazukuni Kobara and Hideki Imai

Institute of Industrial Science, The University of Tokyo
Roppongi, Minato-ku, Tokyo 106, Japan
TEL : +81-3-3402-6231 Ext 2327
FAX : +81-3-3402-7365
{kobara,imai}@iis.u-tokyo.ac.jp

Abstract. Almost all of the current public-key cryptosystems (PKCs) are based on number theory, such as the integer factoring problem and the discrete logarithm problem (which will be solved in polynomial-time after the emergence of quantum computers). While the McEliece PKC is based on another theory, i.e. coding theory, it is vulnerable against several practical attacks. In this paper, we carefully review currently known attacks to the McEliece PKC, and then point out that, without any decryption oracles or any partial knowledge on the plaintext of the challenge ciphertext, no polynomial-time algorithm is known for inverting the McEliece PKC whose parameters are carefully chosen. Under the assumption that this inverting problem is hard, we propose slightly modified versions of McEliece PKC that can be proven, in the random oracle model, to be semantically secure against adaptive chosen-ciphertext attacks. Our conversions can achieve the reduction of the redundant data down to $1/3 \sim 1/4$ compared with the generic conversions for practical parameters.

1   Introduction

Since the concept of public-key cryptosystem (PKC) was introduced by Diffie and Hellman [5], many researchers have proposed numerous PKCs based on various problems, such as integer factoring, discrete logarithm, decoding a large linear code, knapsack, inverting polynomial equations and so on. While some of them are still alive, most of them were broken by cryptographers due to their intensive cryptanalysis. As a result, almost all of the current (so-called) secure systems employ only a small class of PKCs, such as RSA and elliptic curve cryptosystems, which are all based on either integer factoring problem (IFP) or discrete logarithm problem (DLP). This situation would cause a serious problem after someone discovers one practical algorithm which breaks both IFP and DLP in polynomial-time. No one can say that such an algorithm will never be found. Actually, Shor has already found a (probabilistic) polynomial-time algorithm in [25], even though it requires a quantum computer that is impractical so far. In

K. Kim (Ed.): PKC 2001, LNCS 1992, pp. 19–35, 2001.

order to prepare for that unfortunate situation, we need to find another secure scheme relying on neither IFP nor DLP.

The McEliece PKC, proposed by R.J. McEliece in [18], is one of few alternatives[1] for PKCs based on IFP or DLP. It is based on the decoding problem of a large linear code with no visible structure which is conjectured to be an NP-complete problem.[2] While no polynomial-time algorithm has been discovered yet for decoding an arbitrary linear code of large length with no visible structure, a lot of attacks (some of them work in polynomial-time) are known to the McEliece PKC [1,3,4,12,15,28,17,13].

In this paper, we carefully review these attacks in Section 3, and then point out that all the polynomial-time attacks to the McEliece PKC require either decryption oracles or partial knowledge on the corresponding plaintext of the challenge ciphertext. And then without them, no polynomial-time attack is known to invert the McEliece PKC (whose parameters are carefully chosen). Under the assumption that this inverting problem is hard, we convert this problem into semantically secure McEliece PKCs against adaptive chosen-ciphertext attacks (CCA2) by introducing some appropriate conversions. We discuss which conversions are appropriate for the McEliece PKC in Section 4. While some of the generic conversions proposed in [24,9] are also applicable to the McEliece PKC, they have a disadvantage in data redundancy (which is defined by the difference between the ciphertext size and the plaintext size). A large amount of redundant data is needed for the generic conversions since the block size of the McEliece PKC is relatively large. Our conversions in Section 4.4 need less redundant data than the generic ones.

2   McEliece Public-Key Cryptosystem

In this section, we briefly describe the McEliece PKC.

Key generation: Generate the following three matrices G,S,P:

G: $k \times n$ generator matrix of a binary Goppa code which can correct up to t errors, and for which an efficient decoding algorithm is known. The parameter t is given by $\lceil \frac{d_{min}-1}{2} \rceil$ where d_{min} denotes the minimum Hamming distance of the code.

S: $k \times k$ random binary non-singular matrix

P: $n \times n$ random permutation matrix.

Then, compute the $k \times n$ matrix $G' = SGP$.

Secret key: (S,G,P)

Public key: (G',t)

Encryption: The ciphertext c of a message m is calculated as follows:

$$c = mG' \oplus z \tag{1}$$

---

[1]   Another alternative may be a quantum public-key cryptosystem [21] which will be available after the emergence of quantum computers.

[2]   The complete decoding problem of an arbitrary linear code is proven to be NP-complete in [29].

where m is represented in a binary vector of length k, and z denotes a random binary error vector of length n having t 1's.

Decryption: First, calculate cP^{-1}

$$cP^{-1} = (mS)G \oplus zP^{-1} \tag{2}$$

where P^{-1} denotes the inverse of P. Second, apply the decoding algorithm EC for G to cP^{-1}. Since the Hamming weight of zP^{-1} is t, one can obtain mS

$$mS = \mathrm{EC}(cP^{-1}). \tag{3}$$

The plaintext of c is given by

$$m = (mS)S^{-1}. \tag{4}$$

3   Attacks to McEliece PKC

In this section, we review currently known attacks to the McEliece PKC.

While no efficient algorithm has been discovered yet for decomposing G' into (S, G, P) [19], a structural attack has been discovered in [17]. This attack reveals part of structure of a weak G' which is generated from a "binary" Goppa polynomial. However, this attack can be avoided simply by avoiding the use of such weak public keys. (This implies G should not be a BCH code since it is equivalent to a Goppa code whose Goppa polynomial is $1 \cdot x^{2t}$, i.e. "binary". [3]) Next case we have to consider is that an equivalent Goppa code of G' (which is not necessarily G) and whose decoding algorithm is known happens to be found. This probability is estimated in [1][10], and then shown to be negligibly small.

All the other known attacks are for decrypting ciphertexts without breaking public-keys. We categorize them into the following two categories, critical attacks and non-critical attacks, according to whether these attacks can be avoided simply by enlarging the parameter size or not. If avoided, we categorize it in the non-critical attacks. Otherwise, in the critical ones. Interestingly, all the critical attacks require either additional information, such as partial knowledge on the target plaintexts, or an decryption oracle which can decrypt arbitrarily given ciphertexts except the challenge ciphertexts. And then without this additional information and this ability, no efficient algorithm is known to decrypt an arbitrarily given ciphertext of the McEliece PKC.

3.1   Non-critical Attacks

The following two attacks can be avoided simply by enlarging the parameter size or by applying Loidreau's modification [16] without enlarging the parameter size. Thus, not critical.

---

[3] In [14], a variant of McEliece PKC, where G is a BCH code, was broken. However it is not clear their attack works correctly since further information has failed to appear.

Generalized Information-Set-Decoding Attack. Let G'_k, c_k and z_k denote the k columns picked from G', c and z, respectively. They have the following relationship

$$c_k = mG'_k \oplus z_k. \tag{5}$$

If $z_k = 0$ and G'_k is non-singular, m can be recovered by [1]

$$m = c_k G'^{-1}_k. \tag{6}$$

Even if $z_k \neq 0$, m can be recovered by guessing z_k among small Hamming weights [15] (we call this the generalized information-set-decoding (GISD) attack). The correctness of the recovered plaintext m is verifiable by checking whether the Hamming weight of $c \oplus mG'$ is t or not.

The computational cost of this generalized version (where z_k is guessed) is slightly faster than the original one (where z_k is supposed to be 0), but it is still infeasible for appropriate parameters since its computational cost is asymptotically lower bounded by $C(n,k)/C(n-t,k)$.

Finding-Low-Weight-Codeword Attack. This attack uses an algorithm which finds a low-weight codeword among codewords generated by an arbitrary generator matrix using a database obtained by pre-computation [26,4]. Since the minimum-weight codeword of the following $(k+1) \times n$ generator matrix

$$\begin{bmatrix} G' \\ c \end{bmatrix} \tag{7}$$

is the error vector z of c where $c = mG' \oplus z$, this algorithm can be used to recover m from a given ciphertext c.

The precise computational cost of this attack is evaluated in [4], and then shown to be infeasible to invert c for appropriate parameters, e.g. $n \geq 2048$ and optimized k and t, even though the original parameters $(n,k,t) = (1024, 524, 50)$ suggested in [18] is feasible with the work factor of $2^{64.2}$. (Under the assumption that each iteration is independent, the expected computational cost of this attack is asymptotically lower bounded by $C(n,k+1)/C(n-t,k+1)$ and therefore it is infeasible for appropriate parameters.)

3.2   Critical Attacks

The following attacks cannot be avoided by enlarging the parameter size or by applying Loidreau's modification [16]. Therefore critical.

Known-Partial-Plaintext Attack. The partial knowledge on the target plaintext drastically reduces the computational cost of the attacks to the McEliece PKC [4,13].

For example, let m_l and m_r denote the left k_l bits and the remaining k_r bits in the target plaintext m, i.e. $k = k_l + k_r$ and $m = (m_l || m_r)$. Suppose that an adversary knows m_r. Then the difficulty of recovering unknown plaintext m_l in the McEliece PKC with parameters (n, k) is equivalent to that of recovering the full plaintext in the McEliece PKC with parameters (n, k_l) since

$$c = mG' \oplus z$$
$$c = m_l G'_l \oplus m_r G'_r \oplus z$$
$$c \oplus m_r G'_r = m_l G'_l \oplus z$$
$$c' = m_l G'_l \oplus z, \tag{8}$$

where G'_l and G'_r are the upper k_l rows and the remaining lower k_r rows in G', respectively.

If k_l is fixed to a small value, the computational cost of recovering the unknown k_l bits from c, m_r and G' is a polynomial of n since even if non-critical attacks are used, it is asymptotically bounded by $k_l^3 C(n, k_l)/C(n - t, k_l)$ where k_l is a small constant.

Related-Message Attack. This attack uses the knowledge on the relationship between the target plaintexts [3].

Suppose two messages m_1 and m_2 are encrypted to c_1 and c_2, respectively, where $c_1 = m_1 G' \oplus z_1$, $c_2 = m_2 G' \oplus z_2$, and $z_1 \neq z_2$. If an adversary knows their linear relation between the plaintexts, e.g. $\delta m = m_1 \oplus m_2$. Then the adversary can efficiently apply the GISD attack to either c_1 or c_2 by choosing k coordinates whose values are 0 in $(\delta m G' \oplus c_1 \oplus c_2)$. Since $z_1 \oplus z_2 = \delta m G' \oplus c_1 \oplus c_2$ and the Hamming weight t of the error vector z is far smaller than $n/2$. Therefore a coordinate being 0 in $(\delta m G' \oplus c_1 \oplus c_2)$ should also be 0 in both z_1 and z_2 with the high probability of

When the same message is encrypted twice (or more) using different error vectors z_1 and z_2, the value $z_1 \oplus z_2$ is simply given by $c_1 \oplus c_2$. This case is referred to as the message-resend attack [3].

Reaction Attack. This attack might be categorized as a chosen-ciphertext attack (CCA), but uses a weaker assumption [12] than the CCA: the adversary observes only the reaction of the receiver who has the private-key, but does not need to receive its decrypted plaintext. (Similar attack is independently proposed in [28]. In this attack, an adversary receives the corresponding plaintexts. Therefore this attack is categorized as a CCA.)

The idea of this attack is the following. The adversary flips one or a few bits of the target ciphertext c. Let c' denote the flipped ciphertext. The adversary transmits c' to the proper receiver and observes his/her reaction. The receiver's reactions can be divided into the following two:

Reaction A: Return a repeat request to the adversary due to uncorrectable error or due to the meaningless plaintext.

Reaction B: Return an acknowledgment or do nothing since the proper plaintext m is decrypted.

If the total weight of the error vector does not exceed t after the flipping, the reaction B is observed. Otherwise the reaction A is observed. Therefore by repeating the above observations polynomial times of n, the adversary can determine the error vector. Once the error vector is determined, the corresponding plaintext is easily decrypted using the GISD attack.

Malleability Attack. This attack allows an adversary to alter any part of the corresponding plaintext of any given ciphertext c without knowing the plaintext m, i.e. the adversary can generate a new ciphertext c' whose plaintext is $m' = m \oplus \delta m$ from any given ciphertext c without knowing m [13,28].

This attack is described as follows. Let $G'[i]$ denote the i-th row of the public matrix G' and $I = \{i_1, i_2, \cdots\}$ denote a set of coordinates i_j whose value is 1 in δm. The ciphertext c' is calculated by

$$c' = c \bigoplus_{i \in I} G'[i] = (m \oplus \delta m)G' \oplus z = m'G' \oplus z. \tag{9}$$

This attack tells us that the McEliece PKC does not satisfy non-malleability[6] even against passive attacks, such as chosen-plaintext attacks. And then under chosen-ciphertext scenario where an adversary can ask an decryption oracle to decrypt a polynomial number of ciphertexts (excluding the challenge ciphertext c), the adversary can decrypt any given ciphertext c by the following way. First the adversary asks the oracle to decrypt c', then the oracle returns $m' = m \oplus \delta m$. Thus he/she can recover the target plaintext of c by $m = m' \oplus \delta m$.

4   Conversions for McEliece PKC

As mentioned in Section 3, without any decryption oracles and any partial knowledge on the corresponding plaintext of the challenge ciphertext, no polynomial-time algorithm is known for inverting the McEliece PKC (whose parameters are carefully chosen). Under the assumption that this inverting problem is hard, this problem can be converted into the hard problem of breaking the indistinguishability of encryption against critical attacks (or more generally against adaptive chosen-ciphertext attacks) by introducing appropriate conversions in the random oracle mode. In this section, we discuss which conversions are appropriate for the McEliece PKC and which are not.

4.1   Notations

We use the following notations in this paper:

$C(n,t)$: The number of combinations taking t out of n elements.

$Prep(m)$: Preprocessing to a message m, such as data-compression, data-padding and so on. Its inverse is represented as $Prep^{-1}()$.

$Hash(x)$: One-way hash function of an arbitrary length binary string x to a fixed length binary string. When the output domain is Z_N where $N = C(n,t)$, we use $Hash_z(x)$ instead of $Hash(x)$.

$Conv(\bar{z})$: Bijective function which converts an integer $\bar{z} \in Z_N$ where $N = C(n,t)$ into the corresponding error vector z. Its inverse is represented as $Conv^{-1}()$.

$Gen(x)$: Generator of a cryptographically secure pseudo random sequences of arbitrary length from a fixed length seed x.

$Len(x)$: Bit-length of x.

$Msb_{x_1}(x_2)$: The left x_1 bits of x_2.

$Lsb_{x_1}(x_2)$: The right x_1 bits of x_2.

$Const$: Predetermined constant used in public.

$Rand$: Random source which generates a truly random (or computationally indistinguishable pseudo random) sequence.

$\mathcal{E}^{McEliece}(x, z)$: Encryption of x using the original McEliece PKC with an error vector z.

$\mathcal{D}^{McEliece}(x)$: Decryption of x using the original McEliece PKC.

4.2   Insufficient Conversions for McEliece PKC

OAEP Conversion. In [2], Bellar and Rogaway proposed a generic conversion called OAEP (Optimal Asymmetric Encryption Padding) which converts a OWTP (One-Way Trapdoor Permutation), such as RSA primitive, into a PKC which is indistinguishable against adaptive chosen-ciphertext attacks (CCA2). The McEliece PKC with this OAEP conversion is given in Fig.1.[4] Unfortunately, this conversion does not work correctly since the reaction attack is still applicable. This does not mean the OAEP conversion has a fault, but the McEliece primitive is not a permutation.

Fujisaki-Okamoto's Simple Conversion. In [8], Fujisaki and Okamoto proposed a generic and simple conversion from a PKC which is indistinguishable against CPA (Chosen-Plaintext Attacks) into a PKC which is indistinguishable against CCA2. The McEliece PKC with this conversion is given in Fig.2.[4] Unfortunately, this conversion does not work correctly since the known-partial-plaintext attack efficiently works unless $Len(r)$ is close to k.

This does not mean Fujisaki-Okamoto's simple conversion has a fault, but the original McEliece PKC is distinguishable even against CPA. Any passive adversary (who do not use decryption oracle) can guess which message of m_0 and m_1 corresponding plaintext of the given ciphertext $\bar{c}$ of the original McEliece PKC by seeing whether the Hamming weight of $m_b G' \oplus \bar{c}$ is t or not, where $b \in \{0,1\}$.

---

[4] Due to the limitation of pages, we omit the corresponding decryption process.

Encryption of m:

$$r, \bar{z} := Rand$$
$$\bar{m} := Prep(m)$$
$$y_1 := (\bar{m}||Const) \oplus Gen(r)$$
$$y_2 := r \oplus Hash(y_1)$$
$$z := Conv(\bar{z})$$
$$c := \mathcal{E}^{McEliece}((y_1||y_2), z)$$
$$\text{return} \quad c$$

Fig. 1. OAEP conversion + McEliece PKC

Encryption of m:

$$r := Rand$$
$$\bar{m} := Prep(m)$$
$$z := Conv(Hash_z(\bar{m}||r))$$
$$c := \mathcal{E}^{McEliece}((\bar{m}||r), z)$$
$$\text{return} \quad c$$

Fig. 2. Fujisaki-Okamoto's simple conversion + McEliece PKC

Encryption of m:

$$r, r' := Rand$$
$$\bar{m} := Prep(m)$$
$$z := Conv(Hash_z(\bar{m}||r))$$
$$y_1 := \mathcal{E}^{McEliece}(r', z)$$
$$y_2 := Gen(r') \oplus (\bar{m}||r)$$
$$c := y_1||y_2$$
$$\text{return} \quad c$$

Fig. 3. Pointcheval's generic conversion

Encryption of m:

$$r := Rand$$
$$\bar{m} := Prep(m)$$
$$z := Conv(Hash_z(\bar{m}||r))$$
$$y_1 := \mathcal{E}^{McEliece}(r, z)$$
$$y_2 := Gen(r) \oplus \bar{m}$$
$$c := y_1||y_2$$
$$\text{return} \quad c$$

Fig. 4. Fujisaki-Okamoto's generic conversion

4.3   Generic Conversions Being Applicable to McEliece PKC

Pointcheval's Generic Conversion. In [24], Pointcheval proposed a generic conversion from a PTOWF (Partially Trapdoor One-Way Function) to a PKC which is indistinguishable against CCA2.

The definition for $f(x, y)$ to be PTOWF is the following:

– For any polynomial-time adversary and for any given $z = f(x, y)$, it is computationally infeasible to get back the partial preimage x,
– With some extra secret information, it is easy to get back the x.

Not only ElGamal[7], Okamoto-Uchiyama[22], Naccache-Stern[20] and Paillier[23] primitives, but also McEliece primitive can be categorized in PTOWF. Therefore Pointcheval's generic conversion is also applicable to the McEliece PKC with the same proof in [24]. The McEliece PKC with this conversion is given in Fig.3.[4]

Fujisaki-Okamoto's Generic Conversion. In [9], Fujisaki and Okamoto proposed a generic conversion from OWE (One-Way Encryption), which includes both OWTP and PTOWF, into a PKC being indistinguishable against ACC2.

Encryption of m:	Decryption of c:
$r := Rand$	$y_1 := \mathcal{D}^{McEliece}(Msb_n(c))$
$\bar{m} := Prep(m)$	$z := Msb_n(c) \oplus y_1 G'$
$\bar{z} := Hash_z(r\|\|\bar{m})$	$\bar{z} := Conv^{-1}(z)$
$(y_1\|\|y_2) := Gen(\bar{z}) \oplus (r\|\|\bar{m})$	$(r\|\|\bar{m}) := Gen(\bar{z}) \oplus (y_1\|\|y_2)$
$z := Conv(\bar{z})$	If $\quad \bar{z}=Hash_z(r\|\|\bar{m})$
$c := \mathcal{E}^{McEliece}(y_1, z)\|\|y_2$	$\quad$ return $Prep^{-1}(\bar{m})$
$\quad$ return $\quad c$	Otherwise $\quad$ reject c

Fig. 5. Conversion α : $Len(y_1) = k$ and $Len(y_2) = Len(r\|\|\bar{m}) - k$. If $Len(r\|\|\bar{m}) = k$, remove y_2.

Needless to say, McEliece primitive can be categorized in the OWE, and therefore their generic conversion is applicable to the McEliece PKC with the same proof in [9]. The McEliece PKC with this conversion[5] is given in Fig.4.[4]

4.4 Our Specific Conversions

While one can design semantically-secure McEliece PKCs by simply employing the above generic conversions, they are not necessarily suited for the McEliece PKC. Since the block size of the McEliece PKC is larger than the well-known PKCs, such as RSA, elliptic curve cryptosystems and so on, the redundancy of data (which is defined by the difference between the bit length of a plaintext and its corresponding ciphertext) becomes large. For example, for $(n, k) = (4096, 2560)$, the generic conversions require more than or equal to 4096 bits for the overhead data. On the other hand, our conversions described in Fig. 5 $\sim$ 7 require less overhead data than the generic ones. For example, for the same settings and $Len(r) = 160$ and $Len(Const) = 160$, our conversion γ requires only 1040 bits. (This might still be large but interestingly this value is smaller than the original McEliece PKC.) The comparison results are summarized in Table 1.

The point of the conversion γ is that not only a plaintext but also an error vector is taken from a part of y_1 (or $(y_2\|\|y_1)$). This reduces the data overhead even than the original McEliece PKC when $Len(r) + Len(Const) < \lfloor \log_2 C(n,t) \rfloor$. The study to reduce the overhead data (and simultaneously to improve the security against related-message attacks) has been performed in [27]. While his conversions do not provide provable security against CCA2 (since either known-partial-plaintext attacks or reaction attacks are applicable at least), his approach to reduce the overhead data should be appreciated.

Indistinguishability of Our Conversions. It is intuitively clear that our conversions resist all the critical attacks in Section 3.2 since it is hard for ad-

---

[5] They originally proposed to use symmetric encryption (instead of $Gen(r)$). The conversion described here is a variant mentioned in [9].

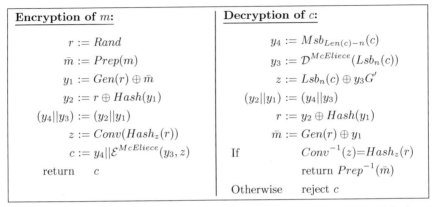

Encryption of m:	Decryption of c:
$r := Rand$	$y_4 := Msb_{Len(c)-n}(c)$
$\bar{m} := Prep(m)$	$y_3 := \mathcal{D}^{McEliece}(Lsb_n(c))$
$y_1 := Gen(r) \oplus \bar{m}$	$z := Lsb_n(c) \oplus y_3 G'$
$y_2 := r \oplus Hash(y_1)$	$(y_2||y_1) := (y_4||y_3)$
$(y_4||y_3) := (y_2||y_1)$	$r := y_2 \oplus Hash(y_1)$
$z := Conv(Hash_z(r))$	$\bar{m} := Gen(r) \oplus y_1$
$c := y_4||\mathcal{E}^{McEliece}(y_3, z)$	If $\quad Conv^{-1}(z)=Hash_z(r)$
return $\quad c$	return $Prep^{-1}(\bar{m})$
	Otherwise $\quad$ reject c

Fig. 6. Conversion β : $Len(y_3) = k$ and $Len(y_4) = Len(r||\bar{m}) - k$ If $Len(r||\bar{m}) = k$, remove y_4.

Encryption of m:	Decryption of c:
$r := Rand$	$y_5 := Msb_{Len(c)-n}(c)$
$\bar{m} := Prep(m)$	$y_3 := \mathcal{D}^{McEliece}(Lsb_n(c))$
$y_1 := Gen(r) \oplus (\bar{m}||Const)$	$z := y_3 G' \oplus Lsb_n(c)$
$y_2 := r \oplus Hash(y_1)$	$\bar{z} := Conv^{-1}(z)$
$(y_5||y_4||y_3) := (y_2||y_1)$	$y_4 := Lsb_{\lfloor \log_2 C(n,t) \rfloor}(\bar{z})$
$z := Conv(y_4)$	$(y_2||y_1) := (y_5||y_4||y_3)$
$c := y_5||\mathcal{E}^{McEliece}(y_3, z)$	$r := y_2 \oplus Hash(y_1)$
return $\quad c$	$(\bar{m}||Const') := y_1 \oplus Gen(r)$
	If $\quad Const'=Const$
	return $Prep^{-1}(\bar{m})$
	Otherwise $\quad$ reject c

Fig. 7. Conversion γ : $Len(y_3) = k$, $Len(y_4) = \lfloor \log_2 C(n,t) \rfloor$, $Len(y_5) = Len(\bar{m}) + Len(Const) + Len(r) - Len(y_4) - k$. If $Len(\bar{m}) + Len(Const) + Len(r) = Len(y_4) + k$, remove y_5.

versaries to abuse decryption oracles because of the difficulty of generating an appropriate ciphertext without knowing its plaintext, and to guess the input to the original McEliece PKC in our conversions even if they know the plaintext to our conversions.

More formally, the following theorem is true for our conversions in the random oracle model (where Gen, $Hash$ and $Hash_z$ are assumed to be ideal).

Theorem 1 *To break the indistinguishability of encryption of our specific conversions in an adaptive-chosen-ciphertext scenario is polynomial equivalent to decrypt the whole plaintext of an arbitrarily given ciphertext of the original McEliece PKC without any help of decryption oracles and any knowledge on the target plaintext.*

Table 1. Comparison between Data Redundancy and Conversions

Conversion Scheme	Conversion Type	Complexity*2 $\geq 2^{56.3}$ $\geq 2^{101.9}$ $\geq 2^{186.2}$		
		Data Redundancy*1 = Ciphertext Size - Plaintext Size		
		(n,k)	$(1024, 644)$	$(2048, 1289)$	$(4096, 2560)$
		t	38	69	128
Pointcheval's [24]	Generic	$n + Len(r)$	1184	2208	4256
Fujisaki -Okamoto's [9]	Generic	n	1024	2048	4096
Our proposal α and β	Specific	$n - k + Len(r)$	540	919	1696
Our proposal γ	Specific	$n - k + Len(r)$ $+ Len(Const)$ $- \lfloor \log_2 C(n,t) \rfloor$	470	648	1040
Original McEliece	None	n-k	380	759	1536

*1: The numerical results are obtained under the setting that $Len(r) = 160$ and $Len(Const) = 160$.

*2: The asymptotic lower bound of the expected number of iterations to invert an arbitrary ciphertext of the original McEliece PKC using the finding-low-weight-codeword attack. The exact complexity is estimated in [4].

Note that, as mentioned in Section 3, it is still infeasible to decrypt the whole plaintext of an arbitrarily given ciphertext of the original McEliece PKC with appropriate parameters (without any help of decryption oracles and any knowledge on the target plaintext).

This theorem can be proven, in the random oracle model, by showing how to construct an algorithm which decrypts an arbitrary ciphertext of the original McEliece PKC using an algorithm which distinguishes a ciphertext of our converted versions in the adaptive-chosen-ciphertext scenario. (It is obvious that an algorithm, which can decrypt the original McEliece PKC, can also distinguish a ciphertext of our converted versions.) Details are described in Appendix A.

5   Conclusion

We carefully reviewed the currently known attacks to the McEliece PKC, and then confirmed that, without any decryption oracles and any partial knowledge on the corresponding plaintext of the challenge ciphertext, no polynomial-time algorithm is known for inverting the McEliece PKC whose parameters are carefully chosen. Under the assumption that this inverting problem is hard, we investigated, in the random oracle mode, how to convert this hard problem into the hard problem of breaking the indistinguishability of encryption with CCA2. While some of the generic conversions are applicable to the McEliece PKC, they have a disadvantage in data redundancy. A large amount of redundant data is needed for the generic conversions since the block size of the McEliece PKC is relatively large. Our specific conversions can achieve the reduction of the redundant data down to $1/3 \sim 1/4$ compared with the generic conversions for practical parameters. This means about 3K bits can be saved for $n = 4096$, with providing semantic security against CCA2.

Acknowledgments

The authors would like to thank Hung-Min Sun, Pierre Loidreau, Kwangjo Kim and Yuliang Zheng for useful discussions and comments.

References

1. C. M. Adams and H. Meijer. "Security-Related Comments Regarding McEliece's Public-Key Cryptosystem". In *Proc. of CRYPTO '87, LNCS 293*, pages 224–228. Springer–Verlag, 1988.
2. M. Bellare and P. Rogaway. "Optimal Asymmetric Encryption". In *Proc. of EUROCRYPT '94, LNCS 950*, pages 92–111, 1995.
3. T. Berson. "Failure of the McEliece Public-Key Cryptosystem Under Message-Resend and Related-Message Attack". In *Proc. of CRYPTO '97, LNCS 1294*, pages 213–220. Springer–Verlag, 1997.
4. A. Canteaut and N. Sendrier. "Cryptoanalysis of the Original McEliece Cryptosystem". In *Proc. of ASIACRYPT '98*, pages 187–199, 1998.
5. W. Diffie and M. Hellman. "New directions in cryptography". *IEEE Trans. IT*, 22(6):644–654, 1976.
6. D. Dolve, C. Dwork, and M. Naor. "Non-Malleable Cryptography". In *Proc. of the 23rd STOC*. ACM Press, 1991.
7. T. ElGamal. "A public-key cryptosystem and a signature scheme bsed on discrete logarithms". In *Proc. of CRYPTO '84*, pages 10–18, 1985.
8. E. Fujisaki and T. Okamoto. "How to Enhance the Security of Public-Key Encryption at Minimum Cost". In *Proc. of PKC'99, LNCS 1560*, pages 53–68, 1999.
9. E. Fujisaki and T. Okamoto. "Secure Integration of Asymmetric and Symmetric Encryption Schemes". In *Proc. of CRYPTO '99, LNCS 1666*, pages 535–554, 1999.
10. J. K. Gibson. "Equivalent Goppa Codes and Trapdoors to McEliece's Public Key Cryptosystem". In *Proc. of EUROCRYPT '91, LNCS 547*, pages 517–521. Springer–Verlag, 1991.
11. S. Goldwasser and S. Micali. "Probabilistic encryption". *Journal of Computer and System Sciences*, pages 270–299, 1984.
12. C. Hall, I. Goldberg, and B. Schneier. "Reaction Attacks Against Several Public-Key Cryptosystems". In *Proc. of the 2nd International Conference on Information and Communications Security (ICICS'99), LNCS 1726*, pages 2–12, 1999.
13. K. Kobara and H. Imai. "Countermeasure against Reaction Attacks (in Japanese)". In *The 2000 Symposium on Cryptography and Information Security : A12*, January 2000.
14. V.I. Korzhik and A.I. Turkin. "Cryptanalysis of McEliece's Public-Key Cryptosystem". In *Proc. of EUROCRYPT '91, LNCS 547*, pages 68–70. Springer–Verlag, 1991.

15. P. J. Lee and E. F. Brickell. "An Observation on the Security of McEliece's Public-Key Cryptosystem". In *Proc. of EUROCRYPT '88, LNCS 330*, pages 275–280. Springer–Verlag, 1988.

16. P. Loidreau. "Strengthening McEliece Cryptosystem". In *Proc. of ASIACRYPT 2000*. Springer–Verlag, 2000.

17. P. Loidreau and N. Sendrier. "Some weak keys in McEliece public-key cryptosystem". In *Proc. of IEEE International Symposium on Information Theory, ISIT '98*, page 382, 1998.

18. R. J. McEliece. "A Public-Key Cryptosystem Based on Algebraic Coding Theory". In *Deep Space Network Progress Report*, 1978.

19. A. J. Menezes, P. C. Oorschot, and S. A. Vanstone. "McEliece public-key encryption". In *"Handbook of Applied Cryptography"*, page 299. CRC Press, 1997.

20. D. Naccache and J. Stern. "A New Cryptosystem based on Higher Residues". In *Proc. of the 5th CCS*, pages 59–66. ACM Press, 1998.

21. T. Okamoto, K. Tanaka, and S. Uchiyama. "Quantum Public-Key Cryptosystems". In *Proc. of CRYPTO 2000, LNCS 1880*, pages 147–165. Springer–Verlag, 2000.

22. T. Okamoto and S. Uchiyama. "A New Public Key Cryptosystem as Secure as Factoring". In *Proc. of EUROCRYPT '98, LNCS 1403*, pages 129–146, 1999.

23. P. Paillier. "Public-Key Cryptosystems Based on Discrete Logarithms Residues". In *Proc. of EUROCRYPT '99, LNCS 1592*, pages 223–238. Springer–Verlag, 1999.

24. D. Pointcheval. "Chosen-Ciphertext Security for Any One-Way Cryptosystem". In *Proc. of PKC 2000, LNCS 1751*, pages 129–146. Springer–Verlag, 2000.

25. P.W. Shor. "Polynomial-Time Algorithms for Prime Factorization and Discrete Logarithms on a Quantum Computer". *SIAM Journal on Computing*, 26:1484–1509, 1997.

26. J. Stern. "A method for finding codewords of small weight". In *Proc. of Coding Theory and Applications , LNCS 388*, pages 106–113. Springer–Verlag, 1989.

27. H. M. Sun. "Improving the Security of the McEliece Public-Key Cryptosystem". In *Proc. of ASIACRYPT '98*, pages 200–213, 1998.

28. H. M. Sun. "Further Cryptanalysis of the McEliece Public-Key Cryptosystem". *IEEE Trans. on communication letters*, 4:18–19, 2000.

29. A. Vardy. "The Intractability of Computing the Minimum Distance of a Code". *IEEE Trans. on IT*, 43:1757–1766, 1997.

A   Proof of Theorem 1

A.1   Indistinguishability of Encryption

Recall a security notion called indistinguishability of encryption [11]. In this notion, an adversary $\mathcal{A}$ selects two distinct plaintexts m_0 and m_1 of the same length in the find stage, and then, in the guess stage, $\mathcal{A}$ is given c which is the encryption of m_b where b is either 0 or 1 with the probability of $1/2$. Then $\mathcal{A}$ tries to guess b. The advantage of $\mathcal{A}$ is defined by $2Pr(\text{Win}) - 1$ where $Pr(\text{Win})$ denotes the expected probability of $\mathcal{A}$ guessing b correctly. If $\mathcal{A}$ has a decryption oracle D (which decrypts any other ciphertexts than the target ciphertext c), it is called that this experiment is in the adaptive-chosen-ciphertext scenario. Otherwise, if $\mathcal{A}$ does not have it, it is called that this experiment is in the adaptive-chosen-plaintext scenario.

A.2   Random Oracle

A random oracle is an ideal hash or an ideal generator which returns truly random numbers distributed uniformly over the output region for a new query, but it returns the same value for the same query. On such random oracles, the following lemma is true.

Lemma 1 *Suppose that f is a random oracle. Then it is impossible to get any significant information on $f(x)$ without asking x to the oracle, even if one knows all the other outputs of f except one corresponding to x.*

It is obvious that Lemma 1 is true since the output value of f is truly random.

A.3   Adaptive-Chosen-Ciphertext Security

The proof of Theorem 1 for the conversion α is given by showing Lemma 3 is true. Before we show it, we prove Lemma 2 first.

Lemma 2 (Adaptive-Chosen-Plaintext Security) *Suppose that there exists, for any $Hash_z$ and any Gen, an algorithm $\mathcal{A}$ which accepts m_0, m_1 and c of conversion α where c is the ciphertext of m_b and $b \in \{0,1\}$, asks at most q_G queries to Gen, asks at most q_H queries to $Hash_z$, runs in at most t steps and guesses b with advantage of ϵ. Then one can design an algorithm $\mathcal{B}$ which accepts a ciphertext $\bar{c}$ of the original McEliece PKC, runs in t' steps and decrypts it with probability ϵ' where*

$$\epsilon' \geq \epsilon - \frac{q_H}{2^{Len(r)+1}},$$

$$t' = t + Poly(n, q_G, q_H)$$

and $Poly(n, q_G, q_H)$ denotes a polynomial of n, q_G and q_H.

Proof.
    The algorithm $\mathcal{B}$ can be constructed as follows. First the algorithm $\mathcal{B}$ simulates both Gen and $Hash_z$ referred by the algorithm $\mathcal{A}$. From the assumption of $\mathcal{A}$ in Lemma 2, $\mathcal{A}$ must be able to distinguish b with the advantage of ϵ for any Gen and any $Hash_z$ as long as the algorithm $\mathcal{B}$ simulates them correctly. Then, $\mathcal{B}$ chooses b, r and y_2 at random, and then defines both $Hash_z$ and Gen so that the ciphertext of $(r||m_b)$ should be $(\bar{c}||y_2)$ where $\bar{c}$ is a ciphertext of the original McEliece PKC which $\mathcal{B}$ wants to decrypt. That is,

$$Gen(\bar{z}) \stackrel{\text{def}}{=} (r||m_b) \oplus (y_1||y_2) \tag{10}$$

$$Hash_z(r||m_b) \stackrel{\text{def}}{=} Conv^{-1}(z) = \bar{z}. \tag{11}$$

For the other queries than $\bar{z}$ to Gen and $(r||m_b)$ to $Hash_z$, they return random values, respectively. Even for these Gen and $Hash_z$, $\mathcal{A}$ must be able to distinguish b with the advantage of ϵ from the assumption in Lemma 2 as long as $\mathcal{B}$ simulates them correctly.[6]

---

[6] If $\mathcal{A}$ distinguishes b only for certain combinations of $Hash_z$ and Gen, then the fault must be in either Gen or $Hash_z$ or in both used in the combinations, and therefore

Then, can $\mathcal{B}$ simulate them correctly for any queries? The answer is no since $\mathcal{B}$ does not know $\bar{z}$, and therefore $\mathcal{B}$ cannot simulate $Hash_z$ correctly when $(r\|m_b)$ is asked to $Hash_z$. We define the following two events AskG and AskH.

Definition 1 *Let AskG denote the event that $\bar{z}$ is asked to Gen among the q_G queries to Gen and this query is performed before $(r\|m_b)$ is asked to $Hash_z$. Let AskH denote the event that $(r\|m_b)$ is asked to $Hash_z$ among the q_H queries to $Hash_z$ and this query is performed before $\bar{z}$ is asked to Gen.*

Since $Pr(\text{AskG} \wedge \text{AskH}) = 0$ in this definition, the following holds

$$Pr(\text{AskG} \vee \text{AskH}) = Pr(\text{AskG}) + Pr(\text{AskH}). \tag{12}$$

Next, we estimate the upper-limit of $Pr(\text{Win})$, the probability of $\mathcal{A}$ guessing b correctly. From Lemma 1, without asking either $\bar{z}$ to Gen or asking $(r\|m_b)$ to $hash_z$, one cannot get any information on the connectivity between $(z, y_1\|y_2)$ and $(r\|m_b)$, and therefore cannot guess b with a significant probability after the event $(\neg\text{AskG}\wedge\neg\text{AskH})$. After the other event, i.e. after the event $(\text{AskG}\vee\text{AskH})$, $\mathcal{A}$ might guess b with more significant probability. By assuming this probability to be 1, the upper-limit of $Pr(\text{Win})$ is obtained as follows:

$$Pr(\text{Win}) \leq Pr(\text{AskG} \vee \text{AskH}) + \frac{(1 - Pr(\text{AskG} \vee \text{AskH}))}{2}$$
$$\leq \frac{Pr(\text{AskG} \vee \text{AskH}) + 1}{2}. \tag{13}$$

From the definition of advantage, i.e. $Pr(\text{Win}) = (\epsilon + 1)/2$, the following relationship holds

$$Pr(\text{AskG} \vee \text{AskH}) \geq \epsilon. \tag{14}$$

Since both r and b are chosen at random by $\mathcal{B}$, $\mathcal{A}$ cannot know them without asking $\bar{z}$ to Gen or asking $(r\|m_b)$ to $Hash_z$. Thus the probability of one query to $Hash_z$ accidentally being $(r\|m_b)$ is $1/2^{Len(r)+1}$, and then that of at most q_H queries is given by

$$Pr(\text{AskH}) \leq 1 - \left(1 - \frac{1}{2^{Len(r)+1}}\right)^{q_H} \leq \frac{q_H}{2^{Len(r)+1}}. \tag{15}$$

The algorithm $\mathcal{B}$ can simulate both Gen and $Hash_z$ correctly unless the event AskH happens. And then, after the event AskG, $\mathcal{B}$ can recover the whole plaintext of the target ciphertext $\bar{c}$ of the original McEliece PKC using $\bar{z}$ asked to $\mathcal{B}$. Thus, after the event $(\text{AskG} \wedge \neg\text{AskH})$, $\mathcal{B}$ can recover it. The lower-limit of this probability is given by

---

this fault can be easily removed just avoiding using the combinations. Otherwise, i.e. if $\mathcal{A}$ distinguishes b for any combinations of $Hash_z$ and Gen, the fault must be in the conversion structure.

$$Pr(\text{AskG} \wedge \neg \text{AskH}) = Pr(\text{AskG})$$
$$= Pr(\text{AskG} \vee \text{AskH}) - Pr(\text{AskH})$$
$$\geq \epsilon - \frac{q_H}{2^{Len(r)+1}} \tag{16}$$

from (12), (14) and (15).

The number of steps of $\mathcal{B}$ is at most $t + (T_{Dec} + T_G) \cdot q_G + T_H \cdot q_H$ where T_{Dec} is the number of steps for decrypting the original McEliece PKC using a new query to Gen as $\bar{z}$, T_G is both for checking whether a query to Gen is new or not and for returning the corresponding value, and T_H is both for checking whether a query to $Hash_z$ is new or not and for returning the corresponding value. Since these parameters, T_{Dec}, T_G and T_H can be written in a polynomial of n, q_G and q_H, the total number of steps of $\mathcal{B}$ is also written in a a polynomial of them.

$\square$

Lemma 3 (Adaptive-Chosen-Ciphertext Security) *Suppose that there exists, for any $Hash_z$ and Gen, an algorithm $\mathcal{A}$ which accepts m_0, m_1 and c of conversion α where c is the ciphertext of m_b and $b \in \{0, 1\}$, asks at most q_G queries to Gen, asks at most q_H queries to $Hash_z$, asks at most q_D queries to a decryption oracle D, runs in at most t steps and guesses b with advantage of ϵ. Then one can design an algorithm $\mathcal{B}$ which accepts a ciphertext $\bar{c}$ of the original McEliece PKC, runs in t' steps and decrypts it with probability ϵ' where*

$$\epsilon' \geq \epsilon - \frac{q_H}{2^{Len(r)+1}} - \frac{q_D}{C(n,t)},$$
$$t' = t + Poly(n, q_G, q_H, q_D)$$

and $Poly(n, q_G, q_H, q_D)$ denotes a polynomial of n, q_G, q_H and q_D.

Proof.

The algorithm $\mathcal{B}$ can be constructed as follows. First, the algorithm $\mathcal{B}$ simulates random oracles Gen, $Hash_z$ and the decryption oracle D referred by $\mathcal{A}$. As long as $\mathcal{B}$ simulates them correctly, $\mathcal{A}$ must be able to distinguish the given ciphertext with advantage of ϵ. How to simulate both Gen and $Hash_z$ is the same as in the proof of Lemma 2. The decryption oracle D can be simulated using the following plaintext-extractor [2]. The plaintext-extractor accepts a ciphertext, e.g. $(\bar{c}'||y_2')$ where $\bar{c}'$ denotes a ciphertext of the original McEliece PKC, and then outputs either the corresponding plaintext of $(\bar{c}'||y_2')$, or reject it as an inappropriate ciphertext.

Let g_i and G_i denote the i-th pair of query and its answer for Gen. And then let h_j and H_j denote the j-th pair of query and its answer for $Hash_z$. From the queries and the answers obtained while simulating Gen and $Hash_z$, the plaintext-extractor finds a pair of (g_i, G_i) and (h_j, H_j) satisfying $Conv(g_i) = z'$, $Conv(H_j) = z'$ and $G_i \oplus (y_1'||y_2') = h_j$ where y_1' and z' denote the plaintext and the error vector of $\bar{c}'$, respectively. If found, $\mathcal{B}$ outputs $Lsb_{Len(m')}(h_i)$ as the plaintext of $(\bar{c}'||y_2')$ where $Len(m') = Len(\bar{c}') + Len(y_2') - n + k - Len(r')$. Otherwise $\mathcal{B}$ rejects it as an inappropriate ciphertext.

The plaintext-extractor can simulate D unless $\mathcal{A}$ asks an appropriate ciphertext to D without asking both $\bar{z}'$ and $G_i \oplus (y_1'||y_2')$ to Gen and $Hash_z$, respectively. In this case, the plaintext-extractor rejects the appropriate ciphertext, and therefore does not simulate D correctly. However it is a small chance that $\mathcal{A}$ could generate an appropriate ciphertext without asking them. Since the definition of appropriate is to satisfy

$$Hash_z(Gen(\bar{z}') \oplus (y_1'||y_2')) = \bar{z}', \tag{17}$$

and it is impossible for $\mathcal{A}$ to know whether (17) is true or not without asking $\bar{z}'$ to Gen and asking $Gen(\bar{z}') \oplus (y_1'||y_2')$ to $Hash_z$, respectively, from Lemma 1.

We define AskD as the following event that at least one query out of at most q_D queries to D accidentally becomes an appropriate ciphertext before the queries used in (17) are asked. Since the probability of one query to D being accidentally an appropriate ciphertext is $1/C(n,t)$, the upper-limit of $Pr(\text{AskD})$ is given by

$$Pr(\text{AskD}) \le 1 - \left(1 - \frac{1}{C(n,t)}\right)^{q_D} \le \frac{q_D}{C(n,t)}. \tag{18}$$

Unless either AskD or AskH happens, $\mathcal{B}$ can correctly simulate the oracles referred by $\mathcal{A}$. In addition, when AskG happens, $\mathcal{B}$ can recover the whole plaintext of $\bar{c}$, the ciphertext of the original McEliece PKC. The lower-limit of this probability $Pr(\text{AskG} \wedge \neg\text{AskD} \wedge \neg\text{AskH})$ is given by

$$
\begin{aligned}
&Pr(\text{AskG} \wedge \neg\text{AskH} \wedge \neg\text{AskD}) \\
&= Pr(\text{AskG} \wedge \neg\text{AskH}) - Pr(\text{AskG} \wedge \neg\text{AskH} \wedge \text{AskD}) \\
&\ge Pr(\text{AskG} \wedge \neg\text{AskH}) - Pr(\text{AskD}) \\
&\ge \epsilon - \frac{q_H}{2^{Len(r)+1}} - \frac{q_D}{C(n,t)}.
\end{aligned} \tag{19}
$$

The number of steps of $\mathcal{B}$ is at most $t + (T_{Dec} + T_G) \cdot q_G + T_H \cdot q_H + T_D \cdot q_D$ where T_{Dec}, T_G and T_H are the same as the parameters in the proof of Lemma 2. The number of steps T_D is for the knowledge-extractor to verify whether (17) holds and then to return the result. Since these parameters, T_{Dec}, T_G, T_H and T_D can be written in a polynomial of n, q_G, q_H and q_D, the total number of steps of $\mathcal{B}$ is also written in a polynomial of them.

□

Using the similar discussion to the conversion α, the lower limit of ϵ's for conversions β and γ are given by

$$\epsilon' \ge \epsilon - \frac{(q_G + q_{H_z} + q_D)}{2^{Len(r)}} \tag{20}$$

and

$$\epsilon' \ge \epsilon - \frac{q_G}{2^{Len(r)}} - \frac{q_D}{2^{Len(Const)}}, \tag{21}$$

respectively.

IND-CCA Public Key Schemes Equivalent to Factoring $n = pq$

Kaoru Kurosawa, Wakaha Ogata, Toshihiko Matsuo, and Shuichi Makishima

Tokyo Institute of Technology,
2-12-1 O-okayama, Meguro-ku, Tokyo 152-8552, Japan
{kurosawa,wakaha,tossy,maxima}@ss.titech.ac.jp

Abstract. Indistinguishability against adaptive chosen ciphertext attack (IND-CCA2) is the strongest notion for security of public key schemes. In this paper, we present the first IND-CCA2 schemes whose securities are equivalent to factoring $n = pq$ under the random oracle model, where p and q are prime numbers. Our first scheme works for long messages and our second scheme is more efficient for short messages.

1 Introduction

Indistinguishability against adaptive chosen ciphertext attack (IND-CCA2) is the strongest notion of security for public key schemes. Bellare and Rogaway showed that a trapdoor one-way permutation f can be converted into a IND-CCA2 public key scheme in the random oracle model [1]. They further presented another IND-CCA2 scheme [2], called OAEP, which is more efficient than their first scheme for short messages.

RSA is believed to be a trapdoor one-way permutation. However, it is not known that inverting RSA is equivalent to factoring $n = pq$, where p and q are prime numbers.

On the other hand, Okamoto and Uchiyama showed a probabilistic public key scheme such that inverting the encryption function is equivalent to factoring a special modulus $n = p^2q$ [3]. Fujisaki, Okamoto and then Pointcheval showed some conversions of Okamoto and Uchiyama scheme into IND-CCA2 public key schemes in the random oracle model [4,5,6]. Paillier presented a trapdoor one-way permutation by modifying Okamoto and Uchiyama scheme [7].

Paillier presented a probabilistic public key scheme which is IND-CPA under the composite residuosity assumption [8, Sec.4], where IND-CPA stands for indistinguishability against chosen plaintext attack. Paillier also showed a variant of his scheme which is a trapdoor one-way permutation if and only if inverting RSA is hard [8, Sec.5]. Paillier and Pointcheval gave a conversion of Paillier's scheme [8, Sec.4] into a IND-CCA2 public key scheme in the random oracle model [9].

However, no IND-CCA2 scheme is known whose security is equivalent to factoring $n = pq$. In this paper, we present the first IND-CCA2 schemes whose

K. Kim (Ed.): PKC 2001, LNCS 1992, pp. 36–47, 2001.

securities are equivalent to factoring $n = pq$ in the random oracle model by using Kurosawa et al's public key cryptosystem. Our first scheme works for long messages. Our second scheme is more efficient for short messages.

Rabin's public key cryptosystem [10] is as hard as factorization. However, it is not uniquely deciphered because four different plaintexts produce the same cipher. Williams showed that this disadvantage can be overcome if the secret two prime numbers, p and q, satisfy $p = 3 \bmod 8, q = 7 \bmod 8$ [11]. Kurosawa et al. [12] showed a public key cryptosystem such that (i) inverting is equivalent to factoring $n = pq$, (ii) the decryption is unique and (iii) p and q are arbitrary prime numbers.

Related works: Cramer and Shoup showed an IND-CCA2 scheme in the standard model under the decision Diffie-Hellman problem [13]

2   Preliminaries

Let k be a security parameter. Let $n(k)$ denote the length of a plaintext, where $n(k)$ is bounded by some polynomial on k.

2.1   Definitions

Definition 1. *A public key encryption scheme with a plaintext length function* $n(\cdot)$ *is a triple of algorithms,* $\Pi = (\mathcal{G}, \mathcal{E}, \mathcal{D})$, *where*

- $\mathcal{G}$, *the key generation algorithm, is a probabilistic algorithm that takes a security parameter k and returns pair of (pk, sk) of matching public and secret keys,*
- $\mathcal{E}$, *the encryption algorithm, is a probabilistic algorithm that takes a public key pk and a message $x \in \{0,1\}^n$ to produce a ciphertext y,*
- $\mathcal{D}$, *the decryption algorithm, is a deterministic algorithm that takes a secret key sk and a ciphertext y to produce a message $x \in \{0,1\}^n$ or a special symbol $\perp$ to indicate that the ciphertext was invalid.*

Our goal is to construct an encryption scheme which is indistinguishable secure (or semantically secure). We consider an adversary $A = (A_1, A_2)$ who runs in two stages. In the find-stage A_1 is given an encryption algorithm $\mathcal{E}$ and outputs a pair (x_0, x_1) of messages. It also outputs some string str, for example, its history and its inputs. In the guess-stage A_2 is given the outputs of A_1, (x_0, x_1) and str, and also y which is a ciphertext of a message x_b for random bit b. A_2 guesses a bit b' from x_0, x_1 and y, and outputs a guessing bit b'.

A simple A_2 who always outputs 0 (or 1) can succeed guessing b with probability 1/2. This shows that the minimal probability with which any A_2 can outputs correct bit is 1/2. We measure how well A is doing by the difference between 1/2 and the probability in which A_2 can guess b correctly. Formally, we define the advantage of A as follows.

$$Adv_{A,\Pi}(k) \stackrel{\triangle}{=} |\Pr[(pk, sk) \leftarrow \mathcal{G}(1^k); (x_0, x_1, str) \leftarrow A_1(pk); b \leftarrow \{0,1\};$$
$$y \leftarrow \mathcal{E}_{pk}(x_b); A_2(x_0, x_1, str, y) = b] - 1/2|$$

We consider two attack models, adaptive plaintext attack and adaptive ciphertext attack, in which an adversary can repeatedly use encryption and decryption oracle, respectively.

Definition 2 (IND-CPA). *Let $\Pi = (\mathcal{G}, \mathcal{E}, \mathcal{D})$ be an encryption scheme and let $A = (A_1, A_2)$ be an adversary who can use the encryption oracle. If*

$$Adv_{A,\Pi}(k) \geq \epsilon(k)$$

and A runs at most $t(k)$ steps, we say that A (t, ϵ)-breaks $\Pi(1^k)$ in the sense of IND-CPA.

If $Adv_{A,\Pi}(k)$ is negligible for any adversary A, we say that Π is secure in the sense of IND-CPA.

Definition 3 (IND-CCA2). *Let $\Pi = (\mathcal{G}, \mathcal{E}, \mathcal{D})$ be an encryption scheme and let $A = (A_1, A_2)$ be an adversary who can use the decryption oracle. If*

$$Adv_{A,\Pi}(k) \geq \epsilon(k)$$

and A runs at most $t(k)$ steps with at most q_D queries to decryption oracle, we say that A (t, ϵ, q_D)-breaks $\Pi(1^k)$ in the sense of IND-CCA2. If $Adv_{A,\Pi}(k)$ is negligible for any adversary A, we say that Π is secure in the sense of IND-CCA2.

Some literatures use an other notion IND-CCA1 in which an adversary $A = (A_1, A_2)$ can use the decryption oracle only in its find-stage: A_1. Since the secrecy in the sense of IND-CCA2 is stronger than that of IND-CCA1 (and IND-CPA) [14], we focus on the security in the sense of IND-CCA2.

2.2 Kurosawa et al's Public Key Cryptosystem [12]

Kurosawa et al. [12] showed a public key cryptosystem such that (i) inverting is equivalent to factoring $n = pq$, (ii) the decryption is unique and (iii) p and q are arbitrary prime numbers. Their scheme is described as follows.

Key generation algorithm $\mathcal{G}$: Choose two large primes p and q whose lengths are both $k/2$ bits. The secret key is a pair of p and q.
The public key is $pk = (N, c)$ such that

$$N = pq \text{ and } \left(\frac{c}{p}\right) = \left(\frac{c}{p}\right) = -1,$$

where $\left(\frac{c}{p}\right)$ denotes Legendre symbol.

Encryption algorithm $\mathcal{E}$: For a message $x \in Z_N^*$, let

$$Y_{pk}(x) = x + c/x \bmod N$$

$$U_{pk}(x) = \begin{cases} 0 & \text{if } \left(\frac{x}{N}\right) = 1 \\ 1 & \text{otherwise} \end{cases}$$

$$V_{pk}(x) = \begin{cases} 0 & \text{if } x < c/x \\ 1 & \text{otherwise,} \end{cases}$$

where $\left(\frac{x}{N}\right)$ denotes Jacobi symbol. Then the ciphertext is

$$Y_{pk}(x)||U_{pk}(x)||V_{pk}(x),$$

where $||$ denotes concatenation.

Decryption algorithm $\mathcal{D}$: Suppose that a receiver is given a ciphertext $y||u||v$. He first solves the following equations by using p and q.

$$x^2 - yx + c \equiv 0 \pmod{p},$$
$$x^2 - yx + c \equiv 0 \pmod{q}.$$

He then obtains four solutions x_1, x_2, x_3 and x_4 since $Y_{pk}(x)$ is a four-to-one function. Among the four roots, just one x_i satisfies $u = U_{pk}(x_i)$ and $v = V_{pk}(x_i)$. The receiver finally decides that such x_i is the message the sender sent.

3   Proposed Scheme for Long Messages

In this section, we present our first IND-CCA2 scheme whose security is equivalent to factoring $n = pq$ in the random oracle model, where p and q are arbitrary prime numbers. It works for long messages. We combine Kurosawa et al's scheme with Bellare and Rogaway's scheme of [1]. Note that the conversion of [1] requires a one-way permutation f while $Y_{pk}(x)$ of Sec. 2.2 is a four-to-one function.

Remember that k is a security parameter and $n(k)$ denotes the length of a plaintext. Let $k_0(k)$ be an integer valued function bounded by some polynomial on k. Let G be a mapping from k bit strings to n bit strings and let H be a mapping from $n + k$ bit strings to k_0 bit strings. They are treated as random oracles.

Then our scheme is described as follows.

Key generation algorithm $\mathcal{G}$:   Choose two large primes p and q whose lengths are both $k/2$ bits. The secret key is a pair of p and q.
The public key is $pk = (N, c)$ such that

$$N = pq \text{ and } \left(\frac{c}{p}\right) = \left(\frac{c}{p}\right) = -1,$$

Encryption algorithm $\mathcal{E}$:   Suppose that the input is a message x which is a n bit string. First, $\mathcal{E}$ chooses a random number $r \in Z_N^*$ such that $U_{pk}(r) = 0$ and $V_{pk}(r) = 0$, where

$$U_{pk}(r) = \begin{cases} 0 & \text{if } \left(\frac{r}{N}\right) = 1 \\ 1 & \text{otherwise} \end{cases}$$

$$V_{pk}(r) = \begin{cases} 0 & \text{if } r < c/r \\ 1 & \text{otherwise.} \end{cases}$$

Let

$$Y_{pk}(r) = r + c/r \bmod N.$$

The output which is the ciphertext of x is given as

$$x \oplus G(r)||Y_{pk}(r)||H(x||r).$$

Decryption algorithm $\mathcal{D}$: Suppose that an input is $z||y||s$. $\mathcal{D}$ first solves the following equations by using p and q.

$$r^2 - yr + c \equiv 0 \pmod{p},$$
$$r^2 - yr + c \equiv 0 \pmod{q}.$$

If there is no root, then it outputs $\perp$, which means that the input ciphertext is illegal. Otherwise, it obtains four solutions r_1, r_2, r_3 and r_4 since $Y_{pk}(r)$ is a four-to-one function. Among the four roots, just one r_i satisfies $U_{pk}(r_i) = 0$ and $V_{pk}(r_i) = 0$. let us denote such r_i by r without subscription. It computes

$$x = z \oplus G(r_i).$$

If $H(x||r_i) = s$ then it outputs x as the plaintext. Otherwise, outputs $\perp$.

See Fig.1.

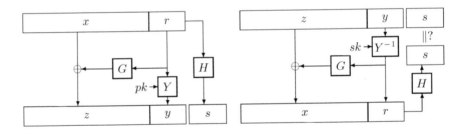

Fig. 1. Proposed scheme for long messages

Theorem 1. *Suppose that there exists an adversary A which $(t^{(A)}, \epsilon^{(A)}, q_D)$-breaks our first scheme in the sense of IND-CCA2 with at most q_G queries to G and at most q_H queries to H. Then there exists M which runs at most $t^{(M)}$ steps and can factor $N = pq$ with probability $\epsilon^{(M)}$, where*

$$t^{(M)} = t^{(A)} + (q_G + q_H + q_D)(T_Y(k) + \lambda(n + k)) + T_{Eu}(k)$$
$$\epsilon^{(M)} = \epsilon^{(A)}(1 - q_D 2^{-k_0})/2,$$

where $T_Y(k)$ denotes the time complexity of $Y_{pk}(x)$ and $T_{Eu}(k)$ denotes that of $\gcd(x, y)$.

The proof of Theorem 1 will be given in the final version.

4   Proposed Scheme for Short Messages

In this section, we present our second IND-CCA2 scheme whose security is equivalent to factoring $n = pq$ in the random oracle model, where p and q are arbitrary prime numbers. It is more efficient than our first scheme for short messages. We combine Kurosawa et al's scheme with Bellare and Rogaway's scheme of [2]. Note that [2] requires a one-way permutation f while $Y_{pk}(x)$ of Sec. 2.2 is four to one.

4.1   Scheme

Remember k is a security parameter. Let $k_0(\cdot)$ and $k_1(\cdot)$ be positive integer valued functions such that $k_0(k) + k_1(k) < k$ for all $k \geq 1$. Let $n(k) = k - k_0(k) - k_1(k)$ be the length of a plaintext.

Let G be a mapping from k_0 bit strings to $n + k_1$ bit strings and let H be a mapping from $n + k_1$ bit strings to k_0 bit strings. They are treaded as random oracles.

Then our scheme is described as follows.

Key generation algorithm: Choose two large primes p and q whose lengths are both $k/2$ bits. The secret key is a pair of p and q.
The public key is $pk = (N, c)$ such that

$$N = pq \text{ and } \left(\frac{c}{p}\right) = \left(\frac{c}{p}\right) = -1,$$

Encryption algorithm: Suppose that input message is $x \in \{0,1\}^n$. $\mathcal{E}$ at first chooses a random bit string r of length k_0, computes

$$s = (x||0^{k_1}) \oplus G(r), \quad t = r \oplus H(s), \quad w = s||t.$$

Let

$$U_{pk}(w) = \begin{cases} 0 & \text{if } \left(\frac{w}{N}\right) = 1 \\ 1 & \text{otherwise} \end{cases}$$

$$V_{pk}(w) = \begin{cases} 0 & \text{if } w < c/w \\ 1 & \text{otherwise.} \end{cases}$$

If $(U_{pk}(w), V_{pk}(w)) = (0,0)$, it outputs $y = Y_{pk}(w)$ as the ciphertext of x. Otherwise, it repeats choosing r untill w satisfies $U_{pk}(w) = V_{pk}(w) = 0$.

Decryption algorithm: Suppose that the input ciphertext is $y \in \{0,1\}^k$. $\mathcal{D}$ solves

$$\left. \begin{array}{l} w^2 - yw + c \equiv 0 \pmod{p} \\ w^2 - yw + c \equiv 0 \pmod{q}. \end{array} \right\} \tag{1}$$

If there is no solution it outputs $\perp$. Otherwise there are four solutions w_1, w_2, w_3 and w_4. Just one of them satisfies $U_{pk}(w) = V_{pk}(w) = 0$. It finds such w_i and sets $w_i = s||t$ where s and t are n and k_0 bits, respectively. It computes $x||z = s \oplus G(t \oplus H(s))$ where x is n bit string and z is the rest. If z is all zeros it outputs x, otherwise $\perp$.

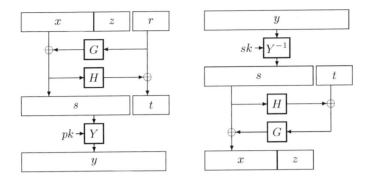

Fig. 2. Proposed scheme for short messages

See Fig.2.

Theorem 2. *Suppose that there exists an adversary A such that it $(t^{(A)}, \epsilon^{(A)})$-breaks our second scheme in the sense of IND-CPA with at most q_G queries to G and at most q_H queries to H. Then there exists M which runs at most $t^{(M)}$ steps and can factor $N = pq$ with probability $\epsilon^{(M)}$, where*

$$t^{(M)} = t^{(A)} + q_G \, q_H(T_Y(k) + \lambda k) + T_{Eu}(k)$$
$$\epsilon^{(M)} = \epsilon^{(A)} \, (1 - q_G 2^{-k_0} - q_H 2^{-(n+k_1)})/2 - q_G 2^{-k}$$

for some constant λ where $T_Y(k)$ denotes the time complexity of $Y_{pk}(x)$ and $T_{Eu}(k)$ denotes that of $\gcd(x, y)$.

Theorem 3. *Suppose that there exists an adversary B such that it $(t^{(B)}, \epsilon^{(B)}, q_D)$-breaks our second scheme in the sense of IND-CCA2 with at most q_G queries to G and at most q_H queries to H. Then there exists A which $(t^{(A)}, \epsilon^{(A)})$-breaks our second scheme in the sense of IND-CPA with at most q_G queries to G and at most q_H queries to H, where*

$$t^{(A)} = t^{(B)} + q_G q_H q_D(T_Y(k) + \lambda k)$$
$$\epsilon^{(A)} = \epsilon^{(B)}(1 - q_D 2^{-k_1}) - q_D 2^{-k_1}/2$$

for some constant λ.

The proof of Theorem 2 and 3 are given in the next subsections. From Theorem 2 and 3, we straightforward obtain the following corollary.

Corollary 1. *If there exists an adversary B such that it $(t^{(B)}, \epsilon^{(B)}, q_D)$-breaks our public encryption scheme in the sense of IND-CCA2 with at most q_G queries to G and at most q_H queries to H, then there exists M which runs at most $t^{(M)}$ steps and can factor $N = pq$ with probability $\epsilon^{(M)}$, where*

$$t^{(M)} = t^{(B)} + q_G q_H(q_D + 1)(T_Y(k) + \lambda k) + T_{Eu}(k)$$
$$\epsilon^{(M)} = \epsilon^{(B)}(1 - q_D 2^{-k_1})(1 - q_G 2^{-k_0} - q_H 2^{-(n+k_1)})/2$$
$$- q_D 2^{-k_1}(1 - q_G 2^{-k_0} - q_H 2^{-(n+k_1)})/4 - q_G 2^{-k}$$

4.2   Proof of Theorem 2

First, we construct M which factors its input N efficiently using $A = (A_1, A_2)$. This is done by finding a random m' with $(m'/N) = -1$ and then using the attacker to extract a preimage m of $y = f(m')$ inequivalent to m' by using the Bellare/Rogaway inversion algorithm. Since the latter does not use the permutation property, our method works.

Firstly, M randomly chooses c from Z_N^* which satisfies $(\frac{c}{N}) = 1$ and sets $pk = (N, c)$. M chooses randomly $\hat{m}$ from Z_N^* which satisfies $U_{pk}(\hat{m}) = 1$ and $V_{pk}(\hat{m}) = 0$ and computes $\hat{y} = Y_{pk}(\hat{m})$. Then it runs $A_1(pk)$. After this, A_1 will make G-queries and/or H-queries. To answer them M prepares two empty lists, G-list and H-list, and performs the following.

G-**query for** g: If G-list includes an entry $(g, G(g))$, return $G(g)$. Otherwise, for all entry $(h, H(h))$ in H-list compute

$$m = h || (g \oplus H(h)). \tag{2}$$

If there exists h such that

$$\hat{y} = Y_{pk}(m), \ U_{pk}(m) = V_{pk}(m) = 0, \tag{3}$$

then obtain p, q from $\gcd(N, m - \hat{m})$. Choose $G(g)$ which is a random bits string with length $n + k_1$, add an entry $(g, G(g))$ into G-list, and return $G(g)$.

H-**query for** h: If there is an entry $(h, H(h))$ in H-list, return $H(h)$. Otherwise, choose $H(h)$ which is a random bits string with length k_0 and add an entry $(h, H(h))$ into H-list. For all entry $(g, G(g))$ in G-list computes Eq.(2). If there exists g which satisfies Eq.(3), then obtain p, q from $\gcd(N, m - \hat{m})$. Finally, return $H(h)$.

Then A_1 will outputs (x_0, x_1, str).

Next, M chooses a random bit b, and runs $A_2(x_0, x_1, str, \hat{y})$. If A_2 makes G-queries and H-queries, M answers in the following ways.

G-**query for** g: If there exists an entry $(g, G(g))$ in G-list, return $G(g)$. Otherwise, compute Eq.(2) for all entry $(h, H(h))$ in H-list. If there exists h which satisfies Eq.(3), then obtain p, q from $\gcd(N, m - \hat{m})$ and return $G(g) = (x_b || 0^{k_1}) \oplus h$. Otherwise, choose $G(g)$ which is a random bits string with length $n + k_1$, add an entry $(g, G(g))$ into G-list, and return $G(g)$.

H-**query for** h: If there exists an entry $(h, H(h))$, return $H(h)$. Otherwise, choose $H(h)$ which is a random bits string with length k_0 and add an entry $(h, H(h))$ into H-list. For all entry $(g, G(g))$ in G-list compute Eq.(2). If there exists g which satisfies Eq.(3), then obtain p, q from $\gcd(N, m - \hat{m})$. Finally return $H(h)$.

A_2 will outputs a bit b'. If M finds p and q then it outputs them, otherwise outputs $\perp$.

If (N, c) is a legal public key of the proposed scheme and there is a pair of (g, h) which satisfies Eq.(2) and (3), $\gcd(N, m - \hat{m})$ always presents p or q. For randomly chosen c, the probability with which (N, c) is a legal public key is $1/2$. Therefore we can estimate $\epsilon^{(M)}$ similarly with the proof of Theorem 3 in [2] without the factor $1/2$.

The running time of M is also similar with the proof of Theorem 3 in [2] except M needs additional time to compute p and q using gcd. When (N, c) is not a legal public key, it is possible that A never finish. In such a case M waits during $t^{(A)}$ and halts A.

4.3   Proof of Theorem 3

First, we show how to construct A_1/A_2 which uses B_1/B_2 as subroutine. This is done by showing that the chosen-ciphertext attacker is answered invalid plaintext with high probability for a decryption query unless the attacker has previously asked the random oracles G and H the queries corresponding to an encryption of the plaintext, the knowledge of which allows the recovery of the plaintext (i.e. the attacker is already aware of the plaintext of the decryption he is asking for).

(A_1 : find stage)
    On input pk A_1 initializes G-list and H-list with empty and runs $B_1(pk)$. After this, B_1 will make G-query, H-query and decryption query. A_1 answers these queries in the following ways:

G-**query for** g: A_1 makes the same query to G oracle, obtains $G(g)$, gives it to B_1, and then adds an entry $(g, G(g))$ into G-list.
H-**query for** h: A_1 answers to it in similar way to the case of G-query and adds an entry into H-list.

The most troublesome task is to answer decryption queries for y. To simulate the decryption oracle without knowing the secret key, A_1 runs Dec-simulator :

Dec-simulator: On input y, for all entry $(h, H(h))$ and $(g, G(g))$ in H-list and G-list, compute $m = h||(g \oplus H(h))$ and check $y = Y_{pk}(m)$ and $U_{pk}(m) = V_{pk}(m) = 0$. If the check is not passed, return $\perp$ which means that y is an illegal ciphertext. Otherwise set $x||z = h \oplus G(g)$ where x is n bits and z is the rest. If $z = 0^{k_1}$ then return x, otherwise $\perp$.

Finally, B_1 outputs (x_0, x_1, str). A_1 outputs $(x_0, x_1, str||G\text{-list}||H\text{-list})$.

(A_2 : guess stage)
    On input $(x_0, x_1, str||G\text{-list}||H\text{-list}, y)$ A_2 runs B_2 on input (x_0, x_1, str, y). After this, B_2 will make G-query, H-query and decryption query. A_2 answers these queries in the same way as A_1. Finally, A_2 outputs a bit b' or $\perp$ which B_2 outputs.

We will estimate the probability $Adv_{A,\Pi}(k)$. Let us denote the event "Dec-simulator can simulate decryption oracle correctly for all queries" with $success_D$. Clearly,

$$\Pr(b' = b) \geq \Pr(b' = b | success_D) \times \Pr(success_D).$$

From the definition of $Adv_{A,\Pi}$ and the hypothesis of the theorem,

$$\epsilon^{(B)} = |\Pr(b' = b|success_D) - 1/2|.$$

Wlog., we assume that

$$\epsilon^{(B)} = \Pr(b' = b|success_D) - 1/2.$$

Then

$$\Pr(b' = b|success_D) = 1/2 + \epsilon^{(B)},$$
$$Adv_{A,\Pi}(k) = |\Pr(b' = b) - 1/2|$$
$$\geq |\Pr(b' = b|success_D) \times \Pr(success_D) - 1/2|$$
$$= |(1/2 + \epsilon^{(B)})\Pr(success_D) - 1/2|$$
$$= |\epsilon^{(B)}\Pr(success_D) - \frac{1 - \Pr(success_D)}{2}|$$

Now then, we need to estimate $\Pr(succeed_D)$. Assume that B_1 or B_2 makes a query for a ciphertext y. We consider three cases.

1. If there exists no m such that $y = Y_{pk}(m)$, then both Dec-simulator and decryption oracle will output $\perp$, that is, Dec-simulator can simulate correctly.
2. If there is $m = s\|t$ such that $y = Y_{pk}(m)$ and $U_{pk}(m) = V_{pk}(m) = 0$, and there are $(g, G(g))$ and $(h, H(h))$ in G-list and H-list such that $h = s, g = t \oplus H(h)$, Dec-simulator returns a correct plaintext (or $\perp$) with probability one.
3. If there is $m = s\|t$ such that $y = Y_{pk}(m)$ and $U_{pk}(m) = V_{pk}(m) = 0$, but there is no $(g, G(g))$ and/or $(h, H(h))$ in G-list and/or H-list such that $h = s, g = t \oplus H(h)$, Dec-simulator returns always outputs $\perp$. On the other hands, the legal decryption oracle will make H-query for $h = s$ and G-query for $g = t \oplus H(h)$, and check whether z is all zeros where $x\|z = h \oplus G(g)$. Since $G(g)$ is random, $h \oplus G(g)$ is random. Then the decryption oracle outputs a message with probability 2^{-k_1}.

Consequently,

$$\Pr(success_D \text{ for one query}) \geq 1 - 2^{-k_1},$$
$$\Pr(success_D) \geq 1 - q_D 2^{-k_1},$$

and

$$Adv_{A,\Pi}(k) \geq \epsilon^{(B)}(1 - q_D 2^{-k_1}) - \frac{q_D 2^{-k_1}}{2}.$$

Finally, we will estimate the time complexity. To answer one decryption query A needs to compute $Y_{pk}(m)$ and to compare for every h and g. Then, it is clear that

$$t^{(A)}(k) = t^{(B)}(k) + q_G q_H q_D(T_Y(k) + \lambda k).$$

5 Discussion

In this section, we discuss about some variations of our schemes.

First, we can reduce the running time of encryption four times in average if we add two bits (U_{pk}, V_{pk}) to the ciphertexts. In this case, we do not have to choose random numbers such that $U_{pk} = V_{pk} = 0$ while the ciphertext becomes two bits longer.

Next, we can replace $Y_{pk}(r)$ with $r^2 \bmod N$. In this case, however, the ciphertexts are not uniquely decrypted with small probabilities such as

$$P_1 = 3/2^{k_0} \text{ in the scheme of Sec. 3,}$$

$$P_2 = 3/2^{k_1} \text{ in the scheme of Sec. 4.}$$

References

1. Bellare, M., Rogaway, P.: Random Oracles are Practical: a Paradigm for Designing Efficient Protocols. Proc. of the 1st CCS (1993) 62–73
2. Bellare, M., Rogaway, P.: Optimal Asymmetric Encryption — How to encrypt with RSA. Proc. of Eurocrypt'94, Lecture Notes in Computer Science, **950** (1994) 92–111
3. Okamoto, T., Uchiyama, S.: A New Public-Key Cryptosystem as Secure as Factoring. Proc. of Eurocrypt'99, Lecture Notes in Computer Science, **1403** (1998) 308–318
4. Fujisaki, E., Okamoto, T.: How to Enhance the Security of Public-Key Encryption at Minimum Cost. Proc. of PKC'99, Lecture Notes in Computer Science, **1560** (1999) 53–68
5. Fujioka, E., Okamoto, T.: Secure integration of asymmetric and symmetric encryption schemes. Proc. of Crypto'99, Lecture Notes in Computer Science, **1666** (1999) 537–554
6. Pointcheval, D.: Chosen-Ciphertext Security for any One-Way Cryptosystem. Proc. of PKC 2000, Lecture Notes in Computer Science, **1807** (2000) 129–146
7. Paillier, P.: A Trapdoor Permutation Equivalent to Factoring. Proc. of PKC'99, Lecture Notes in Computer Science, **1560** (1999) 217–222
8. Paillier, P.: Public-Key Cryptosystems Based on Composite Degree Residuosity Classes. Proc. of Eurocrypt'99, Lecture Notes in Computer Science, **1592** (1999) 223–238
9. Paillier, P., Pointcheval, D.: Deficient Public-Key Cryptosystems Provably Secure Against Active Adversaries. Proc. of Asiacrypt'99, Lecture Notes in Computer Science, **1716** (1999) 165–179
10. Rabin, M.O.: Digitalized signatures and public key cryptosystems as intractable as factorization. MIT/LCS/TR-212, Technical Report MIT (1979)
11. Williams, H.C.: A modification of the RSA public-key encryption procedure. IEEE, IT, **IT-26** No.6 (1980) 726–729
12. Kurosawa, K., Itoh, T., Takeuchi, M.: Public key cryptosystem using a reciprocal number with the same intractability as factoring a large number. CRYPTOLOGIA, **XII** (1988) 225–233

13. Cramer, R., Shoup, V.: A practical public key cryptosystem provably secure against adaptive chosen ciphertext attack. Proc. of Crypto'98, Lecture Notes in Computer Science, **1462** (1998) 13–25

14. Bellare, M., Desai, A., Pointcheval, D., Rogaway, P.: Relations among notations of security for public key encryption schemes. Crypto'98, Lecture Notes in Computer Science, **1462** (1998) 26–45

Identification, Signature and Signcryption Using High Order Residues Modulo an RSA Composite

Yuliang Zheng

LINKS - Laboratory for Information and Network Security
Monash University, McMahons Road, Frankston, VIC 3199, Australia
yuliang.zheng@infotech.monash.edu.au
www.netcomp.monash.edu.au/links/

Abstract. Signcryption is a public key cryptographic primitive that fulfills the functions of digital signature and public key encryption concurrently, with a cost smaller than that required by the traditional signature followed by encryption method. The concept of signcryption, together with an implementation based on the discrete logarithm problem, was proposed in 1996. In this work, we demonstrate how to implement efficient signcryption using high order (power) residues modulo an RSA composite. This contributes to the research of extending computational underpinnings of signcryption schemes to problems related to integer factorization. In the course of achieving our goal, we also show efficient protocols for user identification, and fast and compact digital signature schemes.

Keywords: High Order Residues, Public Key Encryption, RSA, Signature, Signcryption.

1 Introduction

The idea of using (power) residues in public key cryptography first appeared in [5] where Goldwasser and Micali showed how to use quadratic residues in randomized encryption in a bit-by-bit fashion. This early work was followed by Benaloh and Yung's paper [3] where it was proposed to use r^{th} residues, where r was a *small* [1] *prime*, to construct a more efficient randomized public key encryption scheme. In [21] Zheng, Matsumoto and Imai proved that the requirement of r being a *small prime* could be relaxed to a small odd integer. This was further relaxed in [9] where Kurosawa and co-workers showed that r could take the form of a *small even* integer. In [2] (see also [14]), Benaloh observed that one could employ the Chinese Remainder Theorem in decryption, which further relaxed requirements of the number r — it could be a *large odd* integer, provided that it contains only *small and distinct* prime factors. More recently, Pailier [15]

---

[1] By "small" one generally means that the relevant parameter is bounded from above by a *poly-logarithmic* function of a security parameter. Likewise, a "large" parameter is one bounded from above by a *polynomial* function of a security parameter.

K. Kim (Ed.): PKC 2001, LNCS 1992, pp. 48–63, 2001.

discussed how to construct probabilistic public key encryption schemes involving n^{th} residues modulo n^2, where n is an RSA composite.

In all the public key encryption schemes presented in these successive papers, except those special schemes proposed in [15], decryption involves exhaustive search over a space whose size is dictated by a prime factor of r. This explains why these randomized encryption schemes do not work when r has a *large* prime factor.

While all the prior work on the use of rth residues had been mainly limited to the construction of randomized public key encryption (requiring the number r contains only small prime factors), the present work demonstrates applications of rth residues, with r being a *large* prime, in constructing efficient user identification, digital signature and more important, signcryption schemes. [2]

Signcryption was first proposed in [19] as an efficient public key cryptographic primitive that achieves both message confidentiality and non-repudiation with a much smaller cost than that required by digital signature followed by public key encryption. The first implementation of signcryption was based on the discrete logarithm problem over a finite field, which admitted a natural analogue on an elliptic curve over a finite field [20]. The same observation applies also to other sub-group based public key cryptosystems such as the XTR [12]. This early effort left as an interesting research topic to find a signcryption scheme that relies for its security on other computationally hard problems such as factoring large integers. Progress in this line of research has been made recently in [17]. Results presented in this paper represent yet another approach to building signcryption schemes on the integer factorization problem.

Section 2 provides background knowledge on high order (power) residues. Section 3 shows how to construct user identification protocols (also called passport protocols) that are based on high order residues modulo an RSA composite. This is followed by Section 4 where the identification protocols are converted into efficient digital signature schemes. The usefulness of high order residues is highlighted in Section 5 where a signcryption scheme called HORSE is presented. Efficiency of the identification, signature and signcryption schemes, both in terms of computation costs and expanded bits, is analyzed in Section 6. Finally the paper is closed with a summary in Section 7.

2   High Order (Power) Residues

The intension of this section is to summarize some of the core mathematical background that is required in understanding the identification, signature and signcryption schemes to be presented in this paper. Some useful further information on higher order residuosity can be found in [21]

---

[2] Identification and signature schemes proposed in [10,16] rely on properties of a subgroup related to an RSA modulus, and hence appear to be technically different from the present work. Furthermore, schemes in [10] work only when r is "small", as they require in their setting up stage the extraction of rth roots and search over a space of r elements.

Let r and n be positive integers, and z be an integer relatively prime to n (i.e., $\gcd(z, n) = 1$). If there exists an integer x such that $z = x^r \bmod n$, z is said to be an rth (power) residue modulo n. Otherwise z is said to be an rth nonresidue modulo n.

The set of integers $[0, 1, \ldots, n-1]$ is denoted by $\mathbb{Z}_n$, and the set of integers in $\mathbb{Z}_n$ that are relatively prime to n is denoted by $\mathbb{Z}_n^*$.

We are interested in the case where r is a prime of at least 120 bits in size or length in binary representation, and n is an RSA modulus, i.e., $n = pq$, where both p and q are large (> 250 bits) primes. We further require that the three primes r, p and q be related by

$$\gcd(r, p-1) = r, \quad \gcd(r, q-1) = 1.$$

In practice, one may choose p and q in such a way that they take the form of

$$p = 2rp' + 1, \quad q = 2q' + 1$$

where both p' and q' are primes that are different from r.

For r and n of the above forms, an element $z \in \mathbb{Z}_n^*$ is necessarily an rth residue modulo q, and it is an rth residue modulo p if and only if $z^{(p-1)/r} = 1 \bmod p$. Thus z is an rth nonresidue modulo n if and only if

$$z^{(p-1)/r} \neq 1 \bmod p.$$

As a consequence, when the factors p and q are known, one can quickly verify whether or not $z \in \mathbb{Z}_n^*$ is an rth residue modulo n.

Note that $1/r$ of the elements in $z \in \mathbb{Z}_n^*$ are r^{th} residues modulo n, and the remaining $(r-1)/r$ of the elements are all r^{th} nonresidues modulo n. This makes easy the task of finding an rth nonresidue modulo n.

Definition 1. *We say that three integers (r, n, h) are a* good *triplet if they fulfill the following requirements:*

1. *r is a prime whose size (length in binary representation) is at least 120 bits.*
2. *$n = pq$ is an RSA modulus of at least 512 bits, satisfying $\gcd(r, p-1) = r$ and $\gcd(r, q-1) = 1$.*
3. *h is an rth nonresidue modulo n, or equivalently, $h^{(p-1)/r} \neq 1 \bmod p$.*

It should be pointed out that there is a slightly more general version of a good triplet (r, n, h) in which r is defined as an odd integer with distinct prime factors $r_1, r_2, \ldots, r_t$. One of the prime factors of r must be large, say of 120 bits in binary representation. n and r are related in the same way as in the above definition. The number h is an r_i^{th} nonresidue modulo p for every factor r_i, i.e., $h^{(p-1)/r_i} \neq 1 \bmod p$ for all $i = 1, 2, \ldots, t$. The identification, signature and signcryption schemes to be proposed in the forthcoming sections will all work with respect to such a more general version of a good triplet, although our discussions will be focused on the case where r is a large prime.

Fact 1 *For a good triplet* (r, n, h), *every element* $x \in \mathbb{Z}_n^*$ *can be presented as*

$$x = h^i \cdot w^r \mod n$$

for a unique integer $i \in \mathbb{Z}_r$, *where* $\mathbb{Z}_n = [0, 1, \ldots, r-1]$ *and a not necessarily unique* $w \in \mathbb{Z}_n^*$. *The number* i *is called the class-index of* x.

Finding the class-index of x with respect to a good triplet appears to be infeasible, *even if one has the knowledge of the factors of* n. Currently known methods for solving the problem require the knowledge of p and q, and involve search over $\mathbb{Z}_r$. The average computation time required by such an algorithm is in the order of $r/2$, which renders the algorithm ineffective when r is a large prime. It should be pointed out that two of the classical methods for solving the discrete logarithm problem in a group, namely Shank's baby-step-giant-step method and Pollard's rho method (see [13]), do not appear to be applicable to the class-index problem under consideration, although both methods run faster than exhaustive search.

Another fact of importance is that the degree of difficulty in solving the class-index finding problem is not effected in any way by the choice of h, as the problem falls into a class of problems that share an interesting property called random self-reducibility (with respect to h). (See [1] for more discussions on random self-reducibility.) This fact will be used later in designing efficient schemes.

These observations form the computational basis of our new identification, digital signature and signcryption schemes to be presented in the coming sections.

3   Identification Using High Order Residues

3.1   Basic Protocol

At the setting up stage, a user Alice first chooses a good triplet (r, n, h). In addition, she also chooses at random x_a from $\mathbb{Z}_r = [0, 1, \ldots, r-1]$ and w_a from $\mathbb{Z}_n^*$. Namely $x_a \in_R \mathbb{Z}_r$ and $w_a \in_R \mathbb{Z}_n^*$, where $\in_R$ indicates an element is chosen uniformly at random from a set.

Alice then forms

$$y_a = \frac{1}{h^{x_a} \cdot w_a^r} \mod n$$

She keeps x_a and w_a as her important private key, and publishes the triplet (r, n, h) and y_a as her public key.

Later when Alice wishes to prove to another user Bob that she is indeed Alice, she first forwards to Bob her (certified) public key. Bob verifies the authenticity of Alice's public key, and if he is satisfied with the verification, the two users then engage in the protocol specified in Table 1. At the end of an execution of the protocol, Bob would accept Alice's claim if and only if the verification at Step 4 is successful.

Table 1. Identification Using High Order Residues

Step	Alice	Channel	Bob
	Public key: r, n, h, y_a Private key: x_a, w_a		
1	Alice chooses $x \in_R \mathbb{Z}_r$ and $u \in_R \mathbb{Z}_n^*$. She then forms $$y = h^x \cdot u^r \bmod n$$ and sends y to Bob.	$\Rightarrow y \Rightarrow$	
2		$\Leftarrow b \Leftarrow$	Bob chooses $$b \in_R \mathbb{Z}_r$$ and forwards it to Alice as a challenge.
3	Alice forms $$s = x + b \cdot x_a$$ $$v = u \cdot w_a^b \bmod n$$ She then passes s and v over to Bob. Note that no modular operation is involved in the calculation of s.	$\Rightarrow s, v \Rightarrow$	
4			Bob verifies whether or not $$h^s \cdot v^r \cdot y_a^b = y \bmod n$$ Bob accepts Alice if and only if the equation passes the test.

3.2 Efficient Variants

A number of methods can be considered to improve the efficiency of the basic identification protocol.

A Small h. As was discussed earlier, the computational difficulty of the class-index finding problem is not dependent on how h, an rth nonresidue modulo n, is chosen. Thus a small h may be selected so that it uses less memory and helps speed-up computations involving h. For a large r, an overwhelming majority $(\frac{r-1}{r})$ of elements in $\mathbb{Z}_n^*$ are r^{th} nonresidues. Hence the smallest r^{th} nonresidue

h can be easily identified by verifying whether

$$h^{(p-1)/r} \neq 1 \bmod p$$

for $h = 2, 3, 4, \ldots$, where p is a factor of n.

Shorter y and b. In Step 1, Alice may choose to send a hashed value of $h^x \cdot u^r \bmod n$ to Bob, that is

$$y = \mathcal{H}(h^x \cdot u^r \bmod n)$$

where $\mathcal{H}$ is a one-way hashing function. Accordingly, the verification by Bob in Step 4 should be modified to

$$\mathcal{H}(h^s \cdot v^r \cdot y_a^b \bmod n) = y$$

In Step 2, Bob may send Alice a shorter b, say of 60 bits, as a challenge. These improvements will reduce the bandwidth of messages exchanged between Alice and Bob.

Shorter w_a and u. As the generation of secure random bits may consume substantial computational resources, Alice may choose to generate w_a and u from a smaller range, say $\mathbb{Z}_{2^{80}} = [0, 1, \ldots, 2^{80} - 1]$.

Generating w_a and u deterministically. Alice may choose to generate w_a and u in the following way:

$$w_a = \mathcal{H}(x_a, r, n, h)$$
$$u = \mathcal{H}(x, r, n, h)$$

where $\mathcal{H}$ is a one-way hash function. This will completely eliminate the need of generating random bits for these two values.

Removing w_a and u altogether. A more efficient variant of the protocol is to fix w_a to 1, while choosing x_a from a range greater than $\mathbb{Z}_r$. More specifically, Alice can choose

$$x_a \in_R \mathbb{Z}_{2^\ell} = [0, 1, \ldots, 2^\ell - 1]$$

where ℓ may be at least 40 bits longer than the size of r. Namely $\ell \geq |r| + 40$, where $|\cdot|$ indicates the number of bits in the binary representation of an integer. Interestingly, with this modification, the number r will be used only in the setting up stage, but not in an identification process afterwards. Thus r no longer needs to be made public.

At the setting up stage, Alice first chooses a good triplet (r, n, h). She then chooses $x_a \in_R \mathbb{Z}_{2^\ell}$, and forms

$$y_a = \frac{1}{h^{x_a}} \bmod n$$

Alice then keeps x_a as her important private key, and publishes n, h and y_a as her public key. (Note that the use of the number r is now limited to the generation of h.)

When Alice wishes to prove to another user Bob that she is indeed Alice, she first forwards to Bob her (certified) public key. Bob verifies the authenticity of Alice's public key, and if he is satisfied with the verification, the two users then engage in the protocol described in Table 2.

Table 2. Identification Using High Order Residues — A More Efficient Version

Step	Alice	Channel	Bob
	Public key: n, h, y_a Private key: x_a		
1	Alice chooses $x \in_R \mathbb{Z}_{2^{1.75\ell}}$ and forms $$y = \mathcal{H}(h^x \bmod n)$$ She then sends y to Bob.	$\Rightarrow y \Rightarrow$	
2		$\Leftarrow b \Leftarrow$	Bob chooses $$b \in_R \mathbb{Z}_{2^{\ell/2}}$$ and forwards it to Alice as a challenge.
3	Alice forms $$s = x + b \cdot x_a$$ and sends it to Bob. Note that no modular operation is involved in the calculation of s.	$\Rightarrow s \Rightarrow$	
4			Bob verifies whether or not $$\mathcal{H}(h^s \cdot y_a^b \bmod n) = y$$ Bob accepts Alice if and only if the equation passes the test.

As $x_a \in \mathbb{Z}_{2^\ell}$ and $\ell \geq |r| + 40$, x_a can be expressed as $x_a = x'_a + f \cdot r$ for some $0 \leq x'_a < r$ and f. ¿From this it follows that

$$h^{x_a} \bmod n = h^{x'_a} \cdot (h^f)^r \bmod n.$$

Thus the efficient protocol in Table 2 can be viewed as one obtained from the protocol in Table 1 by letting $h^f \bmod n$ play the role of $w_a \in \mathbb{Z}_n^*$.

Note that the protocol in Table 2 has also incorporated other ideas discussed in this section, especially on shortening y and b. Also note that since the x chosen in Step 1 essentially plays the role of "masking" the secret key x_a in Step 3, it should be sufficiently long, say $|x| \geq |x_a| + |b| + 40$. Assuming that $|b| \approx \ell/2$ and $\ell \geq 160$, it would be adequate to have $|x| = 1.75\ell$.

4   Digital Signature Using High Order Residues

4.1   A General Signature Scheme

The identification protocol described in Table 1 can be converted to a digital signature scheme by substituting the role of Bob with an one-way hash function.

Alice sets up all the required parameters (including both public and private keys) in the same way as described in Section 3.1. Alice's public key is composed of y_a and a good triplet (r, n, h). Her private key is a pair of numbers x_a and w_a which are chosen, uniformly at random, from $\mathbb{Z}_r = [0, 1, \ldots, r-1]$ and $\mathbb{Z}_n^*$ respectively. The public and private keys are related by $y_a = \frac{1}{h^{x_a} \cdot w_a^r} \bmod n$.

To sign a message m, Alice first chooses at random x from $\mathbb{Z}_r$ and u from $\mathbb{Z}_n^*$, She then generates three numbers (b, j, v) as her signature on the message m as follows:

$$b = \mathcal{H}(h^x \cdot u^r \bmod n, m)$$
$$s = x + b \cdot x_a$$
$$v = u \cdot w_a^b \bmod n$$

Here $\mathcal{H}$ is an one-way hash function, and the calculation of s does not involve a modular operation.

Given m and (b, s, v), one uses Alice's public key to verify the authenticity of the signature by checking

$$\mathcal{H}(h^s \cdot v^r \cdot y_a^b \bmod n, m) = b$$

The signature is deemed authentic only if the equation holds.

We note that while our signature scheme bears some similarities to a scheme proposed in [7], there is an important technical difference. Namely, the scheme in [7] requires that $p-1$ and $q-1$, where p and q are the factors of an RSA composite n, share a large common divisor f which is needed in the generation of a signature.

4.2   A More Efficient Signature Scheme

Techniques for improving the efficiency of the identification protocol that have been discussed in Section 3.2 can be employed to make the signature scheme more efficient. To highlight the improvements, in the following we specify the digital signature scheme that corresponds to the efficient identification protocol presented in Section 3.2.

As in Section 3.2, Alice's private key is $x_a \in_R \mathbb{Z}_{2^\ell}$, where $\ell \geq |r| + 40$, and her public key consists of three numbers n, h and y_a. The public and private keys are related by $y_a = \frac{1}{h^{x_a}} \bmod n$. There is no need to publish the number r, hence it can be erased at the completion of the setting up stage.

To sign a message m, Alice first chooses $x \in_R \mathbb{Z}_{2^{1.75\ell}}$. She then forms her signature on the message m, which is composed of two numbers (b, s), as follows:

$$b = \mathcal{H}(h^x \bmod n, m)$$
$$s = x + b \cdot x_a$$

The authenticity of Alice's signature can be confirmed by verifying

$$\mathcal{H}(h^s \cdot y_a^b \bmod n, m) = b$$

Table 3 summarizes the two signature schemes. Note that with the efficient version of the signature schemes, it is important that $|x|$ is sufficiently large, namely, $|x| \geq |x_a| + |b| + 40$. Once again assuming that $|b| \approx \ell/2$ and $\ell \geq 160$, it would suffice to have $|x| = 1.75\ell$.

Table 3. Signature Schemes Using High Order (Power) Residues

Signature scheme	Generation of signature	Verification of signature	Length of signature
General scheme Public key: r, n, h, y_a Private key: x_a, w_a	$m \to (m, b, s, v):$ $x \in_R \mathbb{Z}_r$ $u \in_R \mathbb{Z}_n^*$ $b = \mathcal{H}(h^x \cdot u^r \bmod n, m)$ $s = x + b \cdot x_a$ $v = u \cdot w_a^b \bmod n$	$(m, b, s, v):$ $y = h^s \cdot v^r \cdot y_a^b \bmod n$ accept only when $\mathcal{H}(y, m) = b$	$2|\mathcal{H}(\cdot)| + |r| + |n|$
Efficient scheme Public key: n, h, y_a Private key: x_a	$m \to (m, b, s):$ $x \in_R \mathbb{Z}_{2^{1.75\ell}}$ $b = \mathcal{H}(h^x \bmod n, m)$ $s = x + b \cdot x_a$	$(m, b, s):$ $y = h^s \cdot y_a^b \bmod n$ accept only when $\mathcal{H}(y, m) = b$	$|\mathcal{H}(\cdot)| + 1.75\ell$

5   HORSE — An Efficient Hight Order Residue Signcryption Engine

Using the technique for constructing signcryption schemes that was first developed in [19], the efficient signature scheme described in Table 3 can be used to design a new signcryption scheme whose security is related to the hardness of factoring large RSA moduli.

Like the signcryption schemes in [19], some of the parameters for HORSE are required to be shared among all users. The only difference with [19] is that with the present scheme, these shared parameters must be generated either by trusted authorities, possibly in a distributed manner, or by a "black-box" computer mimicking the function of trusted authorities.

To be more specific, the trusted authorities choose, on behalf of all users, a good triplet (r, n, h). The authorities may also choose an integer ℓ so that it is at least 40 bits longer than the size of r (in binary representation). Once (r, n, h) and ℓ are chosen, the authorities publish h and n, as well as ℓ. They then make the prime factors of n, i.e., p and q, and the number r inaccessible to users. Typically, this is done by erasing all the traces about p, q and r.

Alice must first set up her own pair of public and private keys y_a and x_a. This is done by

$$x_a \in_R \mathbb{Z}_{2^\ell},$$
$$y_a = h^{x_a} \bmod n$$

Alice publishes y_a in a public key directory, while keeping x_a as her matching private key.

Likewise Bob must also set up his pair of public and private keys y_b and x_b:

$$x_b \in_R \mathbb{Z}_{2^\ell},$$
$$y_b = h^{x_b} \bmod n$$

Table 4 summarizes the setting up of signcryption.

For Alice to signcrypt a message m to be sent to Bob, she carries out the signcryption operations detailed in Table 5. On receiving a signcrypted message from Alice, Bob can extract the original message by following the unsigncryption steps indicated in the same table. Note that in describing the signcryption scheme, it is assumed that $|KH.(\cdot)| \approx \ell/2$ and $\ell \geq 160$. This results in the choice of $|x| = 1.75\ell$, ensuring that $|x| \geq |x_a| + |b| + 40$.

To close this section, we point out that the way public and private keys are set up in the HORSE signcryption scheme also admits a system reminiscent to the ElGamal public key encryption scheme [4].

When a user Cathy wishes to send to Bob a message m in a secure way, she first chooses $x \in_R \mathbb{Z}_{2^\ell}$, and computes $k = \mathcal{H}(y_b^x \bmod n)$. Cathy then forms $c_1 = E_k(m)$, and $c_2 = h^x \bmod n$, and forwards to Bob the pair (c_1, c_2) as a ciphertext of m. Note that there is no need for Cathy to set up her public and private keys.

Table 4. Setting up for the Signcryption Scheme HORSE

Parameters public to all:
n — a large RSA modulus (chosen by trusted authorities)
h — an rth nonresidue modulo n (chosen by trusted authorities)
ℓ — size of a secret key (may be chosen by trusted authorities)
$\mathcal{H}$ — a one-way hash function with $|\mathcal{H}(\cdot)| \geq 128$
KH — a keyed one-way hash function with $|KH.(\cdot)| \geq 80$
(E, D) — the encryption and decryption algorithms of a private key cipher
Alice's keys:
x_a — private key $(x_a \in_R \mathbb{Z}_{2^\ell})$
y_a — public key $(y_a = h^{x_a} \bmod n)$
Bob's keys:
x_b — private key $(x_b \in_R \mathbb{Z}_{2^\ell})$
y_b — public key $(y_b = h^{x_b} \bmod n)$

On receiving (c_1, c_2) from Cathy, Bob can recover k by involving his private key x_b in the computation of $k = c_2^{x_b} \bmod n$. He can then proceed to extract the original message m from c_1 by $m = D_k(c_1)$.

6   Efficiency of the Schemes

We examine the efficiency of the identification, signature and signcryption schemes in terms of computational efforts invested and communication overhead required. With a protocol or algorithm employing public key cryptography, the dominant computation is modular exponentiations involving large integers. When computing the product of several modular exponentiations, we can use a very effective technique that was discussed in Knuth's book (see Exercise 27, Pages 465 and 637 of [8]; see also [18]). The same technique was later re-discovered by Shamir (see the last part of [4]).

6.1   Efficiency of Identification

We focus on the more efficient protocol specified in Table 2. Messages communicated between Alice and Bob are very compact: $|\mathcal{H}(\cdot)| + 2\ell$ bits from Alice to Bob and ℓ bits from Bob to Alice.

Alice needs to perform one modular exponentiation which can be pre-computed well before the start of the protocol. Using the classical "square-and-multiply" method, on average the exponentiation takes $1.5 \cdot 1.75\ell = 2.625\ell$ modular multiplications.

Bob needs to compute the product of two modular exponentiations. The size (or length) of the longer exponent s has 1.75ℓ bits. Using the fast method discussed in Knuth's book, Bob can complete, once again on average, the computation in $(1 + 3/4)|s| = 1.75^2\ell \approx 3\ell$ modular multiplications.

Table 5. The Signcryption Scheme HORSE

Signcryption by Alice the Sender:
$$m \rightarrow (c, d, e)$$

1. Pick $x \in_R \mathbb{Z}_{2^{1.75\ell}}$, and let $k = \mathcal{H}(y_b^x \bmod n)$.
2. Split k into k_1 and k_2 of appropriate size.
3. $c = E_{k_1}(m)$.
4. $d = KH_{k_2}(m, bind\_info)$,
   where $bind\_info$ may contain, among other data, the public key (certificate) of the recipient, and optionally the public key (certificate) of the sender.
5. $e = x + d \cdot x_a$.
6. Send to Bob the signcrypted text (c, d, e).

Unsigncryption by Bob the Recipient:
$$(c, d, e) \rightarrow m$$

1. Recover k from d, e, h, n, y_a and x_b:
   $k = \mathcal{H}((h^e \cdot (\frac{1}{y_a})^d)^{x_b} \bmod n)$.
2. Split k into k_1 and k_2.
3. $m = D_{k_1}(c)$.
4. Accept m as a valid message originated from Alice only if $KH_{k_2}(m, bind\_info)$ is identical to d.

6.2   Efficiency of Signature

With the fast signature scheme (the second scheme) in Table 3, its signature is significantly shorter than the RSA signature scheme. More specifically, the size of our signature is $|\mathcal{H}(\cdot)| + 1.75\ell$ bits. Assuming that $|\mathcal{H}(\cdot)| = 80$ and $\ell = 200$, the signature has only 430 bits.

The signing procedure requires one exponentiation, or $1.5 \cdot 1.75\ell = 2.625\ell$ modular multiplications on average. This is much faster than the generation of an RSA signature which involves a full length exponent.

The verification of a signature will take more time than the RSA signature scheme with a small public key, as it requires the computation of the product of two exponentiations, with s being the longer exponent. On average, the product takes $(1 + 3/4)|s| = 1.75^2\ell \approx 3\ell$ modular multiplications.

6.3   Efficiency of Signcryption

The communication overhead, measured in bits, of the signcryption scheme HORSE specified in Table 5, is

$$|d| + |e| = |KH.(\cdot)| + 1.75\ell$$

Recall that the communication overhead of the traditional RSA signature followed by RSA encryption is

$$|n_a| + |n_b|$$

where n_a is Alice's RSA modulus and n_b Bob's. Clearly HORSE represents an significant improvement over RSA.

The computational cost for signcryption is

$$1.5 \cdot 1.75\ell = 2.625\ell$$

modular multiplications on average. The unsigncryption operation involves the computation of the product of two exponentiations. The two exponents are $e \cdot x_b$ and $d \cdot x_b$. It is important to note that as $\phi(n)$, the Euler's ϕ-function, is not known to Bob, the size of the exponents cannot be reduced! Clearly, the longer exponent is $e \cdot x_b$ which has 2.75ℓ bits. Thus on average unsigncryption takes

$$(1 + 3/4) \cdot 2.75\ell \approx 4.8\ell$$

modular multiplications.

Together, signcryption and unsigncryption take

$$7.4\ell$$

modular multiplications.

T compare HORSE with RSA signature followed by RSA encryption, we assume that $|n| = |n_a| = |n_b|$, that the size of r and the size of an output of the key-ed hash function KH are related by $|r| = 1.5|KH.(\cdot)|$, and that $\ell = |r| + 0.5|KH.(\cdot)| = 2|KH.(\cdot)|$.

We further assume that the Chinese Remainder Theorem is used in RSA decryption and signature generation, achieving the theoretically maximum speedup. Namely we assume that the average computational cost for RSA signature generation is $\frac{1.5}{4}|n_a| = 0.375|n_a|$ modular multiplications, and for RSA decryption it is $\frac{1.5}{4}|n_b| = 0.375|n_b|$ modular multiplications. With RSA encryption and signature verification, to simplify our discussions we consider two cases, although there are numerous other possible combinations for one to choose from in practice. These two cases are: (1) small public exponents (say of 10 bits or less), and (2) $\ell/2$-bit public exponents,

In order to examine how signcryption outperforms the signature-then-encryption approach, we define the advantages of signcryption as $(1 - C_{sc}/C_{s+e})$, where C_{sc} indicates the cost of signcryption, while C_{s+e} the cost of signature-then-encryption. More specifically, we have

advantage in   average computational cost

$$= \begin{cases} 1 - \frac{7.4\ell}{0.375(|n_a|+|n_b|)}, & \text{for small public exponents} \\ 1 - \frac{7.4\ell}{0.375(|n_a|+|n_b|)+1.5\ell}, & \text{for } \ell/2\text{-bit public exponents} \end{cases}$$

advantage in   communication overhead

$$= 1 - \frac{|KH.(\cdot)| + 1.75\ell}{|n_a| + |n_b|}$$

Table 6 demonstrates the advantages with respect to various key sizes. While the selection of parameter sizes in Table 6 is admittedly somewhat arbitrary, we note that it is still more conservative than a table suggested in [11].

Table 6. Advantage of Signcryption Scheme HORSE over RSA based Signature-Then-Encryption with *Small Public Exponents*

security parameters				advantage in average computational cost		advantage in communication overhead
$\|n\|$ $(\|n_a\|, \|n_b\|)$	ℓ	$\|KH.(\cdot)\|$	$[\|r\|]$	small public exponent	$\ell/2$-bit public exponent	
1024	160	80	[120]	-54.1%	-17.5%	82.4%
1280	176	88	[132]	-35.6%	-6.4%	84.5%
1536	176	88	[132]	-13.0%	8.0%	87.1%
1792	192	96	[144]	-5.7%	13.0%	88.0%
2048	192	96	[144]	7.6%	22.1%	89.5%
2560	208	104	[156]	19.8%	31.0%	90.9%
3072	224	112	[168]	28.1%	37.2%	91.8%
4096	256	128	[192]	38.3%	45.2%	93.0%
5120	288	144	[216]	44.5%	50.1%	93.7%
8192	320	160	[240]	61.5%	64.3%	95.6%
10240	320	160	[240]	69.2%	71.0%	96.5%

In some applications, one may wish to choose RSA public exponents that are longer than $\ell/2$, or even of full size, while in some other applications the Chinese Remainder Theorem may not be used in RSA decryption or signature generation. Furthermore, one may choose to select key sizes by following the suggestions in [11]. In all these situations, the signcryption scheme HORSE will demonstrate even greater savings in computation time and communication overhead.

7   Concluding Remarks

We have demonstrated applications of rth power residues modulo an RSA composite in constructing efficient identification protocols, digital signature and signcryption schemes. A major difference between this work and prior research is that here r is a *large* prime, or more generally an odd integer containing a *large* prime factor. Efficiency of our schemes is analyzed and compared with some existing solutions. Of particular interest to a practitioner in public key cryptography is the fact that the signcryption scheme HORSE is significantly more advantageous over the traditional "signature followed by encryption" approach using the RSA signature and encryption schemes, both in terms of computational and communication overhead. A formal analysis of the security of the protocols and schemes presented in this paper remains a challenging topic for future research.

To close this paper, we summarize in Table 7 the main variants of signcryption known currently.

Table 7. Currently Known Variants of Signcryption

	Computational Foundation	Reference
1	discrete logarithm on a finite field	Zheng, CRYPTO'97 [19]
2	discrete logarithm on an elliptic curve	Zheng, CRYPTO'97 [19], Zheng & Imai, IPL (1998) [20]
3	factoring / residuosity	Steinfeld & Zheng, ISW2000 [17], Zheng, PKC'01
4	other sub-groups (e.g., XTR)	Gong & Harn, IEEE-IT (2000) [6], Lenstra & Verheul, CRYPTO2000 [12], Zheng, CRYPTO'97 [19]

Acknowledgment

Thanks to Ron Steinfeld for various discussions on selecting security parameters for the schemes. Thanks also to PKC2001 Program Committee members for their helpful comments.

References

1. M. Abadi, J. Feigenbaum, and J. Kilian. On hiding information from an oracle. *Journal of Computer and System Sciences*, 39:21–50, 1989.
2. J. Benaloh. Dense probabilistic encryption. In *Workshop on Selected Areas in Cryptography (SAC'94)*, pages 120–128, Ontario, Canada, 1994. Queen's University.
3. J. Benaloh and M. Yung. Distributing the power of a government to enhance the privacy of voters. In *Proceedings of the 5-th ACM Symposium on Principles of Distributed Computing*, pages 52–62, 1986.
4. T. ElGamal. A public key cryptosystem and a signature scheme based on discrete logarithms. *IEEE Transactions on Information Theory*, IT-31(4):469–472, 1985.
5. S. Goldwasser and S. Micali. Probabilistic encryption. *Journal of Computer and System Sciences*, 28(2):270–299, 1984.
6. G. Gong and L. Harn. Public-key cryptosystems based on cubic finite field extensions. *IEEE Transactions on Information Theory*, 45(7):2601–2605, 2000.
7. S. J. Kim, S. J. Park, and D. H. Won. Convertible group signatures. In *Advances in Cryptology - ASIACRYPT'96*, volume 1163 of *Lecture Notes in Computer Science*, pages 311–321, Berlin, New York, Tokyo, 1996. Springer-Verlag.
8. D. E. Knuth. *Seminumerical Algorithms*, volume 2 of *The Art of Computer Programming*. Addison-Wesley, 2 edition, 1981.
9. K. Kurosawa, Y. Katayama, W. Ogata, and S. Tsujii. General public key residue cryptosystems and mental poker protocols. In *Advances in Cryptology - EUROCRYPT'90*, volume 473 of *Lecture Notes in Computer Science*, pages 374–388, Berlin, New York, Tokyo, 1990. Springer-Verlag.

10. B. Lee, S. Kim, and D. Won. ID-based multisignature scheme based on the high residuosity problem. In *Proceedings of 1997 Joint Workshop on Information Security and Cryptography (JW-ISC'97)*, pages 227–230, Seoul, Korea, 1997. KIISC (Korea).

11. A. Lenstra and E. Verheul. Selecting cryptographic key sizes. In *Public Key Cryptography — The Third International Workshop on Practice and Theory in Public Key Cryptography (PKC2000)*, volume 1751 of *Lecture Notes in Computer Science*, pages 446–465, Berlin, New York, Tokyo, 2000. Springer-Verlag.

12. A. Lenstra and E. Verheul. The XTR public key system. In *Advances in Cryptology - CRYPTO2000*, volume 1880 of *Lecture Notes in Computer Science*, pages 1–19, Berlin, New York, Tokyo, 2000. Springer-Verlag.

13. A. K. Lenstra and H. W. Lenstra. *Algorithms in Number Theory*, volume A of *Handbook in Theoretical Computer Science*, chapter 12, pages 673–715. Elsevier and the MIT Press, 1990.

14. D. Naccache and J. Stern. A new public key cryptosystem based on higher residues. In *Proceedings of the 5th ACM Conference on Computer and Communications Security*, pages 59–66. ACM Press, 1998.

15. P. Paillier. Public-key cryptosystems based on composite degree residuosity classes. In *Advances in Cryptology - EUROCRYPT'99*, volume 1592 of *Lecture Notes in Computer Science*, pages 399–416, Berlin, New York, Tokyo, 1999. Springer-Verlag.

16. D. Pointcheval. The composite discrete logarithm and secure authentication. In *Public Key Cryptography — The Third International Workshop on Practice and Theory in Public Key Cryptography (PKC2000)*, volume 1751 of *Lecture Notes in Computer Science*, pages 113–128, Berlin, New York, Tokyo, 2000. Springer-Verlag.

17. R. Steinfeld and Y. Zheng. A signcryption scheme based on integer factorization. In *Information Security — Proceedings of 2000 Information Security Workshop (ISW2000)*, Lecture Notes in Computer Science, Berlin, New York, Tokyo, 2000. Springer-Verlag. (to appear).

18. S.-M. Yen, C.-S. Laih, and A. K. Lenstra. Multi-exponentiation. *IEE Proceedings - Computers and Digital Techniques*, 141(6):325–326, 1994.

19. Y. Zheng. Digital signcryption or how to achieve cost(signature & encryption) << cost(signature) + cost(encryption). In *Advances in Cryptology - CRYPTO'97*, volume 1294 of *Lecture Notes in Computer Science*, pages 165–179, Berlin, New York, Tokyo, 1997. Springer-Verlag.

20. Y. Zheng and H. Imai. How to construct efficient signcryption schemes on elliptic curves. *Information Processing Letters*, 68:227–233, 1998.

21. Y. Zheng, T. Matsumoto, and H. Imai. Residuosity problem and its applications to cryptography. *Transactions of IEICE*, E71(8):759–767, August 1988.

On the Security of Lenstra's Variant of DSA without Long Inversions

Arjen K. Lenstra[1] and Igor E. Shparlinski[2]

[1] Citibank, N.A., Technical University Eindhoven,
1 North Gate Road, Mendham, NJ 07945-3104, U.S.A.
arjen.lenstra@citicorp.com
[2] Department of Computing, Macquarie University,
Sydney, NSW 2109, Australia
igor@comp.mq.edu.au

Abstract. We use bounds of exponential sums to show that for a wide class of parameters the modification of the DSA signature scheme proposed by A. K. Lenstra at Asiacrypt'96 is as secure as the original scheme.

1 Introduction

Let p and $q \geq 3$ be prime numbers with $q|p-1$. As usual $\mathbb{F}_p$ and $\mathbb{F}_q$ denote fields of p and q elements which we assume to be represented by the elements $\{0, \ldots, p-1\}$ and $\{0, \ldots, q-1\}$, respectively.

For a rational number z and $m \geq 1$ we denote by $\lfloor z \rfloor_m$ the unique integer a, $0 \leq a \leq m-1$ such that $a \equiv z \pmod{m}$ (provided that the denominator of z is relatively prime to m).

The *Digital Signature Algorithm*, or DSA, can be described in the following way. Let $\mathcal{M}$ be the set of messages to be signed and let $h : \mathcal{M} \longrightarrow \mathbb{F}_q$ be an arbitrary hash-function. Let $g \in \mathbb{F}_p$ be a fixed element of multiplicative order q, that is, $g^q = 1$, which is *publicly* known (as well as p and q). Finally, fix a certain element $\alpha \in \mathbb{F}_q^*$ which is the *secret* key known only to the signer. For a *message* $\mu \in \mathcal{M}$ we select a random element $k \in \mathbb{F}_q^*$ called a *nonce* and we define the function

$$r(k) = \left\lfloor \lfloor g^k \rfloor_p \right\rfloor_q \qquad \text{and} \qquad s(k, \mu) = \left\lfloor k^{-1} \left(h(\mu) + \alpha r(k) \right) \right\rfloor_q. \qquad (1)$$

The pair $(r(k), s(k, \mu))$ is the *DSA signature* of the message μ with nonce k.

Modular inversion of the nonce k in (1) is a time consuming operation. To improve the performance several inversion-free modifications of the basic scheme have been proposed, see [13] as well as Sections 11.5.2 and 11.5.4 in [8] and Section 20.4 of [14]. On the other hand, these schemes, although quite close to the original DSA scheme, may not be compatible with it, see the discussion in [6]. Thus to overcome the incompatibility problem (and a large signature size for some of the aforementioned modifications) a very different algorithm has been proposed in [6]. This algorithm follows the basic DSA scheme except that

K. Kim (Ed.): PKC 2001, LNCS 1992, pp. 64–72, 2001.

the nonce k is generated in a special way which allows to generate k and $\lfloor k^{-1} \rfloor_q$ simultaneously at reasonably low computational cost.

The algorithm from [6] works as follows, in a special partial case. Given a prime q and two more integer parameters $T \geq 2$ and $m \geq 1$:

  ○ Select independently and uniformly at random $2m$ integers $t_1, \ldots, t_{2m} \in [2, T]$;
  ○ For $i = 1, \ldots, 2m$, compute $u_i = \lfloor q^{-1} \rfloor_{t_i}$ and $w_i = (qu_i - 1)/t_i$;
  ○ For $i = 1, \ldots, 2m$, using the identity $t_i^{-1} \equiv w_i \pmod{q}$, compute $v_i = \lfloor t_i^{-1} \rfloor_q$;
  ○ Compute and output

$$\kappa = \lfloor t_1 \ldots t_m v_{m+1} \ldots v_{2m} \rfloor_q \qquad \text{and} \qquad \lambda = \lfloor v_1 \ldots v_m t_{m+1} \ldots t_{2m} \rfloor_q.$$

It is easy to see that $\lambda = \lfloor \kappa^{-1} \rfloor_q$. The efficiency of the algorithm is based on the observation that for each arithmetic operation it performs one of the operands is of size T. Furthermore, once $\lfloor q \rfloor_{t_i}$ has been computed, the inversion required for the computation of u_i involves only numbers of size $\leq T$. Thus if the bit length of T is essentially smaller than the bit length of q and m is reasonably small this algorithm is faster than the standard inversion modulo q using the Extended Euclid Algorithm. The efficiency of this algorithm (and its slightly more general form described in [6]) has been numerically verified, see [6] and Section 4.

However, it has remained an open question whether this new way of generating k and $\lfloor k^{-1} \rfloor_q$ undermines the security of the DSA. In [6, Section 3] some heuristic arguments in support of the security of the new scheme are given. At the rumpsession of Asiacrypt'96, S. Vaudenay [16] presented a partial cryptanalysis of the scheme that only affected the security if the t_i are chosen in some particularly bad way that is explicitly excluded in [6, Section 3].

In this paper we show that using bounds of character sums one can establish rigorous security results for the above scheme (for some values of the parameters T and m). In fact we show that the distribution of the value of κ is exponentially close to the uniform distribution. Therefore any algorithm attacking this modification immediately implies an attack on the original scheme with exponentially close probabilities of success.

More precisely, for $k \in \mathbb{F}_q^*$, let $P_{m,T}(k)$ be the probability that the output κ of the above algorithm equals k. We use some known bounds of exponential sums to prove that for a wide range of parameters T and m the *statistical distance*

$$\Delta(m, T) = \sum_{k \in \mathbb{F}_q^*} \left| P_{m,T}(k) - \frac{1}{q-1} \right| \qquad (2)$$

is exponentially small, namely

$$\Delta(m, T) < q^{-\delta}$$

for some constant $\delta > 0$. The range of parameters allowed by this general result do, however, not seem to be of much practical value. We show that under the assumption of the Extended Riemann Hypothesis an essentially stronger result can be obtained that allows parameter choices in a more realistic and practical range.

We stress that the uniformity of distribution of the nonce k is absolutely essential. Indeed, it has been shown in the series of papers [5,10,11] that the knowledge of some bits of k can be used to break the DSA (that is, recovering the private key α) in polynomial time.

2   Preparations

Let $\mathcal{X}$ be the set of multiplicative characters of the multiplicative group $\mathbb{F}_q^*$, see Section 1 of Chapter 5 of [7]. We denote by $\mathcal{X}^*$ the subset of non-trivial characters.

We define

$$\sigma(T) = \max_{\chi \in \mathcal{X}^*} \left| \sum_{t=2}^{T} \chi(t) \right|.$$

Lemma 1. *For any integers $T \geq 2$ and $m \geq 1$ the bound*

$$\Delta(m,T) < q^{1/2} \sigma(T)^{2m-1} T^{-2m+1/2}$$

holds for the statistical distance $\Delta(m,T)$ given by (2).

Proof. Let $N_{m,T}(k)$ be the number of sequences $t_1, \ldots, t_{2m} \in [2,T]$ for which $t_1 \ldots t_m t_{m+1}^{-1} \ldots t_{2m}^{-1} \equiv k \pmod q$. Then $P_{m,T}(k) = N_{m,T}(k) T^{-2m}$.

From the following well-known identity

$$\sum_{\chi \in \mathcal{X}} \chi(z) = \begin{cases} q-1, & \text{if } z = 1, \\ 0, & \text{otherwise,} \end{cases}$$

which holds for any $z \in \mathbb{F}_q^*$ (cf. [7, Theorem 5.4]), we derive

$$N_{m,T}(k) = \frac{1}{q-1} \sum_{t_1, \ldots, t_{2m}=2}^{T} \sum_{\chi \in \mathcal{X}} \chi(t_1 \ldots t_m t_{m+1}^{-1} \ldots t_{2m}^{-1} k^{-1}).$$

We remark that $\chi(\lambda^{-1}) = \overline{\chi(\lambda)}$ for $\lambda \in \mathbb{F}_q^*$ and that $z\bar{z} = |z|^2$, where $\bar{z}$ denotes the conjugate of a complex number z. Therefore, changing the order of summation, separating the term $T^{2m}/(q-1)$ which corresponds to the trivial character, and noting that k^{-1} runs through $\mathbb{F}_q^*$ together with k we obtain

$$\left| N_{m,T}(k) - \frac{T^{2m}}{q-1} \right| = \frac{1}{q-1} \sum_{\chi \in \mathcal{X}^*} \chi(k) \left| \sum_{t=2}^{T} \chi(t) \right|^{2m}.$$

Therefore

$$\sum_{k \in \mathbb{F}_q^*} \left| N_{m,T}(k) - \frac{T^{2m}}{q-1} \right|^2$$

$$= \frac{1}{(q-1)^2} \sum_{k \in \mathbb{F}_q^*} \left(\sum_{\chi \in \mathcal{X}^*} \chi(k) \left| \sum_{t=2}^{T} \chi(t) \right|^{2m} \right)^2$$

$$= \frac{1}{(q-1)^2} \sum_{k \in \mathbb{F}_q^*} \sum_{\chi_1, \chi_2 \in \mathcal{X}^*} \chi_1(k) \chi_2(k) \left| \sum_{t=2}^{T} \chi_1(t) \right|^{2m} \left| \sum_{t=2}^{T} \chi_2(t) \right|^{2m}$$

$$= \frac{1}{(q-1)^2} \sum_{\chi_1, \chi_2 \in \mathcal{X}^*} \left| \sum_{t=2}^{T} \chi_1(t) \right|^{2m} \left| \sum_{t=2}^{T} \chi_2(t) \right|^{2m} \sum_{k \in \mathbb{F}_q^*} \chi_1(k) \chi_2(k).$$

Using that the product of two characters is a character as well and the identity

$$\sum_{k \in \mathbb{F}_q^*} \chi(k) = \begin{cases} q-1, & \text{if } \chi = \chi_0, \\ 0, & \text{otherwise}, \end{cases}$$

where χ_0 is the trivial character (cf. [7, Theorem 5.4]), we see that the inner sum vanishes unless

$$\chi_2(k) = \chi_1(k)^{-1} = \chi_1(k^{-1}) = \overline{\chi_1(k)}, \qquad k \in \mathbb{F}_q^*,$$

in which case it is equal to $q - 1$. Therefore

$$\sum_{k \in \mathbb{F}_q^*} \left| N_{m,T}(k) - \frac{T^{2m}}{q-1} \right|^2 = \frac{1}{q-1} \sum_{\chi \in \mathcal{X}^*} \left| \sum_{t=2}^{T} \chi(t) \right|^{2m} \left| \sum_{t=2}^{T} \overline{\chi(k)} \right|^{2m}$$

$$= \frac{1}{q-1} \sum_{\chi \in \mathcal{X}^*} \left| \sum_{t=2}^{T} \chi(t) \right|^{4m} \le \frac{\sigma(T)^{4m-2}}{q-1} \sum_{\chi \in \mathcal{X}^*} \left| \sum_{t=2}^{T} \chi(t) \right|^2.$$

We have

$$\frac{1}{q-1} \sum_{\chi \in \mathcal{X}^*} \left| \sum_{t=2}^{T} \chi(t) \right|^2 < \frac{1}{q-1} \sum_{\chi \in \mathcal{X}} \left| \sum_{t=2}^{T} \chi(t) \right|^2 = T.$$

Hence

$$\sum_{k \in \mathbb{F}_q^*} \left| P_{m,T}(k) - \frac{T^{2m}}{q-1} \right|^2 \le T^{-4m} \sum_{k \in \mathbb{F}_q^*} \left| N_{m,T}(k) - \frac{T^{2m}}{q-1} \right|^2$$

$$\le \sigma(T)^{4m-2} T^{-4m+1}.$$

From the Cauchy inequality we obtain the desired result.

Thus to estimate the statistical distance we need upper bounds on $\sigma(T)$. The simplest and the most well known bound is given by the *Polya–Vinogradov* inequality

$$\sigma(T) \leq q^{1/2} \ln q,$$

see [9, Theorem 2.2], which is non-trivial only for $T \geq q^{1/2+\varepsilon}$. However such values of T are too large to be useful for our application. Instead we use the *Burgess* bound, see [9, Theorem 2.3].

Lemma 2. *For any $\varepsilon > 0$ there exists $\gamma > 0$ such that*

$$\sigma(T) \leq Tq^{-\gamma}$$

for $T \geq q^{1/4+\varepsilon}$ and sufficiently large q.

It is known that the *Extended Riemann Hypothesis*, or ERH, implies nontrivial upper bounds for much shorter sums. We therefore use a result that relies on the assumption of the ERH. In particular, we use a bound which follows from one of the results of [3].

Lemma 3. *Let*

$$v = \frac{\ln T}{\ln \ln q} \to \infty.$$

Then, assuming the ERH, the bound

$$\sigma(T) \leq Tv^{-v/2+o(v)}$$

holds.

Proof. We recall that an integer $n \geq 1$ is called Y-smooth if all primes dividing it are $\leq Y$. Let $\Psi(X, Y)$ denote the total number of Y-smooth numbers $\leq X$. The following estimate is a substantially relaxed and simplified version of [4, Corollary 1.3]. Let $X = Y^u$; then for any $u \to \infty$ with $u \leq Y^{1/2}$ we have the bound

$$\Psi(X, Y) \ll Xu^{-u+o(u)}. \tag{3}$$

It has been proved in [3, Theorem 2] that

$$\sigma(T) = O\left(\Psi\left(T, \ln^2 q \ln^{20} \ln q\right)\right),$$

provided that $u \to \infty$. One easily verifies that the bound (3) can be applied to the last function with $u = v/2 + o(v)$, producing the desired result.

3   Main Results

Now we are prepared to prove our main results.

Theorem 1. *For any $\varepsilon > 0$ and $A \geq 0$ there exists a constant $m_0(\varepsilon, A) > 0$ such that for any integers $T \geq 2$ and $m \geq 1$ satisfying the inequalities*

$$T \geq q^{1/4+\varepsilon} \qquad and \qquad m \geq m_0(\varepsilon)$$

the statistical distance $\Delta(m, T)$ given by (2) satisfies the bound $\Delta(m, T) \leq q^{-A}$.

Proof. From Lemmas 1 and 2 we obtain the bound

$$\Delta(m, T) < q^{1/2}T^{-1/2}q^{-\gamma(2m-1)} \leq q^{1/4-\gamma(2m-1)} \leq q^{-A}$$

provided that $m \geq (4A + 1)/8\gamma + 1$.

Unfortunately the range of parameters allowed by Theorem 1 does not seem to be of any practical value. However under the ERH an essentially stronger result can be obtained.

Theorem 2. *Assume the ERH. Then for any $A > 0$ and any integers $T \geq 2$ and $m \geq 1$ such that*

$$v = \frac{\ln T}{\ln \ln q} \to \infty \qquad and \qquad m \geq (2A + 1)\frac{\ln q}{v \ln v} + 1$$

for sufficiently large q, the statistical distance $\Delta(m, T)$ given by (2) satisfies the bound $\Delta(m, T) \leq q^{-A}$.

Proof. From Lemmas 1 and 3 we obtain the bound

$$\Delta(m, T) < q^{1/2}T^{-1/2}v^{-(v/2+o(v))(2m-1)} \leq q^{1/2}v^{-v(2m-1)/3}$$
$$\leq q^{1/2-(4A+2)/3} \leq q^{-A},$$

provided that q is large enough.

In particular, if q is about n bits long and T is selected about ℓ bits long with $\ell \geq \ln n^{1+\varepsilon}$, then for m of order $n/\ln \ell$ the algorithm of [6] generates a secure sequence of pairs $\kappa, \lambda = \lfloor \kappa^{-1} \rfloor_q$. Thus the values of T used in this algorithm can be rather small.

4   Practical Considerations

In [6] it was shown that generating k and $\lfloor k^{-1} \rfloor_q$ simultaneously as indicated in Section 1 and with $m = 3$ is about as fast as the regular method of computing $\lfloor k^{-1} \rfloor_q$ given a random k, for the common values $n = 160$ and $\ell = 32$ where n and ℓ are the bit lengths of q and T, respectively. In the analysis of [6] it was assumed that the regular method makes use of Lehmer's method for the inversion. Thus, in environments where Lehmer's inversion is available there does not seem to be any good reason not to generate k and $\lfloor k^{-1} \rfloor_q$ in the regular way.

Lehmer's method is about twice faster than regular modular inversion (which is based directly on the Extended Euclidean Algorithm) because it replaces most of the extended precision integer divisions by floating point approximations. The disadvantage of Lehmer's method is, however, that it takes substantially more code and memory than regular modular inversion (or than the method from [6]). For computation in more restricted environments (such as a credit card chip) where the space and size needs of Lehmer's method cannot be met, the method of [6] may therefore be an option, because it would be faster than regular modular inversion, even if m is taken as large as 6.

Theorem 2, however, indicates that for $n = 160$ and $\ell = 32$ security can be guaranteed (under the ERH) only for substantially larger choices for m, namely m should be at least about 100. Obviously, such large m severely limit the practical applicability of the method from [6] reviewed in Section 1, assuming that provable security of the choice of k is required: implementation of the method makes sense only if very limited space is available, and division of extended precision integers (as required for regular modular inversion) is not available. It should be kept in mind, however, that the results presented in this paper are just theoretical lower bounds for the security and that in practice much smaller values of m should give satisfactory results, as also indicated in [6]. In fact even our theoretical results can be improved and extended; some further possibilities are indicated in Section 5. We do not present them here because our main motivation has been to indicate a possible way to establish rigorous proofs of security of the approach proposed in [6], rather than deriving all possible results of this kind.

An alternative way of using the idea behind the method from [6] in the vein of the method of [1], as informally and independently proposed by several different people, is as follows. Compute and store $S_1 = \{t_1, \ldots, t_{2r}\}$ and the corresponding $S_2 = \{v_1, \ldots, v_{2r}\}$ for some large value of r and compute the products over the four relevant random subsets of size m of $S_1 \bigcup S_2$ for each pair k, $\lfloor k^{-1} \rfloor_q$ to be generated, where r is substantially larger than m. Given the successful attack (cf. [12]) on the method from [1], however, this approach cannot be recommended.

5   Remarks

The algorithm itself as well as all our main tools, can be extended to composite moduli. The only difference is that Lemma 2 holds in the present form only for square-free moduli, however a slightly weaker result is known in the general case as well (which is nontrivial for $T \geq q^{3/8+\varepsilon}$).

One can also remark that if $T^{2\nu} < q$ for an integer $\nu \geq 1$ then

$$\sum_{\chi \in \mathcal{X}} \left| \sum_{t=2}^{T} \chi(t) \right|^{2\nu} = (q-1)M_\nu(T),$$

where $M_\nu(T)$ is the number of solutions of the equation (rather than a congruence)

$$t_1 \ldots t_\nu = t_{\nu+1} \ldots t_{2\nu}, \quad t_1, \ldots, t_{2\nu} \in [2, T]$$

which can be estimated using various number theoretic tools. In particular, the bound

$$M_\nu(T) \leq T^\nu \left(1 + (\nu - 1)\ln T\right)^{\nu^2 - 1}$$

has been given in [15, Lemma 4].

It is also worth mentioning that, under the ERH, one can improve Theorem 1 (and Theorem 2 for larger values of T). Namely, for any $\varepsilon > 0$, the ERH implies the bound

$$\sigma(T) = O(T^{1/2}q^\varepsilon). \tag{4}$$

In fact, using the so-called "large sieve" method one can probably obtain quite strong unconditional results for "almost all" q rather than for all of them (which still suffices for cryptographic applications).

On the other hand, there are infinitely many primes q such that for $T = O(\log q)$ and any $m \geq 1$ the statistical distance $\Delta(m, T)$ is very large. Indeed, it has been shown in [2] that there exists a constant $c > 0$ such that for infinitely many primes q the smallest quadratic non-residue modulo q is at least $c \log q \log \log \log q$ (under the ERH the same result is known with $c \log q \log \log q$). Therefore for such q, $T = \lfloor c \log q \log \log \log q \rfloor$ and any $m \geq 1$ we have $P_{m,T}(k) = 0$ whenever k is one of the $(q-1)/2$ quadratic non-residues modulo q. Therefore, in this case $\Delta(m, T) \geq 1/2$. It should be noted that a large statistical distance does not imply that the corresponding signature scheme is insecure.

A more general modification of the algorithm from [6] (where some of the t_i and v_i are alternated in a random fashion in the expressions for κ and λ) can be studied quite analogously.

Acknowledgement

We thank Hugh Montgomery for indicating a proof of the bound (4).

References

1. V. Boyko, M. Peinado and R. Venkatesan, *Speeding up discrete log and factoring based schemes via precomputations,* Proc. EUROCRYPT'98, Lect. Notes in Comp. Sci., Springer-Verlag, Berlin, **1403** (1998), 221–235.
2. S. W. Graham and C. J. Ringrose, *Lower bounds for least quadratic nonresidues,* Analytic number theory, Progr. Math., 85, Birkhäuser, Boston, MA, 1990, 269–309.

3. A. Granville and K. Soundararajan, *Large character sums*, J. Amer. Math. Soc. (to appear); available from http://www.ams.org/jams/.
4. A. Hildebrand and G. Tenenbaum, *Integers without large prime factors*, J. de Théorie des Nombres de Bordeaux, **5** (1993), 411–484.
5. N. A. Howgrave-Graham and N. P. Smart, *Lattice attacks on digital signature schemes*, Designs, Codes and Cryptography (to appear).
6. A. K. Lenstra, *Generating standard DSA signatures without long inversions*, Proc. ASIACRYPT'96, Lect. Notes in Comp. Sci., Springer-Verlag, Berlin, **1163** (1996), 57–64.
7. R. Lidl and H. Niederreiter, *Finite fields*, Cambridge University Press, Cambridge, 1997.
8. A. J. Menezes, P. C. van Oorschot and S. A. Vanstone, *Handbook of Applied Cryptography*, CRC Press, Boca Raton, FL, 1996.
9. W. Narkiewicz, *Classical problems in number theory*, Polish Sci. Publ., Warszawa, 1986.
10. P. Nguyen, *The dark side of the Hidden Number Problem: Lattice attacks on DSA*, Proc. Workshop on Cryptography and Computational Number Theory, Singapore 1999, Birkhäuser, 2000 (to appear).
11. P. Nguyen and I. E. Shparlinski, *The insecurity of the Digital Signature Algorithm with partially known nonces*, Preprint, 2000, 1–26.
12. P. Nguyen and J. Stern, *The hardness of the hidden subset sum problem and its cryptographic implications*, Proc. CRYPTO'99, Lect. Notes in Comp. Sci., Springer-Verlag, Berlin, **1666** (1999), 31–46.
13. K. Nyberg and R. A. Rueppel, *Message recovery for signature schemes based on the discrete logarithm problem*, J. Cryptology, **8** (1995), 27–37.
14. B. Schneier, *Applied cryptography*, John Wiley, NY, 1996.
15. P. J. Stephens, *An average result for Artin's conjecture*, Mathematika, **16** (1969), 178–188.
16. S. Vaudenay, *On the security of Lenstra's DSA variant*, Presented at the Rump Session of ASIACRYPT'96; available from http://lasecwww.epfl.ch/pub/lasec/doc/lenstra.ps

Fast Irreducibility
and Subgroup Membership Testing in XTR

Arjen K. Lenstra[1] and Eric R. Verheul[2]

[1] Citibank, N.A., Technical University Eindhoven, 1 North Gate Road, Mendham,
NJ 07945-3104, U.S.A.
arjen.lenstra@citicorp.com
[2] PricewaterhouseCoopers, GRMS Crypto Group, Goudsbloemstraat 14, 5644 KE
Eindhoven, The Netherlands
Eric.Verheul@[nl.pwcglobal.com, pobox.com]

Abstract. We describe a new general method to perform part of the set-up stage of the XTR system introduced at Crypto 2000, namely finding the trace of a generator of the XTR group. Our method is substantially faster than the general method presented at Asiacrypt 2000. As a side result, we obtain an efficient method to test subgroup membership when using XTR.

1 Introduction

XTR is an efficient and compact method to work with order $p^2 - p + 1$ subgroups of the multiplicative group $\mathrm{GF}(p^6)^*$ of the finite field $\mathrm{GF}(p^6)$. It was introduced at Crypto 2000 (cf. [4]), followed by several practical improvements a Asiacrypt 2000 (cf. [5]). In this paper we present some further improvements of the methods from [4] and [5]. Given the rapidly growing interest in XTR our new methods are of immediate practical importance.

Let p and q be primes such that $p \equiv 2 \bmod 3$ and q divides $p^2 - p + 1$, let g be a generator of the order q subgroup of $\mathrm{GF}(p^6)^*$, and let $Tr(g) = g + g^{p^2} + g^{p^4} \in \mathrm{GF}(p^2)$ be the trace over $\mathrm{GF}(p^2)$ of g. In [4] it is shown that the conjugates over $\mathrm{GF}(p^2)$ of elements of the XTR group $\langle g \rangle$ can conveniently be represented by their trace over $\mathrm{GF}(p^2)$, and it is shown how this representation can efficiently be computed given $Tr(g)$.

Given p and q the trace of a generator of the XTR group can be found as follows, as shown in [4]. First one finds a value $c \in \mathrm{GF}(p^2)$ such that $F(c, X) = X^3 - cX^2 + c^p X - 1 \in \mathrm{GF}(p^2)[X]$ is irreducible over $\mathrm{GF}(p^2)$. Given an irreducible $F(c, X)$, there exists an element $h \in \mathrm{GF}(p^6)^*$ of order > 3 and dividing $p^2 - p + 1$ such that $Tr(h) = c$. Actually, h is a root of $F(c, X)$. This implies that $Tr(g)$ can be computed as $Tr(h^{(p^2-p+1)/q})$, assuming that this value is $\neq 3$; if $Tr(h^{(p^2-p+1)/q}) = 3$ another c has be to found such that $F(c, X)$ is irreducible. Because $F(c, X)$ is irreducible for about one third of the c's in $\mathrm{GF}(p^2)$, on average $3q/(q - 1)$ different c's have to be tried before a proper c is found.

Thus, for the XTR parameter set-up process one needs to be able to test irreducibility of polynomials of the form $F(c, X) = X^3 - cX^2 + c^p X - 1 \in \mathrm{GF}(p^2)[X]$

K. Kim (Ed.): PKC 2001, LNCS 1992, pp. 73–86, 2001.

for random $c \in \mathrm{GF}(p^2)$. The irreducibility test given in [4] takes $8\log_2(p)$ multiplications in $\mathrm{GF}(p)$; finding an irreducible $F(c,X)$ using this method thus takes an expected $24\log_2(p)$ multiplications in $\mathrm{GF}(p)$. In the follow-up paper [5] a method is described that tests irreducibility of $F(c,X)$ for random $c \in \mathrm{GF}(p^2)$ in $2.4\log_2(p)$ multiplications in $\mathrm{GF}(p)$ on average, so that an irreducible $F(c,X)$ can on average be found in $7.2\log_2(p)$ multiplications in $\mathrm{GF}(p)$. In this paper we present a further refinement of this last method that results in an $F(c,X)$-irreducibility test that takes, on average for random $c \in \mathrm{GF}(p^2)$, only $0.9\log_2(p)$ multiplications in $\mathrm{GF}(p)$. As a result, an irreducible $F(c,X)$ can be found in an expected $2.7\log_2(p)$ multiplications in $\mathrm{GF}(p)$.

The test from [4] takes $8\log_2(p)$ multiplications in $\mathrm{GF}(p)$, irrespective of the outcome. The test from [5], on the other hand, is effectively free for half the c's, and takes $4.8\log_2(p)$ multiplications in $\mathrm{GF}(p)$ for the other half (two thirds of which lead to an irreducible $F(c,X)$). Similarly, the refined test in the present paper is effectively free for half the c's, and takes $1.8\log_2(p)$ multiplications in $\mathrm{GF}(p)$ for the other half. Thus, if during a cryptographic application of XTR a value c is transmitted for which, if the protocol is carried out correctly, $F(c,X)$ is supposed to be irreducible, then the irreducibility of $F(c,X)$ can be verified at the cost of $1.8\log_2(p)$ multiplications in $\mathrm{GF}(p)$ using our new method. This is more than 60% faster than the method from [5] and implies that this verification by the recipient of XTR related values does not cause severe additional overhead. Note that such checks are required because many cryptographic protocols are vulnerable if 'wrong' data are used (cf. [1], [2], [6], [11], and Section 4).

As the irreducibility test from [5] our new irreducibility test is based on Scipione del Ferro's method. Instead of applying it directly to test $F(c,X) \in \mathrm{GF}(p^2)[X]$ for irreducibility, however, we reformulate the problem as an irreducibility problem for a third-degree polynomial $P(c,X) \in \mathrm{GF}(p)[X]$. This is done in Section 2. We then show in Section 3 how the irreducibility of the resulting polynomial $P(c,X)$ can be verified. In Section 4 we discuss subgroup membership testing, and in Section 5 we show how this can be done in XTR. We present a method that is based on the $F(c,X)$-irreducibility test and costs a small amount of additional computation but no additional communication, and another method that takes only a constant number of $\mathrm{GF}(p)$-operations but causes some additional communication overhead.

2   From $F(c,X) \in \mathrm{GF}(p^2)[X]$ to $P(c,X) \in \mathrm{GF}(p)[X]$

Let $c \in \mathrm{GF}(p^2)$ and let $h_j \in \mathrm{GF}(p^6)$ for $j = 0,1,2$ be the roots of $F(c,X) \in \mathrm{GF}(p^2)[X]$. Because $F(c, h_j^{-p}) = 0$ for $j = 0,1,2$ (cf. [4, Lemma 2.3.2.iv]) we can distinguish three cases:

I. $h_j = h_j^{-p}$ for $j = 0,1,2$.

II. $h_0 = h_0^{-p}$ and $h_j = h_{3-j}^{-p}$ for $j = 1,2$.

III. $h_j = h_{j+1 \bmod 3}^{-p}$ for $j = 0,1,2$.

In cases I and II we have that $h_j \in \mathrm{GF}(p^2)$ so that $F(c, X)$ is reducible over $\mathrm{GF}(p^2)$. In case III all h_j have order dividing $p^2 - p + 1$ and > 3 so that $F(c, x)$ is irreducible over $\mathrm{GF}(p^2)$ (cf. [4, Lemma 2.3.2.vi]). Thus, if case III can quickly be distinguished from the other two cases, then the irreducibility of $F(c, X)$ can quickly be tested. Actually, we only have to be able to distinguish between cases I and III, because case II can quickly be recognized since it applies if and only if $\Delta \in \mathrm{GF}(p)$ as in [5, Step 2 of Algorithm 3.5] is a quadratic non-residue in $\mathrm{GF}(p)$ (cf. [5, Lemma 3.6]).

Definition 2.1 Let $G(c, X) = F(c, X) \cdot F(c^p, X)$, and let

$$P(c, X) = X^3 + (c^p + c)X^2 + (c^{p+1} + c^p + c - 3)X + c^{2p} + c^2 + 2 - 2c^p - 2c.$$

The following lemma describes some of the immediate properties of the polynomials $G(c, X)$ and $P(c, X)$ and their interrelation.

Lemma 2.2 Both $G(c, X)$ and $P(c, X)$ are in $\mathrm{GF}(p)[X]$. Furthermore $P(c, X)$ can be written as the product $\prod_{j=0}^{2}(X - G_j)$ of three linear polynomials if and only if $G(c, X)$ can be written as the product $\prod_{j=0}^{2}(X^2 + G_j X + 1)$ of three quadratic polynomials, where $G_j \in \mathrm{GF}(p^6)$ for $j = 0, 1, 2$. In particular, this decomposition of $G(c, X)$ is unique modulo permutation and either all G_j are in $\mathrm{GF}(p^2)$ or all G_j are in $\mathrm{GF}(p^3)$.

Proof. It follows from Definition 2.1 and a straightforward computation that $G(c, X)$ equals

$$X^6 - (c^p + c)X^5 + (c^{p+1} + c^p + c)X^4 - (c^{2p} + c^2 + 2)X^3 + (c^{p+1} + c^p + c)X^2 - (c^p + c)X + 1.$$

All coefficients of $G(c, X)$ and $P(c, X)$ equal their own p^{th} power, so that $G(c, X)$ and $P(c, X)$ are in $\mathrm{GF}(p)[X]$. Because $\prod_{j=0}^{2}(X^2 + G_j X + 1)$ equals

$$X^6 + (G_0 + G_1 + G_2)X^5 + (G_0 G_1 + G_0 G_2 + G_1 G_2 + 3)X^4 + (2G_0 + 2G_1 + 2G_2$$

$$+ G_0 G_1 G_2)X^3 + (G_0 G_1 + G_0 G_2 + G_1 G_2 + 3)X^2 + (G_0 + G_1 + G_2)X + 1,$$

it follows that $G(c, X) = \prod_{j=0}^{2}(X^2 + G_j X + 1)$ is equivalent to $G_0 + G_1 + G_2 = -c^p - c \in \mathrm{GF}(p)$, $G_0 G_1 + G_0 G_2 + G_1 G_2 = c^{p+1} + c^p + c - 3 \in \mathrm{GF}(p)$, and $G_0 G_1 G_2 = 2c^p + 2c - c^{2p} - c^2 - 2 \in \mathrm{GF}(p)$. That is, G_0, G_1, G_2 are the roots of $P(c, X)$. The proof now follows from the fact that $\prod_{j=0}^{2}(X - G_j) = X^3 - (G_0 + G_1 + G_2)X^2 + (G_0 G_1 + G_0 G_2 + G_1 G_2)X - G_0 G_1 G_2$, Definition 2.1, and the well known result that the roots of a third degree polynomial over $\mathrm{GF}(p)$ are either in $\mathrm{GF}(p^2)$ or in $\mathrm{GF}(p^3)$.

Lemma 2.3 $G(c, X) = \prod_{j=0}^{2}(X^2 + G_j X + 1)$ where, depending on cases I, II, and III as identified above, the following holds:

I. $G_j \in \mathrm{GF}(p)$ for $j = 1, 2, 3$.
II. $G_0 \in \mathrm{GF}(p)$ and $G_j \in \mathrm{GF}(p^2)$ for $j = 1, 2$.

III. $G_j \in \mathrm{GF}(p^3)$ *for* $j = 0, 1, 2$ *and* $G(c, X)$ *is irreducible over* $\mathrm{GF}(p)$.

Proof. Immediate. For completeness we present the details. It follows from [4, Lemmas 2.3.4.*ii* and 2.3.2.*v*] that $F(c^p, h_j^p) = 0$ for $j = 0, 1, 2$, so that h_j^i for $j = 0, 1, 2$ and $i = 1, p$ are the roots of $G(c, X)$, in cases I, II, and III.

In case III (i.e., $F(c, X)$ is irreducible over $\mathrm{GF}(p^2)$) the h_j are conjugates over $\mathrm{GF}(p^2)$, i.e., $h_j = h_{j+1 \bmod 3}^{p^2}$. It follows that h_0 and its conjugates over $\mathrm{GF}(p)$ are the zeros of $G(c, X)$ so that $G(c, X)$ is irreducible over $\mathrm{GF}(p)$. Furthermore, $h_j^{p^3} = h_j^{p^3 \bmod p^2 - p + 1} = h_j^{-1} = h_{j+1 \bmod 3}^p$ and $h_{j+1 \bmod 3}^{p^4} = h_{j+2 \bmod 3}^{-p^5} = h_j^{p^6} = h_j$. Therefore $(h_j + h_{j+1 \bmod 3}^p)^{p^3} = h_j + h_{j+1 \bmod 3}^p$, so that $h_j + h_{j+1 \bmod 3}^p \in \mathrm{GF}(p^3)$. With $h_j \cdot h_{j+1 \bmod 3}^p = h_{j+1 \bmod 3}^{-p} \cdot h_{j+1 \bmod 3}^p = 1$ and defining $G_j = -h_j - h_{j+1 \bmod 3}^p \in \mathrm{GF}(p^3)$ for $j = 0, 1, 2$ we find that in case III the polynomial $G(c, X)$ factors as $\prod_{j=0}^{2}(X^2 + G_j X + 1)$ over $\mathrm{GF}(p^3)[X]$.

In case I we have for $j = 0, 1, 2$ that $h_j \cdot h_j^p = h_j^{-p} \cdot h_j^p = 1$ and $(h_j + h_j^p)^p = h_j^p + h_j^{p^2} = h_j^p + h_j$ so that $h_j + h_j^p \in \mathrm{GF}(p)$. Defining $G_j = -h_j - h_j^p \in \mathrm{GF}(p)$ for $j = 0, 1, 2$, we find that in case I the polynomial $G(c, X)$ factors as $\prod_{j=0}^{2}(X^2 + G_j X + 1)$ over $\mathrm{GF}(p)[X]$.

In case II we define $G_0 = -h_0 - h_0^p$, so that $G_0 \in \mathrm{GF}(p)$ as in case I. Furthermore, we define $G_j = -h_j - h_{3-j}^p$ for $j = 1, 2$. In this case $(h_j + h_{3-j}^p)^{p^2} = h_j^{p^2} + h_{3-j}^{p^3} = h_j + h_{3-j}^p$ so that $G_j \in \mathrm{GF}(p^2)$ for $j = 1, 2$. Because furthermore $h_j \cdot h_{3-j}^p = h_{3-j}^{-p} \cdot h_{3-j}^p = 1$ we find that $G(c, X)$ is the product of $X^2 + G_0 X + 1 \in \mathrm{GF}(p)[X]$ and $X^2 + G_j X + 1 \in \mathrm{GF}(p^2)[X]$ for $j = 1, 2$. This concludes the proof of Lemma 2.3.

Corollary 2.4 *Depending on cases I, II, and III, the following holds:*

I. $P(c, X)$ *has three roots in* $\mathrm{GF}(p)$.
II. $P(c, X)$ *has one root in* $\mathrm{GF}(p)$ *and two roots in* $\mathrm{GF}(p^2)$.
III. $P(c, X)$ *has three roots in* $\mathrm{GF}(p^3) \setminus \mathrm{GF}(p)$.

Corollary 2.5 $F(c, X)$ *is irreducible over* $\mathrm{GF}(p^2)$ *if and only if* $P(c, X)$ *is irreducible over* $\mathrm{GF}(p)$.

In the next section we show that we can determine irreducibility for $P(c, X)$ faster than for $F(c, X)$. Note that $P(c, X)$ can be computed from $F(c, X)$ at the cost of a small constant number of multiplications in $\mathrm{GF}(p)$.

3   Testing $P(c, X) \in \mathrm{GF}(p)[X]$ for irreducibility

Let $P(c, X) \in \mathrm{GF}(p)[X]$ as in Definition 2.1. We base our method to test $P(c, X)$ for irreducibility over $\mathrm{GF}(p)$ on Scipione del Ferro's method, cf. [5, Algorithm 3.1]. We recall this algorithm as it applies to $P(c, X) \in \mathrm{GF}(p)[X]$.

Algorithm 3.1 To find the roots of $P(c, X) = X^3 + p_2 X^2 + p_1 X + p_0 \in \mathrm{GF}(p)[X]$ in a field of characteristic unequal to 2 or 3, do the following.

1. Compute the polynomial $P(c, X - p_2/3) = X^3 + f_1 X + f_0 \in \mathrm{GF}(p)[X]$ with $f_1 = p_1 - p_2^2/3$ and $f_0 = (27p_0 - 9p_2 p_1 + 2p_2^3)/27$.
2. Compute the discriminant $\Delta = f_0^2 + 4f_1^3/27 \in \mathrm{GF}(p)$ of the polynomial $X^2 + f_0 X - (f_1/3)^3$, and compute its roots $r_{1,2} = (-f_0 \pm \sqrt{\Delta})/2$.
3. If $r_1 = r_2 = 0$, then let $u = v = 0$. Otherwise, let $r_1 \neq 0$, compute a cube root u if r_1, and let $v = -f_1/(3u)$.
4. The roots of $P(c, X)$ are $u + v - p_2/3$, $u\alpha + v\alpha^2 - p_2/3$, and $u\alpha^2 + v\alpha - p_2/3$, with α as in [4, Section 2.1].

Lemma 3.2 *With cases I, II, and III as identified in Section 2 and Algorithm 3.1 applied to the polynomial $P(c, X) \in \mathrm{GF}(p)[X]$, we have that case III applies if and only if Δ as in Step 2 of Algorithm 3.1 is a quadratic non-residue in $\mathrm{GF}(p)$ and r_1 as in Step 2 of Algorithm 3.1 is not a cube in $\mathrm{GF}(p^2)$.*

Proof. If Δ as in Step 2 of Algorithm 3.1 is a quadratic residue in $\mathrm{GF}(p)$, then r_1 is in $\mathrm{GF}(p)$. From $p \equiv 2 \bmod 3$ it follows that all elements of $\mathrm{GF}(p)$ are cubes, so u as in Step 3 of Algorithm 3.1 is in $\mathrm{GF}(p)$ as well. It follows that $P(c, X)$ has at least one root in $\mathrm{GF}(p)$ so that with Corollary 2.4 case III does not apply.

If Δ is a quadratic non-residue in $\mathrm{GF}(p)$, then $r_1 \in \mathrm{GF}(p^2) \setminus \mathrm{GF}(p)$. If r_1 is a cube in $\mathrm{GF}(p^2)$ then $P(c, X)$ cannot have three roots in $\mathrm{GF}(p^3) \setminus \mathrm{GF}(p)$ so that, with Corollary 2.4, case III does not apply. The proof now follows by observing that if Δ is a quadratic non-residue in $\mathrm{GF}(p)$ and r_1 is not a cube in $\mathrm{GF}(p^2)$, then $P(c, X)$ cannot have a root in $\mathrm{GF}(p)$ so that, with Corollary 2.4, case III must apply.

Lemma 3.2 reduces $P(c, X)$-irreducibility (and thus $F(c, X)$-irreducibility, cf. Corollary 2.5) to the computation of a quadratic residue symbol, possibly followed by an actual square-root computation and a cubic residuosity test. We show that the square-root computation can be avoided by combining it with the cubic residuosity test. We first sketch our approach.

In [5] it was shown (just before Algorithm 3.5 in [5]) that an element x of $\mathrm{GF}(p^2)$ is a cube if and only if $x^{(p^2-1)/3} = 1$, i.e., if and only if $(x^{p-1})^{(p+1)/3} = 1$. It is easily shown that for $y \in \mathrm{GF}(p^2)$ of order dividing $p+1$ the trace over $\mathrm{GF}(p)$ of $y^{(p+1)/3}$ equals 2 if and only if $y^{(p+1)/3} = 1$. The trace over $\mathrm{GF}(p)$ of $y^{(p+1)/3}$ can be computed at the cost of $1.8 \log_2(p)$ multiplications in $\mathrm{GF}(p)$ if the trace over $\mathrm{GF}(p)$ of y is known (cf. Algorithm 3.4). In our application, $y = x^{p-1}$ and $x = r_1$ with $r_1 = -f_0/2 + \sqrt{\Delta}/2$ (cf. Step 2 of Algorithm 3.1) where Δ is a quadratic non-residue. We show that for x of this form the trace over $\mathrm{GF}(p)$ of x^{p-1} is given by an easy expression in which $\sqrt{\Delta}$ does not occur. Thus, the only substantial computation that remains to be done is the computation of the trace over $\mathrm{GF}(p)$ of $y^{(p+1)/3}$ at the cost of $1.8 \log_2(p)$ multiplications in $\mathrm{GF}(p)$. We now present this method in more detail.

Lemma 3.3 *Let $t \in \mathrm{GF}(p)$ be a quadratic non-residue in $\mathrm{GF}(p)$ and $a, b \in \mathrm{GF}(p)$. Then $a^2 - b^2 t \neq 0$ and*

$$\left((a + bX)^{p-1} + (a + bX)^{1-p}\right) \bmod (X^2 - t) = 2\frac{a^2 + b^2 t}{a^2 - b^2 t}.$$

Proof. Because t is a quadratic non-residue we find that $a^2 - b^2 t \neq 0$ and that $t^{(p-1)/2} = -1$. The latter implies that $X^p = -X \mod (X^2 - t)$, so that

$$\left(\frac{(a+bX)^p}{a+bX} + \frac{a+bX}{(a+bX)^p} \right) \mod (X^2 - t) = \left(\frac{a-bX}{a+bX} + \frac{a+bX}{a-bX} \right) \mod (X^2 - t).$$

The result follows with

$$\frac{a-bX}{a+bX} + \frac{a+bX}{a-bX} = \frac{(a-bX)^2 + (a+bX)^2}{(a+bX)(a-bX)} = 2\frac{a^2 + b^2 X^2}{a^2 - b^2 X^2}.$$

The following algorithm is well known in the context of primality testing, more specifically the $p+1$-test for primality (cf. [10, Section 4]).

Algorithm 3.4 To compute the trace $Tr(y^n) \in GF(p)$ over $GF(p)$ of $y^n \in GF(p^2)$, given an integer $n > 0$ and the trace $Tr(y) \in GF(p)$ over $GF(p)$ of some $y \in GF(p^2)$ of order dividing $p+1$. This algorithm takes $1.8 \log_2(p)$ multiplications in $GF(p)$ assuming a squaring in $GF(p)$ takes 80% of the time of a multiplication in $GF(p)$.

1. Let $n = \sum_{i=0}^{k} n_i 2^i$ with $n_i \in \{0,1\}$ and $n_k \neq 0$, let $v = Tr(y) \in GF(p)$ and compute $w = (x^2 - 2) \in GF(p)$.
2. For $i = k-1, k-2, \ldots, 0$ in succession, do the following.
   - If $n_i = 1$, then first replace v by $vw - Tr(y)$ and next replace w by $w^2 - 2$.
   - If $n_i = 0$, then first replace w by $vw - Tr(y)$ and next replace v by $v^2 - 2$.
3. Return $Tr(y^n) = v$.

Algorithm 3.5 To test $P(c, X) = X^3 + p_2 X^2 + p_1 X + p_0 \in GF(p)[X]$ for irreducibility over $GF(p)$, with p unequal to 2 or 3, do the following.

1. Compute the polynomial $P(c, X - p_2/3) = X^3 + f_1 X + f_0 \in GF(p)[X]$ with $f_1 = p_1 - p_2^2/3 \in GF(p)$ and $f_0 = (27p_0 - 9p_2 p_1 + 2p_2^3)/27 \in GF(p)$.
2. Compute the discriminant $\Delta = f_0^2 + 4f_1^3/27 \in GF(p)$ of the polynomial $X^2 + f_0 X - (f_1/3)^3$.
3. Compute the Jacobi symbol of Δ. If Δ is a quadratic residue in $GF(p)$, then $P(c, X)$ is not irreducible (cf. Lemma 3.2).
4. Otherwise, if Δ is a quadratic non-residue in $GF(p)$, compute the trace of r_1^{p-1} over $GF(p)$ as $s = 2\frac{f_0^2 + \Delta}{f_0^2 - \Delta} \in GF(p)$, where $r_1 = -f_0/2 + \sqrt{\Delta}/2$ (cf. Lemma 3.3).
5. Apply Algorithm 3.4 to $Tr(y) = s$ and $n = (p+1)/3$ to compute the trace over $GF(p)$ of $(r_1^{p-1})^{(p+1)/3}$. If the result equals 2, then r_1 is a cube in $GF(p^2)$ and thus $P(c, X)$ is not irreducible (cf. Lemma 3.2).
6. Otherwise, Δ is a quadratic non-residue and r_1 is not a cube in $GF(p^2)$ so that $P(c, X)$ is irreducible over $GF(p)$ (cf. Lemma 3.2).

Theorem 3.6 *For $c \in \mathrm{GF}(p^2)$ the irreducibility of the polynomial $F(c, X) = X^3 - cX^2 + c^p X - 1$ over $\mathrm{GF}(p^2)$ can be tested at the cost of $m + 1.8 \log_2(p)$ multiplications in $\mathrm{GF}(p)$, for some small constant m.*

Proof. The proof follows from Section 2, Algorithm 3.5, and Algorithm 3.4.

Corollary 3.7 *Finding the trace of a generator of the XTR group can be expected to take about $\frac{q}{q-1}(2.7 \log_2(p) + 8 \log_2((p^2 - p + 1)/q))$ multiplications in $\mathrm{GF}(p)$ (cf. [5, Theorem 3.7]).*

Proof. Immediate from the proof of [5, Theorem 3.7] and Theorem 3.6 above.

Note that the result from Corollary 3.7 is only about $2.7 \log_2(p)$ multiplications in $\mathrm{GF}(p)$ slower than [5, Algorithm 4.5], but more general since it applies to all $p \equiv 2 \bmod 3$ and not only to $p \equiv 2, 5 \bmod 9$.

4   Subgroup Attacks

Many cryptographic protocols can be tricked into undesirable behavior if data is used that does not have the properties prescribed by the protocol. For instance, elements of a certain group may be exchanged, but if membership of the proper group is not tested before the elements are operated upon, security may be endangered. A prominent example is the following. Let G be a cyclic, multiplicative group of prime order q (of size ≥ 160 bits) where the discrete logarithm problem is believed to be intractable, and let g be an element of order q in G. In practice, G is often constructed as a subgroup of an abelian *supergroup* H, such that membership of H is easily verified.

For example, if $H = \mathrm{GF}(p)^*$ for a 1024-bit prime number p and the set $\{0, 1, ..., p - 1\}$ is used to represent $\mathrm{GF}(p)$, then $x \in H$ if and only if $0 < x < p$, which can trivially be tested. Similarly, if H is the group of points (written multiplicatively) of a properly chosen elliptic curve over a finite field, then $x \in H$ can simply be verified by testing that the coordinates of the 'point' x belong to the finite field and that x satisfies the curve equation. In both examples G may be chosen as $\langle g \rangle$ for an element g of prime order q dividing the order $|H|$ of H. But testing if $x \in G$ is less trivial and consists of verifying that $x \in H$ and $x^q = 1$. In the first example $|H|/|G|$ is usually very large compared to q, whereas in the second example this ratio is commonly chosen to be very small.

To review why membership testing of G is crucial to maintain security we consider the Diffie-Hellman protocol. Assume that Alice calculates $v_A = g^{k_A} \in G$ where k_A is secret and sends the result to Bob. Likewise, Bob calculates and sends $v_B = g^{k_B} \in G$ to Alice, where k_B is supposed to be secret for Alice. The shared secret key $g^{k_A k_B}$ can then easily be computed by both Alice and Bob. The security is based on the assumption that k_A or k_B cannot be inferred from g, v_A, and v_B. This assumption may be incorrect if v_A or v_B is replaced by an element not in G, inadvertently or on purpose. As a first illustration, suppose that $\alpha \in H$ is of small order, say 2, and suppose that an active eavesdropper changes v_A into $v_A \cdot \alpha$ in transit. It follows that in this scenario the Diffie-Hellman protocol runs successfully if and only if v_B is even (or, more in general, if the order of α divides k_B). In other words, the eavesdropper obtains information on k_B, which is not supposed to happen.

As a second illustration, suppose that $|H|/|G|$ is a product of small primes (cf. [8]), and that h is an element of order $|H|/|G|$. If Alice somehow convinces Bob to use gh instead of g, and receives $(gh)^{k_B}$ instead of $g^{k_B} \in G$ from Bob, then Alice can easily determine h^{k_B} and thus $k_B \bmod (|H|/|G|)$ by using the Pohlig-Hellman algorithm (cf. [9]). That is, Alice obtains secret information on k_B if Bob naïvely uses a 'wrong' generator provided by Alice and does not check subgroup membership of the results of his own computations either. Another example is the Cramer-Shoup cryptosystem (cf. [3]) whose provable resistance against chosen ciphertext attacks relies on subgroup membership for a substantial number of elements that are exchanged in the course of the protocol.

In this paper, *subgroup attacks* refer to attacks that take advantage of the omission to verify membership of the subgroup G: they attack the security provided by the subgroup by replacing subgroup elements by elements from the supergroup H that do not belong to the proper subgroup. Examples of subgroup and related attacks can be found in [1], [2], [6], and [11]. We implicitly assume that membership of H is verified, i.e., that all alleged elements of H are indeed elements of H, and that this verification can easily be done.

Subgroup attacks can be prevented in roughly three ways:

1. By assuring that alleged subgroup members are indeed subgroup members, i.e., performing a membership test.
2. By ensuring that the ratio $|H|/|G|$ is small, e.g. 2.
3. By slightly adapting protocols.

We discuss these three prevention methods in more detail.

Membership test

In most practical circumstances the supergroup H is cyclic as well (as in systems based on the multiplicative group of a finite field), or the order q of G is a prime number such that H is not divisible by q^2 (as in elliptic curve cryptography, when using non-cyclic curve groups). The following result states that in these cases it suffices to do an *order check*, i.e., checking that $x \in H$ satisfies $x^q = 1$, to test membership of G.

Lemma 4.1 *Let G be multiplicative subgroup of prime order q of a supergroup H. If there exists an element $x \in H \setminus G$ for which $x^q = 1$, then H is not a cyclic group and the order of H is divisible by q^2.*

Proof: Assume to the contrary that H is cyclic. Then the number of elements of order dividing q is equal to q. The set $G \bigcup \{x\}$, however, contains at least $q+1$ elements of order dividing q; it follows that H cannot be cyclic. Furthermore, $\langle x, g \rangle$ is a subgroup of H of q^2 elements; it follows that q^2 divides $|H|$.

Thus, testing membership of G may entail an operation of cost comparable to the regular operations of the protocol. To illustrate that an order check is not sufficient in all cases, let $\tilde{G}$ be any cyclic group of order q and consider the cyclic subgroup $G = \langle(g_1, g_2)\rangle$ of the supergroup $H = \tilde{G}^2$, where g_1, g_2 are randomly chosen in $\tilde{G}$. In this case H is not cyclic and has order q^2. To test membership of G it is not sufficient to check that $(h_1, h_2)^q = (1, 1)$, but one needs to prove that $\log_{g_1}(h_1) = \log_{g_2}(h_2)$ which usually is computationally infeasible. This is known as an instance of the Decision Diffie-Hellman problem which usually is computationally infeasible. The latter example is not common in cryptographic applications, but simply serves as an illustration. From now on we will restrict ourselves to the situation that an order check is sufficient, i.e., H is cyclic or of order not divisible by q^2.

Choosing a small ratio $|H|/|G|$

If one chooses the ratio $r = |H|/|G|$ small then there exist only very few possibilities to perform subgroup based attacks. It seems widely accepted that at most $\log_2(r)$ secret bits are leaked if membership of H is checked but membership of G is not. In ordinary multiplicative groups r can only be small if q is very large, thereby losing the 'short exponents' advantage of working in a small subgroup. The computational overhead of full size exponents can, however, be reduced by using exponents that are only as long as one typically would choose the size of a subgroup of prime order q, i.e., ≥ 160 bits (cf. [8, Lemma 2]). Note that a small $|H|/|G|$ ratio is common in elliptic curve cryptosystems. In XTR the supergroup H is the order $p^2 - p + 1$ subgroup of $\mathrm{GF}(p^6)^*$, and the XTR group G is a subgroup of order q of H. In Section 5 below it is shown how membership of H can quickly be tested. Although the possibility of small values for $|H|/|G| = (p^2 - p + 1)/q$ is not explicitly mentioned in [4] or [5] it can without difficulty be used in the XTR versions of common cryptographic protocols, thereby limiting the risk of XTR subgroup attacks. Note that the risk of subgroup attacks against XTR is also very limited if $|H|/|G|$ is chosen as $3q_2$ for a prime number q_2 of the same order of magnitude as q.

Slightly Adapting Protocols

By adding an additional step to protocols using subgroups it can be ensured that the alleged subgroup element is retracted into the subgroup before secret information is employed to it. We illustrate this for the Diffie-Hellman protocol, using the notation as introduced above. Instead of using $g^{k_A k_B}$ as the shared secret key, one uses $g^{r k_A k_B}$, where $r = |H|/|G|$, which is computed in the following way. Upon receipt of v_B from Bob, Alice calculates $(v_B^r)^{k_A}$ instead of $v_B^{k_A}$. Similarly, Bob calculates $(v_A^r)^{k_B}$. Note that v_A^r is an element of G and that $v_A^{r k_B \bmod q}$ can only be equal to $(v_A^r)^{k_B}$ if $v_A \in G$. That is, performing the operations successively is crucial and, since an attacker may have chosen $v_A \notin G$, it is also crucial not to compute $v_A^{r \bmod q}$ but v_A^r for the 'original' $r = |H|/|G|$. Since, as we assumed, the co-factor $r = |H|/|G|$ is relatively prime with q, breaking this variant of the Diffie-Hellman protocol is as secure as the original one with a membership test incorporated into it. Many other DL based protocols and schemes that are susceptible to subgroup attacks, like the ElGamal scheme, can be adapted in a similar fashion.

Obviously, adaptation of protocols is typically a practical solution only if r is smaller than the prime order q of G, because otherwise a membership test would be more efficient. For instance, in traditional Schnorr-type subgroups systems H is the multiplicative group of a large finite field $\mathrm{GF}(p)$, the subgroup G has substantially smaller size q, and r is often quite large: if $\log_2(p) = 1024$ and $\log_2(q) = 160$ then $\log_2(r) \approx 864$. If $r > q$, as in this example, then the best method we are aware of to verify subgroup membership is to check that the qth power of the element to be tested equals one (after one has verified, of course, that it is an element of H). Else, if $r < q$, then one may choose to slightly adapt the protocols used.

5   Prevention of Subgroup Attacks in XTR

In this section we focus on preventing subgroup attacks for XTR. Let G denote the XTR group and H the XTR supergroup of all elements of $\mathrm{GF}(p^6)^*$ of order > 3 and dividing $p^2 - p + 1$. We describe efficient ways to determine if an element in $\mathrm{GF}(p^2)$ is the trace of an element of H. The results from the previous section, e.g. choosing $|H|/|G|$ small and using short exponents, can then be used to obtain variants of XTR that are not susceptible to subgroups attacks.

Let d be the element of $\mathrm{GF}(p^2) \setminus \mathrm{GF}(p)$ to be verified. The first method consists simply of checking that $F(d, X)$ is irreducible over $\mathrm{GF}(p^2)$ (cf. [4, Remark 2.3.3]), which can be done at the cost of $1.8\log_2(p)$ plus a small constant number of multiplications in $\mathrm{GF}(p)$ (cf. Theorem 3.6).

Our second method is effectively free from a computational point of view because it requires only a small constant number of operations in $\mathrm{GF}(p)$, but it requires a small amount of additional communication. Let p, q, and $Tr(g)$ be as above and let $d \in \mathrm{GF}(p^2)$ be the element to be verified, i.e., the element that is supposedly the trace of an element, say h, of the XTR group $\langle g \rangle$. Corollary 5.9 below shows that if one sends $Tr(h \cdot g)$ along with $d(= Tr(h))$, then one can efficiently verify that d corresponds to the trace of an element of the XTR supergroup H.

Definition 5.1 Let $R(X), S(X) \in \mathrm{GF}(p^2)[X]$ be two monic third-degree polynomials with non-zero constant term. If the roots of R and S are $\alpha_0, \alpha_1, \alpha_2 \in \mathrm{GF}(p^6)$ and $\beta_0, \beta_1, \beta_2 \in \mathrm{GF}(p^6)$, respectively, then the root-product $\Re(R, S)$ is defined as the monic polynomial with the nine roots $\alpha_i \cdot \beta_j$ for $0 \leq i, j \leq 2$.

Lemma 5.2 For $R(X), S(X) \in \mathrm{GF}(p^2)[X]$ the root-product $\Re(R, S)$ is a ninth-degree polynomial over $\mathrm{GF}(p^2)$ with non-zero constant term.

Proof: Fixing $R(X)$ and varying $S(X)$ one finds that the coefficients of the polynomial $\Re(R, S)$ are symmetric polynomials in the roots $\beta_0, \beta_1, \beta_2$ of $S(X)$, and that they can be written (cf. [7]) as linear sums of elementary symmetric polynomials in $\beta_0, \beta_1, \beta_2$ with fixed coefficients depending on $\alpha_0, \alpha_1, \alpha_2$. It also follows that these fixed coefficients are symmetric polynomials in the roots

$\alpha_0, \alpha_1, \alpha_2$. The values of the elementary symmetric polynomials in $\alpha_0, \alpha_1, \alpha_2$ and $\beta_0, \beta_1, \beta_2$ are in $GF(p^2)$ because $R(X), S(X) \in GF(p^2)[X]$, so that the coefficients of the polynomial $\Re(R,S)$ are in $GF(p^2)$. The remainder of the lemma is straightforward.

Lemma 5.3 *Let* $R(X), S(X) \in GF(p^2)[X]$ *and let* $\beta_0, \beta_1, \beta_2 \in GF(p^6)$ *be the roots of* $S(X)$. *Then*

$$\Re(R,S) = (\beta_0 \cdot \beta_1 \cdot \beta_2)^3 R(X \cdot \beta_0^{-1}) \cdot R(X \cdot \beta_1^{-1}) \cdot R(X \cdot \beta_2^{-1}).$$

If $S(X)$ *is irreducible over* $GF(p^2)$ *then*

$$\Re(R,S) = \beta_0^{3(p^4+p^2+1)} R(X \cdot \beta_0^{-1}) \cdot R(X \cdot \beta_0^{-p^2}) \cdot R(X \cdot \beta_0^{-p^4}).$$

Proof: The first part result is a straightforward verification and the second part follows from the fact that the roots of $S(X)$ are conjugate over $GF(p^2)$ if $S(X)$ is irreducible over $GF(p^2)$.

Note that $\beta_0 \cdot \beta_1 \cdot \beta_2$ in Lemma 5.3 equals the constant term of $S(X)$. The crucial aspect of the second part of the lemma is that it describes $\Re(R,S)$ using only $R(X)$ and the conjugates of the roots of $S(X)$. That is, if we consider the representation of $GF(p^6)$ that follows by adjoining a root of $S(X)$ to $GF(p^2)$, we can efficiently determine the root-product of $R(X)$ and $S(X)$, assuming we can efficiently determine the $(p^2)^{th}$ and $(p^4)^{th}$ powers of a root of $S(X)$ in this representation.

In our application $S(X)$ is $F(c,X)$ where $c = Tr(g)$ for some element g in the XTR supergroup H. That is, $F(c,X)$ is irreducible by [4, Remark 2.3.3], and we represent $GF(p^6)$ as $GF(p^2)(g)$, i.e., by adjoining the root g of $F(c,X)$ to $GF(p^2)$. Since $g^{p^2} = g^{p-1}$ and $g^{p^4} = g^{-p}$ and g^{p-1} and g^{-p} easily follow given a representation of g^p, in order to be able to compute the root-product $\Re(R, F(c,X))$ it suffices to have a representation for g^p in $GF(p^2)(g)$. The following result shows how such a representation can be obtained. We abbreviate $Tr(g^i)$ as c_i.

Proposition 5.4 *Let* $c = Tr(g)$ *for some element* $g \in H$. *Given* $c_{m-2} = Tr(g^{m-2})$, $c_{m-1} = Tr(g^{m-1})$, *and* $c_m = Tr(g^m)$, *values* $K, L, M \in GF(p^2)$ *such that* $g^m = Kg^2 + Lg + M \mod F(c,X)$ *can be computed at the cost of a small constant number of operations in* $GF(p)$.

Proof: By raising $g^m = Kg^2 + Lg + M$ to the $(p^i)^{th}$ power for $i = 0, 2, 4$, and by adding the three resulting identities, we find that $c_m = Kc_2 + Lc_1 + Mc_0$. Similarly, from $g^{m-1} = Kg + L + Mg^{-1}$ and $g^{m-2} = K + Lg^{-1} + Mg^{-2}$ it follows that $c_{m-1} = Kc_1 + Lc_0 + Mc_{-1}$ and $c_{m-2} = Kc_0 + Lc_{-1} + Mc_{-2}$ respectively. This leads to the following system of equations over $GF(p^2)$:

$$\begin{pmatrix} c_{m-2} \\ c_{m-1} \\ c_m \end{pmatrix} = \begin{pmatrix} c_{-2} & c_{-1} & c_0 \\ c_{-1} & c_0 & c_1 \\ c_0 & c_1 & c_2 \end{pmatrix} \cdot \begin{pmatrix} M \\ L \\ K \end{pmatrix}.$$

Because c_m, c_{m-1}, and c_{m-2} are given and the matrix on the right hand side is invertible (cf. [4, Lemma 2.4.4]) the proof follows.

Corollary 5.5 *Let* $c = Tr(g)$ *for some element* $g \in H$. *Given* $Tr(g^{p-2})$, *a representation of* $g^p \bmod F(c, X)$ *can be computed at the cost of a small constant number of operations in* $GF(p)$.

Proof: This follows from Proposition 5.4 and the fact that $c_p = c_1^p = c^p$ and $c_{p-1} = c_{p^2} = c_1^{p^2} = c_1 = c$.

Theorem 5.6 *Let* $R(X) \in GF(p^2)[X]$ *be a monic third-degree polynomial with non-zero constant term. Let* $c = Tr(g)$ *for some element* $g \in H$. *Given* $Tr(g^{p-2})$, *the root-product* $\Re(R(X), F(c, X))$ *can be computed at the cost of a small constant number of operations in* $GF(p)$.

Proof: This follows immediately from Lemma 5.3 and Corollary 5.5.

We remark that $c_{p-2} = c_{p+1}$, as $c_{p+1} = c \cdot c_p - c^p \cdot c_{p-1} + c_{p-2}$ (cf. [4, Lemma 2.3.4.i]), $c_p = c^p$, and $c_{p-1} = c$. As the value c_{p-2} plays an important role it could be pre-computed and stored. The following result states that c_{p-2} can quickly be recovered from a single bit.

Proposition 5.7 *Let* $c = Tr(g)$ *for some element* $g \in H$. *Then* $Tr(g^{p-2}) = c_{p-2}$ *can be computed at the cost of a square-root computation in* $GF(p^2)$, *assuming one bit of information to resolve the square-root ambiguity.*

Proof: Write $c_{p-2} = x_1 \alpha + x_2 \alpha^2$ in the representation of $GF(p^2)$ introduced in [4, Section 2.1]. A straightforward verification shows that $(c_{p-2} - c_{p-2}^p)^2 = -3(x_1 - x_2)^2$. Combining this with the identity for $(c_{p-2} - c_{p-2}^p)^2$ given in [4, Lemmas 2.4.4 and 2.4.5] (and using that $c_{p-2} = c_{p+1}$), we find that $-3(x_1 - x_2)^2 = c^{2p+2} + 18c^{p+1} - 4(c^{3p} + c^3) - 27 \in GF(p)$.

On the other hand $c_{p-2} + c_{p-2}^p = -(x_1 + x_2)$. Using that $c_{p-2} = g^{p-2} + g^{(p-2)p^2} + g^{(p-2)p^4} = g^{p-2} + g^{-2p+1} + g^{p+1}$, it follows that $c_{p-2}^p = g^{-p-1} + g^{-p+2} + g^{2p-1}$. Now,

$$c^{p+1} = c \cdot c^p = (g + g^{p-1} + g^{-p})(g^p + g^{-1} + g^{-p+1})$$
$$= g^{p+1} + g^{p-2} + g^{-2p+1} + g^{-p-1} + g^{-p+2} + g^{2p-1} + 3$$
$$= c_{p-2} + c_{p-2}^p + 3.$$

That is, $x_1 + x_2 = 3 - c^{p+1} \in GF(p)$. Combining the two identities involving $x_1 - x_2$ and $x_1 + x_2$ it follows that c_{p-2} and its conjugate over $GF(p)$ can be computed at the cost of a square-root calculation in $GF(p^2)$. To distinguish $c_{p-2} = x_1 \alpha + x_2 \alpha^2$ from its conjugate $x_2 \alpha + x_1 \alpha^2$ a single bit that is on if and only if $x_1 > x_2$ suffices.

Lemma 5.8 *Let* $c = Tr(g)$ *for some element* $g \in H$ *and let* $d, d' \in GF(p^2)$. *Given the value* c_{p-2} *the correctness of the following statement can be checked at the cost of a small, constant number of operations in* $GF(p)$: *there exists an element* $h \in H$ *such that* $d = Tr(h)$ *and* $d' = Tr(h \cdot g)$.

Proof: Consider the following algorithm:

1. By a simple verification check whether 1, α or α^2 are roots of the polynomial $F(d, X)$. If so, then the statement is not true.
2. Otherwise, calculate the root-product $\Re(F(d, X), F(c, X))$ and determine if this is divisible by the polynomial $F(d', X)$. If so, the statement is true, otherwise it is not.

The conclusion of the first step of the algorithm is trivial. For a proof of the conclusion of Step 2 of the algorithm, assume that d is not equal to the trace of an element of H. It follows from [4, Lemma 2.3.2] that the roots of $F(d, X)$ are in $GF(p^2)$. According to Step 1 the roots are not equal to 1, α or α^2, so that the roots of $F(d, X)$ are not members of H either, as the greatest common divisor of $p^2 - p + 1$ and $p^2 - 1$ is 3 and H has order > 3. It easily follows that none of the roots of the root-product $\Re(F(d, X), F(c, X))$ lies in H. Moreover, as the roots of $F(c, X)$ do not lie in $GF(p^2)$, it follows that the roots of the root-product do not lie in $GF(p^2)$ either.

Applying [4, Lemma 2.3.2] once more, the roots of the polynomial $F(d', X)$ are either in $GF(p^2)$ or in H. It follows that $F(d', X)$ cannot divide the root-product $\Re(F(d, X), F(c, X))$. Thus if $F(d', X)$ divides $\Re(F(d, X), F(c, X))$, then d is equal to the trace of an element $h \in H$. In this situation, the roots of the root-product are equal to $h^{p^i} \cdot g^{p^j}$ for $i, j = 0, 2, 4$. It follows that $F(d', h^{p^i} \cdot g) = 0$ for some i in $\{0, 2, 4\}$ and hence that $d = Tr(h^{p^i})$ and $d' = Tr(h^{p^i} \cdot g)$. That is, the statement is true.

We finally observe that the algorithm requires a small constant number of operations in $GF(p^2)$.

Corollary 5.9 *Let $c = Tr(g)$ for some element $g \in H$ and suppose that $Tr(g^{p-2})$ is known. Then accompanying the trace value of an element $h \in H$ by the trace of its 'successor' $h \cdot g$ enables an efficient proof of membership of h in H.*

Corollary 5.10 *Let $c = Tr(g)$ where g is (known to be) a generator of the XTR group, let d be the trace of an element that is (known to be) in the XTR group $\langle g \rangle$, and let d' be some element of $GF(p^2)$. Then it can efficiently be verified if d and d' are of the form $Tr(g^x)$, $Tr(g^{x+1})$, respectively, for some integer x, $0 < x < q$.*

An XTR public key meant for digital signatures takes the form p, q, c, d, and d' where p and q are primes satisfying the usual XTR conditions and where $c = Tr(g)$ for a generator g of the XTR group, $d = Tr(g^k)$ for a secret key k, and $d' = Tr(g^{k+1})$ (cf. [4]). The above corollary implies that a Certificate Authority can efficiently verify the consistency of an XTR signature public key presented by a client, before issuing a certificate on it. More specifically, suppose a client provides a Certificate Authority with XTR public key data containing p, q, c, d, and d' where p and q are primes satisfying the usual XTR conditions and where, supposedly, $c = Tr(g)$ for a generator g of the XTR group, $d = Tr(g^k)$

for a secret key k, and $d' = Tr(g^{k+1})$. The Certificate Authority can easily check that this is indeed the case, in two steps. First the Certificate Authority checks that p and q are well-formed and that c and d are indeed traces of elements of the XTR group using standard XTR arithmetic (cf. [4, Lemma 2.3.4 and Theorem 2.3.8]). Secondly, the Certificate Authority uses Corollary 5.10 to verify that d and d' are traces of consecutive (and unknown, to the Certificate Authority) powers of the generator corresponding to c.

Acknowledgment

Acknowledgments are due to Wei Dai for inspiring us to improve the $F(c, X)$-irreducibility test from [5].

References

1. I. Biehl, B. Meyer, V. Müller, *Differential fault attacks on elliptic curve cryptosystems*, Proceedings of Crypto 2000, LNCS 1880, Springer-Verlag, 2000, 131-146.
2. M.V.D. Burmester, *A remark on the efficiency of identification schemes*, Proceedings of Eurocrypt'90, LNCS 473, Springer-Verlag 1990, 493-495.
3. R. Cramer, V. Shoup, *A practical public key cryptosystem provably secure against adaptive chosen ciphertext attack*, Proceedings of Crypto'98, LNCS 1462, Springer-Verlag 1998, 13-25.
4. A.K. Lenstra, E.R. Verheul, *The XTR public key system*, Proceedings of Crypto 2000, LNCS 1880, Springer-Verlag, 2000, 1-19; available from www.ecstr.com.
5. A.K. Lenstra, E.R. Verheul, *Key improvements to XTR*, Proceedings of Asiacrypt 2000, LNCS 1976, Springer-Verlag, 2000, 220-233; available from www.ecstr.com.
6. C.H. Lim, P.J. Lee, *A key recovery attack on discrete log-based schemes using a prime order subgroup*, Proceedings of Crypto'97, LNCS 1294, Springer-Verlag 1997, 249-263.
7. W.K. Nicholson, *Introduction to abstract algebra*, PWS-Kent Publishing Company, Boston, 1993.
8. P.C. van Oorschot, M.J. Wiener, *On Diffie-Hellman key agreement with short exponents*, Proceedings of Eurocrypt '96, LNCS 1070, Springer-Verlag 1996, 332-343.
9. S.C. Pohlig, M.E. Hellman, *An improved algorithm for computing logarithms over $GF(p)$ and its cryptographic significance*, IEEE Trans. on IT, 24 (1978), 106-110.
10. H. Riesel, *Prime numbers and computer methods for factorization*, Birkhäuser, Boston, 1985.
11. E.R. Verheul, M.P. Hoyle, *Tricking the Chaum-Pedersen protocol*, manuscript, 1998.

A New Aspect for Security Notions: Secure Randomness in Public-Key Encryption Schemes

Takeshi Koshiba

Secure Computing Lab., Fujitsu Laboratories Ltd.,
4-1-1 Kamikodanaka, Nakahara-ku, Kawasaki 211-8588, Japan
koshiba@acm.org

Abstract. In this paper, we introduce a framework in which we can uniformly and comprehensively discuss security notions of public-key encryption schemes even for the case where some weak generator producing seemingly random sequences is used to encrypt plaintext messages. First, we prove that indistinguishability and semantic security are not equivalent in general. On the other hand, we derive some sufficient condition for the equivalence and show that polynomial-time pseudo-randomness is not always necessary for the equivalence.

1 Introduction

One of the important goals in computational cryptography is to provide a public-key encryption scheme that achieves a security level as strong as possible under various circumstances. For this purpose, several security notions have been introduced. In particular, we will discuss in this paper the notions of "semantic security" and "indistinguishability of encryptions" introduced by Goldwasser and Micali [12], which have shown to be equivalent [12,18]. For another major security notion, we have "non-malleability" introduced in [8]. These notions are defined in terms of an adversary who is given only a challenge ciphertext. This attack model is called *ciphertext only attack* (abbreviated COA). Besides COA, three major attack models have been studied in the literature. One is called *chosen plaintext attack* (abbreviated CPA) model, in which the adversary can encrypt any plaintext messages of his choice. For more stronger attack models, *chosen ciphertext attack* [19] and *adaptive chosen ciphertext attack* [20] have been also considered.

Although these security notions have been studied quite well (see, e.g., [1,2,4]), we think that there are still some important issues that have not been addressed in the previous research. Security when used with a "pseudo-random" resource is one of such issues. Usually, security notions are defined assuming that ideal (i.e., true) random resource is available. Furthermore, it has been shown that one can safely use any "polynomial-time pseudo-random" generator for the substitute of the true random resource; that is, most security notions do not change by using the polynomial-time pseudo-randomness for the true randomness. Although we have several "theoretically guaranteed" polynomial-time pseudo-random generators, they are unfortunately not fast enough for practical use, and much faster

K. Kim (Ed.): PKC 2001, LNCS 1992, pp. 87–103, 2001.
© Springer-Verlag Berlin Heidelberg 2001

but less reliable pseudo-random generators have been used in many practical situations. Then the above security notions (and their relations) may be no longer valid with such weak pseudo-randomness. In fact, it has been shown [3] that if DSS is used with a linear congruential generator, then its secret key can be easily detected after seeing a few signatures. (See also [7,9,15,22].) Though this result indicates that the linear congruential generator is unsuitable for cryptographic purposes, it does not mean that the linear congruential generator is useless at all for *all* cryptographic systems. It is certainly important to study more carefully which aspect of the randomness is indeed important for discussing several security levels.

In this paper, we will introduce a framework in which we can uniformly and comprehensively discuss "semantic security" and "indistinguishability" notions even for the case where some weak generator producing seemingly random sequences is used. (In order to avoid confusion, we will use throughout the paper the term "quasi-random" for referring pseudo-randomness including one without any guarantee.) While most of corresponding notions are easily restated from the original definitions, we have to be a bit careful for choosing right definitions in relation to attack models. In the context of public-key encryption scheme, CPA is equivalent to COA because once the adversary obtains the public-key, he can compute ciphertext messages easily. This may not be true any more when quasi-random generators are involved. In this paper, for the model corresponding to COA, we consider the situation in which an adversary cannot access to the quasi-random generator, it is still possible for the adversary to make use of the encryption algorithm. On the other hand, in the model corresponding to CPA, it may be more natural that adversary can invoke the encryption oracle which, given a plaintext message, uses the quasi-random generator in encrypting the message and replies with its ciphertext message. Throughout this paper, we will discuss under this revised COA model.

Next we will study the relationships between these security notions: semantic security and indistinguishability. We first prove that they are not equivalent in general. On the other hand, while the well-known fact can be restated in our framework as the polynomial-time pseudo-randomness is *sufficient* to have the equivalence between semantic security and indistinguishability, the polynomial-time pseudo-randomness is not necessary for the equivalence. It is easy to see that "polynomial-time pseudo-randomness" has two aspects: "efficient samplability" and theoretically guaranteed "pseudo-randomness." We call the former property *samplability* simply and the latter *semi-randomness* to distinguish from both pseudo-randomness and quasi-randomness. Then we derive that semi-randomness *or* samplability is better sufficient condition for the equivalence between semantic security and indistinguishability.

In Section 2, we review the definitions of security notions of public-key encryption scheme. In Section 3, we introduce our new framework and reformulate well-known security notions to fit for the new framework. In Section 4, we discuss the relation between semantic security and indistinguishability in our new framework.

2 Preliminaries

2.1 Notations and Conventions

We introduce some useful notations and conventions for discussing probabilistic algorithms. If A is a probabilistic algorithm, then for any input x, the notation $A(x)$ refers to the probability space which assigns to the string y the probability that A, on input x, outputs y. If S is a probability space, denote by $\Pr_{e \leftarrow S}[e]$ (or $\Pr_S[e]$) the probability that S associates with element e. When we consider a finite probability space, it is convenient to consider separately the corresponding sample set and probability distribution on the set. If S is a finite set and D is a probability distribution on S, denote by $\Pr_{e \in_D S}[e]$ the probability that element $e \in S$ is chosen according to D. If S is a finite set, denote by $\Pr_{e \in_U S}[e]$ the probability that element $e \in S$ is chosen uniformly.

By 1^n we denote the unary representation of the integer n. A function $f : \{0,1\}^* \to \{0,1\}^*$ is *polynomially-bounded* if there exists a polynomial $p(\cdot)$ such that $|f(x)| \leq p(|x|)$ for all $x \in \{0,1\}^*$.

2.2 True Randomness Framework

In this paper, we will introduce a framework in which we can uniformly and comprehensively discuss "semantic security" and "indistinguishability" notions even for the case where some weak generator producing seemingly random sequences is used. (In order to avoid confusion, we will use throughout the paper the term "quasi-random" for referring the pseudo-randomness including one without any guarantee.) Usually any cryptographic notions are defined in the "true randomness framework," where the true randomness is available. We review the notions of semantic security and indistinguishability (in the true randomness framework) and the relation between them. We begin with the definition of public-key encryption schemes (in the true randomness framework).

Definition 1 (public-key encryption scheme). A *public-key encryption scheme* is a quadruple (G, M, E, D), where the following conditions hold.

1. G, called the *key generator*, is a probabilistic polynomial-time algorithm which, on input 1^n, outputs a pair of binary strings.
2. $M = \{M_n\}_{n \in N}$ is a family of message spaces from which all plaintext messages are drawn. In order to make our notation simpler (but without loss of generality), we assume that $M_n = \{0,1\}^n$.
3. For every n, for every pair (e,d) in the support of $G(1^n)$, and for any $\alpha \in M_n$, probabilistic polynomial-time (*encryption*) algorithm E and deterministic polynomial-time (*decryption*) algorithm D satisfy

$$\Pr_{E}[D(d, E(e, \alpha)) = \alpha] = 1,$$

where the probability is over the internal coin tosses of the algorithm E.

The integer n serves as the *security parameter* of the scheme. Each (e, d) in the range of $G(1^n)$ constitutes a pair of corresponding *encryption/decryption keys*. The string $E(e, \alpha)$ is the *encryption of the plaintext message* $\alpha \in \{0, 1\}^*$ using the encryption key e, whereas $D(d, \beta)$ is the *decryption of the ciphertext message* β using the decryption key d.

Hereafter, we write $E_e(\alpha)$ instead of $E(e, \alpha)$ and $D_d(\beta)$ instead of $D(d, \beta)$. We also write $E_e(\alpha; r)$ when we want to express explicitly the randomness r of the encryption algorithm. Also, we let $G_1(1^n)$ denote the first element in the pair $G(1^n)$.

Since Goldwasser and Micali defined semantic security and polynomial security (a.k.a. indistinguishability), several ways to define such notions are shown. In this paper, we adopt a non-uniform formulation as in [10] in order to simplify the exposition. We note that employing such a non-uniform formulation (rather than a uniform one) may strengthen the definitions; yet, it does weaken the implications proven between the definitions, since proofs make free usage of non-uniformity.

A transformation is a uniform algorithm which, on input $\overline{C_n}$, outputs $\overline{C'_n}$, where $\overline{C_n}$ (resp., $\overline{C'_n}$) is the representation of a circuit C_n (resp., C'_n) in some standard encoding. Without loss of generality, we identify a circuit with its representation (in the standard encoding).

Definition 2 (semantic security). An encryption scheme (G, M, E, D) is *semantically secure* if there exists a probabilistic polynomial-time transformation T so that for every polynomial-size circuit family $\{C_n\}_{n \in N}$, for every probability ensemble $\{X_n\}_{n \in N}$ satisfying that X_n is a probability distribution on M_n, for every pair of polynomially-bounded functions $f, h : \{0, 1\}^* \to \{0, 1\}^*$, every polynomial $p(\cdot)$ and sufficiently large n,

$$\Pr_{G, E, X_n}\left[C_n(G_1(1^n), E_{G_1(1^n)}(X_n), 1^n, h(X_n)) = f(X_n)\right]$$
$$< \Pr_{T, G, X_n}\left[C'_n(G_1(1^n), 1^n, h(X_n)) = f(X_n)\right] + \frac{1}{p(n)}$$

where $C'_n = T(C_n)$ is the circuit produced by T on input C_n. (The probability in the above terms is taken over X_n as well as over the internal coin tosses of the algorithms G and E.)

Definition 3 (indistinguishability). An encryption scheme (G, M, E, D) has *indistinguishable encryptions* if for every polynomial-size circuit family $\{C_n\}_{n \in N}$, for every polynomial $p(\cdot)$, for all sufficiently large n, and for every $x, y \in M_n$

$$\left| \Pr_{G, E}\left[C_n(G_1(1^n), E_{G_1(1^n)}(x)) = 1\right] - \Pr_{G, E}\left[C_n(G_1(1^n), E_{G_1(1^n)}(y)) = 1\right] \right| < \frac{1}{p(n)}.$$

The probability in the above terms is taken over the internal coin tosses of the algorithms G and E.

We have seen two notions of security for public-key encryption schemes. The above definitions only refer to the security of a scheme that is used to encrypt a single plaintext message (per key generated). Clearly, in reality, we want to encrypt many massages with the same key. The corresponding definitions of security notions in the multiple message setting have been given and discussed in [10]. Although it is important to consider the security in the multiple message setting, we will omit to discuss them on account of space constraints. The following theorem has been already shown [12,18].

Theorem 1 ([12,18]). *Let (G, M, E, D) be an encryption scheme. In the true randomness framework, (G, M, E, D) is semantically secure if and only if (G, M, E, D) has indistinguishable encryptions.*

The reductions that are used in the proof of the above theorem are randomized. Care must obviously be taken to confirm that the reductions still work for the case where some quasi-random generator is used instead of the true random resource.

3   Quasi-randomness Framework

In this section, we prepare a framework — quasi-randomness framework — in which we can uniformly and comprehensively discuss "semantic security" and "indistinguishability" notions even for the case where some weak quasi-random generator producing seemingly random sequences is used.

3.1   Public-Key Encryption Scheme for Quasi-random Set Family

We begin with introducing the notion of "quasi-randomness" and some notations. In this paper, a quasi-random string is just a string (of certain length) drawn from some subset of strings (of this length) uniformly at random. More specifically, we consider the following family of sets of strings.

Definition 4. Let $q(\cdot)$ be a polynomial. A *$q(n)$-quasi-random set family* (abbreviated QRSF) $\{R_n\}_{n \in N}$ is a family of sets of strings of length $q(n)$.

Below we usually use $\{R_n\}$ to denote some quasi-random set family. On the other hand, *$q(n)$-true-random set family* (abbreviated TRSF) is just a collection of sets $T_n = \{0, 1\}^{q(n)}$. We use $\{T_n\}$ to denote some true-random set family.

Our ultimate purpose is to give a taxonomy of quasi-random set families from a viewpoint of the security of public-key encryption schemes. We have to enumerate some properties over quasi-random set families to begin with.

While the well-known fact can be restated in our framework as the polynomial-time pseudo-randomness is *sufficient* to have the equivalence between semantic security and indistinguishability, we show that the polynomial-time pseudo-randomness is not necessary to have the equivalence. This implies that there may be more usable sufficient conditions for the equivalence. It is easy to consider separately "efficient samplability" and "pseudo-randomness" as some properties on quasi-randomness. We call the former property *samplability* simply and the latter *semi-randomness* to distinguish from both pseudo-randomness and quasi-randomness. "Samplability" is quite a natural property because generators without samplability is, in general, difficult to use. Especially in Monte-Carlo simulation, efficient samplability is required. On the other hand, "semi-randomness" is also one of important properties. Semi-random sequences pass many statistical tests. Some sequences that are obtained from physical sources such as electronic noise or the quantum effects in a semiconductor. When the sequences pass all known statistical tests, it is often that we use the sequences as "random sequences." We may consider that such sequences may have the semi-randomness property. So, in this paper, we study these two properties on QRSF.

We begin with definition of "semi-randomness." Semi-random sequences are ones that are not distinguished by any polynomial-size circuit. More specifically, we consider the following definition.

Definition 5. A $q(n)$-QRSF $\{R_n\}$ is said to be *semi-random* if for every polynomial-size circuit family $\{C_n\}_{n \in N}$, every polynomial $p(\cdot)$, all sufficiently large n,

$$\left| \Pr_{r \in_U R_n} \left[C_n(r) = 1 \right] - \Pr_{r' \in_U T_n} \left[C_n(r') = 1 \right] \right| < \frac{1}{p(n)},$$

where $\{T_n\}$ is $q(n)$-TRSF.

We note that semi-random sequences are different from output sequences by polynomial-time pseudo-random generators. Semi-random sequences need not to be recursive nor generated efficiently.

Next, we give a definition of "samplability." For any samplable sequence, there exists a (polynomial-size) generator $\{S_n\}_{n \in N}$ whose output is statistically close to the samplable sequence. More specifically, we consider the following definition.

Definition 6. A $q(n)$-QRSF $\{R_n\}$ is said to be *samplable* if there exists a polynomial-size circuit family $\{S_n\}_{n \in N}$ so that for every polynomial $p(\cdot)$ and all sufficiently large n,

$$\max_A \left\{ \left| \Pr_{r \in_U \{0,1\}^{q(n)}} \left[S_n(r) \in A \right] - \Pr_{r \in_U R_n} \left[r \in A \right] \right| \right\} < \frac{1}{p(n)},$$

where the maximum is taken all over the subsets of $\{0,1\}^{q(n)}$.

We note that the maximum value in the above definition is so called "statistical difference" between two probability distributions: $\{S_n(r)\}_{r \in_U \{0,1\}^{q(n)}}$ and the uniform distribution on R_n.

We extend the notion of public-key encryption scheme in order to cope with QRSF instead of the true randomness.

Definition 7 (public-key encryption scheme, revisited). A *public-key encryption scheme* is a quadruple (G, M, E, D), where the following conditions hold.

1. G, called the *key generator*, is a probabilistic polynomial-time algorithm which, on input 1^n, outputs a pair of binary strings. (Although the key generator also uses randomness, we disregard it here in order to cast light on roles of randomness in encrypting. So, we assume that randomness in key generator is always ideal.)
2. $M = \{M_n\}_{n \in N}$ is a family of message spaces from which all plaintext messages will be drawn. In order to make our notation simpler (but without loss of generality), we will assume that $M_n = \{0, 1\}^n$.
3. For every $q(n)$-QRSF $\{R_n\}$, for every n, for every pair (e, d) in the support of $G(1^n)$ and for any $\alpha \in M_n$, "deterministic" polynomial-time (*encryption*) algorithm E and deterministic polynomial-time (*decryption*) algorithm D satisfy

$$\Pr_{r \in_U R_n} \left[D_d(E_e(\alpha; r)) = \alpha \right] = 1,$$

where the probability is over the uniform distribution on R_n.

We note that we treat the encryption algorithm as deterministic one fed with a plaintext message and a (random) supplementary input of length $q(n)$.

3.2   Security Notions for Quasi-random Set Family

In this subsection, we reformulate the notions of semantic security and indistinguishability to suit the framework of quasi-random set family.

Definition 8 (semantic security, revisited). An encryption scheme (G, M, E, D) is *semantically secure w.r.t. $q(n)$-quasi-random set family* $\{R_n\}$ if there exists a probabilistic polynomial-time transformation T so that every polynomial-size circuit family $\{C_n\}_{n \in N}$, for every probability ensemble $\{X_n\}_{n \in N}$ satisfying that X_n is a probability distribution on M_n, every pair of polynomially-bounded functions $f, h : \{0, 1\}^* \to \{0, 1\}^*$, every polynomial $p(\cdot)$ and all sufficiently large n,

$$\Pr_{G, X_n; r \in_U R_n} \left[C_n(G_1(1^n), E_{G_1(1^n)}(X_n; r), 1^n, h(X_n)) = f(X_n) \right]$$
$$< \Pr_{T, G, X_n} \left[C'_n(G_1(1^n), 1^n, h(X_n)) = f(X_n) \right] + \frac{1}{p(n)}$$

where $C'_n = T(C_n)$.

Some explanation on the attack model is needed here. In the above definition, an adversary C_n is given only an encryption key $G_1(1^n)$ and a ciphertext message $E_{G_1(1^n)}(X_n; r)$ (and some supplementary information $h(X_n)$). Thus, it is considered as ciphertext only attack (COA) model. But note here that we may consider any polynomial-size circuit C_n for the adversary; hence, we may assume that the encryption algorithm is also included in C_n. In the true random-ness framework, this immediately includes the chosen plaintext attack (CPA) in which model the adversary can encrypt any plaintext messages of his choice. This is not true any more in the quasi-randomness framework because there is no guarantee that some (randomized) polynomial-size circuit can generate quasi-random strings in R_n uniformly at random.

Moreover, we consider our revised COA model. For our COA model, we consider the situation in which an adversary cannot access to the quasi-random generator. The situation means that those who use public-key encryption scheme have their *private* quasi-random generators. In general, they do not have to publicize their quasi-random generators which are used in public-key encryption scheme. In addition, the case where *private* quasi-random generators are used is more secure than the case where *public* quasi-random generators are used. Thus, we can say that our COA model makes sense.

Definition 9 (indistinguishability, revisited). An encryption scheme (G, M, E, D) has *indistinguishable encryptions w.r.t. $q(n)$-quasi-random set family* $\{R_n\}$ if for every polynomial-size circuit family $\{C_n\}_{n \in N}$, every polynomial $p(\cdot)$, all sufficiently large n and every $x, y \in M_n$,

$$\left| \Pr_{G; r \in_U R_n} \left[C_n(G_1(1^n), E_{G_1(1^n)}(x; r)) = 1 \right] \right.$$
$$\left. - \Pr_{G; r' \in_U R_n} \left[C_n(G_1(1^n), E_{G_1(1^n)}(y; r')) = 1 \right] \right| < \frac{1}{p(n)}.$$

We also note that C_n, in the above definition, cannot directly access to QRSF $\{R_n\}$.

The following notion is somewhat artificial. However, it is useful to charac-terize the notions of semantic security and indistinguishability.

Definition 10 (skew-indistinguishability). An encryption scheme (G, M, E, D) has *skew-indistinguishable encryptions w.r.t. $q(n)$-quasi-random set family* $\{R_n\}$ if for every polynomial-size circuit family $\{C_n\}_{n \in N}$, every polynomial $p(\cdot)$, all sufficiently large n and every $x, y \in M_n$,

$$\left| \Pr_{G; r \in_U R_n} \left[C_n(G_1(1^n), E_{G_1(1^n)}(x; r)) = 1 \right] \right.$$
$$\left. - \Pr_{G; r' \in_U T_n} \left[C_n(G_1(1^n), E_{G_1(1^n)}(y; r')) = 1 \right] \right| < \frac{1}{p(n)}$$

where $\{T_n\}$ is $q(n)$-TRSF.

In this paper, we do not consider the non-malleability, However, we only give the corresponding definition. We note that, in the definition below, "$r' \in R_n$" is optional, since the definition without it is alternative.

Definition 11 (non-malleability, revisited). An encryption scheme (G, M, E, D) is *non-malleable w.r.t. $q(n)$-quasi-random set family* $\{R_n\}$ if there exists a probabilistic polynomial-time transformation T so that every polynomial-size circuit family $\{C_n\}_{n \in N}$, for every relation V that is decidable by a polynomial-size circuit family, for every probability ensemble $\{X_n\}_{n \in N}$ satisfying that X_n is a probability distribution on M_n, every polynomially-bounded function $h : \{0,1\}^* \to \{0,1\}^*$, every polynomial $p(\cdot)$ and all sufficiently large n,

$$\Pr_{G, X_n; r \in_U R_n} \left[C_n(G_1(1^n), E_{G_1(1^n)}(X_n; r), 1^n, h(X_n)) = E_{G_1(1^n)}(X'_n; r') \right.$$
$$\text{such that } V(X_n, X'_n) = 1, \ X_n \neq X'_n \text{ and } r' \in R_n \left. \right]$$
$$< \Pr_{T, G, X_n} \left[C'_n(G_1(1^n), 1^n, h(X_n)) = E_{G_1(1^n)}(X'_n; r') \right.$$
$$\text{such that } V(X_n, X'_n) = 1, \ X_n \neq X'_n \text{ and } r' \in R_n \left. \right] + \frac{1}{p(n)}$$

where $C'_n = T(C_n)$.

We note that, in four definitions above, any adversary does not directly access to QRSF $\{R_n\}$ but gets ciphertext messages encrypted using QRSF $\{R_n\}$ as challenge inputs.

4   Properties in Quasi-randomness Framework

4.1   Relations among Security Notions

In this subsection, we consider classes of pairs of QRSF and public-key encryption schemes w.r.t. the QRSF. We will especially show that semantic security and indistinguishability (in the quasi-randomness framework) are separable from each other.

We denote by $\mathcal{SS}_q$ the class of pairs of encryption scheme (G, M, E, D) and QRSF $\{R_n\}$ satisfying that (G, M, E, D) w.r.t. $\{R_n\}$ is semantically secure. We also denote $\langle (G, M, E, D), \{R_n\}\rangle \in \mathcal{SS}_q$ if an encryption scheme (G, M, E, D) which is semantically secure w.r.t. a QRSF $\{R_n\}$. We denote by $\mathcal{IND}_{qq}$ the class of pairs of encryption schemes (G, M, E, D) and QRSF $\{R_n\}$ satisfying that (G, M, E, D) w.r.t. QRSF $\{R_n\}$ has indistinguishable encryptions. We denote by $\mathcal{IND}_{qt}$ the class of pairs of encryption scheme (G, M, E, D) and QRSF $\{R_n\}$ satisfying that (G, M, E, D) w.r.t. QRSF $\{R_n\}$ has skew-indistinguishable encryptions.

Theorem 2. $\mathcal{IND}_{qt} \subsetneq \mathcal{SS}_q \subsetneq \mathcal{IND}_{qq}$.

The above theorem follows the four lemmas below.

Lemma 1. $\mathcal{SS}_q \subseteq \mathcal{IND}_{qq}$.

Lemma 2. $\mathcal{IND}_{qt} \subseteq \mathcal{SS}_q$.

Lemma 3. $\mathcal{IND}_{qq} \setminus \mathcal{SS}_q \neq \emptyset$.

Lemma 4. $\mathcal{SS}_q \setminus \mathcal{IND}_{qt} \neq \emptyset$.

Proof. **(Lemma 1)** We show that if an encryption scheme (G, M, E, D) w.r.t. $\{R_n\}$ is semantically secure then (G, M, E, D) w.r.t. $\{R_n\}$ has indistinguishable encryptions.

Now, we assume that (G, M, E, D) w.r.t. $\{R_n\}$ does not have indistinguishable encryptions; namely, there exist a polynomial-size circuit family $\{D_n\}_{n\in N}$ and a polynomial $p(\cdot)$ such that for infinitely many n, there exist x_n and $\tilde{x}_n$ satisfying

$$\left| \Pr_{G;r\in_U R_n} \left[D_n(G_1(1^n), E_{G_1(1^n)}(x_n; r)) = 1 \right] \right.$$
$$\left. - \Pr_{G;r\in_U R_n} \left[D_n(G_1(1^n), E_{G_1(1^n)}(\tilde{x}_n; r)) = 1 \right] \right| > \frac{1}{p(n)}.$$

Without loss of generality, for infinitely many n, there exist x_n and $\tilde{x}_n$ satisfying

$$\Pr_{G;r\in_U R_n} \left[D_n(G_1(1^n), E_{G_1(1^n)}(x_n; r)) = 1 \right]$$
$$- \Pr_{G;r\in_U R_n} \left[D_n(G_1(1^n), E_{G_1(1^n)}(\tilde{x}_n; r)) = 1 \right] > \frac{1}{p(n)}.$$

Let X_n be a random variable such that $\Pr[X_n = x_n] = \Pr[X_n = \tilde{x}_n] = 1/2$. Let f be a function such that $f(x_n) = 1$ and $f(\tilde{x}_n) = 0$. Now, we consider the following circuit C_n. On input $(e, E_e(x; r))$, the new circuit C_n feeds D_n with input $(e, E_e(x; r))$ and output 1 if D_n outputs 1; otherwise, C_n outputs 0. It is left to estimate the probability that $C_n(e, E_e(x; r)) = f(x)$ when x is drawn according to X_n.

$$\Pr_{\substack{G;x\in X_n\{x_n,\tilde{x}_n\} \\ r\in_U R_n}} \left[C_n(G_1(1^n), E_{G_1(1^n)}(x; r)) = f(x) \right]$$

$$= \frac{1}{2} \cdot \Pr_{G;r\in_U R_n} \left[C_n(G_1(1^n), E_{G_1(1^n)}(x_n; r)) = f(x_n) \right]$$
$$+ \frac{1}{2} \cdot \Pr_{G;r\in_U R_n} \left[C_n(G_1(1^n), E_{G_1(1^n)}(\tilde{x}_n; r)) = f(\tilde{x}_n) \right]$$

$$= \frac{1}{2} \left(\Pr_{G;r\in_U R_n} \left[D_n(G_1(1^n), E_{G_1(1^n)}(x_n; r)) = 1 \right] + 1 \right.$$
$$\left. - \Pr_{G;r\in_U R_n} \left[D_n(G_1(1^n), E_{G_1(1^n)}(\tilde{x}_n; r)) = 1 \right] \right)$$

$$\geq \frac{1}{2} + \frac{1}{2p(n)}.$$

In contrast, for every (randomized) circuit C'_n, $\Pr[C'_n(G_1(1^n)) = f(X_n)] \leq 1/2$. This contradicts the hypothesis that the scheme is semantically secure. $\square$

Proof. **(Lemma 2)** We show that if (G, M, E, D) w.r.t. $q(n)$-QRSF $\{R_n\}$ has skew-indistinguishable encryptions then (G, M, E, D) w.r.t. $q(n)$-QRSF $\{R_n\}$ is semantically secure.

Now, we assume that there exist a polynomial-size circuit family $\{C_n\}_{n \in N}$, a polynomial $p(\cdot)$, and polynomially-bounded functions f, h such that for infinitely many n,

$$\Pr_{\substack{T,G;x \in X_n M_n \\ r \in_U R_n}} \left[C_n(G_1(1^n), E_{G_1(1^n)}(x;r), 1^n, h(x)) = f(x) \right]$$

$$- \Pr_{\substack{G;x \in X_n M_n \\ r \in_U R_n}} \left[C'_n(G_1(1^n), 1^n, h(x)) = f(x) \right] > \frac{1}{p(n)}.$$

Now, we consider the following circuit $C'_{n,r}$. $C'_{n,r}$ feeds C_n with input $(e, E_e(1^n; r)$, $1^n, h(x))$ and outputs a value that C_n outputs. Thus it is easy to transform C_n to $C'_{n,r}$ in probabilistic polynomial time. Then

$$\Pr_{\substack{G;x \in X_n M_n \\ r \in_U R_n}} \left[C_n(G_1(1^n), E_{G_1(1^n)}(x;r), 1^n, h(x)) = f(x) \right]$$

$$- \Pr_{\substack{G;x \in X_n M_n \\ r \in_U T_n}} \left[C_n(G_1(1^n), E_{G_1(1^n)}(1^n; r), 1^n, h(x)) = f(x) \right] > \frac{1}{p(n)},$$

where $\{T_n\}$ is $q(n)$-TRSF. Let x_n be a string for which the difference above is maximum over X_n. Using this x_n, we construct a new circuit D_n as follows. On input $(e, E_e(\alpha; r))$, D_n feeds C_n with input $(e, E_e(\alpha; r), 1^n, h(x_n))$ and outputs 1 if C_n outputs $f(x_n)$; otherwise D_n outputs 0. Then

$$\Pr_{G;r \in_U R_n} \left[D_n(G_1(1^n), E_{G_1(1^n)}(x_n; r)) = 1 \right]$$

$$- \Pr_{G;r \in_U T_n} \left[D_n(G_1(1^n), E_{G_1(1^n)}(1^n; r)) = 1 \right] > \frac{1}{p(n)}.$$

This contradicts the hypothesis that the encryption scheme has skew-indistinguishable encryptions. □

Proof. (**Lemma 3**) Suppose that $\langle (G, M, E, D), \{T_n\} \rangle \in SS_q$, where $\{T_n\}$ is $q(n)$-TRSF. Then there exists an encryption scheme (G, M, E', D') such that $\langle (G, M, E', D'), \{T'_n\} \rangle \in SS_q$, where $\{T'_n\}$ is $(q(n) + 1)$-TRSF, $E'_e(\alpha; r) = E_e(\alpha; r_1)r_2$, $D'_d(\beta) = D_d(\beta')$, $r = r_1 r_2$, $|r_2| = 1$, and β' is the prefix of β of length $|\beta| - 1$. Let V be a non-BPP subset (i.e., tally set) of 1^*. We consider a QRSF $\{R_n\} = \{\{0,1\}^{q(n)}b\}$, where $b = 1$ if $1^n \in V$; $b = 0$ otherwise. Since the last bit of the ciphertext message is always constant of all ciphertext messages specified by security parameter n, any distinguishing circuit cannot use the last bit of the ciphertext message. ¿From Lemma 1, it follows that $\langle (G, M, E, D), \{T_n\} \rangle \in IND_{qq}$. Thus $\langle (G, M, E', D'), \{R_n\} \rangle \in IND_{qq}$.

On the other hand, $\langle (G, M, E', D'), \{R_n\} \rangle \notin SS_q$. We will show this by contradictory. We assume that $\langle (G, M, E', D'), \{R_n\} \rangle \in SS_q$. In other words, there exists a probabilistic polynomial transformation T such that for every polynomial-size circuit $\{C_n\}_{n \in N}$, for every probability ensemble $\{X_n\}_{n \in N}$ satisfying that X_n is a probability distribution on M_n, for every pair of polynomially-bounded functions $f, h : \{0,1\}^* \to \{0,1\}^*$, every polynomial $p(\cdot)$ and sufficiently large n,

$$\Pr_{G,X_n;r\in_U R_n}\left[C_n(G_1(1^n), E_{G_1(1^n)}(X_n;r), 1^n, h(X_n)) = f(X_n)\right]$$
$$< \Pr_{T,G,X_n}\left[C'_n(G_1(1^n), 1^n, h(X_n)) = f(X_n)\right] + \frac{1}{p(n)}$$

where $C'_n = T(C_n)$. Here, we consider a circuit family $\{C_n\}_{n\in N}$, probability ensemble $\{X_n\}_{n\in N}$, polynomially-bounded functions f, h satisfying the following: C_n outputs the last bit of the ciphertext message; $\Pr[X_n = 1^n] = 1$; h is constant; and $f(X_n) = 1$ if $1^n \in V$, $f(X_n) = 0$ otherwise. Then C_n always computes $f(X_n)$ correctly. We can say that there exists a probabilistic polynomial transformation T such that for sufficiently large n,

$$1 - \Pr_{G,T}\left[T(C_n)(G_1(1^n), 1^n) = f(1^n)\right] < \frac{1}{p(n)}.$$

Since $\{C_n\}_{n\in N}$ can be implemented by a (uniform) constant size circuit family, $T(\{C_n\}_{n\in N})$ can be also implemented by a (uniform) probabilistic polynomial-time algorithm B. Thus, we can say that B computes the membership of a non-BPP tally set. This is a contradiction. Therefore $\langle(G, M, E', D'), \{R_n\}\rangle \notin \mathcal{SS}_q$. $\square$

Proof. **(Lemma 4)** Suppose that $\langle(G, M, E, D), \{T_n\}\rangle \in \mathcal{IND}_{qt}$, where $\{T_n\}$ is $q(n)$-TRSF. Then there exists an encryption scheme (G, M, E', D') such that $\langle(G, M, E', D'), \{T'_n\}\rangle \in \mathcal{IND}_{qt}$, where $\{T'_n\}$ is $(q(n)+1)$-TRSF, $E'_e(\alpha; r) = E_e(\alpha; r_1)r_2$, $D'_d(\beta) = D_d(\beta')$, $r = r_1r_2$, $|r_2| = 1$, and β' is the prefix of β of length $|\beta| - 1$. We consider a QRSF $\{R_n\} = \{\{0,1\}^{q(n)}1\}$. It is easy to see that $\langle(G, M, E', D'), \{R_n\}\rangle \notin \mathcal{IND}_{qt}$ because a distinguisher can use the last bit of the ciphertext message.

On the other hand, from Lemma 2, it follows that $\langle(G, M, E, D), \{T_n\}\rangle \in \mathcal{SS}_q$. Since, in the scheme (G, M, E', D'), the last bit of the ciphertext message gives no information on the plaintext message, $\langle(G, M, E', D'), \{R_n\}\rangle \in \mathcal{SS}_q$. $\square$

4.2   Properties of QRSF and Their Effects on the Security

In this subsection, we consider how properties of QRSF affect on the security of encryption schemes. We will especially give a sufficient condition that semantic security and indistinguishability become equivalent in the quasi-randomness framework.

Theorem 3. *Suppose that* $\langle(G, M, E, D), \{R_n\}\rangle \in \mathcal{IND}_{qq}$. *If* $\{R_n\}$ *is semi-random, then* $\langle(G, M, E, D), \{R_n\}\rangle \in \mathcal{IND}_{qt}$.

We note that since the true randomness is semi-random, the equivalence between semantic security and indistinguishability (w.r.t. the true randomness) can be shown as a corollary of Lemmas 1, 2 and Theorem 3. The above theorem says that if an encryption scheme is semantically secure in the true-randomness framework and we use "semi-random" sequence as random inputs to the encryption algorithm then the encryption scheme is still semantically secure in the quasi-randomness framework.

Proof. We show that if an encryption scheme (G, M, E, D) w.r.t. $\{R_n\}$ has indistinguishable encryptions and $\{R_n\}$ is semi-random, then (G, M, E, D) w.r.t. $\{R_n\}$ has skew-indistinguishable encryptions.

Now, we assume that there exist a polynomial-size circuit family $\{D_n\}_{n \in N}$ and a polynomial $p(\cdot)$ such that for infinitely many n and for some $x, \tilde{x} \in M_n$

$$\left| \Pr_{G; r' \in_U T_n} \left[D_n(G_1(1^n), E_{G_1(1^n)}(x; r')) = 1 \right] \right.$$
$$\left. - \Pr_{G; r \in_U R_n} \left[D_n(G_1(1^n), E_{G_1(1^n)}(\tilde{x}; r)) = 1 \right] \right| > \frac{1}{p(n)}.$$

If $x = \tilde{x}$ then it is easy to construct a polynomial-size circuit from D_n and E_e to distinguish r' and r using the circuit. This contradicts that $\{R_n\}$ is semi-random. Thus we have only to consider the case $x \neq \tilde{x}$.

Since $\{R_n\}$ is semi-random, for any polynomial $p'(\cdot)$ such that $p(n) < p'(n)$,

$$\left| \Pr_{G; r' \in_U T_n} \left[D_n(G_1(1^n), E_{G_1(1^n)}(x; r')) = 1 \right] \right.$$
$$\left. - \Pr_{G; r \in_U R_n} \left[D_n(E_{G_1(1^n)}(x; r)) = 1 \right] \right| < \frac{1}{p'(n)}.$$

Therefore, there exists a polynomial $p''(\cdot)$ such that

$$\left| \Pr_{G; r \in_U R_n} \left[D_n(G_1(1^n), E_{G_1(1^n)}(x; r)) = 1 \right] \right.$$
$$\left. - \Pr_{G; r \in_U R_n} \left[D_n(G_1(1^n), E_{G_1(1^n)}(\tilde{x}; r)) = 1 \right] \right| > \frac{1}{p(n)} - \frac{1}{p'(n)} > \frac{1}{p''(n)}.$$

This contradicts the hypothesis that the scheme has indistinguishable encryptions. □

Theorem 4. *Suppose that* $\langle (G, M, E, D), \{R_n\} \rangle \in \mathcal{IND}_{qq}$. *If* $\{R_n\}$ *is samplable, then* $\langle (G, M, E, D), \{R_n\} \rangle \in \mathcal{SS}_q$.

The above theorem says that if the combination of the encryption scheme and quasi-randomness sequences as random inputs to the encryption algorithm has indistinguishable encryptions then the combined encryption scheme is semantically secure in the quasi-randomness framework. Namely, the above theorem offers us another way to show that the encryption scheme is semantically secure (in the quasi-randomness framework). The above theorem also says that the property of "semi-randomness" for random inputs to the encryption algorithm is not essential. It is open to further discussion whether or not the combined encryption schemes are semantically secure in the quasi-randomness framework even though the quasi-random sequences are not semi-random or even though the quasi-random sequences have not been proved to be semi-random yet.

Proof. We show that if (G, M, E, D) w.r.t. $q(n)$-QRSF $\{R_n\}$ has indistinguishable encryptions and $\{R_n\}$ is samplable then (G, M, E, D) w.r.t. $q(n)$-QRSF $\{R_n\}$ is semantically secure.

Now, we assume that, for any transformation T, there exist a polynomial-size circuit family $\{C_n\}$, a polynomial $p(\cdot)$, and polynomially-bounded functions f, h such that for infinitely many n,

$$\Pr_{\substack{G;x\in_{X_n} M_n \\ r\in_U R_n}} \left[C_n(G_1(1^n), E_{G_1(1^n)}(x;r), 1^n, h(x)) = f(x) \right]$$

$$- \Pr_{\substack{T,G;x\in_{X_n} M_n \\ r\in_U R_n}} \left[C'_n(G_1(1^n), 1^n, h(x)) = f(x) \right] > \frac{1}{p(n)},$$

where $C'_n = T(C_n)$. Now, we consider the following circuit $C'_{n,r'}$. $C'_{n,r'}$ feeds C_n with input $(e, E_e(1^n; r))$ and outputs a value that C_n outputs. Since $\{R_n\}$ is samplable, $r \in R_n$ is samplable in polynomial time using the truly random r'. Thus it is easy to transform C_n to $C'_{n,r'}$ in probabilistic polynomial time. Then

$$\Pr_{\substack{G;x\in_{X_n} M_n \\ r\in_U R_n}} \left[C_n(G_1(1^n), E_{G_1(1^n)}(x;r), h(x)) = f(x) \right]$$

$$- \Pr_{\substack{G;x\in_{X_n} M_n \\ r'\in_U \{0,1\}^{q(n)}; r\leftarrow S_n(r')}} \left[C_n(G_1(1^n), E_{G_1(1^n)}(1^n; r), h(x)) = f(x) \right] > \frac{1}{p(n)},$$

where S_n is the sampling circuit. Since the statistical difference between $\{S_n(r)\}$ and the uniform distribution on R_n is less than $1/4p(n)$ (actually it is less than $1/p'(n)$ for any polynomial $p'(\cdot)$), we have,

$$\Pr_{\substack{G;x\in_{X_n} M_n \\ r\in_U R_n}} \left[C_n(G_1(1^n), E_{G_1(1^n)}(x;r), 1^n, h(x)) = f(x) \right]$$

$$- \Pr_{\substack{G;x\in_{X_n} M_n \\ r\in_U R_n}} \left[C_n(G_1(1^n), E_{G_1(1^n)}(1^n; r), 1^n, h(x)) = f(x) \right]$$

$$> \Pr_{\substack{G;x\in_{X_n} M_n \\ r'\in_U \{0,1\}^{q(n)}; r\leftarrow S_n(r')}} \left[C_n(G_1(1^n), E_{G_1(1^n)}(1^n; r), 1^n, h(x)) = f(x) \right]$$

$$- \Pr_{\substack{G;x\in_{X_n} M_n \\ r\in_U R_n}} \left[C_n(G_1(1^n), E_{G_1(1^n)}(1^n; r), 1^n, h(x)) = f(x) \right] + \frac{1}{p(n)}$$

$$> \frac{1}{p(n)} - \sum_r \left(\Pr_{\substack{G;x\in_{X_n} M_n}} \left[C_n(G_1(1^n), E_{G_1(1^n)}(1^n; r), 1^n, h(x)) = f(x) \right] \cdot \right.$$

$$\left. \left| \Pr[r \leftarrow S_n(r')] - \Pr[r \in_U R_n] \right| \right)$$

$$> \frac{1}{p(n)} - \sum_r \left| \Pr[r \leftarrow S_n(r')] - \Pr[r \in_U R_n] \right|$$

$$= \frac{1}{p(n)} - 2 \cdot \max_A \left\{ \left| \Pr_{r'\in_U \{0,1\}^{q(n)}} [S_n(r') \in A] - \Pr_{r\in_U R_n} [r \in A] \right| \right\} > \frac{1}{2p(n)}.$$

Let x_n be a string for which the difference above is maximum over X_n. Using this x_n, we construct a new circuit D_n as follows. On input $(e, E_e(\alpha; r))$, D_n

feeds C_n with input $(e, E_e(\alpha; r), 1^n, h(x_n))$ and outputs 1 if C_n outputs $f(x_n)$; otherwise D_n outputs 0. Then

$$\Pr_{G; r \in_U R_n} \left[D_n(G_1(1^n), E_{G_1(1^n)}(x_n; r)) = 1 \right]$$
$$- \Pr_{G; r \in_U T_n} \left[D_n(G_1(1^n), E_{G_1(1^n)}(1^n; r)) = 1 \right] > \frac{1}{2p(n)}.$$

This contradicts the hypothesis that the scheme has indistinguishable encryptions. □

As a corollary, we have the following. The below gives us a better sufficient condition for the equivalence between semantic security and indistinguishability.

Corollary 1. *Suppose that* $\{R_n\}$ *is semi-random or samplable. Then* $\langle (G, M, E, D), \{R_n\} \rangle \in \mathcal{IND}_{qq}$ *if and only if* $\langle (G, M, E, D), \{R_n\} \rangle \in \mathcal{SS}_q$.

Theorem 5. *There exists* $\langle (G, M, E, D), \{R_n\} \rangle \in \mathcal{IND}_{qt}$ *such that* $\{R_n\}$ *is not semi-random.*

Although we have a better sufficient condition for the equivalence between semantic security and indistinguishability, the condition is not necessary for the equivalence. The above theorem actually says that neither semi-randomness nor polynomial-time pseudo-randomness is necessary for the equivalence.

Proof. Suppose that $\langle (G, M, E, D), \{T_n\} \rangle \in \mathcal{IND}_{qt}$, where $\{T_n\}$ is $q(n)$-TRSF. Then there exists an encryption scheme (G, M, E', D') such that $\langle (G, M, E', D'), \{T'_n\} \rangle \in \mathcal{IND}_{qt}$, where $\{T'_n\}$ is $(q(n)+1)$-TRSF, $E'_e(\alpha; r) = E_e(\alpha; r_1)$, $D'_d(\beta) = D_d(\beta)$, $r = r_1 r_2$ and $|r_2| = 1$. We consider a QRSF $\{R_n\} = \{\{0,1\}^{q(n)}1\}$. It is easy to see that $\langle (G, M, E', D'), \{R_n\} \rangle \in \mathcal{IND}_{qt}$, because the last bit of the supplementary random input is not used in encrypting.

On the other hand, it is easy to see that $\{R_n\}$ and $\{T'_n\}$ are distinguishable. In other words, $\{R_n\}$ is not semi-random. □

5 Concluding Remarks

We have introduced a framework in which we can uniformly and comprehensively discuss security notions of public-key encryption schemes even for the case where some weak generator producing seemingly random sequences is used to encrypt plaintext messages. Since the new framework separates chosen plaintext attack and ciphertext only attack, we consider the security under the COA model in the framework. We have proved that indistinguishability and semantic security are not equivalent in general. On the other hand, we have derived some sufficient condition for the equivalence and shown that polynomial-time pseudo-randomness is not always necessary for the equivalence.

The discussion has been restricted on the case of ciphertext only attack, so we will consider the case of chosen plaintext attack and chosen ciphertext attack. We will also consider non-malleability [8] in the new framework.

Acknowledgments

I would like to thank Osamu Watanabe for helpful comments and suggestions on this paper drafts.

References

1. M. Bellare, A. Boldyreva, and S. Micali. Public-key encryption in a multi-user setting: Security proofs and improvements. In B. Preneel, editor, *Advances in Cryptology — EUROCRYPT 2000*, volume 1807 of *Lecture Notes in Computer Science*, pages 259–274. Springer-Verlag, 2000.
2. M. Bellare, A. Desai, D. Pointcheval, and P. Rogaway. Relations among notions of security for public-key encryption schemes. In H. Krawczyk, editor, *Advances in Cryptology — CRYPTO'98*, volume 1462 of *Lecture Notes in Computer Science*, pages 26–45. Springer-Verlag, 1998.
3. M. Bellare, S. Goldwasser, and D. Micciancio. Pseudo-random number generation within cryptographic algorithms: The DSS case. In B. S. Kaliski Jr., editor, *Advances in Cryptology — CRYPTO'97*, volume 1294 of *Lecture Notes in Computer Science*, pages 277–291. Springer-Verlag, 1997.
4. M. Bellare and A. Sahai. Non-malleable encryption: Equivalence between two notions, and an indistinguishability-based characterization. In M. Wiener, editor, *Advances in Cryptology — CRYPTO'99*, volume 1666 of *Lecture Notes in Computer Science*, pages 519–536. Springer-Verlag, 1999.
5. L. Blum, M. Blum, and M. Shub. A simple unpredictable pseudo-random number generator. *SIAM Journal on Computing*, 15(2):364–383, 1986.
6. M. Blum and S. Micali. How to generate cryptographically strong sequences of pseudo-random bits. *SIAM Journal on Computing*, 13(4):850–864, 1984.
7. J. Boyar. Inferring sequences produced by pseudo-random number generators. *Journal of the Association for Computing Machinery*, 36(1):129–141, 1989.
8. D. Dolev, C. Dwork, and M. Naor. Non-malleable cryptography. In *Proceedings of the 23rd Annual ACM Symposium on Theory of Computing*, pages 542–552. ACM Press, 1991.
9. A. M. Frieze, J. Hastad, R. Kannan, J. C. Lagarias, and A. Shamir. Reconstructing truncated integer variables satisfying linear congruences. *SIAM Journal on Computing*, 17(2):262–280, 1988.
10. O. Goldreich. *Foundation of Cryptography (Fragment of a Book – Version 2.03)*, 1998.
11. O. Goldreich, S. Goldwasser, and S. Micali. How to construct random functions. *Journal of the Association for Computing Machinery*, 33(4):792–807, 1986.
12. S. Goldwasser and S. Micali. Probabilistic encryption. *Journal of Computer and System Sciences*, 28(2):270–299, 1984.
13. D. E. Knuth. *The Art of Computer Programming*, volume 2. Seminumerical Algorithms. Addison-Wesley, 3rd edition, 1998.
14. T. Koshiba. A theory of randomness for public key cryptosystems: The ElGamal cryptosystem case. *IEICE Transactions on Fundamentals of Electronics, Communications and Computer Sciences*, E83-A(4):614–619, 2000.
15. H. Krawczyk. How to predict congruential generators. *Journal of Algorithms*, 13(4):527–545, 1992.
16. M. Luby. *Pseudorandomness and Cryptographic Applications*. Princeton Univ. Press, 1996.

17. A. J. Menezes, P. C. van Oorschot, and S. A. Vanestone. *Handbook of Applied Cryptography*. CRC Press, 1997.
18. S. Micali, C. Rackoff, and B. Sloan. The notion of security for probabilistic cryptosystems. *SIAM Journal on Computing*, 17(2):412–426, 1988.
19. M. Naor and M. Yung. Public-key cryptosystems provably secure against chosen ciphertext attacks. In *Proceedings of the 22nd Annual ACM Symposium on Theory of Computing*, pages 427–437. ACM Press, 1990.
20. C. Rackoff and D. R. Simon. Non-interactive zero-knowledge proof of knowledge and chosen ciphertext attack. In J. Feigenbaum, editor, *Advances in Cryptology — CRYPTO'91*, volume 576 of *Lecture Notes in Computer Science*, pages 433–444. Springer-Verlag, 1992.
21. A. Shamir. On the generation of cryptographically strong pseudorandom sequences. *ACM Transactions on Computer Systems*, 1(1):38–44, 1983.
22. J. Stern. Secret linear congruential generators are not cryptographically secure. In *Proceedings of the 28th Annual IEEE Symposium on Foundations of Computer Science*, pages 421–426. IEEE Computer Society Press, 1987.
23. A. C. Yao. Theory and applications of trapdoor functions. In *Proceedings of the 23rd Annual IEEE Symposium on Foundations of Computer Science*, pages 80–91. IEEE Computer Society Press, 1982.

The Gap-Problems: A New Class of Problems for the Security of Cryptographic Schemes

Tatsuaki Okamoto[1] and David Pointcheval[2]

[1] NTT Labs, 1-1 Hikarinooka, Yokosuka-shi 239-0847 Japan.
okamoto@isl.ntt.co.jp.
[2] Dépt d'Informatique, ENS – CNRS, 45 rue d'Ulm, 75230 Paris Cedex 05, France.
David.Pointcheval@ens.fr – http://www.di.ens.fr/~pointche.

Abstract. This paper introduces a novel class of computational problems, the *gap problems*, which can be considered as a dual to the class of the *decision problems*. We show the relationship among inverting problems, decision problems and gap problems. These problems find a nice and rich practical instantiation with the Diffie-Hellman problems.
Then, we see how the gap problems find natural applications in cryptography, namely for proving the security of very efficient schemes, but also for solving a more than 10-year old open security problem: the Chaum's undeniable signature.

1 Introduction

1.1 Motivation

It is very important to prove the security of a cryptographic scheme under a reasonable computational assumption. A typical reasonable computational assumption is the intractability of an inverting problem such as factoring a composite number, inverting the RSA function [33], computing the discrete logarithm problem, and computing the Diffie-Hellman problem [12]. Here, an inverting problem is, given a problem, x, and relation f, to find its solution, y, such that $f(x, y) = 1$.

Another type of reasonable computational assumptions is the intractability of a decision problem such as the decision Diffie-Hellman problem. Such a decision problem is especially useful to prove the semantical security of a public-key encryption (e.g., El Gamal and Cramer-Shoup encryption schemes [13,11]). Although we have several types of decision problems, a typical decision problem is, given (x, y) and f, to decide whether the pair (x, y) satisfies $f(x, y) = 1$ or not. Another typical example of decision problems is, given x and f, to decide a hard core bit, $H(y)$, of x with $f(x, y) = 1$.

After having studied some open problems about the security of several primitive cryptographic schemes in which we have not found any flaw, we have realized that the existing computational assumptions (or primitive problems) are not sufficient to prove the security of these schemes. For example, Chaum's undeniable signature scheme [9,7] based on the discrete logarithm is the most typical scheme to realize an undeniable signature scheme and is often used for cryptographic

K. Kim (Ed.): PKC 2001, LNCS 1992, pp. 104–118, 2001.

protocols (e.g., Brands' restrictive blind signatures [6,5]), however, we cannot prove the security of Chaum's undeniable signature scheme under any existing computational assumption. That is, we have realized that a new family of computational assumptions (or problems) are necessary to prove several important cryptographic schemes.

1.2   Achievement

To prove the security of these primitive cryptographic schemes, this paper introduces a new family of problems we called the *gap problems*. Intuitively speaking, a gap problem is to solve an inverting problem with the help of the oracle of a related decision problem. For example, a gap problem of f is, given problem x and relation f, to find y satisfying $f(x, y) = 1$, with the help of the oracle of, given question (x', y'), answering whether $f(x', y') = 1$ or not.

Indeed, in some situations, an adversary has to break a specific computational problem to make fail the security, while having a natural access to an oracle which answers a yes/no query, and therefore leaking one bit. For example, in an undeniable signature, an adversary tries to forge a signature (i.e., solve an inverting problem) with being allowed to ask a signer (i.e., oracle) of whether a pair of signature s and message m is valid or not.

We show that the class of gap problems is dual to the class of decision problems. We then prove Chaum's undeniable scheme is secure under the assumption of the related gap problem. Here note that it has been open for more than 10 years to prove the security of Chaum's undeniable scheme.

1.3   Outline of the Paper

This paper has the following organization. First, we formally define this new family of gap-problems, in a general setting and for the particular situation of the random self-reducible problems. Then, we present some interesting examples, derived from the classical problems used in cryptography. Finally, we prove that the security of some very old protocols (undeniable signatures and designated confirmer signatures) is equivalent to some gap problems, while it has been an open problem for a long time.

2   Gap Problems

This section is devoted to the presentation of this new class of problems which can be seen as the dual to the decisional problems. Some theoretical results are proposed together with some practical examples.

2.1   Definitions

Let $f : \{0, 1\}^* \times \{0, 1\}^* \to \{0, 1\}$ be any relation. The inverting problem of f is the classical computational version, while we introduce a generalization of the decision problem, by the R-decision problem of f, for any relation

$$R : \{0,1\}^* \times \{0,1\}^* \times \{0,1\}^* \to \{0,1\},$$

- the *inverting problem* of f is, given x, to compute any y such as $f(x,y) = 1$ if it exists, or to answer Fail.
- the *R-decision problem* of f is, given (x,y), to decide whether $R(f,x,y) = 1$ or not. Here y may be the null string, $\perp$.

Let us see some examples for the relation, R_1, R_2, R_3, R_4:

- $R_1(f,x,y) = 1$ iff $f(x,y) = 1$, which formalizes the classical version of decision problems (*cf.* the Decision Diffie-Hellman problem [4,26]).
- $R_2(f,x,\perp) = 1$ iff there exists any z such that $f(x,z) = 1$, which simply answers whether the inverting problem has a solution or not.
- $R_3(f,x,\perp) = 1$ iff z is even, when z such that $f(x,z) = 1$ is uniquely defined. This latter example models the least-significant bit of the pre-image, which is used in many hard-core bit problems [1,14].
- $R_4(f,x,\perp) = 1$ iff all the z such that $f(x,z) = 1$ are even.

It is often the case that the *inverting problem* is strictly stronger than the *R-decision problem*, namely for all the classical examples we have for cryptographic purpose. However, it is not always the case, and the R-decision problem can even be strictly stronger than the inverting one (the latter R_4-relation above gives the taste of such an example). In this section, we define the *R-gap problem* which deals with the gap of difficulty between these problems.

Definition 1 (Gap Problem). *The R-gap problem of f is to solve the inverting problem of f with the help of the oracle of the R-decision problem of f.*

2.2 Winning Probabilities

For a computational problem (the inverting or the gap problem), the winning probability is the probability of finding the correct solution on input an instance I and a random tape r. While for a decision problem, the winning probability expresses the advantage the algorithm has in guessing the output bit of the relation R above flipping a coin, on input an instance I and a random tape r.

Computational Problems. For an algorithm $\mathcal{A}$ against a computational problem P, we define winning probabilities as follows:

$$\text{for any instance } I \in P, \quad \mathsf{Win}_{\mathcal{A}}^P(I) = \Pr_r[\mathcal{A}(I;r) \text{ wins}],$$
$$\text{in general,} \quad \mathsf{Win}_{\mathcal{A}}^P = \Pr_{I,r}[\mathcal{A}(I;r) \text{ wins}].$$

Decision Problems. For an algorithm $\mathcal{A}$ against a decision problem P, we define winning probabilities as follows, which consider the advantage an adversary gains above flipping a coin:

$$\text{for any instance } I \in P, \quad \mathsf{Win}_{\mathcal{A}}^P(I) = 2 \times \Pr_r[\mathcal{A}(I;r) \text{ wins}] - 1,$$
$$\text{in general,} \quad \mathsf{Win}_{\mathcal{A}}^P = 2 \times \Pr_{I,r}[\mathcal{A}(I;r) \text{ wins}] - 1.$$

2.3 Tractability

Let us now define some specific notions of tractability which will be of great interest in the following:

- a problem P is *tractable* if there exists a probabilistic polynomial time Turing machine $\mathcal{A}$ which can win with non-negligible probability, over the instances and the internal coins of $\mathcal{A}$.

$$\exists \mathcal{A}, \mathsf{Win}_{\mathcal{A}}^{P} \text{ is non-negligible.}$$

- a problem P is *strongly tractable* if there exists a probabilistic polynomial time Turing machine $\mathcal{A}$ which can win, for any instance I, with overwhelming probability, over the internal coins of $\mathcal{A}$.

$$\exists \mathcal{A}, \forall I \in P, \mathsf{Win}_{\mathcal{A}}^{P}(I) \text{ is overwhelming.}$$

Therefore, we have the negation:

- a problem P is *intractable* if it is not *tractable*
- a problem P is *weakly intractable* if it is not *strongly tractable*.

Finally, to compare the difficulty of problems, we use the notion of polynomial time reductions:

- a problem P is *reducible* to problem P' if there exists a probabilistic polynomial time oracle Turing machine $\mathcal{A}^{P'}$ (with an oracle of the problem P') that wins P with non-negligible probability.
- a problem P is *strongly reducible* to problem P' if there exists a probabilistic polynomial time oracle Turing machine $\mathcal{A}^{P'}$ (with an oracle of the problem P') that wins any instance I of P with overwhelming probability.

We can easily obtain the following proposition,

Proposition 2. *Let f and R be any relations.*

- *If the R-gap problem of f is tractable (resp. strongly tractable), the inverting problem of f is reducible (resp. strongly reducible) to the R-decision problem of f.*
- *If the R-decision problem of f is strongly tractable, the inverting problem of f is reducible to the R-gap problem of f.*

Proof. The first claim directly comes from the definition of the gap problem and the definitions of tractability and reducibility. Let us consider the second claim, with a probabilistic polynomial time Turing machine $\mathcal{B}$ that solves the R-decision problem of f, with overwhelming probability. Let us also assume that we have a probabilistic polynomial time oracle Turing machine $\mathcal{A}^D$ that solves the inverting problem of f with the help of a R-decision oracle D. Since $\mathcal{B}$ solves any instance of the R-decision problem with overwhelming probability, it perfectly simulates the D oracle, after polynomially many queries, with non-negligible probability. For this non-negligible fraction of cases, the machine $\mathcal{A}$ can invert f. But one has to remark that after polynomially many calls to $\mathcal{B}$, the success probability cannot be proven more than non-negligible, hence the classical reducibility, and not the *strong* one.   □

This proposition implies a duality between the gap and the decision problems.

2.4   The Random Self-Reducible Problems

Definition 3 (Random Self-Reducibility). *A problem $\mathcal{P} : P \mapsto S$, where P defines the set of the instances and S the set of the possible solutions ($S = \{0, 1\}$ for a decision problem) is said* random self-reducible *(see figure 1) if there exist two probabilistic polynomial time Turing machines $A : P \mapsto P$ and $B : S \mapsto S$, with random tape $\omega \in \Omega$, such that*

- *for any $I \in P$, $A(I; \omega)$ is uniformly distributed in P while ω is randomly drawn from Ω,*
- *for any $s' \in S$, $B(s'; \omega)$ is uniformly distributed in S while ω is randomly drawn from Ω.*
- *for any instance $I \in P$ and any random tape $\omega \in \Omega$, if $I' = A(I; \omega)$ and s' is a solution to I', then $s = B(s'; \omega)$ is a solution to I.*

For such problems, the weak intractability is equivalent to the classical intractability.

Proposition 4. *Let P be any random self-reducible problem:*

- *this problem P is strongly tractable if and only if it is tractable;*
- *this problem P is intractable if and only if it is weakly intractable.*

Proof. It is clear that both claims are equivalent, and furthermore in each, one of the directions is trivial, since any strongly tractable problem is *a fortiori* tractable. For the remaining direction, one can simply use Shoup's construction [35] to obtain the result. ☐

Corollary 5. *Let f and R be any relations. Let us assume that both the inverting problem of f and the R-decision problem of f are random self-reducible.*

- *If the R-gap problem of f is tractable, the inverting problem of f is reducible to the R-decision problem of f.*
- *If the R-decision problem of f is tractable, the inverting problem of f is reducible to the R-gap problem of f.*

For any $\omega \in \Omega$,

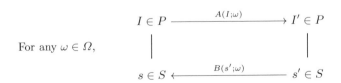

Fig. 1. Random Self-Reducible Problems

Proof. To complete the proof, one just has to remark that if the inverting problem is random self-reducible, then the gap problem is so too.   □

Remark 6. Almost all the classical problems used in cryptography are *random self-reducible*: RSA [33] for fixed modulus n and exponent e, the discrete logarithm and the Diffie-Hellman problems [12] for a fixed basis of prime order, or even over the bases if the underlying group is a cyclic group of prime order, etc.

3   Examples of Gap Problems

Let us review some of these classical problems, with their gap variations. Let us begin with the most famous problem used in cryptography, the RSA problem.

3.1   The RSA Problems

Let us consider $n = pq$ and e relatively prime with $\varphi(n)$, the totient function of n. We have the classical *Inverting RSA problem*: given y, find the e-th root of y modulo n. This corresponds to the relation

$$f(y, x) \stackrel{\text{def}}{=} \left(y \stackrel{?}{=} x^e \bmod n \right),$$

which is a polynomially computable function. Therefore, the default decision problem, $R(f, y, x) = 1$ iff $f(y, x) = 1$, is trivial.

A more interesting relation is the least-significant bit of the e-th root of y:

Definition 7 (The lsb-D-RSA(n, e) Problem). *Given y, decide whether the least-significant bit of the e-th root of y, $x = y^{1/e} \bmod n$, is 0 or 1:*

$$R(f, y) \stackrel{\text{def}}{=} \mathsf{lsb}(x \text{ such that } f(y, x) = 1) = \mathsf{lsb}(y^{1/e} \bmod n).$$

Then, one can define the related gap problem, the lsb-G-RSA(n, e) problem. And therefore, with the results about hard-core bits of RSA [1,14], we know that the lsb-D-RSA is equivalent to the RSA problem, therefore the lsb-G-RSA problem is tractable (and even strongly tractable because of the random self-reducibility of the inverting problem).

3.2   The Diffie-Hellman Problems

The most famous family of problems is definitely the Diffie-Hellman problems [12]. Indeed, it already provides multiple variations (decision and computational versions) as well as interesting environments. Then let us consider any group $\mathcal{G}$ of prime order q. We define three problems as follows:

- *The Inverting Diffie-Hellman Problem (C-DH)* (a.k.a. the Computational Diffie-Hellman problem): given a triple of $\mathcal{G}$ elements (g, g^a, g^b), find the element $C = g^{ab}$.

- *The Decision Diffie-Hellman Problem (D-DH)*: given a quadruple of $\mathcal{G}$ elements (g, g^a, g^b, g^c), decide whether $c = ab \bmod q$ or not.
- *The Gap–Diffie-Hellman Problem (G-DH)*: given a triple (g, g^a, g^b), find the element $C = g^{ab}$ with the help of a Decision Diffie-Hellman Oracle (which answers whether a given quadruple is a Diffie-Hellman quadruple or not).

Note that the decision problem is the default one, when the relation f is defined by

$$f((g, A, B), C) \stackrel{\text{def}}{=} \left(\log_g C \stackrel{?}{=} \log_g A \times \log_g B \bmod q \right),$$

which is *a priori* not a polynomially computable function.

There also exist many possible variations of those problems where the first component, and possibly the second one are fixed:

$$\star\text{-DH}_g(\cdot) = \star\text{-DH}(g, \cdot) \text{ and } \star\text{-DH}_{g,h}(\cdot) = \star\text{-DH}(g, h, \cdot).$$

About the inverting problem, it is believed intractable in many groups (prime subgroups of the multiplicative groups $\mathbb{Z}_n^\star$ or $\mathbb{Z}_p^\star$ [18,23], prime subgroups of some elliptic curves [20], or of some Jacobians of hyper-elliptic curves [21,22]). The decision problem is also believed so in many cases. For example, in generic groups, where only generic algorithms [28] can be used, because of a non-manageable numeration, the discrete logarithm, the inverting Diffie-Hellman and the decision Diffie-Hellman problems have been proven to require the same amount of computation [35]. However, no polynomial time reduction has ever been proposed, excepted in groups with a smooth order [24,25,26]. Therefore, in all these groups used in cryptography, intractability of the gap problem is a reasonable assumption.

However, because of some dual properties in Abelian varieties, the decision Diffie-Hellman problem is easy over the Jacobians of some (hyper)-elliptic curves: namely, in [16], it has been stated the following result

Proposition 8. *Let m be an integer relatively prime to q, and let $\mu_m(\mathbb{F}_q)$ be the group of roots of unity in $\mathbb{F}_q$ whose order divides m. We furthermore assume that the Jacobian $J(\mathbb{F}_q)$ contains a point of order m. Then there is a surjective pairing*

$$\phi_m : J_m(\mathbb{F}_q) \times J(\mathbb{F}_q)/mJ(\mathbb{F}_q) \to \mu_m(\mathbb{F}_q)$$

which is furthermore computable in $\mathcal{O}(\log q)$ (where $J_m(\mathbb{F}_q)$ is the group of m-torsion points).

This pairing, the so-called Tate-pairing, can be used to relate the discrete logarithm in the group $J_m(\mathbb{F}_q)$ to the discrete logarithm in $\mathbb{F}_q^\star$, if $q - 1$ is divisible by m. A particular application [15] is over an elliptic curve, with a trace of the Frobenius endomorphism congruent to 2 modulo m. Indeed, for example, with an elliptic curve $J(\mathbb{F}_q) = E$ of trace $t = 2$ and $m = \#E = q + 1 - t = q - 1$, we have $J_m(\mathbb{F}_q) = J(\mathbb{F}_q)/mJ(\mathbb{F}_q) = E$ and $\mu_m(\mathbb{F}_q) = \mathbb{F}_q^\star$. Then,

$$\phi : E \times E \to \mathbb{F}_q^\star.$$

Let us consider a Diffie-Hellman quadruple, P, $A = a \cdot P$, $B = b \cdot P$ and $C = c \cdot P$,

$$\phi(A, B) = \phi(a \cdot P, b \cdot P) = \phi(P, P)^{ab} = \phi(P, ab \cdot P) = \phi(P, C).$$

And the latter equality only holds with the correct candidate C.

3.3   The Rabin Problems

Let us consider $n = pq$. We define three problems as follows:

- *The Inverting Rabin Problem* (a.k.a. the Factoring Problem): given y, find $x = y^{1/2} \bmod n$ if x exists. This corresponds to the relation

$$f(y, x) \stackrel{\mathsf{def}}{=} \left(x^2 \stackrel{?}{=} y \bmod n \right).$$

- *The Decision Rabin Problem* (a.k.a the Quadratic Residuosity Problem): given y, decide whether x exists or not.
- *The Gap–Rabin Problem*: given a pair y, find $x = y^{1/2} \bmod n$ if x exists, with the help of a Decision Rabin Oracle.

Note that these decision and gap problems correspond to the R relation

$$R(f, y) \stackrel{\mathsf{def}}{=} (\exists x \text{ such that } f(y, x) = 1).$$

Since no polynomial time reduction is known from the Factorization to the Quadratic-Residuosity problem, the Gap–Rabin assumption seems as reasonable as the Quadratic-Residuosity assumption.

It is worth remarking that like in the RSA case, the lsb-G-Rabin problem would be tractable because of hard-core bit result about the least-significant bit [1,14].

4   Application to Cryptography

This notion of gap-problem is eventually not new because it is involved in many practical situations. This section deals with undeniable signatures and designated confirmer signatures. More precisely we show that the security of some old and efficient such schemes is equivalent to a gap-problem, whereas it was just known weaker than the computational version.

4.1   Signatures

An important tool in cryptography is the authentication of messages. It is provided using digital signatures [17]. The basic property of a signature scheme, from the verifier point of view, is the easy verification of the relation between a message and the signature, whereas it should be intractable for anybody, excepted the legitimate signer, to produce a valid signature for a new message: the relation $f(m, \sigma)$, with input a message m and a signature σ, must be computable, while providing an intractable inverting problem. Therefore, an intractable gap-problem is required, with an easy decision problem.

4.2 Undeniable Signatures

In undeniable signatures [9,7], contrarily to plain signatures, the verification process must be intractable without the help of the signer (or a confirmer [8]). And therefore, the confirmer (which can be the signer himself) can be seen as a decision oracle.

Let us study the first example of undeniable signatures [9,7] whose security proof has been an open problem for more than 10 years. We will prove that the full-domain hash [3] variant of this scheme is secure under the Gap-DH problem, in the random oracle model [2].

Definition. First, we just define informally an undeniable signature scheme. For more details, the reader is referred to the original papers [9,7]. An undeniable signature scheme consists of 3 algorithms/protocols:

- key generation algorithm, which on input a security parameter produces a pair of secret/public keys (sk, pk) for the signer.
- signature protocol. It is a, possibly interactive, protocol in which, on input a message m and a signer secret key sk_s, the verifier gets a certificate s on m for which he is convinced of the validity, without being able to transfer this conviction to anybody.
- confirmation/disavowal protocol. It is a, possibly interactive, protocol in which, on input a message m and an alleged certificate s, the signer convinces the verifier whether the certificate s is actually related to m and pk or not, using his secret key sk (in a non-transferable way).

The security notions are similar to the plain signature setting [17]. One wants to prevent existential forgeries under chosen-message attacks. Then, an existential forgery is a certificate that the signer cannot repudiate whereas he did not produce it. But in such a context, the verification protocol can be called many times, on any message-certificate pair chosen by the adversary. We have to take care about this kind of oracle access, hence the gap-problems.

Description. The first proposal was a very nice and efficient protocol. It consists of a non-interactive signature process and an interactive confirmation protocol.

- Setting: g is a generator of a group $\mathcal{G}$ of prime order q. The secret key of the signer is a random element $x \in \mathbb{Z}_q$ while his public key is $y = g^x$.
- Signature of m: in order to sign a message m, the signer computes and returns $s = m^x$.
- Confirmation/Disavowal of (m, s): an interactive proof is used to convince the verifier whether
$$\log_g y = \log_m s \bmod q.$$

In the first paper [9], this proof was not zero-knowledge, but it has been quickly improved in [7].

But we further slightly modify this scheme to prevent existential forgeries, namely by ruling out the basic multiplicative attacks: one uses the classical full-domain hash technique [3,10]. If this hash function is furthermore assumed to behave like a random oracle [2], this scheme can be proven secure. Moreover, to make the analysis easier, we replace the zero-knowledge interactive proof by a non-interactive but non-transferable proof. There are well-known techniques using trapdoor commitments [19] which are perfectly simulatable in the random oracle model [31].

Therefore, we analyze the following variant.

- Setting: g is a generator of a group $\mathcal{G}$ of prime order q. The secret key of the signer is a random element $x \in \mathbb{Z}_q$ while his public key is $y = g^x$. We furthermore need a hash function H which outputs random elements in the whole group $\mathcal{G}$.
- Signature of m: in order to sign a message m, the signer computes $h = H(m)$ and returns $s = h^x$.
- Confirmation/Disavowal of (m, s): the signer uses non-transferable NIZK proofs of either the equality or inequality between

$$\log_g y \text{ and } \log_h s \bmod q, \text{ where } h = H(m).$$

Thus, the confirmation proof answers positively to the D-DH(g, y, h, s) problem whereas the disavowal proof answers negatively.

Security Analysis. Before providing such an analysis, one can state the following theorem:

Theorem 9. *An existential forgery under adaptively chosen-message attacks is equivalent to the Gap Diffie-Hellman problem.*

Proof. For this equivalence, one can easily see that if one can break the C-DH$_{g,y}$ problem, possibly with access to a D-DH$_{g,y}$ oracle (which means that the two first components are fixed to g and y), then one can forge a signature in a universal way: first, a D-DH$_{g,y}$ oracle is simulated (with overwhelming probability) by the confirmation/disavowal protocols. Then, for any message m, one computes $h = H(m)$ as well as C-DH$_{g,y}(m)$. Therefore, the security of this undeniable signature scheme is weaker than the G-DH$_{g,y}$ problem.

In the opposite way, one can use the same techniques as in [3,10] for the security of the full-domain hash signature. Let us consider an adversary that is able to produce an existential forgery with probability ε within time t after q_h queries to the signing oracle, where g is the basis of $\mathcal{G}$ and y the public key of the signer. Then, we will use it to break the G-DH$_{g,y}$ problem. Given $\alpha \in \mathcal{G}$, one tries to extract $\beta = $ C-DH$_{g,y}(\alpha) = $ C-DH(g, y, α). For that, we simulate any interaction with the adversary in an indistinguishable setting from a real attack:

- confirmation/disavowal queries are perfectly simulated by simulating the appropriate proof, correctly chosen thanks to the D-DH$_{g,y}$ oracle.

- any hash query m is answered in a probabilistic way. More precisely, one chooses a random exponent $r \in \mathbb{Z}_q$ and then, with probability p, $H(m)$ is answered by α^r, otherwise it is answered by g^r.
- any signing query m (assumed to has already been asked to H) is answered as follows: if $H(m)$ has been defined as g^r, then $s = y^r$ is a valid signature for m since $s = y^r = g^{xr} = H(m)^x$, for x satisfying $y = g^x$. Otherwise, the simulation aborts.

Finally, the adversary outputs a forgery s for a new message m (also assumed to have already been asked to H). If $H(m)$ has been defined as α^r then $s = H(m)^x = \alpha^{rx}$. Consequently, $s^{1/r} = \mathsf{C\text{-}DH}(g, y, \alpha) = \mathsf{C\text{-}DH}_{g,y}(\alpha)$.

The success probability is exactly the same as for the full-domain hash technique [10]

$$\varepsilon' = \varepsilon(1-p)^{q_h} p \geq \exp(-1) \times \frac{\varepsilon}{q_h}, \text{ while simply choosing } p = \frac{1}{q_h + 1}.$$

$\square$

4.3   Designated Confirmer Signatures

In 1994, Chaum [8] proposed a new kind of undeniable signatures where the signer is not required to confirm the signature, but a designated confirmer, who owns a secret. Furthermore, he proposed a candidate. The same year, Okamoto [29] proved that the existence of such schemes is equivalent to the existence of public-key encryption schemes. He furthermore gave an example, based on the Diffie-Hellman problem [12] (on which relies the security of the El Gamal encryption scheme [13]).

Let us first give a quick definition of this new cryptographic object together with the security notions. Then we study the Okamoto's example, using the Schnorr signature [34], in the random oracle model.

Definition. As for undeniable signatures, we just give an informal definition of designated confirmer signatures. For more details, the reader is referred to [8]. A designated confirmer signature scheme consists of 3 algorithms/protocols:

- key generation algorithm, which on input a security parameter produces two pairs of secret/public keys, the pair $(\mathsf{sk}_s, \mathsf{pk}_s)$ for the signer and the pair $(\mathsf{sk}_c, \mathsf{pk}_c)$ for the confirmer.
- signature protocol. It is a, possibly interactive, protocol in which, on input a message m, a signer secret key sk_s and a confirmer public key pk_c, the verifier gets a certificate s on m for which he is convinced of the validity, without being able to transfer this conviction.
- confirmation/disavowal protocol. It is a, possibly interactive, protocol in which, on input a message m and an alleged certificate s, the confirmer convinces the verifier whether the certificate s is actually related to m and pk_s or not, using his secret key sk_c (in a non-transferable way).

The security notions are the same as for undeniable signatures, excepted that the confirmer may be a privileged adversary: an existential forgery is a certificate that the confirmer cannot repudiate, whereas the signer never produced it. Once again, the confirmation protocol can be called many times, on any message-certificate pair chosen by the adversary. However this kind of oracle is of no help for the confirmer, in forging a certificate.

Description. Let us describe the original Okamoto's example [29], using the Schnorr signature [34]. Because of a flaw remarked by Michels and Stadler [27], one cannot prove the security of this scheme against attacks performed by the confirmer. Then we focus on standard adversaries.

- Setting: g is a generator of a group $\mathcal{G}$ of prime order q. The secret key of the signer is a random element $x \in \mathbb{Z}_q$ while his public key is $y = g^x$. We furthermore need a hash function H which outputs elements in $\mathcal{G}$ (still full-domain hash). The confirmer also owns a secret key $a \in \mathbb{Z}_q$ associated to the public key $b = g^a$.
- Signature of m: in order to sign a message m, the signer chooses random $r, w \in \mathbb{Z}_q$, computes

$$d = g^r, t = g^w, e = b^r \cdot H(m, t) \text{ and } s = w - ex \bmod q$$

and returns (d, e, s). The signer can furthermore prove the validity of this signature by proving, in a non-interactive and non-transferable zero-knowledge way, the equality between

$$\log_g d \text{ and } \log_b z \bmod q, \text{ where } z = e/H(m, g^s y^e).$$

- Confirmation/Disavowal of $(m, (d, e, s))$: the verifier and the confirmer, both compute $z = e/H(m, g^s y^e)$ and the confirmer uses non-interactive and non-transferable zero-knowledge proofs of either the equality or inequality between

$$\log_g b \text{ and } \log_d z \text{ modulo } q.$$

Thus, the confirmation proof by the signer answers positively to D-DH(g, d, b, z), and the confirmation proof by the confirmer answers positively to D-DH(g, b, d, z) whereas the disavowal proof answers negatively.

Therefore, one can get the answer of D-DH(g, b, d, z), which is indeed equivalent to D-DH(b, g, z, d), for any (d, z) of his choice, which looks like to a D-DH$_{b,g}$ oracle.

Security Analysis. Once again, one can state the following theorem:

Theorem 10. *An existential forgery under adaptively chosen-message attacks, for a standard adversary (not the confirmer), is equivalent to the Gap Diffie-Hellman problem.*

Proof. First, if one can break the C-DH$_{b,g}$ problem, possibly with access to a D-DH$_{b,g}$ oracle, then one can forge a signature in a universal way: indeed, a D-DH$_{b,g}$ oracle is simulated, as already seen, by the confirmation/disavowal protocols. Then, for any message m, one chooses random s and e, computes $t = g^s y^e$ and $z = e/H(m,t)$. Then one gets $d = $ C-DH$(b,g,z) = $ C-DH$_{b,g}(z)$ which completes a valid signature (d,e,s). Therefore, the security of this designated confirmer signature scheme is weaker than the G-DH$_{b,g}$ problem.

In the opposite way, one can use a replay technique [32]. Let us consider an adversary that is able to produce an existential forgery with probability ε within time t after q_s queries to the signing oracle and q_h queries to the random oracle H, where g is the basis of $\mathcal{G}$ and b the public key of the confirmer.

Remark 11. We furthermore need to assume that the bit-length k of the notation of $\mathcal{G}$-elements is not too large comparatively to q: $q/2^k$ must be non-negligible.

Then, we will use it to break the G-DH$_{b,g}$ problem. Given $\alpha \in \mathcal{G}$, one tries to extract $\beta = $ C-DH$_{b,g}(\alpha) = $ C-DH(b,g,α). For that, we simulate any interaction with the adversary in an indistinguishable setting from a real attack:

- for setting up the system, we furthermore choose a random $x \in \mathbb{Z}_q$ and define $y = g^x$ to be the public key of the signer.
- confirmation/disavowal queries are perfectly simulated by simulating the appropriate proof, correctly chosen thanks to the D-DH$_{b,g}$ oracle.
- any new hash query is answered by a random element in $\mathcal{G}$.
- any signing query m is perfectly simulated thanks to the secret key x of the signer.

Finally, the adversary outputs a forgery (d,e,s) for a new message m. One computes $t = g^s y^e$, stores $h = H(m,t)$ (which has been defined) and replays the adversary with the same random tape, a new random oracle H' which outputs the same answers than H did until the query (m,t) appears. But this latter query is that time answered by e/α^u for a randomly chosen u. With non-negligible probability, the adversary outputs a new forgery (d',e',s') based on the same query (m,t) to the random oracle H. Since $t = g^s y^e = g^{s'} y^{e'}$

- either $s' = s \bmod q$ and $e' = e \bmod q$
- or the adversary can be used to break the discrete logarithm problem (indeed, the signing answers could be simulated without the secret key x, thanks to the random oracle which makes the non-interaction proof simulatable [32]).

Therefore, one may assume that $s' = s \bmod q$ and $e' = e \bmod q$. Since the answer to (m,t) given by the new random oracle H' is totally independent of e, we furthermore have $e' = e$ in the group $\mathcal{G}$, with probability $q/2^k$, which has been assumed non-negligible. Thus,

$$z' = e'/H'(m, g^{s'} y^{e'}) = e/H'(m,t) = \alpha^u.$$

Consequently,

$$d' = \text{C-DH}(b,g,z'), \text{ and thus, } \beta = d'^{1/u} = \text{C-DH}(b,g,\alpha).$$

$\square$

5   Conclusion

This paper introduced a novel class of computational problems, the *gap problems*, which is considered to be dual to the class of the *decision problems*. We have shown how the gap problems find natural applications in cryptography, namely for proving the security of some primitive schemes like Chaum's undeniable signatures and designated confirmer signatures.

But there are still other clear applications. For example, they appear while considering a new kind of attacks, the *plaintext-checking attacks*, against public-key encryption scheme. And they help us to provide REACT, a Rapid Enhanced-security Asymmetric Cryptosystem Transform [30], which makes into a chosen-ciphertext secure cryptosystem any weakly secure scheme.

Other applications will certainly appear. Anyway, it is worth noting that it had been open for more than 10 years to prove the security of Chaum's undeniable signatures.

References

1. W. Alexi, B. Chor, O. Goldreich, and C. P. Schnorr. RSA and Rabin Functions: Certain Parts are as Hard as the Whole. *SIAM Journal on Computing*, 17:194–209, 1988.
2. M. Bellare and P. Rogaway. Random Oracles Are Practical: a Paradigm for Designing Efficient Protocols. In *Proc. of the 1st CCS*, pages 62–73. ACM Press, New York, 1993.
3. M. Bellare and P. Rogaway. The Exact Security of Digital Signatures – How to Sign with RSA and Rabin. In *Eurocrypt '96*, LNCS 1070, pages 399–416. Springer-Verlag, Berlin, 1996.
4. S. A. Brands. An Efficient Off-Line Electronic Cash System Based on the Representation Problem. Technical Report CS-R9323, CWI, Amsterdam, 1993.
5. S. A. Brands. Off-Line Electronic Cash Based on Secret-Key Certificates. In *LATIN '95*, LNCS 911, pages 131–166. Springer-Verlag, Berlin, 1995.
6. S. A. Brands. Secret-Key Certificates. Technical Report CS-R9510, CWI, Amsterdam, 1995.
7. D. Chaum. Zero-Knowledge Undeniable Signatures. In *Eurocrypt '90*, LNCS 473, pages 458–464. Springer-Verlag, Berlin, 1991.
8. D. Chaum. Designated Confirmer Signatures. In *Eurocrypt '94*, LNCS 950, pages 86–91. Springer-Verlag, Berlin, 1995.
9. D. Chaum and H. van Antwerpen. Undeniable Signatures. In *Crypto '89*, LNCS 435, pages 212–216. Springer-Verlag, Berlin, 1990.
10. J.-S. Coron. On the Exact Security of Full-Domain-Hash. In *Crypto '2000*, LNCS 1880, pages 229–235. Springer-Verlag, Berlin, 2000.
11. R. Cramer and V. Shoup. A Practical Public Key Cryptosystem Provably Secure against Adaptive Chosen Ciphertext Attack. In *Crypto '98*, LNCS 1462, pages 13–25. Springer-Verlag, Berlin, 1998.
12. W. Diffie and M. E. Hellman. New Directions in Cryptography. *IEEE Transactions on Information Theory*, IT–22(6):644–654, November 1976.
13. T. El Gamal. A Public Key Cryptosystem and a Signature Scheme Based on Discrete Logarithms. *IEEE Transactions on Information Theory*, IT–31(4):469–472, July 1985.

14. R. Fischlin and C. P. Schnorr. Stronger Security Proofs for RSA and Rabin bits. *Journal of Cryptology*, 13(2):221–244, 2000.
15. G. Frey, M. Müller, and H. G. Rück. The Tate-Pairing and the Discrete Logarithm Applied to Elliptic Curve Cryptosystems. *IEEE Transactions on Information Theory*, 45:1717–1719, 1999.
16. G. Frey and H. G. Rück. A Remark Concerning m-Divisibility and the Discrete Logarithm in the Divisor Class Group of Curves. *Mathematics of Computation*, 62:865–874, 1994.
17. S. Goldwasser, S. Micali, and R. Rivest. A Digital Signature Scheme Secure Against Adaptive Chosen-Message Attacks. *SIAM Journal of Computing*, 17(2):281–308, April 1988.
18. D. M. Gordon. Discrete Logarithms in GF(p) Using the Number Field Sieve. *SIAM Journal of Discrete Mathematics*, 6(1):124–138, February 1993.
19. M. Jakobsson, K. Sako, and R. Impagliazzo. Designated Verifier Proofs and Their Applications. In *Eurocrypt '96*, LNCS 1070, pages 143–154. Springer-Verlag, Berlin, 1996.
20. N. Koblitz. Elliptic Curve Cryptosystems. *Mathematics of Computation*, 48(177):203–209, January 1987.
21. N. Koblitz. A Family of Jacobians Suitable for Discrete Log Cryptosystems. In *Crypto '88*, LNCS 403, pages 94–99. Springer-Verlag, Berlin, 1989.
22. N. Koblitz. Hyperelliptic Cryptosystems. *Journal of Cryptology*, 1:139–150, 1989.
23. A. Lenstra and H. Lenstra. *The Development of the Number Field Sieve*, volume 1554 of *Lecture Notes in Mathematics*. Springer-Verlag, 1993.
24. U. M. Maurer and S. Wolf. Diffie Hellman Oracles. In *Crypto '96*, LNCS 1109, pages 268–282. Springer-Verlag, Berlin, 1996.
25. U. M. Maurer and S. Wolf. Diffie-Hellman, Decision Diffie-Hellman, and Discrete Logarithms. In *Proceedings of ISIT '98*, page 327. IEEE Information Theory Society, 1998.
26. U. M. Maurer and S. Wolf. The Diffie-Hellman Protocol. *Designs, Codes, and Cryptography*, 19:147–171, 2000.
27. M. Michels and M. Stadler. Generic Constructions for Secure and Efficient Confirmer Signature Schemes. In *Eurocrypt '98*, LNCS 1403, pages 406–421. Springer-Verlag, Berlin, 1998.
28. V. I. Nechaev. Complexity of a Determinate Algorithm for the Discrete Logarithm. *Mathematical Notes*, 55(2):165–172, 1994.
29. T. Okamoto. Designated Confirmer Signatures and Public Key Encryption are Equivalent. In *Crypto '94*, LNCS 839, pages 61–74. Springer-Verlag, Berlin, 1994.
30. T. Okamoto and D. Pointcheval. REACT: Rapid Enhanced-security Asymmetric Cryptosystem Transform. In *RSA '2001*, LNCS. Springer-Verlag, Berlin, 2001.
31. D. Pointcheval. Self-Scrambling Anonymizers. In *Financial Cryptography '2000*, LNCS. Springer-Verlag, Berlin, 2000.
32. D. Pointcheval and J. Stern. Security Arguments for Digital Signatures and Blind Signatures. *Journal of Cryptology*, 13(3):361–396, 2000.
33. R. Rivest, A. Shamir, and L. Adleman. A Method for Obtaining Digital Signatures and Public Key Cryptosystems. *Communications of the ACM*, 21(2):120–126, February 1978.
34. C. P. Schnorr. Efficient Signature Generation by Smart Cards. *Journal of Cryptology*, 4(3):161–174, 1991.
35. V. Shoup. Lower Bounds for Discrete Logarithms and Related Problems. In *Eurocrypt '97*, LNCS 1233, pages 256–266. Springer-Verlag, Berlin, 1997.

A Generalisation, a Simplification and Some Applications of Paillier's Probabilistic Public-Key System

Ivan Damgård and Mads Jurik

University of Aarhus, **BRICS**[*]

Abstract. We propose a generalisation of Paillier's probabilistic public key system, in which the expansion factor is reduced and which allows to adjust the block length of the scheme even after the public key has been fixed, without loosing the homomorphic property. We show that the generalisation is as secure as Paillier's original system.

We construct a threshold variant of the generalised scheme as well as zero-knowledge protocols to show that a given ciphertext encrypts one of a set of given plaintexts, and protocols to verify multiplicative relations on plaintexts.

We then show how these building blocks can be used for applying the scheme to efficient electronic voting. This reduces dramatically the work needed to compute the final result of an election, compared to the previously best known schemes. We show how the basic scheme for a yes/no vote can be easily adapted to casting a vote for up to t out of L candidates. The same basic building blocks can also be adapted to provide receipt-free elections, under appropriate physical assumptions. The scheme for 1 out of L elections can be optimised such that for a certain range of parameter values, a ballot has size only $O(\log L)$ bits.

1 Introduction

In [9], Paillier proposes a new probabilistic encryption scheme based on computations in the group $Z_{n^2}^*$, where n is an RSA modulus. This scheme has some very attractive properties, in that it is homomorphic, allows encryption of many bits in one operation with a constant expansion factor, and allows efficient decryption. In this paper we propose a generalisation of Paillier's scheme using computations modulo n^{s+1}, for any $s \geq 1$. We also show that the system can be simplified (without degrading security) such that the public key can consist of only the modulus n. This allows instantiating the system such that the block length for the encryption can be chosen freely for each encryption, independently of the size of the public key, and without loosing the homomorphic property. The generalisation also allows reducing the expansion factor from 2 for Paillier's original system to almost 1. We prove that the generalisation is as secure as Paillier's original scheme.

[*] Basic Research in Computer Science,
Centre of the Danish National Research Foundation.

K. Kim (Ed.): PKC 2001, LNCS 1992, pp. 119–136, 2001.
© Springer-Verlag Berlin Heidelberg 2001

We propose a threshold variant of the generalised system, allowing a number of servers to share knowledge of the secret key, such that any large enough subset of them can decrypt a ciphertext, while smaller subsets have no useful information. We prove in the random oracle model that the scheme is as secure as a standard centralised implementation.

We also propose a zero-knowledge proof of knowledge allowing a prover to show that a given ciphertext encodes a given plaintext. From this we derive other tools, such as a protocol showing that a ciphertext encodes one out of a number of given plaintexts. Finally, we propose a protocol that allows verification of multiplicative relations among encrypted values without revealing extra information.

We look at applications of this to electronic voting schemes. A large number of such schemes is known, but the most efficient one, at least in terms of the work needed from voters, is by Cramer, Gennaro and Schoenmakers [4]. This protocol provides in fact a general framework that allows usage of any probabilistic encryption scheme for encryption of votes, if the encryption scheme has a set of "nice" properties, in particular it must be homomorphic. The basic idea of this is straightforward: each voter broadcasts an encryption of his vote (by sending it to a bulletin board) together with a proof that the vote is valid. All the valid votes are then combined to produce an encryption of the result, using the homomorphic property of the encryption scheme. Finally, a set of trustees (who share the secret key of the scheme in a threshold fashion) can decrypt and publish the result.

Paillier pointed out already in [9] that since his encryption scheme is homomorphic, it may be applicable to electronic voting. In order to apply it in the framework of [4], however, some important building blocks are missing: one needs an efficient proof of validity of a vote, and also an efficient threshold variant of the scheme, so that the result can be decrypted without allowing a single entity the possibility of learning how single voters voted.

These building blocks are precisely what we provide here. Thus we immediately get a voting protocol. In this protocol, the work needed from the voters is of the same order as in the original version of [4]. However, the work needed to produce the result is reduced dramatically, as we now explain. With the El Gamal encryption used in [4], the decryption process after a yes/no election produces $g^R \bmod p$, where p is prime, g is a generator and R is the desired result. Thus one needs to solve a discrete log problem in order to find the result. Since R is bounded by the number of voters M, this is feasible for moderate size M's. But it requires $\Omega(\sqrt{M})$ exponentiations, and may certainly be something one wants to avoid for large scale elections. The problem becomes worse, if we consider an election where we choose between L candidates, $L \geq 2$. The method given for this in [4] is exponential in L in that it requires time $\Omega(\sqrt{M}^{L-1})$, and so is prohibitively expensive for elections with large L.

In the scheme we propose below, this work can be removed completely. Our decryption process produces the desired result directly. We also give ways to implement efficiently constraints on voting that occur in real elections, such as allowing to vote for precisely t out of the L candidates, or to vote for up to t of them. In each of these schemes, the size of a single ballot is $O(k \cdot L)$, where k is the bit length of the modulus used[1]. We propose a variant using a different technique where ballots have size $O(max(k, L \log M) \cdot \log L)$. Thus for $k \geq L \log M$, this is much more efficient, and even optimal up to a constant factor, since with less than $\log L$ bits one cannot distinguish between the L candidates. Furthermore this scheme requires only 1 decryption operation, even when $L > 2$.

2   Related Work

In work independent from, but earlier than ours, Fouque, Poupard and Stern [6] proposed the first threshold version of Paillier's original scheme. Like our threshold scheme, [6] uses an adaptation of Shoup's threshold RSA scheme [10], but beyond this the techniques are somewhat different, in particular because we construct a threshold version for our generalised crypto system (and not only Paillier's original scheme). In [6] voting was also pointed out as a potential application, however, no suggestion was made there for protocols to prove that an encrypted vote is correctly formed, something that is of course necessary for a secure election in practice.

In work done concurrently with and independent from ours, Baudron, Fouque, Pointcheval, Poupard and Stern [1] propose a voting scheme somewhat similar to ours. Their work can be seen as being complementary to ours in the sense that their proposal is more oriented towards the system architectural aspects of a large scale election, and less towards optimisation of the building blocks. To compare to their scheme, we first note that there the modulus length k must be chosen such that $k > L \log M$. The scheme produces ballots of size $O(k \cdot L)$. An estimate with explicit constants is given in [1] in which the dominating term in our notation is $9kL$.

Because our voting scheme uses the generalised Paillier crypto system, k can be chosen freely, and the voting scheme can still accommodate any values of L, M. If we choose k as in [1], i.e. $k > L \log M$, then the ballots we produce have size $O(k \cdot \log L)$. Working out the concrete constants involved, one finds that our complexity is dominated by the term $11k \log L$. So for large scale elections we have gained a significant factor in complexity compared to [1].

In [8], Hirt and Sako propose a general method for building receipt-free election schemes, i.e. protocols where vote-buying or -coercing is not possible because voters cannot prove to others how they voted. Their method can be applied to make a receipt-free version of the scheme from [4]. It can also be applied to our scheme, with the same efficiency gain as in the non-receipt free case.

---

[1] All complexities given here assume that the length of challenges for the zero-knowledge proofs is at most k. Also, strictly speaking, this complexity only holds if $k > \log M$, however, since $k \geq 1000$ is needed for security anyway, this will always be satisfied in practice.

3   A Generalisation of Paillier's Probabilistic Encryption Scheme

The public-key crypto-system we describe here uses computations modulo n^{s+1} where n is an RSA modulus and s is a natural number. It contains Paillier's scheme [9] as a special case by setting $s = 1$.

We start from the observation that if $n = pq$, p, q odd primes, then $Z^*_{n^{s+1}}$ as a multiplicative group is a direct product $G \times H$, where G is cyclic of order n^s and H is isomorphic to Z^*_n, which follows directly from elementary number theory. Thus, the factor group $\bar{G} = Z^*_{n^{s+1}}/H$ is also cyclic of order n^s. For an arbitrary element $a \in Z^*_{n^{s+1}}$, we let $\bar{a} = aH$ denote the element represented by a in the factor group $\bar{G}$.

Lemma 1. *For any $s < p, q$, the element $n + 1$ has order n^s in $Z^*_{n^{s+1}}$.*

Proof. Consider the integer $(1 + n)^i = \sum_{j=0}^{i} \binom{i}{j} n^j$. This number is 1 modulo n^{s+1} for some i if and only if $\sum_{j=1}^{i} \binom{i}{j} n^{j-1}$ is 0 modulo n^s. Clearly, this is the case if $i = n^s$, so it follows that the order of $1 + n$ is a divisor in n^s, i.e., it is a number of form $p^\alpha q^\beta$, where $\alpha, \beta \leq s$. Set $a = p^\alpha q^\beta$, and consider a term $\binom{a}{j} n^{j-1}$ in the sum $\sum_{j=1}^{a} \binom{a}{j} n^{j-1}$. We claim that each such term is divisible by a: this is trivial if $j > s$, and for $j \leq s$, it follows because $j!$ can then not have p or q as prime factors, and so a must divide $\binom{a}{j}$. Now assume for contradiction that $a = p^\alpha q^\beta < n^s$. Without loss of generality, we can assume that this means $\alpha < s$. We know that n^s divides $\sum_{j=1}^{a} \binom{a}{j} n^{j-1}$. Dividing both numbers by a, we see that p must divide the number $\sum_{j=1}^{a} \binom{a}{j} n^{j-1}/a$. However, the first term in this sum after division by a is 1, and all the rest are divisible by p, so the number is in fact 1 modulo p, and we have a contradiction.

Since the order of H is relatively prime to n^s this implies immediately that the element $\overline{1+n} := (1 + n)H \in \bar{G}$ is a generator of $\bar{G}$, except possibly for $s \geq p, q$. So the cosets of H in $Z^*_{n^{s+1}}$ are

$$H, (1 + n)H, (1 + n)^2 H, ..., (1 + n)^{n^s - 1} H,$$

which leads to a natural numbering of these cosets.

The final technical observation we need is that it is easy to compute i from $(1 + n)^i \mod n^{s+1}$. We now show how to do this. If we define the function $L()$ by $L(b) = (b - 1)/n$ then clearly we have

$$L((1 + n)^i \mod n^{s+1}) = (i + \binom{i}{2} n + ... + \binom{i}{s} n^{s-1}) \mod n^s$$

We now describe an algorithm for computing i from this number.

The general idea of the algorithm is to extract the value part by part, so that we first extract $i_1 = i \mod n$, then $i_2 = i \mod n^2$ and so forth. It is easy to extract $i_1 = L((1 + n)^i \mod n^2) = i \mod n$. Now we can extract the rest by the following induction step: In the j'th step we know i_{j-1}. This means that $i_j = i_{j-1} + k * n^{j-1}$ for some $0 \leq k < n$. If we use this in

$$L((1+n)^i \bmod n^{j+1}) = (i_j + \binom{i_j}{2} n + \ldots + \binom{i_j}{j} n^{j-1}) \bmod n^j$$

We can notice that each term $\binom{i_j}{t+1} n^t$ for $j > t > 0$ satisfies that $\binom{i_j}{t+1} n^t = \binom{i_{j-1}}{t+1} n^t \bmod n^j$. This is because the contributions from $k * n^{j-1}$ vanish modulo n^j after multiplication by n. This means that we get:

$$L((1+n)^i \bmod n^{j+1}) = (i_{j-1} + k * n^{j-1} + \binom{i_{j-1}}{2} n + \ldots +$$
$$\binom{i_{j-1}}{j} n^{j-1}) \bmod n^j$$

Then we just rewrite that to get what we wanted

$$i_j = i_{j-1} + k * n^{j-1}$$
$$= i_{j-1} + L((1+n)^i \bmod n^{j+1}) - (i_{j-1} + \binom{i_{j-1}}{2}) n$$
$$+ \ldots + \binom{i_{j-1}}{j} n^{j-1}) \bmod n^j$$
$$= L((1+n)^i \bmod n^{j+1}) - (\binom{i_{j-1}}{2} n + \ldots + \binom{i_{j-1}}{j} n^{j-1}) \bmod n^j$$

This equation leads to the following algorithm:

$i := 0$;
for j:= 1 **to** s **do**
begin
    $t_1 := L(a \bmod n^{j+1})$;
    $t_2 := i$;
    for k:= 2 **to** j **do**
    begin
        $i := i - 1$;
        $t_2 := t_2 * i \bmod n^j$;
        $t_1 := t_1 - \frac{t_2 * n^{k-1}}{k!} \bmod n^j$;
    end
    $i := t_1$;
end

We are now ready to describe our cryptosystem. In fact, for each natural number s, we can build a cryptosystem CS_s, as follows:

Key Generation. On input the security parameter k, choose an RSA modulus $n = pq$ of length k bits[2]. Also choose an element $g \in Z^*_{n^{s+1}}$ such that $g = (1+n)^j x \bmod n^{s+1}$ for a known j relatively prime to n and $x \in H$. This can be done, e.g., by choosing j, x at random first and computing g; some alternatives are described later. Let λ be the least common multiple of $p-1$ and $q-1$. By the Chinese Remainder Theorem, choose d such that $d \bmod n \in Z^*_n$ and $d = 0 \bmod \lambda$. Any such choice of d will work in the following. In Paillier's original scheme $d = \lambda$ was used, which is the smallest possible value. However, when making a threshold variant, other choices are better - we expand on this in the following section.

Now the public key is n, g while the secret key is d.

Encryption. The plaintext set is Z_{n^s}. Given a plaintext i, choose a random $r \in Z^*_{n^{s+1}}$, and let the ciphertext be $E(i, r) = g^i r^{n^s} \bmod n^{s+1}$.

Decryption. Given a ciphertext c, first compute $c^d \bmod n^{s+1}$. Clearly, if $c = E(v, r)$, we get

$$c^d = (g^i r^{n^s})^d = ((1+n)^{ji} x^i r^{n^s})^d = (1+n)^{jid \bmod n^s} (x^i r^{n^s})^{d \bmod \lambda}$$
$$= (1+n)^{jid \bmod n^s}$$

Now apply the above algorithm to compute $jid \bmod n^s$. Applying the same method with c replaced by g clearly produces the value $jd \bmod n^s$, so this can either be computed on the fly or be saved as part of the secret key. In any case we obtain the cleartext by $(jid) \cdot (jd)^{-1} = i \bmod n^s$.

Clearly, this system is additively homomorphic over Z_{n^s}, that is, the product of encryptions of messages i, i' is an encryption of $i + i' \bmod n^s$.

The security of the system is based on the following assumption, introduced by Paillier in [9] the *decisional composite residuosity assumption* (DCRA):

Conjecture 1. Let A be any probabilistic polynomial time algorithm, and assume A gets n, x as input. Here n has k bits, and is chosen as described above, and x is either random in $Z^*_{n^2}$ or it is a random n'th power in $Z^*_{n^2}$ (that is, a random element in the subgroup H defined earlier). A outputs a bit b. Let $p_0(A, k)$ be the probability that $b = 1$ if x is random in $Z^*_{n^2}$ and $p_1(A, k)$ the probability that $b = 1$ if x is a random n'th power. Then $| p_0(A, k) - p_1(A, k) |$ is negligible in k.

Here, "negligible in k" as usual means smaller than $1/f(k)$ for any polynomial $f()$ and all large enough k.

We now discuss the semantic security of CS_s. There are several equivalent formulations of semantic security. We will use the following:

Definition 1. *An adversary A against a public-key cryptosystem gets the public key pk generated from secuity parameter k as input and outputs a message m. Then A is given an encryption under pk of either m or a message*

---

2   Strictly speaking, we also need that $s < p, q$, but this is insignificant since s is a constant.

chosen uniformly in the message space, and outputs a bit. Let $p_0(A, k)$, respectively $p_1(A, k)$ be the probability that A outputs 1 when given an encryption of m, respectively a random encryption. Define the advantage *of A to be $Adv(A, k) = |p_0(A, k) - p_1(A, k)|$. The cryptosystem is* semantically secure *if for any probabilistic polynomial time adversary A, $Adv(A, k)$ is negligible in k.*

In [9], Paillier showed that semantic security of his cryptosystem (which is the same as our CS_1) is equivalent to DCRA. This equivalence holds for any choice of g, and follows easily from the fact that given a ciphertext c that is either random or encrypts a message i, $cg^{-i} \bmod n^2$ is either random in $Z_{n^2}^*$ or a random n'th power. In particular one may choose $g = n + 1$ always without degrading security. We do this in the following for simplicity, so that a public key consists only of the modulus n. We now show that in fact security of CS_s is equivalent to DCRA:

Theorem 1. *For any s, the cryptosystem CS_s is semantically secure if and only if the DCRA assumption is true.*

Proof. From a ciphertext in CS_s, one can obtain a ciphertext in CS_1 by reducing modulo n^2, this implicitly reduces the message modulo n. It is therefore clear that if DCRA fails, then CS_s cannot be secure for any s. For the converse, we show by induction on s that security of CS_s follows from DCRA. For $s = 1$, this is exact.ly Paillier's result. So take any $s > 1$ and assume that CS_t for any $t < s$ is secure.

The message space of CS_s is Z_{n^s}. Thus any message m can be written in n-adic notation as an s-tuple $(m_s, m_{s-1}, ..., m_1)$, where each $m_i \in Z_n$ and $m = \sum_{i=0}^{s-1} m_{i+1} n^i$. Let $D_n(m_s, ..., m_1)$ be the distribution obtained by encrypting the message $(m_s, ..., m_1)$ under public key n. If one or more of the m_i are replaced by $*$'s, this means that the corresponding position in the message is chosen uniformly in Z_n before encrypting.

Now, assume for contradiction that CS_s is insecure, thus there is an adversary A, such that for infinitely many k, $Adv(A, k) \geq 1/f(k)$ for some polynomial $f()$. Take such a k. Without loss of generality, assume we have $p_0(A, k) - p_1(A, k) \geq 1/f(k)$. Suppose we make a public key n from security parameter k, show it to A, get a message $(m_s, ..., m_1)$ from A and show A a sample of $D_n(*, m_{s-1}, ..., m_1)$. Let $q(A, k)$ be the probability that A now outputs 1. Of course, we must have

$$(*) \quad p_0(A, k) - q(A, k) \geq \frac{1}{2f(k)} \quad \text{or} \quad q(A, k) - p_1(A, k) \geq \frac{1}{2f(k)}$$

for infinitely many k.

In the first case in $(*)$, we can make a successful adversary against CS_1, as follows: we get the public key n, show it to A, get $(m_s, ..., m_1)$, and return m_s as output. We will get a ciphertext c that either encrypts m_s in CS_1, or is a random ciphertext, i.e., a random element from $Z_{n^2}^*$. If we consider c as an element in $Z_{n^{s+1}}^*$, we know it is an encryption of some plaintext, which must have either m_s or a random element in its least significant position. Hence $c^{n^{s-1}} \bmod n^{s+1}$ is an encryption of $(m_s, 0, ..., 0)$ or $(*, 0, ..., 0)$. We then make a random encryption d of $(0, m_{s-1}, ..., m_1)$, give $c^{n^{s-1}} d \bmod n^{s+1}$ to A and return the bit A outputs. Now, if c encrypts m_s, we have shown to A a sample of $D_n(m_s, ..., m_1)$, and otherwise a sample of $D_n(*, m_{s-1}, ..., m_1)$. So by assumption on A, this breaks CS_1 with an advantage of $1/2f(k)$, and so contradicts the induction assumption.

In the second case of $(*)$, we can make an adversary against CS_{s-1}, as follows: we get the public key n, show it to A, and get a message $(m_s, ..., m_1)$. We output $(m_{s-1}, ..., m_1)$ and get back a ciphertext c that encrypts in CS_{s-1} either $(m_{s-1}, ..., m_1)$ or something random. If we consider c as a number modulo n^{s+1}, we know that the corresponding plaintext in CS_s has either $(m_{s-1}, ..., m_1)$ or random elements in the least significant $s - 1$ positions - and something unknown in the top position. We make a random encryption d of $(*, 0, ..., 0)$, show $cd \bmod n^{s+1}$ to A and return the bit A outputs. If c encrypted $(m_{s-1}, ..., m_1)$, we have shown A a sample from $D_n(*, m_{s-1}, ..., m_1)$, and otherwise a sample from $D_n(*, ..., *)$. So by assumption on A, this breaks CS_{s-1} with an advantage of $1/2f(k)$ and again contradicts the induction assumption.

3.1   Adjusting the Block Length

To facilitate comparison with Paillier's original system, we have kept the above system description as close as possible to that of Paillier. In particular, the description allows choosing g in a variety of ways. However, as mentioned, we may choose $g = n + 1$ always without loosing security, and the public key may then consist only of the modulus n. This means that we can let the receiver decide on s when he encrypts a message. More concretely, the system will work as follows:

Key Generation. Choose an RSA modulus $n = pq$. Now the public key is n while the secret key is λ, the least common multiple of $(p - 1)$ and $(q - 1)$.

Encryption. Given a plaintext $i \in Z_{n^s}$, choose a random $r \in Z_{n^{s+1}}^*$, and let the ciphertext be $E(i, r) = (1 + n)^i r^{n^s} \bmod n^{s+1}$.

Decryption. Given a ciphertext c, first compute, by the Chinese Remainder Theorem d, such that $d = 1 \bmod n^s$ and $d = 0 \bmod \lambda$ (note that the length of the ciphertext allows to decide on the right value of s, except with negligible probability). Then compute $c^d \bmod n^{s+1}$. Clearly, if $c = E(i, r)$, we get

$$c^d = ((1 + n)^i r^{n^s})^d = (1 + n)^{id \bmod n^s} (x^i r^{n^s})^{d \bmod \lambda} = (1 + n)^i \bmod n^{s+1}$$

Now apply the above algorithm to compute $i \bmod n^s$.

4   Some Building Blocks

4.1   A Threshold Variant of the Scheme

What we are after in this section is a way to distribute the secret key to a set of servers, such that any subset of at least t of them can do decryption efficiently, while less than t have no useful information. Of course this must be done without degrading the security of the system.

In [10], Shoup proposes an efficient threshold variant of RSA signatures. The main part of this is a protocol that allows a set of servers to collectively and efficiently raise an input number to a secret exponent modulo an RSA modulus n. A little more precisely: on input a, each server returns a share of the result, together with a proof of correctness. Given sufficiently many correct shares, these can be efficiently combined to compute $a^d \bmod n$, where d is the secret exponent.

As we explain below it is quite simple to transplant this method to our case, thus allowing the servers to raise an input number to our secret exponent d modulo n^{s+1}. So we can solve our problem by first letting the servers help us compute $E(i, r)^d \bmod n^{s+1}$. Then if we use $g = n + 1$ and choose d such that $d = 1 \bmod n^s$ and $d = 0 \bmod \lambda$, the remaining part of the decryption is easy to do without knowledge of d.

We warn the reader that this is only secure for the particular choice of d we have made, for instance, if we had used Paillier's original choice $d = \lambda$, then seeing the value $E(i, r)^d \bmod n^{s+1}$ would allow an adversary to compute λ and break the system completely. However, in our case, the exponentiation result can safely be made public, since it contains no trace of the secret λ.

A more concrete description: Compared to [10] we still have a secret exponent d, but there is no public exponent e, so we will have to do some things slightly differently. We will assume that there are l decryption servers, and a minimum of $k < n/2$ of these are needed to make a correct decryption.

Key generation

Key generation starts out as in [10]: we find 2 primes p and q, that satisfies $p = 2p' + 1$ and $q = 2q' + 1$, where p' and q' are primes and different from p and q. We set $n = pq$ and $m = p'q'$. We decide on some $s > 0$, thus the plaintext space will be Z_{n^s}. We pick d to satisfy $d = 0 \bmod m$ and $d = 1 \bmod n^s$. Now we make the polynomial $f(X) = \sum_{i=0}^{k-1} a_i X^i \bmod n^s m$, by picking a_i (for $0 < i < k$) as random values from $\{0, \cdots, n^s * m - 1\}$ and $a_0 = d$. The secret share of the i'th authority will be $s_i = f(i)$ for $1 \leq i \leq l$ and the public key will be n. For verification of the actions of the decryption servers, we need the following fixed public values: v, generating the cyclic group of squares in $Z_{n^{s+1}}^*$ and for each decryption server a verification key $v_i = v^{\Delta s_i} \bmod n^{s+1}$, where $\Delta = l!$.

Encryption

To encrypt a message M, a random $r \in Z_{n^{s+1}}^*$ is picked and the cipher text is computed as $c = g^M r^{n^s} \bmod n^{s+1}$.

Share decryption

The i'th authority will compute $c_i = c^{2\Delta s_i}$, where c is the ciphertext. Along with this will be a zero-knowledge proof that $log_{c^4}(c_i^2) = log_v(v_i)$, which will convince us, that he has indeed raised to his secret exponent s_i [3]

---

[3] A non interactive zero-knowledge proof for this using the Fiat-Shamir heuristic is easy to derive from the corresponding one in [10].

Share combining
If we have the required k (or more) number of shares with a correct proof, we can combine them into the result by taking a subset S of k shares and combine them to

$$c' = \prod_{i \in S} c_i^{2\lambda_{0,i}^S} \bmod n^{s+1} \qquad \text{where } \lambda_{0,i}^S = \Delta \prod_{i' \in S \setminus i} \frac{-i}{i - i'} \in Z$$

The value of c' will have the form $c' = c^{4\Delta^2 f(0)} = c^{4\Delta^2 d}$. Noting that $4\Delta^2 d = 0 \bmod \lambda$ and $4\Delta^2 d = 4\Delta^2 \bmod n^s$, we can conclude that $c' = (1+n)^{4\Delta^2 M} \bmod n^{s+1}$, where M is the desired plaintext, so this means we can compute M by applying the algorithm from Section 3 and multiplying the result by $(4\Delta^2)^{-1} \bmod n^s$.

Compared to the scheme proposed in [6], there are some technical differences, apart from the fact that [6] only works for the original Paillier version modulo n^2: in [6], an extra random value related to the public element g is part of the public key and is used in the Share combining algorithm. This is avoided in our scheme by the way we choose d, and thus we get a slightly shorter public key and a slightly simpler decryption algorithm.

The system as described requires a trusted party to set up the keys. This may be acceptable as this is a once and for all operation, and the trusted party can delete all secret information as soon as the keys have been distributed. However, using multi-party computation techniques it is also possible to do the key generation without a trusted party.

Note that the key generation phase requires that a value of the parameter s is fixed. This means that the system will be able to handle messages encrypted modulo $n^{s'+1}$, for any $s' \leq s$, simply because the exponent d satisfies $d = 1 \bmod n^{s'}$, for any $s' \leq s$. But it will not work if $s' > s$. If a completely general decryption procedure is needed, this can be done as well: If we assume that λ is secret-shared in the key set-up phase, the servers can compute a suitable d by running a secure protocol that first inverts λ modulo n^s to get some x as result, and then computes the product $d = x\lambda$ (over the integers). This does not require generic multi-party computation techniques, but can be done quite efficiently using techniques from [5]. Note that, while this does require communication between servers, it is not needed for every decryption, but only once for every value of s that is used.

We can now show in the random oracle model that this threshold version is as secure as a centralised scheme where one trusted player does the decryption[4], in particular the threshold version is secure relative to the same complexity assumption as the basic scheme. This can be done in a model where a static adversary corrupts up to $k - 1$ players from the start. Concretely, we have:

Theorem 2. *Assume the random oracle model and a static adversary that corrupts up to $k - 1$ players from the beginning. Then we have: Given any cipher-*

---

[4] In fact the random oracle will be needed only to ensure that the non-interactive proofs of correctness of shares will work. Doing these proofs interactively instead would allow us to dispense with the random oracle.

text, the decryption protocol outputs the correct plaintext, except with negligible probability. Given an oracle that on input a ciphertext returns the corresponding plaintext, the adversary's view of the decryption protocol can be efficiently simulated with a statistically indistinguishable distribution.

The full proof will be included in the final version of this paper. Here we only give the basic ideas: correctness of the scheme is immediate assuming that the adversary can contribute bad values for the c_i's with only negligible probability. This, in turn, is ensured by soundness of the zero-knowledge proofs given for each c_i.

For the simulation, we start from the public key n. Then we can simulate the shares $s_{i_1}, ..., s_{i_{k-1}}$ of the bad players by choosing them as random numbers in an appropriate interval. Since d is fixed by the choice of n, this means that the shares of uncorrupted players and the polynomial f are now fixed as well, but are not easy for the simulator to compute.

However, if we choose v as a ciphertext with known plaintext m_0, we can also compute what $v^{f(0)}$ would be, namely $v^{f(0)} = v^d \bmod n^{s+1} = (1+n)^{m_0} \bmod n^{s+1}$. Then by doing Lagrange interpolation "in the exponent" as in [10], we can compute correct values of $v_i = v^{\Delta s_i}$ for the uncorrupted players. When we get a ciphertext c as input, we ask the oracle for the plaintext m. This allows us to compute $c^d = (1+n)^m \bmod n^{s-1}$. Again this means we can interpolate and compute the contributions c_i from the uncorrupted players. Finally, the zero-knowledge property is invoked to simulate the proofs that these c_i are correct.

4.2   Some Auxiliary Protocols

Suppose a prover P presents a sceptical verifier V with a ciphertext c and claims that it encodes plaintext i. A trivial way to convince V would be to reveal also the random choice r, then V can verify himself that $c = E(i, r)$. However, for use in the following, we need a solution where no extra useful information is revealed.

It is easy to see that that this is equivalent to convincing V that $cg^{-i} \bmod n^{s+1}$ is an n^s'th power. So we now propose a protocol for this which is a simple generalisation of the one from [7]. We note that this and the following protocols are not zero-knowledge as they stand, only honest verifier zero-knowledge. However, first zero-knowledge protocols for the same problems can be constructed from them using standard methods and secondly, in our applications, we will always be using them in a non-interactive variant based on the Fiat-Shamir heuristic, which means that we cannot obtain zero-knowledge, we can, however, obtain security in the random oracle model. As for soundness, we prove that the protocols satisfy so called special soundness (see [2]), which in particular implies that they satisfy standard knowledge soundness.

Protocol for n^s'th powers
Input: n, u
Private Input for P: v, such that $u = v^{n^s} \bmod n^{s+1}$

1. P chooses r at random mod n^{s+1} and sends $a = r^{n^s} \bmod n^{s+1}$ to V
2. V chooses e, a random k bit number, and sends e to P.
3. P sends $z = rv^e \bmod n^{s+1}$ to V, and V checks that $z^{n^s} = au^e \bmod n^{s+1}$, and accepts if and only if this is the case.

It is now simple to show

Lemma 2. *The above protocol is complete, honest verifier zero-knowledge, and satisfies that from any pair of accepting conversations (between V and any prover) of form $(a, e, z), (a, e', z')$ with $e \neq e'$, one can efficiently compute an n^s'th root of u, provided 2^t is smaller than the smallest prime factor of n.*

Proof. Completeness is obvious from inspection of the protocol. For honest verifier simulation, the simulator chooses a random $z \in Z^*_{n^{s+1}}$, a random e, sets $a = z^{n^s} u^{-e} \bmod n^{s+1}$ and outputs (a, e, z). This is easily seen to be a perfect simulation.

For the last claim, observe that since the conversations are accepting, we have $z^{n^s} = au^e \bmod n^{s+1}$ and $z'^{n^s} = au^{e'} \bmod n^{s+1}$, so we get

$$(z/z')^{n^s} = u^{e-e'} \bmod n^{s+1}$$

Since $e - e'$ is prime to n by the assumption on 2^t, choose α, β such that $\alpha n^s + \beta(e - e') = 1$. Then let $v = u^\alpha (z/z')^\beta \bmod n^{s+1}$. We then get

$$v^{n^s} = u^{\alpha n^s}(z/z')^{n^s \beta} = u^{\alpha n^s} u^{\beta(e-e')} = u \bmod n^{s+1}$$

so that v is indeed the desired n^s'th root of u

In our application of this protocol, the modulus n will be chosen by a trusted party, or by a multi-party computation such that n has two prime factors of roughly the same size. Hence, if k is the bit length of n, we can set $t = k/2$ and be assured that a cheating prover can make the verifier accept with probability $\leq 2^{-t}$.

The lemma immediately implies, using the techniques from [2], that we can build an efficient proof that an encryption contains one of two given values, without revealing which one it is: given the encryption C and the two candidate plaintexts i_1, i_2, prover and verifier compute $u_1 = C/g^{i_1} \bmod n^{s+1}, u_2 = C/g^{i_2} \bmod n^{s+1}$, and the prover shows that either u_1 or u_2 is an n^s'th power. This can be done using the following protocol, where we assume without loss of generality that the prover knows an n^s'th root u_1, and where M denotes the honest-verifier simulator for the n^s-power protocol above:

Protocol 1-out-of-2 n^s'th power
Input: n, u_1, u_2
Private Input for P: v_1, such that $u_1 = v_1^{n^s} \bmod n^{s+1}$

1. P chooses r_1 at random mod n^{s+1}. He invokes M on input n, u_2 to get a conversation a_2, e_2, z_2. He sends $a_1 = r_1^{n^s} \bmod n^{s+1}, a_2$ to V

2. V chooses s, a random t bit number, and sends s to P.
3. P computes $e_1 = s - e_2 \bmod 2^t$ and $z_1 = r_1 v_1^{e_1} \bmod n^{s+1}$. He then sends e_1, z_1, e_2, z_2 to V.
4. V checks that $s = e_1 + e_2 \bmod 2^t$, $z_1^{n^s} = a_1 u_1^{e_1} \bmod n^{s+1}$ and $z_2^{n^s} = a_2 u_2^{e_2} \bmod n^{s+1}$, and accepts if and only if this is the case.

The proof techniques from [2] and Lemma 2 immediately imply

Lemma 3. *Protocol 1-out-of-2 n^s'th power is complete, honest verifier zero-knowledge, and satisfies that from any pair of accepting conversations (between V and any prover) of form $(a_1, a_2, s, e_1, z_1, e_2, z_2)$, $(a_1, a_2, s', e_1', z_1', e_2', z_2')$ with $s \neq s'$, one can efficiently compute an n^s'th root of u_1, and an n^s'th root of u_2, provided 2^t is less than the smallest prime factor of n.*

Our final building block allows a prover to convince a verifier that three encryptions contain values a, b and c such that $ab = c \bmod n^s$. For this, we propose a protocol inspired by a similar construction found in [3].

Protocol Multiplication-mod-n^s

Input: n, g, e_a, e_b, e_c
Private Input for P: a, b, c, r_a, r_b, r_c such that $ab = c \bmod n$ and $e_a = E(a, r_a)$, $e_b = E(b, r_b)$, $e_c = E(c, r_c)$

1. P chooses a random value $d \in Z_{n^s}$ and sends to V encryptions $e_d = E(d, r_d), e_{db} = E(db, r_{db})$.
2. V chooses e, a random t-bit number, and sends it to P.
3. P opens the encryption $e_a^e e_d = E(ea + d, r_a^e r_d \bmod n^{s+1})$ by sending $f = ea + d \bmod n^s$ and $z_1 = r_a^e r_d \bmod n^{s+1}$. Finally, P opens the encryption $e_b^f (e_{db} e_c^e)^{-1} = E(0, r_b^f (r_{db} r_c^e)^{-1} \bmod n^{s+1})$ by sending $z_2 = r_b^f (r_{db} r_c^e)^{-1} \bmod n^{s+1}$.
4. V verifies that the openings of encryptions in the previous step were correct, and accepts if and only if this was the case.

Lemma 4. *Protocol Multiplication-mod-n^s is complete, honest verifier zero-knowledge, and satisfies that from any pair of accepting conversations (between V and any prover) of form $(e_d, e_{db}, e, f, z_1, z_2)$, $(e_d, e_{db}, e', f', z_1', z_2')$ with $e \neq e'$, one can efficiently compute the plaintext a, b, c corresponding to e_a, e_b, e_c such that $ab = c \bmod n^s$, provided 2^t is smaller than the smallest prime factor in n.*

Proof. Completeness is clear by inspection of the protocol. For honest verifier zero-knowledge, observe that the equations checked by V are $e_a^e e_d = E(f, z_1) \bmod n^{s+1}$ and $e_b^f (e_{db} e_c^e)^{-1} = E(0, z_2) \bmod n^{s+1}$. From this it is clear that we can generate a conversation by choosing first f, z_1, z_2, e at random, and then computing e_d, e_{db} that will satisfy the equations. This only requires inversion modulo n^{s+1}, and generates the right distribution because the values f, z_1, z_2, e are also independent and random in the real conversation. For the last claim, note first that since encryptions uniquely determine plaintexts, there are fixed values a, b, c, d contained in e_a, e_b, e_c, e_d, and a value x contained in e_{db}. The fact that the conversations given are accepting implies that $f = ea + d \bmod n^s$, $f' = e'a + d \bmod n^s$, $fb - x - ec = 0 = f'b - x - e'c \bmod n^s$. Putting this together, we obtain $(f - f')b = (e - e')c \bmod n^s$ or $(e - e')ab = (e - e')c \bmod n^s$. Now, since $(e - e')$ is invertible modulo n^s by assumption on 2^t, we can conclude that $c = ab \bmod n^s$ (and also compute a, b and c).

The protocols from this section can be made non-interactive using the standard Fiat-Shamir heuristic of computing the challenge from the first message using a hash function. This can be proved secure in the random oracle model.

5   Efficient Electronic Voting

In [4], a general model for elections was used, which we briefly recall here: we have a set of voters $V_1, ..., V_M$, a bulletin board B, and a set of tallying authorities $A_1, ..., A_v$. The bulletin board is assumed to function as follows: every player can write to B, and a message cannot be deleted once it is written. All players can access all messages written, and can identify which player each message comes from. This can all be implemented in a secure way using an already existing public key infrastructure and server replication to prevent denial of service attacks. We assume that the purpose of the vote is to elect a winner among L candidates, and that each voter is allowed to vote for $t < L$ candidates.

In the following, h will denote a fixed hash function used to make non-interactive proofs according to the Fiat-Shamir heuristic. Also, we will assume throughout that an instance of threshold version of Paillier's scheme with public key n, g has been set up, with the A_i's acting as decryption servers. We will assume that $n^s > M$, which can always be made true by choosing s or n large enough.

The notation $Proof_P(S)$, where S is some logical statement will denote a bit string created by player P as follows: P selects the appropriate protocol from the previous section that can be used to interactively prove S. He computes the first message a in this protocol, computes $e = h(a, S, ID(P))$ where $ID(P)$ is his user identity in the system and, taking the result of this as the challenge from the verifier, computes the answer z. Then $Proof_P(S) = (e, z)$. The inclusion of $ID(P)$ in the input to h is done in order to prevent vote duplication. To check such a proof, note that all the auxiliary protocols are such that from S, z, c one can easily compute what a should have been, had the proof been correct. For instance, for the protocol for n^s powers, the statement consists of a single number u modulo n^{s+1}, and the verifier checks that $z^{n^s} = au^e \bmod n^{s+1}$, so we have $a = z^{n^s} u^{-e} \bmod n^{s+1}$. Once a is computed, one checks that $e = h(a, S, ID(P))$.

A protocol for the case $L = 2$ is now simple to describe. This is equivalent to a yes/no vote and so each vote can thought of as a number equal to 0 for no and 1 for yes:

1. Each voter V_i decides on his vote v_i, he calculates $E_i = E(v_i, r_i)$, where r_i is randomly chosen. He also creates

$Proof_{V_i}(E_i$ or E_i/g is an n^s'th power modulo $n^{s+1})$

based on the 1-out-of-2 n^s'th power protocol. He writes the encrypted vote and proof to B.

2. Each A_j does the following: first set $E = 1$. Then for all i: check the proof written by V_i on B and if is it valid, then $E := E \cdot E_i \bmod n^{s+1}$. Finally, A_j executes his part of the threshold decryption protocol, using E as the input ciphertext, and writes his result to B.

3. From the messages written by the A_j's, anyone can now reconstruct the plaintext corresponding to E (possibly after discarding invalid messages). Assuming for simplicity that all votes are valid, it is evident that $E = \prod_i E(v_i, r_i) = E(\sum_i v_i \bmod n^s, \prod_i r_i \bmod n^{s+1})$. So the decryption result is $\sum_i v_i \bmod n^s$ which is $\sum_i v_i$ since $n^s > M$.

Security of this protocol (in the random oracle model) follows easily from security of the sub-protocols used, and semantic security of Paillier's encryption scheme. Proofs will be included in the final version of this paper.

There are several ways to generalise this to $L > 2$. Probably the simplest way is to hold L parallel yes/no votes as above. A voter votes 1 for the candidates he wants, and 0 for the others. This means that V_i will send L votes of form $(j = 1, .., L)$

$$E_{ij} = E(v_{ij}, r_{ij}),$$
$$Proof_{V_i}(E_{ij} \text{ or } E_{ij}/g \text{ is an } n^s\text{'th power modulo } n^{s+1})$$

To prove that he voted for exactly t candidates, he also writes to B the number $\prod_j r_{ij} \bmod n^{s+1}$. This allows the talliers to verify that $\prod_j E(v_{ij}, r_{ij})$ is an encryption of t. This check is sufficient, since all individual votes are proved to be 0 or 1. It is immediate that decryption of the L results will immediately give the number of votes each candidate received.

We note that his easily generalises to cases where voters are allowed to vote for *up to* t candidates: one simply introduces t "dummy candidates" in addition to the actual L. We then execute the protocol as before, but with $t+L$ candidates. Each voter places the votes he does not want to use on dummy candidates.

The size of a vote in this protocol is seen to be $O(Lk)$, where k is the bit length of n, by simple inspection of the protocol. The protocol requires L decryption operations. As a numeric example, suppose we have $k = 1000, M = 64000, L = 64, s = 1$ and we use challenges of 80 bits in the proofs. Then a vote in the above system has size about 50 Kbyte.

If the parameters are such that $L \log_2 M < k \cdot s$ and $t = 1$, then we can do significantly better. These conditions will be satisfied in many realistic situations, such as for instance in the numeric example above.

The basic idea is the following: a vote for candidate j, where $0 \le j < L$ is defined to be an encryption of the number M^j. Each voter will create such an encryption and prove its correctness as detailed below. When all these encryptions are multiplied we get an encryption of a number of form $a = \sum_{j=0}^{L} a_j M^j \bmod n^s$, where a_j is the number of votes cast for candidate j. Since $L \log_2 M < k \cdot s$, this relation also holds over the integers, so decrypting and writing a in M-ary notation will directly produce all the a_j's.

It remains to describe how to produce encryption hiding a number of form M^j, for some $0 \leq j < L$, and prove it was correctly formed. Let $b_0, ..., b_l$ be the bits in the binary representation of j, i.e. $j = b_0 2^0 + b_1 2^1 + ... + b_l 2^l$. Then clearly we have $M^j = (M^{2^0})^{b_0} \cdot ... \cdot (M^{2^l})^{b_l}$. Each factor in this product is either 1 or a power of M. This is used in the following algorithm for producing the desired proof (where P denotes the prover):

1. P computes encryptions $e_0, ..., e_l$ of $(M^{2^0})^{b_0}, ..., (M^{2^l})^{b_l}$. For each $i = 0...l$ he also computes $Proof_P(e_i/g$ or $e_i/g^{M^{2^i}}$ is an n^s'th power).
2. Let $F_i = (M^{2^0})^{b_0} \cdot ... \cdot (M^{2^i})^{b_i}$, for $i = 0...l$. P computes an encryption f_i of F_i, for $i = 1..l$. We set $f_0 = e_0$. Now, for $i = 1...l$, P computes

$$Proof_P(\text{Plaintexts corr. to } f_{i-1}, e_i, f_i \text{ satisfy}$$

$$F_{i-1} \cdot (M^{2^i})^{b_i} = F_i \bmod n^s),$$

based on the multiplication-mod-n^s protocol. The encryption f_l is the desired encryption, it can be verified from the e_i, f_i and all the proofs computed.

It is straightforward to see that a vote in this system will have length $O(k \log L)$ bits (still assuming, of course, that $L \log_2 M \leq k \cdot s$).

With parameter values as in the numeric example before, a vote will have size about 8.5 Kbyte, a factor of more than 5 better than the previous system. Moreover, we need only 1 decryption operation as opposed to L before.

6   Efficiency and Implementation Aspects

An implementation of some of the teqniques discussed in this paper can be found at http://www.brics.dk/~jurik/research.html.

Key Generation. The primes p and q are made using the usual techniques, so that n will be as difficult as possible to factor. Since there is no difference in choosing a general g and $(n + 1)$ as generator, we can just use $(n + 1)$ and save some work for finding a suitable g.

Encryption. As mentioned in Paillier we can choose $g = 2$ (provided it satisfies the contraints) to get a speed-up in encryption. But since we can use $(n + 1)$ as generator we can make it even more efficient since calculating $(n + 1)^i$ is the same as calculating:

$$1 + in + \binom{i}{2}n^2 + ... + \binom{i}{s}n^s \bmod n^{s+1}$$

this means raising $(n + 1)$ to i'th power takes about $5s$ multiplications. We can precompute the factors $k!^{-1}n^k \bmod n^{s+1}$ which reduces the number of multiplications to $2s$. We can't get rid of the exponentiation $r^{n^s} \bmod n^{s+1}$, but the random value can be choosen in advance and the exponentiation calculated in advance. If $r^{n^s} \bmod n^{s+1}$ is calculated in advance an encryption will take $2s$ multiplications which is approximately as efficient as RSA for small s.

Decryption. Decryption can be speeded up by calculating the different powers of n, and the $k!^{-1} \bmod n^j$ for $2 \leq k \leq j \leq s$. All this can be calculated $\bmod p^j$ and $\bmod q^j$ instead of $\bmod n^j$ by using

$$L_p(x) = \frac{x-1}{p} \text{ and } L_q(x) = \frac{x-1}{q}$$

instead of the normal L. The decryption algorithm is then executed 2 times, once $\bmod p^j$'s instead of $\bmod n^j$ and with L_p instead of L and once with $\bmod q^j$ and L_q. Then after the 2 parts have been calculated they are combined using Chinese remaindering.

Performance Evaluations. We give here a comparison between the schemes presented in this paper, Paillier's original scheme, RSA with public exponent $2^{16}+1$ and El-Gamal. There are 3 versions of our scheme, namely one without precomputation, one with, and one with $s = 1$ (and no precomputation), since this is equivalent to Paillier's scheme. It is assumed that all numbers has about the same number of 1's and 0's in their binary representation. In figure 1 we compare the different scheme using the same security parameter. It should be noted that it compares the number of multiplications, but these multiplications are made using different modulus size. It should be also be noted that the 2 first columns encrypt sk bits of plaintext instead of k bits in the other columns. The last 2 rows of the table shows the number of bits that are encrypted for each multiplication made. It only makes sense to compare the numbers in these 2 rows if the modulus size is the same and thus the security parameter k is different.

Scheme	General Scheme		Scheme			
	No Precomp.	Precomp.	$s = 1$	Paillier	RSA	El-Gamal
n/p Size (k)	k	k	k	k	k	k
Modulus Size	$(s+1)k$	$(s+1)k$	$2k$	$2k$	k	k
Plaintext Size	sk	sk	k	k	k	k
Multiplications for Encryption	$\frac{3}{2}sk + 5s$	$2s$	$\frac{3}{2}k + 5$	$3k+1$	17	$3k+1$
Multiplications for Decryption	$\frac{5}{2}(s+1)k + 2s(s+1)$	$\frac{5}{2}(s+1)k + s(s+1)$	$5k+8$	$\frac{3}{2}k$	$3k+3$	$\frac{3}{2}k+1$
Multiplications per bit encrypted	$\approx \frac{3}{2}$	$\frac{2}{k}$	$\frac{3}{2}$	3	$\frac{17}{k}$	3
Multiplications per bit decrypted	$\approx \frac{5}{2}$	$\approx \frac{5}{2}$	5	3	$\frac{3}{2}$	$\frac{3}{2}$

Fig. 1. Comparison with equal security parameter k

References

1. Baudron, Fouque, Pointcheval, Poupard and Stern: *Practical Multi-Candidate Election Scheme*, manuscript, May 2000.
2. Cramer, Damgård and Schoenmakers: *Proofs of partial knowledge*, Proc. of Crypto 94, Springer Verlag LNCS series nr. 839.
3. R.Cramer, S.Dziembowski, I. Damgård, M.Hirt and T.Rabin: *Efficient Multiparty Computations Secure against an Adaptive Adversary*, Proc. of EuroCrypt 99, Springer Verlag LNCS series 1592, pp. 311-326.
4. R.Cramer, R.Gennaro, B.Schoenmakers: *A Secure and Optimally Efficient Multi-Authority Election Scheme*, Proceedings of EuroCrypt 97, Springer Verlag LNCS series, pp. 103-118.
5. Frankel, MacKenzie and Yung: *Robust Efficient Distributed RSA-key Generation*, proceedings of STOC 98.
6. P. Fouque, G. Poupard, J. Stern: *Sharing Decryption in the Context of Voting or Lotteries*, Proceedings of Financial Crypto 2000.
7. L. Guillou and J.-J. Quisquater: *A Practical Zero-Knowledge Protocol fitted to Security Microprocessor Minimizing both Transmission and Memory*, Proc. of EuroCrypt 88, Springer Verlag LNCS series.
8. M.Hirt and K.Sako: *Efficient Receipt-Free Voting based on Homomorphic Encryption*, Proceedings of EuroCrypt 2000, Springer Verlag LNCS series, pp. 539-556.
9. P.Pallier: *Public-Key Cryptosystems based on Composite Degree Residue Classes*, Proceedings of EuroCrypt 99, Springer Verlag LNCS series, pp. 223-238.
10. V.Shoup: *Practical Threshold Signatures*, Proceedings of EuroCrypt 2000, Springer Verlag LNCS series, pp. 207-220.
11. J. Bar-Ilan, and D. Beaver: *Non-Cryptographic Fault-Tolerant Computing in a Constant Number of Rounds*, Proceedings of the ACM Symposium on Principles of Distributed Computation, 1989, pp. 201-209.

Marking: A Privacy Protecting Approach Against Blackmailing

Dennis Kügler and Holger Vogt

Department of Computer Science,*
Darmstadt University of Technology,
D-64283 Darmstadt, Germany
{kuegler|hvogt}@cdc.informatik.tu-darmstadt.de

Abstract. Electronic payment systems based on anonymous coins have been invented as a digital equivalent to physical banknotes. However, von Solms and Naccache discovered that such anonymous coins are also very well suited to support criminals in blackmailing.

In this paper we present a payment system, which has an efficient tracing and revocation mechanism for blackmailed coins. The used tracing method is based on the idea of marking coins similar to marking banknotes with an invisible color. In contrast to previous solutions our payment system is unconditionally anonymous and thus protects the privacy of the users.

1 Introduction

Blind signature based anonymous payment systems [Cha83] have been invented for privacy protecting payments over the internet. However, it was discovered by von Solms and Naccache [vSN92] that *unconditional anonymity* may be misused by criminals: A blackmailer can exploit the properties of the used blind signature to receive blackmailed money from his victim so that neither the victim nor the bank are able to recognize the blackmailed coins later. Furthermore, the blackmailed coins can be transferred anonymously via an unobservable broadcast channel (e.g. a newsgroup). This attack is called the *perfect crime*, as it is impossible to identify or trace the blackmailer.

To solve anonymity related problems as blackmailing, money laundering, or illegal purchases, payment systems with *revokable anonymity* have been proposed [CMS96,JY96,FTY96,JY97]. In these payment systems trusted third parties are able to revoke the anonymity of the users at any time.

In our opinion blackmailing is the most serious drawback of the known payment systems offering unconditional anonymity. Attacks like money laundering and illegal purchases aren't a major problem in anonymous electronic payment systems, as these problems are even worse with physical cash [Fro96], because

---

* This work was supported by the Deutsche Forschungsgemeinschaft (DFG) as part of the PhD program (Graduiertenkolleg) "Enabling Technologies for Electronic Commerce" at Darmstadt University of Technology.

K. Kim (Ed.): PKC 2001, LNCS 1992, pp. 137–152, 2001.

in anonymous electronic payment systems the bank always knows how much a customer withdraws and how much a person deposits. Thus the bank is able to detect either the initiator or the recipient of a suspicious transaction.

In this paper we will show how to fight blackmailing without restricting the anonymity of users as it is done in systems with revokable anonymity. We present a new online payment scheme, which offers unconditional anonymity, but does not suffer from the blackmailing attack described above.

We stress that our proposed payment system is very practical as no trusted third parties are needed, and it is especially well suited for payments over the internet and for mobile payments using cellular phones. In our opinion, it is not a drawback that our system is an online system, as these systems minimize the risk of fraud and losses that may be caused by e.g. overspending.

The remainder is structured as follows: A new technique, which we call *marking*, is introduced in the next section. In Section 3 we show how marking is used in several scenarios to fight blackmailing. The implementation of a payment system using the marking technique is presented in section 4. The security and anonymity aspects are discussed in section 5. Furthermore, we sketch several improvements of the payment system in section 6, and we discuss how our approach relates to systems with revokable anonymity in section 7. Finally we conclude the paper with some open issues for further research.

2   Marking: A New Approach Against Blackmailing

Physical cash, particularly banknotes have two important features, which can be used to fight blackmailing:

- The serial numbers of the banknotes can be annotated.
- The banknotes can be marked, e.g. with a special invisible color.

The goal of both approaches is to support the investigation of blackmailings by enabling recognition of blackmailed banknotes after they are spent or discovered somewhere. As precondition for this method of investigation the victim of a blackmailing has to inform the bank and the police about the blackmailing **before** delivering the money.

Using the idea of annotating serial numbers for electronic payments results in payment systems with revokable anonymity, where a hint is kept in a database, which enables a trusted third party to recover the serial number. However, the knowledge of the serial numbers may be misused to trace users even if no blackmailing occurred.

As annotating serial numbers of electronic coins may violate anonymity, we base our approach for an anonymous payment system on the idea of marking coins. No electronic payment system with a similar mechanism has been proposed yet.[1]

---

[1] Note that the notion of marking with an invisible color should not be confused with magic ink signatures introduced in [JY97], which uses the approach of annotating serial numbers.

2.1   Marking of Electronic Coins

Our anonymous payment system implements a reliable marking mechanism for electronic coins and has the following properties:

- For every blackmailing the bank may issue coins with a different marking.
- Only the bank can determine whether a coin is marked or not. For every other person marked coins are indistinguishable from unmarked coins.
- At withdrawal the bank has to prove that a coin is unmarked. This proof cannot be used to convince anybody except the owner of the bank account.
- At deposit the bank can accept or reject marked coins, depending on the choice of the blackmailed person.

It follows directly that the anonymity of a customer is protected, as he always detects unsolicited marking. In case of blackmailing, a customer requests marked coins from the bank, and every spending of marked coins will immediately be noticed by the bank.

Compared to physical cash, our marking mechanism has several advantages:

- All unspent marked coins can be invalidated and refunded to the customer, after he instructs the bank to reject all marked coins. Thus the customer looses only the amount of the already spent marked coins.
- All spent marked coins can efficiently be detected at deposit. This enables tracing of the blackmailer.
- Marking cannot be misused to trace honest users.

2.2   A New Payment System Based on Undeniable Signatures

The typical approach for unconditional anonymous payment systems is based on blind signatures [Cha83]. However, in these systems it is hard to embed an undetectable mark in a coin, because the bank would have to generate a modified signature at the withdrawal, and as the validity of a coin's signature is publicly verifiable, such a modification of a blind signature is easy to detect.

Due to this shortcomings our aim is to restrict the verifiability of coins. We basically suggest the use of blind undeniable signatures [CvA89,Cha90] instead of blind signatures so that the verification of a signature can only be done by interacting with the bank in non-transferable zero-knowledge protocols:

Confirmation protocol: This protocol is used by the signer to prove the *validity* of an undeniable signature to another party.
Disavowal protocol: This protocol is used by the signer to prove the *invalidity* of an undeniable signature to another party.

The main idea of our payment system is that the bank issues coins consisting of undeniable signatures. This has the following consequences:

- At withdrawal, the bank must prove validity of a blindly withdrawn coin with a confirmation protocol. Without the confirmation protocol the bank may issue invalid or marked coins.

– At deposit, if the bank rejects a coin, it must prove the invalidity of this coin with a disavowal protocol. For an accepted coin the bank never proves the validity. Therefore, the bank may accept detected marked coins, but cannot deny a valid coin.

It is not a drawback in an online payment system that a coin cannot be verified without the issuing bank, because due to possible overspendings the validity of coins can only be checked by the bank.

2.3   Implementing Marking in Our Payment System

The bank can issue marked coins by using a different private key (we will also call this a *marking key*) instead of the normal private key to generate the undeniable signature. When the bank receives a coin, which was not generated with the normal private key, the bank has to check whether the coin has been created with a marking key.

Basically, we have to distinguish three different types of coins:

Valid coins: These coins are created with the normal private key of the bank. The bank always proves the validity of this type of coins with the confirmation protocol at withdrawal.

Marked coins: These coins are only issued in case of blackmailing and are created with a different marking key for each blackmailing. The confirmation protocol always fails for marked coins.

Invalid coins: These coins were neither generated with the normal private key nor with any of the marking keys. In other words, they were not generated by the bank. At deposit those coins are always rejected by the bank, which proves the invalidity with the disavowal protocol.

Some problems arise with these three types of coins, as a blackmailer must not be able to distinguish between marked and valid coins. The obvious way to test a coin to be valid, is to execute the confirmation protocol. Thus, we restrict the use of the confirmation protocol only to the withdrawal and we guarantee that for a specific coin the confirmation protocol is executed exactly once.

3   Cheating a Blackmailer to Accept Marked Coins

In this section we show how the customer and the bank together can cheat a blackmailer in the confirmation protocol to accept marked coins as valid coins. Depending on the power of the blackmailer, we have to distinguish three scenarios:

Perfect crime: The blackmailer contacts the victim via an anonymous channel and threatens him to withdraw some coins which are chosen and blinded by the blackmailer. The blackmailer communicates only with the victim but cannot observe the victim's communication with the bank.

Impersonation: The blackmailer gains access to the victim's bank account and withdraws coins by himself. The blackmailer communicates directly with the bank but cannot observe the victim's communication with the bank.

Kidnapping: The blackmailer has physical control over the blackmailed victim and withdraws the coins similar to the impersonation scenario. The blackmailer communicates directly with the bank and prevents the victim from communicating with the bank.

In all these scenarios the blackmailer hides his identity by using anonymous communication channels (e.g. remailer, broadcast communication or an anonymous communication endpoint).

We assume that the customer always tries to inform the bank about a blackmailing. If the customer notifies the bank about a blackmailing, the bank will issue marked coins in future withdrawals of the customer. Furthermore, we assume that the blackmailer is not able to observe the actions of the bank. The bank strictly follows the defined protocols for withdrawal and deposit and never cooperates with a blackmailer.

Next, we describe the different scenarios and their problems in detail and discuss our countermeasures when blackmailing occurs.

3.1   Perfect Crime

In this scenario the blackmailer threatens the victim to withdraw some coins which are chosen and blinded by the blackmailer. The victim contacts his bank and instructs it to mark these blinded coins during the withdrawal. The victim sends the marked coins back to the blackmailer, who unblinds the coins. In the subsequent confirmation protocol the blackmailer can choose the secret parameters and thus the challenge for the bank. Then the blackmailer instructs the customer to execute the confirmation protocol with this challenge to prove whether the coins are valid or marked/invalid.

Basically, we face the problem that the confirmation protocol is necessary to protect the customer from a cheating bank, but it also enables the blackmailer to detect marked coins. We solve this problem with a designated verifier proof [JSI96] in the confirmation protocol. Such a proof for the validity of the coins convinces only the designated verifier, who is in our case the owner of the bank account.

In the following we describe our generic confirmation protocol (see figure 1), which uses public key encryption as a trapdoor to extract the secret parameters of the challenge:

1. The customer generates a challenge from the coin and secretly chosen parameters. These parameters are encrypted with his own public key and sent together with the challenge to the bank.
2. For the given challenge the bank commits to a zero-knowledge proof for the validity of the coin and sends the committed proof to the customer.
3. The customer has to reveal his secret parameters to the bank. Then the bank checks, if the customer's challenge was built correctly.

4. Only then the bank opens the committed proof, which convinces the customer of the validity of the withdrawn coin.

Bank		Customer
		choose parameters $\mathcal{P}$
		$e = E_{PK_C}(\mathcal{P})$
	$\xleftarrow{\quad e, c \quad}$	$c = \text{challenge}(\mathcal{P}, coin)$
$p = \text{proof}(c)$		
$u = \text{commit}(p)$	$\xrightarrow{\quad u \quad}$	
check if:	$\xrightarrow{\quad \mathcal{P} \quad}$	
$\quad e \stackrel{?}{=} E_{PK_C}(\mathcal{P})$		
$\quad c \stackrel{?}{=} \text{challenge}(\mathcal{P}, coin)$		
	$\xrightarrow{\quad p \quad}$	check if:
		$\quad u \stackrel{?}{=} \text{commit}(p)$
		$\quad \text{testproof}(\mathcal{P}, coin, p) \stackrel{?}{=} \text{true}$

Fig. 1. This confirmation protocol convinces only the designated verifier of the validity of a coin.

In the case of a blackmailing the customer receives the challenge from the blackmailer. But as the customer can decrypt the secret parameters of the challenge, he can generate the answer that the blackmailer expects for an unmarked coin although the bank has issued a marked coin. Because the blackmailer cannot distinguish between the simulated and a real transcript of the confirmation protocol, he will always accept the proof.

A different solution for a designated verifier confirmation protocol, which is based on trapdoor commitments, is given in [JSI96]. In contrast to our solution the customer can open the commitment so that the revealed value is the correct answer for an unmarked coin. In the following we will focus on our solution, as it is more generic.

3.2   Impersonation of the Customer

In addition to the perfect crime scenario the blackmailer may even force the victim to reveal any private information including the information to access the victim's bank account. The blackmailer contacts the bank and pretends to be the owner of the victim's account. Thus the blackmailer can withdraw an arbitrary number of coins without the help of the victim.

However, the victim may communicate with the bank, as this is unobservable for the blackmailer. The customer gives his decryption key to the bank, who can cheat the blackmailer as described in the perfect crime scenario. Note that transferring the decryption key to the bank will only enable the bank to mark coins in the future. Previously withdrawn coins are not affected and the privacy of the customer remains untouched. Alternatively, the customer can decrypt the parameters for the bank and keep his decryption key secret.

3.3 Kidnapping the Customer

In addition to the impersonation scenario the blackmailer has now physical control over the blackmailed victim. Thus the victim can only communicate with the blackmailer so that the victim is neither able to directly instruct the bank to issue marked coins nor to generate a faked confirmation protocol.

In this scenario a covert channel is needed to inform the bank about the kidnapping. For implementing such a covert channel we adopt the idea of a distress cash system [DFTY97]. Furthermore, we must enable the bank to generate a faked confirmation protocol by utilizing the trapdoor in the confirmation protocol, which is only possible, if the bank knows the private key for the decryption of the secret parameters.

A simple solution is to use secure hardware for the authentication at the beginning of the withdrawal. The main idea is that the hardware offers two different PINs, where one can be used to indicate a blackmailing. In this case the secure hardware informs the bank about the blackmailing and delivers the decryption key, which enables the bank to utilize the trapdoor to cheat the blackmailer. Due to the use of secure hardware, communication with the bank is encrypted and can be assumed to be unobservable. This means that it is impossible for the blackmailer to detect that his victim used the PIN, which enables the bank to issue marked coins.

A solution that does not depend on secure hardware is more complicated. For simplicity we assume that we use the same key pair for encryption of the challenge and for authentication of the customer. A covert channel is implemented by providing at least two different authentication key pairs. The first key pair should be used for ordinary withdrawals. All other key pairs are used only in the case of blackmailing, where both the public and the private key are already known to the bank, which enables it to decrypt the challenge given by the blackmailer in the confirmation protocol.

We suggest to generate all authentication key pairs dynamically from passphrases. Then it is impossible for the blackmailer to detect that his victim used a passphrase which instructs and enables the bank to issue marked coins.

4   Implementation of Our Payment System

In the following we will assume an attacker trying to commit the perfect crime, as the solution for this scenario can easily be transferred to the impersonation and the kidnapping scenario.

For the implementation of our payment system there are still some problems, which we will solve:

Comparing: A blackmailer can withdraw some coins in a regular withdrawal and the same coins in a blackmailing. For the regular withdrawal he knows that the coins are valid. If the blackmailed coins are marked, he will determine a difference between the blackmailed coins and the regularly withdrawn coins.

Transforming: A blackmailer must not be able to destroy marking. It cannot be assumed that a blackmailer follows the withdrawal protocol (e.g. he may use a different kind of blinding), but it must be guaranteed that marked coins cannot be transformed to invalid coins, while valid coins remain valid.

4.1   The Main Idea of Our Construction

To prevent the comparing attack we have to ensure that withdrawing the same coin two or more times always results in different signatures. This can be achieved with a randomized signature scheme.

We developed a new construction for a randomized undeniable signature, which uses the Okamoto-Schnorr blind signature scheme [Oka92,PS96] combined with the Chaum-van Antwerpen undeniable signature scheme [CvA89]. The main idea is to sign a random value with an undeniable signature, where the random value is a part of the blind signature. However, signing the commitment of a randomized blind signature does not work, as it is susceptible to the transforming attack. Instead we choose a system parameter of the blind signature randomly and sign it with the undeniable signature.

4.2   System Setup

In our payment system the system parameters are prime numbers p and q with $q|(p-1)$ and elements g_1, g_2 and g_3 of $(\mathbb{Z}/p\mathbb{Z})^*$ of order q. The bank chooses a key pair

$$SK_{\mathcal{B}} := (s_1, s_2) \in_R (\mathbb{Z}/q\mathbb{Z})^2$$
$$PK_{\mathcal{B}} := v = g_1^{s_1} g_2^{s_2} \bmod p$$

for the blind signature and a key pair

$$SK_{\mathcal{U}} := x \in_R \mathbb{Z}/q\mathbb{Z}$$
$$PK_{\mathcal{U}} := y = g_3^x \bmod p$$

for the undeniable signature scheme. Then it publishes the public keys $PK_{\mathcal{B}}$ and $PK_{\mathcal{U}}$.

4.3   The Withdrawal Protocol

The withdrawal protocol is shown in figure 2. For every new coin the bank creates a new random generator $\alpha = g_2^r \bmod p$ and sends this value to the customer. Then the bank and the customer interact in a blind Okamoto-Schnorr signature protocol, where the bank uses the generators g_1 and α. The customer transforms p and q are prime numbers such that $q|(p-1)$

g_1, g_2 and g_3 are some elements of $(\mathbb{Z}/p\mathbb{Z})^*$ of order q

$s_1, s_2 \in_R \mathbb{Z}/q\mathbb{Z}$ is the blind signature private key of the bank

$v = g_1^{s_1} g_2^{s_2} \bmod p$ is the blind signature public key of the bank

$x \in_R \mathbb{Z}/q\mathbb{Z}$ is the undeniable signature private key of the bank

$y = g_3^x \bmod p$ is the undeniable signature public key of the bank

Bank	Customer
	random blinding factors:
$r \in_R (\mathbb{Z}/q\mathbb{Z})^*$	$\delta \in_R (\mathbb{Z}/q\mathbb{Z})^*$
$k_1, k_2 \in_R \mathbb{Z}/q\mathbb{Z}$	$\beta_1, \beta_2, \gamma \in_R \mathbb{Z}/q\mathbb{Z}$
$\alpha = g_2^r \bmod p$	$\alpha' = \alpha^\delta \bmod p$
$a = g_1^{k_1} \alpha^{k_2} \bmod p$	$a' = a \cdot g_1^{\beta_1} \alpha'^{\beta_2} v^\gamma \bmod p$
$\xrightarrow{\quad \alpha, a \quad}$	$c' = H(m, \alpha', a')$
	$c = c' - \gamma \bmod q$
	$\xleftarrow{\quad c \quad}$
$S_1 = k_1 - cs_1 \bmod q$	$S_1' = S_1 + \beta_1 \bmod q$
$S_2 = k_2 - cs_2 r^{-1} \bmod q$	$S_2' = \delta^{-1} S_2 + \beta_2 \bmod q$
$w = \alpha^x \bmod p$	$w' = w^\delta = \alpha'^x \bmod p$
$\xrightarrow{\quad (S_1, S_2), w \quad}$	$a' \overset{?}{=} g_1^{S_1'} \alpha'^{S_2'} v^{c'} \bmod p$
	Signature: $(c', S_1', S_2', \alpha', w')$

Fig. 2. Withdrawal of coins based on Okamoto-Schnorr blind signatures combined with Chaum-van Antwerpen undeniable signatures.

this signature to a signature based on the generators g_1 and $\alpha' = \alpha^\delta \bmod p$ using a randomly chosen $\delta \in_R (\mathbb{Z}/q\mathbb{Z})^*$. This transformation is needed, because otherwise the bank could recognize coins at deposit on behalf of the generator α.

Finally the bank issues an undeniable signature $w = \alpha^x \bmod p$ as a certificate for α. Again, the certificate has to be transformed to $w' = w^\delta = \alpha'^x \bmod p$ by the customer to circumvent recognition by the bank and to be a valid undeniable signature for α'. Note that for this transformation we have to omit the hashfunction on α. The impact on the security will be discussed in section 5.

At the end of the withdrawal protocol the customer possesses a valid coin $(m, c', S_1', S_2', \alpha', w')$, and the validity of the undeniable signature w has to be proven in a confirmation protocol. Our confirmation protocol (see figure 3) is a designated verifier variant of the protocols described in [CvA89,Cha90]. If the customer follows the withdrawal protocol correctly, then the given proof is also valid for w'.

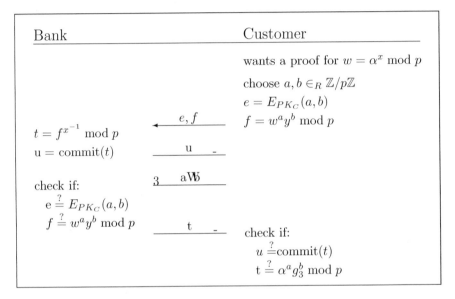

Fig. 3. This confirmation protocol proves the validity of the withdrawn coin only to the designated verifier.

4.4   Marking Blackmailed Coins

In the case of blackmailing marked coins are issued using a different private key $SK_{U_M} := x_M$ to generate the undeniable signature. In order to recognize marked coins the bank has to maintain lists of all used marking keys:

1. The list $\mathbb{M}_A$ contains all marking keys for which the corresponding coins should be *accepted*.
2. The list $\mathbb{M}_R$ contains all marking keys for which the corresponding coins should be *rejected*.

When the customer instructs the bank to reject all his marked coins, the bank moves the corresponding marking key to $\mathbb{M}_R$ and refunds the amount of all unspent marked coins to the customer.

Our confirmation protocol for the Chaum-van Antwerpen undeniable signature used in the case of blackmailing is shown in figure 4. As the customer is able to decrypt the committed secret parameters a and b, he can give the correct answer $t = \alpha^a g_3^b \bmod p$, which the blackmailer expects for an unmarked coin.

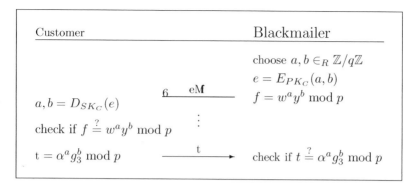

Fig. 4. In case of blackmailing the customer can even prove the validity of a marked coin.

4.5 Spending and Depositing Coins

When a customer spends a coin $(m, c', S_1', S_2', \alpha', w')$, the merchant is not able to check the validity of this coin alone, because he cannot verify the undeniable signature and cannot check for double spending. Thus he immediately has to deposit this coin at the bank.

For every coin to be deposited the bank first checks for double spending and then verifies the Okamoto-Schnorr signature and the corresponding Chaum-van Antwerpen undeniable signature.

Verification of the Okamoto-Schnorr signature: The bank verifies the signature by computing $a' = g_1^{S_1'} \alpha'^{S_2'} v^{c'} \bmod p$ and checking $c' \stackrel{?}{=} H(m, \alpha', a')$. If this test fails, the coin is rejected.

Verification of the Chaum-van Antwerpen undeniable signature: The bank verifies the undeniable signature by checking $w' \stackrel{?}{=} \alpha'^x \bmod p$. If this test also succeeds, then the coin is valid and will be accepted. If the test fails, the bank checks all previously used marking keys.

Checking the marking keys: The bank checks the marking keys $x_{\mathcal{M}} \in \mathbb{M}_A \cup \mathbb{M}_R$ by testing $w' \stackrel{?}{=} \alpha'^{x_{\mathcal{M}}} \bmod p$. If one of the marking keys fulfills this equation, the bank knows to which blackmailing this coin belongs and whether it has to accept or reject this coin. If the test fails for all marking keys, the coin is invalid and will be rejected.

Disavowal protocol: If the bank rejects a coin because of the undeniable signature, it has to prove that the undeniable signature was not generated with x. In our payment system we use Chaum's disavowal protocol [Cha90] for this proof.

5 Discussion of Security and Anonymity

In this section we discuss some aspects of security and anonymity of our payment system.

Unforgability of coins: It is sufficient to show that the blind signature is unforgeable, as this implies the unforgability of coins. Obviously, the security of the blind signature is not affected even if marking keys are published.

Our Okamoto-Schnorr blind signature differs from the original blind signature [Oka92,PS96], as it is possible to modify one generator by computing $\alpha' = \alpha^\delta \bmod p$. However, even if an attacker enforces this generator to be $\alpha' = 1$ by choosing $\delta = 0$ the signature remains witness-indistinguishable [FS90], as k_1 and k_2 are always hidden in a. The security of witness-indistinguishable blind signatures is shown in [PS96]. Also note that no valid signature can be created with $\delta = 0$, as δ has to be invertible.

Undetectability of marking for blackmailers: Blinding of the undeniable signature is only possible as we omit the hashfunction on α, which makes the undeniable signature susceptible to the transforming attack described at the beginning of section 4. The goal of such a transformation is that marked coins are transformed to invalid coins, while valid coins remain valid. In this attack the undeniable signature (α, w) may be transformed to $(\alpha', w') = (\alpha^\delta h \bmod p, w^\delta h^x \bmod p)$ using a value h for which an undeniable signature $h^x \bmod p$ is available. In the verification of the blind signature ($a' = g_1^{S_1'} \alpha'^{S_2'} v^{c'} \bmod p$) the value α' is raised to the power of S_2'. However, $h^{S_2'} \bmod p$ was not known at the time when a' was computed and thus the verification equation can only be fulfilled, if an attacker knows the discrete logarithm of h to the base of g_1 or g_2. As no undeniable signature of g_1 or g_2 is available to an attacker, no suitable h can be constructed. Thus h always has to be 1, which means that blackmailers cannot apply this attack to destroy marking.

Anonymity of customers: A unique property of our payment system is that the decision whether a coin is traceable or not has to be made at withdrawal and is unalterable afterwards.

If the customer receives unmarked coins at withdrawal, the views of the customer and the bank on the coins are unlinkable due to the blind signature. This means that payments with unmarked coins are unconditional anonymous for the customer.

The only way to degrade the anonymity of customers is to mark their coins. However, a polynominal time bounded bank has only a negligible chance to succeed in the confirmation protocol with a marked coin. If the bank is not polynominal time bounded, it may cheat the customer in the confirmation protocol by decrypting his challenge.

6   Improvements and Enhancements

After we described the basic version of our payment system, we now sketch several ideas how the system can be further improved.

- The efficiency of the withdrawal can be improved, if the bank uses the same random α and the same certificate w for all coins of a withdrawal session. This improvement has no impact on the linkability of the coins from one session, as long as the customer uses a different δ for every coin.
- As long as no marked coins are issued by the bank, the bank only needs to verify the blind signature. If this signature is correct, then it must have been issued by the bank, and thus the coin can be accepted without checking the undeniable signature.
- If the bank detects a coin generated with a marking key $x_{\mathcal{M}} \in \mathbb{M}_R$ at deposit, the bank may simply publish the key $x_{\mathcal{M}}$ instead of interacting in a disavowal protocol.
- When a blackmailer has been caught, the marking key used for this blackmailing can be removed from $\mathbb{M}_A$ or $\mathbb{M}_R$. If a coin with such a marking is deposited later, it is always rejected as invalid.
- There also exist other, less efficient implementations of our payment scheme, e.g. an Okamoto-Guillou-Quisquater blind signature [Oka92,PS96] combined with an undeniable RSA signature [GKR97].

7   A Comparison to Systems with Revocable Anonymity

In this section we compare our payment system to systems with revocable anonymity (e.g. [DFTY97,JY96,CMS96,JY97]), which are another well known solution to blackmailing attacks. In contrast to our solution these systems are based on trusted third parties.

The advantage of a system with revocable anonymity is that tracing is possible at any time after the withdrawal. This makes it always possible to trace blackmailed coins. In our system the customer has to decide at withdrawal, whether the coins should be traceable or not. But due to this restriction of our scheme, we do not suffer from *illegal tracing*, which may be possible in systems with revokable anonymity due to the following reasons:

- If the trusted third party illegally cooperates with the bank, they can trace the customer.
- Even if the trusted third party is honest, there is the danger that the bank gains access to the private data of the trusted third party and is able to trace the customer on its own. Vice versa, a dishonest trusted third party might get access to the bank's database and trace customers.
- Even if the private data of an honest trusted third party is protected carefully, the bank may be able to trace the customer alone: If anonymity revocation is implemented by trusted third party decryption (this applies to all offline trusted third parties, e.g. [CMS96,DFTY97]) and the cryptosystem is

broken, then the bank can trace any payment by computing the decryption key of the trusted third party.

In all of these cases illegal tracing is a serious threat for the privacy of a customer, as he has no possibility to detect illegal tracing. Moreover, it is always hard to prove that illegal tracing has happened.

In our payment system illegal tracing is impossible. Even if the cryptosystem used for the encryption in the confirmation protocol can be broken, the bank will not be able to trace previous payments. As long as the customer uses a secure encryption scheme at withdrawal the probability of illegal marking is negligible. Furthermore, any unmarked coin remains unconditionally anonymous in the future.

Last but not least we'd like to mention that most arguments against key escrow [AAB+98] (e.g. risk, complexity, costs) also apply for revocable anonymity.

8   Conclusions

We have sketched a novel anonymous payment system offering unconditional anonymity. In contrast to systems with revocable anonymity our approach does not rely on a trusted third party. In general a trusted third party causes additional costs, which the customer may not be willing to pay for. As the trusted third party manages sensitive personal data, it has to be protected carefully. However, the more secure the trusted third party is, the more expensive is the service of the trusted third party.

Our payment system protects private users against blackmailing attacks, by offering a marking mechanism similar to the well known marking of banknotes. Our marking mechanism is even more effective, because every transaction with a marked coin is immediately recognized by the bank. At deposit a detected marked coin may be accepted or rejected, depending on the choice of the customer.

As coins may only be marked in agreement with the customer, the bank cannot misuse marking to degrade anonymity. Nevertheless marked coins are undetectable for a blackmailer. This enables tracing of blackmailers and allows revocation of marked coins, without sacrificing anonymity.

An open question about our system is how it can be extended to other blackmailing scenarios (e.g. when the bank is blackmailed). Another question is whether the marking mechanism can also be applied to fight money laundering.

Acknowledgments

We like to thank Ingrid Biehl and the anonymous reviewers for their valuable suggestions and comments.

References

AAB+98. H. Abelson, R. Anderson, S. Bellovin, J. Benaloh, M. Blaze, W. Diffie, J. Gilmore, P. Neumann, R. Rivest, J. Schiller, and B. Schneier. The risks of key recovery, key escrow, and trusted third-party encryption. Online available at http://www.cdt.org/crypto/risks98, 1998. An earlier version appeared in World Wide Web Journal, v.2, n.3, 1997, pages 241–257.

Cha83. D. Chaum. Blind signatures for untraceable payments. In *Advances in Cryptology - CRYPTO '82*, pages 199–203. Plenum, 1983.

Cha90. D. Chaum. Zero-knowledge undeniable signatures. In *Advances in Cryptology - EUROCRYPT '90*, volume 473 of *Lecture Notes in Computer Science*, pages 458–464. Springer-Verlag, 1990.

CMS96. J. Camenisch, U. Maurer, and M. Stadler. Digital payment systems with passive anonymity-revoking trustees. In *Computer Security - ESORICS '96*, volume 1146 of *Lecture Notes in Computer Science*, pages 31–43. Springer-Verlag, 1996.

CvA89. D. Chaum and H. van Antwerpen. Undeniable signatures. In *Advances in Cryptology - CRYPTO '89*, volume 435 of *Lecture Notes in Computer Science*, pages 212–216. Springer-Verlag, 1989.

DFTY97. G. Davida, Y. Frankel, Y. Tsiounis, and M. Young. Anonymity control in e-cash systems. In *Financial Cryptography '97*, volume 1318 of *Lecture Notes in Computer Science*, pages 1–16. Springer-Verlag, 1997.

Fro96. A.M. Froomkin. Flood control on the information ocean: Living with anonymity, digital cash, and distributed databases. *15 U. Pittsburgh Journal of Law & Commerce 395*, 1996. Online available at http://www.law.miami.edu/~froomkin/articles/ocean.htm.

FS90. U. Feige and A. Shamir. Witness indistinguishable and witness hiding protocols. In *22nd Symposium on Theory of Computing (STOC '90)*, pages 416–426. ACM Press, 1990.

FTY96. Y. Frankel, Y. Tsiounis, and M. Young. "Indirect discourse proofs": Achieving efficient fair off-line e-cash. In *Advances in Cryptology - ASIACRYPT '96*, volume 1163 of *Lecture Notes in Computer Science*, pages 286–300. Springer-Verlag, 1996.

GKR97. R. Gennaro, H. Krawczyk, and T. Rabin. RSA-based undeniable signatures. In *Advances in Cryptology - CRYPTO '97*, volume 1294 of *Lecture Notes in Computer Science*, pages 132–149. Springer-Verlag, 1997.

JSI96. M. Jakobsson, K. Sako, and R. Impagliazzo. Designated verifier proofs and their applications. In *Advances in Cryptology - EUROCRYPT '96*, volume 1070 of *Lecture Notes in Computer Science*, pages 143–154. Springer-Verlag, 1996.

JY96. M. Jakobsson and M. Yung. Revokable and versatile electronic money. In *3rd ACM Conference on Computer Communication Security (CCCS '96)*, pages 76–87. ACM Press, 1996.

JY97. M. Jakobsson and M. Yung. Distributed "magic ink" signatures. In *Advances in Cryptology - EUROCRYPT '97*, volume 1233 of *Lecture Notes in Computer Science*, pages 450–464. Springer-Verlag, 1997.

Oka92. T. Okamoto. Provably secure and practical identification schemes and corresponding signature schemes. In *Advances in Cryptology - CRYPTO '92*, volume 740 of *Lecture Notes in Computer Science*, pages 31–53. Springer-Verlag, 1992.

PS96.   D. Pointcheval and J. Stern. Provably secure blind signature schemes. In
          Advances in Cryptology - ASIACRYPT '96, volume 1163 of *Lecture Notes
          in Computer Science*, pages 252–265. Springer-Verlag, 1996.
vSN92.   B. von Solms and D. Naccache. On blind signatures and perfect crimes.
          Computers and Security, 11(6):581–583, 1992.

Cryptanalysis of Two Sparse Polynomial Based Public Key Cryptosystems

Feng Bao[1], Robert H. Deng[1], Willi Geiselmann[2], Claus Schnorr[3],
Rainer Steinwandt[2], and Hongjun Wu[1]

[1] Kent Ridge Digital Labs
21 Heng Mui Keng Terrace, Singapore 119613
{baofeng,deng,hongjun}@krdl.org.sg

[2] Institut für Algorithmen und Kognitive Systeme
Arbeitsgruppen Computeralgebra & Systemsicherheit, Prof. Dr. Th. Beth,
Universität Karlsruhe, Am Fasanengarten 5, 76 131 Karlsruhe, Germany
{geiselma,steinwan}@ira.uka.de

[3] Department of Mathematics/Computer Science
Johann Wolfgang Goethe-University, Frankfurt am Main, Germany
schnorr@cs.uni-frankfurt.de

Abstract. The application of sparse polynomials in cryptography has been studied recently. A public key encryption scheme EnRoot [4] and an identification scheme SPIFI [1] based on sparse polynomials were proposed. In this paper, we show that both of them are insecure.

The designers of SPIFI proposed the modified SPIFI [2] after Schnorr pointed out some weakness in its initial version. Unfortunately, the modified SPIFI is still insecure. The same holds for the generalization of EnRoot proposed in [2].

1 Introduction

The commonly used public key cryptosystems today are based on either the factorisation problem or the discrete logarithm [3,7,8]. Some public key cryptosystems based on polynomials have been developed recently, such as the NTRU [6] and PASS [5]. EnRoot [4] and SPIFI [1] are two public key cryptosystems based on so-called sparse polynomials. The sparse polynomials used in EnRoot and SPIFI are of very high degree (as large as $2^{31} - 2$) while most of the terms are with zero coefficients.

EnRoot is a public key encryption scheme and is based on the difficulty of finding a solution to a given system of sparse polynomial equations over certain large rings. SPIFI is an identification scheme and is based on the difficulty of finding a sparse polynomial with specified values at some given points.

In this paper, we break EnRoot and SPIFI. Without dealing with the embedded hard problems, both cryptosytems could be broken easily: the plaintext of the original EnRoot could be recovered (without knowing the private key) faster than the decryption algorithm; the private key of the original SPIFI could

K. Kim (Ed.): PKC 2001, LNCS 1992, pp. 153–164, 2001.
© Springer-Verlag Berlin Heidelberg 2001

be determined faster than the key generation process. We also break the modified SPIFI [2] in this paper. The modified SPIFI was proposed to eliminate the weakness of the original SPIFI pointed out by Schnorr.

This paper is organized as follows. Section 2 introduces the identification scheme SPIFI and the modified version. Section 3 gives the cryptanalysis of the original SPIFI and the modified version. Section 4 describes the public key encryption scheme EnRoot. The attack against EnRoot is given in Section 5. This attack also covers the generalized EnRoot system described in [2]. Section 6 concludes this paper.

2 Description of the Identification Scheme

The original SPIFI [1] (Secure Polynomial IdentiFIcation) and the modified version [2] are introduced in Subsections 2.1 and 2.2, respectively.

2.1 The Original SPIFI

We begin with the introduction of some terminology concerning polynomials.

Definitions. Given a finite field $\mathbb{F}_q$ and a set $S \subseteq \mathbb{F}_q$, we use the following terminology:

> S-polynomial: a polynomial $G(X) \in \mathbb{F}_q[X]$ is an S-polynomial if every coefficient of G belongs to S.
> Essentially S-polynomial: a polynomial $G(X) \in \mathbb{F}_q[X]$ is an essentially S-polynomial if $G(X) - G(0)$ is an S-polynomial.
> τ-sparse: a polynomial $G(X) \in \mathbb{F}_q[X]$ is τ-sparse if it has at most τ non-zero coefficients.

The system parameters of SPIFI include

> $\mathbb{F}_q$: a large finite field (where q is a large prime integer);
> k: a small positive integer;
> r, s, t: three small positive integers.

Key Generation. The key generation process consists of the following steps:

1. Randomly select k elements a_i $(i = 0, 1, \ldots, k - 1)$, where each $a_i \in \mathbb{F}_q$.
2. Randomly select a t-sparse $\{0,1\}$-polynomial $\varphi(X) \in \mathbb{F}_q$ of degree at most $q - 1$.
3. Compute $A = -\varphi(a_0)$, and let $f(X) = \varphi(X) + A$.
4. Compute $C_i = f(a_i)$ for $i = 1, 2, \ldots, k - 1$.
5. The private key is the polynomial f, and the public key consists of the values $A, a_0, a_1, \ldots, a_{k-1}$ and $C_1, C_2, \ldots, C_{k-1}$.

Verification Protocol. It consists of the following steps:

1. The verifier selects at random an s-sparse essentially $\{0,1\}$-polynomial $h(X)$ from $\mathbb{F}_q[X]$ with $h(0) = B$ and sends $h(X)$ to the prover.

2. The prover randomly selects an r-sparse $\{0,1\}$-polynomial $g(X) \in \mathbb{F}_q[X]$ of degree at most $q - 1$ with $g(0) = 1$.
3. The prover computes $F(X)$ and D_i $(i = 1, 2, \ldots, k - 1)$ as

$$F(X) \equiv f(X)g(X)h(X) \mod (X^q - X)$$

$$D_j = g(a_i) \qquad i = 1, \ldots, k - 1$$

Then $F(X)$ and D_i $(i = 1, \ldots, k - 1)$ are sent to the verifier.
4. The verifier computes

$$E_j = h(a_j), \qquad j = 1, 2, \ldots, k - 1$$

and verifies that $F(X)$ is an rst-sparse $\{0,1,A,B,AB\}$-polynomial that satisfies $F(0) = AB$, and

$$F(a_j) = C_j D_j E_j, \qquad j = 0, 1, \ldots, k - 1$$

where $D_0 = E_0 = 1, C_0 = 0$.

Eligibility of F

There is a negligible chance that the constructed polynomial $F(X)$ is not a $\{0, 1, A, B, AB\}$-polynomial. However, if rst is substantially smaller than q, this chance is extremely small. The sparser the polynomials are, the smaller is the chance.

Recommended Parameters

It is claimed in [1] that parameters $q = 2^{31} - 1$, $r = s = t = 5$, and $k = 3$ guarantee a security level of 2^{90} and a fast signature.

Hard Problem

It is claimed that the identification protocol is based on the following hard problem.

> Given $2m$ arbitrary elements $\alpha_1, \ldots, \alpha_m, \gamma_1, \ldots, \gamma_m$ and a set $S \subseteq \mathbb{F}_q$ of small cardinality, it is unfeasible to find a τ-sparse S-polynomial $G(X) \in \mathbb{F}_q[X]$ of degree $deg(G) \leq q - 1$ such that $G(\alpha_j) = \gamma_j$ for $j = 1, \ldots, m$, provided that q is of "medium" size relative to the choice of $m \geq 1$ and $\tau \geq 3$.

This hard problem ensures that it is hard to compute the private key $f(X)$ from the public key (the values of $f(X)$ at some given points).

2.2   The Modified SPIFI

We introduce only the modified SPIFI over the finite field $\mathbb{F}_q$. The general modified SPIFI can be found in [2]. The modified SPIFI differs from the original one only at the key generation process and the first step of the verification protocol.

Modified Key Generation. The key generation process consists of the following steps:

1. Randomly select k elements a_i $(i = 0, 1, \ldots , k - 1)$, where each $a_i \in \mathbb{F}_q$.
2. Randomly select a $\frac{t}{2}$-sparse $\{0,1\}$-polynomial $f_1(X) \in \mathbb{F}_q[X]$ of degree at most $q - 1$, $f_1(0) = 1$.
3. Randomly select a $\frac{t}{2}$-sparse $\{0,1\}$-polynomial $f_2(X) \in \mathbb{F}_q[X]$ of degree at most $q - 1$, $f_2(0) = 0$, $f_2(a_0) \neq 0$ and $f_2(a_0) \neq -f_1(a_0)$.
4. Compute $A = -f_2(a_0)f_1(a_0)^{-1}$, and let $f(X) = Af_1(X) + f_2(X)$. Then $f(X)$ is a t-sparse $\{0, 1, A\}$-polynomial with $f(0) = A$ and $f(a_0) = 0$.
5. Compute $C_i = f(a_i)$ for $i = 1, 2, \ldots , k - 1$.
6. The private key is the polynomial f, and the public key consists of the values $A, a_0, a_1, \ldots , a_{k-1}$ and $C_1, C_2, \ldots , C_{k-1}$.

Only the first step of the verification protocol is modified. It is modified as:

> The verifier selects at random an s-sparse $\{0, 1, B\}$-polynomial $h(X) \in \mathbb{F}_q[X]$ with $h(0) = B$ and sends $h(X)$ to the prover.

Recommended Parameters

It is claimed in [2] that the parameters $q = 2^{31} - 1$, $r = s = t = 5$, and $k = 3$ guarantee a security level of 2^{90}. These recommended parameters are the same as those in the original SPIFI.

3   Cryptanalysis of the Original SPIFI

We give two attacks to break the original SPIFI. One attack is to recover the private key $f(X)$ from $F(X)$ (part of the identification transcript), another one is to forge the identification transcript without knowing the secret key. They are illustrated in Subsection 3.1 and 3.2. We show that the modified SPIFI is still insecure in Subsection 3.3.

3.1   Recover the Private Key

In this subsection, we give an attack to recover the private key $f(X)$ from the identification transcript $F(X)$. Our attack involves only computations over $\mathbb{F}_q$. The direct computation over $\mathbb{F}_q[X]$ is too heavy for extremely large values of q and is thus not used in our attack.

The attack begins with recovering the polynomial $f(X)g(X)$ from $F(X)$. Let the polynomial $h'(X) = h(X) - B$, i.e., $h'(X)$ is a $\{0,1\}$-polynomial. Then the following relationship holds:

$$F(X) = f(X)g(X)h(X) = f(X)g(X)h'(X) + f(X)g(X) \cdot B.$$

Clearly, the product $f(X)g(X)h'(X)$ is a $\{0,1,A\}$-polynomial while $f(X)g(X) \cdot B$ is a $\{0,B,AB\}$-polynomial. It is thus straight forward to separate $Bf(X)g(X)$ from $F(X)$. The product $f(X)g(X)$ is obtained subsequently.

After knowing $f(X)g(X)$, we tend to recover $g(X)$. Denote the polynomial $f'(X) = f(X) - A$. Then

$$f(X)g(X) = f'(X)g(X) + Ag(X).$$

$f'(X)g(X)$ is a $\{0,1\}$-polynomial while $Ag(x)$ is a $\{0,A\}$-polynomial. The polynomial $g(X)$ could thus be obtained easily from $f(X)g(X)$.

We proceed to recover $f(X)$ from $f(X)g(X)$. Denote the set of all the non-zero-coefficient degrees of $f'(X)$ as $U = \{u_1, u_2, \dots, u_t\}$. Denote the set of all the non-zero-coefficient degrees of $f(X)g(X)$ as $V = \{v_1, v_2, \dots, v_{rt}\}$. Let two non-zero-coefficient degrees of $g(X)$ be w_1 and w_2. Then $X^{w_1}f(X)$ and $X^{w_2}f(X)$ are both in $f(X)g(X)$. Denote $U' = U + w_1$ as

$$U' = \{w_1 + u_1, w_1 + u_2, \dots, w_1 + u_t\}$$

where $w_i + u_j$ is set as $(w_i + u_j - q + 1)$ if $w_i + u_j \geq q$. And let $U'' = U + w_2$. It is obvious that $U' \subset V$ and $U'' \subset V$, i.e., $U \subset (V - w_1)$ and $U \subset (V - w_2)$, where $v_i - w_j$ is set as $(v_i - w_j + q - 1)$ if $v_i - w_j \leq 0$. Due to the sparse nature of the problem, it is not difficult to show that $U = (V - w_1) \cap (V - w_2)$ holds with large probability. $f'(X)$ is thus determined and so is the private key $f(X) = f'(X) + A$.

The amount of computation needed in the attack to recover the private key is less than that required by the SPIFI key generation process.

3.2   Forge the Identification Transcript without the Private Key

The identification transcript of the SPIFI [1] could be forged without knowing the private key. Let Catherine be an attacker who does not know the prover's private key. She forges the identification transcript as follows:

1. Catherine receives an s-sparse essentially $\{0,1\}$-polynomial $h(X)$ ($h(0) = B$) from the verifier.
2. Catherine gives an rt-sparse essentially $\{0,1,A\}$-polynomial $e(X) \in \mathbb{F}_q[X]$ such that $e(0) = A$ and $e(a_0) = 0$. (The detail will be discussed later in this subsection.)
3. Catherine computes $F(X) = e(X)h(X) \mod (X^q - X)$, sets $D_j = \frac{F(a_j)}{C_j E_j}$ ($E_j = h(a_j)$) for $j = 1, \dots, k-1$, and sends $F(X)$ and $D_1, \dots, D_{k-1}$ to the verifier.
4. The verifier checks that $F(X)$ is an rst-sparse $\{0, 1, A, B, AB\}$-polynomial with $F(0) = AB$, and $F(a_j) = C_j D_j E_j$ for $j = 1, \dots, k-1$ and $F(a_0) = 0$.
5. Catherine successfully impersonates the prover.

In Step 2, Catherine needs to compute an rt-sparse essentially $\{0,1\}$-polynomial $e(X) \in \mathbb{F}_q[X]$ satisfying $e(0) = A$ and $e(a_0) = 0$. This problem is easy to solve as long as the value of q is not very large, such as the recommended $q = 2^{31} - 1$. Choose randomly an $(rt - 2)$-sparse essentially $\{0,1\}$-polynomial $e'(X)$. The required $e(X)$ is given as

$$e(X) = X(e'(X) + X^w) + A$$

where

$$w = \log_{a_0} \left(-\frac{A + a_0 e'(a_0)}{a_0} \right).$$

It is easy to compute the value of w over $\mathbb{F}_q$ for $q = 2^{31} - 1$.

If the value of q is too large, the attack in this subsection could not be applied. However, in that case, the SPIFI cryptosystem is based on the well-known discrete logarithm, instead of the hard problem related to the sparse polynomials. It is irrelevant for the attack how A and B appear in the polynomials. The attack applies to S-polynomials for any S.

3.3 Cryptanalysis of the Modified SPIFI

The SPIFI is modified to resist the attack in Subsection 3.1, i.e., to prevent the private key from being recovered from the identification transcript. However, our attack given in Subsection 3.2 could be applied (with only slight modification) to break the modified SPIFI, i.e., to forge the identification transcript without the private key (the details to forge the identification transcripts are ignored in this paper). Furthermore, we developed a new attack to recover the private key of the modified SPIFI. Details of this new attack are given in the following.

Recover the Private Key

The modified SPIFI still fails to hide the private key in a secure way. An extremely simple attack to recover the private key is given below.

Suppose now we obtained two identification transcripts. Denote these two polynomials in the transcripts as $F'(X)$ and $F''(X)$, where

$F'(X) \equiv f(X)g'(X)h'(X) \bmod (X^q - X)$ and
$F''(X) \equiv f(X)g''(X)h''(X) \bmod (X^q - X)$.

Let g', h', g'', h'' be randomly chosen sparse polynomials, $f(X)$ would be the only common terms of F' and F'' (with different coefficients). Thus $f(X)$ is recovered with negligible amount of computation. The probability of success of this attack would be very close to one due to the sparse nature of the involved polynomials.

Remarks.

1. To prevent the verifier from gaining the private key information by choosing certain special polynomials h, the SPIFI designers suggest to use two equivalent private keys alternatively [2]. This approach has little effect on our attack above. With at most three identification transcripts, we can recover one of the equivalent private keys and thus break the system. Generally, if r equivalent private keys are used, one of the keys could be determined with at most $r + 1$ identification transcripts.
2. The attack above can be applied directly to recover the private key in the original SPIFI. However, the attack in Subsection 3.1 requires only one identification transcript while the attack in this subsection requires two.

4   Description of the Encryption Scheme EnRoot

The sparse polynomial public key encryption scheme proposed in [4] is called EnRoot. A generalized version of EnRoot is also considered in [2]. As the generalized system can be attacked in the same as the original one proposed in [4], in the sequel we restrict our attention to the original system.
The system parameters of EnRoot include

$\mathbb{F}_q$: a large finite field (where q is a large prime integer);
k: a small positive interger;
t: $t = (t_1, t_2, \ldots, t_k)$ where each t_i is a small positive integer;
s: $s = (s_1, s_2, \ldots, s_k)$ where each s_i is a small positive integer.

Key Generation. The key generation process consists of the following steps:

1. Randomly choose k integers $e_i \in \mathbb{Z}/(q-1)\mathbb{Z}$ $(i = 1, 2, \ldots, k)$.
2. Choose a random element $\vartheta \in \mathbb{F}_q$. Let $a_i = \vartheta^{e_i}$ for $i = 1, 2, \ldots, k$.
3. Select k random polynomials $h_i \in \mathbb{F}_q[X_1, X_2, \ldots, X_k]$ $(i = 1, 2, \ldots, k)$ of degree at most $q - 1$. Each h_i contains at most $t_i - 1$ monomials.
4. For $i = 1, 2, \ldots, k$ compute

$$f_i(X_1, X_2, \ldots, X_k) := h_i(X_1, X_2, \ldots, X_k) - h_i(a_1, a_2, \ldots, a_k) \quad (1)$$

5. The secret key is $a = (a_1, a_2, \ldots, a_k)$. The public key is $f = (f_1, f_2, \ldots, f_k)$.

Encryption. To encrypt a message $m \in \mathbb{F}_q$,

1. Select k random polynomials $g_i \in \mathbb{F}_q[X_1, X_2, \ldots, X_k]$ $(i = 1, 2, \ldots, k)$. Each g_i contains at most s_i monomials and has a non-zero constant coefficient.
2. Compute the reduction Ψ of the polynomial $f_1 g_1 + f_2 g_2 + \ldots + f_k g_k$ modulo the ideal generated by $(X_1^q - X_1, \ldots, X_k^q - X_k)$.
3. The message m is encrypted as the polynomial $\Phi = m + \Psi$.

Decryption. To decrypt the message, compute $m = \Phi(a_1, a_2, \ldots, a_k)$.

Recommended Parameters. It is claimed in [4] that the parameter values $q = 2^{31} - 1$, $k = 3$, $s = t = (4, 4, 4)$ guarantee a security level of 2^{70}.

Moreover, it is claimed in [4] that EnRoot is based on the following hard problem:

> Given a system of sparse polynomial equations of high degree over certain large rings, it is hard to find a solution to this system.

This means that the secret key $a = (a_1, a_2, \ldots, a_k)$ cannot be recovered from the public key $f = (f_1, f_2, \ldots, f_k)$, where a is a common root of those polynomials f_i $(i = 1, 2, \ldots, k)$. However, as is shown in the next section, EnRoot can be broken without knowing the private key.

5   Decryption without Secret Key

First we note, that for decrypting a ciphertext

$$c = m + \sum_{i=1}^{k} f_i \cdot g_i \mod (X_1^q - X_1, \dots, X_k^q - X_k)$$

it is sufficient to reconstruct the constant coefficients $g_i(0)$ of Bob's polynomials g_i: The absolute coefficient of c is

$$c(0) = m + \sum_{i=0}^{k} f_i(0) \cdot g_i(0),$$

because of all non-constant monomials in the expression $\sum_{i=1}^{k} f_i \cdot g_i$ remaining non-constant after reduction modulo $(X_1^q - X_1, \dots, X_k^q - X_k)$. Hence, knowing both Alice's public polynomials f_i and the constant coefficients $g_i(0)$ we can reveal the plaintext m via

$$m = c(0) - \sum_{i=0}^{k} f_i(0) \cdot g_i(0).$$

How can we find the constant coefficients $g_i(0)$? As there are $q^k - 1$ different non-constant terms (monic monomials) which are of degree $< q$ in each variable, with high probability the public polynomials f_i of Alice satisfy the condition

$$\text{Terms}(f_i) \not\subseteq \bigcup_{j \neq i} \text{Terms}(f_j) \quad (1 \leq i \leq k) \tag{2}$$

(here $\text{Terms}(f_j)$ denotes the set of terms occuring in f_j with non-zero coefficient). In other words, for each f_i we can find a term

$$X^{\mu_i} := \prod_{j=1}^{k} X_j^{\mu_{ij}} \in \text{Terms}(f_i)$$

such that X^{μ_i} does not occur in any polynomial f_j with $j \neq i$. Now let $i \in \{1, \dots, k\}$ be arbitrary but fixed, and denote by a_{μ_i} the (non-zero) coefficient of X^{μ_i} in f_i. Then the coefficient of the term X^{μ_i} in the ciphertext $c = \sum_{i=1}^{k} f_i \cdot g_i$ is with high probability equal to $g_i(0) \cdot a_{\mu_i}$: If this coefficient were different from a_{μ_i} we had

$$X^{\alpha} \cdot X^{\beta} \equiv X^{\mu_i} \mod (X_1^q - X_1, \dots, X_k^q - X_k)$$

for some $(X^{\alpha}, X^{\beta}) \in \text{Terms}(f_j) \times \text{Terms}(g_j)$ with $j \in \{1, \dots, k\}$. However, the non-constant terms of the (sparse) polynomials f_j, g_j were chosen at random, and as there are $q^k - 1$ possible non-zero exponent vectors the chance of this to happen is negligible. So in practice we can reveal $g_i(0)$ by simply reading off the coefficient of X^{μ_i} in the ciphertext, followed by dividing this coefficient by a_{μ_i}.

To illustrate this astonishingly simple attack let us consider an example with the parameters $q = 2^{31} - 1$ (a prime number), $k = 3$, $s_1 = t_1 = \dots = s_3 = t_3 = 4$ considered in [4]:

Example 1. By means of the `randpoly` function of the computer algebra system *Maple V Realease 4* we derive the following public polynomials for Alice—the secret common zero is

$$(x_1, x_2, x_3) := (723264497, 1295378210, 230009212) :$$

$$
\begin{aligned}
f_1 = \; & 349502340 \cdot X_1^{809446137} \cdot X_2^{956143141} \cdot X_3^{1600225079} + \\
& 313871617 \cdot X_1^{779070143} \cdot X_2^{727160601} \cdot X_3^{1344053701} + \\
& 1715097824 \cdot X_1^{1172854581} \cdot X_2^{559420076} \cdot X_3^{439722691} + \\
& 116222600
\end{aligned}
$$

$$
\begin{aligned}
f_2 = \; & 200180663 \cdot X_1^{1823184387} \cdot X_2^{1504204554} \cdot X_3^{472267093} + \\
& 1678471703 \cdot X_1^{759656320} \cdot X_2^{273015567} \cdot X_3^{1022563056} + \\
& 10188499 \cdot X_1^{92552998} \cdot X_2^{1050663882} \cdot X_3^{371683973} + \\
& 1218489385
\end{aligned}
$$

$$
\begin{aligned}
f_3 = \; & 942412531 \cdot X_1^{1346986246} \cdot X_2^{1330841188} \cdot X_3^{1657353576} + \\
& 539695881 \cdot X_1^{332026853} \cdot X_2^{273278370} \cdot X_3^{1260893325} + \\
& 1786359577 \cdot X_1^{900024634} \cdot X_2^{592601620} \cdot X_3^{182312333} + \\
& 931260911
\end{aligned}
$$

For our attack we use the following terms (any other combination is possible as well):

$$
\begin{aligned}
X^{\mu_1} &:= X_1^{809446137} \cdot X_2^{956143141} \cdot X_3^{1600225079} \\
X^{\mu_2} &:= X_1^{1823184387} \cdot X_2^{1504204554} \cdot X_3^{472267093} \\
X^{\mu_3} &:= X_1^{1346986246} \cdot X_2^{1330841188} \cdot X_3^{1657353576}
\end{aligned}
$$

Next, we encrypt the plaintext message $1234567890 \in \mathbb{F}_{2^{31}-1}$ with the polynomials g_i below (these were also created by means of *Maple V*'s `randpoly` function):

$$
\begin{aligned}
g_1 = \; & 757504042 \cdot X_1^{1902769822} \cdot X_2^{1021006850} \cdot X_3^{1121824348} + \\
& 1024142914 \cdot X_1^{522845576} \cdot X_2^{176006881} \cdot X_3^{1459236022} + \\
& 1452872129 \cdot X_1^{227645716} \cdot X_2^{24530405} \cdot X_3^{1104197961} + \\
& 1655562558
\end{aligned}
$$

$$
\begin{aligned}
g_2 = \; & 199017912 \cdot X_1^{2009873524} \cdot X_2^{590749267} \cdot X_3^{1358354210} + \\
& 394475909 \cdot X_1^{1337441105} \cdot X_2^{915805516} \cdot X_3^{971137190} + \\
& 497731252 \cdot X_1^{533944316} \cdot X_2^{641808520} \cdot X_3^{85031460} + \\
& 1158943955
\end{aligned}
$$

$$
\begin{aligned}
g_3 = \; & 1552167047 \cdot X_1^{765919171} \cdot X_2^{2067090688} \cdot X_3^{1623699208} + \\
& 140676907 \cdot X_1^{1867678520} \cdot X_2^{717664997} \cdot X_3^{703320394} + \\
& 478601450 \cdot X_1^{99708880} \cdot X_2^{707867631} \cdot X_3^{2047224198} + \\
& 1010407045
\end{aligned}
$$

The constant coefficient of the resulting ciphertext c is $c(0) = 1881347037$. Further on, c contains—among others—the monomials $1290226445 \cdot X^{\mu_1}$, $463293963 \cdot X^{\mu_2}$, and $1216948431 \cdot X^{\mu_3}$. Using these monomials we can reveal the constant coefficients of the secret polynomials g_i as described above:

$$
\begin{aligned}
g_1(0) &= 1290226445 \cdot 349502340^{-1} = 1655562558 \\
g_2(0) &= 463293963 \cdot 200180663^{-1} = 1158943955 \\
g_3(0) &= 1216948431 \cdot 942412531^{-1} = 1010407045
\end{aligned}
$$

Consequently, the plaintext m computes to

$$m = c(0) - f_1(0) \cdot g_1(0) - f_2(0) \cdot g_2(0) - f_3(0) \cdot g_3(0) = 1234567890.$$

5.1 Modifying EnRoot

Grant et al. also mention the following modification of their public key cryptosystem: instead of choosing the polynomials h_i at random in the key generation phase, each h_i is chosen as an $\mathbb{F}_q$-linear combination

$$h_i = \sum_{j=1}^{z} a_{i\nu_j} X^{\nu_j}$$

of a fixed set of (w. l. o. g. non-constant) terms $X^{\nu_1}, \dots, X^{\nu_z}$. The other parts of the cryptosystem, in particular the encryption and decryption phase, remain unaltered.

In this setting the above attack does not immediately apply, because we cannot assume condition (2) to be fulfilled. However, the next section shows that this modified scheme is insecure, too.

5.2 Decryption without Secret Key in the Modified System

W. l. o. g. we may assume that the public polynomials $f_1, \dots, f_k$ are linearly independent over $\mathbb{F}_q$.—In the contrary, it is sufficient to apply the attack described subsequently to a maximal linearly independent subset of $\{f_1, \dots, f_k\}$, because such a subset is in particular a generating set of the ideal $(f_1, \dots, f_k) \trianglelefteq \mathbb{F}_q[X]$.

As Bob chooses the polynomials g_i at random, analogously as in Section 5 we see that the coefficient c_{ν_j} of X^{ν_j} ($1 \le j \le z$) in the ciphertext c equals $\sum_{i=1}^{k} a_{i\nu_j} \cdot g_i(0)$ with high probability. In other words, we obtain the following system of linear equations for the constant coefficients $g_i(0)$:

$$
\begin{pmatrix} a_{1\nu_1} & \cdots & a_{k\nu_1} \\ \vdots & & \vdots \\ a_{1\nu_z} & \cdots & a_{k\nu_z} \end{pmatrix} \cdot \begin{pmatrix} g_1(0) \\ \vdots \\ g_k(0) \end{pmatrix} = \begin{pmatrix} c_{\nu_1} \\ \vdots \\ c_{\nu_z} \end{pmatrix} \tag{3}
$$

¿From $f_1, \dots, f_k$ being linearly independent we can conclude that also $h_1, \dots, h_k$ are linearly independent (cf. the defining equations (1)). Therefore the coefficient matrix on the left-hand side of Equation (3) is of rank k, and applying Gauß' algorithm to this equation yields a unique solution for $g_1(0), \ldots, g_k(0)$. Finally, as in our attack on the original EnRoot cryptosystem the plaintext computes to

$$m = c(0) - \sum_{i=0}^{k} f_i(0) \cdot g_i(0).$$

Remarks.

1. One of the referees brought up the idea that the system might be resistent to our attack, if Bob chooses the random polynomials so that some of the resulting monomials of the ciphertext have an identical exponent vector, say Bob chooses one term X^β of his polynomials in such a way that $X^{\mu_i} = X^\alpha \cdot X^\beta$, where X^{μ_i} and X^α are terms of Alice's public key.
   In this case obviously we cannot reconstruct the plaintext with the above mentioned procedure. But it is easy to detect the number of such "collisions" of monomials just by counting the number of monomials in the ciphertext. Thus in this case one of the randomly chosen terms has to be of the form $X^\beta := X^{\mu_i - \alpha} \mod (X_1^q - X_1, \ldots, X_k^q - X_k)$ for some terms X^{μ_i}, X^α of the public key. Such a term X^β can easily be disclosed, as (with high probability) it is a term of the ciphertext, too. With the knowledge of the coefficient of X^β the above attack can be adapted appropriately and works again.
2. The secret k polynomials used in the encryption process could also be recovered easily. The attack is similar to that in Section 3.1. The details of this attack are ignored here.

6   Conclusions

In this paper we showed that the sparse polynomial based SPIFI (together with the modified SPIFI) and EnRoot (as well as its generalization) are insecure. Whether secure sparse polynomial based public key cryptosystems exist or not is still an open problem.

References

1. W. Banks, D. Lieman and I. Shparlinski, "An Identification Scheme Based on Sparse Polynomials", in Proceedings of PKC'2000, LNCS 1751, Springer-Verlag, pp. 68–74, 2000.
2. W. Banks, D. Lieman and I. Shparlinski, "Cryptographic Applications of Sparse Polynomials over Finite Rings", to appear in ICISC'2000.
3. T. ElGamal. "A Public Key Cryptosystem and a Signature Scheme based on Discrete Logarithms". *IEEE Transactions on Information Theory*, **31** (1985), 469–472.
4. D. Grant, K. Krastev, D. Lieman and I. Shparlinski, "A Public Key Cryptosystem Based on Sparse Polynomials", in Proceedings of an International Conference on Coding Theory, Cryptography and Related Areas, LNCS, Springer-Verlag, pp. 114–121, 2000.

5. J. Hoffstein, D. Lieman and J.H. Silverman, "Polynomial Rings and Efficient Public Key Authentication", Proceedings of the International Workshop on Cryptographic Techniques and E-Commerce, pp. 7–19, M. Blum and C. H. Lee, eds., July 5–8, 1999, Hong Kong. At the time of writing also available at the URL `http://www.ntru.com/technology/tech.technical.htm`.

6. J. Hoffstein, J. Pipher and J.H. Silverman, "NTRU: A Ring Based Public Key System", Proceedings of ANTS III, Porland (1998), Springer-Verlag.

7. V. Miller, "Uses of Elliptic Curves in Cryptography", in *Advances in Cryptology–Crypto'85*, LNCS 218, Springer-Verlag, pp. 417–426, 1986.

8. R. L. Rivest, A. Shamir, and L. Adleman, "A method for Obtaining Digital Signatures and Public-Key Cryptosystems", *Commun. ACM*, vol. 21, no. 2, pp. 158–164, Feb. 1978.

Cryptanalysis of PKP: A New Approach

Éliane Jaulmes and Antoine Joux

DCSSI
18, rue du Dr. Zamenhoff
F-92131 Issy-les-Mx Cedex
France
eliane.jaulmes@wanadoo.fr
Antoine.Joux@ens.fr

Abstract. Quite recently, in [4], a new time-memory tradeoff algorithm was presented. The original goal of this algorithm was to count the number of points on an elliptic curve, however, the authors claimed that their approach could be applied to other problems. In this paper, we describe such an application and show a new way to attack the Permuted Kernel Problem. This new method is faster than any previously known technique but still requires exponential time. In practice, we find that attacking PKP for the original size proposed by Shamir in [6] could be done on a single PC in 125 years.

1 Introduction

The Permuted Kernel Problem was introduced in cryptography by Shamir at Crypto 1989 [6]. This NP–complete problem can be stated as follows:

- Given a $m \times n$ matrix, a n vector V and a prime p
- Find a permutation π such that the permuted vector V_π is in the kernel of the matrix modulo p.

Any instance of the problem with this choice of parameters will be denoted as a $\mathrm{PKP}_p(m, n)$ problem. Without loss of generality, the left part of $m \times n$ matrix can be turned into the identity sub-matrix, as explained in [6].

In [6], it was shown that this problem possesses a nice zero-knowledge proof and can thus be turned into an authentification scheme. Moreover, when used in practice the scheme offers a good level of security using only simple computations which can be efficiently implemented, even in small portable devices. Since PKP is so simple, and uses only basic linear algebra, it is extremely tempting to search for it's weaknesses. This led to many papers [3,1,2,5], which all concluded that the original dimension proposed par Shamir are a bit too small, but the scheme still resists all known attacks. All the proposed attacks combine exhaustive search with some form of time-memory tradeoff. However, none of the classical time-memory tradeoff techniques seems to apply to this problem, and thus specific methods had to be developed in the previous papers. In this paper, we apply a

K. Kim (Ed.): PKC 2001, LNCS 1992, pp. 165–172, 2001.

new time-memory tradeoff from [4] to the permuted kernel problem. This new technique was originally designed to replace the final baby-step/giant-step when counting points on elliptic curves using the Schoof-Elkies-Atkies algorithm.

2   General Description of the Algorithm

In this section, we reformulate the algorithm from [4] in a general setting, without any reference to the specific problem of point counting on elliptic curve. In our general setting, we want to solve the following problem:

- Given a n vector P whose entries are primes, four sets S_1, S_2, S_3 and S_4 of n vectors, and n sets $D_1, \ldots, D_n$
- Find $v^{(1)} \in S_1$, $v^{(2)} \in S_2$, $v^{(3)} \in S_3$, $v^{(4)} \in S_4$, $d_1 \in D_1, \ldots, d_{n-1} \in D_{n-1}$ and $d_n \in D_n$ such that:

$$\forall i \in [1 \cdots n] : \ v_i^{(1)} + v_i^{(2)} + v_i^{(3)} + v_i^{(4)} \equiv d_i \pmod{P_i}$$

Clearly, this problem, which we note $4SET$, can be solved by exhaustively trying the $N_1 N_2 N_3 N_4$ possible values of $v^{(1)}$, $v^{(2)}$, $v^{(3)}$ and $v^{(4)}$, where N_i denotes the cardinality of S_i. We propose here a time-memory tradeoff that allows to solve this problem faster than exhaustive search. Without loss of generality, we assume that:

$$\frac{|D_1|}{P_1} \leq \frac{|D_2|}{P_2} \leq \cdots \leq \frac{|D_n|}{P_n},$$

where $|D_i|$ denotes the size of D_i. Then, let $\alpha_i = \frac{|D_i|}{P_i}$, choose k a positive integer smaller than n and let

$$\Psi = \prod_{i=1}^{k} \alpha_i \ \text{and} \ \Phi = \prod_{i=1}^{k} P_i$$

The algorithm then consists of a precomputation phase and of a main loop containing two enumeration phases, one involving $v^{(1)}$ and $v^{(2)}$, the A-phase, and one involving $v^{(3)}$ and $v^{(4)}$, the B-phase.

Algorithm for solving $4SET$
- **Precomputation step:** Sort the two sets S_2 and S_4, according to the lexicographical order on the vector coordinates.
  In the sequel, this will permit to quickly find vectors in one of these sets given its first k coordinates.

- **Main loop:**
  For $M_1 \in [0 \cdots P_1 - 1]$, $M_2 \in [0 \cdots P_2 - 1]$, $\ldots M_k \in [0 \cdots P_k - 1]$ do:
  - **A phase:**
    * For each $\Theta \in D_1 \times \cdots \times D_k$,
    * For $v^{(1)} \in S_1$ and $v^{(2)} \in S_2$ such that the first k coordinates[1] $v_i^{(1)} + v_i^{(2)}$ match $\Theta_i - M_i$ modulo P_i,

---

[1] Thanks to the precomputation step, such $v^{(2)}$ can be accessed quickly by computing $\Theta_i - M_i - v_i^{(1)} \pmod{P_i}$ before searching the matching entries in the sorted set S_2.

* For all $\ell > k$ compute and store the following set:

$$H_{\Theta, v^{(1)}, v^{(2)}, \ell} = \{\theta - v_\ell^{(1)} - v_\ell^{(2)} | \theta \in D_\ell\}.$$

- **B phase:**
  * For each $v^{(3)} \in S_3$ and $v^{(4)} \in S_4$ such that the first k coordinates $v_i^{(3)} + v_i^{(4)}$ match M_i,
  * If there exists $\Theta \in D_1 \times \cdots \times D_k$, $v^{(1)} \in S_1$ and $v^{(2)} \in S_2$ such that for every $\ell > k$, $v_\ell^{(3)} + v_\ell^{(4)}$ (mod P_ℓ) is in $H_{\Theta, v^{(1)}, v^{(2)}, \ell}$,
  * Then $v_i^{(1)} + v^{(2)} + v_i^{(3)} + v^{(4)}$ is a solution of the *4SET* problem.

  Terminate

2.1   Practical Considerations

In practice, building the sets $H_{\Theta, v^{(1)}, v^{(2)}, \ell}$ in the *A*-phase and checking their intersections in the *B*-phase can be done very efficiently. Indeed, all these sets can be stored in a single array of bits. This array has $\sum_{\ell=k+1}^{n} P_\ell$ lines and one column for each pair $(v^{(1)}, v^{(2)})$. Each line of this array can also be seen as a bit string $B_{\ell, \tau}$ where $\tau \in \{0, \ldots, P_\ell - 1\}$. During the *A*-phase, we store a 1 in $B_{\ell, \tau}$ in the position corresponding to $(v^{(1)}, v^{(2)})$ if $\tau \in H_{\Theta, v^{(1)}, v^{(2)}, \ell}$ and a 0 otherwise. Note that all strings $B_{\ell, \tau}$ have the same length, however this length may vary from one round of the main loop to the next. On average, this length is $\Psi N_1 N_2$.

During the *B*-phase, to check whether $\tau_\ell = v_\ell^{(3)} + v_\ell^{(4)}$ (mod P_ℓ) is in $H_{\Theta, v^{(1)}, v^{(2)}, \ell}$ for every ℓ and some pair $(v^{(1)}, v^{(2)})$, we simply perform a logical AND between the strings B_{ℓ, τ_ℓ}. If the resulting string is non-nil we have a solution, since any bit equal to 1 in this string corresponds to a pair $(v^{(1)}, v^{(2)})$ such that $v^{(1)} + v^{(2)} + v^{(3)} + v^{(4)}$ is a solution of the *4SET* problem.

Note that, when the expected number of solutions of a *4SET* problem is much smaller than 1, it is worthwhile not to test the last conditions. Indeed, in that case, one can simply remove the useless components and build a similar problem with fewer conditions. In fact, this approach was implicitly used in [4] since some of the conditions found by the SEA algorithm where discarded for the final step. On the contrary, PKP problems are usually built in such a way that all conditions are useful and cannot be discarded (see section 4).

2.2   Analysis of the Algorithm

- **Precomputation step :** The number of operations required to sort S_2 is $O(N_2 \log(N_2))$ and to sort S_4 it is $O(N_4 \log(N_4))$. Thus the time needed is $O(\max(N_2, N_4) \log(\max(N_2, N_4)))$. The total memory required in this precomputation step is $O(\max(N_1, N_2, N_3, N_4) \sum_i \log(P_i))$ because S_1 and S_3 must also be stored, and because each vector can be represented with $\sum_i \log(P_i)$ bits.

- **Phase A** : Clearly, the average number of pairs $(v^{(1)}, v^{(2)})$ constructed in each execution of phase A is $\Psi N_1 N_2$. To do this construction, we enumerate all possible values of Θ and $v^{(1)}$ and search for matching values of $v^{(2)}$. This requires $O(N_1 \log(N_2)\Psi\Phi)$ operations. Then for each valid pair $(v^{(1)}, v^{(2)})$, $n - k$ bits are to be set, the total number of operations for this step is $O((n-k)\Psi N_1 N_2)$. All in all, the number of operations required is:

$$O(\max(N_1 \log(N_2)\Psi\Phi, (n-k)\Psi N_1 N_2)).$$

The total memory needed to store all the sets is $O(\Psi N_1 N_2 \sum_{i=k}^{n} P_i)$.

- **Phase B** : In each execution of phase B, $N_3 N_4/\Phi$ pairs $(v^{(3)}, v^{(4)})$ are constructed. This construction requires $O(N_3 \log(N_4))$ operations. Then for each pair the logical AND of $n - k$ of the strings constructed in phase A is computed. Since on average the length of the strings is $\Psi N_1 N_2$ the number of operations is $O((n-k)\Psi N_1 N_2 N_3 N_4/\Phi)$. All in all, each iteration of phase B costs :

$$O(\max(N_3 \log(N_4), (n-k)\Psi N_1 N_2 N_3 N_4/\Phi)).$$

In term of memory complexity, phase B does not require any memory not already used in the precomputation or in phase A.

When the choice of parameters is reasonable, the time complexity is dominated by phase B and can be expressed as :

$$O((n-k)\Psi N_1 N_2 N_3 N_4).$$

Without going too far into the analysis of the parameters, let say that a choice is reasonable if all the N_i are of the same order N, if $\Psi \approx 1/N$ and if Φ does not become too large. Moreover, in that case the memory needed is:

$$O(N \sum_{i=k}^{n} P_i).$$

Note: With the algorithm as presented here Φ should not become larger than $N^{3/2}$. However, if we slightly modify it be transferring half of Θ from phase A to phase B, Φ can grow up to N^2. Moreover, this transformation reduces the amount of memory needed, by shortening the sets stored during phase A. Since we still need to store the sets, the memory requirement becomes:

$$O(N \sum_{i=1}^{n} \log(P_i)).$$

3   Application to PKP

In order to apply the algorithm of the previous section to PKP, we need to build sets S_1, S_2, S_3, S_4 and D_1, D_2, ..., D_n from a PKP instance. Before doing that, we will slightly transform the PKP instance. Following [3], we can add one more linear equation to the PKP instance. This new equation stems from the simple fact that the sum σ of the coordinates of the solution vector does not depend on the permutation π. Applying Gaussian elimination to the extended linear system, we find that the solution vector V_π must verify:

$$(A_0\, I_{m+1})\, V_\pi = \begin{pmatrix} \sigma \\ 0 \\ 0 \\ \vdots \\ 0 \end{pmatrix},$$

where A_0 is a $(m+1)\times(n-m-1)$ matrix and I_{m+1} is the $(m+1)\times(m+1)$ identity matrix. Clearly, in order to find a solution to the permuted kernel problem thus written, it suffices to try all the possible values of the components of V_π that enters A_0, to find the remaining components by Gaussian elimination and to check that the vector found is indeed a permutation of V. This algorithm requires $n!/(n-m-1)!$ trials. In the sequel, we will refer to it as being the exhaustive search technique for PKP, and we will completely forget the simple minded search where one tries all possible values for π, which requires $n!$ trials.

We can now divide A_0 into four roughly equal parts, and we find:

$$(A_1\, A_2\, A_3\, A_4\, I_{m+1})\, V_\pi = \begin{pmatrix} \sigma \\ 0 \\ 0 \\ \vdots \\ 0 \end{pmatrix},$$

where A_i is a $(m+1) \times n_i$ matrix and $n_1 + n_2 + n_3 + n_4 = n - m - 1$.

We then build the sets S_i by computing the product of A_i by all possible choices of the corresponding n_i bits. Clearly, the size of S_i is $N_i = n!/(n-n_i)!$. Once these sets are constructed, we can apply the algorithm from section 2.

Note: In fact, the algorithm from section 2 can be further refined in the case of PKP. The idea is that while merging together an element of S_1 and an element of S_2 in phase A or an element of S_3 and an element of S_4 in phase B, one should check their compatibility, i.e. verify that put together they form a correct subset of V, which is true if and only if they have no nontrivial intersection (assuming that V contains no double). This reduces the term $N_1 N_2$ and $N_3 N_4$ in the complexities respectively to $n!/(n - n_1 - n_2)!$ and $n!/(n - n_3 - n_4)!$.

4 Asymptotical Analysis

In order to make an asymptotical analysis of our algorithm, we first need to describe an asymptotical version of PKP. For defining this version, we will follow the two following criteria:

– Building a strong instance of PKP, should be easy. More precisely, this means that for any random matrix, finding a kernel vector with distinct coordinates should be easy. Since kernel vectors are chosen at random when building a PKP problem, this implies that the probability of a random kernel vector to have all distinct coordinates should not be too low. Taking in account the birthday paradox, this means that n should be no larger that $O(\sqrt{p})$.
– As explained in [6], the expected number of solutions of a PKP instance should be as near to 1 as possible. This leads to the condition $p^m \approx n!$.

Following these criteria let $p = O(n^2)$, then:

$$m \approx n \log n / \log p$$
$$\approx n/2$$

Using these two criteria, we propose $\mathrm{PKP}_p(n, \lfloor n/2 \rfloor)$ as a reasonable asymptotic choice, where p is a prime near n^2. With this choice of parameters, an exhaustive search attack on PKP takes roughly $n!/m! = O((2n/e)^{n/2})$ trials. For the attack described in section 3, we need to choose the parameter k and thus the value of Ψ. A particularly interesting choice is to use the same amount of storage for the sets S_i and the strings. Assuming that $N_1 = N_2 = N_3 = N_4$, this leads to $\Psi \approx 1/N_1$. Since $N_1 = O((((8/7)^7)(n/e))^{n/8})$, we find that the time complexity of the algorithm is

$$O((((8/7)^7)(n/e))^{3n/8+\varepsilon})$$

and the space complexity is

$$O((((8/7)^7)(n/e))^{n/8+\varepsilon}).$$

The value ε in the exponent offers a simple replacement for the non exponential terms that should appear in these two formulas, and permits a simpler expression.

In fact, if we further take into account the note at the end of section 3, we can somewhat reduce the constant $(8/7)^7$ appearing in the time complexity.

5   Practical Results

In practice, it turns out that the previous ideas lead to a faster attack against PKP, than all previously known techniques. The best previous theoretical attacks against PKP are those from [2] and an implementation of these attacks is described in [5]. In the rest of this section we compare the available data for this attack with our results.

In [2], the following results are found:

Results from [2]	Time needed	Memory needed (in tuples)
$PKP_{251}(16, 32)$	2^{54}	2^{17} 6–tuples
	2^{52}	2^{24} 10–tuples
$PKP_{251}(37, 64)$	2^{123}	2^{27}
	2^{119}	2^{52}
	2^{116}	2^{65}

In order to make the same kind of evaluation for our algorithm, we first need to compute the size of the sets S_1, S_2, S_3, S_4. Starting with $PKP(16, 32)$, we take $n_1 = n_2 = n_4 = 4$ and $n_3 = 3$, we find $N_1 = N_2 = N_4 = 863040$ and $N_3 = 29760$. In order to have $\Psi \approx 1/N_1$, we take $k = 6$ and find $\Psi = (24/251)^6$. With these choice, the space needed is dominated by the storage of the four sets S_i, and $32 \times (N_1 + N_2 + N_3 + N_4) \approx 2^{26}$ bytes are needed. This may seem larger than the 2^{24} in the above table, however this size was not in bytes but in 10–tuples, and thus both sizes are equivalent. The basic time estimate is $\Psi N_1 N_2 N_3 N_4 \approx 2^{54}$. However, recalling the note from section 3 it becomes $\Psi n!^2 /((n - n_1 - n_2)!(n - n_3 - n_4)!) \approx 2^{52}$. Once again, this does not seem better than the value 2^{52} in the above table. However, remember than our basic operation is a bit operation and that on most computers we can pack 32 or even 64 bit operations in a single word operation, thus lowering the complexity to 2^{46}.

As the size increases, the advantage of the new algorithm becomes much clearer. Indeed, for $PKP(37, 64)$, we can take $n_1 = n_3 = 6$, $n_2 = n_4 = 7$ and $k = 17$. Then $\Psi = (48/251)^k$, the space needed becomes $2^{48.5}$ and the time needed 2^{106}. However, while better that the estimates from [2], these values are completely unreachable. The following table shows the results of the new attack for various dimensions of PKP.

New Results	k	Time needed	Memory needed
$PKP_{251}(16, 32)$	6	2^{46}	2^{26} bytes
$PKP_{251}(15, 32)$	6	2^{51}	2^{27} bytes
$PKP_{251}(24, 48)$	12	2^{85}	2^{35} bytes
$PKP_{251}(37, 64)$	17	2^{106}	$2^{48.5}$ bytes

In [5], the attack described in [2] was truly implemented, and experiments were made. At that time, a single workstation would have taken 2000 years for $PKP(16, 32)$. In a private communication, the author from [5] told us than on current machines, experiment showed that this estimate was lowered to 700 years. The ratio between the two figures is much worse than expected because all these computations heavily rely on memory usage. Since the speed of memory access did not increase as quickly as the speed of processors, this accounts for the low ratio. By comparison, on the same machine (Pentium II, 400MHz), the new attack would take 125 years (at most) to find the secret key of $PKP(16, 32)$. Quite strangely, in a practical implementation, phase A takes proportionally much longer then phase B because in the former case we make random memory access (on single bits) while in the latter we read the memory in sequential order. Consequently, phase B is cache friendly while phase A isn't. Moreover, we cannot use the theoretically optimal choice for k, because the code that controls the loop then becomes predominant. Thus our practical choices were $n_1 = 3$, $n_2 = 4$, $n_3 = 3$, $n_4 = 5$ and $k = 4$. With these choices, each iteration of the main loop took just under a second, and the total memory needed was 250 megabytes. Since 251^4 iterations of the main loop are needed, a total running time of 125 years is expected.

6   Conclusion

In this paper, we showed that the time-memory tradeoff technique for [4] could be applied to the PKP problem. Very curiously, this leads to an algorithm which presents similarities with the algorithm from [2]. In practice, this new algorithm can attack PKP(16,32) about five times faster than all previous attacks. However, this attack would still require 125 years on a 450MHz PC. Since the algorithm is straightforward to parallelized, this computation is feasible and PKP(16,32) can no longer be considered as secure. Moreover, PKP(15,32) which takes about 24 times as long, is potentially endangered and should no longer be used for long-term applications. However, slightly larger problems such PKP(24,48) or PKP(37,64) are completely out of reach.

References

1. T. Baritaud, M. Campane, P. Chauvaud, and H. Gilbert. On the security on the permuted kernel identification scheme. In *CRYPTO92*, volume 740 of *LNCS*, pages 305–311, 1992.
2. P. Chauvaud and J. Patarin. Improved algorithms for the permuted kernem problem. In *CRYPTO93*, volume 773, pages 391–402, 1994.
3. J. Georgiades. Some remarks on the security of the identification scheme based on permuted kernels. *Journal of Cryptology*, 5:133–137, 1992.
4. A. Joux and R. Lercier. "Chinese & Match", an alternative to atkin's "match and sort" method used in the SEA algorithm. *Mathematics of Computation*, 1999. To appear.
5. G. Poupard. A realistic security analysis of identification schemes based on combinatorial problems. *European transactions on telecommunications*, 8:471–480, 1997.
6. A. Shamir. An efficient identification scheme based on permuted kernels. In *CRYPTO89*, volume 435 of *LNCS*, pages 606–609, 1989.

Cryptanalysis of a Digital Signature Scheme on ID-Based Key-Sharing Infrastructures

Hongjun Wu, Feng Bao, and Robert H. Deng

Kent Ridge Digital Labs
21 Heng Mui Keng Terrace, Singapore 119613
{hongjun,baofeng,deng}@krdl.org.sg

Abstract. At ISW'99, Nishioka, Hanaoka and Imai proposed a digital signature scheme on ID-based key-sharing infrastructures. That signature scheme is claimed to be secure if the discrete logarithm problem is hard to solve. Two schemes (the ID-type and the random-type schemes) based on the linear scheme for the Key Predistribution Systems (KPS) and the discrete logarithm problem (DLP) were given.

In this paper we show that those two schemes fail to meet the non-repudiation requirement: with negligible amount of computation, a signature could be forged. For the ID-type signature scheme, any verifier could forge a signature to raise repudiation between that verifier and the signer. The random type signature scheme has the same weakness. Furthermore, for the random-type signature scheme, once a signer issued a signature, anyone (not only the user in the scheme) could forge that signer's signature for a n arbitrary message.

1 Introduction

Digital signature plays an important role in authenticating digital documents. The commonly used digital signature schemes [5,11,13] are all belong to the public key cryptosystem (PKC). There is a kind of digital signature scheme that is based on the ID-Based cryptosystem [14] instead of on PKC. The first such digital signature scheme was proposed by Shamir [14]. Some other digital signature schemes [3,10,12] are based on the Key Predistribution Systems (KPS). The KPS is a kind of ID-based cryptosystem and it solves the key distribution problem with simple calculation [1,2,4,6,7,8,9].

Nishioka, Hanaoka and Imai recently proposed a new signature scheme [12] on the KPS infrastructure. This scheme is to satisfy the main signature requirements: authenticity, unforgeability, and non-repudiation [12]. Two examples were given and they are claimed to be secure if the discrete logarithm problem is hard to solve. As will be shown in this paper, those two examples are insecure: a signature could be easily forged with negligible amount of computation.

Nishioka, Hanaoka and Imai also claimed that if an ID-based key sharing system exists, an ID-based digital signature system could be easily implemented [12]. By breaking their proposed concrete signature schemes, it is shown that

K. Kim (Ed.): PKC 2001, LNCS 1992, pp. 173–179, 2001.

the implementation of secure ID-based digital signature system might not be as easy as claimed in [12].

This paper is organised as follows. Section 2 introduces the KPS and the linear KPS scheme. Section 3 introduces the KPS based signature scheme. The attacks against the ID-type signature scheme and the random-type signature scheme are given in Section 4 and Section 5, respectively. Section 6 concludes this paper.

2   KPS and the Linear KPS Scheme

2.1   KPS

The KPS Key Predistribution System [9] consists of one centre and a number of users. The KPS centre keeps in secret a bi-symmetric "center-algorithm" $G(\cdot, \cdot)$. The centre computes each user's secret algorithm as $X_i(\cdot) = G(ID_i, \cdot)$, where ID_i is the identifier of the user U_i and is publicly authenticated. The algorithm X_i is pre-distributed to the user U_i secretly and confidentially. The user U_i could establish a secret common key k_{ij} with the user U_j by computing $k_{ij} = X_i(ID_j)$ (the user U_j computes it as $X_j(ID_i)$).

2.2   The Linear KPS Scheme

The linear KPS scheme is one of the basic schemes of the KPS. In this scheme the symmetric centre algorithm is represented as 2nd degree covariant tensor G where each element $G_{ij}(i, j = 0, \cdots, m - 1)$ is in $GF(q)$. A public function f transforms each ID into an m-dimension vector x on $GF(q)$ as $x_i = f(ID_i)$, where $x_i = (x_i^0, x_i^1, \cdots, x_i^{m-1})^T$. The user U_i's secret algorithm is an m-dimension vector X_i over $GF(q)$ and is generated as

$$X_i = G \cdot x_i$$

The common key k_{ij} established between U_i and U_j is computed by U_i as

$$k_{ij} = X_i^T \cdot x_j$$

or computed by U_j as

$$k_{ij} = X_j^T \cdot x_i$$

As long as the number of users is less than m, this linear KPS scheme is secure since no user(s) could recover the centre algorithm G.

3   The KPS-Based Signature Scheme

In [12], two examples based on the linear scheme for the KPS and the discrete logarithm problem (DLP) are given. These two signature schemes are introduced in this section. In the rest of this paper, H denotes an ideal hash function.

3.1   The ID-Type Scheme

Choose two sufficiently large primes p and q such that $p = 2q + 1$.

Signature Generation. The user U_i signs a message M as follows.

1. Compute $h = H(M||ID_i) \bmod p$
2. The signature S is an m-dimension vector on $GF(p)$ computed as $S = h^{X_i}$, i.e., $S_\ell = h^{X_i^\ell} \bmod p$ for $\ell = 0, 1, \cdots, m - 1$.

Verification. The user U_j verifies the signature as follows:

1. Compute $V_1 = \displaystyle\prod_{\ell=0}^{m-1} (S_\ell)^{x_j^\ell} \bmod p$
2. Compute $V_2 = h^{k_{ij}} \bmod p$ where k_{ij} is the common key shared by U_i and U_j.
3. If $V_1 = V_2$ or $V_1 = V_2 \cdot h^q \bmod p$, the signature is accepted; otherwise, it is rejected.

Remarks. In the signature verification process,

$$V_1 = \prod_{\ell=0}^{m-1} (S_\ell)^{x_j^\ell} \bmod p$$

$$= h^{\sum_{\ell=0}^{m-1} X_i^\ell \cdot x_j^\ell \bmod p-1} \bmod p$$

$$= \begin{cases} h^{k_{ij}} \bmod p & \text{if } \widetilde{k}_{ij} < q \\ h^{k_{ij}} \cdot h^q \bmod p & \text{otherwise} \end{cases}$$

where $\widetilde{k}_{ij} = \displaystyle\sum_{\ell=0}^{m-1} X_i^\ell \cdot x_j^\ell \bmod p-1$. Thus for a signature generated by U_i, $V_1 = V_2$ or $V_1 = V_2 \cdot h^q \bmod p$.

3.2   The Random-Type Scheme

Choose two sufficiently large primes p and q satisfying $q|p - 1$. Pick up g with order q on the multiplicative group $\mathbf{Z}_p^*$.

Signature Generation. The user U_i signs the message M as follows:

1. Generate m random numbers $z_\ell \in \mathbf{Z}_q$ ($\ell = 0, 1, \cdots, m - 1$).
2. Let $z = \displaystyle\sum_{\ell=0}^{m-1} z_\ell \bmod q$, and $r_\ell = g^{z_\ell} \bmod p$.
3. Compute $s_\ell = (H(M) \cdot z_\ell + X_i^\ell) \cdot z^{-1} \bmod q$.
4. The signature of the message M is given as (r_ℓ, s_ℓ) ($\ell = 0, 1, \cdots, m - 1$).

Verification. The user U_j verifies the signature as follows:

1. Let $s = \sum_{\ell=0}^{m-1} s_\ell \cdot x_j^\ell \mod q$, and $r = \prod_{\ell=0}^{m-1} r_\ell^{x_j^\ell} \mod p$.

2. Let $k_{ij} = \sum_{\ell=0}^{m-1} X_j^\ell \cdot x_i^\ell \mod q$.

3. Compute $V_1 = r^{H(M)s^{-1}} \cdot g^{k_{ij} \cdot s^{-1}} \mod p$.

4. Compute $V_2 = \prod_{\ell=0}^{m-1} r_\ell \mod p$.

5. The user U_j accepts the signature only if $V_1 = V_2$.

Remarks. It is not difficult to verify that for a signature generated by U_i, $V_1 = V_2$.

4   Cryptanalysis of the ID-type Signature Scheme

In this section, we show that it is easy for a verifier to forge a signature. This signature could pass this verifier's verification process while it could not pass the verification processes of the other verifiers. However it is sufficient to cause repudiation between the signer and the verifier since the signer, on the other hand, can also forge such a signature to cheat that verifier.

Suppose now the signer is U_i and the verifier is U_j. With only the knowledge of k_{ij}, either the user U_i (signer) or U_j (verifier) could forge the signature as follows:

1. Compute $h = H(M||ID_i)$ and $V_2 = h^{k_{ij}} \mod p$.
2. Solve for a_ℓ ($\ell = 0, 1, \cdots, m-1$) from the following equation:

$$V_2 = \prod_{\ell=0}^{m-1} h^{a_\ell \cdot x_j^\ell} \mod p, \text{ or } V_2 \cdot h^q = \prod_{\ell=0}^{m-1} h^{a_\ell \cdot x_j^\ell} \mod p$$

3. Let $S_\ell' = h^{a_\ell} \mod p$. S_ℓ' ($\ell = 0, 1, \cdots, m-1$) are the forged signature.

In step 2, one of the equation is always solvable. And the amount of computation used in this attack is negligible. Thus either the verifier or signer could forge the signature easily.

The attack above deals with only one verifier. In the following, we consider the case in which all the verifiers are involved. All the verifiers may collude to forge a signature that could pass every verifier's verification. And the signer can also forge such a signature to cheat all the verifiers. Suppose there are n ($n < m$) users in the KPS scheme. The user U_0 is the signer and the users U_1 to U_{n-1} are the verifiers. In the KPS scheme, the signer has the knowledge of the common keys k_{0j} ($j = 1, 2, \cdots, n-1$). The colluded verifiers could also obtain the information of such common keys. The following attack shows how such a signature could be forged with the knowledge of the common keys k_{0j} ($j = 1, 2, \cdots, n-1$).

1. Compute $h = H(M \| ID_0)$. Let $V_{2j} = h^{k_{0j}} \bmod p$ for $j = 1, 2, \cdots, n - 1$.
2. Solve for a_ℓ $(\ell = 0, 1, \cdots, m - 1)$ from the following equations:

$$V_{2j} = \prod_{\ell=0}^{m-1} h^{a_\ell \cdot x_j^\ell} \bmod p, \ (\text{or } V_{2j} \cdot h^q = \prod_{\ell=0}^{m-1} h^{a_\ell \cdot x_j^\ell} \bmod p) \ (j = 1, 2, \cdots, n-1)$$

3. Let $S'_\ell = h^{a_\ell} \bmod p$. S'_ℓ $(\ell = 0, 1, \cdots, m - 1)$ are the forged signature.

5 Cryptanalysis of the Random-Type Signature Scheme

The random-type signature scheme is more vulnerable than the ID-type scheme. In this scheme, every verifier could forge the signature. Furthermore, anyone (not only the users in the scheme) could forge a signer's signatures after that signer released a signature. In Subsection 5.1, we show how a verifier could forge a signature. In Subsection 5.2, we show how a signer's signature could be forged after one signature is issued.

5.1 A Verifier Could Forge the Signature

With the knowledge of the common key k_{ij}, either the user U_i (signer) or U_j (verifier) could forge the signature as follows:

1. Choose m random numbers b_i $(i = 0, 1, \cdots, m - 1)$ from $GF(q)$. Let $r_i = g^{b_i}$.
2. Let $r = \prod_{\ell=0}^{m-1} r_\ell^{x_j^\ell} \bmod p$, $v = \prod_{\ell=0}^{m-1} r_\ell \bmod p$.
3. Solve the following equation for s:

$$v = r^{H(M) \cdot s^{-1}} \cdot g^{k_{ij} \cdot s^{-1}} \bmod p$$

4. Choose m numbers s_ℓ $(\ell = 0, 1, \cdots, m - 1)$ to satisfy the following linear equation:

$$s = \sum_{\ell=0}^{m-1} s_\ell \cdot x_j^\ell \bmod q$$

5. (r_ℓ, s_ℓ) $(\ell = 0, 1, \cdots, m - 1)$ are the forged signature.

Remarks In step 3, the equation could be solved without dealing with the discrete log problem. The reason is that we only need to deal with the exponent since all the bases are the same (g). The amount of computation used in the attack is negligible.

5.2   Anyone Could Forge the Signature

After a signer issued a signature, his signatures could be forged by anyone (not only the user in the KPS scheme). Suppose that a user U_i has issued a signature S of message M. We show that anyone could forge the signature of an arbitrary message M' and to convince a verifier U_j that the signature is given by U_i. The attack is given as follows:

1. Recover $g^{k_{ij}}$ from the signature: from the verification process of signature, it is easy to compute the value of $g^{k_{ij}}$ from the signature and the publicly known information.
2. Let $g' = g^{k_{ij}}$.
3. Choose m random numbers b_i $(i = 0, 1, \cdots, m-1)$ from $GF(q)$. Let $r'_i = g'^{b_i}$.
4. Let $r' = \prod_{\ell=0}^{m-1} r'^{x_j^\ell}_\ell \bmod p$, $v' = \prod_{\ell=0}^{m-1} r'_\ell \bmod p$.
5. Solve the following equation for s':

$$v' = r'^{H(M') \cdot s'^{-1}} \cdot g'^{s'^{-1}} \bmod p$$

6. Choose m numbers s'_ℓ $(\ell = 0, 1, \cdots, m-1)$ to satisfy the following linear equation:

$$s' = \sum_{\ell=0}^{m-1} s'_\ell \cdot x_j^\ell \bmod q$$

7. (r'_ℓ, s'_ℓ) $(\ell = 0, 1, \cdots, m-1)$ are the forged signature.

Remarks In step 5, the equation could be solved easily since the bases are all the same (g'), and only the exponent need to be considered.

Conclusion=============================

6   Conclusions

In this paper, we showed that two recently proposed KPS-based signature schemes are not secure. The design of secure signature scheme based on KPS is still an open problem.

References

1. R. Blom, "Non-public Key Distribution", in *Advances in Cryptology–Crypto'82*, Plenum Press (1983), pp. 231-236.
2. C. Blundo, A. De Santis, A. Herzberg, S. Kutten, U. Vaccaro and M. Yung, "Perfectly Secure Key Distribution for Dynamic Conferences", in *Advances in Cryptology–Crypto'92*, LNCS 740, Springer-Verlag, pp.471-486, 1993.
3. Y. Desmedt and J. J. Quisquater, "Public-Key Systems Based on the Difficulty of Tampering (Is There a Difference Between DES and RSA?)", in *Advances in Cryptology Crypto'86*, LNCS 263, Springer-Verlag, pp. 111-117, 1986.

4. Y. Desmedt and V. Viswanathan, "Unconditionally Secure Dynamic Conference Key Distribution", IEEE, ISIT'98, 1998.

5. T. ElGamal. "A Public Key Cryptosystem and a Signature Scheme based on Discrete Logarithms". *IEEE Transactions on Information Theory*, **31** (1985), 469-472.

6. A. Fiat and M. Naor, "Broadcast Encryption", in *Advances in Cryptology–Crypto'93*, LNCS 773, Springer-Verlag, pp. 480-491, 1994.

7. L. Gong and D. J. Wheeler, "A Matrix Key-Distribution Scheme", *Journal of Cryptology*, vol. 2, pp. 51-59, Springer-Verlag (1993).

8. W. A. Jackson, K. M. Martin, and C. M. O'keefe, "Multisecret Threshold Schemes", in *Advances in Cryptology–Crypto'93*, LNCS773, Springer-Verlag, pp. 126-135, 1994.

9. T. Matsumoto and H. Imai, "On the Key Predistribution System: A Practical Solution to the Key Distribution Problem", in *Advances in Cryptology–Crypto'87*, LNCS 293, Springer-Verlag, pp.185-193, 1987.

10. T. Matsumoto and H. Imai, "Applying the Key Predistribution Systems to Electronic Mails and Signatures", in *Proc. of SITA'87*, pp. 101-106, 1987.

11. V. Miller, "Uses of Elliptic Curves in Cryptography", in *Advances in Cryptology–Crypto'85*, LNCS 218, Springer-Verlag, pp. 417-426, 1986.

12. T. Nishioka, G. Hanaoka, and H. Imai, "A New Digital Signature Scheme on ID-Based Key-sharing Infrastructures", in *Information Security–Proc. of ISW'99*, LNCS 1729, Springer-Verlag, pp. 259-270, 1999.

13. R. L. Rivest, A, Shamir, and L. Adleman, "A method for Obtaining Digital Signatures and Public-Key Cryptosystems", *Commun. ACM*, vol. 21, no. 2, pp. 158-164, Feb. 1978.

14. A. Shamir, "Identity-Based Cryptosystems and Signature Schemes", in *Advances in Cryptology–Crypto'84*, LNCS 196, Springer-Verlag, pp. 47-53, 1985.

Loopholes in Two Public Key Cryptosystems Using the Modular Group

Rainer Steinwandt

Institut für Algorithmen und Kognitive Systeme,
Arbeitsgruppen Computeralgebra & Systemsicherheit, Prof. Dr. Th. Beth,
Universität Karlsruhe, Am Fasanengarten 5, 76 131 Karlsruhe, Germany,
steinwan@ira.uka.de

Abstract. We demonstrate that the public key cryptosystems using the modular group suggested in [4,5] are vulnerable to very simple ciphertext-only attacks. Consequently, in the present form both of these systems cannot be considered as sufficiently secure for cryptographic purposes.

1 Introduction

At PKC'98 A. Yamamura proposed a public key cryptosystem using the so-called modular group (see [4]). In this cryptosystem the ciphertext consists of a 2×2 matrix with entries from $\mathbb{C}[X]$. At ACISP'99 he proposed another public key cryptosystem using the modular group where the ciphertext is represented by a single complex number.

In this paper we show that with the given specifications both of these cryptosystems are vulnerable to ciphertext-only attacks. We give several examples which illustrate that it is often possible to decrypt a ciphertext by means of the public data alone, i.e., without requiring the private key. The essential idea is to exploit the message expansion occurring in both of these cryptosystems.

More detailed, the paper is organized as follows: in the next section we shortly recall the set-up of the cryptosystem suggested in [4] to the extent needed for our attack. In Section 3 we describe our attack and demonstrate its practicability through some examples. Thereafter we show how a modification of our attack can be applied successfully to the public key cryptosystem suggested in [5].

2 A Public Key Cryptosystem Using $\mathrm{SL_2}(\mathbb{Z})$

In this section we shortly recall the ingredients of the public key cryptosystem suggested in [4] to the extent necessary for describing our attack—for a complete description we refer to the original work [4].

As usual, for an integral domain R we denote by

$$\mathrm{SL_2}(R) := \left\{ \begin{pmatrix} a & b \\ c & d \end{pmatrix} \in R^{2\times 2} : \ ad - bc = 1 \right\}$$

K. Kim (Ed.): PKC 2001, LNCS 1992, pp. 180–189, 2001.
© Springer-Verlag Berlin Heidelberg 2001

the group of all 2×2 matrices over R with determinant 1; $\mathrm{SL}_2(\mathbb{Z})$ is also known as the *modular group*. To derive a public key we first need generators A, B of $\mathrm{SL}_2(\mathbb{Z})$ subject to the relations

$$A^6 = B^4 = A^3 B^{-2} = \begin{pmatrix} 1 & 0 \\ 0 & 1 \end{pmatrix}.$$

As is shown in [4] one can derive such generators by choosing a matrix $N \in \mathrm{SL}_2(\mathbb{Z})$ arbitrarily and setting

$$A := N^{-1} \cdot \begin{pmatrix} 0 & -1 \\ 1 & 1 \end{pmatrix} \cdot N, \quad B := N^{-1} \cdot \begin{pmatrix} 0 & -1 \\ 1 & 0 \end{pmatrix} \cdot N.$$

Next, one has to choose two products $V_1, V_2 \in \{A, B\}^*$ subject to certain requirements described in [4]. According to Yamamura's paper a concrete instance satisfying these requirements can be obtained by setting

$$V_1 := (BA)^i, \quad V_2 := (BA^2)^j \quad \text{with } i, j \in \mathbb{N} \text{ positive integers.}$$

Finally, for constructing a public key we also need a non-singular 2×2 matrix M with complex entries, i.e., $M \in \mathrm{GL}_2(\mathbb{C})$ and two 2×2 matrices $F_1(X), F_2(X)$ whose entries are taken from the polynomial ring over the complex numbers $\mathbb{C}[X]$. The matrices $F_1(X), F_2(X)$ are to be chosen in such a way that for some $a \in \mathbb{C}$ we have $F_1(a) = V_1$ and $F_2(a) = V_2$. In other words, evaluating the entries of $F_1(X), F_2(X)$ at $X = a$ yields the matrices V_1, V_2—here $V_1, V_2 \in \{A, B\}^*$ are identified with the 2×2 matrix obtained by "multiplying the letters A, B".

With these conventions the private key is the pair $(M, a) \in \mathrm{GL}_2(\mathbb{C}) \times \mathbb{C}$, and the public key consists of two matrices $W_1(X), W_2(X)$ which are constructed as follows:

$$(W_1(X), W_2(X)) := (M^{-1} \cdot F_1(X) \cdot M, M^{-1} \cdot F_2(X) \cdot M)$$

In order to encrypt the bitstring $b_1 \ldots b_n \in \{0, 1\}^*$ with the public key $(W_1(X), W_2(X))$ one has to compute the matrix product

$$C(X) := W_2(X) \cdot \prod_{i=1}^{n} (W_1(X)^{b_i+1} W_2(X)). \tag{1}$$

From the ciphertext $C(X)$ and the private key (M, a) the original bitstring $b_1 \ldots b_n$ can be recovered by means of a procedure described in [4].

3   Attacking the System

Denote by $C(X)$ the ciphertext obtained by encrypting the bitstring $b_1 \ldots b_n \in \{0, 1\}^*$ according to the rule (1). Then the entries of the matrix

$$D(X) := W_2(X)^{-1} \cdot C(X) = \prod_{i=1}^{n} (W_1(X)^{b_i+1} W_2(X))$$

are contained in $\mathbb{C}[X]$, and by construction also the entries of the matrix $\left(W_1(X)^{b_1+1} \cdot W_2(X)\right)^{-1} \cdot D(X)$ are polynomials with complex coefficients. So if at least one of the entries of

$$\left(W_1(X)^2 \cdot W_2(X)\right)^{-1} \cdot D(X)$$

involves a non-constant denominator then we can conclude $b_1 = 0$. This observation motivates the following naïve procedure which either after n iterations of the while-loop yields the correct plaintext or does not terminate:

Procedure 1

In: *Public key* $(W_1(X), W_2(X))$
       Ciphertext $C(X) = W_2(X) \cdot \prod_{i=1}^{n}(W_1(X)^{b_i+1}W_2(X))$
Out: $\bot$ *or the plaintext* $b_1 \dots b_n$

> **begin**
> $D(X) \leftarrow W_2(X)^{-1} \cdot C(X)$ *# remove superfluous factor*
> $l \leftarrow 1$ *# number of plaintext bit to be processed next*
>   **while** $D(X)$ *is not the identity* **do**   *# decryption incomplete*
> $D'(X) \leftarrow \left(W_1(X)^2 \cdot W_2(X)\right)^{-1} \cdot D(X)$ *# Should left-most bit*
>   *# be set?*
>   **if** $D'(X)$ *contains a non-polynomial entry*
>   **then** $b_l \leftarrow 0$ *# no $\rightarrow$ strip off* $(W_1(X) \cdot W_2(X))^{-1}$
>   **else** $b_l \leftarrow 1$ *# yes $\rightarrow$ strip off* $(W_1(X)^2 \cdot W_2(X))^{-1}$
>   **fi**
> $D(X) \leftarrow \left(W_1(X)^{b_l+1} \cdot W_2(X)\right)^{-1} \cdot D(X)$
> $l \leftarrow l + 1$ *# proceed with next bit of plaintext*
>   **od**
>   **return** $b_1 \dots b_{l-1}$
> **end**

Of course, one may think of elaborating the approach taken in Procedure 1 by overriding the decision for certain plaintext bits in the while-loop—e.g., based on the part of the plaintext which has been recovered already. However, the following examples illustrate that already this simple version works quite well; as always in the sequel for the computations we use the computer algebra system MAGMA V2.5-1 (see [1]) on a Linux platform with 800 MHz:

Example 1. This example is based on matrices $F_1(X), F_2(X)$ taken from [4]: setting

$$V_1 := \begin{pmatrix} -1 & 0 \\ 1 & -1 \end{pmatrix}$$

$$V_2 := \begin{pmatrix} -1 & 1 \\ 0 & -1 \end{pmatrix}$$

$$F_1(X) := \begin{pmatrix} -1 & (X - \sqrt{3})(X - 2\sqrt{3}) \\ \frac{1}{3}(X - \sqrt{3})^2 & -1 \end{pmatrix}$$

$$F_2(X) := \begin{pmatrix} -1 & \frac{1}{3}(X - \sqrt{3})^2 \\ (X - \sqrt{3})(X - 2\sqrt{3}) & -1 \end{pmatrix} \tag{2}$$

we obtain $F_1(2\sqrt{3}) = V_1$ and $F_2(2\sqrt{3}) = V_2$. Moreover, we choose the matrix M as

$$M := \begin{pmatrix} -5 & \frac{1}{2} \\ 3 & -\frac{1}{4} \end{pmatrix}.$$

Finally, we define $W_1(X) := M^{-1} \cdot F_1(X) \cdot M$, $W_2(X) := M^{-1} \cdot F_2(X) \cdot M$ and use these parameters to encrypt the bitstring corresponding to the ASCII representation of the text "A small example." (128 bit) with the encryption rule (1): we obtain a matrix $C(X)$ whose entries are (dense) polynomials of degree 626. As already each of the constant terms of the diagonal entries is an integer with 225 decimal digits, we do not write down the matrix $C(X)$ explicitly here (in particular this example supports the hypothesis from [4] that the public key cryptosystem under consideration is only of limited practical value). Nevertheless, applying Procedure 1 to $C(X)$ yields the correct plaintext within a few minutes.

Example 2. Setting

$$V_1 := \begin{pmatrix} -1 & 0 \\ -35 & -1 \end{pmatrix}$$

$$V_2 := \begin{pmatrix} -1 & -61 \\ 0 & -1 \end{pmatrix}$$

$$F_1(X) := \begin{pmatrix} X^2 - 86X + 1847 & X^3 - 126X^2 + 5297X - 74298 \\ 5X^4 - 840X^3 + 52920X^2 - 1481767X + 15558739 & X^2 - 88X + 1931 \end{pmatrix}$$

$$F_2(X) := \begin{pmatrix} X^3 - 126X^2 + 5297X - 74299 & X^4 - 168X^3 + 10588X^2 - 296688X + 3118691 \\ X^2 - 86X + 1848 & X^3 - 126X^2 + 5288X - 73921 \end{pmatrix}$$

we obtain $F_1(42) = V_1$ and $F_2(42) = V_2$. Moreover, we choose the matrix M as

$$M := \begin{pmatrix} -1 & 2 \\ 1 & -3 \end{pmatrix}.$$

Finally, we define $W_1(X) := M^{-1} \cdot F_1(X) \cdot M$, $W_2(X) := M^{-1} \cdot F_2(X) \cdot M$ and use these parameters to encrypt the bitstring corresponding to the ASCII representation of the text "a secret message" (128 bit) with the encryption rule (1): we obtain a matrix $C(X)$ whose entries are (dense) polynomials of degree 1150. Again, applying Procedure 1 to $C(X)$ yields the correct plaintext within a few minutes.

In [4] the possibility is mentioned to replace the univariate polynomial ring $\mathbb{C}[X]$ with a multivariate polynomial ring $\mathbb{C}[X_1, \ldots, X_r]$. Obviously, this modification does not vitiate the above attack, and the question arises which public keys are not vulnerable to the approach of Procedure 1. An obvious way to prevent this kind of attack is to impose an appropriate restriction on the choice of $W_1(X), W_2(X)$: if both $W_1(X), W_2(X)$ and $W_1(X)^{-1}, W_2(X)^{-1}$ are contained in $\mathrm{SL}_2(\mathbb{C}[X])$ already, then Procedure 1 does not terminate, as no non-constant denominators can occur when multiplying $D(X)$ with $\left(W_1(X)^2 \cdot W_2(X)\right)^{-1}$.

Unfortunately, this condition is not sufficient to guarantee the security of the cryptosystem either, as the above attack can be adapted easily: again, the basic idea is to strip off the plaintext from $C(X)$ bit by bit. The loophole we can exploit to do this is the message expansion occurring during encryption: in the cryptosystem under consideration one can expect that a short plaintext encrypts to a matrix with "simple" polynomials and a long plaintext encrypts to a matrix with "complicated" polynomials. Taking the number of terms in a polynomial for a measure of its complexity this idea motivates the following variant of Procedure 1 (for a matrix A we denote by $A_{i,j}$ the entry of A in row i and column j):

Procedure 2

In: *Public key* $(W_1(X), W_2(X))$
  Ciphertext $C(X) = W_2(X) \cdot \prod_{i=1}^{n}(W_1(X)^{b_i+1} W_2(X))$
Out: $\perp$ *or the plaintext* $b_1 \ldots b_n$

```
begin
    D(X) ← W₂(X)⁻¹ · C(X)                    # remove superfluous factor
    l ← 1                         # number of plaintext bit to be processed next
    while D(X) is not the identity do        # decryption still incomplete
        D'(X) ← (W₁(X) · W₂(X))⁻¹ · D(X)
        n₀ ← Σ_{1≤i,j≤2} | Terms(D'(X)_{i,j})|    # number of terms if left-
                                                  # most bit is assumed to be 0
        D'(X) ← (W₁(X)² · W₂(X))⁻¹ · D(X)
        n₁ ← Σ_{1≤i,j≤2} | Terms(D'(X)_{i,j})|       # number of terms if left-
                                                     # most bit is assumed to be 1
        if n₀ < n₁                          # Should left-most bit be reset?
            then bₗ ← 0               # yes → strip off (W₁(X) · W₂(X))⁻¹
            else bₗ ← 1               # no → strip off (W₁(X)² · W₂(X))⁻¹
        fi
        D(X) ← (W₁(X)^{bₗ+1} · W₂(X))⁻¹ · D(X)
        l ← l + 1                        # proceed with next bit of plaintext
    od
    return b₁ … b_{l-1}
end
```

The next example demonstrates that this simple procedure can indeed be applied successfully to the cryptosystem under consideration:

Example 3. Setting

$$V_1 := \begin{pmatrix} -1 & -3 \\ 0 & -1 \end{pmatrix}$$

$$V_2 := \begin{pmatrix} 1 & 0 \\ 2 & 1 \end{pmatrix}$$

$$F_1 := \begin{pmatrix} -X^2 + 2X + 3 & -X^4 + 4X^3 + X^2 - 10X - 7 \\ -X^2 + 2X + 4 & -X^4 + 4X^3 + 2X^2 - 12X - 9 \end{pmatrix}$$

$$F_2 := \begin{pmatrix} 5X^2 - 10X - 19 & 5X^2 - 10X - 20 \\ 5X^2 - 10X - 18 & 5X^2 - 10X - 19 \end{pmatrix}$$

$$M := \begin{pmatrix} -5 & 2 \\ 1 & 4 \end{pmatrix}$$

we obtain $F_1(\sqrt{5} + 1) = V_1$, $F_2(\sqrt{5} + 1) = V_2$, and the public key computes to

$$W_1(X) := \frac{1}{11} \cdot \begin{pmatrix} X^4 - 4X^3 - 5X^2 + 18X + 15 & 4X^4 - 16X^3 + 2X^2 + 28X + 16 \\ -3X^4 + 12X^3 + \frac{41}{2}X^2 - 65X - \frac{167}{2} & -12X^4 + 48X^3 + 16X^2 - 128X - 81 \end{pmatrix}$$

$$W_2(X) := \frac{1}{11} \cdot \begin{pmatrix} 20X^2 - 40X - 79 & -30X^2 + 60X + 124 \\ -60X^2 + 120X + 215 & 90X^2 - 180X - 339 \end{pmatrix}.$$

Encrypting the bitstring corresponding to the ASCII representation of the text "This is the plaintext." (176 bit) with this public key according to the encryption rule (1) yields a matrix $C(X)$ whose entries are (dense) polynomials of degree 1366. By means of Procedure 2 we can recover the plaintext from $C(X)$ within a few minutes—without requiring the private key $(M, \sqrt{5} + 1)$.

In summary, we conclude that the public key cryptosystem suggested in [4] in the present form is not secure, as no possibility for constructing public keys which are immune to the described attacks is provided.

4   Attacking Another Cryptosystem Using the Modular Group

At ACISP'99 A. Yamamura suggested another public key cryptosystem using the modular group which has some similarity with the system considered above. For a full description of this system we refer to the original paper [5]. Here we only recall the aspects of the system which are relevant for the attack described below: as in the cryptosystem of [4], for constructing a public key one starts by choosing appropriate matrices $V_1, V_2 \in \mathrm{SL}_2(\mathbb{Z})$. Moreover, a suitable complex number $p \in \mathbb{C}$ and some non-singular matrix $M \in \mathrm{GL}_2(\mathbb{R})$ have to be chosen. Then the two matrices

$$W_1 := M^{-1} \cdot V_1 \cdot M \in \mathrm{SL}_2(\mathbb{R}), \quad W_2 := M^{-1} \cdot V_2 \cdot M_2 \in \mathrm{SL}_2(\mathbb{R})$$

and the complex number p are made public. To encrypt the bitstring $b_1 \ldots b_n \in \{0,1\}^*$ with the public key one starts by computing the matrix product $C := \prod_{i=1}^{n}(W_{b_i+1}) \in \mathrm{SL}_2(\mathbb{R})$. Then the ciphertext c is given by the complex number

$$c := \frac{C_{1,1} \cdot p + C_{1,2}}{C_{2,1} \cdot p + C_{2,2}}.$$

Equivalently, we can also start by computing

$$c_n := \frac{W_{b_n+1_{1,1}} \cdot p + W_{b_n+1_{1,2}}}{W_{b_n+1_{2,1}} \cdot p + W_{b_n+1_{2,2}}}$$

$$c_{n-1} := \frac{W_{b_{n-1}+1_{1,1}} \cdot c_n + W_{b_{n-1}+1_{1,2}}}{W_{b_{n-1}+1_{2,1}} \cdot c_n + W_{b_{n-1}+1_{2,2}}}$$

$$\vdots$$

and continue in this way until we finally obtain the ciphertext

$$c = c_1 := \frac{W_{b_1+1_{1,1}} \cdot c_2 + W_{b_1+1_{1,2}}}{W_{b_1+1_{2,1}} \cdot c_2 + W_{b_1+1_{2,2}}}.$$

Now the question arises whether we can recover the plaintext $b_1 \ldots b_n \in \{0,1\}^*$ efficiently from the ciphertext c and the public data alone. As all the matrices involved are contained in $\mathrm{SL}_2(\mathbb{R})$ it seems worthwhile to have a look at Procedure 2 again. The essential idea in this procedure was to exploit the message expansion occurring during encryption. To measure this expansion we used the number of terms occurring in the matrix. In the cryptosystem from [5] there is a similar phenomenon: for a long plaintext we expect the matrix C resp. the resulting ciphertext c to be "more complicated" than for a short plaintext.

In order to define a suitable measure of complexity (in analogy to the number of terms used above) it is helpful to have some information about the possible coefficients which can occur—for computational reasons it is not practical to consider coefficients which are arbitrary real or complex numbers. Motivated by the discussion in the last section of [5] here we will restrict our attention to the case that all the real numbers occurring are contained in some number field $\mathbb{Q}(\alpha) = \mathbb{Q}[\alpha]$ already. Hence, we can express each element $\eta \in \mathbb{Q}[\alpha]$ uniquely in the form $\eta = \sum_{i=0}^{r} a_i \cdot \alpha^i$ where $a_0, \ldots, a_r \in \mathbb{Q}$ and $\alpha^0, \ldots, \alpha^r$ is a vector space basis of $\mathbb{Q}[\alpha]$ over $\mathbb{Q}$.

Using this representation we can regard the number of binary digits required for expressing the absolute value of the occurring numerators resp. denominators as a measure for the "complexity" of the number η. This motivates the following procedure:

Procedure 3

In: *Public data* (W_1, W_2, p) *with* $W_1, W_2 \in \mathrm{SL}_2(\mathbb{Q}[\alpha])$ *and* $p \in \mathbb{Q}[\alpha]$
   Ciphertext $c = \frac{C_{1,1} \cdot p + C_{1,2}}{C_{2,1} \cdot p + C_{2,2}}$ *where* $C = \prod_{i=1}^{n} W_{b_i + 1}$
Out: $\perp$ *or the plaintext* $b_1 \ldots b_n$

```
begin
    d ← c                                    # partially decrypted ciphertext
    l ← 1                          # number of plaintext bit to be processed next
    while d ≠ p do                            # decryption still incomplete
        D ← W₁⁻¹          # "complexity" if left-most bit is assumed to be 0
        a₀ + a₁·α + ... + aᵣ·αʳ ← (D₁,₁·d+D₁,₂)/(D₂,₁·d+D₂,₂)
        n₀ ← ∑(aᵢ≠0) log₂|Numerator(aᵢ)·Denominator(aᵢ)|
        D ← W₂⁻¹          # "complexity" if left-most bit is assumed to be 1
        a₀ + a₁·α + ... + aᵣ·αʳ ← (D₁,₁·d+D₁,₂)/(D₂,₁·d+D₂,₂)
        n₁ ← ∑(aᵢ≠0) log₂|Numerator(aᵢ)·Denominator(aᵢ)|
        if n₀ < n₁                            # Should left-most bit be reset?
            then (bₗ, D) ← (0, W₁⁻¹)          # yes → strip off W₁⁻¹
            else (bₗ, D) ← (1, W₂⁻¹)          # no → strip off W₂⁻¹
        fi
        d ← (D₁,₁·d+D₁,₂)/(D₂,₁·d+D₂,₂)
        l ← l + 1                             # proceed with next bit of plaintext
    od
    return b₁ ... bₗ₋₁
end
```

To check the relevance of Procedure 3 we apply it to some examples:

Example 4. Setting

$$V_1 := \begin{pmatrix} -1 & 0 \\ 123 & -1 \end{pmatrix}$$

$$V_2 := \begin{pmatrix} -1 & 321 \\ 0 & -1 \end{pmatrix}$$

$$M := \begin{pmatrix} 1 & 3 \\ 2 & -1 \end{pmatrix}$$

$$p := -\frac{9}{5} \cdot \left(\zeta_7^5 + \zeta_7^4 + \zeta_7^3 + \zeta_7^2 + \zeta_7 + \frac{13}{9} \right)$$

(where ζ_7 is a primitive 7-th root of unity) the public matrices W_1, W_2 compute to

$$W_1 = \frac{1}{7} \cdot \begin{pmatrix} 362 & 1107 \\ -123 & -376 \end{pmatrix}$$

$$W_2 = \frac{1}{7} \cdot \begin{pmatrix} 635 & -321 \\ 1284 & -649 \end{pmatrix}.$$

Encrypting the bitstring corresponding to the ASCII representation of "Yet another plaintext ..." (200 bit) with these parameters yields a ciphertext c, and by applying Procedure 3 to c we obtain the correct plaintext within a few minutes.

Example 5. Setting

$$V_1 := \begin{pmatrix} 1 & 0 \\ -32 & 1 \end{pmatrix}$$

$$V_2 := \begin{pmatrix} -1 & 11 \\ 0 & -1 \end{pmatrix}$$

$$M := \begin{pmatrix} 3 & 2 \\ -\sqrt{-11} & 1 \end{pmatrix}$$

$$p := -\frac{1}{10} \cdot \sqrt{-11} + \frac{12}{5}$$

the public matrices W_1, W_2 compute to

$$W_1 = \frac{1}{53} \cdot \begin{pmatrix} -384 \cdot \sqrt{-11} + 629 & -256 \cdot \sqrt{-11} + 384 \\ 576 \cdot \sqrt{-11} - 864 & 384 \cdot \sqrt{-11} - 523 \end{pmatrix}$$

$$W_2 = \frac{1}{53} \cdot \begin{pmatrix} -33 \cdot \sqrt{-11} - 295 & -22 \cdot \sqrt{-11} + 33 \\ -242 \cdot \sqrt{-11} + 363 & 33 \cdot \sqrt{-11} + 189 \end{pmatrix}.$$

Encrypting the bitstring corresponding to the ASCII representation of "Unfortunately, it is not necessary to know the private key for reading this." (608 bit) with these parameters yields a ciphertext c. Applying Procedure 3 to c yields the correct plaintext within a few seconds.

Analogously as in the previous section, one may think of elaborating the approach taken in Procedure 3 by overriding the decision for certain plaintext bits in the while-loop—e. g., based on the part of the plaintext which has been recovered already. However, the above examples illustrate that already this crude variant works quite well.

5   Related Work and Conclusions

It is worth mentioning that the attacks described in this paper are somewhat reminiscent of a property of the $\mathrm{SL}_2(\mathbb{F}_{2^n})$ hashing scheme of J.-P. Tillich and

G. Zémor [3]. In the latter the hash value of a bitstring is given by a matrix in $SL_2(\mathbb{F}_{2^n})$, and similarly as above for very short bitstrings it is possible to recover the original bitstring from its hash value "bit by bit" (cf. [2, Proposition 2]).

The reason for the vulnerability of the cryptosystems in [4,5] to this kind of attack is the possibility to exploit the message expansion occurring in both of these cryptosystems. Consequently, as the given specifications do not rule out such an attack we conclude that in the present form the public key cryptosystems described in [4,5] must be considered as insecure.

Acknowledgements

The author is indebted to Willi Geiselmann and Markus Grassl for various fruitful discussions and helpful comments.

References

1. W. BOSMA, J. CANNON, AND C. PLAYOUST, *The Magma Algebra System I: The User Language*, Journal of Symbolic Computation, 24 (1997), pp. 235–265.
2. R. STEINWANDT, M. GRASSL, W. GEISELMANN, AND T. BETH, *Weaknesses in the $SL_2(\mathbb{F}_{2^n})$ Hashing Scheme*, in Advances in Cryptology – CRYPTO 2000 Proceedings, M. Bellare, ed., vol. 1880 of Lecture Notes in Computer Science, Springer, 2000, pp. 287–299.
3. J.-P. TILLICH AND G. ZÉMOR, *Hashing with SL_2*, in Advances in Cryptology – CRYPTO '94, Y. Desmedt, ed., vol. 839 of Lecture Notes in Computer Science, 1994, pp. 40–49.
4. A. YAMAMURA, *Public-Key Cryptosystems Using the Modular Group*, in Public Key Cryptography; First International Workshop on Practice and Theory in Public Key Cryptography, PKC '98, H. Imai and Y. Zheng, eds., vol. 1431 of Lecture Notes in Computer Science, Berlin; Heidelberg, 1998, Springer, pp. 203–216.
5. ———, *A Functional Cryptosystem Using a Group Action*, in Information Security and Privacy; 4th Australasian Conference, ACISP'99, J. Pieprzyk, R. Safavi-Naini, and J. Seberry, eds., vol. 1587 of Lecture Notes in Computer Science, Berlin; Heidelberg, 1999, Springer, pp. 314–325.

Efficient Revocation in Group Signatures

Emmanuel Bresson and Jacques Stern

Ecole Normale Supérieure, 45 rue d'Ulm, 75230, Paris, France
{Emmanuel.Bresson,Jacques.Stern}@ens.fr

Abstract. We consider the problem of revocation of identity in group signatures. Group signatures are a very useful primitive in cryptography, allowing a member of a group to sign messages anonymously on behalf of the group. Such signatures must be anonymous and unlinkable, but a group authority must be able to open them in case of dispute. Many constructions have been proposed, some of them are quite efficient. However, a recurrent problem remains concerning revocation of group members. When misusing anonymity, a cheating member must be revoked by the authority, making him unable to sign in the future, but without sacrifying the security of past group signatures. No satisfactory solution has been given to completely solve this problem. In this paper, we provide the first solution to achieve such action for the Camenish-Stadler [6] scheme. Our solution is efficient provided the number of revoked members remains small.

1 Introduction

1.1 Overview of Group Signatures

Digital signatures are becoming a fact of life. They are used in more and more products and protocols and one can find a large amount of literature dealing with their applications, variants and security [12,1,2]. Group signatures were first introduced in 1991 by Chaum and Van Heyst [8]. This recent concept is linked (at least originally) with applications to electronic cash. It tries to combine security (no framing, no cheating) and privacy (anonymity, unlinkability). These two constraints have recently motivated much work and many publications, to make such protocols more realistic and efficient.

A digital group signature scheme deals with a group, possibly a dynamic one, whose users are called *players* (or simply *members*) and most of the time a *group center* (also called *group leader*), who is the authority with ability to "open" a signature in case of later dispute, and to reveal the identity of the actual signer. The underlying group structure is said to be *dynamic* if the number of users can increase by registering and adding new members.

1.2 Previous Work

The concept of group signatures was introduced in 1991 in [8]. That paper proposed four different group signature schemes. The first one provided unconditional anonymity, and the others provided computational anonymity only. However, adding new members was not always possible, and in some schemes, the

K. Kim (Ed.): PKC 2001, LNCS 1992, pp. 190–206, 2001.

leader needed to contact group members in order to open a group signature. See [8] and [13] for a comparison of these schemes.

At Eurocrypt'94, Chen and Pedersen proposed two new schemes, based on undeniable signatures [9]. They used proofs of knowledge of discrete logarithm to build group signatures: proving the knowledge of a discrete logarithm within a collection, without revealing which one is known, corresponds to the requirements of a group signature: proving membership without revealing individual's identity.

Unfortunately, all the above schemes were relatively inefficient due to a growth of the signature size linear with respect to the number of group members. A solution has been proposed by Camenish and Stadler in 1997 [6]. Their scheme provides a constant-size signature a well as a constant-size group public key. The tools they used to build such a scheme are an ordinary digital signature scheme, a probabilistic semantically secure encryption scheme and a one-way function. We recall the description and the functioning on this scheme in section 3.

1.3 Functioning and Security

We now give a more formal definition of a group signature scheme, as well as the related security requirements.

A group signature scheme allows members to sign on behalf of the group. That is, any user (not necessarily a member) should be able to verify that the message has been signed by an authorized member of the group (i.e. a registered member). However, the verifier should learn no information on which member actually signed the message. Moreover, the signatures must be unlinkable, that is, deciding whether two different signatures have been produced by the same person must be (computationaly) infeasible. In case of dispute, the verifier can interact with the group leader to get the real identity of the actual signer.

More formally, a group signature scheme consists of the following algorithms:

- SETUP: a probabilistic algorithm initializing public parameters and providing a secret key to the group leader.
- JOIN: an interactive protocol between the group center and a user becoming a group member. This protocol provides a secret key and a membership key to the new member, and registers his identity.
- SIGN: a probabilistic algorithm, computing from a message m and a member's secrets s a group signature σ.
- VERIF: an algorithm, run by any user, which checks that a signature σ has been produced by an authorized signer.
- OPEN: an algorithm allowing the group leader to obtain the identity of the member who actually signed a given message.

These algorithms are considered in the case of dynamic group. Otherwise, there is no JOIN algorithm, and each member receives his keys in the SETUP algorithm. Note that there exist many variants of group signatures (see [14,13,15,5,3]). Depending on what additional properties are proposed, we could find corresponding variants in the algorithms.

The following conditions must hold for a group signature scheme:

- **Correctness:** Any signature generated by a registered group member is valid.
- **Unforgeability:** Only registered members are able to sign messages.
- **Anonymity** (or untraceability): Identifying the signer of a given signature is computationally hard, except for the group manager.
- **Unlinkability:** Deciding whether two signatures were generated by the same member is computationally hard.
- **Traceability:** Any fairly-generated signature can be opened by the group leader in order to identify the actual signer.
- **Exculpability** (or unforgeability of tracing, or no framing): No coalition of members nor the group leader can sign on behalf of other members, which means that they cannot compute a signature that can be associated to another group member.
- **Coalition-resistance** (or unavoidable traceability): No coalition of members can prevent a group signature from being opened. A scheme offering provable security against coalition resistance was proposed in [1]

One critical point in group signatures is the efficiency of the algorithms. In particular, one wants to avoid the group public key or the signature size to be linear in the number of group members. This is especially true in very large group as well as very dynamic ones. Efficiency of SIGN and VERIF algorithms is also important.

1.4   Motivation of Our Work

Revocation in group signatures is a very delicate problem. In a paper by Ateniese and Tsudik [3], some critical points are put forth: coalition-resistance and member deletion. In this paper, we concentrate on the second one.

In some cases, it can be useful to *delete* members from a group. This can be necessary for many reasons (cheating from the said member, e.g.), and one does not want to change the group public key as well. Revocation of a member should prevent him from generating valid group signatures in the future. At the same time, one generally wants to preserve his past signatures, that is, keeping them indistinguishable from others signatures, unlinkable, openable, etc. The difficulty encountered can be stated as follows. On the one hand, in order to preserve anonymity, group signatures must not need to be opened when checking the legitimity of the signer: verifying that the actual signer is not a revoked member must be feasible by anybody, in a public manner and without the help of the group leader. The verifier must learn nothing about the signer but the fact he is not a deleted member. On the other hand, in order to preserve anonymity and unlinkability of **past** signatures, we require that no private information (who could help somebody to link signatures) concerning revoked members be published. Of course, the guarantee of opening signatures in case of conflict remains.

Our paper is organized as follows. In section 2, we describe the basic tools used in the Camenish/Stadler scheme, this later being exposed in section 3.

In section 4, we explain our technique to achieve revocation of members in that scheme. We propose a solution efficient if the number of deleted member is small, the size of the group signature growing linearly with that number. Finally, we discuss the security of the scheme and conclude.

2   Signatures of Knowledge

Many group signature schemes use the notion of *signature of knowledge*. This cryptographic tool allows one party to prove the knowledge of a secret value, without revealing any information on it. Such tools are zero-knowledge proofs of knowledge and minimum-disclosure proofs. The notion of signature of knowledge is based (originally) on the Schnorr digital signature scheme [16]. We call them signature of knowledge instead of proofs of knowledge to avoid confusion with zero-knowledge proofs while reminding the fact they are based on signature schemes (being message-dependent). Let us review the most important signatures of knowledge one can find in the area of group signatures.

In the following sections, we will denote by Greek letters the values whose knowledge is proven and by Latin or any other symbol the elements that are publicly known. We consider a cyclic group G, of order n (where n is an RSA modulus) and a random element g generating G. We consider also a hash function $\mathcal{H}$ from $\{0,1\}^*$ to $\{0,1\}^k$ (k being typically equal to 160). All security notions are considered in the Random Oracle model [4].

2.1   Knowledge of a Discrete Logarithm

Given an element $y \in G$, a signature of knowledge of the discrete logarithm of y to the base g on the message m is a pair $(c,s) \in \{0,1\}^k \times \mathbb{Z}_n^*$ satisfying:

$$c = \mathcal{H}(m\|y\|g\|g^s y^c)$$

This signature is denoted by:

$$SKLOG[\alpha : y = g^\alpha](m)$$

Suh a pair can be computed by a prover who knows the secret value x (such that $y = g^x$ holds) as follows: first choose a random value $r \in \mathbb{Z}_n$ and compute c as $c := \mathcal{H}(m\|y\|g\|g^r)$. Knowing x, it is possible to compute $s := r - xc$.

2.2   Knowledge of a Representation

Consider another element $h \in G$ whose discrete logarithm to the base g is unknown. Given an element $y \in G$, a signature of knowledge of a representation of y to the bases g and h on the message m is a tuple $(c,s_1,s_2) \in \{0,1\}^k \times \mathbb{Z}_n^{*2}$ satisfying:

$$c = \mathcal{H}(m\|y\|g\|h\|g^{s_1} h^{s_2} y^c)$$

Such a tuple is denoted by:

$$SKREP[\alpha, \beta : y = g^{\alpha} h^{\beta}](m)$$

A prover who knows a representation (x_1, x_2) of y to the bases g and h can compute an accepting tuple as follows: at first, choose two random numbers $r_i \in \mathbb{Z}_n$, $i = 1, 2$ and compute $c = \mathcal{H}(m\|y\|g\|h\|g^{r_1} h^{r_2})$. Then, the values s_i can be constructed as $s_i = r_i - x_i c$, $i = 1, 2$. This construction can easily be extended to more than one element and two bases [6].

2.3   Knowledge of Roots of Representation

Such signatures are used to prove that one knows the e-th root of a part of a representation. That is, given an element $y \in G$, one wants to prove knowledge of a pair (α, β) such that the equation $y = h^{\alpha} g^{\beta^e}$ holds. Such proofs have been proposed by Camenish and Stadler in [6]. They can be used to improve efficiency of signature of knowledge for double discrete logarithm and roots of discrete logarithms, these proofs being bit-to-bit process and then quite inefficient. See [6] for further details.

Given an element $y \in G$ and an small integer e, a signature of knowledge of the e-th root of the g-part of the representation of y to the bases g and h on the message m, consists in an $(e-1)$-tuple $(y_1, \ldots, y_{e-1}) \in G^{e-1}$ and a signature of knowledge of representation of $(y_1, \ldots, y_{e-1}, y)$ to the bases $\{h, g\}, \{h, y_1\}, \ldots, \{h, y_{e-1}\}$ respectively. More precisely, the latter signature of knowledge is:

$$SKREP[\gamma_1, \ldots, \gamma_e, \delta : y_1 = h^{\gamma_1} g^{\delta} \quad \wedge \quad y_2 = h^{\gamma_2} y_1^{\delta} \quad \wedge \quad \cdots$$
$$\wedge \quad y_{e-1} = h^{\gamma_{e-1}} y_{e-2}^{\delta} \quad \wedge \quad y = h^{\gamma_e} y_{e-1}^{\delta}](m)$$

where $\wedge$ is a conjunction's symbol. This means that all relations specified within square brakets [..] are proven. Note that there exist proofs of knowledge for disjunctive relations or more complicated statements.

Knowing secret values a and b such that $y = h^a g^{b^e}$, one can efficiently compute the desired signature. With randomly chosen numbers r_i, for $i = 1, \ldots, e-1$, first calculate the $(e-1)$-tuple: $y_i := h^{r_i} g^{b^i}$. According to the above equations, by identifying the representations of each y_i to the bases h and y_{i-1}, we actually have: $\gamma_1 = r_1$, $\gamma_i = r_i - b r_{i-1}$ for $i = 2, \ldots, e-1$, $\gamma_e = a - b r_{e-1}$ and $\delta = b$. The sub-signature of representation is as follows: c is computed as

$$c = \mathcal{H}(m\|g\|h\|y_1\|\cdots\|y_{e-1}\|h^{t_1} g^d\|h^{t_2} y_1^d\|\cdots\|h^{t_e} v_{e-1}^d)$$

where $t_1, \ldots, t_e, d$ are random numbers in $\mathbb{Z}_n$. Then "answers" are computed as usual:

$$s_1 = t_1 - c\gamma_1$$
$$s_2 = t_2 - c\gamma_2$$
$$\cdots$$

$$s_e = t_e - c\gamma_e$$
$$s_d = d - c\delta$$

This signature of knowledge of a representation of $(y_1, y_2, \ldots, y_{e-1}, y)$ to the respective bases $\{h, g\}, \{h, y_1\}, \ldots, \{h, y_{e-1}\}$ consists in the tuple $(c, s_1, \ldots, s_e, s_d)$ and is checked by verifying the following equation:

$$c = \mathcal{H}(m\|g\|h\|y_1\| \cdots \|y_{e-1}\|y_1^c h^{s_1} g^{s-d}\|y_2^c h^{s_2} y_1^{s_d}\| \cdots \|y^c h^{s_e} y_{e-1}^{s_d})$$

The global signature is denoted by:

$$SKROOTREP[\alpha, \beta : y = h^\alpha g^{\beta^e}](m)$$

The following equations show what is checked by the verifier:

$$y_1 = h^{\gamma_1} g^\delta$$
$$y_2 = h^{\gamma_2} y_1^\delta \quad = h^{\gamma_2 + \gamma_1 \delta} g^{\delta^2}$$
$$y_3 = h^{\gamma_3} y_2^\delta \quad = h^{\gamma_3 + \gamma_2 \delta + \gamma_1 \delta^2} g^{\delta^3}$$
$$\cdots = \cdots$$
$$y = h^{\gamma_e} y_{e-1}^\delta = h^{\gamma_e + \cdots + \gamma_2 \delta^{e-2} + \gamma_1 \delta^{e-1}} g^{\delta^e}$$

Hence, y is actually of the form $h^\alpha g^{\beta^e}$, where α and β are proven to be known by the signer.

2.4   Knowledge of Roots of Discrete Logarithms

We can use the previous tool to construct efficient signature of knowledge of roots of discrete logarithm. Given an element $y \in G$, an small integer e and two generators g and h of G (such that the discrete logarithm of h to the base g is unknown), a signature of knowledge of the e-th root of the discrete logarithm of y to the base g on the message m consists of two signatures:

$$SKREP[\delta : y = g^\delta](m) \quad \text{and} \quad SKROOTREP[\alpha, \beta : y = h^\alpha g^{\beta^e}](m)$$

Such a proof is checked by verifying the correctness of the two underlying signatures. Since the prover can know at most one representation of y to the bases g and h (otherwise, he would be able to compute $\log_g h$), it follows that: $\alpha \equiv 0 \pmod{n}$ and $\delta \equiv \beta^e \pmod{n}$. Hence the verifier must be convinced that the prover knows a e-th root of the discrete logarithm of y to the base g.

Such a signature is denoted:

$$SKROOTLOG[\eta : y = g^{\eta^e}](m)$$

3   Group Signatures by Camenish and Stadler

3.1   System Overview

The system parameters are chosen as follows by the group manager during the setup procedure:

- n is an RSA modulus; e_1 and e_2 are two public RSA exponents (and thus relatively prime to $\varphi(n)$).
- $G = \langle g \rangle$ is a cyclic group generated by g of order n.
- $h \in G$ is an element whose discrete logarithm to the base g is unknown.
- f_1 and f_2 are two elements in $\mathbb{Z}_n \setminus \{0, 1\}$.
- $R = h^w$, for a randomly chosen $w \in \mathbb{Z}_n$ is the manager's public key.

The group leader should keep secret the factorization of n as well as the value of w. All others parameters are public and consitute the group's public key.

Security hypothesis. System parameters should be chosen in such a way that the following conditions hold (see in 5 the proof of security).

- Computing discrete logarithm to the base g should be infeasible in G. This can be achieved by choosing for G a subgroup of $\mathbb{Z}_p^*$, where p is a prime number and $n|(p-1)$.
- The discrete logarithm of h to the base g is unknown (and hard to compute).
- Both e_1-th and e_2-th roots of f_1 as well as those of f_2 are unknown (and hard to compute without the factorization of n).

3.2   Member Registration

Consider a user Alice who wants to become a member of the group. She first has to compute her *membership key*: she chooses a random number $x \in \mathbb{Z}_n^*$. Let $y = x^{e_1} \pmod{n}$. Alice keeps y and x secret as the private parts of her membership key. Then Alice computes $z = g^y$ and publishes it together with her identity. This is the public part of her membership key.

Alice must then register these values to the group manager in order to get a *membership certificate*. She cannot send y to the group manager, otherwise he could forge Alice's signatures as he wants. Thus she sends z, a blinded value of y and a proof that this value actually blinds a well-formed membership key. In order to do that, Alice computes:

$$\tilde{y} := r^{e_2}(f_1 y + f_2) \pmod{n} \quad \text{for } r \in_R \mathbb{Z}_n^*$$
$$U := SKROOTLOG[\alpha : z = g^{\alpha^{e_1}}](\text{` '})$$
$$V := SKROOTLOG[\beta : g^{\tilde{y}} = (z^{f_1} g^{f_2})^{\beta^{e_2}}](\text{` '})$$

and sends $z, \tilde{y}, U, V$ to the manager. If both U and V are correct, the latter should be convinced that $\tilde{y}$ actually blinds a correct membership key, contained in the value z (α and β proving indeed the knowledge of x and r respectively). Then the manager computes a blinded version of the membership certificate as:

$$\tilde{v} := \tilde{y}^{1/e_2} \pmod{n}$$

The (unblinded) membership certificate is

$$v = \tilde{v}/r = (f_1 y + f_2)^{1/e_2}$$

A possible choice for parameters is suggested in [6]: $e_1 = 5, e_2 = 3, f_1 = 1, f_2$ is such that 3rd root is hard to compute. It seems to be difficult to find some tuples (x, v) such that $v^{e_2} = f_1 x^{e_1} + f_2$ holds, without knowing the factorisation of n. This assumption is used in the proof of security of our scheme 5.1.

3.3   Signing Messages

To sign a message m, Alice basically computes, dependent on m, signatures of knowledge proving that she is a registered member (this allows the signature to be verified). At the same time, she encrypts her membership key z with respect to the group manager's public key (this allows the signature to be opened). To this aim, Alice chooses a random number $r \in \mathbb{Z}_n^*$ and sends the following five elements as the signature of m:

$$\tilde{z} := h^r g^y$$
$$d := R^r$$
$$V_1 := SKROOTREP[\alpha, \beta : \tilde{z} = h^\alpha g^{\beta^{e_1}}](m)$$
$$V_2 := SKROOTREP[\gamma, \delta : \tilde{z}^{f_1} g^{f_2} = h^\gamma g^{\delta^{e_2}}](m)$$
$$V_3 := SKREP[\epsilon, \zeta : d = R^\epsilon \quad \wedge \quad \tilde{z} = h^\epsilon g^\zeta](m)$$

The correctness of the group signature is the conjunction of the correctness of V_1, V_2 and V_3. Indeed, considering V_1 together with V_2, and assuming that Alice can know at most one representation of $\tilde{z}^{f_1} g^{f_2}$ to the bases g and h, the verifier is convinced that:

$$\gamma = \alpha f_1 \pmod{n} \quad \text{and} \quad \delta^{e_2} = f_1 \beta^{e_1} + f_2 \pmod{n}$$

The second equation proves that Alice knows a valid membership certificate $v = \delta$ whose related secret membership key is $x = \beta$. Now considering V_3, it proves that the same random number is used in the computation of $\tilde{z}$ and d. Therefore $(d, \tilde{z})$ is an El-Gamal encryption of $z = g^y$ with respect to the leader's public key (h, R) (the secret key being actually $1/w$ rather than w). If V_3 is correct, the encryption is well-formed, ensuring that the signature can be opened if necessary.

3.4   Opening Signatures

As just said, the opening of signature consists of the decryption of $(d, \tilde{z})$ as an ElGamal ciphertext. By computing $\hat{z} = \tilde{z}/d^{1/w}$, the group center obtains the public membership key z of the actual signer. To prove such a fact, he can produce a signature of knowledge of the representation of $\tilde{z}, h$ to the bases $\{z, d\}, \{R\}$ respectively, that is:

$$SKREP[\omega : \tilde{z} = zd^\omega \quad \wedge \quad h = R^\omega](`\ ')$$

where ω holds for $1/w$.

4   Achieving Revocation of Identity

4.1   Introduction

Revocation of identities (or members deletion) is a very delicate problem. Ateniese and Tsudik [3] have suggested that Certificate Revocation Lists (CRLs) is not an appropriate method for group structures. They invoked the following reasons: firstly, since group signatures are based on anonymous and unlinkable mechanisms, the fact that a given signature was made (illegally) by a revoked member can be only proven by the group manager, by opening the signature. This is surely not practical. Secondly, if the group center reveals some informations or secret values concerning a revoked member, in order to immediately detect possible further cheating, how can the anonymity and unlinkability of his past signatures be preserved? Thirdly, decision of changing the group's public-key is clearly not desirable in very large groups, or in groups with frequent membership changes.

4.2   Our Approach

In this section, we propose a solution to delete members from a group without leaking any information about their past signatures. In case of member deletion, the group manager would issue a list of identities (public membership keys "z") and would certify them as being deleted (for instance by signing the list). Any user could continue to sign if he is able to prove, in a zero-knowledge way, that his membership key contained in the signature is not present in the revocation list. It is clear that, while releasing only public informations, the process leaks no extra information and thus does not compromise the past signatures of the deleted members. The drawback is that signature size will grow linearly with respect to the number of members deleted. Providing a constant-size revocation mechanism remains an open and interesting challenge.

4.3   Proving a Non-encryption of a Given Value

We show here how to prove that the encrypted value in an ElGamal ciphertext is not equal to a particular one. More precisely, we can prove that the discrete logarithm of the plaintext is known and that the plaintext differs form a particular value. Consider the ElGamal cryptosystem in a group $H = \langle h \rangle$ of order a large prime number p, and let $y = h^x \pmod{p}$ be the public key associated with the secret key x. A message m is encrypted by $(A, B) = (h^r, y^r m)$, where r is a random number. Let $\bar{m}$ be a particular message. We now explain how the sender can publicly prove that the encrypted message m is different from a value $\bar{m}$, in the case where $m = g^u \pmod{p}$.

We propose a technique using a "witness" value. The idea is quite similar to that used by Canetti and Goldwasser. In [7], they propose a method to distribute the Cramer-Shoup cryptosystem [10]. See [7] for more details. In the context of group members revocation, we first note that the problem can be stated as follows: the signer publishes a random power of $m/\bar{m}$ as a witness together with a proof that this witness is well-constructed and that the plaintext equals the numerator of that underlying fraction, that is m. The fact that the witness value differs from 1 thus proves that the plaintext differs from $\bar{m}$. More formally, the sender computes the following values, where r and r' are random:

$$(A, B) = (h^r, y^r m) \quad : \text{the ciphertext}$$

$$t = (m/\bar{m})^{r'} \quad : \text{the witness}$$

$$V = SKREP[\alpha, \beta, \gamma, \delta : A = h^\alpha \quad \wedge \quad B = y^\alpha g^\beta$$
$$\wedge \quad A^\gamma = h^{-\delta} \quad \wedge \quad t = (B/\bar{m})^\gamma y^\delta](')$$

What does this proof show? The first two equations simply prove that the same value α is used to compute A and B, and thus that (A, B) is an encryption of $m = g^\beta$ with respect to the public key $y = h^x$. This guarantees the ciphertext is fairly computed and that the discrete logarithm of the plaintext is known. Now considering the first and third equations in the proof:

$$A = h^\alpha \quad \text{and} \quad A^\gamma = h^{-\delta},$$

we obtain, taking the discrete logarithm of A^γ to the base h:

$$\delta = -\alpha\gamma \pmod{n}$$

Replacing this value in the last equation, we get:

$$t = \left(\frac{B}{\bar{m}}\right)^\gamma y^{-\alpha\gamma} = \frac{(By^{-\alpha})^\gamma}{\bar{m}^\gamma} = \left(\frac{m}{\bar{m}}\right)^\gamma$$

Being convinced of this equality, the fact that $t \neq 1$ proves that $m \neq \bar{m}$.

4.4 Application to a Revocation Mechanism

In this paragraph, we use the previous technique to construct a revocation mechanism in the group signature scheme by Camenish and Stadler [6]. We first consider the basic case, where only one member has been revoked.

Recall how the mechanism to open group signatures works. The signer (Alice) encrypts her identity (z) according to the ElGamal scheme and with respect to the group manager public key (h, R). Thus, the manager is able to reveal her identity by decrypting this ciphertext. The signature of knowledge V_3 is used to publicly ensure that the encryption is well-formed: the ciphertext is $(d, \tilde{z})$ where $d = R^r$, $\tilde{z} = zh^r$; V_3 convinces any verifier that the same random number r is used in d and $\tilde{z}$.

Using the fact that the plaintext is Alice's identity, and thus can be written in the desired form g^{y_A}, we can apply our technique to slightly modify the proof V_3 in order to convince the verifier of the group signature that the identity of the signer, say z, differs from a publicly revoked value z_1. We also add the "witness" value t (we will have to transmit several witnesses in case of multiple revocations); other items in the group signature remain unchanged.

$$\tilde{z} := h^r g^y$$
$$d := R^r$$
$$t := (z/z_1)^{r'} \text{ for some random number } r'$$
$$V_1 := SKROOTREP[\alpha, \beta : \tilde{z} = h^\alpha g^{\beta^{e_1}}](m)$$
$$V_2 := SKROOTREP[\gamma, \delta : \tilde{z}^{f_1} g^{f_2} = h^\gamma g^{\delta^{e_2}}](m)$$
$$V_3 := SKREP[\epsilon, \zeta, \eta, \lambda : d = R^\epsilon \quad \wedge \quad \tilde{z} = h^\epsilon g^\zeta$$
$$\wedge \quad d^\eta = R^{-\lambda} \quad \wedge \quad t = (\tilde{z}/z_1)^\eta h^\lambda](m)$$

If the three proofs V_1, V_2, V_3 are correct, the verifier is convinced, as in the classical scheme, that the encryption of z is well-formed, that is $(d, \tilde{z})$ is an ElGamal encryption of z. According to V_3, the verifier can deduce as explained above:

$$\lambda = -\eta\epsilon \pmod{n}$$

And then, by replacing these value in the last equation of V_3, he obtains:

$$t = \left(\frac{\tilde{z}}{z_1}\right)^\eta h^{-\eta\epsilon} = \frac{(\tilde{z}h^{-\epsilon})^\eta}{z_1^\eta} = \left(\frac{z}{z_1}\right)^\eta$$

The verifier is convinced of the existence of a value η such that the above equation holds. Granted this, the fact that $t \neq 1$ actually proves that $z \neq z_1$. Hence, Alice is not the revoked member.

4.5   Case of Multiple Revocations

We can easily extend this feature to the scenario of multi-revocations. However, as observed above, the size of the signature will grow linearly with the number of members deleted. More precisely, the number of values t having to been transmitted will be proportional (and even equal) to the number of members revocated. On the other hand, the size of the signature of knowledge V_3 will not grow any more.

Let us consider a list $\mathcal{L}$ of l deleted members, whose identities (or public membership keys) are denoted $z_1, \ldots, z_l$. If a signer Alice wants to sign a message m while proving she is not in the list of revocated members, she will send together with $\tilde{z}$ and d the following l values:

$$t_1 = (z/z_1)^{r'}, \ldots, t_l = (z/z_l)^{r'}$$

where r' is a random number. The proofs V_1 and V_2 remain unchanged, while V_3 becomes:

$$SKREP[\epsilon, \zeta, \eta, \lambda : d = R^\epsilon \quad \wedge \quad \tilde{z} = h^\epsilon g^\zeta \quad \wedge \quad d^\eta = R^{-\lambda}$$

$$\wedge \quad t_1 = (\tilde{z}/z_1)^\eta h^\lambda \quad \wedge \; \ldots \; \wedge \quad t_l = (\tilde{z}/z_l)^\eta h^\lambda](m)$$

It is important to note that the number of "equations" in V_3 does not change the length of V_3 itself. V_3 is made of a tuple (c, s_1, s_2, s_3, s_4) corresponding to a "challenge" and four "answers" since one wants to prove the knowledge of four private values. The only data which grows when increasing the revocation list are the transmitted "witnesses" $t_1, \ldots, t_l$.

It is also important to notice that the constant size of V_3 is due to that we use the same random r' in all the witness values. We claim that this can be done without loss of security. Consider the case $l = 2$; denote $\mathcal{S} = (z_1, z_2, t_1, t_2)$, where $t_1 = (z/z_1)^r, t_2 = (z/z_2)^r$, the distribution which appears to the verifier in the scheme. It is esay to show the distribution $\mathcal{S}$ is as indistinguishable from a random distribution as the Diffie-Hellman distribution $\mathcal{D} = (g, g^a, g^r, g^{ar})$. To do so, let

$$g = \frac{z}{z_1} \quad \text{and} \quad a = \log_g \left(\frac{z}{z_2} \right)$$

Then we have: $z/z_2 = g^a$ and we can rewrite:

$$\mathcal{S} = (z_1, z_2, t_1, t_2) = (zg^{-1}, zg^{-a}, g^r, g^{ar}) \overset{c}{\approx} (g, g^a, g^r, g^{ar}) = \mathcal{D}$$

where $\overset{c}{\approx}$ stands for "computationally indistinguishable".

5 Security of the Enhanced Scheme

5.1 Correctness and Unforgeability

Verifying correctness is trivial. Since the validity of a group signature is checked by verifying the three proofs of knowledge V_1, V_2, V_3, it is obvious that a registered member of the group is able to produce valid sinatures (keep in mind that the quantities $\alpha, \beta, \gamma, \delta, \epsilon, \zeta$ represent r, x, rf_1, v, r, y respectively, as defined in section 3.3).

Unforgeability against Adaptive Chosen-Message Attacks.

We now prove that unforgeability is satisfied against an active adversary. We consider a polynomial-time bounded adversary having access to a signing oracle. A signing oracle for group signatures can be modelled as follow: the adversary makes a query to the oracle and obtains a group signature on a message of his choice. The signing oracle returns a valid group signature, which means that this later can be opened by the manager. We show that the identity revealed by such hypothetical opening does not influence our proof.

In that model, the adversary makes a polynomial number of queries to obtain adaptively some group signatures on messages of his choice. Next, the adversary tries to produce a valid group signature. We say that he is successful if he can output a message m^* and a valid group signature $(\tilde{z}^*, d^*, V_1^*, V_2^*, V_3^*)$ and if m^* was not previously queried to the signing oracle. The security of the group signature scheme states that this occurs with negligible probability.

It can be shown using standard techniques that, in the Random Oracle model, we can efficiently simulate the signing oracle used in a chosen-message attack. For instance, the signature of knowledge denoted by V_3 :

$$SKREP[\epsilon, \zeta, \eta, \lambda : d = R^\epsilon \wedge \tilde{z} = h^\epsilon g^\zeta \wedge d^\eta = R^{-\lambda} \wedge t = (\tilde{z}/z_1)^\eta h^\lambda](m)$$

is a tuple (c, s_1, s_2, s_3, s_4) satisfying:

$$c = \mathcal{H}(m\|d\|\tilde{z}\|R\|h\|g\|d^c R^{s_1}\|\tilde{z}^c h^{s_1} g^{s_2}\|d^{s_3} R^{s_4}\|t^c(\tilde{z}/z_1)^{s_3} h^{s_4})$$

Such a tuple can be simulated as follows (notice than we need the value of t to correctly simulate V_3):

SIMULATE-SKREP
1 Choose s_1, s_2, s_3, s_4, c at random
2 Define $\mathcal{H}(m\|d\|\tilde{z}\|R\|h\|g\|d^c R^{s_1}\|\tilde{z}^c h^{s_1} g^{s_2}\|d^{s_3} R^{s_4}\|t^c(\tilde{z}/z_1)^{s_3} h^{s_4}) := c$
3 **Return** c, s_1, s_2, s_3, s_4 as the signature of knowledge

Now we show the security of the scheme. Assume that, at the end of the previously described game, the adversary outputs a valid group signature

$$(\tilde{z}^*, d^*, V_1^*, V_2^*, V_3^*)$$

for which the verification algorithm outputs "Valid".

The correctness of V_1^* and V_2^* ensures that he knows four values α, β, γ and ζ such that the following equations hold:

$$\tilde{z}^* = h^\alpha g^{\beta^{e_1}} \quad , \quad \tilde{z}^{*f_1} g^{f_2} = h^\gamma g^{\delta^{e_2}}$$

which implies:

$$\tilde{z}^{*f_1} g^{f_2} = h^\gamma g^{\delta^{e_2}} = h^{\alpha f_1} g^{f_1 \beta^{e_1} + f_2}$$

Hence, we have two representations of $\tilde{z}^{*f_1} g^{f_2}$ to the bases g and h. Consequently, either the two representations are different and the adversary can compute $\log_g h$, or they are identical and we have $\gamma = \alpha f_1$, $\delta^{e_2} = f_1 \beta^{e_1} + f_2$, which means that he had computed a certificate, δ, without registering the corresponding key β. Both of these scenarios are assumed to occur with negligible probability. This concludes our proof.

5.2   Anonymity and Unlinkability

Anonymity is ensured by the security of the ElGamal scheme, that is, the hardness of computational Diffie-Hellman problem. It is easy to see that, because, since V_1, V_2, V_3 are zero-knowledge, the only information an adversary has to learn z is the encryption $(\tilde{z}, d)$ of it.

More interesting is unlinkability. We can prove that the signatures are unlinkable by using a signature distinguisher as an oracle to break the decisional Diffie-Hellman problem, or, which is equivalent, the semantic security of ElGamal scheme.

Assume we have an oracle that can distinguish two group signatures, i.e. that can win with non-negligible probability the following game: a message m and two members z_1 and z_2 are chosen. A bit b is secretly and randomly chosen. Then the group member z_b signs the message m. The resulting signature $(\tilde{z}, d, V_1, V_2, V_3)$ is given to the adversary which outputs a bit b'. He wins if $b = b'$.

We now can use such an adversary to break the semantic security of ElGamal [11]. Consider the following two algorithms:

FINDER
1 Randomly choose z_1, z_2 in G

DISTINGUISHER(A, B)
/*$(A, B) = (h^r z_b, R^r)$ is an ElGamal encryption of z_b*/
1 Randomly choose a message m
2 Randomly choose a witness $t \neq 1$
3 Simulate V_1, V_2, V_3 on the message m
4 Give $(m, A, B, t, V_1, V_2, V_3)$ to the adversary
5 **Return** b': the output of the adversary

We first run the FINDER and obtain two members z_1 and z_2. Then a bit b is randomly chosen (out of our view) and we are given an encryption of z_b by ElGamal. Using the adversary through algorithm DISTINGUISHER, we can distinguish which one of z_1 or z_2 has been ElGamal encrypted, which is the break of semantic security.

5.3   Traceability and Framing

The ability to open a group signature for the group manager is ensured by the correctness of V_3. Keep in mind that V_3 proves that the identity of the signer, z, is correctly ElGamal encrypted. Anybody can thus be sure that the group leader would be able to open the signature if asked. Combined with V_1 and V_2, this proof ensures that the revealed member is a registered one: what is shown in these signature of knowledge is the knowledge of a membership certificate corresponding to the identity encrypted. Thus, avoiding traceability is at least as hard as the computation of an unregistered certificate or the break of the underlying signatures of knowledge.

The security against a framing attack is a bit more complicated. It can be stated as follows: no coalition of members nor the group leader can compute a valid group signature which, if opened, would be associated to somebody else.

Since the validity of a signature ensures that the signer knows a membership certificate (i.e. a solution to the equation $v^{e_2} = f_1 x^{e_1} + f_2$), a framing attack is hard if the following assumption holds:

Claim. No (adaptive) coalition can compute $k + 1$ points on the curve $\mathcal{C}$: $Y^{e_2} = f_1 X^{e_1} + f_2$ when knowing only k points on it.

This assumption does not hold for every values of e_1 and e_2, f_1 and f_2. We now deal with what can be done to obtain an equivalent assumption, as well as the description of cases where the claim is false (which implies that a coalition attack is possible).

Case Where $\gcd(e_1, e_2) = 1$. First, we can note that Claim 5.3 is equivalent to a simpler version in case that e_1 and e_2 are relatively prime; in that case, there exist λ and μ such that: $\lambda e_1 + \mu e_2 = 1$. Then the equation of $\mathcal{C}$ can be rewritten:

$$Y^{e_2} = f_1^{\lambda e_1 + \mu e_2} X^{e_1} + f_2$$

$$\left(\frac{Y}{f_1^{\mu}}\right)^{e_2} = \left(f_1^{\lambda} X\right)^{e_1} + f_2 f_1^{-\mu e_2}$$

or, by changing variables,

$$Y'^{e_2} = X'^{e_1} + d , \quad \text{where } d = f_2 f_1^{-\mu e_2}$$

Thus, we just have to consider cases where $f_1 = 1$. Proving Claim 5.3 appears to be mathematically non-trivial, although it seems to be true.

Other Cases. If e_1 and e_2 are not relatively prime, a similar transformation can be performed, which modifies the values of the exponents. Let e be the greatest common divisor of e_1 and e_2, and note $e_1' = e_1/e$, $e_2' = e_2/e$. We now have $\gcd(e_1', e_2') = 1$ and we can write:

$$\begin{cases} Y' = Y^e f_1^{-\mu} \\ X' = X^e f_1^{\lambda} \end{cases}$$

$$Y'^{e_2'} = X'^{e_1'} + d' , \quad \text{where } d' = f_2 f_1^{-\mu e_2'}$$

This does not appear to be interesting, because the transformation used is non-linear.

A Framing Attack When $e_1 = e_2$. If $e_1 = e_2$ the transformation proposed above is useless. However, if $f_1 = 1$, we can show that Claim 5.3 is false. Assuming that the common value $e = e_1 = e_2$ is small, it is possible for a coalition of 2^e registered members to compute a new membership certificate without the help of the group manager.

$\textsc{Framing}(e)$
1 Choose a membership key V_0
2 $i \leftarrow 1$, $k \leftarrow 2^e$
3 **For** $i \leftarrow 1$ **to** k
4     $X_i \leftarrow V_{i-1}$
5     $V_i \leftarrow \textsc{Register}(X_i)$
6 **Return** $(V_k/2, X_1/2)$ as a new certificate

It easy to verify that such an algorithm produce new (unregistered) membership certificate. From k equations $V_i^e = X_i^e + f_2$ coming from registrations, we obtain by summation: $V_k = V_0^e + 2^e f_2$ and then:

$$\left(\frac{V_k}{2}\right)^e = \left(\frac{V_0}{2}\right)^e + f_2$$

This shows how a coalition of $k = 2^e$ members can forge a valid group signature which would be associated to an unexistent member if opened. Although such a problem can easily be avoided by carefully choosing group parameters, it is interesting to mention it as a new possible weakness of the scheme.

6   Conclusion

In this paper, we provide the first efficient solution to delete members from a group without compromising their past signatures or changing the group public key. The security of our mechanism is formally proven, as well as the underlying group signature scheme. However, obtaining members revocation with constant size signatures remains an open problem.

Acknowledgments

The authors especially thank the anonymous referees for helpful comments, including constructive remarks as well as minor corrections.

References

1. G. Ateniese, J. Camenisch, M. Joye, and G. Tsudik. A Practical and Provably Secure Coalition-Resistant Group Signature Scheme. In M. Bellare, editor, *Crypto '2000*, volume 1880 of *LNCS*, pages 255–270. Springer-Verlag, 2000.
2. G. Ateniese and G. Tsudik. Group Signature à la carte. In *10th ACM-SIAM Symposium on Discrete Algorithms (SODA)*, January 1999.
3. G. Ateniese and G. Tsudik. Some Open Issues and New Directions in Group Signature. In *Financial Cryptography '99*, 1999.
4. M. Bellare and P. Rogaway. Random Oracles are Practical: a Paradigm for Designing Efficient Protocols. In *Proc. of the 1st Annual Conf. on Computer and Communications Security*. ACM Press, 1993.
5. J. Camenish and M.Michels. A Group Signature with Improved Efficiency. In K. Ohta and D. Pei, editors, *Asiacrypt '98*, volume 1514 of *LNCS*, pages 160–174. Springer-Verlag, 1999.
6. J. Camenish and M.Stadler. Efficient Group Signatures Schemes for Large Groups. In B. Kaliski, editor, *Crypto '97*, volume 1294 of *LNCS*, pages 410–424. Springer-Verlag, 1997.
7. R. Canetti and S. Goldwasser. An Efficient Threshold PKC Secure Against Adaptive CCA. In J. Stern, editor, *Eurocrypt '99*, volume 1592 of *LNCS*, pages 90–106. Springer-Verlag, 1999.

8. D. Chaum and E. van Heyst. Group Signatures. In D.W. Davies, editor, *Eurocrypt '91*, volume 547 of *LNCS*, pages 257–265. Springer-Verlag, 1992.

9. L. Chen and T.P. Pedersen. New Group Signature Schemes. In A. De Santis, editor, *Eurocrypt '94*, volume 950 of *LNCS*, pages 171–181. Springer-Verlag, 1995.

10. R. Cramer and V. Shoup. A Practical Public-Key Cryptosystem Provably Secure against Adaptive Chosen Ciphertext Attack. In H. Krawczyk, editor, *Crypto '98*, volume 1462 of *LNCS*, pages 13–25. Springer-Verlag, 1998.

11. T. ElGamal. A Public Key Cryptosystem and a Signature Scheme Based on Discrete Logarithms. In G.R. Blakley and D. Chaum, editors, *Crypto '84*, volume 196 of *LNCS*, pages 10–18. Springer-Verlag, 1985.

12. J. Kilian and E. Petrank. Identity Escrow. In H. Krawczyk, editor, *Crypto '98*, volume 1462 of *LNCS*, pages 169–185. Springer-Verlag, 1998.

13. S. Kim, S. Park, and D. Won. Convertible Group Signatures. In S. Kim and T. Matsumoto, editors, *Asiacrypt '96*, volume 1163 of *LNCS*, pages 311–321. Springer-Verlag, 1997.

14. S. Kim, S. Park, and D. Won. Group Signatures for Hierarchical Multigroups. In *Proc. of ISW '97*, volume 1396 of *LNCS*, pages 273–281. Springer-Verlag, 1998.

15. H. Petersen. How to Convert any Digital Signature Scheme into a Group Signature Scheme. In M. Lomas and S. Vaudenay, editors, *Proc. of Security Protocols Workshop '97*, volume 1361 of *LNCS*, pages 67–78. Springer-Verlag, 1997.

16. C. P. Schnorr. Efficient Identification and Signatures for Smart Cards. In G. Brassard, editor, *Crypto '89*, volume 435 of *LNCS*, pages 239–252. Springer-Verlag, 1990.

A Public-Key Traitor Tracing Scheme with Revocation Using Dynamic Shares*

Wen-Guey Tzeng and Zhi-Jia Tzeng

Department of Computer and Information Science
National Chiao Tung University
Hsinchu, Taiwan 30050
{tzeng,zjtzeng}@cis.nctu.edu.tw

Abstract. We proposed a new public-key traitor tracing scheme with revocation capability using the dynamic share and entity revocation techniques. The enabling block of our scheme is independent of the number of subscribers, but dependent on the collusion and revocation thresholds. Each receiver holds one decryption key only. Our traitor tracing algorithm works in a black-box way and is conceptually simple. The *distinct feature* of our scheme is that when the traitors are found, we can revoke their private keys (up to some threshold z) without updating any private key of the remaining subscribers. Furthermore, we can restore the decryption privilege of a revoked private key later. We can actually increase the revocation capability beyond z with dynamic assignment of shares into the enabling block. This property makes our scheme highly practical. Previously proposed public-key traitor tracing schemes have to update all existing private keys even when revoking one private key only. Our scheme is as efficient as Boneh and Franklin's scheme in many aspects. Our traitor tracing scheme is fully k-resilient such that our traitor tracing algorithm can find all traitors if the number of them is k or less. The encryption algorithm of our scheme is semantically secure assuming that the decisional Diffie-Hellman problem is hard. We also proposed a variant traitor tracing scheme whose encryption algorithm is semantically secure against the adaptive chosen ciphertext attack assuming hardness of the decisional Diffie-Hellman problem.

Keywords: broadcast encryption, traitor tracing, revocation.

1 Introduction

A broadcast encryption scheme [10] involves a sender and multiple (authorized) receivers. The sender has an encryption key and each receiver has a decryption (private) key such that the sender can encrypt a message and broadcast the ciphertext so that only the authorized receivers can decrypt the ciphertext.

Consider a situation that a content supplier distributes some digital data to its subscribers by a broadcast channel. To protect the data from eavesdropping,

---

* Research supported in part by the National Science Council grant NSC-89-2213-E-009-180 and by the Ministry of Education grant 89-E-FA04-1-4, Taiwan, ROC.

K. Kim (Ed.): PKC 2001, LNCS 1992, pp. 207–224, 2001.

the content supplier encrypts the data and broadcast the ciphertext such that only its subscribers can decrypt the ciphertext. The content supplier gives each subscriber a decoder (decoding box) for decrypting the broadcast ciphertext. Each decoder consists of a tailored private key and a decryption program. However, a *traitor* (malicious subscriber) may clone his decoder (and the private key in it) and sell the pirate decoders for profits. The traitor may modify the private key and the decryption program in the pirate decoder to avoid leaking his identity. Furthermore, some traitors may together create a new and legal private key that cannot be traced to their creators. To deter the attack, when a pirate decoder is confiscated, the content supplier wants to reveal the private key in it and trace back to its original owners. A traitor tracing scheme is a broadcast encryption scheme with capability of dealing with the above scenario [6]. Furthermore, the content supplier may want to revoke the keys of traitors without too much work, such as, updating each subscriber's key. We focus on providing revocation capability to public-key traitor tracing schemes.

The basic technique of broadcast encryption is: first, to select a (or a set of) session key s for encrypting the broadcast data as the *cipher block* and embed the session key in the *enabling block*; then, to broadcast ⟨*enabling block, cipher block*⟩ to all subscribers. Any decoder with a legal private key can extract the session key from the enabling block and then uses the session key to decrypt the cipher block. A traitor tracing scheme tries to identify traitors by finding out the keys embedded in the confiscated pirate decoder. There are two measures for efficiency: the storage for the private key (or keys) in a decoder and the size of enabling block. Sometimes, encryption and decryption time is also considered.

The secret-key and coding approach has each decoder holding a set of keys (or codewords) such that the keys in the pirate decoder can be identified by the combinatorial methods [4,6,11,15,17,18,20]. There is a trade-off between the size of enabling block and the number of keys held by each decoder [5,14]. Generally speaking, if the number of subscribers is large, say millions, the schemes become impractical as one of the measures grows proportionally with the number of subscribers.

The public-key approach tries to have the size of enabling block independent of the number of subscribers and each decoder holding one key only [3,13]. This is achieved at the expense of tracing capability and computation time, for example only the collusion of k or less traitors can be dealt with for some threshold k. Boneh and Franklin's traitor tracing scheme is algebraic and deterministic such that k or less traitors who create a single-key pirate decoder can be traced efficiently. However, they have to embed a hidden trapdoor in the modulus so that the discrete logarithm problem over $Z_{n^2}^*$ can be solved in polynomial time.

As to other directions, Naor and Pinkas [15] proposes a threshold traitor tracing scheme that can trace the private keys in a pirate decoder if the decoder's decrypting probability is over some threshold. Fiat and Tassa's dynamic traitor tracing scheme [9] uses the watermarking technique. By observing the watermarks output by a pirate decoder on the fly, they can trace the traitors who created the pirate decoder.

Our results. We propose a new public-key traitor tracing scheme with revocation capability using the dynamic share and entity revocation techniques [2]. The enabling block of our scheme is independent of the number of subscribers, but dependent on the collusion and revocation thresholds, which are k and z, respectively. Each decoder stores only one private key. Our traitor tracing algorithm works in a black-box way and is conceptually simple. Our traitor tracing scheme is fully k-resilient, that is, our traitor tracing algorithm can find all traitors if the number of them is k or less. The encryption algorithm of our scheme is semantically secure against the passive adversary assuming hardness of the decisional Diffie-Hellman problem.

The *distinct feature* of our scheme is that when the traitors are found, we can revoke their private keys (up to z keys totally) without updating any private key of the remaining subscribers. Furthermore, we can restore a revoked private key later. We can actually increase the revocation capability beyond the threshold z with dynamic assignment of shares into the enabling block. This property makes our scheme highly practical. Previously proposed public-key traitor tracing schemes have to update all existing private keys even if revoking one private key only.

Our scheme is as efficient as Boneh and Franklin's scheme in many aspects. For example, the encryption and decryption algorithms of our scheme take $O(z)$ modular exponentiations. Our black-box tracing algorithm takes $O(n^k)$ time when $k \ll n$. Note that the encryption key of our scheme is dynamically dependent on the revoked traitors, while that Boneh and Franklin's scheme is fixed.

We also propose a variant traitor tracing scheme whose encryption algorithm is semantically secure against the adaptive chosen ciphertext attack assuming that computing the decisional Diffie-Hellman problem is hard.

Note: some of our results in this paper are independently discovered in [16] by Naor and Pinkas. Our scheme possesses traceability in addition.

2   Preliminaries

In this section we review the polynomial interpolation, the decisional Diffie-Hellman (DDH) problem and the chosen ciphertext attack and provide the definition for a traitor tracing scheme.

Polynomial interpolation. Let $f(x) = \sum_{i=0}^{z} a_i x^i$ be a polynomial of degree $z \geq 1$. Assume that each user i is given a share $(x_i, f(x_i))$. Then, a group of $z+1$ users, say users $0, 1, \dots, z$, can compute the polynomial $f(x)$ by the Lagrange interpolation method, or equivalently solving the system of equations:

$$\begin{pmatrix} 1 & x_0 & \cdots & x_0^z \\ 1 & x_1 & \cdots & x_1^z \\ \vdots & \vdots & \vdots & \vdots \\ 1 & x_z & \cdots & x_z^z \end{pmatrix} \begin{pmatrix} a_0 \\ a_1 \\ \vdots \\ a_z \end{pmatrix} = \begin{pmatrix} f(x_0) \\ f(x_1) \\ \vdots \\ f(x_z) \end{pmatrix}$$

Let $XA = F$ denote the above system of equations. If $\det(X) \neq 0$, we can solve all coefficients of $f(x)$ by $A = X^{-1}F$. The constant term a_0 is equal to the first row vector of X^{-1} multiplying F, which is

$$\sum_{t=0}^{z}\left(f(x_t)\cdot\prod_{0\le j\ne t\le z}\frac{x_j}{x_j-x_t}\right).$$

where $\lambda_t=\prod_{0\le j\ne t\le z}\frac{x_j}{x_j-x_t}, 0\le t\le z$, are the Lagrange coefficients. Furthermore, in the exponent case, if we are given $(x_0,g^{rf(x_0)})$, $(x_1,g^{rf(x_1)})$, $\ldots$, $(x_z,g^{rf(x_z)})$, we can compute

$$g^{ra_0}=\prod_{t=0}^{z}(g^{rf(x_t)})^{\lambda_t}.$$

for arbitrary r. On the other hand, if $\det(X)=0$, we cannot get any information about a_0 or g^{ra_0}.

In traitor tracing, a set of legal users may combine their shares linearly to form a new "share", which is the main threat that haunts some public-key based traitor tracing schemes [13]. For example, the legal users $z+i$ and $z+j$, $i,j\ge 1$ and $i\ne j$, can combine their shares to form a new "share"

$$(a+b, ax_{z+i}+bx_{z+j},\ldots, ax_{z+i}^z+bx_{z+j}^z, af(x_{z+i})+bf(x_{z+j})).$$

Together with the shares $(x_0,f(x_0)),(x_1,f(x_1)),\ldots,(x_{z-1},f(x_{z-1}))$, one can compute a_0 by solving the system of equations:

$$\begin{pmatrix}1 & x_0 & \cdots & x_0^z \\ 1 & x_1 & \cdots & x_1^z \\ \vdots & \vdots & \vdots & \vdots \\ 1 & x_{z-1} & \cdots & x_{z-1}^z \\ a+b & ax_{z+i}+bx_{z+j} & \cdots & ax_{z+i}^z+bx_{z+j}^z\end{pmatrix}\begin{pmatrix}a_0 \\ a_1 \\ \vdots \\ \\ a_z\end{pmatrix}=\begin{pmatrix}f(x_0) \\ f(x_1) \\ \vdots \\ f(x_{z-1}) \\ af(x_{z+i})+bf(x_{z+j})\end{pmatrix}$$

We observe that if a pirate P gets a share by linear combination of m shares of traitors $j_1, j_2,\ldots, j_m, m\le z$, then P and the traitors together cannot compute a_0, or g^{ra_0} in the exponent case. We base our traitor tracing algorithm on this observation. In our system, we give each user i a share $(x_i, f(x_i))$. If we suspect that the users $j_1, j_2,\ldots, j_m, m\le z$, are traitors, we broadcast data encrypted with the session key s, which is embedded in sg^{ra_0}, together with the shares

$$(x_{j_1},g^{rf(x_{j_1})}),\ldots,(x_{j_m},g^{rf(x_{j_m})}),(l_1,g^{rf(l_1)}),\ldots,(l_{z-m},g^{rf(l_{z-m})})$$

where $l_1, l_2,\ldots, l_{z-m}$ are arbitrarily chosen and different from $x_{j_1}, x_{j_2},\ldots, x_{j_m}$. A user who is not a traitor can compute g^{ra_0} and thus s. We confirm the traitors if the pirate decoder cannot decrypt the data properly.

Decisional Diffie-Hellman problem. Let G be a group of a large prime order q. Consider the following two distribution ensembles R and D:

- $R = (g_1, g_2, u_1, u_2) \in G^4$, where g_1 and g_2 are generators of G_q;
- $D = (g_1, g_2, u_1, u_2)$, where g_1 and g_2 are generators of G_q and $u_1 = g_1^r$ and $u_2 = g_2^r$ for $r \in Z_q$.

The DDH problem is to distinguish the distribution ensembles R and D. That is, we would like to find a probabilistic polynomial-time algorithm A such that, for some positive constant c and all sufficiently large complexity parameter n,

$$| \Pr[A(R_n) = 1] - \Pr[A(D_n) = 1] | \geq 1/n^c,$$

where R_n and D_n are the size-n distributions of R and D, respectively.

Chosen ciphertext attack. The chosen ciphertext attack on an encryption scheme works as follows. Let PK be the public key of the scheme. The probabilistic polynomial-time adversary $\mathcal{A}$ of the attack has two algorithms A_1 and A_2. A_1 takes as input PK, makes some queries to the decryption oracle adaptively, and outputs two messages m_0 and m_1. Then, the encryption oracle randomly chooses a bit d and encrypts m_d as $C = E(PK, m_d)$. A_2 takes as input PK, m_0, m_1 and C, makes some queries to the decryption oracle in an adaptive way, and outputs d'. The decryption oracle takes as an input a ciphertext C', $C' \neq C$, and returns its corresponding plaintext m'. We say that A attacks the encryption scheme successfully if the probability of $d = d'$ is $1/2 + \varepsilon$ for some non-negligible function ε, where the probability is taken over all coin tossing of d, A_1 and A_2.

Traitor tracing scheme. A traitor tracing scheme consists of the following functions.

- **System setup.** The content supplier sets up the system algorithms and related parameters.
- **Registration.** After system setup, a user (subscriber) can register to the system and get a data decoder that contains a private key specific to the subscriber. A data decoder with a legal private key can decode the data broadcast by the content supplier.
- **Encryption.** When the content supplier would like to broadcast data M, it uses the encryption algorithm E with an appropriate key s to encrypt the data as the enabling block T and the cipher block $C = E(s, M)$ such that only legal subscribers who have decoders with appropriate keys can decrypt $\langle T, C \rangle$ to get the content M.
- **Decryption.** The data decoder consists of a decryption algorithm D such that with an appropriate private key the decoder can decrypt the broadcast $\langle T, C \rangle$ to get the message.
- **Traitor tracing.** If the content supplier gets a decoder, it wants to determine who is the original owner of the private key in the decoder. It may be that some legal subscribers conspire to compute some key that is not legal, but able to decrypt, maybe with a different decryption algorithm, the broadcast data. The traitor tracing algorithm need be able to reveal the identities of the conspirators. If we trace the owner of the private key in the decoder by observing the relation between input and output of the decoder, it is called *black box* tracing.

A tracing scheme is *k-resilient* if it can find at least one traitor among the k or less traitors. It is *fully k-resilient* if it can find all of them.

Note. In order to simplify presentation, we omit the security parameter (or complexity measure) n from the related parameters. For example, when we say a probability ϵ is negligible, we mean that for any positive constant c, $\epsilon = \epsilon(n) < 1/n^c$ for large enough n. A probability δ is overwhelming if $\delta = 1 - \epsilon$ for some negligible probability ϵ.

3   Our Traitor Tracing Scheme

In this section we present our traitor tracing scheme. Let k be the maximum number of colluded subscribers (traitors) and z be the revocation threshold, ie., at most z private keys of traitors can be revoked. We set $z \geq 2k - 1$.

System setup. Let G_q be a group of a large prime order q. The content supplier selects a degree-z polynomial $f(x) = \sum_{t=0}^{z} a_t x^t \pmod{q}$ with coefficients over Z_q. $f(x)$ is the content supplier's secret key. The content supplier publishes the public key

$$\langle g, g^{a_0}, g^{f(1)}, \dots, g^{f(z)} \rangle$$

for a subscriber to verify his private key.

Registration. When a subscriber $i, i > z$, registers, the content supplier gives the subscriber i a decoder with the private key $(i, f(i))$. The subscriber i verifies whether the received key is correct by checking whether

$$g^{a_0} = \prod_{t=0}^{z} g^{f(x_t)\lambda_t}$$

where $x_0 = 1, x_1 = 2, \dots, x_{z-1} = z, x_z = i$. If it is so, the subscriber i gets a decoder with the private key $(i, f(i))$.

Encryption. The content supplier randomly selects z unused shares, which are not assigned to any subscriber,

$$(j_1, f(j_1)), (j_2, f(j_2)), \dots, (j_z, f(j_z))$$

and a one-time random number $r \in Z_q$, and computes the *enabling block*

$$T = \langle sg^{ra_0}, g^r, (j_1, g^{rf(j_1)}), (j_2, g^{rf(j_2)}), \dots, (j_z, g^{rf(j_z)}) \rangle,$$

where s is the session key of encrypting broadcast data. To broadcast message M, the content supplier broadcasts

$$E(f(x), M) = \langle T, E'(s, M) \rangle$$

where E' is a secret-key cipher, such as DES.

For every possible m-coalition $\{c_1, c_2, \ldots, c_m\}$ of the subscribers, $m \leq k$,
1. Randomly selects $z - m$ unused shares, say, $\{j_1, \ldots, j_{z-m}\}$.
2. Construct a testing message $E(f(x), M) = \langle T, E'(s, M) \rangle$, where

$$T = \langle sg^{ra_0}, g^r, (c_1, g^{rf(c_1)}), (c_2, g^{rf(c_2)}), \ldots, (c_m, g^{rf(c_m)}),$$
$$(j_1, g^{rf(j_1)}), (j_2, g^{rf(j_2)}), \ldots, (j_{z-m}, g^{rf(j_{z-m})}) \rangle.$$

3. Feed $\langle T, E'(s, M) \rangle$ to the decoder.
4. If the decoder does not output the correct data M, we set $\{c_1, c_2, \ldots, c_m\}$ as a possible set of traitors.
Output the smallest of all possible sets of traitors found in Step 4.

Fig. 1. A traitor tracing algorithm

Decryption. When receiving the broadcast data $\langle T, E'(s, M) \rangle$, the subscriber i uses T to compute s and then uses s to decrypt $E'(s, M)$ to get M. The subscriber i computes s with the equation:

$$s = sg^{ra_0} / [(g^r)^{f(i)\lambda_z} \cdot \prod_{t=0}^{z-1} (g^{rf(x_t)})^{\lambda_t}]$$

where $x_0 = j_1, x_1 = j_2, \ldots, x_{z-1} = j_z$ and $x_z = i$.

Traitor tracing. We present two black box traitor tracing algorithms. We can mix their use in tracing traitors.

Assume that m subscribers $\{c_1, c_2, \ldots, c_m\}, m \leq k$, use their shares to create a decoding key in any form. As long as the share indices $\{j_1, j_2, \ldots, j_z\}$ in the enabling block covers $\{c_1, c_2, \ldots, c_m\}$, ie., $\{c_1, c_2, \ldots, c_m\} \subseteq \{j_1, j_2, \ldots, j_z\}$, there is no way that the decoder can use the conspired key and the enabling block to decode the data assuming that computing the discrete logarithm over G_q is hard. Our first traitor tracing algorithm is based on this idea. If we suspect the subscribers $\{c_1, c_2, \ldots, c_m\}, m \leq k$, are traitors, we put their shares in the enabling block

$$\langle sg^{ra_0}, g^r, (c_1, g^{rf(c_1)}), \ldots, (c_m, g^{rf(c_m)}), (j_1, g^{rf(j_1)}), \ldots, (j_{z-m}, g^{rf(j_{z-m})}) \rangle,$$

where $j_1, j_2, \ldots, j_{z-m}$ are unused indices and different from $\{c_1, c_2, \ldots, c_m\}$. Therefore, our black box tracing algorithm is in Figure 1

Our second traitor tracing algorithm uses the opposite direction, that is, the traitors can decrypt the enabling block. If we suspect $\{c_1, c_2, \ldots, c_m\}, m \leq k$, are traitors, we find a degree-z polynomial $h(x) = \sum_{t=0}^{z} b_t x^t$ that passes points $(c_1, f(c_1)), (c_2, f(c_2)), \ldots, (c_m, f(c_m))$. $h(x)$ is significantly different from $f(x)$, ie., they share m common points only. We use $h(x)$ to create the enabling block. Let $\{j_1, j_2, \ldots, j_z\}$ be the indices other than $\{c_1, c_2, \ldots, c_m\}$. We feed $T = \langle sg^{rb_0}, g^r, (j_1, g^{rh(j_1)}), (j_2, g^{rh(j_2)}), \ldots, (j_z, g^{rh(j_z)}) \rangle$ to the decoder. Note that this enabling block is computationally indistinguishable from the one created using $f(x)$, see Lemma 1. A share index x_i that is not in $\{c_1, c_2, \ldots, c_m\}$ cannot decode the enabling block correctly. If the decoder outputs correct data, we confirm that $\{c_1, c_2, \ldots, c_m\}$ are traitors.

Lemma 1. *For degree-z polynomials $f(x)$ and $h(x)$, the distributions of the enabling blocks constructed by $f(x)$ and $h(x)$ are computationally indistinguishable assuming that the DDH problem is hard.*

Proof. Note that the distinguisher does not know $f(x)$ and $h(x)$. Let g be a fixed generator of G_q and $a \in_R S$ denote that a is chosen from the set S uniformly and independently. Consider the following 3 distributions:

1. $T_1 = \langle S, g^r, (c_1, g_1^r), (c_2, g_2^r), \ldots, (c_z, g_z^r) \rangle$, where $r \in_R Z_q$, $S \in_R G_q$, $c_i \in_R G_q$, $g_i = g^{f(c_i)}$. This is the enabling block constructed by $f(x)$.
2. $R = \langle S, g^r, (c_1, u_1), (c_2, u_2), \ldots, (c_z, u_z) \rangle$, where $r \in_R Z_q$, $S \in_R G_q$, $c_i \in_R G_q$, $u_i \in_R G_q$, $1 \leq i \leq z$.
3. $T_2 = \langle S, g^r, (c_1, g_1^r), (c_2, g_2^r), \ldots, (c_z, g_z^r) \rangle$, where $r \in_R Z_q$, $S \in_R G_q$, $c_i \in_R G_q$, $g_i = g^{h(c_i)}$. This is the enabling block constructed by $h(x)$.

We can easily show that T_1 and R, and R and T_2 are computationally indistinguishable. Therefore, T_1 and T_2 are computationally indistinguishable. □

Framing. We now address the framing problem [3]. We show that it is not possible for two disjoint sets of k subscribers to construct the same "new" share by linear combination. Therefore, framing is not possible by linear combination of shares.

Lemma 2. *Let $C = \{c_1, c_2, \ldots, c_k\}$ and $D = \{d_1, d_2, \ldots, d_k\}$ be two disjoint subscriber sets. All linear combination of shares of C and those of D are different except the zero point.*

Proof. We can represent a share i as a $z + 2$-dimensional vector

$$v_i = (1, i, i^2, \ldots, i^z, f(i)).$$

Since it is a point of a degree-z polynomial, any $z + 1$ different shares are linearly independent. If one can use the shares of C and the shares of D to construct the same non-zero share by linear combination, we have

$$\sum_{i=1}^{k} a_i v_{c_i} = \sum_{i=1}^{k} b_i v_{d_i} \neq \mathbf{0}.$$

Therefore, we have

$$\sum_{i=1}^{k} a_i v_{c_i} - \sum_{i=1}^{k} b_i v_{d_i} = \mathbf{0}.$$

This is a contradiction since not all a_i's and b_i's are zero and $C \cup D$ is linearly independent. □

Complexity. To broadcast data, the computing time of creating an enabling block is $O(z)$ modular exponentiations, which can be pre-computed. The runtime of the decryption algorithm for each subscriber is $O(z)$ modular exponentiations also. The traitor tracing algorithm runs in $O(C_k^n)$, where n is the total number of subscribers. When $n \gg k$, the runtime is about $O(n^k)$.

3.1   Revocation of Traitors

After a pirate decoder is confiscated and the traitors are revealed, we would like to revoke the private keys of the traitors since thousands of the pirate decoders may be sold.

Assume that $C = \{c_1, c_2, \ldots, c_m\}$, $m \leq z$, is the set of found traitors or revoked subscribers. We can revoke their shares without updating the private keys of the remaining subscribers. To broadcast data to the remained subscribers, instead of randomly choosing unused shares for the enabling block, the content suppliers fixes the first m shares as

$$(c_1, g^{rf(c_1)}), (c_2, g^{rf(c_2)}), \ldots, (c_m, g^{rf(c_m)})$$

and randomly chooses the rest $z - m$ unused shares

$$(j_1, g^{rf(j_1)}), (j_2, g^{rf(j_2)}), \ldots, (j_{z-m}, g^{rf(j_{z-m})}).$$

We can see that the revoked shares or their combinations cannot be used to decrypt the broadcast data since their shares are in the enabling block. We can revoke at most z shares totally before updating the shares of the remaining subscribers.

3.2   Restoration of a Revoked Key

If for some reason we would like to restore the decryption privilege of a revoked key, we simply do not use it in forming the enabling block. The restored key can decrypt the broadcast ciphertext again.

3.3   Revocation beyond the Threshold

It is possible to revoke more than z traitors. The idea is that if a pirate decoder can get at most c percent of data M, say 95%, the partial part of M is useless [1]. For example, if a pirate decoder can only decrypt 95% of a movie, the traitor is revoked de facto.

Assume that $C = \{c_1, c_2, \ldots, c_m\}$, $m > z$, is the set of found traitors or revoked subscribers. Without loss of generality, let $m = tz$. To broadcast data M to the remained subscribers, we partition M as $M_1 || M_2 || \cdots || M_l$. For each M_i, $1 \leq i \leq l$, we construct an enabling block T_i with shares

$$(c_{i_1}, g^{rf(c_{i_1})}), (c_{i_2}, g^{rf(c_{i_2})}), \ldots, (c_{i_r}, g^{rf(c_{i_z})}),$$

where $c_{i_1}, c_{i_2}, \ldots, c_{i_z}$ are randomly chosen from C. With appropriately chosen r and l, each traitor in C can decrypt at most c percent of M in average.

Let $E_j^{(i)}$ be the probability that c_i is chosen into T_j. We can see that $E_j^{(i)} = z/m = 1/t$. The probability that c_i is not chosen into any T_j, $1 \le j \le l$, is $(1 - 1/t)^l$. With $l = 3t$, $(1 - 1/t)^{3t} \simeq 1/e^3 \simeq 0.05$. That is, to increase the revocation capability by 5 folds, we partition M into 15 parts. Furthermore, we can adjust these values dynamically.

3.4   Speedup of Tracing

Since the runtime of the tracing algorithm is $O(C_k^n)$, when n or k is large, the algorithm is not efficient. In practice, we would like to have a more efficient tracing algorithm.

A practical solution to this problem is to group subscribers into classes C_1, $C_2, \ldots, C_r$. Each class C_i consists of a reasonable number of subscribers by the subscribers' residence, etc. For each class C_i, the content supplier uses a different polynomial $f_i(x)$ as the secret key. A subscriber j in class C_i is given a share $(j, f_i(j))$. The data M broadcast to the subscribers of class C_i are encrypted as $E(f_i(x), M)$. The decryption and tracing algorithms are the same as the original ones except that the keys are different for different classes.

Grouping subscribers can make our revocation mechanism more practical. It will be less frequent to revoke private keys in a class since the size is smaller. Even if the content supplier wants to revoke the $(z + 1)$th private key in a class, only the private keys in the class have to be updated.

4   Security Analysis

We consider both semantic security and security against the z-coalition attack, in which any coalition of z or less legal subscribers cannot compute a legal private key for decryption.

The encryption algorithm of our scheme is semantically secure against a passive adversary if the DDH problem in G_q is hard (or computationally infeasible). Recall that $D = \langle g_1, g_2, g_1^r, g_2^r \rangle$ and $R = \langle g_1, g_2, g_1^a, g_2^b \rangle$ where g_1, g_2 are generators and a, b and r are randomly chosen over Z_q.

Theorem 1 (Semantic security). *Assume that the DDH problem is hard. The encryption algorithm of our traitor tracing scheme is semantically secure against the passive adversary.*

Proof. Suppose that our encryption algorithm is not semantically secure against the passive adversary. We show that there is a probabilistic polynomial-time algorithm $\mathcal{B}$ that distinguishes D from R with a non-negligible advantage ε.

Assume that adversary $\mathcal{A}$ attacks our encryption algorithm successfully in terms of semantic security. $\mathcal{A}$ has two procedures A_1 and A_2. Given the public key $\langle g, g^{a_0}, g^{f(1)}, \ldots, g^{f(z)} \rangle$ of the content supplier, A_1 finds two session keys s_0 and s_1 in G_q such that A_2 can distinguish them by observing the enabling block.

Let $\langle g_1, g_2, u_1, u_2 \rangle$ be an input of the DDH problem. The following algorithm $\mathcal{B}$ shall decide whether $\langle g_1, g_2, u_1, u_2 \rangle$ is from D or R.

1. Randomly choose $a_i \in Z_q$, $1 \leq i \leq z$, and let $f'(x) = \sum_{t=1}^{z} a_t x^t$. Let $g = g_1$, $g^{a_0} = g_2$, $g^{f(1)} = g_2 g_1^{f'(1)}, \ldots, g^{f(z)} = g_2 g_1^{f'(z)}$, where $f(x) = f'(x) + a_0$. Note that we don't know a_0.
2. Feed the public key $\langle g, g^{a_0}, g^{f(1)}, \ldots, g^{f(z)} \rangle$ to A_1. A_1 returns s_0 and s_1 in G_q.
3. Randomly select $d \in \{0, 1\}$ and encrypt s_d as

$$C = \langle s_d u_2, u_1, (j_1, u_2 u_1^{f'(j_1)}), \ldots, (j_z, u_2 u_1^{f'(j_z)}) \rangle$$

   where $j_1, j_2, \ldots, j_z$ are randomly chosen.
4. Feed C to A_2 and get a return d'. Then, the algorithm outputs 1 if and only if $d = d'$.

If $\langle g_1, g_2, u_1, u_2 \rangle$ is from D, $g = g_1, g_2 = g^{a_0}, u_1 = g^r, u_2 = g_2^r = g^{ra_0}$ and $u_2 u_1^{f'(j_i)} = g^{rf(j_i)}$ for $1 \leq i \leq z$. Thus, C is the encryption of s_d and $\Pr[\mathcal{B}(g_1, g_2, u_1, u_2) = 1] = \Pr[A_2(C) = d] = 1/2 + \varepsilon$. Otherwise, since $u_1 = g_1^a$ and $u_2 = g_2^b$, the distribution of C is the same for $d = 0$ and $d = 1$. Thus, $\Pr[\mathcal{B}(g_1, g_2, u_1, u_2) = 1] = \Pr[A_2(C) = d] = 1/2$. Therefore, $\mathcal{B}$ distinguishes D from R with a non-negligible advantage ε. $\square$

The encryption algorithm of our scheme is secure against z-coalition assuming that computing the discrete logarithm is hard.

Theorem 2. *Assume that computing the discrete logarithm over G_q is hard. No coalition of z or less legal subscribers can compute the private key of another legal subscriber with a non-negligible probability.*

Proof. Assume that the probabilistic polynomial-time algorithm $\mathcal{A}$ can compute a new share (private key) $(x_u, f(x_u))$ from the given public key $\langle g, g^{a_0}, g^{f(1)}, g^{f(2)}, \ldots, g^{f(z)} \rangle$ and z shares $(x_1, f(x_1)), \ldots, (x_z, f(x_z))$ with a non-negligible probability ε. We construct another probabilistic polynomial-time algorithm $\mathcal{B}$ to compute the discrete logarithm over G_q with an overwhelming probability.

Let (p, g, y) be the input of the discrete logarithm problem. The following algorithm $\mathcal{B}'$ computes $\log_g y \pmod{p}$ with a non-negligible probability. Let $y = g^{a_0}$ and $f(x)$ be the degree-z polynomial passing $(0, a_0)$ and $(x_i, f(x_i)), 1 \leq i \leq z$. By Lagrange interpolation, we can compute $g^{f(i)}, 1 \leq i \leq z$. We feed the public key $\langle g, g^{a_0}, g^{f(1)}, g^{f(2)}, \ldots, g^{f(z)} \rangle$ and z shares $(x_1, f(x_1)), \ldots, (x_z, f(x_z))$ to $\mathcal{A}$ and shall get a new share $(x_u, f(x_u))$ with a non-negligible probability. With the given z shares and $(x_u, f(x_u))$, we can compute $f(0) = a_0$.

By applying the randomized technique to $\mathcal{B}'$ for a polynomial number of times, we get $\mathcal{B}$. $\square$

5   Chosen Ciphertext Security

It is often desirable to have a cryptosystem secure against the adaptive chosen ciphertext attack. By the technique of [7], we modify our scheme so that it becomes secure against the adaptive chosen ciphertext attack under the standard intractability assumptions. Recall that G_q is a group of order-q and g is its generator. Our variant traitor tracing scheme is as follows.

System setup. The content supplier randomly chooses a degree-z polynomial $f(x) = \sum_{t=0}^{z} a_t x^t$ with coefficients in G_q and $a, b, x_1, x_2, y_1, y_2 \in Z_q$. Its secret key is $\langle f(x), a, b \rangle$ and public key is

$$\langle g, g^{a_0}, g^{f(1)}, \ldots, g^{f(z)}, g^a, g^b, c, d, H \rangle$$

where $c = g^{ax_1} g^{bx_2}$, $d = g^{ay_1} g^{by_2}$, and H is a collision-resistant hash function. Let $f'(x) = a^{-1}(f(x) - b)$ or $f(x) = af'(x) + b$.

Registration. When a subscriber $i, i > z$, registers to the system, the content supplier gives him a private key

$$(i, f'(i), x_1, x_2, y_1, y_2)$$

The subscriber i can verify his share.

Encryption. To broadcast data M, the content supplier randomly selects a session key $s \in G_q$, a one-time number $r \in Z_q$ and z unused indices $j_1, j_2, \ldots, j_z$ and computes the enabling block

$$T = \langle sg^{ra_0}, (j_1, g^{rf(j_1)}), \ldots, (j_z, g^{rf(j_z)}), g^{ra}, g^{rb}, v \rangle$$

where $v = c^r d^{r\alpha}$ and $\alpha = H(sg^{ra_0}, (j_1, g^{rf(j_1)}), \ldots, (j_z, g^{rf(j_z)}), g^{ra}, g^{rb})$. We use $T = \langle S, (j_1, F_{j_1}), \ldots, (j_z, F_{j_z}), F_a, F_b, v \rangle$ to denote the enabling block.

Decryption. When receiving the enabling block $T = \langle S, (j_1, F_{j_1}), \ldots, (j_z, F_{j_z}), F_a, F_b, v \rangle$, the subscriber i with the private key $\langle i, f'(i), x_1, x_2, y_1, y_2 \rangle$ can compute the session key s by the following steps.

- Compute $\alpha = H(S, (j_1, F_{j_1}), \ldots, (j_z, F_{j_z}), F_a, F_b, v)$;
- Check whether $F_a^{x_1 + y_1 \alpha} F_b^{x_2 + y_2 \alpha} = v$;
- If the checking fails, reject the enabling block; otherwise, compute

$$S / [F_a^{f'(i)\lambda_z} \cdot F_b^{\lambda_z} \cdot \prod_{t=0}^{z-1} F_{j_t}^{\lambda_t}] = S / g^{ra_0} = s,$$

where $x_0 = j_1, x_1 = j_2, \ldots, x_{z-1} = j_z$ and $x_z = i$.

Traitor tracing. The traitor tracing algorithm is the same as that in Section 3.

The encryption algorithm of the above traitor tracing scheme is semantically secure against the adaptive chosen ciphertext attack.

Theorem 3. *Assume that the DDH problem is hard. The encryption algorithm of the above traitor tracing scheme is semantically secure against the adaptive chosen ciphertext attack.*

Proof. We assume that there is a probabilistic polynomial-time adversary $\mathcal{A}$ that can break our encryption algorithm with a non-negligible probability ε. $\mathcal{A}$ consists of two algorithms A_1 and A_2. A_1 takes as input of the content supplier's public key and outputs two session keys s_0 and s_1. Let d be a random bit. A_2 takes as input of the enabling block for s_d, makes some chosen ciphertext queries, and outputs d'. The probability of $d = d'$ is $1/2 + \varepsilon$. By A_1 and A_2, we can construct a probabilistic polynomial-time algorithm $\mathcal{B}$ that distinguishes D from R with a non-negligible probability.

Given a quadruple (g_1, g_2, u_1, u_2) in G_q^4, we construct a simulator S that simulates $\mathcal{A}$'s view in its attack on the algorithm. The simulator S includes an encryption oracle and a decryption oracle. We will show that if the quadruple is from D, the simulation of $\mathcal{A}$'s view will be nearly perfect and if the quadruple is from R, $\mathcal{A}$'s advantage is negligible. The simulator S works as follows.

1. **Key setup.** The content supplier's public key is constructed as follows.
   (a) Select two degree-z polynomials $f'(x) = \sum_{t=0}^{z} a_t x^t$ and $f''(x) = \sum_{t=0}^{z} r_t x^t$ and $w, j \in Z_q$ randomly. Let $g = g_1$, $g_2 = g_1^a = g^a$, $f(x) = f'(x) + wa$ and $g^b = g^{f(j)}/g_2^{f''(j)}$. Note that we don't know the constant coefficient of $f(x)$ since a is unknown. We have $f(j) = f'(j) + wa = af''(j) + b$. We don't know b, either.
   (b) Randomly select x_1, x_2, y_1, y_2 and compute
   $$c = g^{ax_1}g^{bx_2}, d = g^{ay_1}g^{by_2}.$$
   (c) The public key of the content supplier is
   $$\langle g, g^{a_0}g_2^w, g^{f'(1)}g_2^w, g^{f'(2)}g_2^w, \ldots, g^{f'(z)}g_2^w, g^a, g^b, c, d, H\rangle.$$

   The above key generation is a bit different from the actual cryptosystem, but the effect is the same. We essentially fix $w = 0$.
2. **Challenge.** Feed the public key of the content supplier to A_1 and get two session keys s_0 and s_1 in G_q.
3. **Encryption.** Randomly pick d and z indices $\{j_1, \ldots, j_z\}$ and compute
   $$S = s_d u_1^{a_0} u_2^w, F_{j_1} = u_1^{f'(j_1)} u_2^w, \ldots, F_{j_z} = u_1^{f'(j_z)} u_2^w, F_a = u_2,$$
   $$F_b = u_1^{f'(j)} u_2^w / u_2^{f''(j)}, \alpha = H(S, (j_1, F_{j_1}), \ldots, (j_z, F_{j_z}), F_a, F_b),$$
   $$v = F_a^{x_1+y_1\cdot\alpha} \cdot F_b^{x_2+y_2\cdot\alpha}.$$

   The ciphertext of s_d is $T = \langle S, (j_1, F_{j_1}), \ldots, (j_z, F_{j_z}), F_a, F_b, v\rangle$.
4. **Decryption.** Given the ciphertext T, the decryption oracle first checks validity of T by verifying $u_1^{x_1+y_1\alpha} u_2^{x_2+y_2\alpha} = v$. If it is not valid, the oracle rejects it; otherwise, the oracle returns
   $$s = S/[\prod_{t=0}^{z-1} F_{j_t}^{\lambda_{t-1}} \cdot F_a^{f''(j)\lambda_z} \cdot F_b^{\lambda_z}],$$

where $x_0 = j_1, x_2 = j_1, \ldots, x_{z-1} = j_z, x_z = j$.

The above completes description of S. The adversary $\mathcal{B}$ takes as input (g_1, g_2, u_1, u_2) and outputs 1 if and only if $d = A_2(T)$, where T is the enabling block of the challenge s_d.

If the input comes from D, the ciphertext T of encryption of s_d is legitimate. If the input comes from R, the distribution of T is almost the same for $d = 0$ and $d = 1$. To complete the proof, we show:

1. If $\langle g_1, g_2, u_1, u_2 \rangle$ is from D, the joint distribution of the simulator S's output (adversary's view) and the hidden bit d is statistically indistinguishable from that in the actual attack.
2. If $\langle g_1, g_2, u_1, u_2 \rangle$ is from R, the distribution of the hidden bit d is (essentially) independent of S's output.

Lemma 3. *If the simulator S's input $\langle g_1, g_2, u_1, u_2 \rangle$ is chosen from D, the joint distribution of the adversary's view and the hidden bit d is statistically indistinguishable from that in the actual attack.*

Lemma 4. *If the simulator S's input $\langle g_1, g_2, u_1, u_2 \rangle$ is chosen from R, the distribution of the hidden bit d is (essentially) independent of the adversary's view.*

Since the proofs of the above two lemmas are similar to those of Cramer and Shoup [7], we put them in Appendix.

This completes the proof of Theorem 3. $\qquad\square$

6   Discussion

Actually, we can drop the content supplier's public key from our traitor tracing schemes if verification of private keys by subscribers is not necessary. This is indeed the case for practicality. Thus, only the content suppblier can do data encryption. Since the enabling blocks are computationally indistinguishable from each other due to the DDH assumption, our scheme should be more secure.

For practicality, we can set $z = k$. In this case, there may be framing problem. The probability that a set of k subscribers can frame a specific set of k subscribers is $1/q$. Assume that there are $m = 10,000,000$ subscribers and k is set as 20. Then, the probability that a set of k subscribers can frame some set of k subscribers is $\leq C_k^m/q \approx m^k/q \approx 1/(10)^{168}$, for q being 1024-bit long.

7   Conclusion

In this work we have proposed a new public-key traitor tracing scheme with revocation capability using dynamic shares. Its distinct feature of revoking private keys makes the protocol highly practical. The scheme's traitor tracing algorithm is fully k-resilient and conceptually simple. The size of the enabling block is independent of the number of subscribers.

Our scheme is semantically secure against the passive adversary assuming that the DDH problem is hard. We also present a variant scheme that is semantically secure against the adaptive chosen ciphertext attack assuming that the DDH problem is hard.

References

1. M. Abdalla, Y. Shavitt, A. Wool, "Key management for restricted multicast using broadcast encryption", *Proceedings of Financial Cryptology 99*, Lecture Notes in Computer Science 1648, Springer Verlag, 1999.
2. J. Anzai, N. Matsuzaki, T. Matsumoto, "A quick group key distribution scheme with "entity revocation"", *Proceedings of Advances in Cryptology - Asiacrypt 99*, Lecture Notes in Computer Science 1716, pp.333-347, Springer Verlag, 1999.
3. D. Boneh, M. Franklin, "An efficient public key traitor tracing scheme", *Proceedings of Advances in Cryptology - Crypto 99*, Lecture Notes in Computer Science 1666, pp.338-353, Springer Verlag, 1999.
4. D. Boneh, J. Shaw, "Collusion-secure fingerprinting for digital data", *IEEE Trasaction on Information Theory* 44(5), pp.1897-1905, 1998. (See also, *Proceedings of Advances in Cryptology - Crypto 95*, Lecture Notes in Computer Science 963, pp.452-465, Springer Verlag, 1995.)
5. R. Canetti, T. Malkin, K. Nissim, "Efficient communication-storage tradeoffs for multicast encryption", *Proceedings of Adnaces in Cryptology - Eurocrypt 99*, Lecture Notes in Computer Science 1592, pp.459-474, 1999.
6. B. Chor, A. Fiat, M. Naor, "Tracing traitor", *Proceedings of Advances in Cryptology - Crypto 94*, Lecture Notes in Computer Science 839, pp.257-270, Springer Verlag, 1994.
7. R. Cramer, V. Shoup, "A practical public key cryptosystem provably secure against adaptive chosen ciphertext attack", *Proceedings of Advances in Cryptology - Crypto 98*, Lecture Notes in Computer Science 1462, pp.13-25, Springer Verlag, 1998.
8. T. ElGamal, "A public-key cryptosystem and a signature scheme based on discrete logarithms", *IEEE Transactions on Information Theory* 31(4), pp.469-472, 1985.
9. A. Fiat, T. Tassa, "Dynamic traitor tracing", *Proceedings of Advances in Cryptology - Crypto 99*, Lecture Notes in Computer Science 1666, pp.354-371, Springer Verlag, 1999.
10. A. Fiat, M. Naor, "Broadcast encryption", *Proceedings of Advances in Cryptology - Crypto 93*, Lecture Notes in Computer Science 773, pp.480-491, Springer Verlag, 1993.
11. E. Gafni, J. Staddon, Y.L. Yin, "Efficient methods for integrating traceability and broadcast encryption", *Proceedings of Advances in Cryptology - Crypto 99*, Lecture Notes in Computer Science 1666, pp.372-387, Springer Verlag, 1999.
12. R. Kumar, S. Rajagopalan, A. Sahai, "Coding constructions for blacklisting problems without computational assumptions", *Proceedings of Advances in Cryptology - Crypto 99*, Lecture Notes in Computer Science 1666, pp.609-623, Springer Verlag, 1999.
13. K. Kurosawa, Y. Desmedt, "Optimum traitor tracing and asymmetric schemes", *Proceedings of Advances in Cryptology - Eurocrypt 98*, Lecture Notes in Computer Science 1403, pp.145-157, Springer Verlage, 1998.
14. M. Luby, J. Staddon, "Combinatorial bounds for braodcast encryption", *Proceedings of Advances of Cryptology - Eurocrypt 98*, Lecture Notes in Compouter Science 1403, pp.512-526, Springer Verlag, 1998.

15. M. Naor, B. Pinkas, "Threshold traitor tracing", *Proceedings of Advances in Cryptology - Crypto 98*, Lecture Notes in Computer Science 1462, pp.502-517, Springer Verlag, 1998.
16. M. Naor, B. Pinkas, "Efficient trace and revoke schemes", *Proceedings of Financial Cryptography 00*, 2000.
17. B. Pfitzmann, "Trials of traced traitors", *Proceedings of Workshop on Information Hiding*, Lecture Notes in Computer Science 1174, pp.49-64, Springer Verlag, 1996.
18. B. Pfitzmann, M. Waidner, "Asymmetric fingerprinting for large collusions", *Proceedings of ACM Conference on Computer and Communication Security*, pp.151-160, 1997.
19. A. Shamir, "How to share a secret", *Communications of the ACM*, 22(11), pp.612-613, 1979.
20. D.R. Stinson, R. Wei, "Combinatorial properties and constructions of traceability schemes and frameproof codes", *SIAM J. on Discrete Math* 11(1), pp.41-53, 1998.

Appendix

Lemma 3. Proof. We need argue two things. One is that the output of the encryption oracle and the decryption oracle has the right distribution. The other is that the decryption oracle rejects all invalid ciphertexts except with a negligible probability.

If the input is from D, we have $u_1 = g_1^r$ and $u_2 = g_2^r$ for some r. Therefore, $F_{j_i} = u_1^{f'(j_i)} u_2^w = g^{f(j_i)}$ for $1 \leq i \leq z$, $F_a = g_2^r = g^{ar}$, $F_b = (u_1^{f'(j)} u_2^w / u_2^{f''(x)}) = g^{br}$, $F_a^{x_1} F_b^{x_2} = c^r$, $F_a^{y_1} F_b^{y_2} = d^r$. Thus, $S = s_d u_1^{a_0} u_2^w = s_d g^{a_0 r} g^{arw} = s_d g^{rf(0)}$ and $v = c^r d^{r\alpha}$, where α is in right form. Hence, the output of the encryption oracle has the right distribution. In addition, $\langle S, (j_1, F_{j_1}), \ldots, (j_z, F_{j_z}), F_a, F_b, v \rangle$ is a valid ciphertext. Therefore, the decryption oracle outputs $s_d = S / \prod_{t=0}^{z-1} F_{j_t}^{\lambda_t - 1} \cdot F_a^{f''(j)\lambda_z} \cdot F_b^{\lambda_z}$.

Moreover, we should prove that the decryption oracle rejects all invalid ciphertexts, except with a negligible probability. Consider the distribution of the point $\mathbf{P} = (x_1, x_2, y_1, y_2) \in Z_q^4$. Recall that $g = g_1$ and $\log_g g_2 = a$. ¿From c and d of the public key, we get two equations:

$$\log_g c = ax_1 + bx_2, \tag{1}$$

$$\log_g d = ay_1 + by_2. \tag{2}$$

¿From the output of the encryption oracle, we get another equation:

$$\log_g v = rax_1 + brx_2 + \alpha ray_1 + \alpha rby_2. \tag{3}$$

If the adversary submits an invalid ciphertext $\langle S', (j_1, F'_{j_1}), \ldots, (j_z, F'_{j_z}), F'_a, F'_b, v \rangle$ to the decryption oracle, ie., $r_1 = \log_g u'_1 \neq \log_{g_2} u'_2 = r_2$. The decryption oracle will reject, unless $\mathbf{P}$ lies on the hyperplane $\mathbf{H}$ defined by

$$\log_g v' = ar_1 x_1 + br_2 x_2 + \alpha' ar_1 y_1 + \alpha' r_2 by_2, \tag{4}$$

where $\alpha' = H(S', (j_1, F'_{j_1}), \ldots, (j_z, F'_{j_z}), F'_a, F'_b)$. Since Equations 1, 2 and 4 are linearly independent, the hyperplane $\mathbf{H}$ and the plane $\mathbf{P}$ intersect at a line.

The first time the adversary submits an invalid ciphertext, the decryption oracle rejects it with probability $1 - 1/q$. This rejection constrains the point P with q less points. Furthermore, the ith invalid ciphertext will be rejected with probability at least $1 - q/(q^2 - q(i-1)) = 1 - 1/(q-i+1)$. Therefore, the decryption oracle rejects all invalid ciphertexts except with a negligible probability.   □

Lemma 4. Proof. We should prove that if the decryption oracle rejects all invalid ciphertexts, the distribution of the hidden bit b is independent of the adversary's view. Furthermore, we still need to prove that the decryption oracle will reject all invalid ciphertexts, except with a negligible probability.

Let $t_1 = \log_g u_1$ and $t_2 = log_{g_2} u_2$. Assume that $t_1 \neq t_2$ since this holds except with a negligible probability $1/q$. The public key $l = g^{a_0} g^{aw}$ determines the equation:

$$\log_g l = a_0 + aw. \tag{5}$$

Since the decryption oracle only decrypts valid ciphertexts, the adversary obtains only linearly dependent equation $r' \log_g l = r'a_0 + r'wa$. Thus, no further information about (a_0, w) is leaked.

Consider that the output of the encryption oracle, we have $S = s_d g_1^{t_1 a_0} g_2^{t_2 w}$. Let $\beta = g_1^{t_1 a_0} g_2^{t_2 w}$. We get the equation:

$$\log_g \beta = t_1 a_0 + t_2 wa. \tag{6}$$

Clearly, Equations 5 and 6 are linearly independent. We can view β as a perfect one-time pad. As a result that d is independent of the adversary's view.

Next, we argue that the decryption oracle will reject all invalid ciphertexts except with a negligible probability. Let us examine the distribution of $P = (x_1, x_2, y_1, y_2) \in Z_q^4$, based on the adversary's view. ¿From the output v of the encryption oracle, we get the equation:

$$\log_g v = at_1 x_1 + bt_2 x_2 + \alpha a t_1 y_1 + \alpha b t_2 y_2. \tag{7}$$

¿From the adversary's view, P is a random point on the line $\mathbf{L}$ formed by intersecting the hyperplanes of Equations 1, 2 and 7. Assume that the adversary submits an invalid ciphertext $\langle S', (j_1, F'_{j_1}), \ldots, (j_z, F'_{j_z}), F'_a, F'_b, v' \rangle$. Let $\log_g u'_1 = t'_1$ and $\log_{g_2} u'_2 = t'_2$. There are three cases to consider:

Case I. $\langle S', (j_1, F'_{j_1}), \ldots, (j_z, F'_{j_z}), F'_a, F'_b \rangle = \langle S, (j_1, F_{j_1}), \ldots, (j_z, F_{j_z}), F_a, F_b \rangle$. Although the hash values are the same, the decryption oracle still reject because of $v' \neq v$.

Case II. $\langle S', (j_1, F'_{j_1}), \ldots, (j_z, F'_{j_z}), F'_a, F'_b \rangle \neq \langle S, (j_1, F_{j_1}), \ldots, (j_z, F_{j_z}), F_a, F_b \rangle$ and the hash values are not the same. Unless the point $\mathbf{P}$ satisfies the hyperplane $\log_g v'$, the decryption oracle will reject. Moreover, Equations 1, 2, 4 and 7 are linearly independent by observing that

$$\det \begin{pmatrix} a & b & 0 & 0 \\ 0 & 0 & a & b \\ t_1 a & t_2 b & \alpha t_1 a & \alpha t_2 b \\ t_1' a & t_2' b & \alpha' t_1' a & \alpha' t_2' b \end{pmatrix} = a^2 b^2 (\alpha - \alpha')(t_2' - t_1')(t_2 - t_1) \neq 0.$$

Thus, the hyperplane and the line **L** intersect at a point. Therefore, the decryption oracle rejects the query except with a negligible probability.

Case III. $\langle S', (j_1, F_{j_1}'), \ldots, (j_z, F_{j_z}'), F_a', F_b' \rangle \neq \langle S, (j_1, F_{j_1}), \ldots, (j_z, F_{j_z}), F_a, F_b \rangle$, but the hash values are the same, which contradicts with the assumption that H is collision-resistant.

This completes the proof. $\qquad\square$

Efficient Asymmetric Self-Enforcement Scheme with Public Traceability

Hirotaka Komaki, Yuji Watanabe, Goichiro Hanaoka, and Hideki Imai

The Third Department, Institute of Industrial Science, the University of Tokyo
7-22-1 Roppongi, Minato-ku, Tokyo 106-8558, Japan
Phone & Fax: +81-3-3402-7365
{komaki,mue,hanaoka}@imailab.iis.u-tokyo.ac.jp
imai@iis.u-tokyo.ac.jp

Abstract. Traitor tracing schemes deter traitors from giving away their keys to decrypt the contents by enabling the data supplier to identify the source of a redistributed copy. In asymmetric schemes, the supplier can also convince an arbiter of this fact.

Another approach to the same goal was suggested by Dwork, Lotspiech and Naor, so called self-enforcement schemes. In these schemes, traitors have to either divulge their private sensitive information or distribute fairly large amount of data. However, the same private information must be revealed to the data supplier, which invokes the necessity of more discussion about the model underlying this scheme.

In this paper, we present an efficient asymmetric self-enforcement scheme, which also supports the asymmetric traceability without any trusted third parties, assuming the situation where the authenticity of the exponent of each subscriber's sensitive information bound to the subject entity is publicly certified, such as PKI derived from discrete logarithm based cryptosystems. In our scheme, the sensitive information needs not to be revealed to any entities. As far as we know, there has never been any proposal of asymmetric self-enforcement schemes. Furthermore, our scheme is as efficient as the previous most efficient symmetric or asymmetric traitor tracing schemes proposed so far.

1 Introduction

In the contents distribution system over a broadcast channel, such as pay TV, online database, DVD distribution, the system authority gives each authorized subscriber a hardware or software decoder containing a decryption key and broadcasts encrypted digital contents, in order to prevent non-subscribers (*pirates*) from accessing the contents. However, some non-subscribers might obtain a decryption key from one or a set of authorized subscribers (*traitors*) and construct a pirate decoder. In practice today, the so-called *secure* hardware solution is commonly used against such piracy, where cryptanalyzing the secret is assumed to be hard. Unfortunately, such assumption about the security is not always correct. There are several *side-channel attacks* that threat to the assumption,

K. Kim (Ed.): PKC 2001, LNCS 1992, pp. 225–239, 2001.

such as the power analysis [7]. Moreover, secure hardware solutions are often expensive.

In the absence of secure hardware, the cryptographic solution cannot prevent the subscribers from copying their decryption keys themselves. Against the piracy of digital data, such as contents or decryption keys, a lot of cryptographic techniques have been proposed that make redistribution either inconvenient or traceable.

Traitor tracing, which was introduced by Chor, Fiat and Naor [5], is an extension of broadcast encryption, in such a way that it can reveal the traitor on the confiscation of a pirate decoder. To offer traceability, each subscriber is given a different set of decryption keys that identify the subscriber. In a sense, traitor tracing can be seen as one of fingerprinting schemes [15,12] where the decryption keys are fingerprinted. A traitor tracing is called *k-resistant* if the scheme can reveal at least one traitor on the confiscation of a pirate decoder which was constructed by up to k traitors.

The schemes in [5] are *symmetric* in the sense that subscribers share all their secrets with the system authority. In symmetric schemes, the authority itself, or malicious employee or someone with illegal access to the authority could incriminate an honest subscriber as a traitor using the secrets. Thus the result of tracing is no real evidence that could unambiguously convince a third party. Pfitzmann [11] pointed out this problem and introduced *asymmetric* traitor tracing schemes, where using an interactive key distribution protocol the system authority cannot construct a pirate decoder that frames an honest subscriber, but if a pirate decoder which was constructed by malicious subscribers is found the authority is able to trace the source of it.

The problem with relying on the traceability is that the authority or other entities must always monitor all over the world for potentially redistributed copies. To overcome such shortcoming, Dwork, Lotspiech and Naor [6] introduced another approach, so-called *self-enforcement scheme*, where the system authority needs not the confiscation of a pirate decoder nor trace the source of it. Instead, traitors have to either divulge their private sensitive information (e.g., a credit card number) or distribute fairly large amount of data in order to succeed the piracy. A similar approach using sensitive information has been suggested by Sander and Ta-Shma [13] in the context of electronic payment systems, in order to make the coin *non-transferable* as a countermeasure to financial crimes, such as the tax evasion.

The scheme in [6] still remains a serious problem that the same private information must be revealed to the data supplier, which invokes the necessity of more discussion about the model underlying this scheme. In [11], Pfitzmann mentioned that one can try to combine those techniques with the ideas of asymmetric traitor tracing, so that the private information can also remain private from the authority. But it is not so easy to construct such *asymmetric self-enforcement scheme* because the authority must confirm that subscriber's decryption key certainly contains his private sensitive information without the knowledge of it. Asymmetric traitor tracing schemes do not need such a verification. As far as we know, there has never been any proposal of asymmetric self-enforcement schemes.

Our Contribution In this paper, we present an efficient asymmetric self-enforcement scheme, which also offers asymmetric traceability. In our scheme, we assume the situation where each subscriber i has a pair of values (d_i, g^{d_i}) such that d_i is i's private sensitive information (e.g., the secret key in Public Key Infrastructure (PKI), biometrical information, code number of the bank account or driver's license number etc.) and g^{d_i} is the exponent of it, and the authenticity of g^{d_i} bound to the subject entity i is publicly certified. If we take each subscriber's secret key in PKI derived from discrete logarithm based cryptosystems as their private sensitive information d_i, then g^{d_i} corresponds to the public key and the Certification Authority (CA) vouches for the authenticity of the public key. Thus such an assumption underlies every cryptosystem based on PKI. For concreteness we consider the situation that each user's private sensitive information is their secret key in PKI derived from discrete logarithm based cryptosystems hereafter unless otherwise mentioned.

In our scheme, even if at most k malicious subscribers collude to construct a pirate decoder, arbitrary entity can obtain all of their secret keys in PKI on the confiscation of it. Thus the redistribution of the decryption key which contains the secret keys damages the traitors very much. For example, if the secret key is used for the signature, a receiver of it can impersonate the owner, e.g. for signing contracts, receiving loans, etc. Thus the owner of the key may not want to give it away.

Furthermore if a pirate decoder which is constructed by at most k traitors is confiscated by any entities, they can trace and reveal the secret of all the traitors and convince any third party of the validity of the tracing results without the participation of the accused traitors and the system authority in the trial phase, unless the system authority plays the role of the tracer (*direct non-repudiation*). Our scheme does not need any trusted third parties (if we assume PKI) and offer *full frameproof* that arbitrary collusion of entities including the system authority cannot frame an honest subscriber. In our scheme, the encryption key of the broadcasted contents can be open to the public and an arbitrary entity can play a role of the data supplier.

Our scheme is very efficient compared with the previous most efficient symmetric or asymmetric traitor tracing schemes proposed so far. Table 1 shows a comparison about the efficiency among related works and our proposal. [1] $1/\rho, 1/\rho_B$ are defined by

$$1/\rho \stackrel{\triangle}{=} max\left\{\frac{log|\mathcal{U}_i|}{log|\mathcal{S}|} : i \in \Phi\right\}$$

---

[1] In the original scheme in [8] $1/\rho_B = k + 2$, but it was not *k-resistant* but $\lfloor\frac{k+1}{2}\rfloor$-*resistant* on the *convex combination attack* [14,3]. If we take $k \to 2k - 1$, then the scheme in [8] offers *k-resistant*. See Section 4 for more details.

Table 1. A comparison of the decryption key size and the data redundancy.

		$1/\rho$	$1/\rho_B$
[12]	Scheme 1	$O(k\log n)$	$O(k^2\log n)$
[12]	Scheme 2	$O(\sigma k)$	$O(\sigma^2 k^2)$
[8]		1	$2k+1$
[18]		2	$4k+3$
[16,17]		2	$3k+3$
Proposal		2	$2k+1$

$$1/\rho_B \stackrel{\triangle}{=} max\left\{\frac{log|\mathcal{B}|}{log|\mathcal{S}|}\right\}$$

where $\mathcal{U}_i$ denotes the set of all possible subsets of decryption keys, $\mathcal{B}$ denotes the set of all possible subsets of the data redundancy, $\mathcal{S}$ denotes the set of all possible subsets of the session keys and Φ denotes the set of subscribers of the system [14]. Thus $1/\rho$ is a parameter on the size of each user's decryption key and $1/\rho_B$ is a parameter on the size of data redundancy. n is the number of subscribers and σ is a parameter where the system authority cannot frame an honest subscriber as a traitor with probability more than $1/2^{\sigma}$. From a brief view of Table 1, one can see that our scheme is one of the most efficient schemes.

Related Works. The asymmetric traitor tracing scheme suggested by Pfitzmann and Waidner in [11,12] used the symmetric scheme in [5] as a building block. The scheme was, however, not efficient because the scheme of [5] on which it is based required large overhead and large decryption key.

Kurosawa and Desmedt [8] proposed a more efficient construction of asymmetric public key traceability scheme where the encryption key could be public. Their scheme is based on the ElGamal type threshold cryptosystem and very efficient. But their approach to the asymmetric traceability was to share the secret information of the system authority among some trusted third parties, which implies that they can still frame an honest subscriber on their conspiracy.

Another constructions of asymmetric public key traceability schemes without any trusted third parties were given in [16,17,18]. In [18], any entities can trace the source of a pirate decoder and can convince any arbiter of the result, but a suspected traitor must participate in trial phase to prove his guilt. The scheme in [16,17] offers the tracer enough information to convince the arbiter and needs not the accused traitor's participation in trial phase. However those schemes do not support self-enforcement as mentioned above.

Organization. In Section 2, we describe the model, the definition and building blocks which include efficient public key traitor tracing schemes and *oblivious polynomial evaluation* protocol. Our construction is described in Section 3. We analyze the security of our proposal in Section 4. Finally, conclusions are given in Section 5.

2   Preliminaries

In this section we describe the model underlying our protocol and define the security requirement. Then we describe an efficient public key traitor tracing scheme and oblivious polynomial evaluation protocol, which are building blocks of our proposal.

2.1   Model

The entities who participate in the proposed protocol are as follows. (Considering the practical case, we describe the model where the data supplier plays a role of the tracer. As mentioned in Section 1, arbitrary entites *can* do it.)

System Authority: The system Authority $\mathcal{SA}$ generates one public key and sells the decoder containing the decryption key (*personal key*) to each user, in a complicated way such that the personal key is constructed by each user's secret key of the PKI and $\mathcal{SA}$ cannot know the value of the key itself.

Data Supplier: The data supplier $\mathcal{T}$ distributes encrypted contents using a public key generated by $\mathcal{SA}$, and if he finds the pirate decoder which was illegally distributed, he traces the source of it. $\mathcal{SA}$ may play the role of $\mathcal{T}$.

Users: Users are authorized subscribers of the system and the set of users is denoted by $\Phi = \{1, \cdots, n\}$. Each user decrypts the encrypted contents with the personal key, which was given by $\mathcal{SA}$ when he subscribed to the system.

Traitors: Traitors are person who redistribute their own personal keys, or colluders to construct the pirate decoder, and the set of traitors is denoted by $\Omega = \{u_1, \cdots, u_t\}$. Then, $\Omega \subset \Phi$.

Arbiter: An arbiter $\mathcal{A}$ is a party that verifies the tracing results. In practice, this can be a court of law or an entity publicly agreed on.

Certification Authority: A certification authority $\mathcal{CA}$ vouches for the authenticity of the public key of PKI bound to the subject user. We consider the case where PKI is derived from discrete logarithm based cryptosystems, such as ElGamal encryption.

Before executing the protocol, $\mathcal{CA}$ generates his signatures on $text_i$ for each user i ($i \in \Phi$), where $text_i$ includes the public key $v_i \overset{\triangle}{=} g^{d_i}$ (d_i is user i's secret key), the identity of subject entity and other information such as serial numbers or algorithm etc. $\mathcal{CA}$ publicizes $text_i$ and the signature denoted by $sig_{CA}(text_i)$. Then, our scheme proceeds as follows:

System initialization – $\mathcal{SA}$ generates some information that he will need with $\mathcal{T}$ and all users, and he makes the encryption key $e_{\mathcal{SA}}$ public.

User initialization – $\mathcal{SA}$ sells the decoder containing the personal key D_i to user i, in a way that D_i is constructed by d_i, and $\mathcal{SA}$ verifies this with zero-knowledge of the value of d_i nor D_i.

Session sending – The content is divided into smaller parts called sessions denoted by M. $\mathcal{T}$ chooses a random session key s, and broadcasts $(e_{\mathcal{SA}}(s)$,

$ENC_s(M))$, where $e_{\mathcal{SA}}(s)$ is called a *header* and ENC is a symmetric encryption function. Each user i can decrypt $e_{\mathcal{SA}}(s)$ to obtain s with D_i, and thus can decrypt M.

Tracing – If a pirate decoder is confiscated, $\mathcal{T}$ analyzes the personal keys D_{u_1}, $\cdots$, D_{u_t} in it and specifies a set of the suspected traitors Ω.

Trial – $\mathcal{T}$ accuses Ω to $\mathcal{A}$ with $(D_{u_j}, text_{u_j}, sig_{\mathcal{CA}}(text_{u_j}))$, $(j \in \Omega)$.

In this paper, the confiscation of a pirate decoder implies the possibility to obtain the value of the decryption key in it. If a non-subscriber obtains a pirate decoder which was constructed by at most k traitors, he can reveal all the secret keys of the traitors. Thus, in the model of our scheme traitors do not willingly give away their personal keys which include their secret keys, and such a situation is not considered in the model of traitor tracing.

2.2   Definition

Security requirements for $\mathcal{SA}$ on our schemes are as follows.

Definition 1 *We say that secrecy is established, if it is hard for non-subscribers to cryptanalyze a new session key from a new header, the public key, the old headers, and the old session keys.*

Definition 2 *When a pirate decoder is confiscated, which was constructed by at most k traitors, and if $\mathcal{T}$ can identify at least one traitor, then we say that traceability is established.*

Definition 3 *If no collusion among at mosk k malicious users can construct a pirate decoder without divulging at least one of the traitors' sensitive information to the entity who obtained the decoder, then we say that self-enforcement is established.*

Definition 4 *We say that direct non-repudiation is established, if $\mathcal{T}$ can convince $\mathcal{A}$ of the validity of the tracing results without the participation of the suspected traitors and $\mathcal{SA}$ in the trial phase, if not $\mathcal{T} = \mathcal{SA}$.*

Next, we define security for users.

Definition 5 *We say full frameproof is established, if no collusion of arbitrary entities including $\mathcal{SA}$ can frame an honest user*

Now we give our security parameters. Let q be a prime such that $q|p - 1$, $q \geq n+1$, where p is a prime power, and let g be a qth root of unity over $GF(p)$. Unless we stated otherwise, all calculation as below is done over $GF(p)$, and all entities agree on p, q and g.

2.3 Building Blocks

Our protocol is based on the efficient public key traitor tracing [8], and Oblivious Polynomial Evaluation (OPE) protocol [10]. Now, we briefly describe them.

Asymmetric Traitor Tracing with Agents [8]. Kurosawa and Desmedt suggested an efficient public key asymmetric traitor tracing scheme. Their scheme offers asymmetric traceability by dividing $\mathcal{SA}$'s secret into some pieces and separately distributing these to multiple trusted third parties, called *agents*, denoted by $\mathcal{A}_1, \cdots, \mathcal{A}_c$. Their scheme is as follows.

- *System initialization:* Each agent $\mathcal{A}_i$ chooses a random polynomial $f_i(x) = a_{i,0} + a_{i,1}x + \cdots + a_{i,k}x^k$ over Z_q and publicizes

$$y_{i,0} = g^{a_{i,0}}, y_{i,1} = g^{a_{i,1}}, \cdots, y_{i,k} = g^{a_{i,k}}$$

  Let

$$y_j \overset{\triangle}{=} \prod_{i=1}^{c} y_{i,j} \quad (j = 0, \cdots, k)$$

  Then, the public encryption key is $(p, g, y_0, \cdots, y_k)$.
- *User initialization:* Each $\mathcal{A}_i$ secretly gives $f_i(j)$ to user j. Let

$$f(x) \overset{\triangle}{=} \sum_{i=1}^{c} f_i(x) = a_0 + a_1 x + \cdots + a_k x^k$$

  Then, $y_j = g^{a_j}$ for $j = 1, \cdots, k$. User j computes $f(j) = \sum_{i=1}^{c} f_i(j)$ and now $D_j = (j, f(j))$ is his personal key.
- *Session sending:* For a session key s, $\mathcal{T}$ computes a header as $h(s, r) = (g^r, b_0, b_1, \cdots, b_k)$, where $b_0 = sy_0{}^r$, $b_1 = y_1{}^r$, $\cdots$, $b_k = y_k{}^r$ and r is a random number. Then $\mathcal{T}$ broadcasts $h(s, r)$. Each user i computes s from $h(s, r)$ and his personal key as follows.

$$\prod_{j=0}^{k} b_j^{i^j} \Big/ (g^r)^{f(i)} = s$$

- *Tracing:* If the pirate decoder contains $(u, f(u))$, and if

$$g^{f(u)} = \prod_{i=0}^{k} y_i^{u^i} \tag{1}$$

  then $\mathcal{T}$ decides u is a traitor.
- *Trial:* $\mathcal{A}$ is convinced if (1) holds.

In the above protocol, the evidence of the piracy of u is $(u, f(u))$ which satisfies (1). However, the collusion of all agents can generate such evidence and thus frame an honest user. Therefore, their scheme does not offer full frameproof in the sense of our definition.

Oblivious Polynomial Evaluation. The Oblivious Polynomial Evaluation (OPE) protocol, which was introduced by Naor and Pinkas [10], is a novel and useful primitive for two party computation. One party Bob knows a polynomial P and he would like to let Alice compute the value $P(\alpha)$ for an input α known to her in such a way that Bob does not learn α and Alice does not gain any additional information about P (except $P(\alpha)$).

We briefly review the protocol. Bob chooses a random bivariate polynomial $Q(x, y)$, such that $Q(0, y) = P(y)$. Alice chooses a random univariate polynomial $S(x)$, such that $S(0) = \alpha$. Alice's plan is to interpolate the univariate polynomial $R(x) \stackrel{\triangle}{=} Q(x, S(x))$ without revealing $S(x)$, then she knows $R(0) = Q(0, S(0))$ $= P(S(0)) = P(\alpha)$. This is done by sending n ($\stackrel{\triangle}{=} \deg(R(x)) + 1$) x_i and a list of random values $y_{i,j}$ except one value $S(x_i)$ ($i = 1, \cdots, n$). Bob computes $Q(x_i, y_{i,j})$ for all these values and Alice retrieves $Q(x_i, S(x_i))$ ($i = 1, \cdots, n$) using 1-out-of-m oblivious transfer. Then, she can interpolate $R(x)$.

In the above protocol, the secrecy of Alice's input depends on the *noisy polynomial interpolation problem* [10,2]. Recently it was proved that the noisy polynomial interpolation problem can be transformed into the lattice shortest vector problem with high probability, when the parameters satisfy a certain condition, and some other attacks to the problem were suggested [2]. However, a little modification on the protocol makes the secrecy of Alice's input dependent on the *polynomial reconstruction problem*, which is one of the well known most intractable problems [2].

The OPE protocol uses 1-out-of-N oblivious transfer (OT) protocol as the building block. Naor and Pinkas also suggested an efficient construction of 1-out-of-N OT protocol in [10], which invokes 1-out-of-2 OT $\log N$ times and evaluates a pseudo-random function $N \log N$ times. If we use non-interactive 1-out-of-2 OT in [1], the number of communication paths in 1-out-of-N OT and OPE protocol is two.

3   Construction

The central idea of our proposal is to reduce the traitor tracing scheme in [8] to the scheme where user i's personal key is represented by $(d_i, f(d_i))$ (d_i is user i's secret key in the PKI) and $\mathcal{SA}$ can verify it using the public information $text_i, sig_{\mathcal{CA}}(text_i)$. To accomplish this, we divide $f(x)$ into two polynomials $f_1(x), f_2(x)$, such that $(f_1(x) + f_2(x) = f(x))$. $\mathcal{SA}$ distributes $f_1(d_i)$ to user i using OPE protocol and then $\mathcal{SA}$ verifies that the user i's input to OPE was really d_i, without the knowledge of d_i itself. If the verification is passed, $\mathcal{SA}$ distributes $f_2(d_i)$ to user i using OPE. In the second invocation of OPE, even if the user inputs the value which is different from d_i adaptively, he cannot gain any useful information. (See Section 4)

Now, we present the construction of our proposal.

Table 2. System and User Initialization Protocol

$\mathcal{SA}$ User $i \in \Phi$

$$f(x) = \sum_{l=0}^{2k-1} a_l x^l \bmod q$$

$$f_{i,1}(x) = \sum_{l=0}^{2k-1} b_{i,l} x^l \bmod q$$

$$f_{i,2}(x) = f(x) - f_{i,1}(x)$$
$$= \sum_{l=0}^{2k-1} c_{i,l} x^l \bmod q$$

                                                                 d_i: User i 's secret key

$$\xrightarrow{\quad f_{i,1}(d_i) \ (\text{by OPE}) \quad}$$

                                          $(w_{i,2}, \cdots, w_{i,2k-1}, w_i) \leftarrow$
                                          $(g^{d_i^2}, \cdots, g^{d_i^{2k-1}}, g^{f_{i,1}(d_i)})$

$$\xleftarrow{\quad (w_{i,2}, \cdots, w_{i,2k-1}, w_i) \quad}$$

check

$$g^{b_{i,0}} v_i^{b_{i,1}} \prod_{l=2}^{2k-1} w_{i,l}^{b_{i,l}}$$
$$\stackrel{?}{=} w_i$$

$$\xrightarrow{\quad f_{i,2}(d_i) \ (\text{by OPE}) \quad}$$

                                          personal key
$$D_i = (d_i, f(d_i))$$
$$= (d_i, f_{i,1}(d_i) + f_{i,2}(d_i))$$

System Initialization. $\mathcal{SA}$ chooses a random polynomial $f(x) = \sum_{l=0}^{2k-1} a_l x^l$ and computes

$$y_l = g^{a_l} \quad (l = 0, 1, \cdots, 2k-1)$$

Then, the public encryption key is $(p, g, y_0, \cdots, y_{2k-1})$.

User Initialization. $\mathcal{SA}$ chooses a random polynomial $f_{i,1}(x) = \sum_{l=0}^{2k-1} b_{i,l} x^l$ for each user i and computes

$$f_{i,2}(x) = f(x) - f_{i,1}(x) = \sum_{l=0}^{2k-1} c_{i,l} x^l$$

$$c_{i,l} = a_{i,l} - b_{i,l} \quad (l = 0, 1, \cdots, 2k - 1)$$

$\mathcal{SA}$ distributes $f_{i,1}(d_i)$ to user i using the OPE protocol, where d_i is the user i's secret key in PKI. Then $\mathcal{SA}$ verifies that the user i's input was really d_i as follows.

User i computes

$$(w_{i,2}, w_{i,3}, \cdots, w_{i,2k-1}, w_i) \stackrel{\triangle}{=} (g^{d_i{}^2}, g^{d_i{}^3}, \cdots, g^{d_i{}^{2k-1}}, g^{f_{i,1}(d_i)})$$

and sends it to $\mathcal{SA}$. $\mathcal{SA}$ verifies whether

$$g^{b_{i,0}} v_i{}^{b_{i,1}} w_{i,2}{}^{b_{i,2}} w_{i,3}{}^{b_{i,3}} \cdots w_{i,2k-1}{}^{b_{i,2k-1}} = w_i.$$

holds. If the verification is passed, then $\mathcal{SA}$ distributes $f_{i,2}(d_i)$ to user i using the OPE protocol. Now, $D_i = (d_i, f(d_i)) = (d_i, f_{i,1}(d_i) + f_{i,2}(d_i))$ is the user i's personal key.

Session Sending. For a session key s, $\mathcal{T}$ computes a header as $h(s, r) = (g^r, b_0, b_1, \cdots, b_{2k-1})$, where $b_0 = sy_0{}^r$, $b_1 = y_1{}^r$, $\cdots$, $b_{2k-1} = y_{2k-1}{}^r$ and r is a random number. Then $\mathcal{T}$ broadcasts $h(s, r)$. Each user i computes s from $h(s, r)$ and his personal key as follows.

$$\prod_{j=0}^{2k-1} b_j{}^{d_i{}^j} \Big/ (g^r)^{f(d_i)} = s$$

Tracing. If the pirate decoder contains $D_{u_j} = (d_{u_j}, f(d_{u_j}))$, $(j \in \Omega)$, and if

$$g^{f(d_{u_j})} = \prod_{l=0}^{2k-1} y_l{}^{d_{u_j}{}^l} \quad (j \in \Omega) \tag{2}$$

$$g^{d_{u_j}} = v_{u_j} \quad (j \in \Omega) \tag{3}$$

holds, then $\mathcal{T}$ identifies Ω as the set of traitors.

Trial, If $\mathcal{T}$ decides that Ω is the set of traitors, then $\mathcal{T}$ gives $\mathcal{A}$ $(D_{u_j} = (d_{u_j}, f(d_{u_j})), text_{u_j}, sig_{\mathcal{CA}}(text_{u_j})), (j \in \Omega)$ as the evidence of piracy. $\mathcal{A}$ is convinced if $(2)(3)$ holds.

4   Security

In this section we analyze the security of our scheme, which consists of the security analysis for the system authority and for users.

4.1 Security for the System Authority

Secrecy In [8], it is proved (Theorem 14) that the computational complexity for an eavesdropper to cryptanalyze a new session key s, after having received previous session keys s_j, $(j = 0, 1, \cdots, l)$, the public key $e_{\mathcal{SA}} = (p, g, g^{a_0}, g^{a_1}, \cdots, g^{a_k})$, the old headers $h(s_j, r_j) = (g^{r_j}, s_j g^{a_0 r_j}, g^{a_1 r_j}, \cdots, g^{a_k r_j})$, $(j = 0, 1, \cdots, l)$ and the new header $h(s, r) = (g^r, s g^{a_0 r}, g^{a_1 r}, \cdots, g^{a_k r})$, is as hard as to cryptanalyze a plaintext in the ElGamal scheme when the order of g is a prime. In our scheme, the information that a passive eavesdropper could get is the same as in the scheme in [8] except for $k \to 2k - 1$, thus secrecy of the proposal also depends on the difficulty of breaking underlying the ElGamal encryption scheme.

Traceability and Self-Enforcement The strategy for malicious users to construct a pirate decoder which is not traceable or which does not divulge any sensitive information of malicious users is classified into two types.

1. to input invalid values in the user initialization phase adaptively
2. to construct a pirate decoder by colluding among up to k traitors after having received legitimate personal keys in the user initialization phase

We demonstrate that such strategies are not effective in our scheme. First, we give some lemmas about the former strategy.

Lemma 1 *In the user initialization phase, a malicious user u cannot pass the verification after the first invocation of OPE protocol if he inputs an invalid value d' different from his secret key d_u assuming the intractability of breaking the OPE protocol.*

Proof (Sketch)
To pass the verification, u must send $(w_{u,2}, w_{u,3}, \cdots, w_{u,2k-1}, w_u)$ for which

$$g^{b_{u,0}} (g^{d_u})^{b_{u,1}} w_{u,2}{}^{b_{u,2}} w_{u,3}{}^{b_{u,3}} \cdots w_{u,2k-1}{}^{b_{u,2k-1}} = w_u$$

holds after having $d_u, d', f_{u,1}(d')$. It is obviously information theoretically intractable. For example, if we assume u knows $b_{u,2}, b_{u,3}, \cdots, b_{u,2k-1}$, then he can obtain $b_{u,0} + b_{u,1} d'$ by $f_{u,1}(d') - (b_{u,2} d'^2 + \cdots + b_{u,k} d'^{2k-1})$. However he cannot compute $g^{b_{u,0}} (g^{d_u})^{b_{u,1}}$ using these values without knowledge of $b_{u,0}$ or $b_{u,1}$. $\diamond$

Thus, if the malicious user u selects the former strategy, all the measures he can take is to input an invalid value d' in the second invocation of the OPE protocol. However it is obviously information theoretically intractable to compute $(d'', f(d''))$ using $(d_u, f_{u,1}(d_u))$ and $(d', f_{u,2}(d'))$ where $d_u \neq d'$, $f = f_{u,1} + f_{u,2}$. If he can divide the header as follows

$$(g^r, s g^{a_0 r}, g^{a_1 r}, \cdots, g^{a_{2k-1} r}) = (g^r, s g^{b_{u,0} r} g^{c_{u,0} r}, g^{b_{u,1} r} g^{c_{u,1} r}, \cdots, g^{b_{u,2k-1} r} g^{c_{u,2k-1} r})$$

then he can compute s by

$$\frac{s g^{b_{u,0} r} g^{c_{u,0} r} (g^{b_{u,1} r})^{d_u} (g^{c_{u,1} r})^{d'} \cdots (g^{b_{u,2k-1} r})^{d_u{}^{2k-1}} (g^{c_{u,2k-1} r})^{d'^{2k-1}}}{(g^r)^{f_{u,1}(d_u) + f_{u,2}(d')}} = s$$

But such a division is obviously information theoretically intractable. Moreover any collusion attacks on the former strategy is meaningless because $(b_{u,0}, b_{u,1}, \cdots, b_{u,2k-1})$ is unique to user u. Therefore the former strategy is ineffective.

Now we discuss the latter strategy. Due to the similar argument to that of [8], the next lemma holds.

Lemma 2 *The computational complexity for $2k-1$ traitors of finding $(d_u, f(d_u))$, where $d_u \notin \{d_{u_1}, \cdots, d_{u_{2k-1}}\}$, when given the public key and their personal keys $(f(u_1), \cdots, f(u_{2k-1}))$ is as hard as the discrete logarithm problem (DLP) when the order g is prime.*

Proof Sketch
In [8] Theorem 15 proves the same lemma where $2k - 1 \to k$. $\diamond$

The above lemma shows that it is hard to construct another legitimate pirate key $(d, f(d))$ by at most k traitors $\Omega = \{u_1, \cdots, u_t\}$, such that $(d, f(d)) \notin \{(d_{u_1}, f(d_{u_1})), \cdots, (d_{u_t}, f(d_{u_t}))\}$, assuming DLP is computationally hard to solve. However the pirate may construct a key which is not a legitimate personal key but can be used to decrypt a session key in such a way that none of the traitors is identified from it. A successful pirate strategy is given in [14,3] which defeats the scheme of [8] by using a convex combination of traitors' personal keys. Fortunately, it is known that by increasing the degree of f from k to $2k - 1$, anyone who confiscated a pirate decoder which was constructed on this strategy can compute all the traitors' personal keys if the number of traitors is at most k [4,3]. This means that in our protocol arbitrary entities can recover all of the traitor's secret keys in the PKI, on the confiscation of a pirate decoder which was constructed by at most k traitors.

We review their convex combination attack and how it is solved when the degree of f is $2k - 1$. Let $\boldsymbol{\beta} = (\alpha, \beta_0, \cdots, \beta_{2k-1})^T$ such that

$$\boldsymbol{\beta} = t_1 \boldsymbol{u}_1 + \cdots + t_k \boldsymbol{u}_k$$

where

$$\boldsymbol{u}_j = (f(d_{u_j}), 1, d_{u_j}, \cdots, d_{u_j}^{2k-1})^T \quad (j = 1, \cdots, k)$$
$$t_1 + \cdots + t_k = 1$$

Then $\boldsymbol{\beta}$ is not a legitimate personal key, but it can be used to decrypt any header $h(s, r) = (g^r, b_0, b_1, \cdots, b_k) = (g^r, sg^{a_0 r}, g^{a_1 r}, \cdots, g^{a_{2k-1}})$ by

$$\prod_{l=0}^{2k-1} b_l^{\beta_l} \bigg/ (g^r)^{\alpha} = \prod_{m=1}^{k} \left(\prod_{l=0}^{2k-1} b_l^{d_{u_m}^{l}} \bigg/ (g^r)^{f(d_{u_m})} \right)^{t_m} = \prod_{m=1}^{k} s^{t_m} = s$$

Those who obtained $\boldsymbol{\beta}$ can construct the following equation with $2k$ unknowns $u_1, \cdots, u_k, t_1, \cdots, t_k$.

$$\begin{pmatrix} 1 \\ \beta_1 \\ \vdots \\ \beta_{2k-1} \end{pmatrix} = \begin{pmatrix} 1 & \cdots & 1 \\ d_{u_1} & \cdots & d_{u_k} \\ \vdots & \ddots & \vdots \\ d_{u_1}^{2k-1} & \cdots & d_{u_k}^{2k-1} \end{pmatrix} \begin{pmatrix} t_1 \\ t_2 \\ \vdots \\ t_k \end{pmatrix}$$

Some efficient solving algorithms of the above equation are already known, such as the Berlekamp-Massey algorithm [9] or the Peterson-Gorenstein-Zierler decoding algorithm etc. (see [19] for example) and everyone can recover $d_{u_1}, \cdots, d_{u_k}$ which are traitors secret keys in PKI. Therefore the latter strategy is also ineffective.

For the discussions stated above we can conclude that our proposal offers traceability and self-enforcement.

Direct Non-repudiation. Let assume that user i is honest, namely, he keeps his personal key $(d_i, f(d_i))$ secret. Then all the information about d_i that the data supplier, malicious users, and the certification authority could obtain is the corresponding public key g^{d_i}. Thus the difficulty of framing a user i by them is the same as DLP. All the information about d_i that the system authority could obtain is $g^{d_i}, g^{d_i^2}, \cdots, g^{d_i^{2k-1}}$ if we assume that breaking the OPE protocol is intractable. The difficulty of deriving d_i from these values is believed to be as hard as DLP. For the discussion stated above, it is computationally hard for the malicious entities to obtain honest user i's secret key d_i *unless* he divulges it.

Thus, $(d_{u_j}, f(d_{u_j}))(u_j \in \Omega)$ could be the enough evidence to prove the redistribution of the personal key by u_j. (2)(3) in Section 3 means d_{u_j} and $f(d_{u_j})$ matching, and user u_j's secret key and public key matching respectively. The verification process only needs pirate key and public information, and does not need the participation of the pirate user and the system authority.

For the discussion stated above, our proposal offers direct non-repudiation.

4.2   Security for Users

Full Frameproof. In order to win the trial, the tracer must submit the suspected traitor's secret key to the arbiter. Due to the same discussion as the one in the proof of direct non-repudiation, if an honest user i keeps his personal key $D_i = (d_i, f(d_i))$ secret, it is computationally hard for the other malicious entities to obtain user i's secret key d_i, which is a part of the proof of piracy.

Thus our proposal offers full frameproof.

5   Conclusion

In this paper we present a concrete construction of an asymmetric self-enforcement scheme. Our proposal also offers asymmetric traceability without trusted third parties, and is very efficient compared to previous traitor tracing schemes. In the model of our scheme, malicious users do not willingly give away their personal keys because our scheme guarantees that each user's personal key includes the user's sensitive information e.g. secret key in PKI, and such situation is not considered in the model of traitor tracing schemes. Furthermore, our protocol offers direct non-repudiation and full frameproof.

Acknowledgments

Part of this work was supported by Research for the Future Program (RFTF), Japan Society for the Promotion of Science (JSPS), under contract number JSPS-RETF 96P00604.

The authors would like to thank Tatsuyuki Matsushita for very useful discussion in preparing this paper. We are grateful to anonymous referees for their valuable comments that improved the presentation of this paper.

References

1. M.Bellare and S.Micali, "Non-interactive oblivious transfer and applications," *Advances in Cryptology - CRYPTO '89*, LNCS 435, Springer-Verlag, pp.547-557, 1990.
2. D.Bleichenbacher and P.Q.Nguyen, "Noisy Polynomial Interpolation and Noisy Chinese Remaindering," *Advances in Cryptology - EUROCRYPT 2000*, LNCS 1807, Springer-Verlag, pp.53-69, 2000.
3. D.Boneh and M.Franklin, "An Efficient Public Key Traitor Tracing Scheme," *Advances in Cryptology - CRYPTO '99*, LNCS 1666, Springer-Verlag, pp.338-353, 1999.
4. Burmester, Desmedt, Kurosawa, Ogata and Okada, *manuscript*.
5. B.Chor, A.Fiat and M.Naor, "Tracing Traitors," *Advances in Cryptology - CRYPTO '94*, LNCS 839, Springer-Verlag, pp.257-270, 1994.
6. C.Dwork, J.Lotspiech and M.Naor, "Digital Signets: Self-Enforcing Protection of Digital Information," *Proc. of 28th ACM Symposium on Theory of Computing(STOC)*, pp.489-498, 1996.
7. P.Kocher, J.Jaffe and B.Jun, "Differential Power Analysis," *Advances in Cryptology - CRYPTO '99*, LNCS 1666, Springer-Verlag, pp.388-397, 1999.
8. K.Kurosawa and Y.Desmedt, "Optimum Traitor Tracing and Asymmetric Schemes," *Advances in Cryptology - EUROCRYPT '98*, LNCS 1403, Springer-Verlag, pp.145-157, 1998.
9. J.L.Massey, "Shift Register Synthesis and BCH Decoding," *IEEE Transactions on Information Theory*, vol. IT-15, No.1, pp.122-127, January 1969.
10. M.Naor and B.Pinkas, "Oblivious Transfer and Polynomial Evaluation," *Proc. of 31th ACM Symposium on Theory of Computing(STOC)*, pp.245-254, 1999.
11. B.Pfitzmann, "Trials of Traced Traitors," *Proc. of Information Hiding, First International Workshop*, LNCS 1174, Springer-Verlag, pp.49-64,1996.
12. B.Pfitzmann and M.Waidner, "Asymmetric Fingerprinting for Lager Collusions," *Proc. of ACM Conference on Computer and Communication Security*, pp.151-160, 1997.
13. T.Sander and A.Ta-Shma, "Flow Control: A New Approach for Anonymity Control in Electronic Cash Systems," *Proc. of Financial Cryptography: Third International Conference, FC'99*, LNCS 1648, Springer-Verlag, pp.46-61, 1999.
14. D.R.Stinson and R.Wei, "Key Preassigned Traceability Schemes for Broadcast Encryption," *Proc. of SAC '98*, LNCS 1556, Springer-Verlag, pp.144-156, 1998.
15. N.R.Wagner, "Fingerprinting," *Proc. of IEEE 1983 Symposium on Security and Privacy*, April, pp.18-22, 1983.
16. Y.Watanabe, G.Hanaoka and H.Imai, "Asymmetric Public-Key Traitor Tracing without Trusted Agents," *Proc. of the Symposium on Information Theory and Its Application (SITA 2000)*, October, 2000.

17. Y. Watanabe, G. Hanaoka and H. Imai, "Efficient Asymmetric Public-Key Traitor Tracing without Trusted Agents," *to appear in Proc. of the RSA Conference Cryptographer's Track*, April, 2001 (to be published in LNCS).
18. Y.Watanabe, H.Komaki, G.Hanaoka and H.Imai, "Asymmetric Traitor Tracing based on Oblivious Polynomial Evaluation," (in Japanese) *IEICE Technical Report, ISEC*, September, 2000.
19. S.B.Wicker, "Error Control Systems for Digital Communication and Storage," Prentice-Hall, Inc., 1995.

Adaptive Security for the Additive-Sharing Based Proactive RSA

Yair Frankel[1], Philip D. MacKenzie[2], and Moti Yung[3]

[1] Ecash Technologies Inc., USA. yfrankel@cs.columbia.edu
[2] Bell Laboratories, Murray Hill, NJ 07974, USA. philmac@research.bell-labs.com
[3] CertCo Inc., New York, NY, USA. moti@cs.columbia.edu

Abstract. Adaptive security has recently been a very active area of research. In this paper we consider how to achieve adaptive security in the additive-sharing based proactive RSA protocol (from Crypto97). This protocol is the most efficient proactive RSA protocol for a constant number of shareholders, yet it is scalable, i.e., it provides reasonable asymptotic efficiency given certain constraints on the corruption threshold. It is based on organizing the shareholders in a certain design (randomly generated, in the asymptotic case) of families of committees and establishing communications based on this organization. This structure is very different than polynomial-based proactive RSA protocols, and the techniques for achieving adaptive security for those protocols do not apply. Therefore, we develop new techniques for achieving adaptive security in the additive-sharing based proactive RSA protocol, and we present complete proofs of security.

1 Introduction

Distributed cryptosystems provide for security and availability of a private key through distribution of shares of the key, coupled with a mechanism in which some number (a threshold) of shareholders are able to jointly compute the cryptographic function using their shares of the key, while a smaller number of possibly misbehaving parties are prevented from disrupting this computation, or computing the cryptographic function on their own. A distributed cryptosystem achieves *proactive security* if at least a threshold of shareholders must misbehave (or be compromised) *in a specified time period* in order to compromise the security or availability of the system. A distributed cryptosystem achieves *adaptive security* if it is secure against an adaptive adversary, that is, an adversary that may take actions based on the entire available history, including ciphertexts sent during the protocol. (We say such distributed cryptosystems are *adaptively-secure*.) More complicated protocols are typically required to achieve adaptive security, and proving that a protocol is adaptively secure is typically more difficult than proving that a protocol is secure against a non-adaptive adversary.

In this paper we consider the additive-sharing based proactive RSA protocol [FGMY97]. This is the most efficient proactive RSA protocol for a constant number of shareholders, and is also scalable. Unlike some solutions, it guarantees

K. Kim (Ed.): PKC 2001, LNCS 1992, pp. 240–263, 2001.
© Springer-Verlag Berlin Heidelberg 2001

that the threshold value is maintained throughout, even when some participants are unavailable. Therefore it is an attractive solution for practical situations. It is based on organizing the shareholders in a "design" consisting of families of committees of shareholders. We modify this protocol to achieve adaptive security while maintaining the same organization and the basic protocol structure.

History of Threshold Proactive and Adaptive Systems:

Threshold schemes for discrete log and RSA based cryptosystems were presented in [DF89,B88,F89,DF91,DDFY92,FD92]. Robust schemes that assure the correctness and timeliness of the cryptographic operation were presented in [GJKR,FGY96,GJKR96,Sh00]. Some of these protocols make additional system requirements or additional constraints on certain cryptographic parameters beyond what is required for the corresponding non-distributed cryptosystems. This is not a criticism, since such constraints sometimes allow a cleaner or more efficient distributed solution. For example, to allow an efficient non-interactive robustness check in [GJKR96], secure keys are required at the combiner. Without this, every participant must have keys to verify the operation of other participant which makes the scheme much more expensive (i.e., quadratic in the number of participants). The solution of [GJKR96], and the algebraically-pleasing solution of [Sh00], also place constraints on the RSA keys which can be used. (We note that RSA keys constrained in such a manner cannot be generated using the distributed key generation methods in [BF97,FMY98].) Similar constraints are made in the early heuristic protocol of [DF91] (which [FMY00] builds on).

The notion of proactive security [OY91,CH94,HJKY95,HJJKY96] was developed to cope with a mobile adversary, i.e., an adversary that may compromise all servers over the lifetime of a system, but fewer than a given threshold at any particular time. An RSA based proactive scheme (which does not achieve optimal resilience in the asymptotic case) was given in [FGMY97]. It is based on additive sharing and is the one we concentrate on herein. A scheme based on polynomial sharing that achieves optimal resilience was given in [FGMY97b]. A scheme that combined additive and polynomial sharing was offered by [R98], but it has the sometimes undesirable property that the threshold value may be dynamically reduced due to occasional unavailability of possibly honest shareholders.

The importance of developing protocols that are provably secure against a fully-adaptive adversary has been discussed in [BeHa92,CFGN96,B97] in the context of general distributed computation. Adaptively secure (polynomial sharing) threshold schemes were given in [FMY99,FMY99b], and in [CGJKR], which is extended in [JL00]. The RSA based scheme in [CGJKR] seems to be an n-out-of-n system, since all parties need to compute together after each signature.

Our Contribution:

We present an adaptively secure version of the original additive-sharing based proactive RSA. We present a complete careful proof of its security and robustness without making any additional system requirements or any constraints on the cryptographic parameters. Our version exploits the organization and protocol structure of the original protocol. It is only slightly less efficient, yet it is provably secure against a fully-adaptive adversary. The scheme is very efficient for small size system, yet it is scalable asymptotically to tolerate any fraction of malicious shareholders bounded away from half (e.g. 1/3). It can be used with general RSA keys and can be initiated distributedly.

Discussion of Techniques Used:

We distribute the RSA private key using many r-out-of-r additive threshold schemes as in [F89]. The additive shares are distributed to certain subsets of servers where the construction of subsets is taken from [AGY95]. By using a simple additive threshold scheme [F89] as the basis of our system, we simplify the domain over which sharing is done (when compared with [DDFY92]), and enable the verification and re-randomization of shares by the servers. Also, this method is what makes the system suitable for settings with a constant number of servers. To provide robustness, we employ the idea of witness-based cryptographic program checking [FGY96] which extends Blum's methodology of program result checking [Bl88] to a system where the checker itself is not trusted by the program. Finally to show that the distribution of shares is secure, we use a simulatability argument similar to one that was put forth in the static distribution of RSA [DDFY92].

For proving security against a fully-adaptive adversary, we must show that the protocol is simulatable. A problem arises if the simulator must simulate the actions of a servers whose shares are unknown, and those actions may commit to the share value. Then if the adversary decides to corrupt that server, it can distinguish between the real protocol and the simulation. In our proactive protocol we use the erasure primitive to maintain security, and we assume that uncorrupted shareholders will erase information when specified by the protocol. In fact, this assumption is required for the system to be secure against a mobile adversary. (In other words, in this security setting, the erasure primitive is as important as any other computational primitive.) Thus, we can substitute non-committing encryption [BeHa92] (which uses erasure) for probabilistic encryption to remove the commitments from the encryptions.

Allowing erasures may seem to be enough to prove security. However, it is not sufficient, since there are other share commitments in the protocol, namely, the partial signatures combined for signing and the witness-based cryptographic program checking used for *robustness*. This is all publicly available information that must be made accessible to any arbitrary party (a gateway) in order for that party to be able to produce the correct function result from the partial results. We thus require new ideas which are developed here. We use information-theoretically secure witnesses for robustness maintenance, which allows a simulator to "spread the fraud" over all servers, instead of concentrating it on a given shareholder with a single "bogus commitment." Then we show how to remove the share commitments from signatures through blinding. In this case, we still have bogus commitments, but we show that the probability of the simulator successfully fooling the adversary is high enough that (limited) backtracking can be employed to generate realistic-looking views for the adversary.

Other then the above changes the adaptively-secure protocol is compatible with the original Crypto97 protocol. (This enables a system designer to implement both and decide at configuration/run time which variant is applicable to his setting).

2   Model and Definitions

2.1   The RSA Function

First we define the RSA function.

Definition 1. *Let η be the security parameter. Let key generator GE define a family of RSA functions to be $(e, d, N) \leftarrow GE(1^\eta)$ such that N is a composite number $N = P * Q$ where P, Q are prime numbers of $\eta/2$ bits each. The exponent e and modulus N are made public while $d \equiv e^{-1} \mod \lambda(N)$ is kept private.*[1]

*The **RSA encryption function** is public, defined for each message $M \in Z_N$ as: $C = C(M) \equiv M^e \mod N$. The **RSA decryption function** (also called signature function) is the inverse: $M = C^d \mod N$. It can be performed by the owner of the private key d. The security of RSA is given in Definition 6.*

For naming convenience, we will assume our system is used for direct RSA signing of messages; however, the same protocol could be used for decryption. Our results simply concern the application of the RSA function in its assumed intractable direction as a one-way function (as assumed in protocols with formal security proofs which employ RSA, e.g. [ACGS]).

2.2   The Model

Now we define our Proactive RSA system.

The Participants: The participants in our system are (1) l servers $\{s_1, \ldots, s_l\}$, (2) a trusted dealer D, and (3) a gateway G. The dealer D generates an RSA instance (e, d, N), distributes shares of d among the l servers during an initialization phase, and then does not participate any further. The gateway G is used to broadcast messages to be signed to the servers and to combine their partial signatures into the final signature. (Note that G is not trusted, and in fact is not really necessary except for convenience.)

As the protocol is running, the servers will be classified as follows: A server is *compromised* if its secret is known to the adversary. A server is *corrupted* if it is controlled by the adversary. (We assume all corrupted servers are compromised.) We refer to a server as *good* if it is uncorrupted, and actively participates in a protocol. We refer to a server as *bad* if it is compromised. (Note that some servers may be neither good nor bad.) We assume

---

[1] $\lambda(N) = \text{lcm}(P-1, Q-1)$ is the smallest integer such that any element in Z_N^* raised by $\lambda(N)$ is the identity element. RSA is typically defined using $\phi(N)$, the number of elements in Z_N^*, but it is easy to see that $\lambda(N)$ can be used instead. We use it because it gives an explicit way to describe an element of maximal order in Z_N^*. Note that $\phi(N)$ is a multiple of $\lambda(N)$, and that knowing any value which is a multiple of $\lambda(N)$ implies breaking the system.

that all uncorrupted servers receive all messages that are broadcast, and retrieve the information from messages encrypted with a public key, if they know the corresponding private key. We also assume that if they are active in a protocol, they participate honestly. We will show that our protocols perform correctly even if only the good servers and corrupted servers are active.

The Communication Model: The communication model presented here is similar to [HJKY95]. All participants communicate via an authenticated bulletin board [CF85] in a synchronized manner. We assume that the adversary cannot jam communication. The board assumption models an underlying basic communication protocol (authenticated broadcasts) and allows us to disregard the low-level technical details.

Time periods: Time is divided into *time periods* which are determined by the common global clock (e.g., a day, a week, etc.). There are two types of time periods repeated in sequence: an **update period** (odd times) and an **operational period** (even times). During an operational period, the servers can cooperatively sign messages using the current key shares. During the update period the servers engage in an interactive *update protocol*. At the end of an update period the servers hold new shares which are used during the following operational period. (Technical note: we consider a server that is corrupted during an update phase as being corrupted during both its adjacent periods. This is because the adversary could learn the shares used in both the adjacent operational periods.)

System Management: We assume that a server that is determined to be corrupted by a majority of active servers can be *refreshed* (i.e., erased and rebooted, or perhaps replaced by a new server with a blank memory) by some underlying system management. This is a necessary assumption for dealing with corrupted servers in any proactive system.

The Adversarial Model: We next define some orthogonal properties of the adversary.

Definition 2. *A* **stationary** *adversary may corrupt servers at different times, but a server that is corrupted remains corrupted for the duration of the protocol. A* **mobile** *adversary (we employ) may corrupt servers at different times, but a server that is corrupted may be refreshed by the underlying system management at some later time, and become "uncorrupted."*

Note that when we deal with a mobile adversary, the set of corrupted servers does not necessarily monotonically increase over time. Also note that the above definitions also apply to compromising or preventing honest participation by servers.

Definition 3. *A* (k', k, l)**-restricted** *adversary is a mobile adversary that can, during any time period, (a) prevent at most $l - k$ servers from honestly participating in a protocol (i.e., there will always be at least k good servers), (b) corrupt (i.e., force to behave in an arbitrary manner) at most $\min\{l - k, k'\}$ servers, and*

(c) compromise (i.e., view the memory of) at most k' servers (including those that it corrupts).

Threshold schemes are often described in terms of withstanding coalitions of "k-out-of-l" corrupted servers. In our notation, that would correspond to withstanding a $(k, k + 1, l)$-restricted adversary.

The actions of an adversary at any time may include submitting messages to the system to be signed, corrupting or compromising servers, and broadcasting arbitrary information on the communication channel. The following definition describes different criteria on which an adversary may base its actions.

Definition 4. A **static** adversary must decide on its actions before the execution of the protocol. A **non-adaptive** adversary (considered earlier) is allowed to base its actions on previous function outputs (i.e., previous message/signature pairs) obtained during the execution of the protocol, but no other information gained during the execution of the protocol. A **fully adaptive** adversary (which we employ) is allowed to base its actions not only on previous function outputs, but on all the information that it has previously obtained during the execution of the protocol, including all messages broadcast on the public channel (ciphertexts exchanged between servers, partial function evaluations, etc.) and the contents of all memories of servers that it has viewed.

We assume that the adversary stores all messages that were broadcast on the public channel and the contents of all memories of servers that it can view. (Naturally, all this information is time-tagged.) Assuming S is the system being attacked, and $\mathcal{A}$ is the adversary, we call this stored information $view^S_{\mathcal{A}, L}$, where L is the list of messages that are submitted to S to be signed. (Note that the signatures will be implicit in the view.)

system, etc.)

2.3   Properties

We say that a function $f(h)$ is *negligible* if for any polynomial $poly(\cdot)$, there is an h' such that for $h > h'$, $f(h) < 1/poly(h)$.

Now we define what it means for a system to be robust. In these definitions we assume the security parameter η is large enough so that the analysis holds.

Definition 5. (Robustness) Let η be the security parameter. A system S is a (k', k, l)-robust proactive RSA system if it contains a polynomial-time protocol SIG (run by the servers) such that for any probabilistic polynomial-time (k', k, l)-restricted adversary $\mathcal{A}$, with all but negligible probability, assuming (e, d, N) is the RSA instance generated by the dealer, for every $\alpha \in [0, N]$ that is submitted to be signed (during an operational period), the servers can compute $\alpha^d \bmod N$ using SIG.

Next we define what it means for the RSA system to be secure (RSA is treated as a one-way function).

Definition 6. (Security) *Let η be the security parameter. Let key generator GE define a family of RSA functions (i.e., $(e, d, N) \leftarrow GE(1^\eta)$ is an RSA instance with security parameter η). Let $S(e, d, N)$ denote a system S in which the RSA instance (e, d, N) was chosen by the trusted dealer D. Then S is a (k', k, l)-secure proactive RSA system if it generates instances of RSA using $GE(1^\eta)$, and if for any probabilistic polynomial-time (k', k, l)-restricted adversary $\mathcal{A}$, for any list L of randomly chosen messages submitted to S to be signed, for any probabilistic polynomial-time function A: $\Pr[u^e \equiv w \bmod N : (e, d, N) \leftarrow GE(1^\eta); w \in_R \{0, 1\}^\eta; u \leftarrow A(1^\eta, w, view_{\mathcal{A},L}^{S(e,d,N)})]$ is negligible.*

In the next section we describe a proactive RSA system which is (k', k, l)-secure and (k', k, l)-robust, assuming a fully adaptive adversary.

3   The Adaptively-Secure Protocol

3.1   Outline

At the start an assignment of servers to committees and families is chosen (as in [AGY95]). Specifically, for given values m, r, and c, servers are randomly assigned to mr committees that are evenly split between m families, such that each committee has c servers assigned to it. (Note that each server may be assigned to multiple committees.) This random assignment may be performed by the trusted dealer, or by the servers themselves. The values m, r, and c are chosen such that with high probability each set of k servers can obtain all the shares from some family, and no set of k' servers can obtain all the shares from any family.

After the assignment of servers to committees, the dealer D generates an RSA instance (e, d, N), and distributes additive shares of d to the committees in each family as in [F89]. Thus each family obtains an r-out-of-r sharing of the key. In the original protocol $a_{i,j}^0$ is the share given to the jth committee in family i by the dealer, and more generally, $a_{i,j}^{2t}$ is the share corresponding to the jth committee in family i during operational period $2t$. During an operational period (say period $2t$), when a message M needs to be signed, the servers possessing $a_{i,j}^{2t}$ can produce the value (the partial signature) $M^{a_{i,j}^{2t}} \bmod N$. Because of the assignment choice above, at least one of the m families will produce correct values for all committees, and therefore, for at least one i, the gateway G can compute the RSA signature of M using the formula $M^d \equiv \prod_{j=1}^r M^{a_{i,j}^{2t}} \bmod N$.

During an update period (a) the good shares are renewed and (b) corrupted shares are recovered. The basic technique to renew and recover shares is by creating shares of shares and distributing the shares of shares appropriately.

To provide for robustness throughout the protocol, we use a witnesses (similar to [FGY96,GJKR96]) for each share. These witness are used to check partial signatures and to check that the renewal of shares in the update period is performed correctly.

To allow adaptive adversary we take a few extra steps, to assure simulatability of the protocol. We use information theoretic commitments and witness process. We carefully evaluate results. But, the protocol organization and structure remains as in the original protocol, which is our main achievement. (We note that sometimes, adapting a protocol may be harder than having the freedom to design it afresh. Also, we do not change the basic model assumptions: threshold requirements, and the notion of threshold as some earlier protocols did).

Remark: In all of these subprotocols, messages are put on an authenticated bulletin board. One implementation is having every message signed by the sender using a secure signature scheme, and ignoring any message with an invalid signature. We include the renewal of individual signature keys in the description of our protocol. Note that we still need an initial authentication token to be available for recovering servers. We will henceforth assume that all the signed messages originate at the correct server; otherwise, the assumption about the security of the underlying signature scheme is violated.

Notation: In our protocol description, messages are presented inside brackets. Messages include a "message-tag" which is a self-explanatory (mnemonic) description of the role of the message, the tag is followed by the message content.

3.2   Initialization Phase

Families and Committees: The assignment we describe is a slight generalization of [AGY95]. This assignment can be performed by the trusted dealer, or by the servers themselves. Let $S = \{s_1, \ldots, s_l\}$ be the set of servers and $\mathcal{F} = \{F_1, \ldots, F_m\}$ be the set of families, where each $F_i = \{C_{i,1}, \ldots, C_{i,r}\}$ is a set of committees of servers. Each committee is of size c. Let $I = \{1, \ldots, m\}$ and $J = \{1, \ldots, r\}$ be the indices of families and committees, respectively. The parameters m, r, and c are chosen such that the result will be a (k', k, l)-terrific assignment, that is, one that obeys the following properties **for any** set of "bad" servers $B \subseteq S$ with $|B| \leq k'$ and any set of "good" servers $E \subseteq S$ with $|E| \geq k$:

1. For all $i \in I$, there exists a $j \in J$ such that $B \cap C_{i,j} = \emptyset$. (For each family there is one committee with no bad servers which we call an *excellent* committee.)
2. For at least 90 percent of $i \in I$, for all j, $E \cap C_{i,j} \neq \emptyset$. (In 90 percent of the families, all committees have at least one good server. We call a family F_i with this property a *good* family.)

Let $\sigma = k'/l$ and let $\tau = k/l$. Given l, q, p, and security parameter $\eta \geq \max\{2l + 2, 100\}$, we will set $c = \lceil \{2 \log \eta / \log(\frac{1-\sigma}{1-\tau})\} \rceil$, $r = (1 - \tau)^{-c}/\eta$, and $m = 10\eta$. Note that all of these values are polynomial in η as long as $\tau - \sigma$ is greater than some constant (i.e., as long as the gap between the number of good servers and bad servers is at least a constant fraction of l).

Lemma 7 ([AGY95]). *A randomly chosen assignment is ϵ-terrific with overwhelming probability.*

The proof is given in the appendix. We can control the probability of obtaining a non-ϵ-terrific assignment to be smaller than that of breaking the RSA function given the security parameter. Note that once we have terrific assignment, any choice of "bad servers" is allowed– which is important in the mobile adversary case.

In practical adaptations where a small (constant) numbers of servers is expected the randomized construction can be replaced be a deterministic design. For example:

- a (1,2,3)-terrific assignment can be made with 1 family with 3 committees: ({1,2},{1,3},{2,3});
- a (2,3,4)-terrific assignment can be made with two families, each with 3 committees: ({1,2},{3},{4}) and ({1},{2},{3,4});
- a (2,3,5)-terrific assignment can be made with three families, each with 3 committees: ({1,2},{3,4},{5}), ({1,3},{2,5},{4}) and ({2,4},{3,5},{1}); and
- a (2,4,6)-terrific assignment can be made with two families, each with 3 committees: ({1,2},{3,4},{5,6}) and ({2,3},{4,5},{6,1}).

3.3 Initialization Phase

In this phase, only the Share Distribution protocol is changed from the Basic Protocol. The change is simply the inclusion of companion shares.

Share Distribution Protocol:

1. The dealer generates p, q, e, d, as in RSA: $N = pq$ and $ed \equiv 1 \bmod \lambda(N)$.
2. The dealer generates $d' \in_R [1, N^2]$.
3. The dealer generates[2] $g, h \in_R [2, N-2]$, sets $y = g^d h^{d'} \bmod N$ (Pedersen commitment to d), and broadcasts $[\text{DISTRIBUTE}.1, N, e, g, h, y]$.
4. The dealer next generates the shares of the secret: For each $(i,j) \in I \times J \setminus \{r\}$, the dealer generates $a_{i,j}^0 \in_R [-\rho, \rho]$ and $w_{i,j}^0 \in_R [-N\rho, N\rho]$. Then it sets $a_{i,r}^0 = d - \sum_{j \in J \setminus \{r\}} a_{i,j}^0$ and $w_{i,r}^0 = d' - \sum_{j \in J \setminus \{r\}} w_{i,j}^0$.
5. The dealer generates the Pedersen commitment to the shares: For each $i \in I$ and $j \in J$, the dealer sets $\epsilon_{i,j} \equiv g^{a_{i,j}^0} h^{w_{i,j}^0} \bmod N$
6. The dealer broadcasts the private check shares and the encrypted shares: $[\text{DISTRIBUTE}.2, \{\epsilon_{i,j}\}_{(i,j) \in I \times J}, \{\text{ENC}_{i,j}(a_{i,j}^0, w_{i,j}^0)\}_{(i,j) \in I \times J}]$.
7. Every server checks for each family $i \in I$ that $\prod_{j \in J} \epsilon_{i,j} \equiv y \bmod N$ and each server in $C_{i,j}$ checks the correctness of its public share, namely that $\epsilon_{i,j} \equiv g^{a_{i,j}^0} h^{w_{i,j}^0} \bmod N$.
8. Every server sets the signature family indicator $f^0 = 0$, and for each $(i,j) \in I \times J$, every server sets $b_{i,j}^0 = \epsilon_{i,j}$.

Recently, a method for generating a distributed RSA key was developed by [BF97]. Later a robust distributed RSA key generation system was developed

---

[2] As in the Basic Protocol we assume here that g and h are of maximal order.

[FMY98]. We note that, given this distributed generation, we could distributively perform steps 2-7 (with the need to replicate super logarithmic number of random elements g's and generate them and their corresponding h's distributedly). Thus, we could remove the trusted dealer assumption from our proactive RSA model. The initial assignment can also be chosen distributedly via a coin flipping protocol by the shareholders. (A discussion on distributed initialization is omitted from this version).

Now that the system is initialized, we have to describe the the signing protocol and the proactive update (renewal) protocol.

Notation: For each $(i, j) \in I \times J$, $\text{ENC}_{i,j}(\alpha)$ will denote an encryption of α using the public key of $C_{i,j}$. For all $s \in S$, $\text{ENC}_s(\alpha)$ will denote a probabilistic encryption of α using the public key of server s. Remember, in our model the adversary is computationally bounded and thus it cannot get more than a negligible advantage in computing any function of α by seeing its encryption. For succinctness, let $\rho = Nm^2r^2c\psi(\eta)$, where $\psi()$ is an agreed upon super-polynomial function. This value ρ will be used to compute the possible range of secret shares in each period.

3.4 Signature Protocol (Operational Period $2t$)

This is the protocol to be followed when the gateway obtains a message M to be signed in period $2t$. It differs from the Basic Protocol in that families work sequentially to try to generate a signature, instead of in parallel. Also, in each family there is a re-randomization of the shares (in steps 2(a)-(h) below, which are just like the share renewal protocol but only involving one family).

As in the Basic Protocol, we use the fact that since $d = \sum_{j \in J} a_{i,j}^{2t}$ then $M^d \equiv \prod_{j \in J} M^{a_{i,j}^{2t}} \bmod N$.

During an operational period (say period $2t$), when a message M needs to be signed, only one family will initially attempt to generate a signature. This will be indicated by the *signature family indicator* f^{2t}. Let $i = f^{2t}$. If F_i is unable to generate a signature, then all its data is erased, f^{2t} is incremented, and the next family will attempt to generate a signature. This is repeated until some family succeeds in generating a signature. (Success is guaranteed by the assignment choice, which was shown to include good families.) When a family attempts to generate a signature, it will randomize its shares, and use the randomized shares for computing the partial signatures. The signal family indicator f^{2t} is set to the family that should be attempting to generate a signature. There are two possible cases: (1) the family has already signed at this stage, and thus the randomized shares have been produced already and the current signature session can reuse them, or (2) the family has to start by re-randomizing the shares.

The protocol proceeds as follows:

1. The gateway broadcasts [SIGN.1, M].
2. Let $i = f^{2t}$. The following steps are performed for family F_i.

(a) If the period's randomized shares $\tilde{a}_{i,j}^{2t}$, $\tilde{w}_{i,j}^{2t}$, and $\tilde{b}_{i,j}^{2t}$ values have already been produced, skip to Step 3.

Otherwise, run share-randomization: the members of the family perform additive re-randomization of shares: for all $j \in J$, each server s in $C_{i,j}$ does the following: s chooses $\tilde{c}_{s,i,j,j'}^{2t} \in_R [-\rho(t+1)^2, \rho(t+1)^2]$ and $\tilde{v}_{s,i,j,j'}^{2t} \in_R [-N\rho(t+1)^2, N\rho(t+1)^2]$ for $j' \in J \setminus \{r\}$. Then it sets $\tilde{c}_{s,i,j,r}^{2t} = a_{i,j}^{2t} - \sum_{j' \in J \setminus \{r\}} \tilde{c}_{s,i,j,j'}^{2t}$ and $\tilde{v}_{s,i,j,r}^{2t} = w_{i,j}^{2t} - \sum_{j' \in J \setminus \{r\}} \tilde{v}_{s,i,j,j'}^{2t}$. Then for all $j' \in J$, s computes $\alpha_{s,i,j,j'} = \text{ENC}_{i,j'}[\tilde{c}_{s,i,j,j'}^{2t}, \tilde{v}_{s,i,j,j'}^{2t}]$ and $\beta_{s,i,j,j'}^{2t} = g^{\tilde{c}_{s,i,j,j'}^{2t}} h^{\tilde{v}_{s,i,j,j'}^{2t}} \bmod N$.

(b) **Share-of-share distribution**: Each server in a committee redistributes the committee's share amongst the other committees. One of the committee's correct resharings will be used. For all $j \in J$, each server s in $C_{i,j}$ broadcasts
[SIGN.RANDOMIZE.1, $s, i, j, \{\beta_{s,i,j,j'}^{2t}\}_{j' \in J}, \{\alpha_{s,i,j,j'}\}_{j' \in J}$].

(c) **Verification of shares of check shares**: Every server verifies, for all $j \in J$ and all $s \in C_{i,j}$, that $\prod_{j' \in J} \beta_{s,i,j,j'}^{2t} = b_{i,j}^{2t} \bmod N$, and informs the system management if it doesn't hold for some s (The servers can easily agree that this s is faulty). From this point on, we only deal with messages from those s where the above equality does hold.

(d) **Verification of shares of shares**: For all $j' \in J$, each $s \in C_{i,j'}$ decrypts shares to $C_{i,j'}$ and verifies $g^{\tilde{c}_{s',i,j,j'}^{2t}} h^{\tilde{v}_{s',i,j,j'}^{2t}} \equiv \beta_{s',i,j,i',j'}^{2t} \bmod N$ for all s'. For all $j' \in J \setminus \{r\}$, each $s \in C_{i,j'}$ also verifies $|\tilde{c}_{s',i,j,j'}^{2t}| \leq \rho(t+1)^2$ and $|\tilde{v}_{s',i,j,j'}^{2t}| \leq N\rho(t+1)^2$ for all s'.

(e) **Dispute resolution**: If server s finds that verification fails for a message from server s', s broadcasts
[SIGN.ACCUSE, s, i, j, j', s'], to which s' responds by broadcasting
[SIGN.DEFEND, $s', i, j, j', \tilde{c}_{s',i,j,j'}^{2t}, \tilde{v}_{s',i,j,j'}^{2t}$].

(f) **Agreement on bad servers**: All servers check all accusations and inform the system management of any bad servers (i.e., those that defended with invalid values of $\tilde{c}_{s',i,j,j'}^{2t}$ and $\tilde{v}_{s',i,j,j'}^{2t}$). Again, from this point on, we only deal with messages from the good servers.

(g) **Reconstructing the family's randomized shares for signing**: For all $j' \in J$, each $s \in C_{i,j'}$, using the lexicographically first servers in each committee with shares that passed verification (call them $s_{i,j}$), computes $\tilde{a}_{i,j'}^{2t} = \sum_{j \in J} \tilde{c}_{s_{i,j},i,j,j'}^{2t}$, $\tilde{w}_{i,j'}^{2t} = \sum_{j \in J} \tilde{v}_{s_{i,j},i,j,j'}^{2t}$, and $\tilde{b}_{i,j'}^{2t} \equiv \prod_{j \in J} \beta_{s_{i,j},i,j,j'}^{2t} \bmod N$.

(h) Everything produced at previous steps in this protocol is erased except $\tilde{a}_{i,j}^{2t}$, $\tilde{w}_{i,j}^{2t}$, and $\tilde{b}_{i,j}^{2t}$ for all $j \in J$.

3. Now the family has re-randomized shares for signing at this period. They follow the procedure below:

(a) **Generating partial signatures based on randomized shares**: For all $j \in J$, each server $s \in C_{i,j}$ computes $r_{i,j} \equiv M^{\tilde{a}_{i,j}^{2t}} \bmod N$ and broadcasts the message [SIGN.2, $s, i, j, M, r_{i,j}$].

(b) **Disputes within committees**: For all $j \in J$, each server $s' \in C_{i,j}$ checks each message $[\text{SIGN.2}, s, i, j, M, r_{i,j}]$. If M is not the same message broadcast by the gateway, then s' disregards the message, else if $r_{i,j} \not\equiv M^{\tilde{a}^{2t}_{i,j}} \bmod N$, then s' broadcasts the challenge $[\text{SIGN.CHALLENGE}, s', i, j, \tilde{a}^{2t}_{i,j}, \tilde{w}^{2t}_{i,j}]$.

(c) **Agreement on bad servers in committees**: All servers verify all challenges (by checking if $\tilde{b}^{2t}_{i,j} \equiv g^{\tilde{a}^{2t}_{i,j}} h^{\tilde{a}^{2t}_{i,j}} \bmod N$) and inform the system management of any bad servers (i.e., those servers that sent a message with $r_{i,j} \not\equiv M^{\tilde{a}^{2t}_{i,j}} \bmod N$).

(d) **Combining the partial signatures and verifying correctness of the final signature**: After the checks are completed, and for the $r_{i,j}$ values that passed the tests, the gateway tests if $(\prod_{j \in J} r_{i,j})^e \equiv M \bmod N$. If this does not hold, then for all $j \in J$, all servers in $C_{i,j}$ erase their shares $a^{2t}_{i,j}$ and $w^{2t}_{i,j}$ and anything else produced at previous steps in this protocol, f^{2t} is incremented, and we go to Step 2 (thus proceeding to the next family). Note that if a signature is not computed, family F_i must already be bad so erasing the remaining shares does not affect the system. Note also that there are good families, and such a family will produce a valid signature.

3.5 Renewal Protocols (Update Period $2t + 1$)

Only the Share Renewal/Lost Share Recovery protocol changes from the Basic Protocol, whereas individual key renewal and committee key renewal do not. If the non-committing encryption scheme from [BeHa92] is used, the key renewal phases include generation of pseudorandom pads, and the actual keys are erased. We refer the reader to [BeHa92] for details.

Share Renewal/Lost Share Recovery: The only change from the Basic Protocol is to perform renewal on the $w^{2t}_{i,j}$ shares (the companion shares) along with the $a^{2t}_{i,j}$ shares.

Now we give the protocol:

1. **Share-resharing**: For all $(i, j, i') \in I \times J \times I$, each server s in $C_{i,j}$ does the following: s chooses $c^{2t}_{s,i,j,i',j'} \in_R [-\rho(t+1)^2, \rho(t+1)^2]$ and $v^{2t}_{s,i,j,i',j'} \in_R [-N\rho(t+1)^2, N\rho(t+1)^2]$ for $j' \in J \setminus \{r\}$. Then it sets $c^{2t}_{s,i,j,i',r} = a^{2t}_{i,j} - \sum_{j' \in J \setminus \{r\}} c^{2t}_{s,i,j,i',j'}$ and $v^{2t}_{s,i,j,i',r} = w^{2t}_{i,j} - \sum_{j' \in J \setminus \{r\}} v^{2t}_{s,i,j,i',j'}$. Then for all $j' \in J$, s computes $e_{s,i,j,i',j'} = \text{ENC}_{i',j'}[c^{2t}_{s,i,j,i',j'}, v^{2t}_{s,i,j,i',j'}]$ and $\epsilon_{s,i,j,i',j'} = g^{c^{2t}_{s,i,j,i',j'}} h^{v^{2t}_{s,i,j,i',j'}} \bmod N$.

2. **Share-of-share distribution**: For all $(i, j) \in I \times J$, each server s in $C_{i,j}$ broadcasts $[\text{UPDATE.1}, s, i, j, \{\epsilon_{s,i,j,i',j'}\}_{(i',j') \in I \times J}, \{e_{s,i,j,i',j'}\}_{(i',j') \in I \times J}]$.

3. **Public verification of of re-shared witnesses against old witnesses**: Every server verifies, for all $(i, j, i') \in I \times J \times I$ and all $s \in C_{i,j}$, that $\prod_{j' \in J} \epsilon_{s,i,j,i',j'} = b^{2t}_{i,j} \bmod N$, and informs the system management if it

doesn't hold for some s. From this point on, we only deal with messages from those s where it does hold.

4. **Private verification re-shared witnesses:** For all $(i', j') \in I \times J$, each $s \in C_{i',j'}$ decrypts shares to $C_{i',j'}$ and verifies $g^{c^{2t}_{s',i,j,i',j'}} h^{v^{2t}_{s',i,j,i',j'}} \equiv \epsilon_{s',i,j,i',j'}$ mod$N$ for all s'. For all $(i', j') \in I \times J \setminus \{r\}$, each $s \in C_{i',j'}$ also verifies $|c^{2t}_{s',i,j,i',j'}| \leq \rho(t+1)^2$ and $|v^{2t}_{s',i,j,i',j'}| \leq N\rho(t+1)^2$ for all s'.

5. **Dispute resolution:** If server s finds that verification fails for a message from server s', s broadcasts [UPDATE.ACCUSE, s, i, j, i', j', s'], to which s' responds by broadcasting
   [UPDATE.DEFEND, $s', i, j, i', j', c^{2t}_{s',i,j,i',j'}, v^{2t}_{s',i,j,i',j'}$].

6. **Agreement on bad servers:** All servers check all accusations and inform the system management of any bad servers (i.e., those that defended with invalid values of $c^{2t}_{s',i,j,i',j'}$ and $v^{2t}_{s',i,j,i',j'}$). Again, from this point on, we only deal with messages from the good servers.

7. **Correct share update:** For all $(i', j') \in I \times J$, each $s \in C_{i',j'}$, using the shares of the lexicographically first family F_i with shares that passed verification, using the lexicographically first servers in each committee in that family with shares that passed verification (call them $s_{i,j}$), computes $a^{2t+2}_{i',j'} = \sum_{j \in J} c^{2t}_{s_{i,j},i,j,i',j'}$, $w^{2t+2}_{i',j'} = \sum_{j \in J} v^{2t}_{s_{i,j},i,j,i',j'}$, and $b^{2t+2}_{i',j'} \equiv \prod_{j \in J} \epsilon_{s_{i,j},i,j,i',j'}$ mod N.

8. **Terminate update:** Everything is erased except $a^{2t+2}_{i,j}$, $w^{2t+2}_{i,j}$, and $b^{2t+2}_{i,j}$ for all $(i, j) \in I \times J$.

9. f^{2t+2} is set to 0.

4   Proof of Adaptive Security

We claim that:

Theorem 8. *The proactive RSA system above is (k', k, l)-secure against a fully adaptive adversary.*

We prove the security of our system in two stages. First, we construct a simulator which produces views of the adversary in polynomial time (in Subsection 4.1). Then (in Subsection 4.2) we show how, using the simulator, one reduces the security of the RSA function to the security of a slightly modified version of our scheme against the adaptive mobile adversary. This slightly modified system simply gives more information to the adversary, so it is trivial to conclude the security of our actual system. Also, we actually use a more stringent definition of security in which not only should it be difficult for an adversary to generate a signature for a random message, but it also should be difficult to generate the discrete log of g with respect to h, and vice-versa. More concretely,

Definition 9. (Security) *Let η be the security parameter. Let key generator GE define a family of RSA functions (i.e., $(e, d, N) \leftarrow GE(1^\eta)$ is an RSA instance with security parameter η). Let $S(e, d, N, g, h)$ denote a system S in which the RSA instance (e, d, N) was chosen by the trusted dealer D using GE and*

$g, h \in_R Z_N^*$. Then S is a (k', k, l)-secure proactive RSA system if it generates instances of RSA using $GE(1^\eta)$, and if for any probabilistic polynomial-time (k', k, l)-restricted adversary $\mathcal{A}$, for any list L of randomly chosen messages submitted to S to be signed, for any probabilistic polynomial-time function A:
$\Pr[(u^e \equiv w \bmod N) \vee (g^\alpha \equiv h^\beta \bmod N) : (e, d, N) \leftarrow GE(1^\eta); g, h \in_R Z_N^*; w \in_R \{0,1\}^\eta; u, \alpha, \beta \leftarrow A(1^\eta, w, view_{\mathcal{A},L}^{S(e,d,N,g,h)})]$ is negligible.

We will use the following lemma, which can be proven using the RSA security assumption.

Lemma 10. Let η be the security parameter. Let modulus generator GE define a family of modulus generating functions (i.e., $N \leftarrow GE(1^\eta)$ be an RSA modulus with security parameter η). For any probabilistic polynomial-time adversary $\mathcal{A}$, $\Pr[u^e \equiv w^d \bmod N; (e \neq 0) \vee (d \neq 0) : N \leftarrow GE(1^\eta); u, w \in_R \{0,1\}^\eta; e, d \leftarrow A(1^\eta, w, u)]$ is negligible.

Proof. Similar to [B84]. ∎

In the slightly modified system we consider, we assume the adversary is given some extra information each time a set of shares is erased. We assume that after the shares are erased for a given family, the adversary is given the values of shares and "randomized signature shares" from all committees in that family except for the highest numbered committee (hereinafter called the *designated committee*) in which no servers were corrupted (up to that point in the period). Additionally, the adversary is given all values used in constructing those shares, and all values produced from those shares, i.e., the c, $\tilde{c}$, v and $\tilde{v}$ values. Finally, for any families that did not generate randomized signature shares, random ones are generated and revealed to the adversary, except for the ones for the designated committee. Thus the adversary always obtains from each family all but one committee's share and "randomized signature share." The choice of this committee is a deterministic function of the adversary's random bits and the adversary's view of the protocol to that point.

4.1 The Simulator

Here we construct SIM to simulate the view of $\mathcal{A}$ in the (secure-channel) system we describe above. We assume the random bits of $\mathcal{A}$ are fixed. The inputs to the simulator are an RSA public key (e, N), generators g and h,[3] the description of the adversary $\mathcal{A}$, and a history H.

Whenever f^{2t} is set to a value i, SIM chooses $j \in_R J$, indicating that SIM is guessing that $C_{i,j}$ is the designated committee in F_i for period $2t$. Note that SIM has exactly a $1/r$ probability of correctly guessing the one designated committee in F_i for period $2t$. If the guess is incorrect, SIM repeatedly backtracks to the point

---

[3] This is for the more stringent definition of security we want to prove for the Adaptive protocol. The simulator for the basic protocol needed to be able to choose the generator g itself, whereas for the adaptive protocol, it will not actually be necessary to choose these generators. This fact is needed in our proof of robustness.

where f^{2t} is set to i, randomly guessing which committee will be the designated committee, until it guesses correctly. Recall that after backtracking, the view of $\mathcal{A}$ could change, and since $\mathcal{A}$ is fully adaptive, it could corrupt different servers. Thus the designated committee may change. Still, SIM will have exactly a $1/r$ probability of guessing correctly each time it backtracks, and thus there will be no bias in the simulation with respect to the corruptions made by $\mathcal{A}$. There are m families, and the guesses are made sequentially. Therefore, SIM backtracks at most an average of mr times per period.

From now on, we will assume that SIM guesses the designated committee correctly. Below we discuss details of the simulations of the subprotocols. Note that the simulations of the key renewal protocol, the lost share detection protocol, and the share renewal/lost share recovery protocol are all exactly the same as the normal protocols.

Share Distribution Simulation: The Share Distribution Simulation is similar to Share Distribution, except that d is chosen to be 0. We let $a_{i,j}^{2t,sim}$, $w_{i,j}^{2t,sim}$, and $b_{i,j}^{2t,sim}$ denote the simulated values corresponding to the shares with the corresponding names.

Signature Simulation: Simulating a signature of some $M \in L$ during period $2t$ is done as in the Signature protocol with the following exception:

- In step 3, for the family F_i that is currently attempting to sign M and designated committee $C_{i,j}$, each $s \in C_{i,j}$ computes (with SIM's help, using the history H) $r_{i,j} \equiv M^d / \prod_{j' \in J, j' \neq j} r_{i,j'} \mod N$.

4.2   Security Proofs

The outline of the full security proof is as follows. We will first prove security in the secure channels model. Specifically, in Lemma 11 we will prove that the view of an adversary attacking our simulation of the protocol is statistically indistinguishable from the view of that adversary attacking the real protocol. Then, in Lemma 16, we show that statistical indistinguishability in the secure channels model implies polynomial indistinguishability when using non-committing encryption for sending private messages. Finally, we prove the theorem by showing that breaking the security of the protocol implies breaking RSA.

Simulation over Secure Channels For the rest of this section, let S be the system from the previous section with the modification described at the beginning of this section, and let SIM be the simulator described above.

Lemma 11. *Assuming secure channels, for any probabilistic (k', k, l)-restricted fully adaptive adversary $\mathcal{A}$, $view_{\mathcal{A},L}^{\text{SIM}(e,N,\mathcal{A},H,g,h)}$ is statistically indistinguishable from $view_{\mathcal{A},L}^{S(e,d,N,g,h)}$, where $H = hist(d, N, L)$.*

Proof. To simplify the proof we assume that $\mathcal{A}$'s random bits are fixed. We will show that, for every assignment of $\mathcal{A}$'s random bits, the two views are indistinguishable. We will assume that the protocol is run through period $2T$.

Say that, for each family F_i, j_i^{2t} is defined so that $C_{i,j_i^{2t}}$ is the designated committee.

For the sake of a consistent representation, let X be the random variable consisting of the cross product of the values from the set

$$
\bigcup_{(i,j)\in I\times J} \{a_{i,j}^0, w_{i,j}^0\} \cup \{y\} \cup \bigcup_{t\in\{0...T-1\},(i,j,i',j')\in I\times J\times I\times J} \{c_{i,j,i',j'}^{2t}, v_{i,j,i',j'}^{2t}\}
$$

$$
\cup \bigcup_{t\in\{0...T-1\},(i,j,j')\in I\times J\times J} \{\tilde{c}_{i,j,j'}^{2t}, \tilde{v}_{i,j,j'}^{2t}\},
$$

with $*$'s in certain positions indicating information the adversary does not see. Let X^{sim} denote the corresponding random variable in the simulated protocol.

Note that $y(= g^d h^{d'} \bmod N)$ along with the other non-$*$ values of a tuple from X or X^{sim} uniquely determine the check shares.

Proposition 12. $\mathit{diff}(\mathit{view}_{A,L}^{SIM(e,N,A,H,g,h)}, \mathit{view}_{A,L}^{S(e,d,N,g,h)}) \leq \mathit{diff}(X, X^{sim}).$

Proof. The remaining parts of the view of A are exactly determined by X (or X^{sim} in the simulation) g, h, the history tape, and A's random bits, and the history tape and A's random bits are assumed fixed. The remaining parts of the view therefore make no contribution to the statistical difference of the views.

We call the cross-products generated by X and X^{sim} *tuples*. Note that they include $*$'s in certain locations to indicate the value is unspecified (unknown to A). Let Z (Z^{sim}) be the completely specified tuples for the real (simulated) protocol. Of course, Z and Z^{sim} can be distinguished simply by examining the initial share values for one family F_i and determining whether they sum to 0 or not.

Say that two tuples are *overlapping*, if for all positions in which neither has a $*$, the values at those positions are the same. Given that A is a fully adaptive adversary, even though the random bits of A are fixed, tuples generated from X and X^{sim} may have $*$'s in differing positions. As an example, assume the tuples generated from X have length 5. Then one tuple might be $(125, *, 30, 39, 27)$. If the adversary were not fully adaptive, the position with the $*$ would be the same for every other tuple in X. However, since the adversary is fully adaptive, another tuple in X might be $(32, 35, *, 39, 27)$. These two tuples are not overlapping, but the tuple $(125, 35, *, 39, 27)$ would overlap with the first tuple.

The tuples in X, X^{sim}, Z, and Z^{sim} can be logically separated into sub-tuples of length r corresponding to the values that the r committees in a family receive during some protocol. In each sub-tuple of length r, there will be either zero or one $*$, and a sub-tuple with no $*$ indicates that the value shared to that committee was previously known. (This can occur during share renewal, for example, when a share known to the adversary is split into shares of shares.)

Proposition 13. *Given that the random bits of A are fixed, no distinct tuples in $X \cup X^{sim}$, may be overlapping.*

Proof. Consider two distinct tuples in $X \cup X^{sim}$, and consider the runs of the protocol that produced those tuples. Consider the first time that the behavior of

$\mathcal{A}$ diverges in these two runs. Before this time, the positions of $*$'s in the tuples must be the same. Remember that the random bits of $\mathcal{A}$ are fixed, so its actions are only dependent on its view, and when a designated committee is chosen, it is a deterministic function of $\mathcal{A}$'s random bits and $\mathcal{A}$'s view of the protocol to that point. Therefore, the values at some position in the two distinct tuples must be different, and thus the tuples are not overlapping.

Proposition 14. *There is a bijection between the tuples in X (X^{sim}) and the tuples in Z (Z^{sim})*

Proof. Naturally, each tuple in X (X^{sim}) corresponds to at least one tuple in Z (Z^{sim}), since it is $\mathcal{A}$'s view of the tuple in Z (Z^{sim}). Now, each tuple in X (X^{sim}) has at most one $*$ in each r-subtuple. But each of those can only be completed in one way, since the sum of the values in each r-tuple is determined. (For instance, for the r-subtuple of initial shares, the sum is d (0).) Thus there is at most one tuple in Z (Z^{sim}) that can correspond to the tuple in X (X^{sim}).

The following lemma completes the proof by showing that $\mathit{diff}(X, X^{sim})$ is sub-polynomial.

Proposition 15.

$$\mathit{diff}(X, X^{sim}) \leq \frac{2}{N} + \frac{6}{\psi(\eta)}$$

Proof. Let $\hat{X}$ be the distribution X restricted to the case where d' is not in the range $\lfloor N^2/\lambda(N) \rfloor \lambda(N)$ to N^2. Let $\hat{Z}$, $\hat{X}^{sim}$, and $\hat{Z}^{sim}$ be defined similarly. Then $\mathit{diff}(X, X^{sim}) \leq \mathit{diff}(\hat{X}, \hat{X}^{sim}) + 2\lambda(N)/N^2 \leq \mathit{diff}(\hat{X}, \hat{X}^{sim}) + 2/N$. Now we bound $\mathit{diff}(\hat{X}, \hat{X}^{sim})$. We will use the fact that in $\hat{X}$ and $\hat{X}^{sim}$, $d' \bmod \lambda(N)$ is uniform for both the actual protocol and the simulation.

Recall that $\rho = Nm^2r^2c\psi(\eta)$. The probability distribution on tuples generated by $\hat{Z}$ is uniform, meaning each tuple is generated with exactly the same probability. The same holds for $\hat{X}$, $\hat{Z}^{sim}$ and $\hat{X}^{sim}$.

Say a tuple is an *unmatched $\hat{X}$ tuple* if it is in $\hat{X} \setminus \hat{X}^{sim}$, and a tuple is an *unmatched $\hat{X}^{sim}$ tuple* if it is in $\hat{X}^{sim} \setminus \hat{X}$. Finally say a tuple is *unmatched* if it is an unmatched $\hat{X}$ tuple or an unmatched $\hat{X}^{sim}$ tuple. Then $\mathit{diff}(\hat{X}, \hat{X}^{sim})$ is the number of unmatched tuples multiplied by the probability of a given tuple. Note that by symmetry, the number of unmatched tuples will be twice the number of unmatched $\hat{X}$ tuples, so $\mathit{diff}(\hat{X}, \hat{X}^{sim})$ can be calculated by simply doubling the fraction of unmatched $\hat{X}$ tuples. In what follows, we will find an upper bound on the fraction of unmatched X tuples.

To determine if a tuple $v \in \hat{X}$ is an unmatched $\hat{X}$ tuple, we determine whether each $*$ in v could be replaced by a value to produce a tuple in $\hat{Z}^{sim}$. Remember that there could be at most one tuple in $\hat{Z}^{sim}$ that corresponds to v. Basically, we can replace any $*$ in v using the following procedure: Say v_z is the tuple in $\hat{Z}$ corresponding to v, and let x be the value at the location of the $*$ in v_z. Say $\Delta = d' - d'^{sim} \bmod \lambda(N)$. If the $*$ is in an r-subtuple of companion shares or shares of companion shares, then replace the $*$ with $x - \Delta$. If the $*$ is in an

r-subtuple of shares or shares of shares, replace the $*$ with $x - d$. Note that the only way we do not end up with a tuple in $\hat{Z}^{sim}$ is (1) if we replace a $*$ in one of the first $r - 1$ shares of the r-subtuple of shares at period 0 with a number not in the range $[-\rho, \rho]$, (1') if we replace a $*$ in one of the first $r - 1$ companion shares of an r-subtuple of companion shares at period 0 with a number not in the range $[-N\rho, N\rho]$, (2) if we replace a $*$ in one of the first $r - 1$ positions of an r-subtuple of update shares with a number not in the range $[-\rho(t+1)^2, \rho(t+1)^2]$, or (2') if we replace a $*$ in one of the first $r - 1$ positions of an r-subtuple of companion update shares with a number not in the range $[-N\rho(t+1)^2, N\rho(t+1)^2]$. Say an r-subtuple is *discriminating* one of these cases holds. (1) and (2) will each hold for d possible values of x. (1') and (2') will each hold for Δ possible values of x. To get a bound on the fraction of unmatched X tuples, we can place an upper bound on the fraction of tuples containing discriminating r-subtuples.

For each r-subtuple containing shares, for each position with a given value α, there are $(2\rho)^{r-2}$ r-subtuples. For each r-subtuple containing companion shares, for each position with a given value α, there are $(2N\rho)^{r-2}$ r-subtuples. For each r-subtuple containing shares of shares from period $2t + 1$, for each position with a given value α, there are $(2\rho(t+1)^2)^{r-2}$ r-subtuples. For each r-subtuple containing shares of companion shares from period $2t + 1$, for each position with a given value α, there are $(2N\rho(t+1)^2)^{r-2}$ r-subtuples.

To simplify the computation of the upper bound we desire, we will count each tuple with more than one discriminating r-subtuple multiple times, once for each discriminating r-subtuple. The fraction of tuples with discriminating subtuples is then bounded by

$$dm(r-1)\left[(2\rho)^{r-2}(2\rho)^{-(r-1)} + mrc\sum_{t=0}^{T-1}\frac{(2\rho(t+1)^2)^{r-2}}{(2\rho(t+1)^2)^{r-1}}\right]$$

$$+\Delta m(r-1)\left[(2N\rho)^{r-2}(2N\rho)^{-(r-1)} + mrc\sum_{t=0}^{T-1}\frac{(2N\rho(t+1)^2)^{r-2}}{(2N\rho(t+1)^2)^{r-1}}\right].$$

Then $diff(\hat{X}, \hat{X}^{sim})$ can be bounded by twice that number, which can be simplified to:

$$2dm(r-1)\left(\frac{1}{2\rho} + \sum_{t=0}^{T-1}\frac{mrc}{2\rho(t+1)^2}\right) + 2\Delta m(r-1)\left(\frac{1}{2N\rho} + \sum_{t=0}^{T-1}\frac{mrc}{2N\rho(t+1)^2}\right)$$

$$= \frac{md(r-1)}{\rho}\left(1 + mrc\sum_{t=0}^{T-1}(t+1)^{-2}\right) + \frac{m\Delta(r-1)}{N\rho}\left(1 + mrc\sum_{t=0}^{T-1}(t+1)^{-2}\right)$$

$$\leq \frac{2mN(r-1)(3mrc)}{\rho} = \frac{2mN(r-1)(3mrc)}{Nm^2r^2c\psi(\eta)} < \frac{6}{\psi(\eta)}.$$

This ends the proof of Lemma 11.

Simulation with Semantically-Secure Encryption

Lemma 16. *Given a probabilistic polynomial time (k', k, l)-restricted fully adaptive adversary adversary $\mathcal{A}$, views of $\mathcal{A}$ from executions of the real and simulated* *protocols using non-committing encryption are polynomial-time indistinguishable.*

Proof. This follows directly from [BeHa92].

Proof of the Theorem Now we finish the proof of Theorem 8.

Let η be the security parameter, and let GE be the key generator described in the definition of a (k', k, l)-secure proactive RSA system. Assume that the Adaptive Protocol (call it S) is not a (k', k, l)-secure proactive RSA system.

Then there exists a probabilistic polynomial-time (k', k, l)-restricted fully adaptive adversary $\mathcal{A}$, and a polynomial-time function A such that for a list L of randomly chosen messages submitted to be signed, $\Pr[(u^e \equiv w \bmod N) \vee (g^\alpha \equiv h^\beta \bmod N) : (e, d, N) \leftarrow GE(1^\eta); g, h \in_R Z_N^*; w \in_R \{0,1\}^\eta; u, \alpha, \beta \leftarrow A(1^\eta, w, \text{view}_{\mathcal{A},L}^{S(e,d,N,g,h)})]$ is non-negligible.

However, no polynomial-time function A could compute a signature u for a random challenge message $w \in_R \{0,1\}^h$ with more than negligible probability given only $\text{view}_{\mathcal{A},L}^{\text{SIM}(e,N,\mathcal{A},H,g,h)}$, (where $H = \text{hist}(d, N, L)$) since then a polynomial-time function could first compute $\text{view}_{\mathcal{A},L}^{\text{SIM}(e,N,\mathcal{A},H,g,h)}$ and then produce a signature for w, contradicting the RSA security assumption. Similarly, no polynomial-time function A could compute α and β such that $g^\alpha \equiv h^\beta \bmod N$ given only $\text{view}_{\mathcal{A},L}^{\text{SIM}(e,N,\mathcal{A},H,g,h)}$, since then a polynomial-time function could first compute $\text{view}_{\mathcal{A},L}^{\text{SIM}(e,N,\mathcal{A},H,g,h)}$ and then produce the desired α and β contradicting Lemma 10.

Therefore (still assuming the system is not secure), one could construct a distinguisher between $\text{view}_{\mathcal{A},L}^{\text{SIM}(e,N,\mathcal{A},H,g,h)}$ and $\text{view}_{\mathcal{A},L}^{S(e,d,N,g,h)}$, which contradicts Lemma 16. Thus S must be (k', k, l)-secure.

5   Robustness of the Adaptively-Secure Protocol

For a public RSA modulus N and two generators $g, h \in Z_N^*$, we say that one *breaks* (g, h, N) if one finds α and β with $(\alpha \neq 0) \vee (\beta \neq 0)$ such that $g^\alpha \equiv h^\beta \bmod N$.

In the following definitions, for each good committee $C_{i,j}$, we only consider the $a_{i,j}^{2t}$ and $w_{i,j}^{2t}$ values agreed on by the good servers in $C_{i,j}$, if they exist.

We say a proactive RSA system is *correct at period* $2t$ if $d \equiv \sum_{j \in J} a_{i,j}^{2t} \equiv \sum_{j \in J} \tilde{a}_{i,j}^{2t} \bmod \lambda(N)$ and $d' \equiv \sum_{j \in J} w_{i,j}^{2t} \equiv \sum_{j \in J} \tilde{w}_{i,j}^{2t} \bmod \lambda(N)$ for all good families F_i. We say a proactive RSA system is *verifiable at period* $2t$ if for each good committee $C_{i,j}$ $b_{i,j}^{2t} = g^{a_{i,j}^{2t}} h^{w_{i,j}^{2t}} \bmod N$ and $\tilde{b}_{i,j}^{2t} = g^{\tilde{a}_{i,j}^{2t}} h^{\tilde{w}_{i,j}^{2t}} \bmod N$. We say a proactive RSA system is *compact at period* $2t$ if all shares at time $2t$ are between $-r\rho(t + 1)^2$ and $r\rho(t + 1)^2$, and all companion shares at time $2t$ are between $-Nr\rho(t + 1)^2$ and $Nr\rho(t + 1)^2$. We say a proactive RSA system is *available at period* $2t$ if, after a signature protocol is run for a message M in operational period $2t$, a gateway G can efficiently identify a good family F_i, identify or compute correct partial (blinded) signatures $(\{M^{\tilde{a}^{2t}_{i,j}} \bmod N\}_{j\in J})$ for that family, and thus compute the correct signature $M^d \bmod N$ for M.

Lemma 17. *With overwhelming probability, for all $t > 0$, the proactive RSA system above is correct, verifiable, and compact at time $2t$.*

Proof. The basic idea is to show that if the system is not correct, verifiable, and compact at a specific time t, then there is a polynomial-time function A that can sign a random message w, or break (g, h, N), using as input the adversary's view of the protocol, thus breaking the security of the system. By Theorem 8 this happens with negligible probability.

We prove the lemma by induction on t. We will prove results related to the $a^{2t}_{i,j}$, $w^{2t}_{i,j}$, and $b^{2t}_{i,j}$ values. Similarly, we can prove the results related to the $\tilde{a}^{2t}_{i,j}$, $\tilde{w}^{2t}_{i,j}$, and $\tilde{b}^{2t}_{i,j}$ values. Since the dealer is trusted, our initial share distribution protocol guarantees the following properties:

- for all good families F_i, $d \equiv \sum_{j\in J} a^0_{i,j} \bmod \lambda(N)$ and $d' \equiv \sum_{j\in J} w^0_{i,j} \bmod \lambda(N)$, i.e., it is correct at period 0,
- for all good committees $C_{i,j}$, $b^0_{i,j} \equiv g^{a^0_{i,j}} h^{w^0_{i,j}} \bmod N$, where g, h are maximal order elements $\bmod N$, i.e., it is verifiable at period 0, and
- all shares are in the range $-r\rho$ to $r\rho$ and all companion shares are in the range $-Nr\rho$ to $Nr\rho$, i.e., it is compact at period 0.

For the inductive step, we will show correctness, verifiability, and compactness for each good family $F_{i'}$. Note that the shares of a family $F_{i'}$ can change only during the Share Renewal/Lost Share Recovery Protocol. Let F_i be the family used by $F_{i'}$ in update period $2t - 1$ to construct the shares $\{a^{2t}_{i',j'}, w^{2t}_{i',j'}\}_{j'\in J}$. In each committee $C_{i',j'}$, it is verified in the Share Renewal protocol that for all $j \in J$, $\epsilon^{2t-2}_{s,i,j,i',j'} \equiv g^{c^{2t-2}_{s,i,j,i',j'}} h^{v^{2t-2}_{s,i,j,i',j'}} \bmod N$. Then $b^{2t}_{i',j'}$ is set to $\prod_{j\in J} \epsilon^{2t-2}_{s,i,j,i',j'} \bmod N$, $a^{2t}_{i',j'}$ is set to $\sum_{j\in J} c^{2t-2}_{s,i,j,i',j'}$, and $w^{2t}_{i',j'}$ is set to $\sum_{j\in J} v^{2t-2}_{s,i,j,i',j'}$. Thus $b^{2t}_{i',j'} \equiv g^{a^{2t}_{i',j'}} h^{w^{2t}_{i',j'}} \bmod N$, which implies verifiability at period $2t$ for family $F_{i'}$.

Now let $\hat{d} = \sum_{j'\in J} a^{2t}_{i',j'} \bmod \lambda(N)$ and $\hat{d}' = \sum_{j'\in J} w^{2t}_{i',j'} \bmod \lambda(N)$. It is also verified in the Share Renewal protocol that for all $j \in J$, $b^{2t-2}_{i,j} \equiv \prod_{j'\in J} \epsilon^{2t-2}_{s,i,j,i',j'} \bmod N$, and by induction, it is guaranteed that $\prod_{j\in J} b^{2t-2}_{i,j} \equiv g^d h^{d'} \bmod N$. Then $g^{\hat{d}} h^{\hat{d}'} \equiv \prod_{j'\in J} b^{2t}_{i',j'} \equiv \prod_{j\in J} b^{2t-2}_{i,j} \equiv g^d h^{d'} \bmod N$. If $\hat{d} \neq d$, then it is easy to see that a polynomial-time function A could use the view of $\mathcal{A}$ to break (g, h, N), and thus the security of the system. This implies correctness at period $2t$ for family $F_{i'}$.

For compactness, we first show that unless the system has been broken, $\sum_{j'\in J} a^{2t}_{i',j'} = d$ and $\sum_{j'\in J} w^{2t}_{i',j'} = d'$. Assume $\sum_{j'\in J} a^{2t}_{i',j'} \neq d$. By correctness (which relies on the fact that (g, h, N) is not broken), $\sum_{j'\in J} a^{2t}_{i',j'} \equiv d \bmod \lambda(N)$, and thus $\sum_{j'\in J} \sum_{j\in J} c^{2t}_{s,i,j,i',j'} = \sum_{j'\in J} a^{2t}_{i',j'} = d + \kappa\lambda(N)$, for some integer constant κ. Note that for all non-corrupted committees $C_{i,j}$, $a^{2t-2}_{i,j} = \sum_{j'\in J} c^{2t-2}_{s,i,j,i',j'}$, and (from the discussion for verifiability and correctness above) for all other committees $C_{i,j}$, $a^{2t-2}_{i,j} \equiv \sum_{j'\in J} c^{2t-2}_{s,i,j,i',j'} \bmod N$. Let J^C_i be the set of corrupted committees in F_i. Then

$$\sum_{j\in J_i^C}\sum_{j'\in J} c_{s_{i,j},i,j,i',j'}^{2t-2} = d + \kappa\lambda(N) - \sum_{j\in J\backslash J_i^C}\sum_{j'\in J} c_{s_{i,j},i,j,i',j'}^{2t-2} =$$

$$d + \kappa\lambda(N) - \sum_{j\in J\backslash J_i^C} a_{i,j}^{2t-2} = d + \kappa\lambda(N) - (d - \sum_{j\in J_i^C} a_{i,j}^{2t-2}) =$$

$$\kappa\lambda(N) + \sum_{j\in J_i^C} a_{i,j}^{2t-2}$$

Since $\mathcal{A}$ knows $\sum_{j\in J_i^C} a_{i,j}^{2t-2}$ and $\sum_{j\in J_i^C}\sum_{j'\in J} c_{s_{i,j},i,j,i',j'}^{2t-2}$, it must know $\kappa\lambda(N)$, a multiple of $\lambda(N)$, which implies that a polynomial-time function A can use the view of $\mathcal{A}$ to break the underlying RSA function, and thus the security of the system. A similar argument shows that $\sum_{j'\in J} w_{i',j'}^{2t} = d'$.

If the security of the system has not been broken, $\sum_{j'\in J} a_{i',j'}^{2t} = d$ and $\sum_{j'\in J} w_{i',j'}^{2t} = d'$ From the verification in step 4 of the Share Renewal protocol, for any good committee $C_{i',j'}$ with $j' \in J \setminus \{r\}$, $-\rho(t+1)^2 \le a_{i',j'}^{2t} \le \rho(t+1)^2$. Thus $d - (r-1)(\rho(t+1)^2) \le a_{i',r}^{2t} \le d + (r-1)(\rho(t+1)^2)$. Since $d \le N$, $-r\rho(t+1)^2 \le a_{i,r}^{2t} \le r\rho(t+1)^2$. Also for any good committee $C_{i',j'}$ with $j' \in J \setminus \{r\}$, $-N\rho(t+1)^2 \le w_{i',j'}^{2t} \le N\rho(t+1)^2$. Thus $d - (r-1)(N\rho(t+1)^2) \le w_{i',r}^{2t} \le d + (r-1)(N\rho(t+1)^2)$. Since $d \le N$, $-Nr\rho(t+1)^2 \le w_{i,r}^{2t} \le Nr\rho(t+1)^2$. This implies compactness at step $2t$ for family $F_{i'}$.

Theorem 18. *The proactive RSA system above is (k', k, l)-robust against a fully adaptive adversary.*

Proof. Recall that by Lemma 7, with all but negligible probability, the assignment is (k', k, l)-terrific, and thus 90 percent of the families will be good in any period $2t$.

Note that the gateway G is given the outputs of all the committees in all the families, the opened shares at the committees with disputed outputs, and the public witnesses $\{b_{i,j}^{2t}\}_{(i,j)\in I\times J}$. It can easily be verified (using the fact that at least one family is good in any operational period $2t$) that correctness, verifiability, compactness, and availability imply robustness.

Lemma 17 proves that with overwhelming probability, the system is correct, verifiable, and compact during each operational period $2t$. Then for each committee $C_{i,j}$ with bad servers, our protocol allows a good server on that committee to prove its partial signature to be correct (by opening the shares $\tilde{a}_{i,j}^{2t}$ and $\tilde{w}_{i,j}^{2t}$ and verifying them using the public value $\tilde{b}_{i,j}^{2t}$, if there is a dispute). Thus, a gateway G can efficiently identify or compute a correct partial signature for each committee $C_{i,j}$ with a good server. Consequently, it can efficiently identify a good family and compute the correct signature. This implies availability at time $2t$.

Thus the system is (k', k, l)-robust.

References

ACGS.   W. Alexi, B. Chor, O. Goldreich and C. Schnorr. RSA and Rabin Functions: Certain Parts are as Hard as the Whole. In *SIAM Journal of Computing*, volume 17, n. 2, pages 194–209, April 1988.

AGY95.   N. Alon, Z. Galil and M. Yung, *Dynamic-resharing Verifiable Secret Sharing*, European Symposium on Algorithms (ESA) 95, Springer-Verlag LNCS.

AS92.   N. Alon and J. H. Spencer, *The Probabilistic Method* Wiley-Interscience, New York, NY, 1992.

B84.   E. Bach, Discrete Logarithms and Factoring. Tech. Report No. UCB/CSD 84/186. Computer Science Division (EECS), University of California, Berkeley, CA. June 1984.

B97.   D. Beaver, Plug and Play Encryption, Crypto 97, pp. 75-89.

BeHa92.   D. Beaver and S. Haber, *Cryptographic protocols provably secure against dynamic adversaries*, EuroCrypt 92, Springer-Verlag, 1993, 307–323.

B79.   G.R. Blakley, *Safeguarding Cryptographic Keys*, AFIPS Con. Proc (v. 48), 1979, 313–317.

Bl88.   M. Blum, *Designing programs to check their work*, ICSI Technical report TR-88-009.

B88.   C. Boyd, *Digital Multisignatures*, IMA Conference on Cryptography and Coding, Claredon Press, 241–246, (Eds. H. Baker and F. Piper), 1986.

BF97.   D. Boneh and M. Franklin, *Efficient Generation of Shared RSA Keys*, Crypto 97, pp. 425-439.

CFGN96.   R. Canetti, U. Feige, O. Goldreich, and M. Naor, *Adaptively Secure Multiparty Computation*, ACM STOC 96, 639–648.

CGJKR.   R. Canetti, R. Gennaro, S. Jarecki, H. Krawczyk, and T. Rabin. Adaptive Security for Threshold Cryptosystems. In CRYPTO 99, pp. 98-115.

CH94.   R. Canetti and A. Herzberg, *Maintaining Security in the presence of transient faults*, Crypto 94, Springer-Verlag, 1994, pp. 425-438.

Che52.   H. Chernoff, *A Measure of the asymptotic efficiency for tests of a hypothesis based on the sum of observations*, Annals of Mathematical Statistics, 23:493–509, 1952.

CF85.   J. Cohen and M. Fischer, *A robust and verifiable cryptographically secure election scheme*, FOCS 85.

DDFY92.   A. De Santis, Y. Desmedt, Y. Frankel, and M. Yung, *How to Share a Function Securely*, ACM STOC 94, pp. 522-533. (First version May 92).

DF89.   Y. Desmedt and Y. Frankel, *Threshold cryptosystems*, Crypto 89,

DF91.   Y. Desmedt and Y. Frankel, *Shared generation of authenticators and signatures*, Crypto 91, Springer-Verlag LNCS 576, 1992, pp. 307–315.

F87.   P. Feldman, *A Practical Scheme for Non-Interactive Verifiable Secret Sharing*, Proc. of the 28th IEEE FOCS, pp. 427-437, 1987

F89.   Y. Frankel, *A practical protocol for large group oriented networks*, Eurocrypt '89, Springer-Verlag LNCS 773, pp. 56-61.

FD92.   Y. Frankel and Y. Desmedt. *Distributed reliable threshold multisignatures*, Tech. Report version TR–92–04–02, Dept. of EE & CS, Univ. of Wisconsin-Milwaukee, April 1992.

FGY96.   Y. Frankel, P. Gemmell, and M. Yung, *Witness-based Cryptographic Program Checking and Robust Function Sharing* Proc. of STOC, 1996, pp. 499–508.

FGMY97.   Y. Frankel, P. Gemmell, P. D. MacKenzie, and M. Yung. Proactive RSA.
           In Crypto 97, pages 440–454.
FGMY97b.   Y. Frankel, P. Gemmell, P. D. MacKenzie, and M. Yung. Optimal-
           resilience proactive public-key cryptosystems. In FOCS'97, pages 384–393.
FMY99.   Y. Frankel, P. D. MacKenzie, and M. Yung. Adaptively-secure distributed
           public-key systems. ESA 99, July 99.
FMY99b.   Y. Frankel, P. D. MacKenzie, and M. Yung. Adaptively-secure Proactive
           RSA. Asiacrypt 99, pp. 180-194.
FMY98.   Y. Frankel, P. MacKenzie, and M. Yung, *Robust Efficient Distributed RSA-
           Key Generation* STOC, 1998, pp. 663–672.
FMY00.   Y. Frankel, P. D. MacKenzie, and M. Yung. "Pseudorandom Intermixing":
           A Tool for Shared Cryptography, PKC'00.
FY93.   M. Franklin and M. Yung, *Secure and Efficient Digital Coin*, ICALP 93,
           Springer Verlag LNCS.
GHY.   Z. Galil, S. Haber, and M. Yung, *Minimum-Knowledge Interactive Proofs
           for Decision Problems*, SIAM Journal on Computing, vol. 18, n.4, pp.
           711–739, 1989. (Previous version in FOCS 85).
GJKR.   R. Gennaro, S. Jarecki, H. Krawczyk, and T. Rabin, *Robust Threshold
           DSS Signatures*, Eurocrypt 96, pp. 354-371.
GJKR96.   R. Gennaro, S. Jarecki, H. Krawczyk, and T. Rabin, *Robust and Efficient
           Sharing of RSA*, Crypto 96, pp. 157-172.
GM84.   S. Goldwasser and S. Micali, *Probabilistic Encryption*, J. Comp. Sys. Sci.
           28, 1984, pp. 270-299.
HJKY95.   A. Herzberg, S. Jarecki, H. Krawczyk, and M. Yung, *How to Cope with
           Perpetual Leakage, or: Proactive Secret Sharing*, Crypto 95, pp. 339-352.
HJJKY96.   A. Herzberg, M. Jakobsson, S. Jarecki, H. Krawczyk, and M. Yung, *Proac-
           tive public key and signature systems*, The 4-th ACM Symp. on Comp. and
           Comm. Security. April 1997.
JJKY95.   M. Jakobsson, S. Jarecki, H. Krawczyk, and M. Yung, *Proactive RSA for
           constant shareholders*, manuscript.
JL00.   S. Jarecki and A. Lysyanskaya, Adaptively Secure Threshold Cryptogra-
           phy: Introducing Concurrency, Removing Erasures. In Eurocrypt 2000,
           pp. 221-242.
L96.   M. Luby, *Pseudorandomness and its Cryptographic Applications*, Prince-
           ton University Press, 1996.
OY91.   R. Ostrovsky and M. Yung, *How to withstand mobile virus attacks*, ACM
           Symposium on Principles of Distributed Computing (PODC), 1991, pp.
           51-61.
P91.   T.P. Pedersen, *Non-interactive and information theoretic secure verifiable
           secret sharing*, Crypto 91, pp. 129-140.
R98.   T. Rabin. A Simplified Approach to Threshold and Proactive RSA. In
           Crypto 98, pp. 89-104.
RSA78.   R. Rivest, A. Shamir and L. Adleman, *A Method for Obtaining Digital
           Signature and Public Key Cryptosystems*, Comm. of the ACM, 21 (1978),
           pp. 120-126.
S79.   A. Shamir. *How to share a secret*, Comm. of the ACM, 22 (1979), pp.
           612-613.
Sh00.   V. Shoup. Practical Threshold Signatures. In Eurocrypt 2000, pp. 207-220.

A   Proof of Lemma 7

First we bound the probability that there is a family without an excellent committee. We start with some easily computed quantities:

- Probability that a committee has no bad servers: $(1 - \sigma)^c$.
- Probability that a committee has at least one non-bad server: $1 - (1 - \sigma)^c$.
- Probability of a given family having at least one non-bad server on each committee: $(1 - (1 - \sigma)^c)^r$.
- Probability of any family having at least one non-bad server on each committee: at most $m(1 - (1 - \sigma)^c)^r$.

The last quantity is the probability that there is a family without an excellent committee. We bound this as follows, using the fact that $1 + x \leq e^x$ for all x:

$$m(1 - (1 - \sigma)^c)^r = 10\eta(1 - (1 - \sigma)^c)^{\frac{(1-\tau)^{-c}}{\eta}} \leq 10\eta(e^{-(1-\sigma)^c})^{\frac{(1-\tau)^{-c}}{\eta}} =$$

$$10\eta \left(e^{\left(\frac{1-\sigma}{1-\tau}\right)^c / \eta} \right) = 10\eta(e^{-\eta^2/\eta}) = 10\eta e^{-\eta}$$

which is negligible in η.

Next we bound the probability that more than 10 percent of the families each have a committee with no good server. Again we start with some easily computed quantities:

- Probability that a committee has no good server: $(1 - \tau)^c$.
- Probability that a committee has at least one good server: $1 - (1 - \tau)^c$.
- Probability that all committees in a family have at least one good server: $(1 - (1 - \tau)^c)^r$.
- Probability that some committee in a family has no good servers: $1 - (1 - (1 - \tau)^c)^r$.

Now we bound $(1 - \tau)^c$.

$$(1 - \tau)^c = (1 - \tau)^{\frac{2 \log \eta}{\log((1-\sigma)/(1-\tau))}} = 2^{\frac{2 \log(1-\tau) \log \eta}{\log((1-\sigma)/(1-\tau))}} = 2^{\frac{-2 \log((1-\tau)^{-1}) \log \eta}{\log((1-\sigma)/(1-\tau))}}$$

$$\leq 2^{-2 \log \eta} \leq \frac{1}{2}$$

Now we bound the probability that some committee in a family has no good servers, using the fact that $1 - x \geq e^{-2x}$ for $0 \leq x \leq \frac{1}{2}$:

$$1 - (1 - (1 - \tau)^c)^r \leq 1 - (e^{-2(1-\tau)^c})^{(1-\tau)^{-c}/\eta} \leq 1 - e^{-2/\eta} \leq \frac{2}{\eta} \leq \frac{1}{50}$$

Now we state a Chernoff bound [AS92,Che52]:

Fact 1 *Let X be a random variable with binomial distribution $B(n, p)$, i.e., n independent trials each with probability of success p. Then $\Pr[X \geq (1 + \epsilon)np] \leq [e^\epsilon(1 + \epsilon)^{-1+\epsilon}]^n p$.*

A simple corollary is: $\Pr[X \geq 5np] \leq 2^{-np}$.

Using this fact, we can bound the probability of more than 10 percent of families having some committee with no good servers by $2^{-m/50} = 2^{-\eta/5}$, which is negligible in η.

Robust Forward-Secure Signature Schemes with Proactive Security*
(Extended Abstract)

Wen-Guey Tzeng and Zhi-Jia Tzeng

Department of Computer and Information Science
National Chiao Tung University
Hsinchu, Taiwan 30050
{tzeng,zjtzeng}@cis.nctu.edu.tw

Abstract. The secret key of a forward-secure signature scheme evolves at regular intervals, but the public key is fixed during the lifetime of the system. This paper enhances the security of Abdalla and Reyzin's forward-secure signature scheme via threshold and proactive mechanisms. In our threshold forward-secure signature scheme, we combine multiplicative and polynomial secret sharing schemes to form a threshold forward-secure signature scheme. We develop a special proof system to prove robustness of our scheme.

Keywords: signature, forward security, threshold, proactive.

1 Introduction

Proactive cryptography combines the concepts of "distributing the secret" and "refreshing the shares" to provide security against the mobile adversary, who attacks the parties of a distributed cryptosystem dynamically. For an adversary, we cannot assume that it cannot break into a particular party, who holds a share of the secret, during the party's lifetime. However, we can assume that the adversary can break into at most t parties during a short period of time, say an hour. Based on this observation, the proactive cryptography "refreshes" each party's share periodically. It divides the time into time periods, starting at 0. At the end of each time period, there is a "refresh phase" during which each party refreshes its share, but the secret they share remains intact. We assume that the mobile adversary can corrupt all parties during the lifetime of the cryptosystem; nevertheless, it can corrupt at most t parties during a time period. The proactive mechanism provides a high level of security for cryptosystems so that we would like to proactivize important cryptographic primitives.

In this paper we are interested in proactivizing the forward-secure signature scheme of Abadalla and Reyzin [3]. The Abadalla and Reyzin's forward-secure signature scheme (See Appendix) is an improvement of the Bellare-Miner

* Research supported in part by the National Science Council grant NSC-89-2213-E-009-180 and by the Ministry of Education grant 89-E-FA04-1-4, Taiwan, ROC.

K. Kim (Ed.): PKC 2001, LNCS 1992, pp. 264–276, 2001.

scheme [5] with a shorter public key. Abadalla, et. al. has proactivized the Bellare-Miner forward-secure signature scheme [2]. They proposed two threshold signature schemes in proactivizing Bellare-Miner forward-secure signature scheme. One scheme uses multiplicative secret sharing and the other uses polynomial secret sharing. In our scheme, we combine both secret sharing schemes for efficiency. We use multiplicative secret sharing in signing a message in threshold and polynomial secret sharing in sharing the signing secret. Our scheme is not only robust, but also efficient.

It is worth mentioning that we propose a new scheme for multiplying two secrets that are shared among parties [4,7,17]. Our multiplication scheme is efficient since it uses the public channel and the private channel once only.

2   Preliminaries

Communication model. We assume that the involved n parties are connected by a broadcast channel such that the messages over the channel cannot be blocked, delayed or altered. Nevertheless, one can inject false messages. Any two parties are connected by a private channel such that a third party cannot get messages sent over the private channel. We also assume that the communication channel is synchronous by rounds, that is, all parties send messages simultaneously in a round.

Time. There is a universal clock such that each party knows the absolute time. Therefore, we can divide time into time periods, starting at 0. Each time period has two phases: the execution phase and the refresh phase. The refresh phase follows the execution phase. The parties sign messages during the execution phase. During the refresh phase, all parties together run the share refresh algorithm to refresh their shares.

Adversary. We consider the static adversary who chooses corrupted parties at the beginning of each time period. The adversary runs three phases: the chosen message attack phase (CMA), the break-in phase (BREAKIN), and the forgery phase (FORGE). The BREAKIN phase for the threshold signature scheme is equivalent to the OVERTHRESHOLD phase of [2].

In the CMA phase, the adversary can corrupt at most t parties for any period of time. The adversary gets all information in the corrupted parties, including their shares, random bits, etc. The adversary can query the signing oracle $\mathcal{S}_x$, where x is the secret signing key. Since we assume the random oracle model [6], the adversary is allowed to query the random oracle $\mathcal{H}$ corresponding to the collision-resistant hash function used in the scheme. At the end of the CMA phase, the adversary can stay in the current phase or enter the next BREAKIN phase. In the BREAKIN phase, the adversary can corrupt *more than* t parties. Let c be the period that the adversary enters the BREAKIN phase and corrupts more than t users. In this phase, the adversary can compute the master secret (the signing key) of period c from the shares of corrupted parties. Then, the adversary enters the FORGE phase, during which the adversary outputs a forged signature of a new message which has not been queried to the signing oracle. We say that the adversary succeeds in attacking the scheme if it outputs a forged signature for a prior time period c', $c' < c$, with non-negligible probability.

Forward security. A signature in the basic signature scheme is independent of time. Once the secret signing key is exposed, one can sign arbitrary messages. For forward-secure signature, the signing key evolves along time periods. At time period j, the signing key is SK_j. In the next time period $j + 1$, the signing key is updated to SK_{j+1} and SK_j is deleted immediately. Although, the signing key evolves, the public key is the same for the whole lifetime. If one gets the signing key SK_c of time period c, he can fake the signatures of later time periods, but cannot fake the signatures of earlier time periods. Bellare and Miner [5] proposed the first forward-secure signature scheme based on difficulty of computing the square roots modulus a Blum integer. The scheme is actually converted from Fiat and Shamir's identification scheme [13]. To achieve security strength of level l, their scheme uses l public keys and l secret keys. Later, Abdalla and Reyzin [3] proposed an improvement based on the 2^l-th root problem [16,21,23,22]. With the same level of security strength, their scheme uses one public key and one secret key only.

Proactive security. Ostrovsky and Yung [24] proposed proactive security for distributed cryptographic schemes to deter mobile adversaries. For proactive security, the share in each party is refreshed at the end of each time period, but the signing secret key the parties share is unchanged at all time. A proactive cryptosystem remains secure as long as the adversary does not corrupt more than t parties in each time period. The shares of corrupted parties become useless when time enters the next time period. There is much literature about proactive cryptosystems [1,14,15,19,18,10,11,25,12].

3   Building Blocks

The following system setting is used throughout the rest of the paper.

- Let $p = 4p'q' + 1$ be a prime, where p' and q' are large primes and $p' \equiv q' \equiv 3 \pmod 4$.
- Let $N = p'q'$ and g a generator of the order-N subgroup of Z_p^*. All operations hereafter will be over the order-N subgroup, unless stated otherwise.
- The involved parties are dealers D_i, $1 \le i \le n$.

(t, n)-VSS PROCEDURE. If dealer D_i wants to share a random secret with other dealers, it runs the following steps.

1. Select a random polynomial $f_i(x)$ of degree t over Z_N^*. The constant coefficient of $f_i(x)$ is the random secret.
2. Send share $f_i(j)$ to dealer D_j, $j \ne i$ via the private channel.
3. Publish the verification values $\langle g^{a_{i,0}}, \dots, g^{a_{i,t}} \rangle$.
4. Dealer D_j verifies validity of its received share $f_i(j)$ by $\prod_{k=0}^{k=t} g^{a_{i,k}j^k} = g^{f_i(j)}$.

If the verification fails, D_j requests D_i to publish $f_i(j)$. If D_i does not cooperate or posts an inconsistent $f_i(j)$, D_i is disqualified.

RECOVERY PROCEDURE. We use Lagrange's interpolation method to recover the secret with at least $t + 1$ shares.

PROOF-SS PROCEDURE. Given (g, t, N, F, T), prover P wants to convince verifier V two things: (1) $a = \log_g F \bmod p = T^{1/t} \bmod N$ and (2) it knows this a. This is a combination of proofs of membership and knowledge.

1. The prover P selects random $w \in Z_N^*$ and sends $H = F^w$ and $B = w^t \bmod N$ to V.
2. The verifier V selects a random challenge $c \in \{0, 1\}$ and sends it to P.
3. The prover P sends $r = a^c w \bmod N$ to V.
4. The verifier V checks (1) $H = F^r$ and $B = r^t \bmod N$ if $c = 0$; and (2) $H = g^r$ and $B = r^t/T \bmod N$ if $c = 1$.

We use PROOF-SS(g, t, g^a, a^t) to denote the above interactive proof system.

Theorem 1. PROOF-SS *is complete, sound and zero-knowledge.*

Proof. (Sketch) The completeness property can be verified easily. For soundness of proof of knowledge, if any prover P^* can convince V with a non-negligible probability ϵ, P^* and V together can compute a with an overwhelming probability. By a probabilistic argument, there is a set W of w's of probability $\epsilon/2$ such that for every $w \in W$, P^* can answer two different challenges c_1 and c_2 with probability $\epsilon/2$. Therefore, we can get two responses $r_1 = a^{c_1} w \bmod N$ and $r_2 = a^{c_2} w \bmod N$ for the same commitments H and B. We can compute $a = r_2/r_1 \bmod N$ assuming, without loss of generality, $c_1 = 0$ and $c_2 = 1$. For soundness of proof of membership, we can easily show that if F and T are not of right form, the probability that P^* can cheat V is 0.5 (and is negligible after a polynomial number of rounds.)

For zero-knowledge, we construct a simulator S to simulate the view of any verifier V^*. S first selects $c' \in \{0, 1\}$ and $r \in Z_N^*$ randomly and computes $H = F^r$ and $B = r^t \bmod N$ if $c' = 0$ and $H = g^r$ and $B = r^t/T \bmod N$ if $c' = 1$. S then simulates $V^*(H, B)$ to get c. If $c = c'$, S outputs (H, B, c, r); otherwise S outputs $\perp$. The output of S conditioned on that the output is not $\perp$ and the view of V^* are statistically indistinguishable. $\square$

We convert PROOF-SS into a non-interactive version by using a collision-resistant hash function $\mathcal{H} : \{0, 1\}^* \to \{0, 1\}^l$ to replace V [9], where l be the security parameter. The message $(c, r_1, \cdots, r_l)$ sent by P for non-interactive PROOF-SS, denoted by NIPROOF-SS, satisfies

$$c = \mathcal{H}(t||g||N||F||T||H_1||B_1|| \cdots ||H_l||B_l),$$

where $||$ is the concatenation operator of strings. Let c_i denote the i-th bit of c. If c_i is 1, $H_i = g^{r_i}$ and $B_i = r_i^t/T \bmod N$; otherwise $H_i = F^{r_i}$ and $B_i = r_i^t \bmod N$. P can compute $(c, r_1, \cdots, r_l)$ by choosing $w_i \in Z_N^*$ for $i = 1, \cdots, l$, computing $c = \mathcal{H}(t||g||N||F||T||F^{w_1}||w_1{}^t|| \cdots ||F^{w_l}||w_l{}^t)$, and setting $r_i = a^{c_i} w_i \bmod N$. NIPROOF-SS releases no useful information under the random oracle model assuming hardness of discrete logarithm and factoring.

PROOF-DH PROCEDURE. Given (g, H, F) and the prover P wants to convince V that $H = g^s$ and $F = g^{s^2}$ are of right form and it knows the secret s. The interactive proof system is as follows [8].

1. P randomly selects $w \in Z_N^*$ and sends $A = g^w$ and $B = H^w$ to V.
2. V sends a random challenge $c \in \{0, \cdots, 2^k - 1\}$ to P.
3. P sends the response $r = w + cs \mod N$ to V.
4. V checks $g^r = A \cdot H^c$ and $H^r = B \cdot F^c$.

The above PROOF-DH procedure is complete, sound, and zero knowledge. We use NIPROOF-DH to denote its non-interactive version.

SQ PROCEDURE. Let $h(x)$ be a degree-t polynomial over Z_N^* with $h(0) = s$ and shared by the dealers D_i, $1 \le i \le n$. SQ's goal is to make the dealers share a degree-t polynomial $h'(x)$ over Z_N^* with $h'(0) = s^2 \mod N$. SQ procedure is as follows.

1. Dealer D_i selects two degree-t polynomials $f_i(x)$ and $e_i(x)$ over Z_N^* at random, where $e_i(0)=0$. It sends shares $f_i(j)$ and $e_i(j)$ to D_j via the private channel, $1 \le j \le n$. Using (t, n)-VSS PROCEDURE, D_j checks if the received shares are correct. If so, all dealers share two degree-t polynomial $F(x) = \sum_{i=1}^n f_i(x) \mod N$ and $E(x) = \sum_{i=1}^n e_i(x) \mod N$. Each dealer D_i holds shares $F(i)$ and $E(i)$.
2. Each dealer D_i publishes $u_i = h(i)^2 + F(i) \mod N$ and NIPROOF-DH$(g, g^{h(i)}, g^{h(i)^2})$ and checks validity of the published values of other dealers by checking $g^{u_j} = g^{h(j)^2} \cdot \prod_{k=0}^t g^{A_k j^k}$, where $g^{A_0}, g^{A_1}, \dots, g^{A_t}$, computed from the verification values of $f_i(x)$'s, are the verification values of $F(x)$.
3. Each dealer D_i computes the degree-$2t$ polynomial $T(x)=h(x)^2 + F(x) = \sum_{k=0}^{2t} t_k x^k$ over Z_N from u_j, $1 \le j \le n$. Let $T''(x) = \sum_{k=0}^t t_k x^k$, which is $h''(x) + F(x) \mod N$ for some degree-t polynomial $h''(x)$. Note that $h''(0) = h(0)^2 \mod N$.
4. Each dealer D_i computes its share $h''(i) = T''(i) - F(i) \mod N$ and randomizes it to become $h'(i) = h''(i) + E(i)$. The hidden polynomial becomes $h'(x) = h''(x) + E(x) \mod N$ whose constant coefficient is still $s^2 \mod N$.

We use SQ$(C, h(x), h'(x))$ to denote the above procedure, where C is the dealer set, $h(x)$ is the shared polynomial initially and $h'(x)$ is the shared polynomial at the end.

Theorem 2. SQ PROCEDURE *is correct, robust and secure if there are at most $n/3$ corrupted dealers.*

Proof. (Sketch) We can check correctness easily. Since there are at most t corrupted dealers, $t < n/3$, honest dealers can smoothly finish the procedure. This is guaranteed by the (t, n)-VSS procedure.

We present a simulator to show that a malicious adversary, who corrupts at most t dealers, gets no information. Let $\mathcal{B}$ be the corrupted set of dealers.

Input: $\langle g^s, g^{a_1}, \cdots, g^{a_t} \rangle$, $h(i)$ for every dealer $D_i \in \mathcal{B}$, where $h(x) = s + \sum_{k=1}^t a_k x^k$;

1. Randomly select degree-t polynomials $\hat{f}_i(x)$ and $\hat{e}_i(x)$ with $\hat{e}_i(0) = 0$, $1 \leq i \leq n$. Let $\hat{F}(x) = \sum_{i=1}^{n} \hat{f}_i(x)$ and $\hat{E}(x) = \sum_{i=1}^{n} \hat{e}_i(x)$.
2. Run (t, n)-VSS PROCEDURE.
3. For each $D_i \notin \mathcal{B}$, randomly select $\hat{u}_i$ over Z_N^*, compute $g^{h(i)^2} = g^{\hat{u}_i}/g^{\hat{F}(i)}$, and simulate NIPROOF-DH$(g, g^{h(i)}, g^{h(i)^2})$, where $g^{h(i)} = g^s \cdot \prod_{j=1}^{t} g^{a_j i^j}$.
4. For each $D_i \in \mathcal{B}$, publish $u_i = h(i)^2 + \hat{F}(i) \bmod N$ and simulate NIPROOF-DH$(g, g^{h(i)}, g^{h(i)^2})$.

The above simulation produces a distribution computationally indistinguishable from that of the real run. □

Assume that the dealers share two degree-t polynomial $h_1(x)$ and $h_2(x)$ initially. We can modify the SQ procedure so that the dealers share a degree-t polynomial $h'(x)$ whose constant coefficient is $h_1(0)h_2(0) \bmod N$ at the end. Let MULT$(C, h_1(x), h_2(x), h'(x))$ denote the procedure of sharing a degree-t polynomial $h'(x)$ whose constant coefficient is $h_1(0)h_2(0) \bmod N$.

4   Our Threshold Forward-Secure Signature Scheme

Our threshold forward-secure signature scheme, denoted by **TFSS**, is a key-evolving (t, s, n)-threshold signature scheme that consists of four procedures: TFSS.KEY, TFSS.UPDATE, TFSS.SIGN, and TFSS.VERIFY, where t is the maximum number of corrupted dealers, s is the minimum number of alive dealers so that signature computation is possible, and n is the total number of dealers. In our scheme, we set $s = t + 1$ and $n \geq 2t + 1$. There is a manager presiding the scheme.

TFSS.KEY: it generates the public key and each dealer D_i's initial secret-key share $S_{i,0}$ and public-key share $PK_{i,0}$ at time period 0.

1. Select N as that in the system setting.
2. The manager randomly selects $S_{i,0} \in Z_N^*$, $1 \leq i \leq n$ and sets $U_{i,0} = 1/S_{i,0}^{2^{l(T+1)}} \bmod N$, $S_0 = \prod_{i=1}^{n} S_{i,0} \bmod N$, and $U = 1/S_0^{2^{l(T+1)}} \bmod N$.
3. The system's initial secret key at time period 0 is $SK_0 = (N, T, 0, S_0)$ and the public key $PK = (N, U, T)$.
4. Each dealer D_i's initial secret-key share is $SK_{i,0} = (N, T, 0, S_{i,0})$ and public-key share is $PK_{i,0} = (N, U_{i,0}, T)$.
5. Each dealer D_i shares its $S_{i,0}$ with other dealers by the (t, n)-VSS PROCEDURE.

TFSS.UPDATE: at the end of time period j, each dealer updates its secret-key and public-key shares from $S_{i,j}$ and $PK_{i,j}$ to $S_{i,j+1}$ and $PK_{i,j+1}$.

1. Each dealer D_i randomly selects $n-1$ numbers $s_{i,1}, s_{i,2}, \ldots, s_{i,n-1}$ over Z_N^* and computes $s_{i,n} = S_{i,j}/\prod_{k=1}^{n-1} s_{i,k} \bmod N$.
2. Each dealer D_i sends $s_{i,k}$ to D_k privately and publishes $\hat{s}_{i,k} = 1/s_{i,k}^{2^{l(T+1-j)}} \bmod N$, $1 \leq k \leq n$.

3. Each dealer D_k checks validity of the published values by $U_{i,j} = \prod_{r=1}^{n} \hat{s}_{i,r} \bmod N$, $1 \le i \le n, i \ne k$. Dealer D_k also checks validity of its received secret $s_{i,k}$ by $1/s_{i,k}^{2^{l(T+1-j)}} \bmod N = \hat{s}_{i,k}$. If any of the checks fails, all other dealers recover the secret $S_{i,j}$ by RECOVERY PROCEDURE.

4. Dealer D_i's new secret-key share is $S_{i,j+1} = (\prod_{k=1}^{n} s_{k,i})^{2^l} \bmod N$ and the corresponding public-key share is $U_{i,j+1} = \prod_{k=1}^{n} \hat{s}_{k,i} \bmod N$.

5. Dealer D_i shares $S_{i,j+1}$ with other dealers by (t,n)-VSS PROCEDURE. We use NIPROOF-SS$(g, t, g^{S_{i,j+1}}, S_{i,j+1}^t)$ to verify whether D_i's action is correct, where $t = -2^{l(T-j)}$ and $S_{i,j+1}^t = U_{i,j+1}$. If the proof is correct and (t,n)-VSS PROCEDURE succeeds, all dealers delete their old secret-key shares; otherwise, the secret of D_i is reconstructed.

TFSS.SIGN: at time period j, all dealers sign a messages M in a distributed way with the following steps.

1. Each dealer D_i selects $R_i \in Z_N^*$ randomly and publishes $Y_i = R_i^{2^{l(T+1-j)}} \bmod N$ and NIPROOF-SS$(g, 2^{l(T+1-j)}, g^{R_i}, Y_i)$. Then, it shares R_i to other dealers via (t,n)-VSS PROCEDURE with polynomial $f_i(x)$. If NIPROOF-SS or (t,n)-VSS PROCEDURE fails, set $R_i = 1$ and run RECOVERY PROCEDURE to recover the secret-key share $S_{i,j}$ of D_i.

2. Each dealer D_i computes $Y = \prod_{i=1}^{n} Y_i$ and $\sigma = \mathcal{H}(j, Y, M)$ and publishes its partial signature $Z_i = R_i S_{i,j}^\sigma \bmod N$.

3. Each dealer D_i verifies validity of another dealer D_k's partial signature by computing

$$Y_i' = Z_i^{2^{l(T+1-j)}} U_{i,j}^\sigma \bmod N$$

and checking whether Y_i' and Y_i are equal. If the verification fails, all other alive dealers run RECOVERY PROCEDURE to recover the secret-key share $S_{k,j}$ and R_k of D_k and compute the partial signature Z_k.

4. Combine all partial signatures as a signature (j, Z, σ) for M at time j, where $Z = \prod_{i=1}^{n} Z_i \bmod N$. All dealers erase their R_i's.

TFSS.VERIFY: We can use the public key $PK = (N, U, T)$ of the system to verify validity of a signature (j, Z, σ) for M.

1. If $Z = 0$, return '0'.

2. Otherwise, compute $Y' = Z^{2^{l(T+1-j)}} U^\sigma \bmod N$ and output '1' if and only if $\sigma = H(j, Y', M)$.

5   Security Analysis

In this section, we show the correctness and security of our proposed scheme.

Theorem 3 (Correctness). *Assume that $SK_j = (N, T, j, S_j)$ and $PK = (N, U, T)$ are key pairs of the system at time period j. Each dealer D_i holds the secret-key share $SK_{i,j} = (N, T, j, S_{i,j})$ and public-key share $PK_{i,j} = (N, U_{i,j}, T)$. If (j, Z, σ) is generated by TFSS.SIGN for M, TFSS.VERIFY$(PK, j, Z, \sigma)) = 1$.*

Proof.   We have $S_j = \prod_{i=1}^{n} S_{i,j} \bmod N$, $U = \prod_{i=1}^{n} U_{i,j} \bmod N = \prod_{i=1}^{n} S_{i,j}^{-2^{l(T+1-j)}} \bmod N$, $Y = \prod_{i=1}^{n} R_i^{2^{l(T+1-j)}} \bmod N = \prod_{i=1}^{n} Y_i \bmod N$ and $Z = \prod_{i=1}^{n} Z_i \bmod N = \prod_{i=1}^{n} R_i S_{i,j}^{\sigma} \bmod N$. Since

$$Y' = Z^{2^{l(T+1-j)}} U^{\sigma} \bmod N = \prod_{i=1}^{n} (R_i S_{i,j}^{\sigma})^{2^{l(T+1-j)}} \prod_{i=1}^{n} U_{i,j}^{\sigma} \bmod N$$

$$= \prod_{i=1}^{n} [R_i^{2^{l(T+1-j)}} S_{i,j}^{\sigma 2^{l(T+1-j)}} U_{i,j}^{\sigma}] \bmod N = \prod_{i=1}^{n} R_i^{2^{l(T+1-j)}} \bmod N$$

$$= \prod_{i=1}^{n} Y_i \bmod N = Y,$$

we have $\mathcal{H}(j, Y', M) = \mathcal{H}(j, Y, M) = \sigma$.   □

Theorem 4. TFSS.UPDATE *procedure is secure against malicious adversaries.*

Proof. (Sketch) We construct a simulator S to simulate TFSS.UPDATE procedure assuming existence of malicious adversaries. Let $\mathcal{B} = \{D_{b_1}, \ldots, D_{b_t}\}$ be the set of corrupted servers at current time j. For simplicity, the secrets of corrupted dealers are treated as inputs. S simulates each dealer D_i's behavior as follows.

Input: $PK = (N, U, T)$, $S_{b_k, j}, 1 \le k \le t$, $\hat{f}_k(b_i), 1 \le i \le t, 1 \le k \le n$, $PK_{i,j} = (N, U_{i,j}, T), 1 \le i \le n$, and $\langle g^{S_{i,j}}, g^{a_{i,1}} \cdots, g^{a_{i,t}} \rangle, 1 \le i \le n$;

1. Randomly select $\hat{s}_{i,1}, \ldots, \hat{s}_{i,(i-1)}, \hat{s}_{i,(i+1)}, \ldots, \hat{s}_{i,n-1}$ from Z_N^*, compute

$$1/(\hat{s}_{i,i}^{2^{l(T+1-j)}}) = U_{i,j} / \prod_{k=1, k \ne i}^{n} 1/(\hat{s}_{i,k}^{2^{l(T+1-j)}}) \bmod N,$$

and publish $\hat{S}_{i,k} = 1/(\hat{s}_{i,k}^{2^{l(T+1-j)}}) \bmod N$ for $k = 1, \ldots, n$. Note that we do not know the value $\hat{s}_{i,i}$ for $D_i \notin \mathcal{B}$.

2. Randomly select polynomial $\hat{h}_i(x)$ over Z_N^*. Let $\hat{h}_i(0) = S'_{i,j+1}$, which is a random value in Z_N^* for $D_i \notin \mathcal{B}$. Simulate NIPROOF-SS$(g, -2^{l(T-j)}), g^{S'_{i,j+1}}, U_{i,j+1})$, where $U_{i,j+1} = \prod_{k=1}^{n} \hat{S}_{k,i} \bmod N$. For $D_i \in \mathcal{B}$, compute its new secret-key share $S_{b_k, j+1}$ by $\prod_{i=1}^{n} \hat{s}_{i,b_k}^{2^l} \bmod N$ and simulate NIPROOF-SS$(g, -2^{l(T+1-(j+1))}, g^{S_{b_k, j+1}}, U_{b_k, j+1})$, where $U_{b_k, j+1} = \prod_{i=1}^{n} \hat{S}_{i,b_k} \bmod N$. Then, simulate (t, n)-VSS PROCEDURE.

If D_j forces D_i to disclose $\hat{s}_{i,j}$, since D_j has it, we can simulate $\hat{s}_{i,j}$.   □

Theorem 5. *The* TFSS *scheme is a key-evolving* (t, s, n)*-threshold signature scheme for* $s = t + 1$ *and* $n = 2t + 1$.

Proof. (Sketch) Since there are at most t corrupted servers, their secret-key shares are not sufficient to recover the secret-key shares of honest dealers. The others follow the scheme.   □

Theorem 6 (Forward secrecy). *Let* FS-DS *denote the single-user signature scheme in [3].* TFSS *is a threshold forward-secure signature scheme as long as* FS-DS *is a forward-secure signature scheme in the single-user sense.*

Proof. (Sketch) Let F be the adversary who attacks TFSS successfully by forging a signature (c', Z, α). We construct an algorithm that uses this F to forge a signature for the single-user FS-DS. As stated at Section 2, the attacking procedure contains three phases: CMA, BREAKIN, and FORGE. Our algorithm can query from the two oracles: the hashing oracle $\mathcal{H}$ and the singing oracle $\mathcal{S}$.

In the CMA phase, F guesses a particular time period c during which F breaks more than t dealers and gets the secret S_c. Let $U = 1/v^{2^{l(T+1-c)}}$ and $PK = (N, U, T)$, where $v = S_c$. We randomly select $U_{i,0}, \cdots, U_{n-1,0} \in_R Z_N^*$ and compute public-key share $U_{n,0} = U/\prod_{i=1}^{n-1} U_{i,0} \bmod N$. The public key is $PK_{i,0} = (N, U_{i,0}, T)$, $1 \leq i \leq n$. We simulate F by choosing a random tape for F, feeding all public keys to F, and running F in the CMA phase. F can corrupt at most t dealers except the time period c. Since F can corrupt at most t dealers except at time period c, we simply give all necessary secret-key shares and exchanged shares as F's input. F decides either to stay at the CMA phase or to switch to the BREAKIN phase, and then enter the FORGE phase.

We now we simulate the views of corrupted dealers during the key update phase. Let $\mathcal{B} = \{D_{b_1}, \cdots, D_{b_t}\}$ be the set of corrupted dealers at time period j. The simulation is the same as that of Theorem 4, which simulates the key update procedure. Note that the set of corrupted servers is decided in advance.

We can simulate the hash and signing oracles of F. For each query (j, Y, M) made by F, we query $\mathcal{H}$ on the same input and return the answer to F. We simulate the signing oracle of F by using $\mathcal{S}$. Let M be the message queried to $\mathcal{S}$. We give the direct answer (j, Z, σ) of S to F.

Now, we simulate F's view of the signing procedure. The input consists all secrets of the corrupted dealers and public information. For the input M and its signature $(j, Z, \sigma))$ seen by F, we construct the same probability distribution of F's real view as follows.

1. For $D_i \in \mathcal{B}$, we directly choose $R_i \in Z_N^*$ and publish $Y_i = R_i^{2^{l(T+1-j)}} \bmod N$ and NIPROOF-SS$(g, 2^{l(T+1-j)}, g^{R_i}, Y_i)$. Then, we simulate (t, n)-VSS PROCEDURE to share R_i with other dealers. Furthermore, we computes the partial signature $Z_i = R_i S_{i,j}^\sigma \bmod N$.

2. For $D_i \notin \mathcal{B}$, we computes its partial signature as follows. Let $Z' = Z/\prod_{i=1}^t Z_i \bmod N$. We randomly select $n - t - 1$ numbers from Z_N^*, says $Z_{c_1}, \ldots, Z_{c_{n-t-1}}$. We compute $Z_{c_{n-t}} = Z'/\prod_{i=1}^{n-t-1} Z_{c_i} \bmod N$.

3. We compute $Y_{c_i} = Z_{c_i}^{2^{l(T+1-j)}} U_{c_i,j}^\sigma \bmod N$ for $1 \leq i \leq n - t$, and randomly select $(n-t)$ numbers from Z_N^*, says $R_{c_1}, \cdots, R_{c_{n-t}}$. We simulate NIPROOF-SS$(g, 2^{l(T+1-j)}, g^{R_{c_i}}, R_{c_i}^{2^{l(T+1-j)}})$ and run (t, n)-VSS PROCEDURE to share R_{c_i}, $1 \leq i \leq n - t$, with other dealers.

4. Finally, we compute $Y = \prod_{i=1}^t Y_{b_i} \prod_{j=1}^{n-t} Y_{c_j} \bmod N$ and sets $\mathcal{H}(j, Y, M) = \sigma$.

We can show that the above simulated view is statistically indistinguishable from the real view.

Obtaining a forgery. Let c be the time period that F switches to the BREAKIN phase. We provide the secret key S_c to F and run F to output a forged signature (c', Z, α) for M', where $c' < c$. (c', Z, α) is the forged signature for the single-user FS-DS, which is a contradiction. Therefore, our TFSS is secure.   □

6   Discussion

Proactive security. We can easily add the proactive mechanism to TFSS.UPDATE. The only difference is to compute $\hat{s}_{i,k} = 1/s_{i,k}^{2^{l(T-j)}}$ in step 2, instead of $\hat{s}_{i,k} = 1/s_{i,k}^{2^{l(T-j+1)}}$, and new secret-key share $S'_{i,j} = \prod_{k=1}^{n} s_{k,i} \bmod N$ in the refresh phase. Furthermore, $s_{i,k}$ can be encrypted and sent to dealer D_k using D_k's public-key share $P_{k,j}$. This saves the private channel.

New construction. We can use polynomial secret sharing in our scheme, though it is less efficient. Our new construction is as follows. Initial setting is a bit different from that in Section 4. Let $f(x)$ be a degree-t polynomial with $f(0) = S_0$ and shared by all dealers by (t, n)-VSS PROCEDURE. To update the key S_j to S_{j+1}, all dealers compute the multiplication of two secrets for l times, where l is the security parameter. The robustness property is achieved by our MULT PROCEDURE. MULT PROCEDURE uses a proof to show that a dealer is honest. To compute a signature for a message, all dealers compute $l(T + 1 - j) + \log_2 \sigma$ times of distributed multiplication of secrets for $Y = R^{2^{l(T+1-j)}} \bmod N$ and $Z = RS_j^\sigma \bmod N$.

Efficiency. In our *new construction* based on polynomial secret sharing, dealers perform l multiplications of shares to update the key. That is, they exchange messages l times and compute l proofs for MULT PROCEDURE. To compute a signature, dealers exchange $l(T + 1 - j) + \log_2 \sigma$ messages and compute $l(T + 1 - j) + \log_2 \sigma$ proofs. As we can see, the computation and communication costs are quite expensive.

In *our main scheme* in Section 4, we combine the techniques of polynomial secret sharing and multiplicative secret sharing to reduce the cost. Each dealer exchanges messages twice in the key update stage, and once in the signing message stage. Each dealer needs to compute one proof in both key update and signing message stages. Therefore, our main scheme is quite efficient.

7   Conclusion

We have proposed a threshold forward-secure signature scheme, which is based on the 2^l-th root problem. Our scheme is robust and efficient in terms of the number of rounds so that the amount of exchanged messages among dealers is low. We show forward-secure security of our scheme based on that of the single-user scheme.

References

1. N. Alon, Z. Galil, M. Yung, "Dynamic-resharing verifiable secret sharing", *European Symposium on Algorithms 95 (ESA 95)*, Lecture Notes in Computer Science 979, pp.523-537, Springer-Verlag, 1995.
2. M. Abdalla, S. Miner, C. Namprempre, "Forward security in threshold signature schemes", manuscripts.
3. M. Abdalla, L. Reyzin, "A new forward-secure digital signature scheme", *Proceedings of Advances in Cryptology – Asiacrypt 2000*, Springer-Verlag, 2000.
4. M. Ben-Or, S. Goldwasser, A. Wigderson, "Completeness theorems for non-cryptographic fault-tolerant distributed computations", *Proceedings of the 20th ACM Symposium on Theory of Computing*, pp.1-10, 1988.
5. M. Bellare, S. Miner, "A forward-secure digital signature scheme", *Proceedings of Advances in Cryptology – Crypto 99*, Lecture Notes in Computer Science 1666, pp.431-448, Springer-Verlag, 1999.
6. M. Bellare, P. Rogaway, "Random oracles are practical: a paradigm for designing efficient protocols", *Proceedings of the First ACM Conference on Computer and Communications Security*, pp.62-73, 1993.
7. D. Chaum, C. Crepeau, I. Damgard, "Multiparty unconditionally secure protocols", *Proceedings of the 20th ACM Symposium on Theory of Computing*, pp.11-19, 1988.
8. D. Chaum, T. Pedersen, "Wallet databases with observers", *Proceedings of Advances in Cryptology – Crypto 92*, pp.90-105, 1992.
9. U. Feige, A. Fiat, A. Shamir, "Zero-knowledge proof of identity", *Journal of Cryptology*, Vol. 1, pp.77-94, 1988.
10. Y. Frankel, P. Gemmell, P. MacKenzie, M. Yung, "Optimal-resilience proactive public-key cryptosystems", *Proceedings of 38th Annual Symposium on Foundations of Computer Science*, pp.384-393, IEEE, 1997.
11. Y. Frankel, P. Gemmell, P. MacKenzie, M. Yung, "Proactive RSA", *Proceedings of Advances in Cryptology – Crypto 97*, Lecture Notes in Computer Science 1294, pp.440-454, Springer-Verlag, 1997.
12. Y. Frankel, P. MacKenzie, M. Yung, "Adaptively-secure optimal-resilience proactive RSA", *Proceedings of Advances in Cryptology – Asiacrypt 99*, Lecture Notes in Computer Science 1716, pp.180-194, Springer-Verlag, 1999.
13. A. Fiat, A. Shamir, "How to prove yourself: practical solutions to identification and signature problems", *Proceedings of Advances in Cryptology – Crypto 86*, Lecture Notes in Computer Science 263, pp.186-194, Springer-Verlag, 1986.
14. R. Gennaro, S. Jarecki, H. Krawczyk, T. Rabin, "Robust threshold DSS signatures", *Proceedings of Advances in Cryptology – Eurocrypt 96*, Lecture Notes in Computer Science 1070, pp.354-371, Springer-Verlag, 1996.
15. R. Gennaro, S. Jarecki, H. Krawczyk, T. Rabin, "Robust and efficient sharing of RSA functions", *Proceedings of Advances in Cryptology – Crypto 96*, Lecture Notes in Computer Science 1109, pp.157-172, Springer-Verlag, 1996.
16. L. Guillou, J. Quisquater, "A practical zero-knowledge protocol fitted to security microprocessor minimizing both transmission and memory", *Proceedings of Advances in Cryptology – Eurocrypt 88*, Lecture Notes in Computer Science 330, pp.123-128, Springer-Verlag, 1988.
17. R. Gennaro, M. Rabin, T. Rabin, "Simplified VSS and fast-track multiparty computations with applications to threshold cryptography", *Proceedings of the 17th ACM Symposium on Principles of Distributed Computing (PODC)*, 1998.

18. A. Herzberg, M. Jakobsson, S. Jarecki, H. Krawczyk, M. Yung, "Proactive public key and signature systems", *Proceedings of the 4th ACM Symposium on Computer and Communication Security*, 1997.

19. A. Herzberg, S. Jarecki, H. Krawczyk, M. Yung, "Proactive secret sharing or: how to cope with perpetual leakage", *Proceedings of Advances in Cryptology – Crypto 95*, Lecture Notes in Computer Science 963, pp.339-352, Springer-Verlag, 1995.

20. I. Ingemarsson, G. Simmons, "A protocol to set up shared secret schemes without the assistance of a mutually trusted party", *Proceedings of Advances in Cryptology – Eurocrypt 90*, Lecture Notes in Computer Science 473, pp.266-282, Springer-Verlag, 1990.

21. S. Micali, "A secure and efficient digital signature algorithm," *Technical Report MIT/LCS/TM-501*, Massachusetts Institute of Technology, Cambridge, MA, 1994.

22. H. Ong, C. Schnorr, "Fast signature generation with a Fiat-Shamir like scheme", *Proceedings of Advances in Cryptology – Eurocrypt 90*, Lecture Notes in Computer Science 473, pp.432-440, Springer-Verlag, 1990.

23. K. Ohta, T. Okamoto, "A modification of the Fiat-Shamir scheme", *Proceedings of Advances in Cryptology – Crypto 88*, Lecture Notes in Computer Science 403, pp.232-243, Springer-Verlag, 1988.

24. R. Ostrovsky, M. Yung, "How to withstand mobile virus attacks", *Proceedings of the 10th ACM Symposium on Principles of Distributed Computing (PODC)*, pp. 51-61, 1991.

25. T. Rabin, "A simplified approach to threshold and proactive RSA", *Proceedings of Advances in Cryptology – Crypto 98*, Lecture Notes in Computer Science 1462, pp.89-104, Springer-Verlag, 1998.

26. A. Shamir, "How to share a secret", *Communications of the ACM*, 22(11), pp.612-613, 1979.

Appendix

ABDALLA AND REYZIN'S FORWARD-SECURE SIGNATURE SCHEME. It has four procedures: key generation, key update, signing and verification. Let k and l be security parameters, T the largest time period, and $H : \{0,1\}^* \to \{0,1\}^l$ a collision-resistant hash function.

Key generation: generate the initial secret key SK_0 and public key PK.

1. Select two large primes p and q such that $p \equiv q \equiv 3 \pmod 4$, $2^{k-1} \leq (p-1)(q-1)$, and $pq < 2^k$. Let $N = pq$.
2. Randomly select S_0 from Z_N^* and compute $U = 1/S_0^{2^{l(T+1)}} \bmod N$.
3. Set the initial secret key $SK_0 = (N, T, 0, S_0)$ and the public key $PK = (N, U, T)$.

Key update: update the secret key SK_j to SK_{j+1}.

1. If $j = T$, set $SK_j = null$; otherwise, set $SK_{j+1} = (N, T, j+1, S_j^{2^l} \bmod N)$, where $SK_j = (N, T, j, S_j)$.

Signing: sign message M at time period j using key SK_j.

1. Randomly select $R \in Z_N^*$ and compute $Y = R^{2^{l(T+1-j)}} \mod N$, $\sigma = H(j, Y, M)$, and $Z = RS_j^\sigma \mod N$.
2. The signature is (j, Z, σ).

Verification: verify validity of signature (j, Z, σ) for M.

1. If $Z \equiv 0$, return 0; otherwise compute $Y' = Z^{2^{l(T+1-j)}} U^\sigma \mod N$.
2. Output 1 if and only $\sigma = H(j, Y', M)$.

Equitability in Retroactive Data Confiscation versus Proactive Key Escrow

Yvo Desmedt[*,1,2], Mike Burmester[*,1,2], and Jennifer Seberry[3]

[1] Department of Computer Science, Florida State University, 206 Love Building,
Tallahassee, FL 32306-4530, USA
desmedt@cs.fsu.edu, mikeb@dcs.rhbnc.ac.uk
[2] Information Security Group, Royal Holloway, University of London, Egham
Surrey TW20 OEX, UK
[3] Centre for Computer Security Research, TITR, University of Wollongong
Australia
Jennifer_seberry@uow.edu.au

Abstract. The British Regulations of Investigatory Powers (RIP) Act 2000 is one of the first modern bills for mandatory disclosure of protected data in a democratic country. In this paper we compare this bill from a technical point of view with the US key escrow proposal (EES) and its variants and then, more generally we compare the merits of data confiscation vs key escrow.

A major problem with key escrow is that once a private key is recovered it can be used to decipher ciphertexts which were sent well before a warrant was issued (or after its expiration). Several alternative key escrow systems have been proposed in the literature to address this issue. These are equitable, in the sense that the control of society over the individual and the control of the individual over society are fairly shared. We show that equitability is much easier to achieve with data confiscation than with key escrow. Consequently, although the RIP act was heavily criticized in the press and on the internet, it inherently maintains a better level of privacy than key escrow.

Finally we present some practical deniable decryption variants of popular public key systems.

Key words: RIP, key escrow, data confiscation.

1 Introduction

Key escrow was proposed as a mechanism to protect society from criminals who use encryption to block access to evidence of crime [5,25,11] (for a taxonomy of key escrow systems see [13]). While the US key escrow proposal (EES) [11] was never mandatory, the British Regulations of Investigatory Powers (RIP) Act 2000 [29] has been enacted and is now law. The RIP act has been heavily criticized in the press and over the internet (see e.g. [31]). Indeed some internet

---

[*] Research undertaken while visiting the University of Wollongong.

K. Kim (Ed.): PKC 2001, LNCS 1992, pp. 277–286, 2001.
© Springer-Verlag Berlin Heidelberg 2001

societies have considered boycotting Britain [23]. Moreover, the RIP act is being used as a test case by several other countries who are considering similar acts [27], so it could be used as an excuse by less democratic countries to weaken the privacy that encryption provides. A critical analysis is therefore crucial.

The RIP act differs in several respects from the EES. With RIP, it is the person to whom protected (encrypted) material is addressed who should disclose the material, if a warrant for this purpose has been issued [29]. Compliance may be achieved by "simply making a disclosure of the relevant information in an intelligent form" [29, section 50(1,a)], but "shall require the disclosure of the (decryption) key, if the disclosure can only be complied with the disclosure of the key itself" [29, section 51(1)].

Most of the efficient encryption systems currently used (e.g. the SSL [34]) employ a public key cryptosystem to distributed the session keys for symmetric encryption (such as triple DES). For these systems it would not be possible to comply with the disclosure notice unless the (symmetric) session keys are revealed. Therefore it is most likely that with such schemes, key disclosure will be required. However this is not the case with public key encryption schemes. For example, with the RSA encryption scheme [30] compliance can be achieved by simply disclosing the message(s) (the ciphertext must be the encryption of the message). For the ElGamal encryption scheme [16] disclosing the message is not sufficient: in this case the receiver must also, either reveal the key or prove that the ciphertext is the encryption of the message with the public key of the receiver (see Section 3.1).

It is important to note that with the RIP act, disclosure of the decryption key(s) (or the decrypted ciphertext(s)) may only be required *after* an investigation has started. This is in contrast to key escrow, for which shares of the decryption keys must be given to the escrow agencies *before* any investigation.

The RIP act clearly has some controversial aspects. For example, the penalty for *knowingly* failing to complywith a disclosure notice is "imprisonment for a term not exceeding two years ... " [29, section 53(5,a)], whereas tipping off (e.g. an employee who tips off his security manager) can lead "to imprisonment for a term not exceeding five years ... " [29, section 54(4,a)].

Although the RIP act may be somewhat controversial, the idea of confiscating data is worth comparing with the concept of key escrow. There are several good reasons for this. The most important one being that numerous papers have already been published on key escrow (see e.g. [20,22,2,19,7,1]), and most of its problems have been addressed. Furthermore, "key recovery" has often been used as a synonym for key escrow and there are also several papers published on this topic (e.g. in [9]). As far as we know there are no scientific papers on data confiscation.

We do not claim that our study of data confiscation covers all aspects. Indeed, the idea of key escrow is by now (at least) 10 years old [5] and it has taken many years to reach the present state of knowledge. Obviously current research on key escrow will facilitate research on data confiscation, but the fact that these notions are quite different may imply new problems, still to be discovered.

We focus on a particular problem of key escrow that has received some attention. This problem has to do with the fact that, once the key has been recovered, it can be used to decipher ciphertexts sent well before the warrant was issued and/or well after the warrant has expired. Several researchers have pointed out this problem. Lenstra-Winkler-Yacobi [22] state that:

> the key is supposed to be "returned" (!) at the expiration of the warrant, but non-compliance with this or other Dept. of Justice procedures explicitly "shall not provide the basis for any motion to suppress or other objection to the introduction of electronic surveillance evidence lawfully acquired" [14].

It is no surprise therefore that alternative key escrow systems have been proposed to address, to a certain extent, this issue (see e.g. [25,22,19,7,1]).

The strongest model proposed so far guarantees time-limited decryption even when the escrow agencies are taken over unlawfully. For example, encrypted data (ciphertexts) of law abiding citizens in a democratic society is protected even if at a later date a dictatorship takes full control of the escrow agencies. Burmester-Desmedt-Seberry have proposed a scheme with this property [7] and give credit to Gus Simmons [33] for having first observed the problem. The scheme in [7] however needs some interaction: with each public key updating, the receiver must send this key to the sender (the escrow agencies do not need to do this).

In this paper we examine how to achieve such a time limitation when working with data confiscation. We focus on proven security. This means that we shall not consider the following popular scheme in which a public key encryption scheme is used as a transport mechanism to distribute session keys of a symmetric encryption scheme (such as triple DES or IDEA) [24]. For this scheme, compliance with a disclosure notice is achieved by simply disclosing the session key, without having to reveal anything else. The problem with this scheme is that this is not proven secure. For example, given a ciphertext, it may be possible for the parties involved to disclose a spurious key and a spurious message which produce the same ciphertext. The one-time pad allows such deniable encryption [8]. Other deniable cryptosystems have been studied in [8]. The question whether this is possible for DES (or triple DES) is not known.

Our paper is organized as follows. In Section 2 we discuss attacks by different parties in the context of data confiscation. Since deniable encryption undermines data confiscation, we analyze it in Section 2.1. In Section 3 we discuss the issues to guarantee equitable data confiscation. Solutions are discussed in Section 4. Before we end, in Section 5 we describe new methods to obtain practical deniable encryption.

2   Attacks on Data Confiscation

In this section we discuss some possible types of attack by different parties, and in particular those attacks which to a large extent affect the privacy of the citizens.

2.1 Attacks by Citizens

There are several ways to bypass data confiscation. As in the case of key escrow, data confiscation can be bypassed by using, for example, information hiding techniques (see e.g., [28]). However this approach does not not scale well and indeed most private information is sent by parties who may not (or cannot) use information hiding technologies. It is therefore important to analyze data confiscation for the case when such technologies are not used.

Deniable encryption was proposed by Canetti-Dwork-Naor-Ostrovsky [8], and makes it possible to open a ciphertext in different ways. This kind of encryption can therefore be used to undermine data confiscation. The simplest example of a deniable encryption scheme is the one-time pad. For this scheme, intercepted encrypted data can be opened to produce any cleartext (for an appropriate key).

It is clear that data confiscation is only effective when the encryption is *not* deniable, in other words when the encryption scheme corresponds to a commitment scheme.

2.2 Active Attacks by Law Enforcement Agencies

Active attacks by law enforcement agencies may seem unrealistic. However, the RIP act clearly stipulates the involvement of the Secret Intelligence Service, the GCHQ, and the Defence Intelligence (see e.g. [29, section 6]). Their mission may not force them to limit themselves to passive attacks. Protection against active attacks is therefore important.

To attack time-limited data confiscation, law enforcement agencies can use malleable attacks [15]. Let us consider such a type of attack in more detail. Suppose that an agency wants to get hold of the plaintext M_1 of a ciphertext C_1, sent before the time-limited warrant was granted, and suppose that a party (e.g. an insider) is willing to help the law enforcement agency. For this purpose the party can send a ciphertext C_2 whose plaintext M_2 leaks some information about M_1. A particular case of this attack is a replay attack, for which $C_2 = C_1$.

3 Requirements

Although it is often common in modern cryptography to give formal models, we will see that many of the models we need already exists. We therefore discuss the requirements in a more informal way.

3.1 An Introduction

It is obvious that for a public key encryption scheme which is also a commitment scheme, the sender can comply with disclosure by simply revealing the message and the randomness used.

If no randomness is used, as for example with RSA, then disclosure of the message it is sufficient. If randomness is used, as for example with ElGamal, then the receiver does not know the randomness (if the discrete logarithm is hard). However in this case it is still possible for the receiver to comply with the disclosure notice without revealing any private keys. For this purpose the receiver must use an interactive zero-knowledge proof [18] to prove that the ciphertext is the encryption of the plaintext with the public key of the receiver (a proof of knowledge of the discrete logarithm [10] can be used for ElGamal).

Note that the RIP act states that [29, Section 50(5)]:

> It shall not be necessary, for the purpose of complying with the requirement, for the person given notice to make a disclosure of any keys in addition to those the disclosure of which is, alone, sufficient to enable the person to whom they are disclosed to obtain access to the information and to put it into an intelligible form.

So with public key encryption schemes the receiver can comply with the RIP act without having revealing the decryption keys.

If public keys are used to distribute the session keys of a symmetric encryption scheme (as in SSL), then disclosure is complied by simply revealing the session keys.

3.2   Undeniable Data Confiscation

Revealing the randomness used, or proving that the message and ciphertext are properly linked with the public key of the receiver, is only an effective means of disclosure from the point of view of enforcement agency if the encryption scheme is not deniable. We call such schemes, *undeniable*. As mentioned earlier, undeniable encryption schemes are also commitment schemes. For the sake of completeness and to avoid any ambiguity (due to the definition of blobs in [6]) we give the definition below.

Definition 1. Let C be the ciphertext and E be the encryption function with k the receiver's public key. The encryption system E is *undeniable* if, for all ciphertexts C, for all plaintexts m, m', and for all random choices r, r',

$$C = E_k(m, r) = E_k(m', r') \ \text{ implies } \ m = m'.$$

If no randomness is used, as in the case of RSA, we take the randomness to be the empty string. So the definition is sufficiently general. As we know RSA does not offer the security of schemes that use randomness [17].

3.3   Sender and Receiver Coercibility

Canetti-Dwork-Naor-Ostrovsky[8] observed that both the sender and the receiver can be coerced into revealing the message. Since this is the goal of data confiscation, we define the following.

Definition 2. An undeniable encryption scheme is *receiver coercible* if, given a ciphertext $C = E_k(m, r)$, with k the public key of the receiver, the receiver can produce the randomness r and the plaintext m. An undeniable encryption scheme which does not have this property is only *sender coercible*.

Although receiver coercibility is an important property for fair data confiscation, a weaker form allows the receiver to *prove* that the revealed message is the correct one.

Definition 3. An undeniable encryption scheme is *receiver coercible with proof* if, given $C = E_k(m, r)$ the receiver can prove in zero-knowledge that the revealed plaintext m is correct.

Note that the ElGamal scheme is an example of an undeniable encryption scheme which is receiver coercible with proof, but it is *not* receiver coercible (if the discrete logarithm is hard).

We are now in a position to discuss equitable data confiscation.

3.4   Equitable Data Confiscation

Since we do not have escrow agencies with data confiscation, it may seem that one should not be concerned with the possibility of unlawful government action. This would make our analysis much simpler.

However, this impression is wrong. After a coup all senders of messages may be forced to reveal the plaintext-randomness pairs (m, r) of ciphertexts $C = E_k(m, r)$ sent long before the coup. A scheme that protects against such an attack is called *equitable*.

A weaker form of equitability requires that the revealing of randomness does not leak anything additional about an unrevealed plaintext m of a ciphertext $C = E_k(m, r)$. We call this *weak equitability*.

4   Solutions

We now consider two solutions.

Solution 1. *A probabilistic public key encryption scheme which is,*

(i)   secure against chosen-ciphertext attacks, and
(ii) a commitment scheme,

is an undeniable data confiscation scheme which is sender equitable against active attacks by the law enforcment agency. The receiver is coercible with proof.

This follows immediately from the definitions, e.g. of chosen-ciphertext attack. For equitability, we assume that it is legal for all the senders to erase the randomness used after a certain time limit.

Examples of such schemes are the Cramer-Shoup cryptosystem [12] (an adaptation of the ElGamal system [16]) and the Okamoto-Uchiyama cryptosystem modified to get semantic security [26, p. 311]. For another example see [35]. The security of some these schemes is proven only in the Random Oracle model [3].

Solution 2. *The Goldwasser-Micali encryption scheme [17] is an undeniable data confiscation scheme which is sender/receiver coercible, with sender equitability.*

In this case the trapdoor (the factorization of n) can be used to find the randomness the sender used. However, equitability is restricted to the passive case, when the law enforcement agency does not coerce the receiver. Indeed the receiver knows the trapdoor that is needed to compute the randomness. So we only have weak equitability for the receiver.

5   New Deniable Encryption Schemes

Before we conclude we discuss some new ways to achieve deniable encryption.

A deniable encryption scheme [8] allows the sender to open the ciphertext as any message. Canetti-Dwork-Naor-Ostrovsky's work focused on the case when the message space is $\{0,1\}$. A weaker definition of deniability would allow the sender to be able to deny having sent a specific message by opening a different message, not just any message. If the message space is $\{0,1\}$, then of course the two definitions are identical. In many practical encryption schemes the cardinality of the message space is larger than two.

5.1   A Heuristic Scheme

Our scheme is a variant of the RSA encryption scheme. Our technique can be viewed as a subliminal data transmission [32].

Set-up: Alice chooses 4 different large primes p_1, p_2, p_3 and p_4. She then computes $n_1 = p_1 * p_2$, $n_2 = p_3 * p_4$, $n = p_1 * p_2 * p_3 * p_4$, $\lambda(n_1)$ (the Carmichael function[1] of n [21]), $\lambda(n_2)$. Alice then chooses $e_1 \in_R Z_{\lambda(n_1)}$ and $e_2 \in_R Z_{\lambda(n_2)}$. Since $\lambda(n) = \mathrm{lcm}(\lambda(n_1), \lambda(n_2))$ she can compute the unique e modulo $\lambda(n)$ such that:

$$e = e_1 \bmod \lambda(n_1)$$
$$e = e_2 \bmod \lambda(n_2)$$

Alice publishes (e, n) as her public key and gives (e_1, n_1) and (e_2, n_2) to her friends.

Encryption:

For Bob who is not a friend of Alice: Bob uses the normal RSA encryption. The scheme is undeniable for Bob.

For Carol who is a friend of Alice: Carol uses the key (e_1, n_1) instead of (e, n).

---

[1] $\lambda(n)$ is the least positive integer for which we have $b^{\lambda(n)} = 1 \bmod n$ for all $b \in Z_n^*$. If $n = pq$, the product of two different odd primes, then $\lambda(n) = \mathrm{lcm}(p-1, q-1)$.

Let M_1 be the message that Carol wants to encrypt. Carol first computes $C_1 = M_1^{e_1} \bmod n_1$. Then she chooses a C_2 at random from Z_{n_2} and uses the Chinese Remainder Theorem to combine C_1 and C_2 uniquely into a $C \bmod n$. This is the ciphertext she sends to Alice. If Alice is coerced, she produces the unique message M which is such that $C = M^e \bmod n$, which looks likely as random.

Observe that the RSA cryptosystem is not a proven secure. To get semantic security (in the random Oracle model [3]) we can use the technique in [4]. Also, with this protocol the effective bandwidth for Carol is reduced. Can our techniques be used to make high-bandwidth proven secure deniable encryption?

6   Conclusion

Although data confiscation may not be constitutional in countries that protect citizens against self incrimination, we have shown that it clearly has some privacy advantages over key escrow.

In this paper we focused on the time-limited properties of data confiscation and observed that deniable encryption prevents undeniable data confiscation. This paper also opens several new research problems, in particular:

1. Since the US key escrow proposal is not mandatory while the British RIP act is, it is worth studying the properties of key confiscation in greater details. In particular what other advantages/disadvantages does data confiscation have over key escrow?
2. The question on how to obtain equitability relative to the receiver for a scheme which is also receiver coercible seems hard to address. A trivial, but unacceptable solution would be for the sender to destroy his/her secret key. Another trivial solution would be to update the public key on a regular basis, but such a solution is too impractical.

Disclaimer

The authors have focused on technical aspects of privacy. It is not the goal of this paper to endorse the British Regulations of Investigatory Powers Act 2000.

References

1. M. Abe. A key escrow scheme with time-limited monitoring for one-way communication. In E. Dawson, A. Clark, and C. Boyd, editors, *Information Security and Privacy, 5th Australian Conference, ACISP 2000*, Lecture Notes in Computer Science 1841, Springer 2000, 163–177.
2. M. Bellare and S. Goldwasser. Verifiable partial key escrow. In *Proceedings of the 4th ACM Conference on Computer and Communications Security*, April 1997.
3. M. Bellare and P. Rogaway. Random oracles are practical: a paradigm for designing efficient protocols. In *First ACM Conference on Computer and Communications Security*, 1993, 62–73

4. M. Bellare and P. Rogaway. Optimal Asymmetric Encryption. In A. De Santis, editor, *Advances in Cryptology — Eurorypt '94*, Lecture Notes in Computer Science #950, Springer 1995, 92–111
5. T. Beth. Zur Sicherheit der Informationstechnik. *Informatik-Spektrum*, 13, 1990, 204–215. (In German)
6. G. Brassard, D. Chaum, and C. Crépeau. Minimum disclosure proofs of knowledge. *Journal of Computer and System Sciences*, 37(2), 1998, 156–189
7. M. Burmester, Y. Desmedt, and J. Seberry. Equitable key escrow with limited time span. In K. Ohta and D. Pei, editors, *Advances in Cryptology — Asiacrypt '98, Proceedings* Lecture Notes in Computer Science #1514, Springer 1998, 380–391
8. R. Canetti, C. Dwork, M. Naor, and R. Ostrovsky. Deniable encryption. In B. S. Kaliski, editor, *Advances in Cryptology — Crypto '97, Proceedings*, Lecture Notes in Computer Science #1294, Springer 1997, 90–104
9. Key recovery alliance (KRA) technology papers. Special Issue of Computer & Security, 2000, **19**(1).
10. D. Chaum and J.-H. Evertse and J. van de Graaf and R. Peralta. In A. Odlyzko, editor, *Advances in Cryptology, Proc. of Crypto '86*, Lecture Notes in Computer Science #263, Springer-Verlag 1987, 200–212
11. A proposed federal information processing standard for an escrowed encryption standard (EES). Federal Register, July 30, 1993.
12. R. Cramer ans V. Shoup. A Practical Public Key Cryptosystem Provably Secure against Adaptive Chosen Ciphertetx Attack. In H. Krawczyk, editor, *Advances in Cryptology — Crypto '98*, Lecture Notes in Computer Science #1462, Springer 1998, 13–25.
13. D. E. Denning and D. K. Branstad. A taxonomy of key escrow encryption systems. *Commun. ACM*, 39(3), 1996, 34–40
14. Department of Justice Briefing Re Escrowed Encryption Standard, Department of Commerce, Washington D.C., February 4, 1994.
15. D. Dolev, C. Dwork, and M. Naor. Non-malleable cryptography. In *Proceedings of the Twenty third annual ACM Symp. Theory of Computing, STOC*, 1991, 542–552
16. T. ElGamal. A public key cryptosystem and a signature scheme based on discrete logarithms. *IEEE Trans. Inform. Theory*, 1985, 31, 469–472
17. S. Goldwasser and S. Micali. Probabilistic encryption. *Journal of Computer and System Sciences*, 28(2), 1984, 270–299
18. S. Goldwasser and S. Micali and C. Rackoff. The Knowledge Complexity of Interactive Proof Systems. *Siam J. Comput.*, **18**(1), 1989, 186–208
19. J. He and E. Dawson. A new key escrow cryptosystem. In E. Dawson and. J. Golic, editor, *Cryptography Policy and Algorithms, Proceedings*, Lecture Notes in Computer Science #1029, Springer 1996, 105–114
20. J. Kilian and T. Leighton. Failsafe key escrow, revisited. In D. Coppersmith, editor, *Advances in Cryptology — Crypto '95, Proceedings*, Lecture Notes in Computer Science# 963, Springer 1995, 208–221
21. D. E. Knuth. *The Art of Computer Programming, Vol. 2, Seminumerical Algorithms*. Addison-Wesley, Reading, MA, 1981.
22. A. K. Lenstra, P. Winkler, and Y. Yacobi. A key escrow system with warrant bounds. In D. Coppersmith, editor, *Advances in Cryptology — Crypto '95, Proceedings*, Lecture Notes in Computer Science #963, Springer 1995, 197–207
23. C. D. Marsan. Internet organization opposes new u.k. wiretapping law. http://www.cnn.com/2000/TECH/computing/08/04/wiretap.flap.idg/index.html
24. A. Menezes. P.C van Oorscot and S.A. Vanstone. Handbook of applied cryptography. *CRC Press*, 1997

25. S. Micali. Fair public-key cryptosystems. In E. F. Brickell, editor, *Advances in Cryptology — Crypto '92, Proceedings*, Lecture Notes in Computer Science 740, Springer 1993, 113–138

26. T. Okamoto and S. Uchiyama. A new Public-Key Cryptosystem as Secure as Factoring. In K. Nyberg, editor, *Advances in Cryptology — Eurocrypt '98*, Lecture Notes in Computer Science #1403, Springer 1998, 308–318.

27. R. Perera. Dutch secret service accused of e-mail snooping. http://www.cnn.com/2000/TECH/computing/08/02/netherlands.email.idg/index.htm

28. A. Pfitzmann, editor. *Information Hiding, Third International Workshop, Proceedings* Lecture Notes in Computer Science #1768, Springer 1999.

29. Regulation of Investigatory Powers Act 2000. http://www.homeoffice.gov.uk/ripa/ripact.htm.

30. R. L. Rivest and A. Shamir and L. Adleman. A method for obtaining digital signatures and public key cryptosystems. *Commun. ACM*, 1978 **21**, 294–299

31. L. Rohde. U.K. E-mail Snooping Bill passed. http://www.cnn.com/2000/TECH/computing/07/28/uk.surveillance.idg/index.html

32. G. J. Simmons. The prisoners' problem and the subliminal channel. In D. Chaum, editor, *Advances in Cryptology. Proc. of Crypto 83*, pp. 51–67. Plenum Press N.Y., 1984. Santa Barbara, California, August 1983.

33. G. J. Simmons, observation made at the Workshop on Key Escrow, June 22–24, 1994.

34. SSL vs 3.0, http://home.netscape.com/eng/ssl3/

35. Y. Tsiounis and M. Yung. The security of ElGamal based encryption. In H. Imai and Y. Zheng, editors, *Public Key Cryptography, First International Workshop on Practice and Theory in Public Key Cryptography, PKC'98*, Springer 1998, 117–134

A PVSS as Hard as Discrete Log
and Shareholder Separability

Adam Young[1] and Moti Yung[2]

[1] Columbia University, New York, NY, USA.
ayoung@cs.columbia.edu
[2] CertCo, New York, NY, USA.
moti@cs.columbia.edu

Abstract. A Publicly Verifiable Secret Sharing (PVSS) scheme allows
a prover to verifiably prove that a value with specific properties is shared
among a number of parties. This verification can be performed by anyone. Stadler introduced a PVSS for proving that the discrete log of an
element is shared [S96], and based the PVSS on double-decker exponentiation. Schoenmakers recently presented a PVSS scheme that is as hard
to break as deciding Diffie-Hellman (DDH) [Sch99]. He further showed
how a PVSS can be used to improve on a number of applications: fair
electronic cash (with anonymity revocation), universally verifiable electronic voting, and software key escrow schemes. When the solution in
[Sch99] is used for sharing a key corresponding to a given public key, the
double-decker exponentiation method and specific assumptions are still
required. Here we improve on [Sch99] and present a PVSS for sharing
discrete logs that is as hard to break as the Discrete-Log problem itself,
thus weakening the assumption of [Sch99]. Our solution differs in that it
can be used directly to implement the sharing of private keys (avoiding
the double decker methods). The scheme can therefore be implemented
with any semantically secure encryption method (paying only by a moderate increase in proof length). A major property of our PVSS is that
it provides an algebraic decoupling of the recovering participants (who
can be simply represented by any set of public keys) from the sharing
operation. Thus, our scheme diverts from the traditional polynomial-
secret-sharing-based VSS. We call this concept *Separable Shareholders*.

1   Introduction

Secret sharing schemes were introduced to enable the distribution of trust among
several participants. In a secret sharing scheme a secret is split into several pieces
and is shared among several participants. Only when the shares are put together,
or in the case of threshold sharing schemes when some subset of the shares are put
together, is the secret reconstructed. To protect against cheating participants,
the notion of Verifiable Secret Sharing was introduced [CGMA,F85]. In VSS,
a verification protocol allows the participants to verify that the unique secret
can be reconstructed when needed. A property of a VSS which was emphasized
by Stadler [S96] is that "not only the participants, but anyone can verify that

K. Kim (Ed.): PKC 2001, LNCS 1992, pp. 287–299, 2001.

the secret is shared properly". When a VSS scheme has this public verifiability property, it is called a Publicly Verifiable Secret Sharing (PVSS) scheme.

The original PVSS needed the double-decker discrete log assumption [S96]. Other special assumptions for PVSS schemes were given in [FO98] (in particular a special RSA assumption which allows partial recovery), whereas [Sch99] managed to reduce the assumption of a discrete log PVSS to regular Decision DH (DDH). Here we manage to reduce the required assumptions even further, which simplifies the scheme and enhances its usability and availability as we will explain. It is worth noting in this context the interesting work of [PS00], where they develop a nice approach to short non-interactive proofs. However this is a new approach of a somewhat different flavor and obviously of different optimization goals (i.e., their very short elegant proof scheme does not assure asymptotic inverse exponential reduction in security, but relies on the state of the art of certain algorithms. Also, the recovery of secrets in their case may be delayed).

We note that a random oracle assumption for making proofs transferable (NIZK a la Fiat-Shamir) and secure encryption assumptions for implementing secure authenticated channels are also employed whenever a PVSS scheme is designed. For our scheme it is possible to use any probabilistic encryption. Our new scheme enables the use of schemes other than these based on DDH. In particular, for DH based schemes, a practical scheme which is based on a computational Diffie-Hellman assumption, namely, the partial-trapdoor property of DH (and a random oracle) but that *does not require* the DDH assumption can be employed [FO99,P00].

Several useful applications can be built using PVSS schemes. Among the applications of PVSS are voting [Sch99], anonymity-revocation in e-cash systems (e.g., [FTY96]), escrow systems [Mi,S96,VT,YY98], and certified e-mail [Mi98].

A major general advantage of our design (which we bring to the above applications) is a separation of the structure and organization of the recipients (share-holders, election officials, authorities, etc.) from the rest of the world. Thus, the share-holder group can be viewed as an organization which can be managed internally and be presented implicitly (keeping the internal structure hidden) or explicitly (specified access structure and keys) to the rest of the world. This allows a dynamic (and also parallel) share-holder organization. The separation of internal organizational workings and the external world (and its importance to managing evolving commercial entities and consortium bodies) was put forth in [FY99] for general PKI, and, in the context of election schemes it was implemented in [CGS97]. In particular, [FY99] suggests to employ "proactive key maintenance" methods to change the share holder group, while keeping the shared information intact. Our constructions when used with implicitly shared keys, support such operations.

2   The Definition of a PVSS

We will now present the informal definition of a PVSS taken directly from section 2 of [S96] (here s is the value being shared).

Let $\mathcal{A}$ be a monotone access structure. Since $\mathcal{A}$ is a monotone access structure, it follows that if $A \in \mathcal{A}$ and $A \subseteq B$, then $B \in \mathcal{A}$.

Definition 1. *A PVSS consists of a dealer, n participants $P_1,...,P_n$ such that each has a public encryption function E_i and such that each has a corresponding secret decryption function D_i, a monotone access structure $\mathcal{A} \subseteq 2^{\{1,...,n\}}$, and algorithms Share, Recover, and PubVerify which operate as follows:*

Share: The dealer uses the public encryption functions to distribute the shares by calculating $S_i = E_i(s_i)$ for $1 \leq i \leq n$. The dealer then publishes each share S_i.

Recover: If a group of participants want to recover the secret, they run Recover, which has the property that $\forall A \in \mathcal{A}: Recover(\{S_i | i \in A\}) = s$, and that for all $A \notin \mathcal{A}$ it is computationally infeasible to calculate s from $\{S_i | i \in A\}$.

PubVerify: To verify the validity of all encrypted shares, PubVerify is run by any inquiring party. This algorithm has the property that $\exists u \; \forall A \in 2^{\{1,...,n\}}$:

$$(PubVerify(\{S_i | i \in A\}) = 1) \Rightarrow Recover(\{D_i(S_i) | i \in A\}) = u$$

and $u = s$ if the dealer was honest.

A PVSS is called non-interactive if PubVerify requires no interaction with the dealer at all.

Properties of PVSS:

Completeness: We say that a PVSS is **complete** if whenever the dealer is honest (and the (unique) value for s is recoverable by the participant(s)), the verifier accepts the prover's proof as valid (with overwhelming probability).

Soundness: A PVSS is **sound** if whenever the unique s is not recoverable, the verifier accepts the prover's proof only with negligible probability.

The last two properties are important for the notion of a PVSS to be correct. The necessary notion of completeness was omitted from the informal definition of [S96]. We note that the above properties put together also imply that the dealer which encrypts with a group's key (even though it encrypts to a group of servers which it does not even interact with directly), does not have to use chosen ciphertext secure encryption (as our complete proof below demonstrates). This is in contrast to other recent applications of proving properties of encryption.

Secrecy: Finally, another property of a PVSS is **secrecy**, which means that any group not in the access structure should not be able to retrieve s (but perhaps with negligible probability) given the public output of Share.

Observe that the above definition does not state that s must be of any particular form. For example, this definition does not state that s must be a private key, and that PubVerify must be able to verify that s is the private key corresponding to some public key. In fact we may distinguish between the cases in which a value, private key, or encryptions under a shared public key are recovered. These are interesting sub-cases which are required for various applications of PVSSs [1].

Also, the monotone access structure in the original definition may be extended to include threshold schemes [Sch99] (see [D92,FY98]). In fact, we will employ any semantically secure encryption function by the participants, which will enhance the applicability of our scheme.

3   PVSS for Discrete Logs Based on the DL Problem

We will now present a PVSS for discrete logs (DL) which is based on the difficulty of computing discrete logs. This contrasts with the PVSS scheme in [Sch99] which assumes the difficulty of Deciding Diffie-Hellman.

The following are the cryptographic primitives that are used in our system. enc is a a semantically secure probabilistic public key encryption algorithm that takes three arguments, m, s, and PUB. Here m is a message to be encrypted, s is a randomly chosen string to make the encryption probabilistic, and PUB is the public key of the participant (or shared among a set of participants or created by individual public keys of participants). Thus, $c = enc(m, s, PUB)$ is the ciphertext of the message m. Let dec be the corresponding decryption function. Thus, $m = dec(c, PRIV)$, where $PRIV$ is the private key corresponding to PUB. It could be that $PRIV$ is shared distributively, in which case $m = dec(c, PRIV_1, PRIV_2, ..., PRIV_m)$. This can model either a threshold scheme or a polynomial-size monotone access structure composed of nested encryptions of the value by the keys of members of groups in the access structure.

The prover who is the dealer generates a private value x and its corresponding public commitment $y = g^x \bmod p$. We can insist that p is a safe prime and that g has order $p-1$, or we can insist that g has order q where q is a large prime dividing $p-1$. For this section we will w.l.o.g. assume that g has order $p-1$. Informally, the system then works as follows. The dealer commits to knowing two shares that sum to the dealer's private exponent $x \bmod p-1$. This commitment is performed using the envelope method in which additive pieces of the secret are committed to separately [2]. The method employs a public homomorphic commitment for each piece, and a further commitment to a piece which is performed using the arbitrary probabilistic encryption function enc under the participants public keys(s) (shared or explicitly combined key(s) that is). Thus, enc provides a semantically secure encryption relative to the public homomorphism, and hence

---

[1] Of course, sharing a public-key implies sharing a value (which can be encrypted under that key) and sharing the key implies recovery of messages encrypted under that key as well, and we leave as open other implications and separations which may be needed in applications.

[2] The envelope method is different from the usual polynomial sharing which is extensively used; since we are going to use additional shared encryption (owned by the recovery participants) we found that there is no need to employ, prior to the encryption, explicit sharing techniques like polynomial sharing schemes.

provides a secure commitment with respect to the verifier, who can be anyone including the participants. A total of M additive envelope pairs are committed to using *enc*. Using challenge bits, the dealer is forced to reveal a share, not of his choosing, for each pair of additive shares. So, the system in some sense constitutes a proof that at least one pair of shares that sum to x has been committed to under *enc*. Thus, with overwhelming probability, the transcript of the proof itself can be used by the participant(s) to recover x.

We will next review the algorithm in detail.

Share: The following is the non-interactive (transferable) transcript generation algorithm based on H being a random oracle. It is this transcript that forms the verifiable encryption of the prover's secret x.

1. $P = ()$
2. for $i = 1$ to $2k(n)$ do
3. $r_i \in_R Z_{p-1}$
4.   choose two random strings $s_{i,1}$ and $s_{i,2}$ for use in *enc*
5. $Q_i = g^{r_i} \bmod p$
6. $C_{i,1} = enc(r_i, s_{i,1}, PUB)$
7. $C_{i,2} = enc(r_i - x \bmod p - 1, s_{i,2}, PUB)$
8.   add $(Q_i, C_{i,1}, C_{i,2})$ to the end of P
9. val $= H(P)$
10. set $b_1, b_2, ..., b_{2k(n)}$ to be the $k(n)$ least significant bits of val, where $b_i \in Z_2$
11. for $i = 1$ to $2k(n)$ do
12. $w_i = r_i - b_i x$
13. $z_i = (w_i, s_{i,j})$ where $j = 1 + b_i$
14.   add z_i to the end of P

Thus, $P = ((Q_1, C_{1,1}, C_{1,2}), ..., (Q_{2k(n)}, C_{2k(n),1}, C_{2k(n),2}), z_1, ..., z_{2k(n)})$. Here P denotes the non-interactive proof, or transcript. Note that the b_i's can be recovered from P. The algorithm outputs (y, x, P) to the dealer.

PubVerify: To verify that x is recoverable by the participant(s) who own(s) y, the verifier takes y, the corresponding P, and the public key PUB. The verifier first checks that $y < p$. The verifier checks that all of the values in P lie in the correct sets. The verifier also checks that the values $C_{i,j}$ for all i and j, do not contain any repetitions. The verifier checks that none of the Q_i for all i are repetitious. If any of these verifications fail, then false is returned (the prover can easily avoid repetitions by checking that the chosen values are not repeating which is a negligible probability event for the honest prover). The verifier then computes $b_1, b_2, ..., b_{2k(n)}$ in the same way as in the "share" computation. For $i = 1$ to $2k(n)$, the verifier verifies the following things:

1. $enc(w_i, s_{i,j}, PUB) = C_{i,j}$ where $j = 1 + b_i$
2. $Q_i/(y^{b_i}) \bmod p = g^{w_i} \bmod p$

The verifier concludes that x is recoverable as long as all the verifications pass and as long as both 1 and 2 above are satisfied for $1 \le i \le 2k(n)$.

Recover: When the shareholder(s) obtain(s) the non-interactive proof P all values are decrypted and the second cleartext value is subtracted from the first cleartext value mod $p - 1$ for each pair to obtain a value. To verify that such a value is x, the shareholder(s) raise(s) g to this value mod p and compares it with y. We remark that the ability to do this in a shared fashion depends on the algorithms used for enc and dec. Some schemes may use threshold encryption, whereas general semantically secure algorithms can always support a shared dec algorithm in which decryption is performed by each participant in turn, giving the result to the next participant for decryption. The trust model in the later case has to be such that the last participant to decrypt has to be trusted to share its information. Verification of the value is public due to the public homomorphic commitments.

4   Security and Correctness

The non-interactive PVSS for sharing x was constructed based on a 3-round atomic computational ZKIP with error probability $1/2$. To see this, note that it directly corresponds to the following interactive 3-round protocol[3]:

1. For $i = 1$ to $k(n)$ do:
2.   P chooses $r_i \in_R Z_{p-1}$
3.   P chooses $s_{i,1}$ and $s_{i,2}$ randomly for use in enc
4.   P computes $Q_i = g^{r_i} \bmod p$
5.   P computes $C_{i,1} = enc(r_i, s_{i,1}, PUB)$
6.   P computes $C_{i,2} = enc(r_i - x \bmod p - 1, s_{i,2}, PUB)$
7.   P sends $(Q_i, C_{i,1}, C_{i,2})$ to V
8.   V sends $b_i \in_R \{0,1\}$ to P
9.   P computes $w_i = r_i - b_i x \bmod p - 1$
10.   P sends $z_i = (w_i, s_{i,j})$ where $j = 1 + b_i$ to V
11.   V verifies that:
12. $enc(w_i, s_{i,j}, PUB) = C_{i,j}$ where $j = 1 + b_i$
13. $Q_i / (y^{b_i}) \bmod p = g^{w_i} \bmod p$

Here n be a security parameter and $k(n) = \omega(log\ n)$ is given. The proof achieves error $2^{-k(n)}$. Soundness of the above protocol can be seen by the fact that if P does not know x then in a given round P can respond to only one possible outcome, otherwise P can compute discrete logarithms. It differs from standard zero-knowledge proofs in that, in addition to a commitment value being sent in the first round (i.e., using Q_i to commit to the base g logarithm of Q_i mod p), the prover sends two semantically secure encryptions (which must be consistent with the commitment in Q_i and x). The first of these encryptions

---

[3]   We comment that an interactive variant which is based on parallel execution (using claw-free function commitments by the verifier) exists and that allows the entire proof to be conducted in a small (constant) number of rounds [GK,BMO,IS93,BJY97].

can be thought of as yet another commitment of the base g logarithm of Q_i. The second encryption is a commitment to the base g logarithm of Q_i/y. Since these are both semantically secure encryptions, they give nothing to a poly-time bounded adversary that the adversary couldn't compute himself. They are, in some sense, redundant commitments of Q_i and Q_i/y (they are useful since they provide recoverability by the participants). In the second round, the verifier sends a randomly chosen bit to the prover, as in standard zero-knowledge proofs. In the third round, the verifier either opens the commitment r_i (for Q_i) or opens $r_i - x \bmod p - 1$ (for Q_i/y), as in standard zero-knowledge proofs. The only difference is that exactly one of the two semantically secure encryptions is also opened, and verified for consistency (to insure that "recover" works). In arguing zero-knowledge of the interactive procedure, r_i is chosen at random and if b_i is expected to be 0, Q_i is computed as in the protocol. In this case $C_{i,1}$ is encrypted correctly and $C_{i,2}$ is formed by encrypting the string with each bit being zero (indistinguishable from a correct encryption). On the other hand, if b_i is expected to be 1, then again r_i is chosen at random, $C_{i,1}$ is made to be an encryption of zeros, and $C_{i,2}$ is made to encrypt r_i. In addition $Q_i = g^{r_i}y$ is published (so that the verification checks pass). Standard zero-knowledge, assuming commitment (encryption in our case) implies that the simulation can be conducted in expected polynomial time. Completeness follows a standard argument. Thus, given y the above is a complete and sound and computational zero-knowledge (simulatable) interaction.

Lemma 2. *The PVSS scheme is computational zero-knowledge and therefore secure in the random oracle model (with error $1/2^{k(n)}$).*

Proof. (sketch). In section 5.2 of [BRa], a reduction is given that shows how to transform any three move ZKIP for $L \in NP$ with error probability $1/2$ into a non-interactive ZK proof in the random oracle model. The reduction accounts for a set of envelopes being sent in the first round, and having some subset of the envelopes opened according to a randomly chosen challenge bit b. The reduction therefore applies to our protocol above for discrete logs. The transformation that is given in [BRa] is the same transformation that was used to obtain the non-interactive version given above. Since semantically secure encryptions yield nothing that can't be computed efficiently without the encryptions, the lemma then follows from the transformation. Note that since the transcript is zero-knowledge (simulatable) given $y = g^x$ then whatever is derivable from the public key y about the private key x without the transcript, can be derived with the transcript with related probability (the relation is given by the simulation argument given in the transformation). In particular, if x can be derived from y and the transcript by a party that does not hold $PRIV$ (namely, violation of secrecy), then if enc is semantically secure, we can use the successful derivation to break the discrete log assumption. QED.

We will now prove that the non-interactive PVSS for DL based keys is a proof of knowledge in the random oracle model. This will imply that the PVSS itself is, with respect to shares, complete and sound. This part does not need the assumption that computing discrete logs is intractable but we still need the fact that the encryption is indeed a commitment scheme and we still need to use the random oracle model (for the protocol to be non-interactive and produce a transferable transcript). We do not give in this version a formal definition for a non-interactive proof to be a proof of knowledge in the random oracle model. However, in a nutshell, it is a continuation of the formalization of the Fiat Shamir [FS86] notion (which was formalized but not for proofs of knowledge in [BRa,PS96]). We would like that possible unpredictable different (forking of) values of a polynomial portion of the oracle answers imply the extractability of the witness value. We then extend extraction, to extraction by a third party who can recover the commitment. (Familiarity with proof of knowledge, extractors, and the random oracle model is assumed).

Lemma 3. *The non-interactive PVSS for DL based keys constitutes a proof of knowledge with knowledge error* $1/2^{k(n)}$.

Proof. It is easy to see (similar to the zero-knowledge proof being complete) that the non-triviality condition holds. We will now consider the validity condition. The common input α is $y = g^x \bmod p$. The auxiliary input (witness) β is $x \bmod p - 1$. We have that $x_i = (Q_i, C_{i,1}, C_{i,2})$, $y_i = z_i$, $t = 2k(n)$, and the b_i's in the proof are the same as the b_i's in the definition. Suppose that P makes a total of $T(n)$ oracle queries when given H and H' (e.g., in an attempt to fool V). If the prover doesn't know a witness then the prover will convince V of the validity of the proof with probability at most $T(n)2^{-2k(n)}$ which is at most $1/2^{k(n)}$ for sufficiently long n (see [BRa] section 5.2). Thus, the knowledge error is at most $1/2^{k(n)}$. It follows that $p(\alpha)$ is at least $1 - 1/2^{k(n)}$.

Let $T = P_{\alpha,\beta,r}(H)$ and $T' = P_{\alpha,\beta,r}(H')$ Consider the following knowledge extractor K. Suppose that in round i, b_i in T is 0 and b_i in T' is 1. K then subtracts the w_i in T' from the w_i in T mod $p - 1$ to get x_c, a candidate value for x. The operation of K when the bits are inverted is similar.

We will now give a lower bound on K's probability of extracting a witness from T and T' (we won't derive an exact probability, since using $T(n)$ oracle queries, P may always try to make the first half of the b_i's 0 to try to fool the prover, for example). Assuming no extra oracle queries are made, with probability $1/2$ we have that b_i in T equals b_i in T', since the b_i's are chosen randomly for both T and T' (H and H' serve as honest verifiers). So, with probability $1/2$, the b_i's in each transcript differ and the knowledge extractor can extract x from both de-committed values. To see this recall that P for both transcripts is using: the same common-input α, the same auxiliary input β, and *the same random tape* r. The probability that x isn't extracted in any of the $2k(n)$ rounds is $2^{-2k(n)}$. Now consider the case where P makes $T(n)$ additional oracle queries. It can be shown that the probability that x isn't extracted is at most $T(n)2^{-2k(n)}$. For sufficiently large n this probability is at most $2^{-k(n)}$. Thus, the probability that the witness $s = x$ is extracted by K is at least $1 - 2^{-k(n)}$. Taking this worst case value, along with the worst case values for $p(\alpha)$ and the knowledge error, we get the claimed knowledge error.a QED.

Theorem 4. *The PVSS above is a complete, sound, and secure protocol.*

Completeness holds since any decrypted pair can give the correct secret that is shared. The proof of knowledge (extraction) which is done by verifying the commitments (which are in fact encryptions openable by the owners of the encryption's private keys) implies that with the same probability of extraction (as in Lemma 2), the owner of the encryption method can decrypt both envelopes of the correct shared secret (and verifies its value against its public witness), and the owner is fooled only with a negligible probability (that of the knowledge error). This implies soundness. Lemma 1, in turn, implies secrecy.

5 Applications

Shareholder Separability:
The simplified PVSS here treated the encryption keys of the shareholding authorities as a given black box. This enables many applications in an extended setting where the public key schemes of authorities/shareholders/agencies are managed and organized separately from the users who only have access to an agency's public key; various authorities, in fact, may have different types of public keys. This principle of separation of management of various roles is key in evolving organizations. Cryptographic designs in critical commercial and financial settings should follow such principles, as advocated in [FY99] in the context of PKI. The structure and composition of the shareholder group can be changed using "proactive maintenance" [OY91] and the secret is not revealed while the shareholders change as discussed in [FGMY].

E-cash with anonymity revocation:
Various schemes have been used to implement e-cash where the authorities are off-line and the user performs a proof of encryption with the trusted authority keys (e.g. [FTY96]). In these schemes the trustees' key is a shared ElGamal key. Since our PVSS decouples the receivers' key (it can be any public key, have any access structure, and have any organization), we can extend the above schemes by allowing the user to commit to the value of the coin based on the discrete log problem while encrypting using any scheme. The PVSS becomes a generalized "indirect discourse proof." This may be a significant extension which enables the development of the structure of the trustees and their organizational and operational changes independently from the underlying scheme. The changes may be done implicitly or explicitly (notions described in detail in [FY99]). If an explicit change is performed, the trustees' keys are publicly changed and the users have to be notified to spend or replace their coins for the coins to maintain their value. An implicit change does not change the external view of the trustees and seems preferable in this setting.

Universally-verifiable secure ballot election:
We can use our PVSS to obtain a simplified scheme for secure ballot election (in the setting of [CF85]) or with distributed tallying authorities (as in [BY86]). Here we assume that the exponents are taken from a prime order subgroup generated by g (say $p = 2q + 1$, where q is a large prime and g generates the quadratic

residues G_q). Voter i commits to a random $G_i = g^s$ and to $H_i = y^s$ or $y^{(s+1)}$, depending on whether it casts 0 or 1, respectively (the discrete log of y mod g is globally unknown, the security here relies on the semantic security of ElGamal in the subgroup which is equivalent to DDH [TY,NR]). The voter proves (in NIZK) the relationship between G_i and H_i (see [Sch99]). It then PVSS's the value of s in $G_i = g^s$. The tallying authorities can recover s and the ballot (s or $s + 1$) for each voter but will keep it secure. The voting is robust (each user's PVSS proof is publicly verifiable) and can be made independent of other users (by changing the hashing procedure for users based on the unique user ID). The authorities can present and prove the correctness of the results. Everyone can compute the product of the values of $G = \prod_i G_i$ and that of $H = \prod_i H_i$. The discrete logs of G, H and their difference *mod q* (the exact tally) is available to the authorities, who can claim the result and present a NIZK proof of knowledge of this value based on the public availability of G, H and the result (and the private knowledge of the discrete log values). Of course the exponent additive group size, q, is larger than the number of voters which, together with the NIZK of the users being verified, prevents wrap-arounds of the difference above.

Once again, the keys and organization of the tallying authorities and their structure is independent of the ballot construction. This has some advantages such as: a number of parallel tallying authorities can be easily implemented (by encrypting in parallel with their keys), authorities organized as a general linear access structure is possible, dynamic changes in the tallying authorities between and during elections [FY99] is possible, etc. A somewhat more specific separation was given already in the scheme of [CGS97].

Software key escrow applications:
In [YY98] a model and solution for key recovery in the context of a public-key infrastructure was given and implementation based on double-decker exponentiation was given. In this model, each user is responsible for escrowing his or her own private key and is responsible for constructing a proof to this effect. Such a user is granted a digital certificate by a CA only if a public key, an encryption of the corresponding private key, and a proof that the encryption is correct is supplied to the CA during key certification (and only during certification). The PVSS scheme can be used to solve this problem as follows. The user computes the public key $y = g^x$ *mod p* where p is cryptographically secure (e.g. $p - 1$ is a multiple of a large prime). The prover, who is the dealer in the PVSS scheme then shares the private key x among the participants which are the escrow authorities (just by knowing the keys of the authorities which are public). For verification, since the CAs know the shared public key of the participants, the user can send y along with the proof to any CA for key certification. The CA is thus the verifier in the PVSS. The recover procedure is run by the authorities given the transcript from the CA. The authorities recover the private key (or even better they recover encryptions of session keys encrypted under the user's public key without ever recovering the user's private key itself (as advocated in [LWY95,FY95]) which is possible in various threshold cryptography settings).

In contrast, in [Sch99] a similar key escrow solution based on [YY98] was given that makes use of a value f which generates a high order subgroup of Z_p, and which uses a fixed element g with high order in Z_p^*. In that solution the value $C_0 = g^s$ is published (in the distribution protocol of section 3 in that paper). Thus, the escrow solution is secure only if computing discrete logs in a subgroup is intractable (as well as the DH assumption). Note that the parameters g and h require that $p = 2tq + 1$ and $q = 2wr + 1$ where p, q, and r are primes and t and w are positive integers. Also, the public key in that solution is $H = f^{(G^s)}$, where f is an appropriate generator (as in [S96]). Since both H and C_0 are public, this escrow solution makes a cryptographic assumption above and beyond the new PVSS, and this assumption is missing from the paper. The cryptographic assumption is that given (H, C_0) it is intractable to recover G^s (and therefore s too). Note that the exact same assumption was made in [YY98], where it was refereed to as "problem 1" (which is a DH-Dlog combined problem). This is *not* the standard DH assumption. It is important to distinguish between the assumptions made for the security of the PVSS *protocol*, and the assumptions made for the security of the published *trapdoor values*. This is especially true when a PVSS is used for software key escrow, since the requirements for a secure software key escrow solution exceed the requirements of a PVSS (e.g., sharing a public key, or recovering only values encrypted under that key; we can achieve both in the last application).

Certified mail:

When an escrow system and signature scheme are in place a simple "optimistic" certified mail system is possible with an off-line post-office (an idea due to Micali [Mi98]). The sender commits to the encrypted mail and the mail key, signs this message, and sends it to the receiver together with a proof of that everything was constructed correctly, which in our case is just the PVSS escrowing the message key (as above) under the post-office key. The receiver sends back a receipt acknowledging the above message and signs this message. The sender then sends the mail decrypted (by sending the key). If the last message is not received promptly (under an agreeable definition of "promptly") the receiver gets the post-office involved. The PVSS assures the receiver that the encrypted key is recoverable by the post office (under any organization of the post office agents).

References

BJY97. M. Bellare, M. Jakobsson, M. Yung. Round-Optimal Zero-Knowledge Arguments Based on Any One-Way Function. Eurocrypt'97 pp. 280–305.

BRa.   M. Bellare, P. Rogaway. Random Oracles are Practical In *ACM CCCS '94*.

BMO.   M. Bellare, S. Micali, R. Ostrovsky. Perfect Zero-Knowledge in Constant Rounds. In *ACM STOC '90*.

CF85.   J. Cohen (Benaloh) and M. Fischer, *A robust and verifiable cryptographically secure election scheme*, FOCS 1985, pp. 372–382.

BY86.   J. C. Benaloh and M. Yung, *Distributing the Power of a Government to Enhance the Privacy of Voters*, PODC 1986, pp. 52-62.

CGS97. R. Cramer, R. Gennaro and B. Schoonmakers. A Secure and Optimally Efficient Multi-Authority Election Scheme. In Eurocrpt'97, pages 103–118.

CGMA.   B. Chor, S. Goldwasser, S. Micali, B. Awerbuch. Verifiable Secret Sharing and Achieving Simultaneity in the Presence of Faults. In *FOCS '85*.

D92.   Y. Desmedt. Threshold cryptosystems. AUSCRYPT '92, 3–14.

F85.   P. Feldman. A Practical Scheme for Non-interactive Verifiable Secret Sharing. In *FOCS '87*.

FGMY.   Y. Frankel, P. Gemmell, P. MacKenzie, M. Yung. Optimal Resilience Proactive Public Key Systems. In *FOCS '97*.

FS86.   A. Fiat, A. Shamir. How to Prove Yourself: Practical Solutions to Identification and Signature Problems. Crypto'86 pages 186–194.

FTY96. Y. Frankel, Y. Tsiounis, M. Yung. Indirect Discourse Proofs: Achieving Efficient Fair Off-Line Cash. In *Advances in Cryptology—Asiacrypt '96*.

FY95.   Y. Frankel, M. Yung. Escrow Encryption Systems Visited: Attacks, Analysis and Designs. In *Advances in Cryptology—Crypto '95*, pages 222–235.

FY98.   Y. Frankel and M. Yung. Distributed public-key cryptosystems. In *Advances in Public Key Cryptography—PKC '98*, volume 1431 LNCS, 1–13.

FY99.   Y. Frankel, M. Yung. Cryptosystems Robust against "Dynamic Faults" Meet Enterprise Needs for Organizational "Change Control." In *Financial Cryptology 99*.

FO98.   E. Fujisaki and T. Okamoto, A Practical and Provably Secure Scheme for Publicly Verifiable Secret Sharing and Its Applications. Eurocrypt'98.

FO99.   E. Fujisaki and T. Okamoto, Secure Integration of Asymmetric and Symmetric Encryption Schemes. In Crypto'99.

GK.   O. Goldreich, A. Kahan. How to Construct Constant-Round Zero-Knowledge Proof Systems for NP. *Journal of Cryptology*, 9(3), pp. 167–190, 1996.

GM.   S. Goldwasser, S. Micali. Probabilistic Encryption. In *JCSC '84*.

IS93.   T. Itoh, K. Sakurai. On the complexity of constant round ZKIP of possession of knowledge. In *IEICE Transactions on Fundamentals of Electronics, Communications, and Computer Sciences*, vol. E76-A, No. 1, Jan. 1993.

Luby.   M. Luby. Pseudorandomness and its Cryptographic Applications. Princeton Press.

LWY95. A. Lenstra, P. Winkler, Y. Yacobi. A Key Escrow System with Warrant Bounds. In *Advances in Cryptology—Crypto '95*, pages 197–207.

Mi.   S. Micali. Fair Public-Key Cryptosystems. Crypto'92, pp. 113–138.

Mi98.   S. Micali. Certified E-mail with Invisible Post Offices. Weizmann Institute Workshop, talk, June 98.

NR.   M. Naor, O. Reingold, Efficient Cryptographic Primitives based on Decision Diffie-Hellman. In *FOCS '97*.

OY91.   R. Ostrovsky and M. Yung, *How to withstand mobile virus attacks*, PODC 1991, pp. 51-61.

P00.   D. Pointcheval, Chosen-Ciphertext Security for Any One-Way Cryptosystem. PKC'00.

PS96.   D. Pointcheval, J. Stern. Security Proofs for Signature Schemes. Eurocrypt'96.

PS00.   G. Poupard, J. Stern. Fair Encryption of RSA keys, Eurocrypt'00.

S96.   M. Stadler. Publicly Verifiable Secret Sharing. Eurocrypt'96.

Sch99. B. Schoenmakers. A simple Publicly Verifiable Secret Sharing Scheme and its Application to Electronic Voting. Crypto'99.

TY.   Y. Tsiounis, M. Yung. On the Security of ElGamal based Encryption. *PKC '98*.

VT.   E. Verheul, H. van Tilborg. Binding ElGamal: A Fraud-Detectable Alternative to Key-Escrow Proposals. Eurocrypt '97, pages 119–133.

YY98.   A. Young, M. Yung. Auto-Recoverable and Auto-Certifiable Cryptosystems. Eurocrypt'98.

One Round Threshold Discrete-Log Key Generation without Private Channels

Pierre-Alain Fouque and Jacques Stern

École Normale Supérieure, Département d'Informatique
45, rue d'Ulm, F-75230 Paris Cedex 05, France
{Pierre-Alain.Fouque,Jacques.Stern}@ens.fr

Abstract. Pedersen designed the first scheme for generating Discrete-Log keys without any trusted dealer in 1991. As this protocol is simple and efficient, it appeared to be very attractive. For a long time, this robust algorithm has been trusted as being secure. However, in 1999, Gennaro *et al.* proved that one of the requirements is not guaranteed : more precisely, the property that the key is uniformly distributed in the key space.
Their main objective was to repair the security flaw without sacrificing on efficiency. As a result, the protocol became secure but somehow unpractical. In particular, the "complaint phase", in which cheaters are thrown out, makes the scheme overly complex and difficult to deal with in practical situations. In order to avoid this phase and other drawbacks such as the initialization phase where private channels have to be created, we present a *one round* scheme which generates a discrete-log key with public channels only. Finally, we show how to improve the efficiency of our algorithm when the number of servers increases.

Key words: Threshold DLK Generation, Publicly Verifiable Encryption, Adaptive and Concurrent Adversary

1 Introduction

In order to design threshold cryptosystems such as signature or public key encryption schemes, the first stage consists in sharing the key generation procedure. Indeed, if a trusted dealer is used in the key generation protocol, the security of the overall distributed scheme depends on a unique server. Key generation protocols are based on random distribution processes. The servers jointly generate a random key such that, at the end of the process, all honest servers have a share of the secret key.

Improvements to the random generation of private keys for public key cryptography usually fall into two areas : the distribution of a secret for discrete-log based cryptosystems and the distribution of RSA keys.

The latter case is partially solved by the nice paper of Boneh and Franklin [4]. However, the protocol does not allow to efficiently share RSA modulus with

K. Kim (Ed.): PKC 2001, LNCS 1992, pp. 300–316, 2001.
© Springer-Verlag Berlin Heidelberg 2001

strong primes and is not robust against cheaters. Following this paper, two articles provide robustness using different techniques. The first one by Frankel *et al.* [11], is based on the same methods as [4] and uses the protocol of Ben-Or, Goldwasser and Widgerson [2] with private channels between each pair of participants. Frankel *et al.* also propose protocols that make the scheme proactive in [11,10,12]. In [22] Poupard and Stern present a protocol for two players which avoids private channels. They introduce a new technique simpler and more efficient that does not need to perform many rounds of communication. It is based on a trapdoor version of the discrete logarithm problem. This kind of protocol is well-suited to small group of participants which, from a practical point of view, is the usual case. Gilboa has followed this method in [14].

Methods for distributing keys for discrete-log cryptosystems have been known for a long time, starting with Feldman and Pedersen papers [9,20,21]. However, a flaw in the requirements has been discovered and a first solution as well as a security model for DKG protocols have been defined by Gennaro *et al.* in [13]. The solution has been improved by Canetti *et al.* in [7] to withstand adaptive attacks. In [16], Lysyanskaya and Jarecki have proposed two new models of security for this kind of attacks. The first one dealt also with concurrent adversaries whereas the second presents erasure-free adaptive security with persistently inconsistent players. The schemes are based on Pedersen Verifiable Secret Sharing and consequently use private channels. Only, Jarecki's solution uses public channels but it needs non-committing encryption scheme which makes the protocol less efficient.

Whereas previous solutions to DKG prove security in the information-theoretic model, we use here a computational model as the goal of such protocol is to construct a public key. Therefore, we eliminate the committing values of [16,7] which are needed to prove the security against adaptive adversaries. To cope with such adversaries, we design a one round protocol.

Following the new approach proposed by Poupard and Stern, the contribution of this paper is to introduce public channels in order to reduce the communication rounds to a unique phase. If we use non-interactive protocol, we can also ignore concurrent and adaptive adversaries as this kind of attackers make no sense in a one round protocol. To achieve a non-interactive protocol, we need primitives such that all servers can decide whether the other servers have correctly performed their tasks and synchronous network to prevent "rushing attacks". Consequently, we need NIZK proofs secure in the random oracle model and public channels. In appendix 8.1, we relax the assumption of synchronous network and present a model where we can easily prevent the "rushing attack" and adaptive adversaries at the price of a particular player.

1.1 Background and Related Work

Pedersen scheme [20] is a non-interactive scheme with broadcast and private channels. The scheme is organized in two phases : in the first stage, the participants select the key while in the second, the key is distributed between servers.

In the distributed phase, each server acts as the dealer in a Feldman protocol [9] which uses verifiable secret sharing.

Participant P_i chooses $x_i \in \mathbb{Z}_q$ at random and picks t random numbers $a_{i,k}$ in $\mathbb{Z}_q$. Then, he sets $f_i(X) = \sum_{k=0}^{t} a_{i,k} X^k$ where $a_{i,0} = x_i$. He privately sends a secret share $s_{i,j} = f_i(j) \bmod q$ to participant P_j and broadcasts as public information $y_{i,j} = g^{s_{i,j}} \bmod p$, and $A_{i,k} = g^{a_{i,k}} \bmod p$ for $k = 0, \ldots, t$. These data can be used by all servers to check whether the random, x_i chosen by P_i, has been correctly distributed. Let

$$y_{i,j} = \prod_{k=0}^{t} A_{i,k}^{j^k} \bmod p$$

If $s_{i,j}$ is not the discrete logarithm of $y_{i,j}$, participant P_j broadcasts a complaint against P_i.

The complaints are managed through different strategies. A possible one is the following : if more than t participants complain against server P_i, that server is clearly faulty and is disqualified. Otherwise, P_i reveals the share $s_{i,j}$ for each complaining player P_j. If any of the revealed shares fails the equation $y_{i,j} = g^{s_{i,j}} \bmod p$, P_i is disqualified, otherwise P_i can still be qualified. One can then define QUAL as the set of non-disqualified players. The public key is defined as $y = \prod_{i \in \text{QUAL}} y_i$ where $y_i = A_{i,0} = g^{x_i} \bmod p$.

In the previous scheme, participant P_i chooses a random secret x_i and shares it between the other servers. Consequently, since disqualifications may occur after the distribution phase, the selection phase which aims at unambiguously fixing the public key, is not completed before the beginning of the distribution phase. Hence, an adversary can compute the public key at the end of the distribution phase using the values $A_{i,0}$. Depending on this intended value and on the goal of the adversary, this player can, for example, disqualify some members in order to modify the public key distribution. Gennaro *et al.* describe an attack in which two malicious members can create a bias in the distribution of the last bit of the public key with probability 3/4 rather than 1/2. Their attack relies on the fact that the following scheme uses secret channels between each member such that we cannot know whenever an error appears which party has cheated if both players are corrupted.

To avoid this attack, Gennaro *et al.* duplicate the scheme: in the first part, the honest group is selected and in a second phase, the public value associated to the shared secret is made public. In this case, the qualified group is determined at the end of the first phase. In the first selection phase, each server commits a random value with the unconditional scheme of Pedersen in [21] ; whereas in the distribution phase, players release information enabling everyone to compute the public value. If a player cheats in the second phase, but belongs to QUAL, the other players run an error-correcting algorithm with the values that the cheating player had distributed during the first phase.

The need for two phases comes from the fact that the private channels used hide faulty players. Consequently, after the first phase which uses a symmetric algorithm, we do not know if the cheating player is :

- the sender who has sent a false share within the private channel, or
- the receiver who claims that he has received a bad share.

Therefore, the second phase is needed to solve the "complaints". However, we can expect that in general no server will be corrupted. Thus this second phase appears to be redundant and useless. Moreover, it is the most time consuming phase of the protocol.

1.2   Our Solution

Our approach is focused on simplifying previous protocols. In a real implementation of private channels, an additional previous round must be executed to share the secret key between each pair of servers. This first round is usually put as a requirement for the channel but this phase involves penalties in practical implementations.

Moreover, in private channels, we cannot know whether the faulty player is the sender or the receiver in the first phase. The second phase of [13] is therefore needed to solve the complaints coming from this ambiguity. Hence, if we use a Publicly Verifiable Secret Sharing scheme (PVSS) and Publicly Verifiable Encryption scheme (PVE) [5], we are able to immediately detect whether the sender has sent faulty parts. Then, malicious players are caught and we do not allow them in the group of qualified members. Consequently, our scheme consists of only one phase where each participant shares his random number with a PVSS scheme and transfers the share to the intended party with a PVE scheme in such a way that all parties can verify that the receiver is able to recover his share. As we use only one phase with a PVSS, all users must be able to determine the public key at the end of this stage. Consequently, we use a synchronous network to avoid "rushing attacks", where an adversary waits until all other servers have played before defining its own value. In this scenario, an adversary can choose a public key or at least bias the distribution. Therefore, the release of values $A_{i,0}$ will be made at a fixed time for each server. In 8.1 we show how to avoid synchronous network with a new kind of player.

Complexity of the Protocol. In our scheme, all users have to verify a lot of proofs. Particularly, if the numbers of participants is ℓ and each of them shares his secret random in ℓ pieces, we have $O(\ell^2)$ shares in the scheme. Moreover, in our scenario, all of these pieces are broadcast and must be verified by all participants. We do not use a "complaint phase" in which a misleading player informs the others that a verification does not work. Hence, the computation complexity is $O(k\ell^2)$, whereas other schemes have a complexity in $O(k\ell)$. However, we believe that it does not tamper practicality since the number of participants is usually limited. Finally, the hidden constant in the O-notation of other protocols makes the comparison a bit meaningless.

Improvement of the Complexity. At first glance, our scheme seems to be costly in terms of computations since all servers have to check the shares of the others. However, as noted above in practical situations we have to deal only with few servers. Furthermore, if we want to execute our protocol with more servers, we provide in appendix 8.2 a solution to speed-up the verification phase. Thanks to a fast batch verification, we prove that the computation complexity of our scheme is comparable with previous ones.

1.3   Outline of the Paper

In section 2, we define the security model for the distributed key generation of discrete-log keys. In section 3, we recall some cryptographic primitives and present a proof of fairness. In section 4, we describe the scheme and in section 5 the security proof. Finally, we discuss the complexity of our protocol in section 6.

2   The Security Model

2.1   The Network and the Players

Our game includes the following players connected through a synchronous broadcast channel : a set of ℓ servers $P_1, \dots, P_\ell$ and an adversary who may control up to t servers. A player P_i is considered *good* as long as he has followed the protocol and *faulty* once he has deviated from the protocol.

2.2   Formal Definition

A t-out-of-ℓ *threshold key generation scheme* is a protocol that allows any subset of $t + 1$ players out of ℓ to generate the secret key, but disallows the generation if fewer than t players participate to the protocol.

A t-out-of-ℓ threshold key generation is composed by a *key generation algorithm* that takes as input a security parameter k, the number ℓ of generation servers, and the threshold parameter t ; it outputs a public key PK, and a list $SK_1, \dots, SK_\ell$ of shares of the private key associated to the list $PK_1, \dots, PK_\ell$ of shares of the public key.

2.3   Security Requirements

The security requirements for a threshold key generation scheme are *correctness* and *secrecy*. We present here the requirements for discrete logarithm public key $PK = y = g^x \bmod p$ and $SK = x$. The SK is shared among the ℓ servers.

The *correctness* property consists of the three followings items.

- All subsets of $t+1$ shares provided by honest players define the same unique secret key x.
- All honest parties have the same value of public key $y = g^x \bmod p$, where x is the unique secret guaranteed by the previous item.
- The value x is uniformly distributed in $\mathbb{Z}_q$, and hence y is uniformly distributed in the subgroup generated by g.

The *secrecy* property means that no information on x can be learned by an adversary beyond what follows from equality $y = g^x \bmod p$. The secrecy condition can be more formally expressed in terms of simulatability. The simulation enables to prove that the attacker $\mathcal{A}$ learns nothing on the random numbers of the uncorrupted servers. More precisely, if $\mathcal{A}$ has knowledge of the t random numbers of the corrupted servers and knows the public value y, a program called simulator $\mathcal{S}$ can be executed in expected polynomial time, so that the view of the adversary during a real run is indistinguishable from the output of the simulator. Hence, the adversary cannot see if the distribution comes from a simulator or from a real run. Consequently, as the simulator does not know the secret information, the output of the simulator cannot be used by the adversary to learn knowledge on the secret numbers of the uncorrupted players.

2.4   The Adversarial Game

To define *correctness and security against a static adversary*, we consider the following game played against such adversary.

A1 The adversary $\mathcal{A}$ has knowledge of the intended output of the distributed discrete-log public key algorithm : the public key y.

A2 The attacker chooses to corrupt t servers. $\mathcal{A}$ learns all their secrets and she actively controls their behavior.

A3 Each participant chooses a random number and shares it using a Publicly Verifiable Secret Sharing scheme among the others.

3   Cryptographic Primitives

3.1   The Paillier Cryptosystem

Various cryptosystems based on randomized encryption schemes $E(M)$, which encrypt a message M by raising a basis g to the power M and suitably randomizing the result, have been proposed so far [15,3,17,18,19]. Their security is based on various "residuosity" assumptions and the trapdoor is a hidden subgroup where discrete log computations are feasible. We call those cryptosystems *trapdoor discrete logarithm schemes*. As an important consequence of this encryption technique, those schemes have homomorphic properties that can be informally stated as follows:

$$E(M_1 + M_2) = E(M_1) \times E(M_2) \quad \text{and} \quad E(k \times M) = E(M)^k$$

Paillier has presented three closely related such cryptosystems in [19]. We only recall the first one.

This cryptosystem is based on the properties of the Carmichael lambda function $\lambda(N)$ in $\mathbb{Z}_{N^2}^*$. We refer to $\lambda(N)$ as λ. We recall here the main two theorems: for any $w \in \mathbb{Z}_{N^2}^*$,

$$w^\lambda = 1 \bmod N, \quad \text{and} \quad w^{N\lambda} = 1 \bmod N^2$$

Key Generation. Let N be an RSA modulus $N = pq$, where p and q are prime integers. Let G be an integer whose order is a large multiple of N modulo N^2. The public key is $PK = (N, G)$ and the secret key is $SK = \lambda$.

Encryption. To encrypt a message $M \in \mathbb{Z}_N$, randomly choose u in $\mathbb{Z}_N^*$ and compute the ciphertext $c = G^M u^N \bmod N^2$.

Decryption. To decrypt c, compute $M = \dfrac{L(c^\lambda \bmod N^2)}{L(G^\lambda \bmod N^2)} \bmod N$ where the L-function takes in input elements from the set $\mathcal{S}_N = \{x < N^2 | x = 1 \bmod N\}$ and computes $L(x) = \frac{x-1}{N}$.

The integers $c^\lambda \bmod N^2$ and $G^\lambda \bmod N^2$ are equal to 1 when they are raised to the power N so they are N^{th} roots of unity. Furthermore, such roots are of the form $(1+N)^\beta = 1 + \beta N \bmod N^2$. Consequently, the L-function allows to compute such values $\beta \bmod N$ and $L((G^M)^\lambda \bmod N^2) = M \times L(G^\lambda \bmod N^2) \bmod N$.

The Residuosity Class Problem. Assume the order of G is a multiple of N. A number v is said to be a Nth residue modulo N^2 if there exists a number $u \in \mathbb{Z}_{N^2}^*$ such that $v = u^N \bmod N^2$. For $w \in \mathbb{Z}_{N^2}^*$, we call N^{th} residuosity class of w with respect to G the unique integer $r \in \mathbb{Z}_N$ for which there exists $u \in \mathbb{Z}_N^*$ such that $G^r u^N = w \bmod N^2$.

The Composite Residuosity Class Problem is defined to be the computational problem of computing the class of a random element in $\mathbb{Z}_{N^2}^*$.

Security. This problem that exactly consists in inverting the cryptosystem, is believed to be intractable. The semantic security is based on the difficulty to distinguish N^{th} residues modulo N^2. We refer to [19] for details.

3.2   A Proof of Fairness

In this section, we present a proof in the style of [23] which enables to prove that decryption of $Y = G^x u^N \bmod N^2$ in base G allows to recover the discrete logarithm of $y = g^x \bmod p$ in base g, where g is of order a prime q in $\mathbb{Z}_p^*$.

We describe a non-interactive statistical zero-knowledge proof of the existence of two small numbers σ and τ so that $|\sigma| < A$ and $|\tau| < B$ which verify that $G^\sigma Y^{-\tau}$ is a Nth residue for $\sigma \tau^{-1} = \log_g y$. We prove the security of the proof in the random oracle model.

Description of the Proof. Let $x \in [0, S[$ be the secret value, and A, B and S three integers such that $|A| \geq |B| \cdot |S| + k'$ where k' is a security parameter. The value B is the output length of a hash function H.

The prover chooses a random r in $[0, A[$ and a random $s \in \mathbb{Z}_N^*$. Then, he computes $t = (g^r \bmod p, G^r s^N \bmod N^2)$. Let e be the hash value $H(g, G, y, Y, g^r \bmod p, G^r s^N \bmod N^2)$. Next, the prover computes $z = r + ex$ and $w = su^e \bmod N$. If $z \notin [0, A[$, the prover restarts with another random values r and s until $z \in [0, A[$. The proof is the triple $(e, z, w) \in [0, B[\times [0, A[\times [0, N[$. It is checked by the equations $e = H(g, G, y, Y, g^z y^{-e} \bmod p, G^z w^N Y^{-e} \bmod N^2)$, $z \in [0, A[$, and $y^q = 1 \bmod p$.

Completeness. *The execution between a prover who knows the secret x and a verifier is successful with overwhelming probability if $SB/A < 1/2^{k'}$ is negligible.*

Proof: The verifier has access to (e, z, w) where $z = r + ex < A$, $w = su^e \bmod N$, and $e = H(g, G, y, Y, g^r \bmod p, G^r s^N \bmod N^2)$. He can check whether $z < A$, $g^r = g^{r+ex}(g^x)^{-e} = g^z y^{-e} \bmod p$, and $G^r s^N = G^{r+ex}(su^e)^N(G^x u^N)^{-e} = G^z w^N Y^{-e} \bmod N^2$.

If the prover follows the protocol, the proof fails only if $z \geq A$. The probability of failure of such an event taken over all possible choice of r is smaller than SB/A. Consequently, the execution of the protocol is successful with probability greater than $1 - \frac{SB}{A}$. Thus, if SB/A is negligible, the probability of success is overwhelming. □

Soundness. *If the verifier accepts the proof, with probability $\geq 1/B + \epsilon$ where ϵ is a non-negligible quantity, then using the prover as a "black-box" it is possible to compute σ and τ such that $|\sigma| < A$ and $|\tau| < B$ such that $\sigma\tau^{-1} = x \bmod q$, $g^x = y \bmod p$ and $G^\sigma Y^\tau$ is a Nth residue modulo N^2.*

Proof: For a given t, if a prover can find two triples (e, z, w) and (e', z', w') which pass the proof with non-negligible probability, he can obtain the following equalities : $G^{z-z'}(w/w')^{Ne} = Y^{e-e'} \bmod N^2$ and $g^{z-z'} = y^{e-e'} \bmod p$.

Hence, if we note $\sigma = z - z'$ and $\tau = e - e'$:

$$G^\sigma(w/w')^{Ne} = Y^\tau \bmod N^2 \quad \text{and} \quad g^\sigma = y^\tau \bmod p \tag{1}$$

and $|\sigma| < A$ and $0 < |\tau| < B$.

As $y^q = 1 \bmod p$ and as there is a unique subgroup of order q in $\mathbb{Z}_p^*$, the value y is in $\langle g \rangle$. Hence, from the second equality, we deduce that $\sigma\tau^{-1} \bmod q$ is the discrete log of y.

We note $d = \gcd(\sigma, \tau)$. As q is a prime number, we get $\sigma/d = \tau/d \times x \bmod q$. Let $\sigma_0 = \sigma/d$, $\tau_0 = \tau/d$. Knowledge of (σ_0, τ_0) enables to compute the secret $x = \sigma_0 \tau_0^{-1} \bmod q$.

Let $\tilde{x}$ be the result of the decryption of Y. If $g^{\tilde{x}} = y \bmod p$, we are done. Otherwise, we search the values σ_0 and τ_0 where $\sigma_0 = \sigma/d$, $\tau_0 = \tau/d$ and $d = \gcd(\sigma, \tau)$ to find x. In [23], Poupard and Stern describe how to find σ_0 and τ_0 from $\tilde{x}$ and N provided that the proof is correct. They show that the smallest vector of the lattice of dimension two where a basis is $((N, 0), (\tilde{x}, 1))$ corresponds to the vector (σ_0, τ_0) whenever $N \geq 2\sqrt{2}AB$. Hence, as the dimension of the lattice is two, Gauss algorithm can be used to efficiently recover the smallest vector in $O(\log N)$.

Consequently, if the proof is well-formed, participant P_i can always recover the intended share x which matches $y = g^x \bmod p$. This fairness property is useful to guarantee that the receiver will receive the correct data. □

Zero-Knowledge. *This proof is a non-interactive statistical zero-knowledge proof.*

Proof: We can construct a simulator that simulates the adversary's view without knowing the value x in the random oracle model. When an uncorrupted player is supposed to generate a proof for a given y, Y, the simulator chooses $e \in [0, B[$, $z \in [0, A[$ and $w \in \mathbb{Z}_N{}^*$ at random, and defines the value of the random oracle at $(g, G, y, Y, g^z y^{-e} \bmod p, G^z w^N Y^{-e} \bmod N^2)$ to be e. With overwhelming probability, the simulator has not yet defined the random oracle at this point. The proof is just (z, w, e). It is straightforward to verify that the distribution produced by this simulator is statistically close to perfect provided that BS/A is negligible. □

4   The Scenario

Each server has to verify all proofs broadcast by other players and to select the qualified group of servers. All players are considered as probabilistic polynomial time Turing machines. In the initialization stage, each participant performs the key generation algorithm of Paillier's cryptosystem. For $i = 1$ to ℓ, the public keys $PK_i = (G_i, N_i)$ are published and the server P_i secretly stores SK_i. The value N_i is a RSA modulus, G_i is an element in $\mathbb{Z}_{N_i^2}{}^*$ of order a multiple of N_i and $SK_i = \lambda(N_i)$.

We consider the following scenario :

- Participant P_i generates a random $s_{i,0}$, sets $a_{i,0} = s_{i,0}$ and chooses $a_{i,k}$ at random from $\mathbb{Z}_q$ for $1 \le k \le t$. The numbers $a_{i,0}, \ldots, a_{i,t}$ define the polynomial $f_i(X) = \sum_{k=0}^{t} a_{i,k} X^k \in \mathbb{Z}_q[X]$. Then, he computes $s_{i,j} = f_i(j) \bmod q$. He broadcasts : for $k = 0, \ldots, t$, $A_{i,k} = g^{a_{i,k}} \bmod p$ and $y_{i,j} = g^{s_{i,j}} \bmod p$, $Y_{i,j} = G_j^{s_{i,j}} u_{i,j}^{N_j} \bmod N_j^2$, and a proof $(e_{i,j}, w_{i,j}, z_{i,j})$.
- Then, for each $1 \le i, j \le \ell$, the servers verify that :

$$\prod_{k=0}^{t} A_{i,k}^{j^k} = \prod_{k=0}^{t} g^{a_{i,k} j^k} = g^{\sum_{k=0}^{t} a_{i,k} j^k} = g^{f_i(j)} \bmod p$$

and check whether $g^{f_i(j)} \bmod p$ is equal to $y_{i,j}$ in order to verify that the distribution is correct. The servers also verify the proofs $(e_{i,j}, w_{i,j}, z_{i,j})$ and if $y_{i,j}^q = 1 \bmod p$ for $1 \le i, j \le \ell$.
- The set QUAL of qualified servers is defined from the players who have correctly played. The others are disqualified.
- Participant P_j decrypts $Y_{i,j}$ and obtains $s_{i,j}$ for $1 \le i \le \ell$. He stores the parts $s_{i,j}$ for $i \in$ QUAL and computes the public key as $\prod_{i \in \text{QUAL}} A_{i,0} = g^{f(0)} \bmod p$ if we note $f(X) = \sum_{i \in \text{QUAL}} f_i(X)$. The share of the key obtained by participant P_j is equal to

$$\sum_{i \in \text{QUAL}} s_{i,j} = f(j) \bmod q$$

The secret key s is shared in polynomial form with $f(j) \bmod q$ and in additive form with $x_j \bmod q$ between all participants belonging to the set QUAL.

5   Security Proof

In this section, we prove the security of the scheme following the security model defined in section 2.4. We have to ensure the correctness and the secrecy of the scheme.

Correctness means that all players obtain the same key at the end of the protocol, that $t + 1$ correct shares allow to recover the secret key and that the secret value is uniformly distributed in the subgroup generated by g modulo p.

Secrecy means that no information on x can be learned by the adversary except what follows from equation $y = g^x \bmod p$.

Theorem 1 *The sharing scheme is correct against adversaries.*

Proof: Let us assume the existence of an adversary $\mathcal{A}$ able to break t servers.

Correctness. It is clear that, at the end of the protocol, each server obtains the same public key because each honest server has received the same information and deduced the same set QUAL.

At the end of the protocol, the secret value is shared in polynomial form such that any $t + 1$ correct shares enable to interpolate the polynomial f of degree t whose constant coefficient represent the secret key s.

Finally, the public key y is uniformly distributed in the subgroup $\langle g \rangle$ because if one of the honest server is not disqualified and has selected his additive share x_i at random, the secret $\sum_{i \in \text{QUAL}} x_i \bmod q$ is randomized uniformly in $\mathbb{Z}_q$. Therefore, the value y is uniformly randomized in $\langle g \rangle$.   □

Theorem 2 *Under the decisional composite residuosity assumption and in the random oracle model, the sharing scheme is secure against static adversaries.*

Proof: Secrecy. We describe a simulator $\mathcal{S}$ which takes as input an element $y \in \mathbb{Z}_p^*$ in the subgroup generated by g and produces an output distribution which is polynomially indistinguishable from $\mathcal{A}$'s view of a run of the protocol that ends with y as its public key output.

Let $\mathcal{A}$ the adversary who knows y in phase **A1** and corrupts t servers at the beginning of the protocol in phase **A2**. $\mathcal{A}$ learns all their secrets and she actively controls their behavior.

Here, we can take advantage of the synchronized network. We have to simulate the distribution of all servers. However, when we simulate the run of the protocol, the synchronization is not needed and we can wait until all malicious servers play. This allows us to determine the public value y_i^* of a specific good server P_i^* such that we do not know its internal state.

Hence, each server P_i, except P_i^*, chooses at random $x_i \bmod q$ and t other values $a_{i,k}$ for $k = 1, \ldots, t$. He sets $f_i(X) = \sum_{k=0}^{t} a_{i,k} X^k \in \mathbb{Z}_q[X]$. Then, he computes $A_{i,k} = g^{a_{i,k}} \bmod p$ for $k = 0, \ldots, t$ and calculates $y_{i,j} = g^{f_i(j)} \bmod p$ and $Y_{i,j} = G_j^{f_i(j)} u_{i,j}^{N_j} \bmod N_j^2$. The distribution of these values and the distribution of those of the real protocol are equal.

Now, we have to simulate the distribution of player P_i^*. If we want the ending value to be y, let $y_i^* = A_{i,0}^* = y \cdot \prod_{i \in \text{QUAL} \setminus \{P_i^*\}} (y_i)^{-1} \bmod p$, as the set QUAL is defined at the end of the synchronization. We choose at random t values $f_i^*(i_j)$ for the t corrupted servers $\{i_1, \ldots, i_t\}$ and send these values to these servers. With the Lagrange interpolation formula, we can compute the public values $y_{i,j}^*$ of all other shares as :

$$y_{i,j}^* = g^{f_i^*(j)} = (y_i^*)^{\lambda_{j,0}^S} \cdot \prod_{j=1}^{t} g^{\lambda_{j,i_j}^S f_i^*(i_j)}$$

where $\lambda_{i,j}^S = \prod_{j' \in S \setminus \{j\}} \frac{i - j'}{j - j'}$ and $S = \{0, i_1, \ldots, i_t\}$.

Here we use an assumption which seems weaker than the assumption used in order to prove the semantic security of the Paillier cryptosystem. In fact, we have $g^x \bmod p$ and $G^x u^N \bmod N^2$ whereas the semantic security has to decide whether the value $G^x u^N \bmod N^2$ encrypts x or not. To simulate $Y_{i,j}^*$, we can therefore choose at random $x_{i,j} \in \mathbb{Z}_{N_j}$ and $u_j \in \mathbb{Z}_{N_j}^*$, and set $Y_{i,j}^* = G_j^{x_{i,j}} u_j^{N_j} \bmod N_j^2$.

Player P_i^* has an inconsistent internal state because he does not know the discrete-log of y_i in basis g modulo p. However, this player will not be attacked because in this model all corrupted servers are chosen at the beginning of the game A.

Finally, in the simulation, the distribution produced by the simulator is statistically close to perfect. In the random oracle model, where the simulator has a full control of the values returned by the hash function H, we define the value of H at $(g, G, y, Y, g^z y^{-e}, G^z w^N Y^{-e})$ to be e. With overwhelming probability, the simulator has not yet defined the random oracle at this point so the adversary $\mathcal{A}$ cannot detect the twist. □

6 On the Complexity of The Protocol

All servers must perform $\ell \times (\ell - 1)$ verifications of the form $y_{i,j} = \prod_{k=0}^{t} A_{i,k}^{j^k} \bmod p$ for $1 \leq i \leq \ell$ and for $1 \leq j \leq \ell$ except for the ℓ shares generated by themselves. Finally, each server must decrypt its part of the secret x.

In this case, P_i has computed the $t + 1$ values $A_{i,k} = g^{a_{i,k}} \bmod p$ and the 3ℓ values $s_{i,j} = f_i(j)$, $y_{i,j} = g^{s_{i,j}} \bmod p$, $Y_{i,j} = G_j^{s_{i,j}} u_{i,j}^{N_j} \bmod N_j^2$.

For the proofs, each server P_j has to check whether $e_{i,j} = H(g, G_j, y_{i,j}, Y_{i,j}, g^{z_{i,j}} y^{-e_{i,j}} \bmod p, G_j^{z_{i,j}} w_{i,j}^{N_j} Y_{i,j}^{-e_{i,j}} \bmod N_j^2)$ and $y_{i,j}^q = 1 \bmod p$ for each $1 \leq j \leq \ell$ and for each $1 \leq i \leq \ell$ except for the proofs generated by P_i.

In this case, P_i has to compute the proofs $(e_{i,j}, z_{i,j}, w_{i,j})$ where the heavy calculation is to compute $w_{i,j} = s_{i,j} u_{i,j}^{e_{i,j}} \bmod N_j$.

Finally, each server decrypts its own part x_j of the common secret x. To make this operation in an efficient way, the server P_j computes the product $Y_j = \prod_i Y_{i,j} = G_j^{\sum_i x_{i,j}} \bmod N_j^2$ using $\ell - 1$ multiplications and performs a single decryption on Y_j to recover $x_j \bmod N_j$. This operation consists in a single exponentiation as seen in 3.1. As $x_j = \sum_i x_{i,j}$ is upper bounded by $\ell^{\ell+2} \times q$, and $\ell \times \log_2(q\ell) < \log_2(N_j)$ for all j, the share $x_j \bmod N_j$ is equal to x_j.

The complexity of our scheme is in $O(k\ell^2)$ modular exponentiations where ℓ is the number of servers and k a security parameter whereas the complexity of [13,7] is in $O(k\ell)$. However, for a small number of participants, our protocol is more efficient. In an appendix 8.2, we provide an improvement of the computation cost when ℓ becomes large and show that the complexity is of the same order as previous schemes.

7 Conclusion

In this paper, we have proposed a threshold discrete-log key generation scheme. We have described a distributed key generation with public channels using one round of communication. Since the communication has been reduced, the computational cost of the scheme increases, but if the number of servers is limited, the overhead is not significant.

Our approach tends to simplify previous work in an area where recent works have resulted in making schemes complex. Moreover, a second phase is not necessary if we use public channel instead of private channel as was done before. Our protocol is well-suited for small groups of servers. It runs in one round and does not require interaction between servers.

References

1. M. Bellare, J. A. Garay, and T. Rabin. Fast Batch Verification for Modular Exponentiation and Digital Signatures. In *Eurocrypt '98*, LNCS 1403, pages 236–250. Springer-Verlag, 1998. Available at http://www-cse.ucsd.edu/users/mihir/.
2. M. Ben-Or, S. Goldwasser, and A. Widgerson. Completeness theorems for non-cryptographic fault-tolerant distributed computing. In *Proceedings of the 20th STOC*, ACM, pages 1–10, 1988.
3. J. Benaloh. *Verifiable Secret-Ballot Elections*. PhD thesis, Yale University, 1987.
4. D. Boneh and M. Franklin. Efficient Generation of Shared RSA Keys. In *Crypto '97*, LNCS 1294, pages 425–439. Springer-Verlag, 1997.
5. J. Camenisch and I. Damgård. Verifiable Encryption and Applications to Group Signatures and Signature Sharing. Available at http://philby.ucsd.edu/cryptolib/1999/99-08.html, march 1999.
6. R. Canetti. Security and Composition of Multiparty Cryptographic Protocols. In *Journal of Cryptology*, Volume 13, pages 143–202. Springer-Verlag, 2000.
7. C. Canetti, R. Gennaro, S. Jarecki, H. Krawczyk, and T. Rabin. Adaptive Security for Threshold Cryptosystems. In *Crypto '99*, LNCS 1666, pages 98–115. Springer-Verlag, 1999.
8. Y. Dodis and S. Micali. Parallel Reducibility for Information-Theretically Secure Computation. In *Crypto '00*, LNCS 1880, pages 74–92. Springer-Verlag, 2000.
9. P. Feldman. A practical scheme for non-interactive verifiable secret sharing. In *Proceedings of the 28th annual Symposium on the Foundations of Computer Science*. IEEE, 1987.
10. Y. Frankel, P. Gemmel, Ph. MacKenzie, and M. Yung. Optimal-Resilience Proactive Public-Key Cryptosystems. In *Proc. 38th FOCS*, pages 384–393. IEEE, 1997.

11. Y. Frankel, P. Gemmel, Ph. MacKenzie, and M. Yung. Proactive RSA. In *Crypto '97*, LNCS 1294, pages 440–454. Springer-Verlag, 1997.

12. Y. Frankel, P. MacKenzie, and M. Yung. Adaptively-Secure Optimal-Resilience Proactive RSA. In *Asiacrypt '99*, LNCS. Springer-Verlag, 1999.

13. R. Gennaro, S. Jarecki, H. Krawczyk, and T. Rabin. Secure Distributed Key Generation for Discrete-Log Cryptosystems. In *Eurocrypt '99*, LNCS 1592, pages 295–310. Springer-Verlag, 1999.

14. N. Gilboa. Two Party RSA Key Generation. In *Crypto '99*, LNCS 1666, pages 116–129. Springer-Verlag, 1999.

15. S. Goldwasser and S. Micali. Probabilistic Encryption. *Journal of Computer and System Sciences*, 28:270–299, 1984.

16. S. Jarecki and A. Lysyanskaya. Adaptively Secure Threshold Cryptography : Introducing Concurrency, Removing Erasures. In *Eurocrypt' 00*, LNCS 1807, pages 221–242. Springer-Verlag, 2000.

17. D. Naccache and J. Stern. A New Cryptosystem based on Higher Residues. In *Proc. of the 5th CCS*, pages 59–66. ACM press, 1998.

18. T. Okamoto and S. Uchiyama. A New Public Key Cryptosystem as Secure as Factoring. In *Eurocrypt '98*, LNCS 1403, pages 308–318. Springer-Verlag, 1998.

19. P. Paillier. Public-Key Cryptosystems Based on Discrete Logarithms Residues. In *Eurocrypt '99*, LNCS 1592. Springer-Verlag, 1999.

20. T.P. Pedersen. A Threshold Cryptosystem without a Trusted Party. In *Eurocrypt'91*, LNCS 547, pages 522–526. Springer-Verlag, 1991.

21. T.P. Pedersen. Non-Interactive and Information-Theoretic Secure Verifiable Secret Sharing. In *Crypto'91*, LNCS 576, pages 129–140. Springer-Verlag, 1991.

22. G. Poupard and J. Stern. Generation of Shared RSA Keys by Two Parties. In *Asiacrypt '98*, LNCS 1514, pages 11–24. Springer-Verlag, 1998.

23. G. Poupard and J. Stern. Fair Encryption of RSA Keys. In *Proceedings of Eurocrypt 2000*, Lecture Notes in Computer Science. Springer-Verlag, 2000.

8   Appendix

8.1   Asynchronous Network

In some cases the synchronous network seems to be a strong requirement. We use such network to cope with "rushing attacks". A simple solution is to force a Incorruptible Third Party (ITP) to play at the end. We call this third party "incorruptible" since we do not require a "trusted" party, but only honest. At the beginning, this server picks a random value a in $\mathbb{Z}_q$ and commits $H(a)$ using the hash function H. The servers play and compute $y' = g^{x'}$. At the end, the ITP releases a to all players. The secret value is $x = x' + a \bmod q$. Each server can compute its share of the secret as $x_i = x'_i + a \bmod q$. This is due to the Lagrange interpolation since the sum of the Lagrange coefficients is equal to 1. Indeed, if S is a subset of cardinality $t + 1$,

$$f(0) = \sum_{i \in S} \lambda_{i,0}^S f(i) \bmod q$$

Therefore, if we share the constant polynomial $c(x) = 1$ for all x, the value in 0 is always 1 and we obtain $1 = \sum_{i \in S} \lambda_{i,0}^S 1$. Consequently, if we write $f(i) = x'_i$,

$$f(0) + a = \left(\sum_{i \in S} \lambda_{i,0}^S f(i) \right) + a = \sum_{i \in S} \lambda_{i,0}^S (f(i) + a) \bmod q$$

Note 1. In this model, simulations against adaptive adversaries are easy since we can fix the value of the ITP in the random oracle model. We can see it as the "persistently inconsistent player" of [16].

Note 2. Dodis and Micali in [8] proved that a class of Secure Function Evaluation (SFE) remains secure if we compose simple and secure protocols in sequence or in parallel in the information-theoretic model. They use two models of parallel reducibility (or parallel composition of protocols) that they called concurrent reducibility and synchronous reducibility. The *Concurrent reducibility* applies when the order of sub-protocol calls is not important whereas the *Synchronous reducibility* applies when the sub-protocols must be executed simultaneously. Their results [8] hold only in the "information-theoretic model" where we allow private channels and not in the "computational model" that we need in our protocol. In [6], Canetti proved the same results in the computational model but only for concurrent reducibility and not for synchronous reducibility. Therefore, the asynchronous network scheme that we propose in this appendix can be also proved using Canetti's theorem.

8.2   Improvement of the Complexity

When the number of servers is relatively small, our protocol is practical. However, it can be unpractical when the number ℓ of servers becomes larger. Here, we provide methods to reduce the computation cost in this situation. We present the computation cost in term of multiplications and we show that asymptotically our protocol has the same order of magnitude than others, i.e. $O(\ell^3 \log(\ell))$ multiplications. This is achieved by reducing all verifications of our protocol to three computations which are used in all protocols. This last calculation represents the heavy part of the computation cost and cannot be avoided in the verifiable interpolation phase.

Since bad players only appear in rare situations, we aim to design efficient protocols when all players are honest. However, we must be able to detect whenever bad players try to cheat and therefore, we require fast detection of active malicious servers. When a malicious server is detected, we need to carry out the protocol of section 6 or to reboot the system as our protocol is state-free.

The first remark is that we cannot avoid the complexity factor $O(\ell^2 k)$, where k is the bit-length of $|p|$ or $|N_j|/2$, from the communication point of view, since in one round, all servers must be able to test whether other servers have correctly played. But, as today's networks have large bandwidth and high speed performance, the bottleneck is not the network communication but the computation load. Consequently, our main objective is to decrease the computation complexity for detecting bad servers.

It is straightforward to see that the larger complexity factor comes from the verifications of $g^{f_i(j)} = \prod_{k=0}^{t} A_{i,k}^{j^k} \bmod p$. We have to check ℓ^2 such equations while the previous schemes only require ℓ. Here we reduce the computation of each player to 3ℓ such equations.

Batch Verification. Bellare *et al.* in [1] describe algorithms to perform fast batch verification for modular exponentiation and digital signatures. In this paper, they present techniques to test whether many instantiations $(x_i, y_i)_{i=1}^{n}$ satisfy the equations $g^{x_i} = y_i \bmod p$. The naive method requires n exponentiations. However, if we use probabilistic batch tests, the sequence of modular exponentiations can be computed significantly faster than the naive re-computation method.

They also describe an efficient algorithm to compute $\prod_{i=1}^{n} a_i^{b_i}$ where the cost is $k + nk/2$ modular multiplications if we note k the greatest bit-length of the elements b_i ($b_i = b_i[k] \ldots b_i[1]$). This number is strictly less than n exponentiations followed by $n-1$ multiplications where the cost of a single exponentiation a^b can be estimated as $3k/2$ multiplications if k is the bit-length of b. This algorithm is hereafter called FastMult.

Algorithm FastMult$((a_1, b_1), \ldots, (a_n, b_n))$
$\quad a := 1;$
$\quad$ for $j = k$ downto 1 do
$\quad\quad$ for $i = 1$ to n do if $b_i[j] = 1$ then $a := a.a_i;$
$\quad\quad a := a^2;$

return a

This algorithm does k multiplications in the outer loop and $nk/2$ multiplications on the average in the inner loop. Hence, for computing y we get a total of $k + nk/2$ multiplications.

Finally, they also provide a batch verification of the following form: given a set of points, determine whether there exists a polynomial of a certain degree, which passes through all these points. More formally, let $S = (\alpha_1, \alpha_2, \ldots, \alpha_m)$ denote a set of points. We define the relation $\mathrm{DEG}_{\mathcal{F}, t, (\beta_1, \beta_2, \ldots, \beta_m)}(S) = 1$ iff there exists a polynomial $f(x)$ such that the degree of $f(x)$ is at most t, and for all $i \in \{1, \ldots, m\}$, $f(\beta_i) = \alpha_i$, assuming that all the computations are carried out in the finite field $\mathcal{F}$. Let the batch instance of this problem be $S_1, \ldots, S_n$, where $S_i = (\alpha_{i,1}, \ldots, \alpha_{i,m})$. The batch instance is correct if $\mathrm{DEG}_{\mathcal{F}, t, (\beta_1, \ldots, \beta_m)}(S_i) = 1$ for all $i = 1, \ldots, n$; incorrect otherwise. This test is called RANDOM LINEAR COMBINATION TEST.

Random Linear Combination Test. This algorithm takes as input n sets $S_1, \ldots, S_n$ where $S_i = (\alpha_{i,1}, \ldots, \alpha_{i,m})$; $\beta_1, \ldots, \beta_m$, security parameter k, and a value t and checks whether for all $i \in \{1, \ldots, n\}$ there exists a polynomial $f_i(x)$ such that $deg(f_i) \le t$ and $f_i(\beta_1) = \alpha_{i,1}, \ldots, f_i(\beta_m) = \alpha_{i,m}$.

The algorithm works as follows:

1. Pick $r \in_R \mathcal{F}$
2. Compute $\gamma_i = r^n \alpha_{n,i} + \ldots + r\alpha_{1,i}$. This can be efficiently computed with the Horner algorithm.

3. If $\mathrm{DEG}_{\mathcal{F},t,(\beta_1,\dots,\beta_m)}(\gamma_1,\dots,\gamma_m) = 1$, then output "correct", else output "incorrect".

NOTATION If $f_i(x) = a_m x^m + \dots + a_0$, where $a_m \neq 0$, we denote by $f_i(x)|^{t+1}$ the polynomial $a_m x^m + \dots + a_{t+1} x^{t+1}$. Consequently, for $m \le t$, $f_i(x)|^{t+1}$ must be equal to 0.

The polynomial $F(x) = \sum_{i=1}^{n} r^i f_i(x)$ is of degree at most t, and, therefore, it holds that $\sum_{i=1}^{n} r^i f_i(x)|^{t+1}$ must be equal to 0. This is an equation of degree n in the unknown r and hence has at most n roots. Therefore, to output "correct" when in fact the instance is incorrect, r must be one of the roots of the equation. This algorithm fails with probability at most $\frac{n}{|\mathcal{F}|}$, which is a negligible quantity. The running time of this algorithm is $O(nm)$ while the naive method which consists in computing the polynomial interpolation with $t+1$ points and checking for each of them requires $O(m^2 n)$ multiplications.

Application to Our Situation. First of all, we note that the computation cost of checking whether the ℓ^2 values $y_{i,j}$ encrypt $g^{f_i(j)}$, require ℓ^2 exponentiations. In fact, we do not need to exactly test whether these equations hold but rather whether a server send false shares. Obviously, each server must verify its own shares but can only check whether the others are correct with high probability.

To this end, we can use the RANDOM LINEAR COMBINATION TEST. We need to run this algorithm "in the exponents" and the proof follows from the fact that g is a primitive element in the subgroup of $\mathbb{Z}_p^*$ of order q. In our situation, we have values $\alpha_{i,j}$ correspond to $y_{i,j}$ and values β_i to i.

The algorithm works as follows:

1. Pick $r \in_R \mathbb{Z}_q$
2. Compute $\gamma_i = \alpha_{\ell,i}^{r^\ell} \times \dots \times \alpha_{1,i}^r$. This can be efficiently computed from the values $y_{i,1}, \dots, y_{i,\ell}$ using ℓ times the FastMult algorithm.
3. If $\mathrm{DEG}_{\mathbb{Z}_q,t,(1,\dots,\ell)}(\gamma_1,\dots,\gamma_\ell) = 1$, then output "correct", else output "incorrect".

The DEG consists in checking whether for all $j = 1,\dots,\ell$, $g^{F(j)} = \prod_{k=0}^{t} A_{F,k}^{j^k}$ is equal to γ_j. The values $A_{F,k}$ correspond to the coefficients of the polynomial F and are equal to $g^{\sum_{i=1}^{\ell} a_{i,k} r^i} = \prod_{i=1}^{\ell} A_{i,k}^{r^i}$. In fact, γ_j is equal to $y_{\ell,j}^{r^\ell} \times \dots \times y_{1,j}^r = g^{f_\ell(j)r^\ell + \dots + f_1(j)r} = g^{\sum_{i=1}^{\ell} r^i f_i(j)} = g^{F(j)} \bmod p$.

Consequently, we have to compute the ℓ values γ_j, the $t+1$ values $A_{F,k}$ and the ℓ relations DEG.

This algorithm fails with probability at most $\frac{\ell}{q}$ which is a negligible quantity.

As usual, we estimate t as $\ell/2$ and accordingly, the complexity of the scheme in the number of multiplications is:

1. To compute the values γ_j, we need ℓ times calls to the FastMult algorithm for ℓ products of powers where the size of the exponents are in $\ell|q|$; hence, $\ell \times [\ell|q| + \frac{\ell}{2}\ell|q|] = O(\ell^3|q|)$.
2. To compute the coefficients of $g^{F(x)}$, we need $(t+1)$ calls to the FastMult algorithm for ℓ products of powers where the size of the exponents are in $|q|\ell$; hence, $(t+1) \times [|q|\ell + \frac{\ell^2}{2}|q|] = O(\ell^3|q|)$.

3. To check the relation DEG, we need ℓ calls to the FastMult algorithm for $(t+1)$ products of powers where the size of the exponents are in $t\log(\ell)$; hence $\ell \times [t\log(\ell) + \frac{t(t+1)}{2}\log(\ell)] = O(\ell^3 \log(\ell))$.

This algorithm requires $O(\ell^3|q| + \ell^3 \log(\ell))$ multiplications.

The previously proposed algorithms cannot used this trick as they have only one value in all set S_i. Therefore, each server j has to perform ℓ calls to the FastMult algorithm to verify whether $y_j = \prod_{k=0}^{t} A_{i,k}^{j^k}$ for $i = 1$ to ℓ. This leads to ℓ times the $t+1$ products of powers where the size of the exponents are in $t\log(\ell)$; hence, $\ell[t\log(\ell) + \frac{t(t+1)}{2}\log(\ell)] = O(\ell^3 \log(\ell))$. If we have used this method whereas the RANDOM LINEAR COMBINATION TEST "in the exponents", the complexity will have to be $O(\ell^4 \log(\ell))$.

In general, $|q| = 160$ and if we take $\ell = 32 = 2^5$, $\ell\log(\ell) = 160$. Therefore, when the number of server is greater than 32, our batch verification method becomes to be more efficient than the standard method.

In order to be self-contained, we provide here an estimation of the complexity of the proofs. The verifications of the ℓ^2 proofs has a complexity negligible in relation to the previous operation. We can essentially summarize the proofs as checking whether the precomputed value g^r is equal to $g^z \times y^{-e} \bmod p$ and G^r is equal to $G^z w^N Y^{-e} \bmod N^2$. We have to carry out ℓ^2 products of two or three numbers where the size of the exponents are in $|A|$ or $|N|$. Therefore, if we call the FastMult algorithm, we obtain $|A|\ell^2$ for the verifications in $\mathbb{Z}_p^*$ and $|N|\ell^2$ for the proofs in N^2. Consequently, the computation complexity is upper bounded by the Random Linear Combination Test in the exponent for all schemes.

Remarks on Mix-Network
Based on Permutation Networks

Masayuki Abe and Fumitaka Hoshino

NTT Laboratories
Nippon Telegraph and Telephone Corporation
1-1 Hikari-no-oka, Yokosuka-shi, Kanagawa-ken, 239-0847 Japan
{abe,fhoshino}@isl.ntt.co.jp

Abstract. This paper addresses the security and efficiency issues of the Mix-net based on permutation networks introduced in [1]. We first show that the original construction results in a Mix-net that yields biased permutation, so it gives some advantage to adversaries. A simple repair is provided. We then observe that one of the original schemes can be improved so that the servers and verifier enjoy more efficient computation and communication.

1 Introduction

Secure networks will need to provide data integrity and authenticity, and existing networks like the Internet are pursuing these goals. In some applications, however, sending data in an anonymous way plays a central role. Anonymous voting, payments, or donations are typical examples of applications that concern user's privacy. Mix-net is a cryptographic technique that offers anonymity over non-anonymous, i.e., traceable networks; it hides the source of a message by mixing it with other message sources.

Since the notion of Mix-net was introduced by Chaum [3], much work has been done on providing more secure, efficient and widely applicable schemes [15,19,13,2,8,9,1,10,14]. Some of them are cryptoanalyzed and plausibly fixed [17,11,18,16,6,12].

In [1], Abe introduced an efficient construction of robust and publicly verifiable Mix-nets based on permutation networks. Since the resulting schemes provide $O(tN \log N)$ efficiency for N inputs and t tolerable corrupt mix-servers, they suit a small to moderate number of inputs. Those schemes are considered to be the most efficient ones that provide robustness and public verifiability.

This paper addresses the security and efficiency issues of the schemes in [1]. We first show that the construction results in a Mix-net that yields biased permutation, so an adversary can have more advantage in violating anonymity than random guessing. We provide a sure and simple solution that achieves uniform distribution over all permutations. We then observe that one of the original schemes can be improved so that the servers and a verifier enjoy more efficient computation and communication.

K. Kim (Ed.): PKC 2001, LNCS 1992, pp. 317–324, 2001.

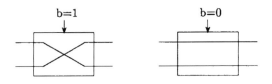

Fig. 1. Settings of a switching gate.

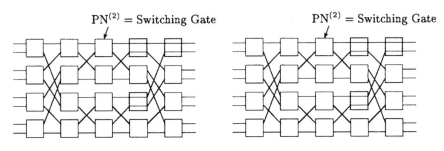

Fig. 2. $\text{PN}^{(8)}$ with $\text{PN}^{(4)}$ **Fig. 3.** $\text{PN}^{(8)}$ after decomposing $\text{PN}^{(4)}$

2   Review

We begin by reviewing the Benes permutation network [20]. Consider a switch that transposes two input signals according to a binary control signal as illustrated in Fig 1. The Benes permutation network is a network of such switches. It yields arbitrary permutation of the inputs by setting the switches. For N inputs, which is restricted to be a power of 2, $N \log_2 N - N + 1$ switches are necessary and sufficient to produce arbitrary permutation. Fig. 2 and 3 illustrate recursive construction of the Benes permutation network for 8 inputs, denoted by $\text{PN}^{(8)}$. Boxes represent switching gates, and the dotted ones indicate fixed gates that simply output the inputs.

Next we review the Mix-net in [1], which they call MiP-1. It consists of m servers. Up to $t(< m/2)$ of them can be malicious and colluding. Let p, q be primes. Let g be an element of Z_p^* that generates a prime subgroup of order q denoted by $\langle g \rangle$. Let x be the decryption key of the Mix-net and $y(= g^x)$ be the corresponding public key (all arithmetic operations in this paper are done in Z_p unless otherwise noted). The input to the Mix-net is a list of N ElGamal ciphertexts encrypted with y. An ElGamal ciphertext of message $msg \in \langle g \rangle$ is a pair (M, G) computed as $(M, G) = (msg \cdot y^s, g^s)$ where $s \in_R Z_q$. The servers logically simulate a series of $t+1$ permutation networks that take N ciphertexts as inputs. Let ξ denote the total number of columns in $t+1$ $\text{PN}^{(N)}$'s. That is, $\xi = (t+1)(2 \log_2 N + 1)$. Each server is assigned some (or all) columns of switches in a permutation network in such a way that m servers are assigned ξ columns in total. Let $y_1, \ldots, y_\xi$ be shares of y such that $y = \prod_{i=1}^{\xi} y_i$. Let x_i be private key for y_i, i.e. $y_i = g^{x_i}$. The server that is in charge of the i-th column privately holds x_i. For the sake of robustness, x_i is shared among all servers by using $t+1$

threshold secret sharing. Let $\hat{y}_j$ denote $\prod_{i=j+1}^{\xi} y_i$. (Let $\hat{y}_0 = y$ and $\hat{y}_\xi = 1$.) At each switching gate in the j-th column, each input ciphertext (M, G) is partially decrypted and randomized as

$$(M', G') = (MG^{-x_j}\hat{y}_j^r, Gg^r)$$

for $r \in_U Z_q$, and output according to the *randomly selected* setting of the switch. (For all fixed gates and the switching gates in the ξ-th column, let $(M', G') = (MG^{-x_j}, G)$.) A zero-knowledge proof is then used to prove that the the outputs are correct. The proof can be done efficiently by using Chaum-Pedersen technique [4] combined with the OR-proof technique of [5]. Observe that (M', G') is an ElGamal ciphertext for public key $\hat{y}_j$. Accordingly, the outputs from the last column, which are $M' = MG^{-x_\xi}$, are the plaintexts that correspond to the input ciphertexts.

This scheme provides $O(tN \log N)$ efficiency and is known to best suit small numbers of inputs as the previous robust verifiable schemes, e.g., [19,13] require $O(mN\kappa)$ for error probability $2^{-\kappa}$.

It was proven in [1] that, under the decision Diffie-Hellman assumption, any poly-time adversary can guess the setting of each switch with probability only negligibly better than $1/2$ since ElGamal encryption is indistinguishable and the proof is zero-knowledge with regard to switch setting. Hence, it was claimed that the scheme provides anonymity.

3   Security Issue

3.1   Biased Permutations

We show that randomly selecting each control signal results in a biased permutation even if all servers behave correctly. Let η be the number of switching gates in $\mathrm{PN}^{(N)}$, that is $\eta = N \log_2 N - N + 1$. Observe that $N! < 2^\eta$ holds for $N > 2$. So there are $2^\eta - N!$ permutations that have two or more different representations (switch settings). Accordingly, permutations with multiple representations are more likely to be generated than those with single representations if control signals are randomly set.

Indeed, the bias is even worse. Let ζ_N be the number of representations of $\mathrm{PN}^{(N)}$ for the identity permutation, which straightforwardly outputs the inputs. The identity permutation is clearly produced when $b = 0$ for all switching gates. Observe that the identity permutation can also be obtained by setting $b = 1$ for two gates located in the same row of the leftmost and rightmost columns such as gate 2 and 5 in Figure 2. Since there are $N/2 - 1$ such pairs of gates in $\mathrm{PN}^{(N)}$, we have

$$\zeta_N = \zeta_{N/2}^2 \cdot 2^{N/2-1}. \tag{1}$$

¿From the above recursive formula and the fact that $\zeta_2 = 1$, we obtain

$$\zeta_N = 2^{(N/2) \log_2(N/2) - N/2 + 1}. \tag{2}$$

Furthermore, as we will discuss in Section 3.2, there exist permutations that have only one representation. Thus, when each control signal is chosen randomly, the identity permutation appears with probability exponentially higher than the ones that have only one representation.

Table 1 shows the number of permutations that have more than two representations for $PN^{(8)}$. It can be observed that some permutations are likely to be chosen with 32 times higher probability.

Table 1. Number of permutations in $PN^{(8)}$ that have multiple switch settings. 128 of 8! permutations have 32 different switch settings.

#(equivalent settings)	#(permutations)
32	128
16	512
8	2816
5	2048
4	12288
2	14336
1	8192

3.2   Generating Non-biased Permutations

This bias can be eliminated in a simple way; first choose a permutation uniformly and then compute a proper setting of switches that represents the permutation. Clearly, this results in uniform distribution over all permutations. As in the original scheme, the setting of switches remains concealed.

A drawback is the increase of computation needed to transform a permutation to a switch setting. According to Waksman's algorithm [20], such a computation incurs $O(N \log N)$ time and memory.

The following description might be easier to follow if readers keep Figure 2 in mind. Let $I_1, \cdots, I_n$ be inputs to $PN^{(n)}$ and $\tilde{O}_1, \cdots, \tilde{O}_n$ be the corresponding outputs from the switching gates in the first column of the permutation network. Similarly, let $O_1, \cdots, O_n$ be outputs of the network and $\tilde{I}_1, \cdots, \tilde{I}_n$ be the corresponding inputs to the switching gates in the last column. All switches are set to be straight, i.e. b=0, as the initial state.

The following algorithm sets the switching gates so that the network represents a given permutation $\sigma : \{1, \cdots, n\} \to \{1, \cdots, n\}$ that results in $O_i = I_{\sigma(i)}$ for $i = 1, \ldots, n$. Indeed, we describe the algorithm so that it sets the gates in only the first and last column of $PN^{(n)}$, i.e., the numbered gates in Figure 2. Applying the algorithm repeatedly to the next inner set of gates, eventually sets all switching gates.

In the following, for some index j, $\bar{j}$ denotes the index such that I_j and $I_{\bar{j}}$ (or O_j and $O_{\bar{j}}$) are connected to the same gate. Let F_i be a flag, associated with O_i, which is initially unset. The algorithm starts with $i = 1$.

Step 1 Find the smallest i such that F_i is unset. If $i \neq 1$, arbitrarily set $b \in \{0,1\}$ for the switch O_i comes from.

Step 2 Repeat the following steps.

    2-1 Set F_i.

    2-2 Identify j such that $\tilde{I}_j = O_i$ by examining the switching gate that O_i comes from.

    2-3 For k such that $I_k = \tilde{I}_j$ (i.e, $k = \sigma(i)$), if either j or k is even while the other is odd, then set $b = 1$ for the switch I_k enters.

    2-4 Identify ℓ such that $\tilde{O}_\ell = I_{\bar{k}}$ by examining the switching gate $I_{\bar{k}}$ enters.

    2-5 For t such that $O_t = \tilde{O}_\ell$ (i.e, $t = \sigma^{-1}(\bar{k})$), if either t or ℓ is even while the other is odd, then set $b = 1$ for the switch that O_t comes from.

    2-6 Set F_t and let i be $\bar{t}$.

    2-7 If F_i is already set, exit Step 2.

Step 3 Repeat Step 1-2 until all flags have been set.

The switches in the first and the last column are now configured and the internal permutation produced by the remaining switches can be computed from the current configuration. By recursively applying the above procedure to the remaining switches, taking the internal permutation as σ, one can configure all switches.

By using the above conversion algorithm, we can show that there exists a permutation with a unique representation. Observe that for any switch setting, there exists an execution of the above algorithm that results in the setting. Thus, the algorithm can yield all possible switch settings. Observe that Step 1 is deterministic when $i = 1$, and Step 2 is always deterministic. Thus, if a permutation has two or more representations, corresponding executions of the above algorithm must select different b at Step 1 in some level of recursion. Conversely, a permutation has a unique representation if Step 1 is executed only once in every recursive execution during the conversion. And clearly, one can manipulate the switch setting so that it happens.

4   Efficiency and Availability Issues

Here we observe that the original scheme reviewed in Section 2 unnecessarily uses many keys. In that scheme, decryption is incorporated into the task of *every* switching gate so that one layer of encryption is removed each time a ciphertext passes a gate. The following drawbacks arise.

- The servers have to securely maintain ξ private keys and m times many shares of the keys.
- The number of inputs has to be fixed before generating $y_1, \ldots, y_\xi$ as ξ depends on N.
- The zero-knowledge proof at each switching gate is expensive.

Our solution to eliminating these drawbacks is to incorporate the partial decryption only into the switching gates in the last column of each permutation network; the remaining switching gates perform randomization only such as

$(M', G') = (M\hat{y}_{i+1}^r, Gg^r)$. Although computational efficiency is asymptotically unchanged, this surely saves running time for computing factor G^{-x_i} in most switching gates and corresponding proofs. Furthermore, since the number of y_i becomes $t + 1$, which is independent of the number of inputs, the number of inputs need not be fixed before key generation.

5   Refined Scheme

The refined scheme, which reflects all the remarks in the previous sections, is given below.

[**Preparation**]
Let $\{1, \ldots, m\}$ denote servers. The servers agree on a subset of servers, say $W \subset \{1, \ldots, m\}$ that contains $t + 1$ servers.

[**Key Generation**]
The servers generate key pairs (y_i, x_i) for $i = 1, \ldots, t + 1$ by executing the key generation protocol of [7]. Public key y_i is published and private key x_i is shared in a threshold manner so that x_i can be re-constructed by $t + 1$ honest servers. Working server i, which refers to the i-th server listed in W, is given shares from other servers and computes x_i privately.

[**Mix processing**]
Let L_0 be a list of input ElGamal ciphertexts. Working server i takes list L_{i-1} and outputs list L_i. Working server i simulates the i-th permutation network in the following way.

1. Randomly choose a permutation $\pi : \{1, \ldots, N\} \to \{1, \ldots, N\}$.
2. Compute the switch setting that corresponds to π following the algorithm shown in Section 3.2.
3. For each switching gate except for the ones in the last column of the simulating permutation network, randomize each input ciphertext (M, G) as $(M', G') = (M\hat{y}_{i+1}^r, Gg^r)$ with random factor $r \in_R Z_q$. For each switching gate in the last column, perform randomization and decryption at the same time as $(M', G') = (MG^{-x_i}\hat{y}_i^r, Gg^r)$. (The last server only perform decryption as $M' = MG^{-x_{t+1}}$.) Then, output the resulting ciphertexts in order according to the switch setting defined in the previous step. For the fixed gate in the last column, decrypt the inputs as $(M', G') = (MG^{-x_i}, G)$ and simply output them. Then prove that the output is correct by using zero-knowledge proof. The proof protocol is unchanged from the original one in [1] (also see [10] for a slightly more efficient proof protocol).

All servers verify the proofs given by server i. If more than t servers agree that any of the proofs is faulty, then server i is disqualified. All servers then cooperatively reconstruct x_i and decrypt the ciphertexts in L_{i-1} in public.

The security of this scheme can be argued in the same way as shown in the original paper with the additional consideration that this scheme yields a uniform distribution over all permutations. (One missing argument in the security proof of [1] was about the distribution of the resulting permutation.)

Acknowledgment

The authors thank Tetsutaro Kobayashi for leading us to the security issue. Invaluable comments from Koutaro Suzuki are appreciated, too.

References

1. M. Abe. Mix-networks on permutation networks. In K. Lam, E. Okamoto, and C. Xing, editors, *Advances in Cryptology – Asiacrypt '99*, volume 1716 of *Lecture Notes in Computer Science*, pages 258–273. Springer-Verlag, 1999.
2. M. Abe. Universally verifiable mix-net with verification work independent of the number of mix-servers. *IEICE Transaction of Fundamentals of electronic Communications and Computer Science*, E83-A(7):1431–1440, July 2000. Presented at Eurocrypt'98.
3. D. L. Chaum. Untraceable electronic mail, return address, and digital pseudonyms. *Communications of the ACM*, 24:84–88, 1981.
4. D. L. Chaum and T. P. Pedersen. Wallet databases with observers. In E. F. Brickell, editor, *Advances in Cryptology — CRYPTO '92*, volume 740 of *Lecture Notes in Computer Science*, pages 89–105. Springer-Verlag, 1993.
5. R. Cramer, I. Damgård, and B. Schoenmakers. Proofs of partial knowledge and simplified design of witness hiding protocols. In Y. G. Desmedt, editor, *Advances in Cryptology — CRYPTO '94*, volume 839 of *Lecture Notes in Computer Science*, pages 174–187. Springer-Verlag, 1994.
6. Y. Desmedt and K. Kurosawa. How to break a practical MIX and design a new one. In B. Preneel, editor, *Advances in Cryptology — EUROCRYPT 2000*, volume 1807 of *Lecture Notes in Computer Science*, pages 557–572. Springer-Verlag, 2000.
7. R. Gennaro, S. Jarecki, H. Krawczyk, and T. Rabin. Secure distributed key generation for discrete-log based cryptosystems. In J. Stern, editor, *Advances in Cryptology — EUROCRYPT '99*, volume 1592 of *Lecture Notes in Computer Science*, pages 295–310. Springer-Verlag, 1999.
8. M. Jakobsson. A practical mix. In K. Nyberg, editor, *Advances in Cryptology — EUROCRYPT '98*, volume 1403 of *Lecture Notes in Computer Science*, pages 448–461. Springer-Verlag, 1998.
9. M. Jakobsson. Flash mixing. In *PODC99*, pages 83–89, 1999.
10. A. Juels and M. Jakobsson. Millimix. Technical Report 99-33, DIMACS Technical Report, June 1999.
11. M. Michels and P. Horster. Some remarks on a receipt-free and universally verifiable mix-type voting scheme. In K. Kim and T. Matsumoto, editors, *Advances in Cryptology — ASIACRYPT '96*, volume 1163 of *Lecture Notes in Computer Science*, pages 125–132. Springer-Verlag, 1996.
12. M. Mitomo and K. Kurosawa. Attack for flash MIX. In *Asiacrypt 2000* (to appear), 2000.
13. W. Ogata, K. Kurosawa, K. Sako, and K. Takatani. Fault tolerant anonymous channel. In *ICICS98*, volume 1334 of *Lecture Notes in Computer Science*, pages 440–444. Springer-Verlag, 1998.

14. M. Ohkubo and M. Abe. A length-invariant hybrid mix. In *Asiacrypt2000* (to appear), 2000.
15. C. Park, K. Itoh, and K. Kurosawa. Efficient anonymous channel and all/nothing election scheme. In T. Helleseth, editor, *Advances in Cryptology — EURO-CRYPT '93*, volume 765 of *Lecture Notes in Computer Science*, pages 248–259. Springer-Verlag, 1994.
16. B. Pfitzmann. Breaking an efficient anonymous channel. In A. D. Santis, editor, *Advances in Cryptology — EUROCRYPT '94*, volume 950 of *Lecture Notes in Computer Science*, pages 339–348. Springer-Verlag, 1995.
17. B. Pfitzmann and A. Pfitzmann. How to break the direct RSA implementation of MIXes. In J.-J. Quisquater and J. Vandewalle, editors, *Advances in Cryptology – Eurocrypt '89*, volume 434 of *Lecture Notes in Computer Science*, pages 373–381. Springer-Verlag, 1989.
18. K. Sako. An improved universally verifiable mix-type voting schemes. Unpublished Manuscript, 1995.
19. K. Sako and J. Kilian. Receipt-free mix-type voting scheme — a practical solution to the implementation of a voting booth —. In L. C. Guillou and J.-J. Quisquater, editors, *Advances in Cryptology — EUROCRYPT '95*, volume 921 of *Lecture Notes in Computer Science*, pages 393–403. Springer-Verlag, 1995.
20. A. Waksman. A permutation network. *Journal of the Association for Computing Machinery*, 15(1):159–163, January 1968.

New Key Recovery in WAKE Protocol

Chong Hee Kim and Pil Joong Lee

Pohang University of Science & Technology (POSTECH),Korea
chhkim@oberon.postech.ac.kr, pjl@postech.ac.kr
http://ist.postech.ac.kr/

Abstract. Wireless authentication and key establishment (WAKE) protocols are essential in mobile communications. The key recovery mechanism may also be required in mobile communication systems for the investigation of serious crimes and for national security. Recently some protocols that give key recovery in the WAKE protocol have been published. In this paper we propose new key recovery protocols that improve previous protocols in security and efficiency.

1 Introduction

Mobile communications comprises one of the fastest growing sectors of the IT industry. Current second generation services such as cellular and PCS are worldwide used. The next generation of mobile communication systems, such as UMTS (Universal Mobile Telecommunications System) [1] and IMT-2000 (International Mobile Telecommunications-2000) [2,3] will provide a wider spectrum of services, including high quality multimedia and Internet services.

The security features for mobile communication systems include: confidentiality on the air interface (which is much more vulnerable to eavesdropping than a wired interface), anonymity of the user and authentication of the user to network administration in order to prevent fraudulent use of the system [11]. As the number of network operators (NOs) or value-added service providers (VASPs, e.g. a bank in electronic commerce) grows, a user may want to ensure that he is connected to the NO/VASP that he trusts. Further, users and NOs/VASPs may want to establish a shared session key to encrypt the subsequent message exchange. This is achieved through the successful execution of wireless authentication and key establishment (WAKE) protocol between the user and the NOs/VASPs.

As mobile communications increase, the key recovery mechanism may be required in mobile communication system for the investigation of serious crime and national security. Key recovery, although still a matter of debate, is expected to be deployed in the UMTS security architecture to satisfy government requirements concerning lawful interception [4].

In this paper, we briefly review the background on key recovery in Section 2. This is followed by previous key recovery systems in WAKE protocol of ASPeCT project [11] in Section 3. New key recovery systems will be described in Section 4. Finally Section 5 contains concluding remarks.

K. Kim (Ed.): PKC 2001, LNCS 1992, pp. 325–338, 2001.

2   Background on Key Recovery

The history of key recovery started in April 1993, with the proposal by the U.S. government of the Escrow Encryption Standard [5], EES, also know as the CLIPPER project. Afterwards, many key recovery schemes have been proposed.

To protect user privacy, the confidentiality of data is needed. For this, key recovery (KR) seems useless, but there are some scenarios where key recovery may be needed [6,7]:

- when the decryption key has been lost or the user is not present to provide the key
- where commercial organizations want to monitor their encrypted traffic without alerting the communicating parties; to check that employees are not violating an organization's policies, for example
- when a national government wants to decrypt intercepted data for the investigation of serious crimes or for national security reasons.

In this paper we use following terminology, as in [6]:

Key Recovery Agent (KRA). A trusted third party that performs KR in response to an authorized request.

Key Recovery Information (KRI). An aggregate of data that is needed by the KRA in order to complete a KR request, e.g. a session key encrypted under the KRA's public key.

Key Recovery Requester (KRR). An authorized entity that requests KR from the KRA. The KRR would usually be a LEA (Law Enforcement Agency) in possession of a valid warrant.

Interception Agent. An entity that acts in response to an authorized request for interception of a target identity by filtering out the communications traffic corresponding to the target identity. This function would usually be performed by NOs [8,9]

In [10], two different enforceability levels are defined in key recovery:

Level 1. At this level, the enforceability mechanism ensures that no user of the system (including VASP) can succeed in circumventing the KR mechanism unilaterally, i.e. without the cooperation of the other communication party.

Level 2. At this level, enforceability mechanisms ensure that no user of the system (including VASP) can succeed in circumventing the KR mechanism, even with the cooperation of the other communicating party.

If a user in the KR system sends a bogus value instead of KRI, the KR cannot succeed and the session key will be unrecoverable. Here, the level 1 condition is not satisfied. In order to satisfy the level 1 condition, the KR system needs additional verifiable information to prove validity of KRI before KR occurs. However, KR system cannot satisfy the level 2 condition because of super-encryption [10]. Therefore, we do not consider level 2 condition here.

3   Previous Protocols

In this section we review the ASPeCT WAKE protocol [11,12], the KR enhanced ASPeCT protocol [7], and the modified KR enhanced ASPeCT protocol [6]. We mainly use notations and definition in [6] to describe these protocols.

3.1   ASPeCT WAKE Protocol

The most well-known public key based WAKE protocol for UMTS is proposed by the ASPeCT project, which is responsible for the research and development of security technologies to be used in the UMTS system. The ASPeCT protocol [11] is proposed for user-to-NO/VASP interfaces to achieve the following goals:

1. mutual explicit authentication of A and B;
2. agreement between A and B on a secret session key K_{AB} with mutual implicit key authentication;
3. mutual key confirmation between A and B;
4. mutual assurance of key freshness (mutual key control);
5. non-repudiation of origin by A for relevant data sent from A to B;
6. confidentiality of relevant data sent by A to B.

Two protocols have been designed for these purposes (B- and C- variant) [11,12]. Their main difference is the existence in the C-variant of an on-line TTP of user A. For brevity we describe the B-variant and mainly consider key recovery in B-variant, but the same solutions can be applied to C-variant.

The message flows of the ASPeCT protocol are shown in Figure 1, where all the charging related data field are omitted for simplicity. The detailed description can be found in [11,12]. The notations used in this, and subsequent protocol descriptions, are shown below.

A	the identity of the user
B	the identity of the VASP
TTP_A	the identity of the TTP that user A trusts
g	a generator of a finite group
r_A	a random nonce chosen by user A

r_B a random nonce chosen by user B

K_{AB} a secret session key established between A and B

K_A^{-1} A's private signature key

A_{Cert} public key certificate of the user A that is signed by TTP_A

B_{Cert} public key certificate of the user B that is signed by TTP_A

b the private key component of the public-private key-agreement key pair of the B

g^b the public key component of the public-private key-agreement key pair of the B

$\{m\}_{K_A^{-1}}$ the message m signed by the user with his private signature key K_A^{-1}

$\{m\}_{K_{AB}}$ the symmetric encryption of a message m using the session key K_{AB}

h, h_1, h_2, h_3 one-way hash functions

A: user, B: VASP, TTP_A: TTP of A, $K_{AB} = h_1(r_B, g^{br_A})$

1. $A \to B$: g^{r_A}, TTP_A
2. $A \leftarrow B$: $r_B, h_2(K_{AB}, r_B, B), B_{Cert}$
3. $A \to B$: $\{\{h_3(g^{r_A}, g^b, r_B, B)\}_{K_A^{-1}}, A_{Cert}\}_{K_{AB}}$

Fig.1 The ASPeCT protocol

A generates a random number r_A, computes g^{r_A}, and sends it to B with the identity TTP_A. On receipt of the first token, B generates a random number r_B and computes a session key $K_{AB} = h_1(r_B, (g^{r_A})^b)$. B then sends Token 2 to A. On the receipt of the second token, A computes the key $K_{AB} = h_1(r_B, (g^b)^{r_A})$ and compares the hashed value $h_2(K_{AB}, r_B, B)$ with the one received. If the check succeeds, A generates the signature (shown in Figure 1) and sends Token 3 to B.

3.2   KR Enhanced ASPeCT Protocol

Rantos and Mitchell proposed a KR enhanced ASPeCT protocol [7]. Their strategy was to modify the already designed and well-studied ASPeCT WAKE protocol [11,12] without any overhead at the user end and without introducing any vulnerability.

In their protocol, each entity A and B registers with a KRA, KRA_A and KRA_B in their respective domain. The same TTP is assumed to act both as the certification authority (CA) and the KRA for each entity. Two different KR schemes are proposed that are applicable to both B- and C-variants of the

ASPeCT protocol. For brevity, we describe the B-variant protocol with KR. The application to C-variant ASPeCT protocol is straightforward. The first KR scheme is described in Figure 2.

A: user, B: VASP, TTP_A: TTP of A, $K_{AB} = h_1(r_B, g^{br_A})$
A: $r_A = f(w_A, s_A)$, $L = (g^{x_A})^{r_A}$

1. $A \rightarrow B$: $g^{r_A}, s_A, \{A\}_L, TTP_A$
2. $A \leftarrow B$: $r_B, h_2(K_{AB}, r_B, B), B_{Cert}$
3. $A \rightarrow B$: $\{\{h_3(g^{r_A}, g^b, r_B, B)\}_{K_A^{-1}}, A_{Cert}\}_{K_{AB}}$

Fig.2 KR enhanced B-variant ASPeCT protocol

The ASPeCT protocol is given a key recovery capability by slightly modifying the way that A's random nonce, r_A is generated. In the ASPeCT protocol, r_A is chosen at random by A prior to the start of protocol. But in the KR enhanced protocol, r_A is computed as:

$$r_A = f(w_A, s_A)$$

where f is a one-way function, s_A is a one-time random seed, and w_A is a secret value shared between A and KRA_A. The user A registers w_A with his KRA_A during the key recovery registration phase. In order for the KRA_A to be able to compute the value s_A, the user A must send s_A and his own identity A encrypted under $L = (g^{x_A})^{r_A}$, where g^{x_A} is the KRA_A's public key-agreement key.

In the key recovery phase of A's domain, intercepted values include s_A, $\{A\}_L$, r_B, and g^b. With these values, KRA_A decrypt $\{A\}_L$ and, from A's identity, obtain the corresponding secret value w_A, which, in turn, can be used to recompute K_{AB}. In B's domain, however, the procedure is slightly different. In key recovery registration phase, B escrows his private key b to KRA_B. Thus KRA_B can recover K_{AB} when presented with r_B and g^{r_A}. Other fields from the protocol also must be submitted to KRA to check that the request is within the scope of the warrant. However, we omit these fields for brevity.

To increase flexibility, Rantos and Mitchell [7] proposed that w_A could be a temporary secret, computed as:

$$w_A = f^*(w_A^*, TT)$$

Where f^* is a second one-way function, w_A^* is a long-term secret shared between KRA_A and A, and TT is a time stamp.

The second KR scheme does not require any shared secret between A and KRA_A. The only difference is that the first token is changed as:

1. $A \rightarrow B$: $g^{r_A}, \{A, r_A\}_L, TTP_A$

where r_A is a random number generated by A. KRA_A can compute K_{AB} directly by decrypting $\{A, r_A\}_L$.

3.3 Modified KR Enhanced ASPeCT Protocol

Nieto et al. identified security flaws with the KR enhanced ASPeCT protocol [7], and proposed a modified KR enhanced ASPeCT protocol [6]. They pointed out that the inclusion of $\{A\}_L$ in Token 1 of the KR enhanced ASPeCT protocol was unnecessary (see Figure 2). In the KR enhanced ASPeCT protocol, A's identity allows KRA_A to obtain the corresponding secret key w_A. In order to preserve the anonymity of the user, the identity is further encrypted under L. However, the identification of the encrypted data is performed before the actual submission of the KRI to the KRA. Therefore, Nieto et al. dropped the unnecessary $\{A\}_L$ from Token 1 in their modified protocol.

Nieto et al. also pointed out that the mutual authentication property, which was originally provided in the ASPeCT protocol, was not provided in the KR enhanced ASPeCT protocol. They explained how an impersonation attack can be mounted in the KR enhanced ASPeCT protocol in the case w_A is a temporary secret. Futher, user A cannot be sure whether the protocol tokens are being exchanged with B or KRA_B, since both B and KRA_B know b. Therefore, in their modified protocol the escrow of b is avoided and the protocol token is changed slightly to protect the impersonation attack. They also enforced the KR protocol by providing a *public KRI validation function* in the domain A. According to their definition, a *public KRI validation function* is a validation function that can be executed to verify the integrity of KRI by anyone using only public available information.

The modified KR enhanced protocol is described in Figure 3.

A: user, B: VASP, TTP_A: TTP of A, $K_{AB} = h_1(r_B, g^{b r_A})$

A: $s_A = (w_A h(g^{r_A}) + r_A) \bmod q$, B: $r_B = f_B(w_B, s_B)$

1. $A \rightarrow B$: g^{r_A}, TTP_A
2. $A \leftarrow B$: $r_B \oplus g^{b r_A}, h_2(K_{AB}, r_B, B), \{s_B\}_{K_{AB}}, B_{Cert}$
3. $A \rightarrow B$: $\{\{h_3(g^{r_A}, g^b, r_B, B)\}_{K_A^{-1}}, A_{Cert}\}_{K_{AB}}, s_A, s_B$

Fig.3 Modified KR enhanced B-variant ASPeCT protocol

In the description of the protocol, we use the following notation: p a large prime, q a prime with $q|(p-1)$, and g an element in the multiplicative group Z_p^* of order q.

KRI Generation Phase. The user A generates w_A, $1 \leq w_A \leq q - 1$, and shares with KRA_A. The value $\phi_A = g^{w_A}$ is made publicly available. A selects a random integer r_A, $1 \leq r_A \leq q - 1$, and compute $u_A = g^{r_A}$ and calculates s_A as:

$$s_A = (w_A h(u_A) + r_A) \bmod q$$

B generates a random number $r_B = f_B(w_B, s_B)$, where f_B is a one-way function, w_B is a secret value shared with KRA_B, and s_B is a random number.

KR Phase. In A's domain, KRA_A first computes r_A as:

$$r_A = s_A - w_A h(u_A) \bmod q,$$

Next, KRA_A compute $K_{AB} = h_1(r_B, (g^b)^{r_A})$.

In B's domain, KRA_B computes g^{br_A} by first calculating

$$r_B = f_B(w_B, s_B)$$

and therefore

$$g^{br_A} = (r_B \oplus g^{br_A}) \oplus r_B.$$

Next, KRA_B computes $K_{AB} = h_1(r_B, g^{br_A})$.

Public KRI Validation Phase in A's Domain. Given the public data u_A, s_A, and A, a monitoring third party V can check the integrity of the KRI fields generated by A, as follows:

- obtain authentic public value ϕ_A
- compute $c' = h(u_A) \bmod q$
- V resolve the validation process as successful if and only if $g^{s_A} = \phi_A^{c'} u_A$

Problems on Modified KR Enhanced ASPeCT Protocol. In Figure 3, s_A and s_B are withheld until the last token exchange in order to prevent impersonation attack. This insertion of s_A, s_B, and $\{s_B\}_{K_{AB}}$ may occure transimission and computation overhead. Due to the different manner in which B authenticates to A, a *public KRI validation property* cannot be applied in B's domain in the modified KR enhanced ASPeCT protocol. If r_B and s_B are generated in a similar manner to A, whoever knows r_A can restore w_B, which is secret between B and KRA_B. For example, A knows r_A and he can obtain r_B from the token $r_B \oplus g^{br_A}$. Next, from the following equation w_B can be restored:

$$s_B = (w_B h(g^{r_B}) + r_B) \bmod q.$$

When designing KR schemes, it is common practice to distribute shares among multiple KRAs. However, the KR enhanced ASPeCT protocol specifies only one KRA. Nieto et al. showed simple (but not efficient) example of how to allow multiple KRAs using the modified KR enhanced ASPeCT protocol that doesn't give public KRI validation property.

4   New Key Recovery in WAKE Protocol

In this section, we propose some improved KR enhanced WAKE protocols which improve on the previous protocols described in Section 3. First, we improved Nieto et al.'s protocol [6] by adding the public KRI validation property in domain B. Secondly, we consider multiple KRAs. The use of multiple KRAs is more practical and increases the user's acceptability on the KR system over that of only one KRA. Finally, we considered key recovery on the more general WAKE protocol with the property of *perfect forward secrecy*.

4.1   Public Verifiable Key Recovery in Both A's and B's Domains

As already seen in Section 3.3, Nieto et al.'s protocol [6] doesn't provide public KRI validation property in B's domain. However if we slightly modify the protocol, we can provide this property. In Nieto et al.'s protocol (see Figure 3), user A knows r_B from the Token 2. This eventually makes the public KRI validation in B's domain to be impossible. Therefore if we modify the session key to $K_{AB} = h_1(g^{br_A + r_B})$ and use g^{r_B} instead of r_B, we can resolve this problem. The proposed protocol (we call this type 1) is described in Figure 4.

A: user, B: VASP, TTP_A: TTP of A, $K_{AB} = h_1(g^{br_A + r_B})$
A: $s_A = (w_A h(g^{r_A}) + r_A) \bmod q$, B: $s_B = (w_B h(g^{r_B}) + r_B) \bmod q$

1. $A \to B$: g^{r_A}, TTP_A
2. $A \leftarrow B$: $g^{r_B}, w_B \oplus r_B \oplus g^{br_A}, h_2(K_{AB}, g^{r_B}, B), \{s_B\}_{K_{AB}}, B_{Cert}$
3. $A \to B$: $\{\{h_3(g^{r_A}, g^b, g^{r_B}, B)\}_{K_A^{-1}}, A_{Cert}\}_{K_{AB}}, s_A, s_B$

Fig.4 Proposed KR enhanced protocol - type 1

In this proposed protocol, the modification of session key, K_{AB}, does not break any property that WAKE protocol should have (see Section3.1). The user A generate session key K_{AB} by first calculating

$$(g^b)^{r_A}$$

and therefore

$$K_{AB} = h_1(g^{br_A} g^{r_B}).$$

The user B generate session key K_{AB} by first calculating

$$(g^{r_A})^b$$

and therefore

$$K_{AB} = h_1(g^{r_A b} g^{r_B}).$$

KRI Generation Phase. Each user A and B generates w_A and w_B, and shares with KRA_A and KRA_B respectively. The value $\phi_A = g^{w_A}$ and $\phi_B = g^{w_B}$ are made publicly available. The user A selects a random integer, r_A, compute $u_A = g^{r_A}$, and calculates s_A as:

$$s_A = (w_A h(u_A) + r_A) \bmod q$$

Similarly the user B generates r_B, u_B, and s_B.

KR Phase. In A's domain, KRA_A computes firstly r_A as:

$$r_A = s_A - w_A h(u_A) \bmod q,$$

KRA_A computes $(g^b)^{r_A}$ and computes $K_{AB} = h_1(g^{br_A} g^{r_B})$.

In B's domain, KRA_B computes firstly r_B as:

$$r_B = s_B - w_B h(u_B) \bmod q,$$

KRA_B computes g^{br_A} from $w_B \oplus r_B \oplus g^{br_A}$. Then KRA_B computes $K_{AB} = h_1(g^{r_B} g^{br_A})$.

Public KRI Validation Phase. Given the public data u_A, s_A, and A, a monitoring third party V can check the integrity of the KRI fields generated by A, by doing the following:

- obtain authentic public value ϕ_A
- compute $c' = h(u_A) \bmod q$
- V resolve the validation process as successful if and only if $g^{s_A} = \phi_A^{c'} u_A$

In B's case, the same procedure is applied.

Analysis of the Protocol. The user A does not know the real value of r_B. Therefore, a public KRI validation in B's domain as well as A's domain can be achieved without any computational overhead at the user's end. In B's end, additional one modular exponentiation, g^{r_B}, is required. However, this can be precomuputed, and usually the computation power of the server is expected to be great. Therefore, this is unlikely to pose serious problems.

4.2 Multiple KRAs

If we use multiple KRAs, the KR protocol can be more efficient in transmission bandwidth. In the proposed protocol (we call this type 2), the user B shares private key-agreement key, b, with multiple KRAs and then the session key, K_{AB}, can be recovered without revealing the value of b in KR phase. Before we describe the proposed protocol, we review verifiable secret sharing (VSS) scheme [13].

VSS Scheme The secret $s \in Z_q$ is distributed to n trusted entities, $T_i, 1 \leq i \leq n$. The dealer selects $(k-1)$ th polynomial $f(x) = f_0 + f_1 x + ... + f_{k-1} x^{k-1}$ that satisfies $f(0) = s$ and computes $s_i = f(x_i)$, where x_i is public number associated with T_i. The s_i and $(g^{f_1}, ...g^{f_{k-1}})$ are sent to each T_i, where g is a generator in Z_q. The secret s can be recovered when (for notational convenience the first) k trusted entities are merged:

$$s = \sum_{i=1}^{k} a_i s_i$$

$$a_i = \prod_{h \neq i} \frac{x_h}{x_h - x_i}$$

Each trusted entity, T_i, could also verify that the received s_i is a valid share. For brevity we omit the validation process of s_i. For a detailed description, see [13].

A: user, B: VASP, TTP_A: TTP of A, $K_{AB} = h_1(r_B, g^{br_A})$
A: $s_A = (w_A h(g^{r_A}) + r_A) \bmod q$

1. $A \rightarrow B$: g^{r_A}, TTP_A
2. $A \leftarrow B$: $r_B, h_2(K_{AB}, r_B, B), B_{Cert}$
3. $A \rightarrow B$: $\{\{h_3(g^{r_A}, g^b, r_B, B)\}_{K_A^{-1}}, A_{Cert}\}_{K_{AB}}, s_A$

Fig.5 Proposed KR enhanced protocol - type 2

The proposed protocol is described in Figure 5. It is same with ASPeCT protocol without sending s_A in the third token. We consider multiple KRA's only in B's domain for brevity. In the case of multiple KRA's in A's domain, the secret, w_A, which is shared between A and only one KRA in the protocol, has to be shared with multiple KRA's by using a publicly verifiable secret sharing scheme.

KRI Generation Phase. User A generates w_A, $1 \leq w_A \leq q - 1$, and shares with KRA_A. The value $\phi_A = g^{w_A}$ is made publicly available. A selects a random integer r_A, $1 \leq r_A \leq q - 1$, and compute $u_A = g^{r_A}$ and calculates s_A as:

$$s_A = (w_A h(u_A) + r_A) \bmod q$$

User B shares his private key-agreement key b with KRA_B's using VSS scheme. In practice, any VSS scheme can be used if the session key K_{AB} can be recovered without revealing the value of b in KR phase.

KR and Public KRI Validation Phase. In B's side, each KRA_B gives $(g^{r_A})^{a_i b_i}$ and then the value of $g^{r_A b}$ is recovered as:

$$g^{r_A b} = g^{r_A a_1 b_1} g^{r_A a_2 b_2} \cdots g^{r_A a_k b_k}$$
$$= g^{r_A (a_1 b_1 + a_2 b_2 + \cdots + a_k b_k)}$$

Because the real value of b is not recovered in KR phase, A can be sure only B knows b, i.e. authentication of B to A can be achieved. Futher, public KRI validation can be achieved if we use public verifiable secret sharing (PVSS) scheme instead of VSS scheme.

Analysis of the Protocol. The proposed protocol has reduced transmission overhead by dropping $\{s_B\}_{K_{AB}}$ in Token 2 and s_B in Token 3. Further, the symmetric encryption/decryption process, which are needed to encrypt s_B in B and decrypting $\{s_B\}_{K_{AB}}$ in A, is not required. Furthermore public verifiability on both A and B's domain can be achieved. By using multiple KRA's, it is more practical and applicable.

4.3   Comparison of Protocols

In this section, we compare existing protocols and our proposed protocols. In Table 1, we calculate the number of modular exponentiation in A's and B's side. The number within the bracket refers to the number of the required online modular exponentiation when precomputation is allowed.

Table 1. Comparison of protocols

protocol	modular exp.		additional	public KRI
	A	B	transmission overhead	validation
ASPeCT	2(1)	1(1)		
KR enhanced	3(1)	1(1)	s_A, $\{A\}_L$ or $\{A, r_A\}_L$	None
Modified KR enhanced	2(1)	1(1)	$\{s_B\}_{K_{AB}}$, s_A, s_B	A
Proposed type 1	2(1)	2(1)	$\{s_B\}_{K_{AB}}$, s_A, s_B, g^{r_B}	A, B
proposed type 2	2(1)	1(1)	s_A	A, B

The proposed protocol type 1 requires one more modular exponentiation in B's side. However this can be precomputed and usually the computation power of B is expected to be great. So it can be serious problem. The proposed protocol type 2 reduces the transmission overhead remaining same computation load. Also both the proposed protocols provide public KRI validation property in A's and B's side.

4.4   Problem of Perfect Forward Secrecy

The original ASPeCT protocol [11] described in Section 3.1 does not provide *perfect forward secrecy*. A protocol is said to have *perfect forward secrecy* if compromise of long-term keys does not compromise past session keys (ch.12, [14]).

In the original ASPeCT protocol, if the long term key, b, is disclosed, then all the previous session keys can be calculated by keeping g^{r_A}, r_B which used in previous protocol. To solve this perfect forward secrecy problem, the generation method of the session key must to be changed. We improved the original ASPeCT protocol by changing the session key to $K_{AB} = h(g^{r_A r_B})$ and using g^{r_B} instead of r_B in the protocol.

The modified protocol is shown in Figure 6. The g^{br_A} is inserted in the hashed value $h_2(K_{AB}, g^{r_B}, g^{br_A}, B)$ of Token 2 to provide the authentication of B to A. This protocol is similar to the protocols in [15], although the protocols were developed independently.

A: user, B: VASP, TTP_A: TTP of A, $K_{AB} = h_1(g^{r_A r_B})$

1. $A \rightarrow B$: g^{r_A}, TTP_A
2. $A \leftarrow B$: $g^{r_B}, h_2(K_{AB}, g^{r_B}, g^{br_A}, B), B_{Cert}$
3. $A \rightarrow B$: $\{\{h_3(g^{r_A}, g^b, g^{r_B}, B)\}_{K_A^{-1}}, A_{Cert}\}_{K_{AB}}$

Fig.6 Modified ASPeCT protocol with perfect forward secrecy property

---

Considering the key recovery system in this modified protocol. Each KRA, KRA_A and KRA_B, must know r_A or r_B in order to recover K_{AB} in KR phase. We can achieve this easily by the method used in previous protocols. The resulting protocol is described in Figure 7.

A: user, B: VASP, TTP_A: TTP of A, $K_{AB} = h_1(g^{r_A r_B})$
A: $s_A = (w_A h(g^{r_A}) + r_A) \bmod q$, B: $s_B = (w_B h(g^{r_B}) + r_B) \bmod q$

1. $A \rightarrow B$: g^{r_A}, TTP_A
2. $A \leftarrow B$: $g^{r_B}, h_2(K_{AB}, g^{r_B}, g^{br_A}, B), \{s_B\}_{k_{AB}}, B_{Cert}$
3. $A \rightarrow B$: $\{\{h_3(g^{r_A}, g^b, g^{r_B}, B)\}_{K_A^{-1}}, A_{Cert}\}_{K_{AB}}, s_A, s_B$

Fig.7 Proposed KR system on the modified ASPeCT protocol

5   Conclusion

In this paper, we proposed improved KR enhanced WAKE protocols that are both efficient in transmission and have improved security. First, we provided a publicly verifiable key recovery protocol that holds on both sides that communicate each other. Secondly, we improved the efficiency of protocol in the case of multiple key recovery agents. In general, the use of multiple key recovery agents helps increasing the user's acceptability on the key recovery system. Finally, we modified the existing ASPeCT WAKE protocol to add the perfect forward secrecy. We also gave this modified protocol to have key recovery property.

Acknowledgment

The authors wish to thank anonymous referees for their critical comments.

References

1. U. Black, "Third Generation Mobile Systems (TGMSs)", *Second Generation Mobile & Wireless Networks*, Prentice Hall, 1999
2. T. Ojanpera and R. Prasad, "IMT-2000 Applications", *Wideband CDMA for Third Generation Mobile Communication*, T. Ojanpera and R. Prasad (ed.), Artech House Publishers, pp.65-76, , 1998
3. K. Buhanal et al., "IMT-2000: Service Providers Perspective", *IEEE Personal Communications*, August 1997
4. ETSI SMG10, "Universal Mobile Telecommunications System (UMTS): Security Requirement", *Draft UMTS 33.21 version 2.0.0*, Feb., 1999
5. NIST, "Escrow Encryption Standard (EES)", *Federal Information Processing Standard Publication (FIPS PUB)* 185, 1994
6. J. Nieto, D. Park, C. Boyd, and E. Dawson, "Key Recovery in Third Generation Wireless Communication Systems", *Public Key Cryptography-PKC2000*, LNCS 1751, pp.223-237, 2000
7. K. Rantos and C. Mitchell, "Key Recovery in ASPeCT Authentication and Initialization of Payment protocol", *Proceedings of ACTS Mobile Summit*, Sorrento, Italy, June 1999
8. ETSI TC Security, "Specification for Trusted Third Party Services: Part1 Key Management and Key Escrow/Recovery", *DEN/SEC-003001x, Draft Version 1.0 (edition2)*, 11th Nov, 1997
9. ETSI TC-STAG, "Security Techniques Advisory Group (STAG); Definition of User Requirements for Lawful Interception of telecommunications: Requirements of the Law Enforcement Agencies", *ETR 331*, December 1996.
10. B. Pfitzmann and M. Waidner, "How to Break Fraud-Detectable Key Recovery", *Operating Systems Review*, 21, 1998, pp.23-28
11. G. Horn and B. Preneel, "Authentication and payment in future mobile systems", *Computer Security - ESORICS'98*, LNCS, 1485, pp.277-293, 1998
12. ACTS AC095, ASPeCT Deliverable D02, "Initial Report on Security Requirements", *AC095/ATEA/W21/DS/P/02/B*, Feb., 1997, Available from *htttp://www.esat.kuleuven.ac.be/cosic/aspect/*

13. T. Pederson, "Distributed provers with application to undeniable signatures", *Advances in Cryptology-Eurocrypt'91*, LNCS vol. 963, pp.222-242, 1991
14. A. Menezes, P. Oorshot, and S.Vanstone, *Handbook of Applied Cryptographay*, 1997
15. DongGook Park, Colin Boyd and Sang-Jae Moon, "Forward Secrecy and Its Application to Future Mobile Communications Security", *PKC2000*, Springer-Verlag, pp.433-445, 2000

Redundant Representation of Finite Fields

Willi Geiselmann and Harald Lukhaub

Institut für Algorithmen und Kognitive Systeme,
Arbeitsgruppen Computeralgebra & Systemsicherheit, Prof. Dr. Th. Beth,
Universität Karlsruhe, Am Fasanengarten 5, 76 128 Karlsruhe, Germany.

Abstract. A redundant representation of finite fields with 2^n elements is presented. It unifies the advantages of polynomial and normal bases by the cost of redundancy. The arithmetic, especially exponentiation, in this representation is perfectly suited for low power computing: multiplication can be built up with reversible gates very efficient and squaring is a cyclic shift.

1 Introduction

Hardware implementations of cryptographic schemes based on the Discrete Logarithm Problem in $\mathbf{F}_{2^n}$, the field with 2^n elements, (see e.g. [1,2]), require efficient exponentiation architectures.

On the one hand, research has been particularly attracted to the choice of the representation of the field. Dual basis multipliers in $\mathbf{F}_{2^n}$ were first suggested by Berlekamp [14] for encoding Reed-Solomon codes. A representation in a polynomial basis is the standard representation, usually the best choice for general-purpose applications. A very promising approach is the use of a normal basis, where squaring is an extremely simple operation [6,8,11,13]. However, normal basis multiplication can become very complex and good normal bases have to be selected carefully [13]. Especially for exponentiation with low weight exponents the advantage of a normal basis is pronounced.

On the other hand, work on low power computing is coming up more and more. One reason is the problem of cooling of the chips with the increasing integration; another problem in cryptology is the resistance of encrption units against differential power analysis [9].

1.1 Classical Multiplication

In this section a brief overview on different representations of finite fields and the resulting circuits is given. More details can be found in [5,8,15].

Polynomial Basis Multiplication The standard representation of an extension field is the polynomial basis:

Definition 1. For $n \in \mathbf{N}, n \geq 2$ it holds $\mathbf{F}_{2^n} \simeq \mathbf{F}_2[x]/f(x)$ where $f(x) \in \mathbf{F}_2[x]$ is an irreducible polynomial of degree n. Let $\alpha \in \mathbf{F}_{2^n}$ be a zero of $f(x)$, then $(1, \alpha, \ldots, \alpha^{n-1})$ is an $\mathbf{F}_2$ (vector space) basis of $\mathbf{F}_{2^n}$, called a polynomial basis.

K. Kim (Ed.): PKC 2001, LNCS 1992, pp. 339–352, 2001.
© Springer-Verlag Berlin Heidelberg 2001

In this representation multiplication can easily be performed by linear feedback shift registers (LFSRs), where $f(x)$ is used as the feedback polynomial. One of the possible realizations is given in Figure 1.

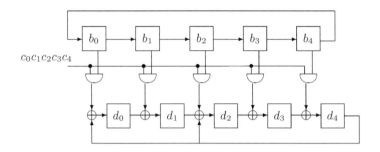

Fig. 1. A polynomial basis multiplier for $\mathbf{F}_{2^5} : \mathbf{F}_2 \bmod f(x) := x^5 + x^2 + 1$.

Normal Basis Multiplication A normal basis of $\mathbf{F}_{2^n}$ is defined as follows.

Definition 2. *A basis* $N = (\alpha_0, \alpha_1, \ldots, \alpha_{n-1})$ *of* $\mathbf{F}_{2^n}$ *is called a* normal basis *(over* $\mathbf{F}_2$*) if there exists some* $\alpha \in \mathbf{F}_{2^n}$ *with* $\alpha_i = \alpha^{2^i}$ *for all* i, $0 \le i < n$.

In a normal basis $(\alpha_0, \alpha_1, \ldots, \alpha_{n-1})$ of $\mathbf{F}_{2^n}$ squaring is a cyclic shift of coefficients due to

$$\left(\sum_{i=0}^{n-1} u_i \alpha_i \right)^2 = \sum_{i=0}^{n-1} u_i \alpha_{i+1} \quad \text{and} \quad \alpha_n := \alpha^{2^n} = \alpha_0. \tag{1}$$

Multiplication is more difficult as the products $\alpha_i \alpha_j$ are, in general, not elements of the normal basis. The cost of normal basis multiplication is frequently measured by the complexity of the linear combinations needed to represent the elements $\alpha_0 \alpha_i$ in the normal basis [13]. The efficiency of any normal basis multiplier suggested uses field extensions in which good (optimal) normal bases exist [3,13]; in many fields such good normal bases are not available.

1.2 Reversible Computing

From physics it is known that erasure of information (deleting or resetting of storage cells) results in heating up the system. Therefore one approach to design low power computing devices is to use reversible gates [4,12,10]. These gates keep all information, i. e. they are bijections.

Permutations and shifts obviously fulfill this condition.

One basic gate is the Fredkin gate: the inputs (a, b, c) are mapped to the outputs (a, b, c) if a = 0; if the input a = 1 the outputs b, c are exchanged, i.e. the output is (a, c, b).

Another reversible gate is the CNOT (Controlled NOT), the reversible version of the XOR ((a, b) ↦ (a, a⊕b)). It is self inverse and can be built up with Fredkin gates.

The generalization of the CNOT is the Toffoli gate, it is a "double controlled NOT" ((a, b, c) ↦ (a, b, c⊕(a∧b))) and is self inverse.

All these gates are shown in Figure 2.

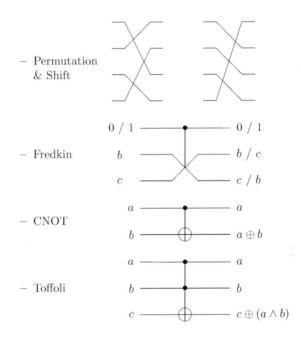

- Permutation
  & Shift

- Fredkin

- CNOT

- Toffoli

Fig. 2. Basic reversible gates

A polynomial basis multiplier, built up with reversible gates can be found in Figure 3. There are $n = 5$ steps required, each step needs

- 2 shift(n) operations;
- wgt($f(x)$) $- 2 = 1$ CNOT gates (the feedback operation) and
- $n = 5$ Toffoli gates.

The normal basis multiplier suggested by Massey and Omura [11], modified for reversible gates, is shown in Figure 4. There are $n = 5$ steps required, each step needs

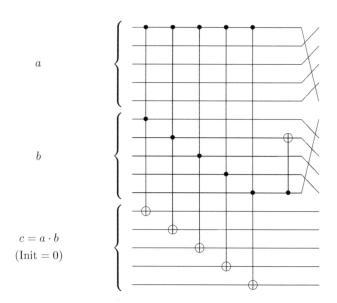

Fig. 3. A polynomial basis multiplier modulo $f(x) = x^5 + x^2 + 1$

- 3 shift(n) operations and
- "normal basis complexity $(f(x))$" $= 9$ Toffoli gates.

There are other realizations of normal basis multipliers, but the "normal basis complexity", as defined in [13], is a lower bound for the number of gates needed. This bound is for optimal normal bases of $\mathbf{F}_{2^n}$ equal to $2n - 1$. In most field extensions such a basis does not exist and in some cases the best known normal basis of $\mathbf{F}_{2^n}$ is not much smaller than $n^2/2$. More details in this topic can be found in [6,8].

2   Redundant Representation of Finite Fields

The representation of $\mathbf{F}_{2^n}$ given in this section can perfectly be used in reversible circuits; but the representation can as well be used for very efficient classical circuits.

The main reason to use a normal basis is the easy procedure for squaring as a cyclic shift. The advantage of a polynomial basis is the easy realization of the multiplication as linear feedback shift register.

A representation that merges these two advantages is the following:

Theorem 1. *Let $m \in \mathbf{N}$ be minimal with $x^m - 1 \in \mathbf{F}_2[x]$ has an irreducible factor $f(x)$ of degree n; let $\alpha \in \mathbf{F}_{2^n}$ be a zero of $f(x)$. Then the elements of $\mathbf{F}_{2^n}$ can be represented as $\mathbf{F}_2$-vectors of size m according to the following embedding:*

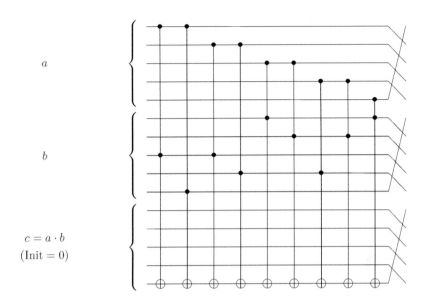

Fig. 4. The Massey-Omura normal basis multiplier with $f(x) = x^5 + x^4 + x^2 + x + 1$

$$\mathbf{F}_2[x]\Big/_{f(x)} \simeq \mathbf{F}_2[\alpha] \hookrightarrow \mathbf{F}_2[x]\Big/_{(x^m - 1)}$$

$$\phi: \quad \sum_{i=0}^{n-1} a_i \cdot \alpha^i \mapsto \sum_{i=0}^{n-1} a_i \cdot x^i \quad \hat{=} \ (a_0, \ldots, a_{n-1}, 0, \ldots, 0)$$

$$\overline{\phi}: \quad \sum_{i=0}^{m-1} b_i \cdot \alpha^i \hookleftarrow \sum_{i=0}^{m-1} b_i \cdot x^i \quad \hat{=} \quad (b_0, \ldots, b_{m-1}).$$

It holds:

(a) $\overline{\phi}(\phi(a) + \phi(b)) = a + b \quad$ *for* $a, b \in \mathbf{F}_2[\alpha]$,
(b) $\overline{\phi}(\phi(a) \cdot \phi(b)) = a \cdot b \quad$ *for* $a, b \in \mathbf{F}_2[\alpha]$.

Proof. Property (a) obviously holds.
To prove (b), note that $f(x) \mid (x^m - 1)$ and thus $\alpha^m = 1$. ∎

The arithmetic in $\mathbf{F}_2[x]\Big/_{(x^{n+1} + 1)}$, can be performed as follows:

- Addition: Is the XOR of the vectors.
- Multiplication with x: Is a cyclic shift.
  With $b := \sum_{i=0}^{m-1} b_i \cdot x^i$ it holds: $b \ \hat{=} \ (b_0, b_1, \ldots, b_{m-1})$
  $$\Rightarrow x \cdot b \ \hat{=} \ (b_{m-1}, b_0, \ldots, b_{m-2}).$$
- Multiplication: Is performed with an LFSR with trivial feedback polynomial $x^m - 1$.

- Squaring: Is a permutation ("stretching").
  (Note m is odd, because of m being minimal with $f(x) \mid (x^m - 1)$.) Let
  $$b := \sum_{i=0}^{m-1} b_i \cdot x^i, \text{ then}$$

$$b^2 = \sum_{i=0}^{m-1} b_i \cdot x^{2i} = \sum_{i=0}^{(m-1)/2} b_i \cdot x^{2i} + \sum_{i=(m+1)/2}^{m-1} b_i \cdot x^{2i-m}.$$

Written as vectors this is:

$$b \; \hat{=} \; (b_0, b_1, b_2, \ldots, b_{m-1})$$
$$\Rightarrow b^2 \; \hat{=} \; (b_0, b_{(m+1)/2}, b_1, b_{(m+3)/2}, b_2, \ldots, b_{m-1}, b_{(m-1)/2}).$$

Example 1. The elements of the field $\mathbf{F}_{2^4}$ can be represented as vectors of length 5 according to the factorization of $x^5 + 1 \in \mathbf{F}_2[x]$ to $x^5 + 1 = (x + 1)(x^4 + x^3 + x^2 + x + 1)$. Let α be a zero of $x^4 + x^3 + x^2 + x + 1$, then $(1 + \alpha^3)^3$ can be calculated as follows:

$$\mathbf{F}_2[\alpha] \hookrightarrow \mathbf{F}_2[x] \big/ (x^5 + 1)$$
$$1 + \alpha^3 \; \hat{=} \; (1, 0, 0, 1, 0)$$
$$(1 + \alpha^3)^2 \; \hat{=} \; (1, 1, 0, 0, 0) \quad \text{(by stretching)}$$
$$(1 + \alpha^3)^2 \cdot (1 + \alpha^3) \; \hat{=} \; (1, 1, 0, 0, 0) \oplus (0, 0, 0, 1, 1)$$
$$\hat{=} \; (1, 1, 0, 1, 1) \quad \text{(with } \alpha^4 = \alpha^3 + \alpha^2 + \alpha + 1$$
$$\text{this reduces to)}$$
$$\alpha^2 \; \hat{=} \; (1, 1, 0, 1, 1).$$

In the appendix a list of the minimal required length m of the redundant representation is given for $n \leq 250$ and for primes $n \leq 2000$.

3   Multiplication with a Fixed Element

For crypto systems based on a discrete logarithm problem in $\mathbf{F}_{2^n}$ exponentiation of one fixed element $a \in \mathbf{F}_{2^n}$ is one of the operations required. This is an operation perfectly suited to reversible computing when squaring is a permutation. The multiplication with a is a linear mapping and can be performed without any intermediate results that need to be deleted.

One way to generate a reversible implementation of a linear mapping (represented as multiplication $\phi(a) \mapsto A \cdot \phi(a)$ with A an $m \times m$ matrix and $\phi(a)$ a vector of size m) is to decompose A into $A = P \cdot L \cdot U$ with P a permutation matrix, L a lower triangular matrix and U an upper triangular matrix.

For the multiplication $U \cdot \phi(a)$ first calculate the first component by adding the required components to it (first row of U). After this step one bit of the result is stored in the first component – the previous value is lost, but not needed any more because of the trinagular structere of U. Proceeding with the other components of $\phi(a)$ in the same way gives $U \cdot \phi(a)$ without any intermediate result to be deleted. The number of CNOT gates required is the weight of $U - I_m$, where I_m denotes the unity matrix of size m.

The multiplication with L is performed in the same way, but the resulting bits are calculated in the reverse order.

In the rest of this section we give some examples for normal basis multiplication and the multiplication in the corresponding redundant representation with reversible gates according to the decomposition of matrices.

Example 2. For the smaller examples the decomposition of the matrices is given, for the larger ones we restrict ourself to the complexity only.

– $\mathbf{F}_{2^4}$:
Let α be a zero of $x^4 + x^3 + x^2 + x + 1$, then α generates a normal basis with the multiplication matrix

$$A_4 := \begin{pmatrix} 0\,1\,0\,0 \\ 0\,0\,0\,1 \\ 1\,1\,1\,1 \\ 0\,0\,1\,0 \end{pmatrix}.$$

Then $\alpha + 1$ is a primitive element and the multiplication with $A_4 + I_4$ decomposes as follows:

$$A_4 + I_4 = \begin{pmatrix} 1\,0\,0\,0 \\ 0\,1\,0\,0 \\ 0\,0\,0\,1 \\ 0\,0\,1\,0 \end{pmatrix} \cdot \begin{pmatrix} 1\,0\,0\,0 \\ 0\,1\,0\,0 \\ 0\,0\,1\,0 \\ 1\,0\,0\,1 \end{pmatrix} \cdot \begin{pmatrix} 1\,1\,0\,0 \\ 0\,1\,0\,1 \\ 0\,0\,1\,1 \\ 0\,0\,0\,1 \end{pmatrix}.$$

This decomposition results in a multiplication circuit with $1 + 3 = 4$ CNOT gates and 1 permutation of two elements.

For the redundant representation $m = 5$ (note: $x^5 = (x + 1)(x^4 + x^3 + x^2 + x + 1)$). The matrix $R_4 \in \mathbf{F}_2^{5 \times 5}$ corresponding to multiplication with x has to perform a cyclic shift and thus is the circulant matrix with first row $(0, 1, 0, 0, 0)$. The element $1 + x + x^2$ is primitive, and the decomposition of the corresponding matrix is:

$$I_5 + R_4 + R_4^2 = \begin{pmatrix} 1\,0\,0\,0\,0 \\ 0\,1\,0\,0\,0 \\ 0\,0\,1\,0\,0 \\ 0\,0\,0\,0\,1 \\ 0\,0\,0\,1\,0 \end{pmatrix} \cdot \begin{pmatrix} 1\,0\,0\,0\,0 \\ 0\,1\,0\,0\,0 \\ 0\,0\,1\,0\,0 \\ 1\,0\,1\,1\,0 \\ 1\,1\,0\,0\,1 \end{pmatrix} \cdot \begin{pmatrix} 1\,1\,1\,0\,0 \\ 0\,1\,1\,1\,0 \\ 0\,0\,1\,1\,1 \\ 0\,0\,0\,1\,0 \\ 0\,0\,0\,0\,1 \end{pmatrix}.$$

Here the multiplication circuit requires $4 + 6 = 10$ CNOT gates and 1 permutation of two elements.

− $\mathbf{F}_{2^6}$:

In this field an optimal normal basis exists with the multiplication matrix:

$$A_6 := \begin{pmatrix} 0\,1\,0\,0\,0\,0 \\ 1\,0\,0\,0\,1\,0 \\ 0\,0\,0\,1\,1\,0 \\ 0\,0\,1\,0\,0\,1 \\ 0\,1\,1\,0\,0\,0 \\ 0\,0\,0\,1\,0\,1 \end{pmatrix}$$

The corresponding field element is primitive and A_6 decomposes to:

$$A_6 = \begin{pmatrix} 0\,1\,0\,0\,0\,0 \\ 1\,0\,0\,0\,0\,0 \\ 0\,0\,0\,1\,0\,0 \\ 0\,0\,1\,0\,0\,0 \\ 0\,0\,0\,0\,0\,1 \\ 0\,0\,0\,0\,1\,0 \end{pmatrix} \cdot \begin{pmatrix} 1\,0\,0\,0\,0\,0 \\ 0\,1\,0\,0\,0\,0 \\ 0\,0\,1\,0\,0\,0 \\ 0\,0\,0\,1\,0\,0 \\ 0\,0\,0\,1\,1\,0 \\ 0\,1\,1\,0\,0\,1 \end{pmatrix} \cdot \begin{pmatrix} 1\,0\,0\,0\,1\,0 \\ 0\,1\,0\,0\,0\,0 \\ 0\,0\,1\,0\,0\,1 \\ 0\,0\,0\,1\,1\,0 \\ 0\,0\,0\,0\,1\,1 \\ 0\,0\,0\,0\,0\,1 \end{pmatrix},$$

giving a reversible realization with $3+4 = 7$ CNOT gates and 3 permutations of two elements.

For the redundant representation $m = 9$ (note: $x^9 + 1 = (x + 1)(x^2 + x + 1)(x^6 + x^3 + 1)$). The element $1 + x + x^3$ is primitive, and the decomposition of the corresponding matrix is:

$$I_9 + R_6 + R_6^3 = \begin{pmatrix} 1\,0\,0\,0\,0\,0\,0\,0\,0 \\ 0\,1\,0\,0\,0\,0\,0\,0\,0 \\ 0\,0\,1\,0\,0\,0\,0\,0\,0 \\ 0\,0\,0\,1\,0\,0\,0\,0\,0 \\ 0\,0\,0\,0\,1\,0\,0\,0\,0 \\ 0\,0\,0\,0\,0\,1\,0\,0\,0 \\ 0\,0\,0\,0\,0\,0\,1\,0\,0 \\ 0\,0\,0\,0\,0\,0\,0\,1\,0 \\ 0\,0\,0\,0\,0\,0\,0\,0\,1 \end{pmatrix} \cdot \begin{pmatrix} 1\,0\,0\,0\,0\,0\,0\,0\,0 \\ 0\,1\,0\,0\,0\,0\,0\,0\,0 \\ 0\,0\,1\,0\,0\,0\,0\,0\,0 \\ 0\,0\,0\,1\,0\,0\,0\,0\,0 \\ 0\,0\,0\,0\,1\,0\,0\,0\,0 \\ 0\,0\,0\,0\,0\,1\,0\,0\,0 \\ 1\,1\,1\,0\,1\,0\,1\,0\,0 \\ 0\,1\,1\,1\,0\,1\,0\,1\,0 \\ 1\,1\,0\,1\,0\,0\,1\,0\,1 \end{pmatrix} \cdot \begin{pmatrix} 1\,1\,0\,1\,0\,0\,0\,0\,0 \\ 0\,1\,1\,0\,1\,0\,0\,0\,0 \\ 0\,0\,1\,1\,0\,1\,0\,0\,0 \\ 0\,0\,0\,1\,1\,0\,1\,0\,0 \\ 0\,0\,0\,0\,1\,1\,0\,1\,0 \\ 0\,0\,0\,0\,0\,1\,1\,0\,1 \\ 0\,0\,0\,0\,0\,0\,1\,0\,0 \\ 0\,0\,0\,0\,0\,0\,0\,1\,0 \\ 0\,0\,0\,0\,0\,0\,0\,0\,1 \end{pmatrix}.$$

Here the multiplication circuit requires $12 + 12 = 24$ CNOT gates and no permutation.

− $\mathbf{F}_{2^{54}}$:

In $\mathbf{F}_{2^{54}}$ a good normal basis (with complexity 209) exists. The generator α is not primitive, thus we choose the primitive Element: $1 + \alpha$. The decomposition of the corresponding matrix gives us a circuit with $236 + 255 = 491$ CNOT gates and a very irregular permutation.

The redundant representation with $m = 81$ and the primitive element $x + x^3 + x^4$ gives a circuit with $135 + 159 = 294$ CNOT gates and a very regular permutation, a cyclic shift on all but 3 elements.

- $\mathbf{F}_{2^{121}}$:

  In $\mathbf{F}_{2^{121}}$ a good normal basis (with complexity 705) exists. The generator α is primitive and the decomposition of the corresponding matrix gives us a circuit with $1183 + 1126 = 2309$ CNOT gates and a very irregular permutation.

  The redundant representation with $m = 727$ and the primitive element $x + x^2 + x^3$ gives a circuit with $968 + 550 = 1518$ CNOT gates and a very regular permutation, close to a cyclic shift.

- $\mathbf{F}_{2^{239}}$:

  In $\mathbf{F}_{2^{239}}$ a good normal basis (with complexity 477) exists. The generator α is primitive and the decomposition of the corresponding matrix gives us a circuit with $233 + 234 = 467$ CNOT gates and a very irregular permutation.

  The redundant representation with $m = 479$ and the primitive element $x + x^2 + x^3$ gives a circuit with $637 + 955 = 1592$ CNOT gates and a very regular permutation, close to a cyclic shift.

- $\mathbf{F}_{2^{240}}$:

  In $\mathbf{F}_{2^{240}}$ no good normal basis exists. We chose the best we found, with complexity 28433. The generator α is primitive and the decomposition of the corresponding matrix gives us a circuit with $14213 + 14370 = 28583$ CNOT gates and a very irregular permutation.

  The redundant representation with $m = 1067$ and the primitive element $1 + x + x^2$ gives a circuit with $1420 + 2130 = 3550$ CNOT gates and a very regular permutation, close to a cyclic shift.

  If a good normal bases exists in a field extension, it depends very much on the degree of redundancy required, if the normal basis representation or the redundant representation is better. If an optimal normal basis of type 1 (see. [13]) exists for the extension degree n, the redundant representation with $m = n+1$ is the best choice for implementation; if an optimal normal basis of type 2 (see. [13]) exists, the best redundant representation is with $m = 2n - 1$ and the normal basis multiplication (with complexity $2n - 1$) is the better choice.

  If no good normal basis exists in the field in question even a high degree of redundancy will result in a better performance than a normal basis multiplier.

4   General Multiplication

The general multiplication (with two variable inputs) can be realized with reversible gates in a straight forward manner. There are exactly m Toffoli gates and 2 cyclic shifts of m signals needed. It corresponds directly to a LFSR with trivial feedback polynomial.

The major problem of any normal basis multiplier is the irregular structure. In hardware it results in additional area needed for wiring, in software unregular access to the bits causes additional operations. With the redundant representation these problems do not occure at all. The highly regular structure can be seen best in some example: The field $\mathbf{F}_{2^4}$ is represented as $\mathbf{F}_2[x]\big/(x^5 - x)$:

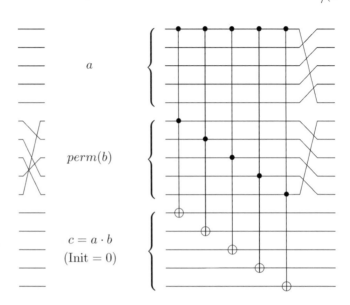

The corresponding normal basis multiplier needs "normal basis complexity $(f(x))$" many Toffoli gates, in this example this is 9. The permutation of the input b seems to reduce the advantage of the redundant representation; in cryptography in most cases an exponentiation is required, and thus the permutation has to be performed only once and not for each multiplication.

In this setting the redundant representation has often a better performance than a normal basis representation if the number of gates is the measure to be used. If the regularity of the design is taken into account the advantage is even more pronounced.

5   Conclusion

The presented redundant representation of finite extension fields via roots of unity joins the two good properties of normal and polynomial bases. On the one hand squaring can be performed by a simple and very structured permutation – a stretching; on the other hand multiplication can be performed with an LFSR with trivial feedback polynomial.

The price to pay is the additional place required for storage of the redundancy. The level of redundancy depends very much on the degree of the field and in many cases it is a perfect choice for exponentiation.

A   Degree of Redundancy

In the following table for all fields $\mathbb{F}_{2^n}$ with $n \leq 250$ and extension degrees with $n \leq 2000$ beeing a prime, the smallest degree of redundancy m is given, that allows a representation with roots of unity. In some cases even the field $\mathbb{F}_{2^{n_1}} \supset \mathbb{F}_{2^n}$ can be represented with the smallest m-th roots of unity where $\mathbb{F}_{2^n}$ can be embedded.

n	n_1	m	n	n_1	m	n	n_1	m	n	n_1	m
			41	82	83	81	162	163	121	121	727
2	2	3	42	42	147	82	82	83	122	244	733
3	3	7	43	172	173	83	83	167	123	246	581
4	4	5	44	44	115	84	84	203	124	372	373
5	10	11	45	180	181	85	340	1021	125	500	625
6	6	9	46	138	139	86	172	173	126	378	379
7	28	29	47	94	283	87	348	349	127	508	509
8	8	17	48	48	97	88	88	353	128	384	769
9	18	19	49	196	197	89	178	179	129	258	1033
10	10	11	50	100	101	90	180	181	130	130	131
11	11	23	51	51	103	91	546	547	131	131	263
12	12	13	52	52	53	92	92	235	132	132	299
13	52	53	53	106	107	93	372	373	133	532	1597
14	28	29	54	54	81	94	94	283	134	268	269
15	60	61	55	110	121	95	95	191	135	135	271
16	48	97	56	224	449	96	96	193	136	136	289
17	51	103	57	342	361	97	388	389	137	411	823
18	18	19	58	58	59	98	196	197	138	138	139
19	95	191	59	708	709	99	99	199	139	556	557
20	20	25	60	60	61	100	100	101	140	140	319
21	21	49	61	183	367	101	303	607	141	564	1129
22	66	67	62	372	373	102	102	307	142	284	569
23	23	47	63	378	379	103	618	619	143	858	859
24	48	97	64	64	641	104	104	901	144	144	577
25	100	101	65	130	131	105	210	211	145	290	649
26	52	53	66	66	67	106	106	107	146	292	293
27	54	81	67	268	269	107	214	643	147	147	343
28	28	29	68	68	137	108	108	405	148	148	149
29	58	59	69	138	139	109	1090	1091	149	298	1193
30	60	61	70	210	211	110	110	121	150	300	707
31	155	311	71	284	569	111	444	1043	151	906	907
32	96	193	72	72	323	112	224	449	152	152	1217
33	66	67	73	292	293	113	226	227	153	612	613
34	68	137	74	148	149	114	342	361	154	154	617
35	35	71	75	300	707	115	460	461	155	155	311
36	36	37	76	76	229	116	116	295	156	156	169
37	148	149	77	231	463	117	117	937	157	1570	1571
38	76	229	78	156	169	118	708	709	158	316	317
39	39	79	79	316	317	119	119	239	159	318	749
40	40	187	80	240	1067	120	120	1037	160	480	2123

n	n_1	m	n	n_1	m	n	n_1	m	n	n_1	m
161	483	967	206	618	619	251	251	503	523	2615	5231
162	162	163	207	828	829	257	771	1543	541	3246	9739
163	652	653	208	1040	2081	263	526	1579	547	547	5471
164	164	415	209	418	419	269	1076	2153	557	557	3343
165	660	661	210	210	211	271	542	1627	563	7882	7883
166	166	499	211	1055	2111	277	1108	1109	569	6828	6829
167	2338	2339	212	212	535	281	562	563	571	571	5711
168	168	833	213	852	853	283	566	1699	577	2308	2309
169	676	677	214	214	643	293	586	587	587	8218	8219
170	340	1021	215	1290	1291	307	1228	1229	593	1186	1187
171	342	361	216	648	1297	311	1866	1867	599	2396	4793
172	172	173	217	651	1303	313	939	1879	601	601	3607
173	346	347	218	1090	1091	317	8242	8243	607	3642	3643
174	348	349	219	876	877	331	1986	1987	613	6130	6131
175	700	701	220	220	575	337	3370	3371	617	1234	4937
176	704	1409	221	442	443	347	2082	2083	619	2476	2477
177	708	709	222	444	1043	349	3490	3491	631	3155	6311
178	178	179	223	2676	2677	353	2471	4943	641	1282	1283
179	179	359	224	224	449	359	359	719	643	7716	7717
180	180	181	225	900	1919	367	734	2203	647	9058	9059
181	543	1087	226	226	227	373	1492	1493	653	1306	1307
182	546	547	227	908	5449	379	1516	4549	659	659	1319
183	183	367	228	228	1603	383	1532	4597	661	1983	3967
184	184	799	229	916	2749	389	2334	9337	673	2692	2693
185	370	1481	230	460	461	397	397	2383	677	2708	5417
186	372	373	231	231	463	401	1604	3209	683	683	1367
187	1122	1123	232	464	929	409	1636	1637	691	3455	6911
188	940	941	233	466	467	419	419	839	701	12618	12619
189	378	379	234	468	1007	421	842	4211	709	2836	2837
190	190	573	235	940	941	431	431	863	719	719	1439
191	191	383	236	708	709	433	1732	1733	727	2908	2909
192	384	769	237	237	1423	439	2195	4391	733	7330	7331
193	772	773	238	238	717	443	443	887	739	2956	2957
194	388	389	239	239	479	449	1796	3593	743	743	1487
195	390	869	240	240	1067	457	6855	13711	751	4506	4507
196	196	197	241	723	1447	461	461	2767	757	6056	12113
197	3546	3547	242	1210	1331	463	5556	5557	761	1522	1523
198	198	437	243	243	487	467	2802	2803	769	7690	7691
199	796	797	244	244	733	479	958	3833	773	2319	4639
200	200	401	245	490	491	487	1948	1949	787	4722	4723
201	201	1609	246	246	581	491	491	983	797	2391	4783
202	404	809	247	1482	1483	499	1996	1997	809	1618	1619
203	812	841	248	744	1489	503	3018	3019	811	4055	8111
204	204	409	249	249	1169	509	1018	1019	821	1642	6569
205	820	821	250	500	625	521	2084	16673	823	4115	8231

n	n_1	m	n	n_1	m	n	n_1	m	n	n_1	m
827	11578	11579	1097	7679	15359	1423	5692	5693	1693	1693	10159
829	8290	8291	1103	1103	2207	1427	8562	8563	1697	6788	13577
839	10068	10069	1109	4436	13309	1429	5716	5717	1699	6796	20389
853	3412	3413	1117	3351	6703	1433	4299	8599	1709	20508	20509
857	857	6857	1123	4492	4493	1439	1439	2879	1721	34420	34421
859	18898	18899	1129	4516	4517	1447	17364	34729	1723	1723	17231
863	5178	5179	1151	6906	6907	1451	1451	2903	1733	3466	3467
877	7016	14033	1153	12683	25367	1453	5812	5813	1741	19151	38303
881	15858	15859	1163	4652	37217	1459	1459	14591	1747	8735	17471
883	3532	3533	1171	7026	7027	1471	5884	23537	1753	7012	7013
887	1774	5323	1181	14172	14173	1481	2962	2963	1759	15831	31663
907	5442	5443	1187	4748	9497	1483	7415	14831	1777	7108	7109
911	911	1823	1193	3579	7159	1487	8922	8923	1783	21396	21397
919	3676	3677	1201	3603	7207	1489	14890	14891	1787	10722	10723
929	3716	7433	1213	14556	14557	1493	10451	20903	1789	17890	17891
937	2811	5623	1217	3651	29209	1499	1499	2999	1801	21612	21613
941	2823	5647	1223	1223	2447	1511	1511	3023	1811	1811	3623
947	5682	5683	1229	2458	2459	1523	3046	21323	1823	3646	10939
953	1906	1907	1231	9848	19697	1531	3062	9187	1831	10986	10987
967	7736	15473	1237	2474	19793	1543	6172	6173	1847	11082	11083
971	5826	5827	1249	12490	12491	1549	6196	6197	1861	18610	74441
977	1954	7817	1259	17626	17627	1553	4659	9319	1867	9335	18671
983	13762	13763	1277	25540	25541	1559	1559	3119	1871	1871	14969
991	8919	17839	1279	6395	12791	1567	6268	6269	1873	5619	11239
997	3988	3989	1283	2566	7699	1571	3142	12569	1877	1877	15017
1009	10090	10091	1289	2578	2579	1579	6316	6317	1879	7516	7517
1013	2026	2027	1291	6455	12911	1583	1583	3167	1889	3778	3779
1019	1019	2039	1297	5188	5189	1597	6388	6389	1901	3802	3803
1021	2042	10211	1301	26020	26021	1601	3202	3203	1907	11442	11443
1031	1031	2063	1303	10424	20849	1607	9642	9643	1913	13391	26783
1033	4132	4133	1307	2614	10457	1609	3218	16091	1931	1931	3863
1039	4156	4157	1319	3957	23743	1613	4839	9679	1933	23196	23197
1049	2098	2099	1321	1321	7927	1619	6476	12953	1949	35082	35083
1051	12612	12613	1327	5308	5309	1621	3242	29179	1951	42922	42923
1061	3183	6367	1361	1361	8167	1627	4881	29287	1973	3946	3947
1063	4252	4253	1367	1367	10937	1637	31103	62207	1979	39580	39581
1069	10690	10691	1373	16476	16477	1657	6628	26513	1987	7948	7949
1087	4348	4349	1381	1381	8287	1663	6652	6653	1993	1993	11959
1091	6546	6547	1399	12591	25183	1667	1667	13337	1997	87868	87869
1093	4372	4373	1409	2818	2819	1669	3338	16691	1999	9995	19991

References

1. ElGamal, T. (1985). *A public key cryptosystem and a signature scheme based on discrete logarithms.* IEEE Trans.Inform.Theory, **IT-31**, 469-472
2. Odlyzko, A.M. (1985). *Discrete logarithms in finite fields and their cryptographic significance.* Proc. of Eurocrypt'84, T.Beth, N.Cot, I.Ingemarsson (eds.), Springer LNCS 209, 224–314.

3. Agnew, G.B., Mullin, R.C., Onyszchuk, I.M., Vanstone, S.A. (1991). *An Implementation for a Fast Public Key Cryptosystem.* Journal of Cryptology, **3**, 63-79.
4. Bennet, C.H. (1982). *The thermodynamics of computation – a review.* International Journal of Theoretical Physics, 21, **12**, 905–940.
5. Beth, T., Gollmann, D. (1989). *Algorithm Engineering for Public Key Algorithms.* IEEE JSAC, **7**, 458–466.
6. Geiselmann, W., Gollmann, D. (1990). *VLSI design for exponentiation in $GF(2^n)$.* Proc. of Auscrypt'90, Seberry, J., Pieprzyk, J. (eds.), Springer LNCS 453, 398–405.
7. Haining, F.; *Simple multiplication algorithms for a class of $GF(2^n)$.* Electronics Letters, 28th March 1996; Vol 32, No 7, 636–637.
8. Hsu, I.S., Truong, T.K., Deutsch, L.J., Reed, I.S. (1988). *A Comparison of VLSI Architecture of Finite Field Multipliers Using Dual, Normal, or Standard Bases.* IEEE Trans. Comp., **C-37**, 735–739.
9. Kocher, P., Jaffe, J., Jun, B. (1999). *Differential Power Analysis.* Advances in Cryptology - CRYPTO'99, Wiener, M. (ed.). Springer, LNCS 1666, 388–397.
10. Koller, C.G., Athas, W.C., (1993). *Adiabatic Switching, Low Energy Computing, and the Physics of Storing and Erasing Information.* Proceedings of the Workshop on Physics and Computation, PhysCmp '92, IEEE Press.
11. Massey, J.L., Omura, J.K. (1981). *Computational method and apparatus for finite field arithmetic.* U.S. Patent application.
12. Merkle, R.C. (1993). *Reversible electronic logic using switches.* Nanotechnology, **4**, 21–40.
13. Mullin, R.C., Onyszchuk, I.M., Vanstone, S.A., Wilson, R.M. (1988) *Optimal Normal Bases in $GF(p^n)$.* Discrete Applied Mathematics, **22**, 149–161.
14. Berlekamp, E.R. (1982). *Bit-Serial Reed-Solomon Encoders.* IEEE Trans.Inf.Th., **IT-28**, 869–874.
15. Lidl, R., Niederreiter, H. (1986). *Introduction to Finite Fields and Their Applications.* Cambridge University Press.
16. MacWilliams, F.J., Sloane, N.J.A. (1977). *The Theory of Error-Correcting Codes.* North Holland.

Compact Encoding of Non-adjacent Forms with Applications to Elliptic Curve Cryptography*

Marc Joye[1] and Christophe Tymen[2]

[1] Gemplus Card International
Parc d'Activités de Gémenos, B.P. 100, 13881 Gémenos, France
marc.joye@gemplus.com
[2] Gemplus Card International
34 rue Guynemer, 92447 Issy-les-Moulineaux, France
christophe.tymen@gemplus.com

Abstract. Techniques for fast exponentiation (multiplication) in various groups have been extensively studied for use in cryptographic primitives. Specifically, the coding of the exponent (multiplier) plays an important role in the performances of the algorithms used. The crucial optimization relies in general on minimizing the Hamming weight of the exponent (multiplier). This can be performed optimally with non-adjacent representations. This paper introduces a compact encoding of non-adjacent representations that allows to skip the exponent recoding step. Furthermore, a straightforward technique for picking random numbers that already satisfy the non-adjacence property is proposed. Several examples of application are given, in particular in the context of scalar multiplication on elliptic curves.

Keywords. Public-key cryptography, non-adjacent forms, elliptic curves, smart-cards.

1 Introduction

Most public-key cryptographic primitives rely on group exponentiations (or multiplications for additively written groups). We refer the reader to [3] for an excellent survey on exponentiation techniques. Many implementations are based on the square-and-multiply methods or one of their numerous improvements, for computing g^x. One of these uses Reitwiesner's recoding algorithm [11], which requires the knowledge of g^{-1}. This supposes that the value of g^{-1} is already available (i.e., precomputed) or easily computable, as is the case for elliptic curves [8].

Reitwiesner's algorithm expresses exponent x with the set of digits $\{-1, 0, 1\}$. Because of the sign "$-$", each digit is usually encoded with two bits and so, *twice* the size of the usual binary representation of x is needed to store its Reitwiesner's representation. That's why it is suggested to compute it "on the fly" when needed [4]. In this paper, we exploit the non-adjacency property of

---

* Some techniques presented in this paper are patent pending.

K. Kim (Ed.): PKC 2001, LNCS 1992, pp. 353–364, 2001.

Reitwiesner's representation to encode the exponent with the *same* efficiency (up to 1 bit) as the binary representation.

Moreover, we present a straightforward method to pick a r-bit random number so that it already satisfies the non-adjacency property. In this case too, NAF-recoding is thus useless. We prove that the numbers we generate in this way are *exactly* the elements of $\{0,1\}^r$; there is therefore no loss of security for cryptographic applications. We then extend our method to τ-NAF recoding for use on Koblitz curves and conjecture, based on numerical evidences, that the numbers we generate are *almost perfectly* distributed in the set $\{0,1\}^r$.

The rest of this paper is organized as follows. In Section 2, we briefly review elliptic curves and Koblitz curves. Section 3 presents our new encoding method. In Section 4, we explain how to pick a random number satisfying the non-adjacency property. Section 5 highlights the benefits of our techniques in a Diffie-Hellman key exchange and for El Gamal encryption on a smart-card implementation. Finally, we conclude in Section 6.

2   Elliptic Curves

Up to a birational equivalence, an *elliptic curve* over a field $\mathbb{K}$ is a plane nonsingular cubic curve with a $\mathbb{K}$-rational point [12, Chapter III]. Elliptic curves are often expressed in terms of Weierstraß equations:

$$E/\mathbb{K} : y^2 + a_1 xy + a_3 y = x^3 + a_2 x^2 + a_4 x + a_6 \tag{1}$$

where $a_1, \ldots, a_6 \in \mathbb{K}$. In characteristic $\mathrm{Char}(\mathbb{K}) \neq 2, 3$, the equation may be simplified to $y^2 = x^3 + a_4 x + a_6$, and in characteristic $\mathrm{Char}(\mathbb{K}) = 2$ the equation (for a non-supersingular curve) may be simplified to $y^2 + xy = x^3 + a_2 x^2 + a_6$.

2.1   Scalar Multiplication

Together with an extra point $\mathcal{O}$, the points on an elliptic curve form an Abelian group. We use the additive notation. The computation of

$$[k]P := \underbrace{P + P + \cdots + P}_{k \text{ times}}$$

is usually carried out through the binary method. However, noting that if $P = (p_x, p_y)$ its inverse is given by $-P = (p_x, -p_y - a_1 p_x - a_3)$, we see that the computation of an inverse is virtually free. So we can use a binary *signed-digit* representation for k, i.e., $(\ldots, k_2, k_1, k_0)$ with $k_i \in \{0, 1, -1\}$. This speeds up the scalar multiplication by a factor of 11.11% compared to the binary method [8] (see also §3.1), on average.

2.2   Frobenius Expansions

In [6], Koblitz suggested the use of so-called *anomalous binary curves*. These are elliptic curves over $GF(2^n)$ given by

$$E_n : y^2 + xy = x^3 + x^2 + 1 \quad \text{or} \quad \tilde{E}_n : y^2 + xy = x^3 + x^2 + 1 \; . \tag{2}$$

The Frobenius map, $\varphi : (x, y) \mapsto \varphi(x, y) = (x^2, y^2)$, satisfies the characteristic equation $T^2 - T + 2 = 0$ for E_n, and $T^2 + T + 2 = 0$ for $\tilde{E}_n$. It corresponds to multiplication by $\tau = (1 + \sqrt{-7})/2$ on E_n, and by $-\bar{\tau} = (-1 + \sqrt{-7})/2$ on $\tilde{E}_n$.

Since multiplication by τ is cheap (i.e., $[\tau](x, y) = (x^2, y^2)$), it is advantageous to write k in τ-adic expansion (i.e., $k = \sum k_i \tau^i$) when computing $[k](x, y)$ on E_n. Note also that since $\tau^n = 1$, we can first reduce k modulo $(\tau^n - 1)$ [7]. The advantage resides in that the norm of k, as an element of the Euclidean domain $\mathbb{Z}[\tau]$, is $k^2 = O(2^{2n})$ and the norm of $k \bmod (\tau^n - 1)$ is smaller than $\mathrm{Norm}(\tau^n - 1) = \#E_n = O(2^n)$ by Hasse Theorem [12, Theorem 1.1, Chapter V]. Consequently, k reduced modulo $(\tau^n - 1)$ has a τ-NAF representation of length almost equal to the length of its binary representation.

3   How to Represent the Multiplier?

3.1   Non-adjacent Forms

A *b-non-adjacent form* (or *b*-NAF in short) of length n for an element x in a ring $\mathbb{A}$ is a sequence of digits $(d_{n-1} \cdots d_0)$ such that

$$x = \sum_{i=0}^{n-1} d_i \, b^i \tag{3}$$

and

$$d_i \cdot d_{i+1} = 0, \quad \forall i \; . \tag{4}$$

Equation (4) captures the property of non-adjacency. In the sequel, a *b*-NAF representation for x will be denoted by $\mathrm{NAF}_b(x)$. Moreover, the integer associated to a *b*-NAF, say d, will be denoted by $\vartheta(d)$; i.e., if $d = (d_{n-1} \cdots d_0)$ then $\vartheta(d) := \sum_{i=0}^{n-1} d_i b^i$.

Reitwiesner [11] proved that each integer has exactly one 2-NAF representation. More importantly, he proved that the 2-NAF minimizes the Hamming weight amongst all the binary signed-digit representations. NAFs are thus particularly suitable for fast exponentiations [3]. See also [8,13] for applications to elliptic curves. Another representation minimizing the Hamming weight is described in [5].

3.2   New Compact Encoding

An r-bit integer has a 2-NAF representation of $(r + 1)$ digits in $\{0, 1, -1\}$ [11] and hence needs $2(r + 1)$ bits to be encoded, that is, *twice* more than the binary representation. However, we can exploit the non-adjacency property (Eq. (4)), that is, a '1' or a '−1' is always followed by a '0'. We therefore suggest the following simple right-to-left encoding:[1]

$$\mathcal{R} : \begin{cases} 01 \mapsto 01 \\ 0\bar{1} \mapsto 11 \\ 0 \mapsto 0 \end{cases}, \qquad \mathcal{R}^{-1} : \begin{cases} 01 \mapsto 01 \\ 11 \mapsto 0\bar{1} \\ 0 \mapsto 0 \end{cases}. \tag{5}$$

With conversion $\mathcal{R}$, a 2-NAF representation requires only one bit more than the binary representation to be encoded. For example, by right-to-left applying $\mathcal{R}$, $\mathrm{NAF}_2(29) = (100\bar{1}01)$ is encoded into 101101:

$$(1\,0\,0\,\bar{1}\,01) \mapsto (1\,0\,11\,01)$$

Moreover, the inverse right-to-left transformation, $\mathcal{R}^{-1}$, unambiguously gives back the NAF representation.

It is also possible to design a left-to-right encoding. The previous encoding implicitly assumes that the NAF begins with a '0'. For the left-to-right transformation, we add an artificial ending '0', e.g., $\mathrm{NAF}_2(29) = (100\bar{1}01.0)$. Then we left-to-right apply transformation

$$\begin{cases} 10 \leftrightarrow 10 \\ \bar{1}0 \leftrightarrow 11 \\ 0 \leftrightarrow 0 \end{cases}. \tag{6}$$

(Note that if the last obtained digit is '0', we may discard it.) Again with our example, $\mathrm{NAF}_2(29)$ is left-to-right encoded into 100111:

$$(10\,0\,\bar{1}0\,1.0) \mapsto (10\,0\,11\,1.0)$$

and the inverse transformation gives back the NAF representation.

3.3   Frobenius Expansions

On a Koblitz curve E_n (see Eq. (2)), it can be shown ([3, Theorems 5 and 6]) that every (rational) integer $0 \le k < \#E_n$ has a (non-unique) τ-NAF representation

$$k \equiv \sum_{i=0}^{n+1} k_i\,\tau^i \pmod{(\tau^n - 1)}, \quad k_i \in \{0, 1, -1\}, \tag{7}$$

and that this NAF representation has $1/3$ of nonzero digits, on average. The same also holds for the twisted curve $\tilde{E}_n$.

Consequently, the proposed encodings (5) and (6) can be used to efficiently store k (or more exactly $k \bmod (\tau^n - 1)$) in the computation of $[k](x, y)$ on an anomalous binary curve, as well.

---

[1] For convenience, we write $\bar{1}$ for -1.

4 How to Pick a Random Number?

4.1 Generating a Random Integer

Cryptographic applications frequently require random numbers of a given length. We show here how to obtain an r-bit random number already in the non-adjacent form. Our technique is based on transformation $\mathcal{R}^{-1}$ (cf. Eq. (5)).

First, pick a random number k in $\{0,1\}^r$. Next, right-to-left apply $\mathcal{R}^{-1}$ to the binary representation of k. If the most significant digit of the resulting representation is $\bar{1}$, pad the representation with '0' until position $(r-1)$ and add a '1' in position r. The representation resulting from the whole transformation is referred to as the $\mathcal{R}^*$-representation.

Here is an example to illustrate the technique. Let $r = 3$. So the set of 3-bit numbers, their 2-NAF representations and their $\mathcal{R}^*$-representations are respectively given by

k	$\mathrm{NAF}_2(k)$	$\mathcal{R}^*(k)$
0	(0)	(0)
1	(1)	(1)
2	(10)	(10)
3	$(10\bar{1})$	$(100\bar{1})$
4	(100)	(100)
5	(101)	(101)
6	$(10\bar{1}0)$	$(10\bar{1}0)$
7	$(100\bar{1})$	$(10\bar{1})$

From this example, we see that:

Theorem 1. *Transformation $\mathcal{R}^*$ induces a permutation on the set $\{\mathrm{NAF}_2(k) \mid k \in \{0,1\}^r\}$.*

Proof. By construction, transformation $\mathcal{R}^{-1}$ uniquely maps the representation of a r-bit number k to a binary signed-digit representation. When the leading digit is $\bar{1}$, a '1' is added in position r; the corresponding representations are the only ones having exactly $(r+1)$ digits. Therefore, each r-bit binary representation is transformed by $\mathcal{R}^*$ into a different $(r+1)$-digit representation. Noting that all these $\mathcal{R}^*$-representations verify the NAF property (Eq. (4)), are all different, and represent numbers smaller than 2^r , the theorem follows. □

4.2 Generating a Random Multiplier on a Koblitz Curve

Solinas proposed in [13] an algorithm to compute a τ-NAF of length less than $n + 2$ for a multiplier on a Koblitz curve (cf. Eq. (7)). This algorithm involves two steps: an Euclidean division in the ring $\mathbb{Z}[\tau]$ and the computation of the τ-NAF itself. The idea here is simply to generate directly a random NAF of the required length using transformation (5), and then to use the associated integer as a multiplier.

Let P be a base-point on a Koblitz curve E_n. For some primes n, one has $\#E_n = 2 \cdot \text{prime}$ (or $\#\tilde{E}_n = 4 \cdot \text{prime}$) [6]. So w.l.o.g. we suppose that P has prime order p and that $p \geq 2^{n-2}$.

Now, in order to randomly generate a multiplier for P we proceed as follows. We pick a random x in $\{0,1\}^{n+3}$. Next, using transformation $\mathcal{R}^{-1}$ we set $g := \vartheta(\mathcal{R}^{-1}(x))$ and use it as a random multiplier when computing $[g]P$ on E_n. (Note here that the length of x is chosen to be $n+3$ since the leading digit of $\mathcal{R}^{-1}(x)$ is always 0.) The arising question is to determine the distribution of g in $[0,p)$. First, it is clear that $\mathcal{R}^{-1}$ generates all the NAF representations of length smaller than or equal to $n+2$. Hence, from the discussion in §3.3, $\vartheta(\mathcal{R}^{-1}(x))$ reaches all the elements in $\{0, \ldots, p-1\}$; or equivalently

$$\{0, \ldots, p-1\} \subseteq \left\{ g = \vartheta(\mathcal{R}^{-1}(x)) \mid x \in \{0,1\}^{n+3} \right\} .$$

To estimate the quality of g, we bound the statistical difference of $\vartheta(\mathcal{R}^{-1}(x))$ where x is considered as a random variable uniformly distributed in $\{0,1\}^{n+3}$. The following argument does not conclude but gives evidences to conjecture that the distribution g is close to the uniform one.

The statistical difference of g is defined as

$$\delta(g) := \frac{1}{2} \sum_{i=0}^{p-1} \left| \Pr(g = i) - \frac{1}{p} \right| . \tag{8}$$

The next lemmas respectively give a bound on the statistical difference in term of exponential sums and a formula to approximate it numerically. Their proofs are given in appendix. In the sequel, we let $\Im$ denote the usual complex number verifying $\Im^2 = -1$, whereas i is merely used as an index.

Lemma 1. *Let p be a prime and let X be a random variable in $[0, \ldots, p-1]$. Then,*

$$\delta(X) \leq \frac{1}{2} \sqrt{\sum_{i=1}^{p-1} |E[\chi(iX)]|^2}$$

where $\chi(x) = e^{\frac{2\Im\pi x}{p}}$.

Lemma 2. $E[\chi(ig)]$ *is equal to a_0, where $(a_0, \ldots, a_{n+2})$ is the sequence recursively defined by*

$$a_j = \frac{1}{2} \left[a_{j+1} + \cos(2i\pi\tau^j/p) \, a_{j+2} \right] \quad \forall 0 \leq j \leq n , \tag{9}$$

with $a_{n+1} = \frac{1}{2}[\cos(2i\pi\tau/p) + 1]$ *and* $a_{n+2} = 1$.

Letting $f(i) = E[\chi(ig)]$, Lemmas 1 and 2 imply that

$$\delta(g) \leq B := \sqrt{\sum_{i=1}^{p-1} f(i)^2} . \tag{10}$$

The numerical computation of this sum becomes untractable for large values of p. Nevertheless, considering numerical experiments, we conjecture an estimated bound for $\delta(g)$.

Theorem 2 (Conjectured). *On a Koblitz curve E_n, for $n \geq 100$, we have*

$$\delta(g) \leq 2^{-n/5} .$$

Table 1 summarizes different values of $B_{\text{samp}} := \frac{p-1}{N_{\text{samp}}} \sqrt{\sum_{j=1}^{N_{\text{samp}}} f(i_j)}$ for random points i_j. The values are obtained using various n and p corresponding to Koblitz curves. The list of the primes used is given in appendix. We took $N_{\text{samp}} = 10000$. Of course, N_{samp} is completely negligible compared to p, and these experiments do not prove anything about the exact value of the bound. Nevertheless, we remark that $B_{\text{samp}} \leq 2^{-n/\alpha_n}$ where α_n seems to decrease as n grows. This fact indicates that our conjecture seems reasonable.

Table 1. Estimated bounds for $\delta(g)$.

n	$\lfloor \log_2 B_{\text{samp}} \rfloor$	α_n
109	-23	4.7
113	-27	4.2
131	-39	3.6
163	-40	4.1
233	-75	3.1
239	-80	3.0
277	-93	3.0
283	-87	3.3
359	-120	3.0
409	-158	2.6
571	-196	3.0

5 Applications

This section gives a non-exhaustive list of practical applications of the new encodings (Eqs (5) and (6)), namely the Diffie-Hellman key exchange and the El Gamal encryption. Finally, we discuss the implications for a smart-card implementation.

5.1 Diffie-Hellman Key Exchange

Let E be an elliptic curve over $\mathbb{F}_q$ and let G be a base-point on E. To exchange a key, Alice and Bob choose a random number x_A and x_B, respectively. Alice computes $Y_A = [x_A]G$ and sends it Bob. Likewise, Bob computes $Y_B = [x_B]G$

and sends it to Alice. Their common key is $K_{AB} = [x_A \cdot x_B]G$. Alice computes it as $[x_A]Y_B$ and Bob as $[x_B]Y_A$.

The advantage of using the proposed encodings is that randoms x_A and x_B can be seen as NAF representations and so the computations are speeded up since subtraction has the same cost as an addition over an elliptic curve. Moreover, if uniformity is desired, Section 4 shows that the proposed encodings can easily be adapted to meet this additional requirement (under a reasonable conjecture for Koblitz curves).

5.2   El Gamal Encryption

Again, let E be an elliptic curve over $\mathbb{F}_q$ and let G be a point on E. The private key of Alice is x_A and her public key is $Y_A = [x_A]G$. To encrypt a message m for Alice, Bob first represents m as a point $M \in E$. Next, for a randomly chosen k, he computes $C_1 = [k]G$ and $C_2 = [k]Y_A + M$. The ciphertext is the pair $\{C_1, C_2\}$. To decrypt $\{C_1, C_2\}$, using her private key, Alice recovers $M = C_2 - [x_A]C_1$ and so message m.

Here too, the proposed encodings are advantageous since the NAFs do not have to be computed. When computing multiples of points on E, Alice and Bob just consider the binary expansion of the scalar multiplier as a representation given by encoding (5) or (6). Note that since the mappings are 1-to-1, there is no loss of security; moreover as before, if desired, uniformity can be achieved.

5.3   Smart-Card Implementation

The proposed methods are particularly suitable for smart-cards. A direct generation of the multiplier avoids the precomputations proposed in [13]. Furthermore, the RAM space needed for the scalar multiplication is smaller, because the multiplier can be generated on the fly, and does not need to be stored beforehand. Besides, the code space required for the routines that precompute the NAF is quite large. Consequently, the proposed encodings enable to save a non-negligible amount of space in ROM or EEPROM.

6   Conclusion

We proposed a new method to encode in a compact way the non-adjacent form of an integer. We gave several applications of this encoding, including the generation of a random multiplier in the context of elliptic curves. For Koblitz curves, we gave an argument to conjecture a bound on the distribution of this generator. Finally, we exposed practical examples of this encoding for some widely used cryptographic schemes.

References

1. W. Diffie and M. E. Hellman, "New directions in cryptography," *IEEE Trans. on Information Theory*, vol. 22, pp. 644–654, 1976.

2. T. El Gamal, "A public key cryptosystem and a signature scheme based on discrete logarithms," *IEEE Trans. on Information Theory*, vol. 31, pp. 469–472, 1985.

3. D. M. Gordon, "A survey of fast exponentiation methods," *J. Algorithms*, vol. 27, pp. 129–146, 1998.

4. IEEE Std P1363-2000, *IEEE Standard Specifications for Public-Key Cryptography*, IEEE Computer Society, August 20, 2000.

5. M. Joye and S.-M. Yen, "Optimal left-to-right binary signed-digit recoding," *IEEE Trans. Computers*, vol. 49, pp. 740–748, 2000.

6. N. Koblitz, "CM-curves with good cryptographic properties," *Advances in Cryptology – CRYPTO '91*, LNCS 576, pp. 279–287, Springer-Verlag, 1992.

7. W. Meier and O. Staffelbach, "Efficient multiplication on certain non-supersingular elliptic curves," *Advances in Cryptology – CRYPTO '92*, LNCS 740, pp. 333–344, Springer-Verlag, 1993.

8. F. Morain and J. Olivos, "Speeding up the computations on an elliptic curve using addition-subtraction chains," *Theoretical Informatics and Applications*, vol. 24, pp. 531–543, 1990.

9. P. Nguyen and J. Stern, "The hardness of the hidden subset sum problem and its cryptographic implications," *Advances in Cryptology – CRYPTO '99*, LNCS 1666, pp. 31–46, Springer-Verlag, 1999.

10. A. Pinkus and S. Zafrany, *Fourier Series and Integral Transforms*, Cambridge University Press, 1997.

11. G. W. Reitwiesner, "Binary arithmetic," *Advances in Computers*, vol. 1, pp. 231–308, 1960.

12. J. H. Silverman, *The Arithmetic of Elliptic Curves*, GTM 106, Springer-Verlag, 1986.

13. J. A. Solinas, "An improved algorithm for arithmetic on a family of elliptic curves," *Advances in Cryptology – CRYPTO '97*, LNCS 1294, pp. 357–371, Springer-Verlag, 1997.

14. J. H. van Lint, *Introduction to Coding Theory*, GTM 86, Springer-Verlag, 3rd edition, 1999.

A   Proof of Lemmas 1 and 2

Similarly to [9], we make use of the Fourier transform in our proofs. We first recall some basic notions (see [10, Chapter 1]).

Let p be a natural number. For each $m = 0, \ldots, p - 1$, we define a vector in $\mathbb{C}^p$ by

$$\boldsymbol{u_m} = \left(1, e^{\frac{2\pi \Im m}{p}}, e^{\frac{4\pi \Im m}{p}}, \ldots, e^{\frac{2(p-1)\pi \Im m}{p}}\right) .$$

We also define $\boldsymbol{e_m} = \frac{\boldsymbol{u_m}}{\|\boldsymbol{u_m}\|} = \frac{\boldsymbol{u_m}}{\sqrt{p}}$. The system of vectors $\{\boldsymbol{e_m}\}_{m=0}^{p-1}$ is an orthonormal system in $\mathbb{C}^p$ with the standard inner product.[2] So, for every vector $\boldsymbol{v} \in \mathbb{C}^p$, we can write

$$\boldsymbol{v} = \sum_{m=0}^{p-1} \langle \boldsymbol{v}, \boldsymbol{e_m} \rangle \boldsymbol{e_m} .$$

---

[2] That is, $\langle (a_0, \ldots, a_{p-1}), (b_0, \ldots, b_{p-1}) \rangle = \sum_{j=0}^{p-1} a_j \overline{b_j}$.

For $m = 0, \ldots, p - 1$, the coefficients $FT(\boldsymbol{v})_m := \langle \boldsymbol{v}, \boldsymbol{e_m} \rangle$ are called the *Fourier coefficients of $\boldsymbol{v}$*. The sequence $FT(\boldsymbol{v}) = \{FT(\boldsymbol{v})_m\}_{m=0}^{p-1}$ is called the *transform Fourier of $\boldsymbol{v}$*.

Lemma 1. *Let p be a prime and let X be a random variable in $[0, \ldots, p - 1]$. Then,*

$$\delta(X) \leq \frac{1}{2} \sqrt{\sum_{i=1}^{p-1} |E[\chi(iX)]|^2}$$

where $\chi(x) = e^{\frac{2\Im \pi x}{p}}$.

Proof. We let $\boldsymbol{a} = (a_i)_{1 \leq i \leq p-1}$ and $\boldsymbol{u} = (u_i)_{1 \leq i \leq p-1}$ denote the sequences defined by $a_i = \Pr(X = i)$ and $u_i = \frac{1}{p}$, respectively. The Cauchy-Schwarz inequality yields

$$\sum_{i=0}^{p-1} |(\boldsymbol{a} - \boldsymbol{u})_i (\boldsymbol{u})_i| \leq \sqrt{\sum_{i=0}^{p-1} |(\boldsymbol{a} - \boldsymbol{u})_i|^2} \sqrt{\sum_{i=0}^{p-1} |(\boldsymbol{u})_i|^2}$$

$$\iff \delta(X) \leq \frac{\sqrt{p}}{2} \sqrt{\sum_{i=0}^{p-1} |(\boldsymbol{a} - \boldsymbol{u})_i|^2} = \sqrt{\sum_{i=0}^{p-1} |FT(\boldsymbol{a} - \boldsymbol{u})_i|^2},$$

by noting that the Fourier transform is an isometry when p is prime.

Furthermore, since $FT(\boldsymbol{a})_0 = \frac{1}{\sqrt{p}}$, $FT(\mathbf{a})_i = \frac{1}{\sqrt{p}} \sum_{j=0}^{p-1} \Pr(X = j)\chi(ij) = \frac{1}{\sqrt{p}} E[\chi(iX)]$, and $FT(\boldsymbol{u}) = (\frac{1}{\sqrt{p}}, 0, \ldots, 0)$, we finally obtain

$$\delta(X) \leq \frac{\sqrt{p}}{2} \sqrt{\sum_{i=1}^{p-1} |FT(\mathbf{a})_i|^2} = \frac{1}{2} \sqrt{\sum_{i=1}^{p-1} |E[\chi(iX)]|^2},$$

as required. $\qquad\square$

Lemma 2. *$E[\chi(ig)]$ is equal to a_0, where $(a_0, \ldots, a_{n+2})$ is the sequence recursively defined by*

$$a_j = \frac{1}{2}[a_{j+1} + \cos(2i\pi\tau^j/p)\, a_{j+2}] \quad \forall 0 \leq j \leq n,$$

with $a_{n+1} = \frac{1}{2}[\cos(2i\pi\tau/p) + 1]$ and $a_{n+2} = 1$.

Proof. Recall that g is obtained from x by right-to-left applying $\mathcal{R}^{-1}$ to $x = (x_{n+2} \cdots x_0)$, that is, by right-to-left applying the rules

$$\begin{cases} 01 \mapsto 01 \\ 11 \mapsto 0\bar{1} \\ 0 \mapsto 0 \end{cases}.$$

If we denote by $y = (d_{n+1} \cdots d_0)$ the result of this transformation, the independence of the x_i's implies that for $j > 0$

$$\begin{cases} \Pr(d_j = 0 | d_{j-1} = 0) = \Pr(x_j = 0) = 1/2 \\ \Pr(d_j = 1 | d_{j-1} = 0) = \Pr(x_j = 1; x_{j+1} = 0) = 1/4 \\ \Pr(d_j = \bar{1} | d_{j-1} = 0) = \Pr(x_j = 1; x_{j+1} = 1) = 1/4 \\ \Pr(d_j = 0 | d_{j-1} \neq 0) = 1 \end{cases},$$

and

$$\begin{cases} \Pr(d_0 = 0) = \Pr(x_0 = 0) = 1/2 \\ \Pr(d_0 = 1) = \Pr(x_0 = 1; x_1 = 0) = 1/4 \\ \Pr(d_0 = \bar{1}) = \Pr(x_0 = 1; x_1 = 1) = 1/4 \end{cases}.$$

In particular, the sequence of digits d_i forms a Markov chain. Now, for $d \in \{-1, 0, 1\}$ and $1 \leq j \leq n+1$, we define

$$x_{j,d} = E\left[\chi\left(i \sum_{l=j}^{n+1} d_l \tau^l\right) \mid d_{j-1} = d\right].$$

By convention, we also define $x_{n+2,0} = 1$ and $x_{0,0} = E[\chi(ig)]$. Using Bayes's formula and the definition of a Markov chain, we have

$$x_{j,0} = \sum_{d' \in \{\bar{1},0,1\}} \Pr(d_j = d' | d_{j-1} = 0) \chi(i \tau^j d') E\left[\chi\left(i \sum_{l=j+1}^{n+1} d_l \tau^l\right) \mid d_{j-1} = 0; d_j = d'\right]$$

$$= \sum_{d' \in \{\bar{1},0,1\}} \Pr(d_j = d' | d_{j-1} = 0) \chi(i \tau^j d') x_{j+1,d'}$$

$$= \frac{1}{4}\left(x_{j+1,\bar{1}} \chi(-i \tau^j) + 2x_{j+1,0} + x_{j+1,1}\chi(i \tau^j)\right).$$

Furthermore, $x_{j,1} = x_{j,\bar{1}} = x_{j+1,0}$ if $j \leq n$, and $x_{n+1,1} = x_{n+1,\bar{1}} = 1 = x_{n+2,0}$ because of the non-adjacency property. Therefore, for $0 < j \leq n$,

$$x_{j,0} = \frac{1}{2}\left(x_{j+2,0} \cos(2i\pi\tau^j/p) + x_{j+1,0}\right). \tag{11}$$

Bayes's formula applied to $\chi(ig)$ yields

$$E[\chi(ig)] = \Pr(d_0 = \bar{1})\chi(-i)x_{1,\bar{1}} + \Pr(d_0 = 0)x_{1,0} + \Pr(d_0 = 1)\chi(i)x_{1,1}.$$

Consequently, as $x_{1,1} = x_{1,\bar{1}} = x_{2,0}$, the recursion formula (11) holds for all $0 \leq j \leq n$. It remains to compute $x_{n+1,0} = E[\chi(i \, d_{n+1}\tau^{n+1})|d_n = 0]$. By definition of partial expectation, this is equal to

$$x_{n+1,0} = \Pr(d_{n+1} = \bar{1}|d_n = 0) \chi(-i\tau^{n+1}) + \Pr(d_{n+1} = 0|d_n = 0) + \\ \Pr(d_{n+1} = 1|d_n = 0) \chi(i\tau^{n+1})$$

$$= \frac{1}{2}[\cos(2i\pi\tau/p) + 1],$$

as $\tau^{n+1} \equiv \tau \pmod{p}$. Thus, setting $a_j = x_{j,0}$ for all $0 \leq j \leq n+2$ concludes the proof. $\qquad\square$

B Values of p and τ Used in Table 1

n	p, τ
109	$p = 324518553658426701487448656461467$
	$\tau = 138423345589698157369693034392981$
113	$p = 5192296858534827627896703833467507$
	$\tau = 3126605487954413221319732774018522$
131	$p = 680564733841876926932320129493409985129$
	$\tau = 196511074115861092422032515080945363956$
233	$p = 3450873173395281893717377931138512760570940988862252126328087024741343$
	$\tau = 2598851043790259083579160746211533789223151387669521214510026908255781$
239	$p = 220855883097298041197912187592864814948216561321709848887480219215362213$
	$\tau = 112828630731959940948877831557777689652816470033386308605701621931818 52$
277	$p = 60708402882054033466233184588234965832575110498786508764884175561891 6221 \backslash$
	$\qquad 65064650683$
	$\tau = 353992045507433384574068525952839139632658201745749716048780945143046006 \backslash$
	$\qquad 18244376699$
283	$p = 388533778445145814183892381364703781328481173379306132429587499752981582 \backslash$
	$\qquad 9704422603873$
	$\tau = 162253735759432174230582978486606377514699833490883648184574795706225844 \backslash$
	$\qquad 1461142295062$
359	$p = 587135645693458306972370149197334256843920637227079966811081824609485917 \backslash$
	$\qquad 2441244948823651724787481656489986 63$
	$\tau = 162253735759432174230582978486606377514699833490883648184574795706225844 \backslash$
	$\qquad 1461142295062$
359	$p = 587135645693458306972370149197334256843920637227079966811081824609485917 \backslash$
	$\qquad 2441244948823651724787481656489986 63$
	$\tau = 180233645531928689293637781182435953315044566263288800836105166268336446 \backslash$
	$\qquad 405029570298350415645598109280911691$
409	$p = 330527984395124299475957654016385519914202341482140609642324395022880711 \backslash$
	$\qquad 289249191050673258457777458014096366590617731358671$
	$\tau = 953774549173500098520882611070108682320029172836475855985603040002899322 \backslash$
	$\qquad 913171795482260879911514950355696416282468418 74340$
571	$p = 193226876150862917234767594546599367214946366485321749932861762572575957 \backslash$
	$\qquad 114478021226813397852270671183470671280082535146127367497406661731192 9 \backslash$
	$\qquad 68242161709250355573368 5276673$
	$\tau = 173761715345266710045062065436101013657569621494943574842405832235085200 \backslash$
	$\qquad 340670770727839066098031150677230979331850875126277848269385615419123 7 \backslash$
	$\qquad 9125948894463071467320 63445937$

Efficient Implementation of Elliptic Curve Cryptosystems on the TI MSP430x33x Family of Microcontrollers

Jorge Guajardo[1]*, Rainer Blümel[2], Uwe Krieger[2], and Christof Paar[1]

[1] ECE Department, Worcester Polytechnic Institute, Worcester, MA 01609, USA
{guajardo,christof}@ece.wpi.edu
[2] cv cryptovision gmbh, Munscheidstr. 14, 45886 Gelsenkirchen, Germany
{Rainer.Bluemel,Uwe.Krieger}@cryptovision.com

Abstract. This contribution describes a methodology used to efficiently implement elliptic curves (EC) over $GF(p)$ on the 16-bit TI MSP430x33x family of low-cost microcontrollers. We show that it is possible to implement EC cryptosystems in highly constrained embedded systems and still obtain acceptable performance at low cost. We modified the EC point addition and doubling formulae to reduce the number of intermediate variables while at the same time allowing for flexibility. We used a Generalized-Mersenne prime to implement the arithmetic in the underlying field. We take advantage of the special form of the moduli to minimize the number of precomputations needed to implement inversion via Fermat's Little theorem and the k-ary method of exponentiation. We apply these ideas to an implementation of an elliptic curve system over $GF(p)$, where $p = 2^{128} - 2^{97} - 1$. We show that a scalar point multiplication can be achieved in 3.4 seconds without any stored/precomputed values and the processor clocked at 1 MHz.

1 Introduction

It is widely recognized that data security will play a central role in the design of future IT systems. Until a few years ago, the PC had been the major driver of the digital economy. PCs have processors with large RAM memories and fast CPUs that make most cryptographic algorithms practical from a user's satisfaction point of view. Recently, however, there has been a shift towards IT applications realized as embedded systems. In fact, 98% of all microprocessors sold today are embedded in household appliances, vehicles, and machines on factory floors [12,6]. Not only are embedded devices already ubiquitous in our lives, but it is predicted that in the very near future, we will be able to add to these devices two simple technologies: reliable wireless communication and sensing and actuation functions [6]. On the other hand, these new applications represent many challenges among which security and privacy will play an important role [6].

---

* Part of this work was performed while the author was at cv cryptovision gmbh.

K. Kim (Ed.): PKC 2001, LNCS 1992, pp. 365–382, 2001.
© Springer-Verlag Berlin Heidelberg 2001

Embedded devices are very different from PCs from the computational resources and memory availability point of view. Generally, embedded computers possess CPUs with very slow clock rates and a relatively small pool of memory. In addition, embedded systems are usually designed to consume small amounts of energy. Despite these constraints, we want to be able to run the same (or similar) types of applications that we run today in a fast computer. These applications often need to talk to each other and transmit information over wireless channels which are insecure by nature. Thus, cryptographic algorithms, which are computationally intensive by design, are imperative for embedded applications. In particular, it is important to show that it is feasible to implement cryptographic algorithms in constrained environments and, at the same time, be able to obtain acceptable levels of performance.

Our contribution deals with the implementation of Elliptic Curve (EC) cryptosystems [25,20] on the TI MSP430x33x family of devices. These 16-bit microcontrollers are one example of embedded device used for extremely low-power and low-cost applications, running at a maximum frequency of 3.8 MHz. Elliptic curves, on the other hand, are a particularly attractive option because of their relatively short operand length as compared to RSA and systems based on the discrete logarithm (DL) in finite fields.

The remaining of this contribution is organized as follows. Section 2 gives a survey of previous implementations of public-key algorithms on embedded processors. Section 3 describes the choice of parameters used in our EC implementation and a modification to the point addition and doubling algorithms which allow for a reduction in the memory requirements. The architecture of the TI MSP430x33x family of devices is covered in Section 4. In Section 5, we modify the k-ary algorithm to take advantage of the special form of the moduli and compute the inverse of an element in $GF(p)$ via Fermat's Little theorem. We also describe ways to tailor multiplication, squaring, and modular reduction algorithms to the architecture of the processor, thus, making the algorithms more efficient. Finally, Sections 6 and 7 summarize our implementation results and provide recommendations for possible enhancements.

2   Previous Work

Most of the cryptographic research conducted to date has been independent of hardware platforms, and little research has focused on algorithm optimization for specific processors. In the following, we will review previous implementations of public-key algorithms on embedded processors.

In [5], the Barret modular reduction method is introduced. The author implemented RSA on the TI TMS32010 DSP. A 512-bit RSA exponentiation took on the average 2.6 seconds running at the DSP's maximum speed of 20 MHz. Reference [11] describes the implementation of a cryptographic library designed for the Motorola DSP56000 which was clocked at 20 MHz. The authors focused on the integration of modular reduction and multi-precision multiplication according to Montgomery's method [26,7]. This RSA implementation achieved a data rate of 11.6 Kbits/s for a 512-bit exponentiation using the Chinese Remainder Theorem (CRT) and 4.6 Kbits/s without using it.

The authors in [16] described an ECDSA implementation over $GF(p)$ on the M16C, a 16-bit 10 MHz microcomputer. Reference [16] proposes the use of a field of prime characteristic $p = e2^c \pm 1$, where e is an integer within the machine word size and c is a multiple of the machine word size. This choice of field allows to implement multiplication in $GF(p)$ in a small amount of memory. Notice that [16] uses a randomly generated curve with the a coefficient of the elliptic curve equal to $p - 3$. This reduces the number of operations needed for an EC point doubling. They also modify the point addition algorithm in [29] to reduce the number of temporary variables from 4 to 2. This contribution uses a 31-entry table of precomputed points to generate an ECDSA signature in 150 msec. On the other hand, scalar multiplication of a random point takes 480 msec and ECDSA verification 630 msec. The whole implementation occupied 4 Kbyte of code/data space.

In [17], two new methods for implementing public-key cryptography algorithms on the 200 MHz TI TMS320C6201 DSP are proposed. The first method is a modified implementation of the Montgomery variant known as the Finely Integrated Operand Scanning (FIOS) algorithm [7] suitable for pipelining. The second approach suggests a method for reducing the number of multiplications and additions used to compute $2^m P$, for P a point on the elliptic curve and m some integer. The final code implemented RSA and DSA combined with the k-ary method for exponentiation, and ECDSA combined with the improved method for multiple point doublings, sliding window exponentiation, and signed binary exponent recoding. The total instruction code was 41.1 Kbytes. They achieved 11.7 msec for a 1024-bit RSA signature using the CRT (1.2 msec for verification assuming a 17-bit exponent) and 1.67 msec for a 192-bit ECDSA signature over $GF(p)$ (6.28 msec for verification and 4.64 msec for general point multiplication).

Recently, two papers have introduced fast implementations on 8-bit processors over Optimal Extension Fields (OEFs), originally introduced in [3]. Reference [9] reports on an ECC implementation over the field $GF(p^m)$ with $p = 2^{16} - 165$, $m = 10$, and $f(x) = x^{10} - 2$ is the irreducible polynomial. The authors use the column major multiplication method for field multiplication and squaring, for the specific case in which $f(x)$ is a binomial. They achieve better performance than when using Karatsuba multiplication because in this processor additions and multiplications take the same number of cycles. Modular reduction is done through repeated use of the division step instruction. For inversion, they use the variant of the Itoh and Tsujii Algorithm [18] proposed in [4]. For EC arithmetic they combine the mixed coordinate system methods of [10] and [22]. These combined methods allow them to achieve 122 msec for a 160-bit point multiplication on the CalmRISC with MAC2424 math coprocessor running at 20 MHz. The second paper [34] describes a smart card implementation over the field $GF((2^8 - 17)^{17})$ without the use of a coprocessor.

Reference [34] focuses on the implementation of ECC on the 8051 family of microcontrollers, popular in smart cards. The authors compare three types of fields: binary fields $GF(2^k)$, composite fields $GF((2^n)^m)$, and OEFs. Based on multiplication timings, the authors conclude that OEFs are particularly well suited for this architecture. A key idea of this contribution is to allow each of the 16 most significant coefficients resulting from a polynomial multiplication to accumulate over three 8-bit words instead of reducing modulo $p = 2^8 - 17$ after each 8-bit by 8-bit multiplication. Fast field multiplication allows the implementation to have relatively fast inversion operations following the method proposed in [4]. This, in turn, allows for the use of affine coordinates for point representation. Finally, the authors combine the methods above with a table of 9 precomputed points to achieve 1.95 sec for a 134-bit fixed point multiplication and 8.37 sec for a general point multiplication using the binary method of exponentiation.

3   Elliptic Curves over $GF(p)$

In this paper, we will only be concerned with non-supersingular elliptic curves over $GF(p)$, $p > 3$. Thus, an elliptic curve E will be defined to be the set of points $P = (x, y)$ with $x, y \in GF(p)$ and satisfying the cubic equation $y^2 = x^3 + ax^2 + b$, where $a, b \in GF(p)$ with $4a^2 + 27b^2 \neq 0 \pmod{p}$, together with the point at infinity $\mathcal{O}$. The points (x, y) form an abelian group under "addition" where the group operation is defined as in [23]. It is a well known fact that in *affine* representation, one needs to compute the inverse of an element in $GF(p)$ to perform an addition or a doubling of a point $P \in E$. Inversion can be a very time consuming operation (when compared to multiplication, addition, and subtraction in the finite field) and thus, to avoid inversion in the group operation, one can represent points in *projective* coordinates. Given a point $P = (x, y)$ in affine coordinates, one obtains the projective coordinate representation of $P = (X, Y, Z)$ by:

$$X = x; \quad Y = y; \quad Z = 1 \tag{1}$$

On the other hand, the projective coordinates of a point are not unique and they require more bandwidth. Thus, for transmission/exchange of data, affine coordinate representation is the method of choice. Given a point $P = (X, Y, Z)$ in projective coordinates, the corresponding affine coordinate representation of $P = (x, y)$ is given by:

$$x = \frac{X}{Z^2} \quad y = \frac{Y}{Z^3} \tag{2}$$

where we have chosen the Jacobian representation [8,10].

3.1   Addition and Doubling Formulae in Jacobian Representation

Using the representation in (1) and (2) is equivalent to using a curve equation of the form:

$$E: \quad Y^2 = X^3 + aXZ^4 + bZ^6 \tag{3}$$

Then, one can define addition and doubling of points as follows. Let $P_0 = (X_0, Y_0, Z_0), P_1 = (X_1, Y_1, Z_1), P_2 = (X_2, Y_2, Z_2) \in E$, then if $P_0 = P_1$:

$$P_2 = 2P_1 = \begin{cases} X_2 = M^2 - 2S \\ Y_2 = M(S - X_2) - T \\ Z_2 = 2Y_1 Z_1 \end{cases} \tag{4}$$

where $M = 3X_1^2 + aZ_1^2$, $S = 4X_1Y_1^2$, and $T = 8Y_1^4$. On the other hand, if $P_0 \neq P_1$:

$$P_2 = P_0 + P1 = \begin{cases} X_2 = R^2 - TW \\ 2Y_2 = VR - MW^3 \\ Z_2 = Z_0 Z_1 W \end{cases} \tag{5}$$

where $W = X_0Z_1^2 - X_1Z_0^2$, $R = Y_0Z_1^3 - Y_1Z_0^3$, $T = X_0Z_1^2 + X_1Z_0^2$, $M = Y_0Z_1^3 + Y_1Z_0^3$, and $V = TW^2 - 2X_2$.

Based on (4) and (5) one can implement doubling of EC points using 5 temporary variables and addition of EC points using 7 temporary variables [29]. The number of temporary variables used in the addition and doubling operation can further be reduced to 2 temporary variables and 3 output variables if one follows the ideas proposed in [16].

3.2   Elliptic Curve Arithmetic Implementation

Our point addition and doubling routines follow closely the formulae in [29] combined with modifications similar to the ones proposed in [16]. In particular, we follow a similar idea to minimize the number of temporary variables used in performing a point addition or a point doubling. Our implementation requires 5 temporary variables but it also allows for greater flexibility. We perform the following computation $P_2 \leftarrow P_0 + P_1$ as opposed to $P_0 \leftarrow P_0 + P_1$ as described in [16]. Another difference is that whenever we have to multiply by 2,3, or 8 in the algorithms, we substitute the multiplication by one, two or three additions respectively. As it will be seen in Section 6 one modular multiplication time is about 10 modular addition times, thus it makes sense to exchange multiplications for additions whenever possible. Similarly, we have used a special squaring routine whenever possible since squaring is 24% more efficient than regular multiplication. Finally, notice that because point addition and doubling will never occur simultaneously, it is possible to use the temporary memory space available for the point addition routine in the point doubling routine, effectively reducing the memory required by a factor of 2.

For scalar point multiplication, which is the most important operation in ECDSA [2,27] signature generation or verification operation we implemented the binary method for exponentiation [19] which is simple to implement and minimizes memory requirements. It is important to point out that signature generation times can be further improved by using point precomputation since the base point in ECDSA is a system parameter. However, this method has the drawback of increasing the memory required for the implementation.

3.3 Elliptic Curve Parameters

In this contribution, we consider two 128-bit elliptic curves, both specified in [31]. Notice that the set of parameters recommended in [31] is also identical to the set of parameters recommended in [1]. Both curves presented in this section are defined over $GF(p)$ and their parameters are verifiable generated at random. The parameters are a sextuple $T = (p, a, b, n, h, G)$, where a, b are the elliptic curve coefficients as defined in (3), G is a base point of prime order n and represented in affine coordinates, and h is the cofactor $\#E(GF(p))/n$, where $\#E(GF(p))$ denotes the number of points in the curve E. We also include the seed S used to choose E according to [2].

Parameters secp128r1.

$p = (\text{FFFFFFFD FFFFFFFF FFFFFFFF FFFFFFFF})_{16} = 2^{128} - 2^{97} - 1$

$a = (\text{FFFFFFFD FFFFFFFF FFFFFFFF FFFFFFFC})_{16} = p - 3$

$b = (\text{E87579C1 1079F43D D824993C 2CEE5ED3})_{16}$

$n = (\text{FFFFFFFE 00000000 75A30D1B 9038A115})_{16}$

$h = (01)_{16}$

$G = ((\text{161FF752 8B899B2D 0C28607C A52C5B86})_{16},$
$\qquad (\text{CF5AC839 5BAFEB13 C02DA292 DDED7A83})_{16}) = (x, y)$

$S = (\text{000E0D4D 696E6768 75615175 0CC03A44 73D03679})_{16}$

Parameters secp128r2.

$p = (\text{FFFFFFFD FFFFFFFF FFFFFFFF FFFFFFFF})_{16} = 2^{128} - 2^{97} - 1$

$a = (\text{D6031998 D1B3BBFE BF590C9B BFF9AEE1})_{16}$

$b = (\text{5EEEFCA3 80D02919 DC2C6558 BB6D8A5D})_{16}$

$n = (\text{3FFFFFFF 7FFFFFFF BE002472 0613B5A3})_{16}$

$h = (04)_{16}$

$G = ((\text{7B6AA5D8 5E572983 E6FB32A7 CDEBC140})_{16},$
$\qquad (\text{27B6916A 894D3AEE 7106FE80 5FC34B44})_{16}) = (x, y)$

$S = (\text{004D696E 67687561 517512D8 F03431FC E63B88F4})_{16}$

4 The TI MSP430x33x Family of Microcontrollers

The TI MSP430x33x is a 16-bit RISC based family of microcontrollers with a 16-by-16, 16-by-8, 8-by-16, and 8-by-8 bit hardware multiplier. This family of devices is commonly used in low-cost and low-power applications involving electronic gas, water, and electric meters and other sensor systems that capture analog signals, convert them to digital values, and then process, display, or transmit the data to a host system. It is important to point out that they have been specially designed for ultra-low power applications. Family members include the MSP430C336 with 24 Kbytes of ROM and the MSP430C337, MSP430P337A, MSP430P337A and PMS430E337A with 32 Kbytes of ROM (or EPROM/OTP). All of the MPS430x33x family members include 1 Kbyte of on-chip RAM and can be clocked to a maximum frequency of 3.8 MHz. The total addressable space is 64 Kbytes [32].

Instruction fetches from program memory (ROM) are always 16-bit access, whereas data memory can be accessed using 16-bit (word) or 8-bit (byte) instructions. In addition to program code, data can also be placed in the ROM area of the memory map and it can be accessed using word or byte instructions. This is useful for storing data tables, for example. At the top of the 64 kilobytes of addressable space 16 words of memory are reserved for the interrupt and reset vectors. The remaining address space (after ROM, RAM, and interrupts) is used for peripherals.

The architecture of the MSP430 family is based on a memory-to-memory architecture, a common address space for all functional blocks and a reduced instruction set. The MSP430 RISC CPU includes sixteen 16-bit registers $R0 - R15$. Registers $R0 - R3$ are special function registers or SFRs and have the dedicated functions of Program Counter, Status Register, Constant Generator, and Stack Pointer. The remaining registers ($R4 - R15$) are general purpose registers and have no restrictions in their usage. All registers except for the Constant Generator can be accessed using the complete instruction set. This includes 27 core instructions and 24 additional emulated instructions (instructions that make programming simpler and that are substituted for core instructions by the assembler). All instructions are single or double operand instructions. The MSP430 devices support 7 different addressing modes. They include: register mode, indexed mode, symbolic mode, absolute mode, indirect register mode, indirect auto-increment, and immediate mode. Depending on the addressing mode the instructions take between 1 cycle and 6 cycles to execute. As a final remark, notice that the result of a multiply instruction is available one clock cycle after loading the two operands into the hardware multiplier [33].

5   Finite Field Arithmetic

In this section we summarize the rational behind some of our design choices. We emphasize the description of a new inversion algorithm specially suited for primes of special form. We also describe how our implementation was tailored to take the most advantage of the architecture of the MSP430 family of processors.

5.1   Modular Reduction

Reduction Modulo $p = 2^{128} - 2^{97} - 1$. One of the critical operations when implementing finite field arithmetic is modular reduction. We chose the field $GF(p)$ where $p = 2^{128} - 2^{97} - 1$, for the underlying arithmetic of our EC implementation. The first thing to notice is that p is a generalized Mersenne prime and that this type of fields allow for efficient reduction as described in [28]. Following [28], we first notice that any number $A \in GF(p)$ such that $A < p^2$ can be written as:

$$A = \sum_{i=0}^{i=15} a_i 2^{16i} \quad 0 \le a_i \le 2^{16} - 1 \tag{6}$$

where we have chosen $2^{16} - 1$ to be the maximum digit value because of the MSP430 16-bit based architecture. Then, it is easy to see that only the 8 most significant digits a_i need to be modulo reduced. Using the fact that $p = 2^{128} - 2^{97} - 1$, one obtains the following identities:

$$a_8 2^{128} \equiv 2a_8 2^{96} + a_8 \pmod{p} \tag{7}$$

$$a_9 2^{144} \equiv 2a_9 2^{112} + a_9 2^{16} \pmod{p} \tag{8}$$

$$a_{10} 2^{160} \equiv 4a_{10} 2^{96} + a_{10} 2^{32} + 2a_{10} \pmod{p} \tag{9}$$

$$a_{11} 2^{176} \equiv 4a_{11} 2^{112} + a_{11} 2^{48} + 2a_{11} 2^{16} \pmod{p} \tag{10}$$

$$a_{12} 2^{192} \equiv 8a_{12} 2^{96} + a_{12} 2^{64} + 2a_{12} 2^{32} + 4a_{12} \pmod{p} \tag{11}$$

$$a_{13} 2^{208} \equiv 8a_{13} 2^{112} + a_{13} 2^{80} + 2a_{13} 2^{48} + 4a_{13} 2^{16} \pmod{p} \tag{12}$$

$$a_{14} 2^{224} \equiv (16+1)a_{14} 2^{96} + 2a_{14} 2^{64} + 4a_{14} 2^{32} + 8a_{14} \pmod{p} \tag{13}$$

$$a_{15} 2^{240} \equiv (16+1)a_{15} 2^{112} + 2a_{15} 2^{80} + 4a_{15} 2^{48} + 8a_{15} 2^{16} \pmod{p} \tag{14}$$

Adding up the first 8 words from A, relations (7) through (14), and reducing modulo p, one readily obtains $A \bmod p$. Notice that one only needs single precision additions to perform this operation. In general, whenever a product of the form $2^i a_j$ happens in relations (7) through (14), it is more efficient to compute the product and then add it to the partial result than adding a_j $(2^i - 1)$-times. Notice that the final result after adding relations (7) through (14) and the first 8 words of A, only needs nine 16-bit words to be represented and that one will need at most 2 subtractions to reduce this result modulo p. Thus, we kept all the partial sums in 9 of the 12 general purpose registers to minimize the fetches to memory during the modular reduction operation.

Modular Reduction for Arbitrary p. In both ECDSA signature and ECDSA verification operations, one needs to perform modular reductions modulo the order of the base point G. In general, $\mathrm{ord}(G) = n$ is not of special form and, thus, one needs to implement modular reduction for arbitrary moduli. We used Montgomery modular reduction [26]. In particular, we implemented the Separated Operand Scanning (SOS) method as proposed in [7]. Algorithm 1 summarizes the SOS method for Montgomery reduction.

Algorithm 1 SOS Method of Montgomery Reduction

$INPUT:$ $t = \bar{a} \cdot \bar{b} = (a \cdot r \bmod n) \cdot (b \cdot r \bmod n) = (t_{2s-1}, \ldots, t_0)$
                $n = (n_{s-1}, \ldots, n_0)$

$r = 2^{sw}$ and w is typically the word size of the processor

n'_0 where $n' = (n'_{s-1}, \ldots, n'_0)$, satisfies $(r)(r^{-1}) + (-n)(n') = 1$

OUTPUT: $\bar{c} = (\bar{c}_{s-1}, \ldots, \bar{c}_0) = a \cdot b \cdot r \bmod n$

```
01          for i = 0 to s − 1
02              c = 0
03              m = t_i · n'_0 mod 2^w
04              for j = 0 to s − 1
05                  (c, t_{i+j}) = t_{i+j} + m · n_j + c
06              endfor
07              while (c ≠ 0)
08                  (c, t_{i+s}) = t_{i+s} + c
09                  i = i + 1
10              endwhile
11          endfor
12
13          for j = 0 to s
14              u_j = t_{j+s}
15          endfor
16
17          if u ≥ n
18              return c̄ = u − n
19          else
20              return c̄ = u
21          endif
```

First, we notice that in our particular implementation $s = 128/16 = 8$, thus it is possible to load all of n into 8 of the 12 general purpose registers. This simple observation saves 2 cycles per iteration when loading n_j in line 05 of Algorithm 1 into the multiplier. Since the j-loop executes s-times and this in turn is executed s-times by the i-loop, it gives a total of $8 \cdot 8 \cdot 2 = 128$ cycles in savings. In addition, since m stays constant within the j-loop, we can load m into the multiplier before starting the execution of the j-loop and only load n_j each time we execute line 05 in Algorithm 1. This observation saves $4 \cdot 8 \cdot 7 = 224$ cycles.

5.2   Multiplication and Squaring

Multiplication and squaring operations for long number arithmetic are described in [24]. For completeness Algorithm 2 summarizes the school-book method for multiplication. We notice Algorithm 2 has a similar structure to that of Algorithm 1. In particular, in line 04, for a fixed word a_i we compute s inner products. Thus, the same optimizations that were applied to Algorithm 1 are applicable to Algorithm 2. Finally, we notice that a squaring operation is 24% cheaper to compute than a regular multiplication because, in the squaring case, we do not need to fetch from memory the words from the second operand.

Algorithm 2 School-book Method for Multiplication

$INPUT:$ $A = (a_{s-1}, \ldots, a_0)$
             $B = (b_{s-1}, \ldots, b_0)$
$OUTPUT:$ $C = (c_{2s-1}, \ldots, c_0) = a \cdot b$

```
01          for i = 0 to s − 1
02              c = 0
03              for j = 0 to s − 1
04                  (c, t_{i+j}) = t_{i+j} + a_i · b_j + c
05              endfor
06              t_{i+s} = c
07          endfor
```

5.3 Modular Addition and Subtraction

We followed the methods described in [24] to implement modular addition and modular subtraction. Given two elements $A, B \in GF(p)$, $C = A + B \bmod p$ can be obtained by first adding A and B and reducing modulo p. This last step can be accomplished by simply subtracting p from the partial result $A + B$, rather than using the method described in Section 5.1. The same comments apply to modular subtraction.

5.4 A New Inversion Algorithm for Moduli of Special Form

Several methods to compute the inverse of an element in $GF(p)$ exist. They include methods based on the extended Euclidean algorithm [19] such as the binary Euclidean algorithm and the Almost Inverse algorithm [30], methods based on Itoh and Tsujii's inversion algorithm and its variants [18,14,4], and methods based on Fermat's Little theorem. Despite the fact that on the average Fermat based inversion is slower than methods based on the Euclidean algorithm, it has several advantages. First, Fermat based inversion is easier to implement and it allows for implementations that occupy less code space than those implementations based on Euclid's algorithm. Second, in an ECC implementation that uses projective coordinates, inversion is not time critical.

The new inversion algorithm is based on Fermat's Little theorem, i.e., on the observation that for any non-zero element $A \in GF(p)$, $A^{-1} \equiv A^{p-2} \bmod p$. In particular, the algorithm that we are proposing in this section is only applicable to the computation of inverses when p is a Mersenne or Generalized-Mersenne prime. Despite this apparent constraint on the applicability of the algorithm, it is our opinion that the algorithm is highly relevant given the recent parameter recommendations by NIST [28] and SECG [31], both of which include Generalized-Mersenne primes. The basic idea of the new algorithm is to minimize the number of precomputations in the k-ary method for exponentiation [24,13] used to compute the inverse via Fermat's Little theorem. This is possible because of the special form of Mersenne and Generalized-Mersenne primes and, as a consequence, of $p-2$. Algorithm 3 describes the k-ary method for exponentiation.

Algorithm 3 k-ary Method for Exponentiation

INPUT: $A \in GF(p)$

           $e = (e_s e_{s-1} \ldots e_1 e_0)_b$, where $b = 2^k$ for some $k \geq 1$

OUTPUT: $C = A^e$

```
01              Precomputation
02                      A_0 = 1
03                      for i = 1 to (2^k − 1)
04                          A_i = A_{i−1} · A (Thus, A_i = A^i)
05                      endfor
06              A = 1
07              for i = s down to 0
08                      A = A^{2^k}
09                      A = A · A_{e_i}
10              endfor
11              C = A
```

Notice that given a window size k, the precomputation stage of Algorithm 3 computes all the possible values A^i for $i = 1, \ldots, 2^k - 1$ (observe that the Improved k-ary algorithm can reduce the number of precomputed values in half [24]). These values are then used in line *09* of the k-ary algorithm. In addition, the number of precomputed values (i.e., k) is determined by two factors: the amount of RAM memory (or the size of the cache) available in the processor and the number of operations (multiplications) used to compute the table values . In particular, the table of precomputed values should fit in RAM memory (or in the cache), if we want to ensure that memory accesses to the table are fast. Reference [13] also gives the following complexity formula for the number of multiplications (assuming squarings and multiplications take the same time) performed in the k-ary method, in the worst case:

$$\#\text{Multiplications} = 2^k - 2 + \left(1 + \frac{1}{k}\right) \lfloor \log_2 e \rfloor \tag{15}$$

Equation (15) gives an easy way to find the optimum value of k for a given exponent size. In particular, $k = 4$ minimizes (15) for a 128-bit exponent. We also notice that in general not all the precomputed values will be used. In particular, only the values A^{e_i} which correspond to the e_i digits happening in the exponent will be used. For the case $k = 4$ these values correspond to the hexadecimal digits present in the exponent when e is in radix-16 representation. The above discussion leads us to believe that it would be of great help if we find a way to reduce the number of precomputations performed in the k-ary method.

Next, we turn our attention to the exponent. Notice, that to compute the inverse of any element in $GF(p)$ we need to raise to the $p - 2$ power, where p is a Mersenne prime or Generalized-Mersenne prime. Thus, our exponent has a very special form. We first consider the case in which $p = 2^r - 1$.

Theorem 1. *Let $p = 2^r - 1$ be a prime. Then, one can compute the inverse of an element $A \in GF(p)$ using Algorithm 3, with only two precomputed values.*

Proof. If $p = 2^r - 1$, then $p - 2 = 0xFF \ldots FFD$ in hexadecimal representation. But, the hexadecimal representation of $p - 2$ (the exponent) corresponds exactly to the values that will be used in line *09* of Algorithm 3, which for the case $k = 4$ are A^{13} and A^{15}. Thus, we only need to precompute and store 2 values.   □

For the Generalized-Mersenne prime used here the case is very similar.

Theorem 2. *Let $p = 2^r - 2^t - 1$ be a prime, with $r = 4 \cdot d$ for some d. Then, one can compute the inverse of an element $A \in GF(p)$ using Algorithm 3, with at most 3 precomputed values.*

Proof. If $p = 2^r - 2^t - 1$ with $r = 4 \cdot d$ then we can rewrite it as $p = 2^r - 2^u \cdot 2^{4 \cdot v} - 1$ where $u = 0, 1, 2, 3$, $t = u + 4 \cdot v$, and v is any positive integer less than $d - 1$. Notice that the value $2^r - 1$ can be written as $\sum_{i=0}^{i=r/4-1} \left(2^4 - 1\right) 2^{4 \cdot i}$ Then, it follows that we can write $p - 2$ as:

$$\left(2^4 - 1\right) 2^{r-4} + \left(2^4 - 1\right) 2^{r-8} + \cdots + \left(2^4 - 2^u - 1\right) 2^{4 \cdot v} +$$
$$\left(2^4 - 1\right) 2^{4 \cdot v - 4} + \cdots + \left(2^4 - 1\right) 2^4 + \left(2^4 - 3\right)$$

Looking at the coefficients of the powers of 2^4, we see that there are three: $2^4 - 1$, $2^4 - 2^u - 1$, and $2^4 - 3$. This ends the proof.   □

Notice, that Theorems 1 and 2 suggest an improved algorithm to compute the inverse of a non-zero element $A \in GF(p)$. Algorithm 4 describes the new algorithm.

Algorithm 4 Inversion Algorithm for Mersenne and Generalized-Mersenne Primes

INPUT:	$A \in GF(p)$ with $p = 2^r - 1$ (Mersenne) or
	$p = 2^r - 2^u 2^{4 \cdot v} - 1$ (Generalized-Mersenne prime
	From Theorem 2)
	$e = (e_s e_{s-1} \ldots e_1 e_0)_b = p - 2$, with $b = 2^4$ and $0 \le e_i \le 2^4 - 1$
OUTPUT:	$C = A^{-1} = A^e$

01	Precomputation
02	if $p = 2^r - 1$
02	$A_{13} = A^{13}$
03	$A_{15} = A^{15}$
04	if $p = 2^r - 2^u \cdot 2^{4 \cdot v} - 1$
05	$A_{2^4 - 2^u - 1} = A^{2^4 - 2^u - 1}$
06	$A_{13} = A^{13}$
07	$A_{15} = A^{15}$
08	$A = 1$
09	for $i = s$ down to *0*
10	$A = A^{2^4}$
11	$A = A \cdot A_{e_i}$
12	endfor
13	$C = A$

5.5   A Word about the Security of a 128-bit EC Implementation

In recent work, Lenstra and Verheul show that under particular assumptions, 952-bit RSA and DSS systems may be considered to be of equivalent security to 132-bit ECC systems [21]. The authors further argue that 132-bit ECC keys are adequate for commercial security in the year 2000. This notion of commercial security is based on the hypothesis that a 56-bit block cipher offered adequate security in 1982 for commercial applications.

This estimate has more recently been confirmed by the breaking of the ECC2K-108 challenge [15]. First, note that the field $GF(2^{128} - 2^{97} - 1)$ has an order of about 2^{128}. Breaking the Koblitz (or anomalous) curve cryptosystem over $GF(2^{108})$ required slightly more effort than a brute force attack against DES. Hence, an ECC over a 128-bit field which does not use a subfield curve is by a factor of $\sqrt{108} \cdot \sqrt{2^{20}} \approx 10000$ harder to break than the ECC2K-108 challenge or DES. Thus, based on current knowledge of EC attacks, the system proposed here is roughly security equivalent to a 69-bit block cipher. This implies that an attack would require about 10000 times as much effort as breaking DES. Note also that factoring the 512-bit RSA challenge took only about 2% of the time required to break DES or the ECC2K-108 challenge. This implies that an ECC over the proposed field $GF(2^{128} - 2^{97} - 1)$ offers far more security than the 512-bit RSA system which has been popular, for example, for fielded smart card applications. We would also like to point out that due to the shorter size of the operands (128 bits vs. 160 bits) one could potentially attack a signature scheme by trying to find collisions in the hash function. Nevertheless, we feel that our selection of field order provides medium-term security which is sufficient for many applications intended for the MSP430x33x family of microcontrollers.

6   Implementation and Results

6.1   Software Architecture

The EC arithmetic library for the MSP430x33x devices was designed with modularity in mind. Thus, the design consists of three levels as depicted in Figure 1. Level 1 includes basic arithmetic functions such as addition, subtraction, multiplication, and squaring routines; modulo arithmetic functions such as modular reduction for $p = 2^{128} - 2^{97} - 1$, addition and subtraction modulo p, Montgomery reduction; and other support routines such as memory copying and setting routines, long number comparisons $(>,<,=)$, and shift-right operations. It is important to point out that many of the modular arithmetic routines were optimized for the prime that we chose. Level 2 consists of macros. The assembly language for the TI MSP430 allows the programmer to use macros which are substituted by the compiler at compile time. This enables the programmer to write the Level 3 routines in terms of the macros from Level 2, thus, making the elliptic curve arithmetic routines independent of the chosen field. In the future, this will allow us to change the underlying arithmetic without changing the top level routines. It is important to point that this could have been accomplished

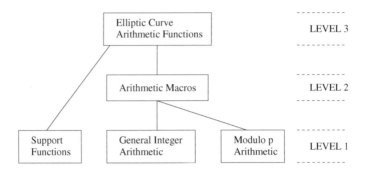

Fig. 1. Library Architecture

by using functions in Level 2 but this would increase the overhead (5 cycles per function call) which would impact negatively on the performance of our implementation. Finally, Level 3 routines included addition and doubling of elliptic curve points and scalar point multiplication.

6.2   Timings

The critical functions of the elliptic curve library were timed using the MSP430 TI Simulator version 2.30. The code was compiled using the MSP430 TI Macro Assembler version 1.08 and the MSP430 COFF TI Linker version 1.01. These tools are all part of the TI MSP-EVK430S330 Evaluation Kit which includes the PMS430E337HFD (UV EPROM) chip. Arithmetic is always assumed to be for 128-bit long operands. The actual timings are calculated for two frequencies: 1 MHz which seems to be a commonly used frequency in applications and 3 MHz which is close to the highest frequency that the MSP430 device can be clocked at. Table 1 summarizes the timings corresponding to basic arithmetic operations.

Some of the times reported are exact times. These include the execution times for multiplication and squaring Montgomery reduction. On the other hand, the times reported for modular addition, modular subtraction, and inversion modulo $p = 2^{128} - 2^{97} - 1$ using the modified k-ary method were computed by averaging out the worst and best times observed during the execution of these routines. Modular addition and modular subtraction, for example, perform the modular reduction by subtracting p from the intermediate result. In some cases, one can obtain the final result with only one subtraction, other times two subtractions are necessary. Best and worst case timings correspond to one or two subtractions performed in the reduction step, respectively. The remaining timings in Table 1 are the result of performing several computations with a given routine (Montgomery reduction, Montgomery exponentiation, etc.) and then averaging over the total number of operations performed. Finally, notice that the timings do not include the loading of the operands onto the registers where the routines expect their inputs. However, this operation can at most take 6 cycles for routines with 3 operands, so its impact on the overall performance

Table 1. Timings for basic arithmetic operations with 128-bit long operands.

Arithmetic Operation	Average Timing @ 1 MHz(usec)	Average Timing @ 3 MHz(usec)
addition modulo $p = 2^{128} - 2^{97} - 1$	164	55
subtraction modulo $p = 2^{128} - 2^{97} - 1$	156	52
multiplication	1425	475
squaring	998	333
reduction modulo $p = 2^{128} - 2^{97} - 1$	343	114
Montgomery reduction	1626	542
inversion modulo $p = 2^{128} - 2^{97} - 1$ via modified k-ary method.	235.9 msec	78.6 msec

of an elliptic curve operation is negligible. Table 2 presents the timings for the elliptic curve operations. The point doubling timings depend on whether the coefficient a of the elliptic curve is equal to $p - 3$ or not. So both timings have been included. The longer timing corresponds to the case $a \neq p - 3$. The point addition timings depend on whether the Z coordinate of the second point is equal to 1 or not. If it is equal to one then the number of operations is smaller and, thus, the addition operation takes less time. In this case we have also included both timings. The fulladd operation (a wrapper routine that can perform both point addition and point doubling) if used only for adding ($P0 \neq P1$) takes less time than when a doubling ($P0 = P1$) is performed. The reason for this is that fulladd first performs an add and if the output is $P0 + P1 = (0, 0, 0)$ (which is not a point on the elliptic curve but rather a pointer indicating that the doubling routine must be used), it performs a point doubling. Only timings for the case $P0 \neq P1$ are included. It is important to point out that this is the case of most relevance in practice since one can always make the Z coordinate of the second operand equal to 1. In fact, it should not occur that we perform a double with a fulladd when implementing point multiplication using the binary, k-ary, sliding window, or addition-subtraction algorithms since the point G is usually of prime order and in general the multiplier is chosen to be less than the order of G. In all cases, it makes no sense to average the two values because the timings correspond to situations which will not occur at the same time or in the same implementation. For example, one either chooses a curve with the a coefficient equal to $p - 3$ or one does not. Finally, the timings for 128-bit point multiplication were computed using a 128-bit long exponent.

7   Conclusions

In this contribution, we have described a practical implementation of an EC cryptosystem over a prime field, where the prime is a Generalized-Mersenne prime, on the TI MSP430x33x family of low-cost and low-power microprocessors. We show how the special form of the Generalized-Mersenne prime can be used to

Table 2. Timings for elliptic curve operations assuming a 128-bit base field.

Elliptic Curve Operation	Average Timing @ 1 MHz (msec)	Average Timing @ 3 MHz (msec)
point doubling $a = p - 3$	15.1	5.0
point doubling $a \neq p - 3$	17.7	5.9
point addition $Z = 1$	20.7	6.9
point addition $Z \neq 1$	29.1	9.6
point fulladd $(P0 \neq P1)$ $Z = 1$	21.1	7.0
point fulladd $(P0 \neq P1)$ $Z \neq 1$	29.5	9.8
point subtraction $(P0 \neq P1)$ $Z = 1$	21.2	7.2
point multiplication using the binary method of exponentiation $(a = p - 3)$	3.4 sec	1.1 sec
point multiplication using the binary method of exponentiation $(a \neq p - 3)$	3.8 sec	1.3 sec

implement a new inversion algorithm, based on Fermat's Little theorem and the k-ary method for exponentiation, which minimizes the number of precomputed values, thus, also minimizing the memory requirements of the inversion operation. We would like to point out that even though $k = 4$ minimizes (15), this value might not be the optimum for our algorithm. Since we only required two (or three) precomputed values it is possible to increase the size of k, thus making the algorithm more efficient. In fact, it is easy to verify that a value of $k = 16$ will reduce in half the number of multiplications required to perform the inversion.

In addition, we tailor the field arithmetic algorithms to the processor architecture to achieve acceptable timings for a scalar point multiplication. Running at 1 MHz we can perform a 128-bit random point multiplication in 3.4 sec using projective coordinates (this time includes transforming back to affine coordinates) using the binary method for exponentiation. Notice that these timings can be further improved by using addition-subtraction methods. Finally, it is possible to dramatically reduce the time required for a point multiplication if the point is known ahead of time, like in the ECDSA signature generation operation. This can be accomplished by using precomputation methods. However, these methods require additional memory which in embedded systems is not always freely available.

References

1. ANSI X9.62-1-xxxx. Public Key Cryptography for the Financial Services Industry: the Ellip tic Curve Digital Signature Algorithm (ECDSA) (Revised). Technical report, American Bankers Association, October 1999.
2. ANSI X9.62-1999. The Elliptic Curve Digital Signature Algorithm. Technical report, ANSI, 1999.

3. D. V. Bailey and C. Paar. Optimal Extension Fields for Fast Arithmetic in Public-Key Algorithms. In H. Krawczyk, editor, *Advances in Cryptology — CRYPTO '98*, volume LNCS 1462, pages 472–485, Berlin, Germany, 1998. Springer-Verlag.

4. D. V. Bailey and C. Paar. Inversion in Optimal Extension Fields. In A. Odlyzko, G. Walsh, and H. Williams, editors, *Conference on The Mathematics of Public Key Cryptography*, The Fields Institute for Research in the Mathematical Sciences, Toronto, Canada, June 1999.

5. P. Barrett. Implementing the Rivest Shamir and Adleman Public Key Encryption Algorithm on a Standard Digital Signal Processor. In A. M. Odlyzko, editor, *Advances in Cryptology – CRYPTO '86*, volume LNCS 263, pages 311–323, Berlin, Germany, August 1986. Springer-Verlag.

6. G. Borriello and R. Want. Embedded computation meets the world wide web. *Communications of the ACM*, 43(5):59–66, May 2000.

7. Ç. K. Koç, T. Acar, and B. Kaliski. Analyzing and Comparing Montgomery Multiplication Algorithms. *IEEE Micro*, pages 26–33, June 1996.

8. D.V. Chudnovsky and G.V. Chudnovsky. Sequences of numbers generated by addition in formal groups and new primality and factorization tests. *Advances in Applied Mathematics*, 7:385–434, 1986.

9. Jae Wook Chung, Sang Gyoo Sim, and Pil Joong Lee. Fast Implementation of Elliptic Curve Defined over $GF(p^m)$ on CalmRISC with MAC2424 Coprocessor. In Çetin K. Koç and Christof Paar, editors, *Workshop on Cryptographic Hardware and Embedded Systems — CHES 2000*, pages 57–70, Berlin, 2000. Springer-Verlag.

10. Henry Cohen, Atsuko Miyaji, and Takatoshi Ono. Efficient Elliptic Curve Exponentiation Using Mixed Coordinates. In Kazuo Ohta and Dingyi Pei, editors, *Advances in Cryptology — ASIACRYPT'98*, volume LNCS 1514, pages 51–65, Berlin, 1998. Springer-Verlag.

11. S. R. Dussé and B. S. Kaliski. A Cryptographic Library for the Motorola DSP56000. In I. B. Damgård, editor, *Advances in Cryptology — EUROCRYPT '90*, volume LNCS 473, pages 230–244, Berlin, Germany, May 1990. Springer-Verlag.

12. D. Estrin, R. Govindan, and J. Heidemann. Embedding the Internet. *Communications of the ACM*, 43(5):39–41, May 2000.

13. D. M. Gordon. A survey of fast exponentiation methods. *Journal of Algorithms*, 27:129–146, 1998.

14. J. Guajardo and C. Paar. Efficient Algorithms for Elliptic Curve Cryptosystems. In B. Kaliski, editor, *Advances in Cryptology — CRYPTO '97*, volume LNCS 1294, pages 342–356, Berlin, Germany, August 1997. Springer-Verlag.

15. R. Harley, D. Doligez, D. de Rauglaudre, and X. Leroy. http://cristal.inria.fr/%7Eharley/ecdl7/.

16. Toshio Hasegawa, Junko Nakajima, and Mitsuru Matsui. A Practical Implementation of Elliptic Curve Cryptosystems over $GF(p)$ on a 16-bit Microcomputer. In Hideki Imai and Yuliang Zheng, editors, *First International Workshop on Practice and Theory in Public Key Cryptography — PKC'98*, volume LNCS 1431, pages 182–194, Berlin, 1998. Springer-Verlag.

17. K. Itoh, M. Takenaka, N. Torii, S. Temma, and Y. Kurihara. Fast Implemenation of Public-Key Cryptography on a DSP TMS320C6201. In Çetin K. Koç and Christof Paar, editors, *Proceedings of the First Workshop on Cryptographic Hardware and Embedded Systems — CHES'99*, volume LNCS 1717, pages 61–72, Berlin, Germany, August 1999. Springer-Verlag.

18. T. Itoh and S. Tsujii. A fast algorithm for computing multiplicative inverses in $GF(2^m)$ using normal bases. *Information and Computation*, 78:171–177, 1988.

19. D. E. Knuth. *The Art of Computer Programming. Volume 2: Seminumerical Algorithms.* Addison-Wesley, Reading, Massachusetts, USA, 2nd edition, 1981.
20. N. Koblitz. Elliptic curve cryptosystems. *Mathematics of Computation,* 48:203–209, 1987.
21. Arjen Lenstra and Eric Verheul. Selecting cryptographic key sizes. In Hideki Imai and Yuliang Zheng, editors, *Third International Workshop on Practice and Theory in Public Key Cryptography — PKC 2000,* volume LNCS 1751, Berlin, 2000. Springer-Verlag.
22. Chae Hoon Lim and Hyo Sun Hwang. Fast Implementation of Elliptic Curve Arithmetic in $GF(p^n)$. In Hideki Imai and Yuliang Zheng, editors, *Third International Workshop on Practice and Theory in Public Key Cryptography — PKC 2000,* volume LNCS 1751, pages 405–421, Berlin, 2000. Springer-Verlag.
23. A. J. Menezes. *Elliptic Curve Public Key Cryptosystems.* Kluwer Academic Publishers, Boston, Massachusetts, USA, 1993.
24. A. J. Menezes, P. C. van Oorschot, and S. A. Vanstone. *Handbook of Applied Cryptography.* CRC Press, Boca Raton, Florida, USA, 1997.
25. V. Miller. Uses of elliptic curves in cryptography. In H. C. Williams, editor, *Advances in Cryptology — CRYPTO '85,* volume LNCS 218, pages 417–426, Berlin, Germany, 1986. Springer-Verlag.
26. P. L. Montgomery. Modular multiplication without trial division. *Mathematics of Computation,* 44(170):519–521, April 1985.
27. U.S. Department of Commerce/National Institute of Standard and Technol ogy. *Digital Signature Standard (DSS),* January 27 2000.
28. National Institute of Standard and Technology. Recommended elliptic curves for federal government use. available at http://csrc.nist.gov/encryption, May 1999.
29. *IEEE P1363 Standard Specifications for Public Key Cryptography,* November 1999. Last Preliminary Draft.
30. R. Schroeppel, H. Orman, S. O'Malley, and O. Spatscheck. Fast key exchange with elliptic curve systems. In D. Coppersmith, editor, *Advances in Cryptology — CRYPTO '95,* volume LNCS 963, pages 43–56, Berlin, Germany, 1995. Springer-Verlag.
31. Standards for Efficient Cryptography Group. SEC2: Recommended Elliptic Curve Domain Parameters. Working draft, version 0.7, September 2000.
32. Texas Instruments, Inc., Dallas, Texas 75265 USA. *MSP430C33x,MSP430P337A Mixed Signal Microcontrollers,* October 1999 (Revised June 2000).
33. Texas Instruments, Inc., Dallas, Texas 75265 USA. *MSP430x3xx Family – User's Guide,* July 2000.
34. A. Woodbury, D. V. Bailey, and C. Paar. Elliptic curve cryptography on smart cards without coprocessors. In *IFIP CARDIS 2000, Fourth Smart Card Research and Advanced Application Conference,* Bristol, UK, September 20–22 2000. Kluwer.

Secure Server-Aided Signature Generation

Markus Jakobsson and Susanne Wetzel

Bell Laboratories, Lucent Technologies
Information Sciences Research Center
Murray Hill, NJ 07974, USA
{markusj,sgwetzel}@research.bell-labs.com

Abstract. We study how to reduce the local computational cost associated with performing exponentiation. This involves transforming a large computational task into a large set of small computational tasks that are to be performed by a set of external servers who may all be controlled by one and the same adversary. In order to attack our problem, we introduce and employ the three principles of duplication, distribution and delegation. We apply our exponentiation scheme to performing inexpensive server-aided batch signature generation, and show noticeable efficiency improvements for batches of size 20 and up.

Keywords: Batch, DSS, delegation, duplication, error-detection.

1 Introduction

It is unfortunate that in spite of increasing processor speeds, the most important design criteria for many security protocols remains the computational complexity of the protocols, and not their security. To some extent, this is a mere reflection of human greed, as the relationship between efficiency and cost is well understood, whereas the impact of security problems is harder to quantify. With this in mind, it is clear that the development and understanding of efficient cryptographic building blocks is a vital contribution to protocol security, as only efficient tools will be employed for all but a few applications. On one hand, this prompts research into the development and usage of symmetric key cryptography; on the other hand, it suggests efforts to provide improved techniques for versatile but expensive operations, such as those relating to public key cryptography. In this paper, we focus on the latter.

One of the most common – and expensive – operations in public key cryptography is that of exponentiating. Its costs hover around 200 modular multiplications per exponentiation for exponent sizes around 160 bits, using standard window based methods. Clearly, any advance that allows its cost to be reduced is valuable. For very small batches, currently known techniques do not give any noteworthy speedups, while for large batches, various amortization techniques are known. An example of an amortization method is addition chains [6,5], which to day is the most efficient way of performing exponentiation for large batches, with a cost around a mere 10 multiplications per item [5]. The methods suggested in this paper allow for a local reduction of computational costs for both small

K. Kim (Ed.): PKC 2001, LNCS 1992, pp. 383–401, 2001.

batches (compared to window based methods) and large batches (compared to addition chain methods.)

In the above, the importance of the word *local* is imperative. Namely, we take the approach (so commonly used in most hierarchical organizations) of *delegation*: Instead of *performing* the task in question, it is handed off to somebody else. Whereas this can safely be done for most everyday life tasks (such as making coffee), one has to be very careful about how it is performed for tasks that involve security. In particular, if an enemy server learns an exponent used in a signature, and later intercepts the signature, he may be able to determine the secret key of the signer. A second problem is that of robustness, i.e., making sure that the computation performed is correct. The methods introduced in this paper are aimed at overcoming these and related problems, and thereby allowing the safe and robust delegation of exponentiation work to a set of untrusted servers. It is important to notice here that the security does not rely on sending different portions of a query to different servers that are assumed not to communicate. (In contrast to some work on how to compute with oracles.) Rather, we assume that *all* the delegated work may be performed or seen by one and the same malicious party. We argue security of our solution in this setting.

Our methods, which constitute a new approach to an old problem, involve as a first step some amount of pre-processing by the server wishing to have the computation to be performed. Let us call this party the *originator*. As a second step, they involve some computation by untrusted *external servers*, and finally, some post-processing by the originator. Generally speaking, the significance of the first step is to appropriately blind the request and to insert sufficient redundancy in the request, so that in the third step, errors and other deviations can be detected. Note, however, that standard methods for blinding cannot be used, as they involve the use of exponentiation (which, of course, is what we want to perform in the first place.) A contribution of this paper is therefore the development of inexpensive methods for blinding batches of queries. A second contribution is the development of methods that inexpensively allow for error detection and error correction in settings like ours. However, whereas these may be contributions of independent interest, we feel that the main importance is the move towards lowering exponentiation costs, along with the introduction of the idea of delegation to the setting considered.

While most batch methods require large batches, ours does well for small ones as well, which is particularly useful in a setting involving computationally limited devices such as smartcards.

For batches of size 20, we achieve local computational savings of approximately 81% over window-based methods, while batches of 100000 give us savings of 20%. When we talk about small batches, such as batches of size 20, we assume the use of a larger *cumulative* batch size, where the cumulative batch size corresponds to the number of elements to be processed over the lifetime of the device, as opposed to the number processed at one occasion. This is important to note as it allows for preprocessing corresponding to the cumulative batch size, which is performed externally, thus resulting in further savings.

Outline: We begin by discussing the related work in section 2. We then introduce the model and define our goals in section 3. This is followed by a high-level discussion of our methods in section 4, after which we delve into our solution (tailored for large batches) in section 5. In section 5.4 we make security claims corresponding to this scenario, with a corresponding security and efficiency analysis in the appendix. In section 6 we briefly discuss a variant of our solution applied to a smartcard scenario (corresponding to reduced quantities of local storage and use of small batches.)

2   Related Work

The general ideas of server-aided computation and batching are not new (c.f. [1,3,9,21,24,25,29]). While the server-aided RSA computation protocols proposed in [9,24,25] have been found not to be secure [28,22], the methods introduced in [29,21] are believed to be secure against passive attacks, i.e., attacks performed by honest-but-curious servers.

Our work differs from the above in several ways. First, while most of the previous work focuses on modular exponentiation for composite moduli (i.e., RSA), we target computation with prime moduli, and in particular, discrete log protocols like DSA [26] and Schnorr [32]. A second difference is that we make more pessimistic trust assumptions, and introduce methods for achieving robustness under such assumptions, and under active attacks. In this sense, we position ourselves much closer to work on oracle computation [1], which can be seen as a theoretical relative of server-aided computation, and where robustness is a core issue.

However, we make computational assumptions that are closer related to those typically made for server-aided computation, as we adopt the setting of a polynomial-time limited adversary. This makes particular sense in the context of generating standard signatures, which in turn is one of the focal points of our work. Therefore, on the one hand, we make stronger security assumptions than what is done for much of the work relating to computing with oracles, which allows us more efficient results. On the other hand, some of our other assumptions are *weaker* (and more realistic, we believe), as we allow the adversary to see the *entire* query string, independently of whether one or more servers are employed in practice. This is in contrast to what is assumed for some of the work on computing with oracles (e.g., [2,16]), where it is assumed that there is a separation between servers.

Our work is related to [7] in terms of the goal it achieves. However, a noteworthy difference is that the exponents for which computation is performed are random (according to some near-random diatribution) in [7], while they can be chosen arbitrarily in our scheme.

Technically, our work is influenced by a whole array of well understood methods. Whereas the type of blinding we perform is novel, it is related in spirit to existing blinding techniques performed for discrete log based signature schemes, such as was done in [8]. While the solutions in [9,25,24] are vulnerable to active and passive attacks [22,28], we introduce various error detecting techniques to achieve robustness. These techniques, which depend closely on the use of blinding, also draw on several previously proposed methods. One method is to duplicate the set of queries, and to permute and blind each item individually, forcing an adversary to guess the location of related portions in order to successfully attack the system. This idea has previously been employed for robustness of mix networks [20,15]. Another method is to introduce known values in the query string, and verify that these are computed correctly. Together with the permutation performed, this becomes an inexpensive and powerful way of protecting against an attack in which the adversary offsets all the queries in the same manner (which in principle would be possible were only the duplication method to be used.) A third method, of a more traditional error-detecting type, is to introduce values that depend on other values, and to verify that these values, when returned, have the expected relationship. A drawback of this approach is the increased cost per item; however, it could be a useful method in a setting with very small batches (in which case the duplication methods becomes less powerful.) Finally, a fourth method is to introduce dependencies in how the computation is performed. In other words, this chains the partial results in a manner that spreads any inconsistency, thereby making it easier to detect. (While this is related in spirit to the avalanche effect used in symmetric cipher design, the actual methods employed differ substantially.) This method becomes a powerful (but also rather expensive) error-detecting tool in conjunction with the previously outlined methods. However, the error-spreading functionality not only allows easy detection of errors, but has the flip side of spreading the effects of any error to otherwise good portions of computation.

3   Model and Requirements

Participants. We assume all participants to be modeled by polynomial-time limited Turing machines. The scheme has two types of "desired" participants: an *originator* (who in our signature setting is the party who holds the secret key for generating signatures) and *external servers*. The latter are used by the originator to have computation performed.

We assume that all the external servers may be controlled by an "unwanted" entity, the adversary. It is the primary goal of the adversary to improve his chances of computing some known function of the secret signing key of the originator (such as forging a signature.) A secondary goal is to corrupt the computation the originator wishes to perform, without this being noticed by the the originator.

Informally, a protocol for outsourcing computation should be *private* (not leak secret information) and *robust* (not allow incorrect computation to go undetected). Moreover, it has to be *efficient*, i.e., reduce the amount of local computation to be performed given some assumptions on the probability that a computational portion is correctly performed when outsourced. More formally, we can define these as follows:

Definition: *Let T be a computational task, and f an arbitrary function. We say that a delegation of T is ϵ-private with respect to f if the adversary has only a negligible advantage ϵ in computing $f(i)$ for some input i if performing the delagated work and seeing the public input and output of the originator, compared to a setting where he only sees the public input and output of the originator.*

It has to be noted that in the setting we study, we are – in terms of privacy – only directly concerned with the privacy of the exponent values for the signatures (which indirectly corresponds to the privacy of the secret signing key). If this context it may be more appropriate to denote the property *security*, although we will use the more general (and generally applicable) *privacy*.

The robustness of the scheme deals with a different kind of attack, namely the adversary trying to corrupt the computations. In the following, we consider the robustness of a signature generation:

Definition: *We say that a delegation of T is ϵ-robust if an adversary who controls all the external servers performing computation for the signer cannot corrupt the computation but for a probability ϵ. (The above is over all random strings of the signer, and over all computational tasks T.)*

Turning to efficiency, note that we are primarily concerned with the amount of computation performed by the signer, and not with that performed by the external servers (as long as their computational tasks are feasible.) We define the efficiency of an outsourced computation as follows:

Definition: *We say that a delegation of a computational task T is (ϵ, ν)-efficient, if the signer's computational load if performing the computation T himself is a fraction ϵ of that required by him if outsourcing T. This is relative to a certain fraction ν of incorrect responses that are scheduled by the adversary, and where the probability is over all random coins of the signer.*

In the following we present a solution which allows the efficient delegation of signature generation. This proposed solution meets the requirements of robustness and privacy, as will be shown in the analysis section.

4   Delegation

The type of work we strive to delegate in this paper, namely generating DSA signatures [26], is characterized by a large amount of exponentiation. We will use the standard denotation for DSA, in which one of the computational tasks is to compute $r = g^k \bmod p$, where $k \in Z_q$, primes p and q such that $p = lq + 1$, and $|p| = 1024$, $|q| = 160$. As usual, all operations are assumed to be performed modulo p, where applicable, unless otherwise noted.

Clearly, it is easy to delegate the exponentiation of values simply by transmitting the bases, exponents, and moduli to a server performing the computation. However, this simplistic approach has several potential weaknesses; in the following, we will discuss these, along with the constructions we will employ to avoid them.

The issues of robustness and defense against information leaks are closely related in that the methods to achieve these two goals are largely overlapping. Let us consider what these methods are:

1. *Permutation.* A first method is to randomly permute the order of the partial tasks in the batch of requests sent to the external servers. Permutation is helpful as it forces the adversary to guess what exponentiation(s) corresponds to what signature. The costs incurred by the originator to perform this operation are insignificant. Similarly, the permutation does not affect the amount of computation to be performed by the external servers.

2. *Blinding.* A second method we use is to transform the exponents in a way that closely corresponds to a traditional blinding. This is done by applying a random (and secret) offset to each exponentiation in the batch where offsets are selected in a particular way to keep the costs of the operation down. (We elaborate on how this is done below.) The additional local cost incurred by blinding consists of a first cost corresponding to applying the offsets to the exponents, and a second cost of removing the resulting offsets from the values returned by the external servers. The blinding does not affect the global costs, i.e., the amount of computations performed by the external servers, at all.

3. *Error-detection and error-correction.* Finally, a third method we use (and which to some extent is a novel method for this type of application) employs error detection and error correction methods to spot and remedy inconsistencies. This is done by introducing what we call *known values, replication, dependencies* and *checksums.* These methods manipulate the vector of queries and verify that certain relationships hold for the returned results. The methods are as follows:

   (a) *Known values.* We let the originator insert some w tasks into the batch of computations to be delegated, where he already knows the results of these computational tasks. (For example, $x = 0$, resulting in $g^x = 1$; note that such simple computational tasks can not be distinguished from other tasks once they are blinded.) This allows the detection of so-called offset attacks, in which the adversary correctly computes all tasks, and then offsets all of the replies using the same multiplicative offset. Both the additional local and global costs are negligible.

   (b) *Replication.* A second method for error-detection is replication, according to which one instead of delegating a computational task only once delegates it some τ times. We will apply this transformation before blinding and permutation are performed. Since each task is delegated τ times, both local and global costs increase by a factor τ (not considering minor amortization gains.)

(c) *Dependency.* Including dependencies in the computations performed by the clients results in serious error propagation, which reduces the success probability of attacks in which an adversary provides some incorrect replies. Together with duplication, this allows easy detection of errors and malicious responses. We implement dependencies by "linking" tasks to each other, making one result depend on two or more other results, which in turn depend on others. We introduce dependencies by transforming a query consisting of the exponents $k_1, \ldots, k_n$ to a query consisting of the the exponents $k'_1, \ldots, k'_n$, where

$$k'_i = \begin{cases} k_1 & : i = 1 \\ k_i + \alpha \cdot k_{i-1} + \beta \cdot k'_{i-1} \bmod q & : 1 < i \le n \end{cases}$$

where $\alpha, \beta \in \{-1, 0, 1\}$. Depending on the values of α and β, different levels of error propagation can be achieved. While error propagation is very useful for detecting forgery, it also requires recomputation of many exponentiations. For efficiency reasons, this method needs to be combined with the other mechanisms.

(d) *Checksums.* A fourth method is that of inserting checksums. These are values that depend on subsets of the other values (potentially all of these), and which are checked by multiplying the results together and comparing to the corresponding checksum values. Whereas it is an expensive operation to verify the checksums (requiring roughly one multiplication per item selected for the checksum) it can be used as a recovery method to locate good sections of a corrupted set of computed values. (Where we use other methods to *detect* errors.) This may be beneficial given the negligible precomputation costs of the operation. The operation results in a minor blow-up in the size of the query string; namely, introducing u checksums each of length v with $u \cdot v = n$ (i.e., each element is part of one checksum) results in u additional computational tasks to be delegated to the servers.

It is important to note that in order to achieve maximum security, one should perform the error detection and error correction before performing the blinding and permutation steps.

Detailed Blinding Description. In detail, the blinding for the exponent vector $(k_1, \ldots, k_n)$ is done by first choosing e random numbers $r_1, \ldots r_e \in \{0, \ldots, \frac{q-1}{2}\}$. Then, for each exponent k_j with $1 \le j \le n$, d elements are chosen and the new exponents are computed as

$$k'_j = k_j - \sum_{i=1}^{e} \gamma_{i,j} r_i \bmod q$$

with $\gamma_{i,j} \in \{0, 1\}$ and $\sum_{i=1}^{e} \gamma_{i,j} = d$. The choice of what blinding values to combine in order to obtain the various blinding elements, we must not select two equal sets of blinding values, or they can be cancelled by randomly guessing these two resulting blinded portions, which could leak the secret key. In fact, we select what blinding values to use by enumeration over all sets with a particular minimum Hamming distance (where the Hamming distance of two sets $\mathcal{S}_1, \mathcal{S}_2$ is defined as the number of elements of $(\mathcal{S}_1 \cup \mathcal{S}_2) \backslash (\mathcal{S}_1 \cap \mathcal{S}_2)$). The Hamming distance in turn determines how many portions have to be combined by the adversary in order to cancel blinding factors. The sets of blinding factors form a so-called constant weight code with length n and weight d. We refer to [12,30] for a description of these codes, their properties and how they can be constructed. Computing the actual signatures corresponding to the exponents $k_1, \ldots, k_n$ requires the computation of the $g^{\sum_{i=1}^{e} \gamma_{i,j} r_i \bmod q}$ for $1 \leq j \leq n$ by the signer. Using standard methods, the g^{r_i} for $1 \leq i \leq e$ can be computed with ≈ 200 multiplications and the precomputation of all possible pairs $g^{r_i + r_j \bmod q}$ with $1 \leq i < j \leq e$ requires $\leq \frac{e(e-1)}{2}$ multiplications. Thus, the additional costs for the signer computing the original signature amount to

$$\approx 1 + (\lceil \frac{d}{2} \rceil - 1) + \frac{1}{n}(200e + \frac{e(e-1)}{2}).$$

Remark on dependencies: In a more general setting, the dependencies can be introduced on blocks of size $b \leq n$ where $b \cdot b' = n$ as follows:

$$k_i' = \begin{cases} k_i & : i = l \cdot b + 1 \\ k_i + \alpha \cdot k_{i-1} + \beta \cdot k_{i-1}' \bmod q & : l \cdot b + 1 < i \leq (l+1) \cdot b \end{cases}$$

for $1 \leq l \leq b'$.

5   Solution (Large Batches)

We are now ready to present our solution. At this level of description, we are only concerned with the computation performed on the signer's side. This is broken into two portions, sandwiching the portion performed by the computing servers. These two portions correspond to transforming the problem into a randomized description of the same, and to transform back the corresponding "randomized result" into a result, and check for inconsistencies. The parameters, e.g., the number of signatures to be produced, have been chosen to balance efficiency and security requirements for an Internet scenario (characterized by large batches.)

5.1   Problem Transformation

Let the input consist of the vector $((g, k_1), \ldots, (g, k_n))$ corresponding to an implicit request to compute $(g^{k_1}, \ldots, g^{k_n})$. We denote this input by $\mathcal{G}_1 = (k_1, \ldots, k_n)$. The signer will transform $\mathcal{G}_1$ as follows:

1. **Replication** At first, the above vector is extended by replicating the last element of $\mathcal{G}_1$, i.e., $k_{n+1} = k_n$. Then, the resulting is substituted with a

vector where each element occurs three times. I.e., the original vector $\mathcal{G}_1 = (k_1, \ldots, k_n)$ is transformed into the new vector

$$\mathcal{G}_2 = (k_1, \ldots k_n, k_{n+1}, k_1, \ldots$$
$$\ldots, k_n, k_{n+1}, k_1, \ldots, k_n, k_{n+1}).$$

2. **Dependency.** As a next step, dependency is introduced by transforming the third part of the vector $\mathcal{G}_2$ yielding

$$\mathcal{G}_3 = (K_1, \ldots, K_{3n+3})$$

where $K_i = (\mathcal{G}_2)_i$ for $1 \leq i \leq 2n + 2$ and for $2n + 3 \leq i \leq 3n + 3$ the K_i are inductively defined as

$$K_i = \begin{cases} k_1 & : i = 2n + 3 \\ k_i - k_{i-1} - K_{i-1} \bmod q : 2n + 3 < i \leq 3n + 2 \\ K_{i-1} & : i = 3n + 3 \end{cases}$$

Due that the fact that the dependencies can also be interpreted as checksums, no additional checksums are introduced.

3. **Blinding.** For the blinding, e random numbers $r_1, \ldots, r_e \in \{0, \ldots, \frac{q-1}{2}\}$ are picked. Then, for each element of the vector $\mathcal{G}_3$, 4 elements $\rho_{1,(\mathcal{G}_3)_i}, \ldots, \rho_{4,(\mathcal{G}_3)_i}$ are selected (in the manner previously described) from $R = \{r_1, \ldots, r_e\}$ and the new vector

$$\mathcal{G}_4 = (\kappa_1, \ldots, \kappa_{3n+3})$$

is computed as $\kappa_i = (\mathcal{G}_3)_i - \sum_{j=1}^4 \rho_{j,(\mathcal{G}_3)_i} \bmod q$ for $1 \leq i \leq 3n + 3$.

4. **Random permutation.** A permutation, Π on the vector is selected uniformly at random, resulting in the new vector

$$\mathcal{G}_5 = \Pi(\mathcal{G}_4).$$

5.2   Outsourcing

The vector that constitutes the final output of the above transformation is broken up into blocks of appropriate size, and communicated to computing servers. (We note that one clearly only has to communicate the value g once.) If a vector $(A_1, \ldots, A_k)$ is sent to a computing server, the latter is expected to compute and return the vector $(g^{A_1}, \ldots, g^{A_k})$.

5.3   Result Transformation

Again, we assume the input consists of one vector $\mathcal{G}_6$ whose elements consist of the values returned by the computing servers, arranged in the order in which they were handed out (that is, so that the reply to a query is entered in the same position from which the query was taken). The following steps are performed to transform and verify the result:

1. **Inverse permutation.** The signer constructs a new vector by applying the inverse permutation, compared to the one performed towards the end of the transformation stage. This results in the vector

$$\mathcal{G}_7 = \Pi^{-1}(\mathcal{G}_6).$$

2. **Inverse blinding.** For each $1 \leq i \leq 3n + 3$ the signer computes

$$(\mathcal{G}_8)_i = g^{(\mathcal{G}_7)_i + \sum_{j=1}^{4} \rho_{j,(\mathcal{G}_3)_i}} \bmod q$$

thus resulting in $\mathcal{G}_8$. This computation is performed using methods for addition chains.

3. **Verification of dependencies and redundancy.** As a last step, the redundancies are checked, i.e., if $(\mathcal{G}_8)_{n+2} \overset{?}{=} (\mathcal{G}_8)_{2n+3}$, $(\mathcal{G}_8)_n \overset{?}{=} (\mathcal{G}_8)_{n+1}$, $(\mathcal{G}_8)_{2n+1} \overset{?}{=} (\mathcal{G}_8)_{2n+2}$ and $(\mathcal{G}_8)_{3n+2} \overset{?}{=} (\mathcal{G}_8)_{3n+3}$, as well as if for $1 \leq i \leq n$

$$(\mathcal{G}_8)_{n+1+i} \overset{?}{=} (\mathcal{G}_8)_i.$$

Moreover, for $2 \leq i \leq n$ the signer checks inductively

$$(\mathcal{G}_8)_{2n+2+i} \cdot (\mathcal{G}_8)_{2n+i+1} \cdot (\mathcal{G}_8)_{i-1} \overset{?}{=} (\mathcal{G}_8)_i.$$

If so, $(\mathcal{G}_8)_i$ with $1 \leq i \leq n$ are the correct results of the delegated computations. Otherwise, if $1 \leq j \leq n$ is the index where the check fails, then the computations of $(\mathcal{G}_8)_i$ with $1 \leq i < j$ are correct. The values $(\mathcal{G}_8)_i$ with $i < j < n$ are compared with $(\mathcal{G}_8)_{n+i+1}$. If equality holds, these values are assumed to be correct. Otherwise, recomputation will be necessary as in case of $(\mathcal{G}_8)_j$.

Remark: The above protocol obtains a high degree of robustness (as will be discussed in the following subsection and argued in the appendix). However, in situations in which robustness is not critical, or in which a third party is employed to verify the signatures, our protocol can be altered to substantially reduce the costs. Similarly, if our methods are employed for purposes of decryption instead of signature generation, redundancy checks (of the resulting plaintexts) can be used to obtain robustness at reduced costs.

The protocol costs can be reduced by not performing the verification of dependencies (reducing the amount of work performed in steps 2 and 3 above), or by not using duplication (reducing the amount of work performed in step 2). Note that these changes do not alter the degree of privacy, but only the robustness. We will review the resulting costs and robustness claims of the corresponding protocol versions.

5.4   Security Claims

For concreteness, we analyze the security of our scheme only for the particular parameters proposed.

Privacy. Starting with the privacy aspect, and considering the state of the art in terms of attacks, we argue in Appendix A that if we choose at least $e = 75$ blinding factors, then our scheme is 2^{-80}-private for input sizes larger than 100000 and smaller than $\binom{e}{4} = \binom{75}{4} = 1215450$.

Robustness. For an input size n, our protocol is $(3 \cdot \binom{3n+2}{5})^{-1}$-robust against an adversary who controls all the external servers, for large batch sizes. Thus, for input sizes larger than 47000 elements, an attacker has less than a probability 2^{-80} to corrupt the computation without detection.

   In Appendix B, we argue by case analysis that it is necessary for an adversary to select a "coherent set" of at least six elements among the existing $3n + 3$ elements. Given the random distribution of the elements (described in appendix A) the adversary can only succeed if the five last elements he chooses are "coherent with" the first elements he chose, which gives the claimed probability of success.

Efficiency. In Appendix C, we show that our protocol is approximately $(\frac{5}{4}, 0)$-efficient for batches of size approximately 100000 signatures, with an actual cost per signature of 8 multiplications. This corresponds to a local efficiency improvement of 20%, compared to addition chain methods.

6   Smartcard Setting (Small Batches)

In our smartcard setting, we perform the initial exponentiation as part of the manufacturing or initialization process of the smartcard. (However, we do not precompute all pairs, due to the storage problems that would cause.) Thus, the smartcard stores pairs (r_i, g^{r_i}). While in this smartcard setting the original vector has to be replicated seven times in order to obtain a robustness level corresponding to a probability of failure of 2^{-80} for a batch size of $n = 20$, the dependency is introduced as before. In order to achieve a security level of 2^{-80}, the cumulative batch size will have to be chosen to be at least 80000. Therefore, 75 blinding factors is sufficient, since $\binom{75}{4} > 80000 \cdot 9$, where 9 is the effect of replication and dependencies. We note that the cumulative batch size corresponds to the number of signatures that can be generated by the smartcard without "recharging".

   We see that the local cost per signature is only 42 multiplications per signature, which is in strong contrast to the approximately 200 multiplications that are otherwise needed for such small batches. Thus, our protocol is $(\frac{100}{19}, 0)$-efficient for very small batches, which corresponds to a 81% savings.

7   Conclusions

In this paper we have presented methods to reduce the local computational costs associated with performing exponentiations for signature generation. Using the principles of duplication, distribution and delegation, we achieve a reduction of costs incurred by the use of addition chains which to day is the most efficient method of performing exponentiations. A future direction of interest is to apply our methods to different problems and to research other redundancy methods to obtain robustness. In particular, employing different patterns for the recurrence computation may be of benefit. Furthermore, application of results known from coding theory could give improved methods for selection of blinding values which in turn would improve efficiency by allowing smaller batches and cumulative batches.

References

1. M. Abadi, J. Feigenbaum and J. Kilian, "On Hiding Information from an Oracle", Journal of Computer and System Sciences, Vol. 39, no. 1, Aug 1989, pp. 21–50.
2. D. Beaver, J. Feigenbaum and V. Shoup, "Hiding Instances in Zero-Knowledge Proof Systems," CRYPTO '90, pp. 326–338.
3. M. Bellare, J.A. Garay and T. Rabin, "Fast Batch Verification for Modular Exponentiation and Digital Signatures," EUROCRYPT '98, 1998, pp. 236–250.
4. M. Ben-Or, S. Goldwasser and A. Wigderson, "Completeness Theorems for Non-cryptographic Fault-Tolerant Distributed Computations", STOC '88, pp. 1–10.
5. D. Bleichenbacher, "Addition Chains for Large Sets", preprint, 1999.
6. J. Bos and M. Coster, "Addition Chain Heuristics," CRYPTO '89, pp. 400–407.
7. V. Boyko, M. Peinado and R. Venkatesan, "Speeding up discrete log and factoring based schemes via precomputations. EUROCRYPT '98, pp. 221–235.
8. S. Brands, "Untraceable Off-line Cash in Wallet with Observers," CRYPTO '93, pp. 302–318.
9. J. Burns and C.J. Mitchell, "Parameter Selection for Server-Aided RSA Computation Schemes" IEEE Transactions on Computers, Vol. 43, No. 2, 1994, pp. 163–174.
10. D. Chaum, C. Crépeau and I. Damgård, "Multiparty Unconditionally Secure Protocols", STOC '98, pp. 11–19.
11. R. Canetti, U. Feige, O. Goldreich and M. Naor, "Adaptively Secure Multi-Party Computation", STOC '96, pp. 639–648.
12. J.H. Conway and N.J.A.Sloane, "Sphere Packings, Lattices and Groups", Springer, 1993.
13. M.J. Coster, B.A. LaMacchia, A.M. Odlyzko, C.P. Schnorr and J. Stern, "Improved Low-Density Subset Sum Algorithms", Journal of Computational Complexity, Vol. 2, 1992, pp. 111–128.
14. A. De Santis, Y. Desmedt, Y. Frankel and M. Yung, "How to Share a Function Securely", STOC '94, pp. 522–533.
15. Y. Desmedt and K. Kurosawa, "How to Break a Practical MIX and Design a New One," EUROCRYPT '00, pp. 557–772.
16. J. Feigenbaum and R. Ostrovsky, "A Note on One-Prover Instance-Hiding, Zero-Knowledge Proof Systems", ASIACRYPT '91, pp. 352–359.
17. M.R. Garey and D.S. Johnson, "Computers and Intractability: A Guide to the Theory of NP-Completeness," W.H. Freeman and Company, 1979.
18. R. Gennaro, M. Rabin and T. Rabin, "Simplified VSS and Fast-track Multiparty Computations with Applications to Threshold Cryptography", PODC '98, pp. 101–111.

19. O. Goldreich, S. Micali and A. Wigderson, "How to Play Any Mental Game", STOC '87, pp. 218–229.

20. M. Jakobsson, "A Practical Mix", EUROCRYPT '98, pp. 448–461.

21. S. Kawamura and A. Shimbo, "Fast Server-Aided Secret Computation Protocols for Modular Exponentiation", IEEE Journal on Selected Areas in Communications, Vol. 11, No. 5, 1993, pp. 778–784.

22. C.H. Lim and P.J. Lee, "Security and Performance of Server-Aided RSA Computation Protocols," CRYPTO '95, pp. 70–83.

23. C.H. Lim and P.J. Lee, "More Flexible Exponentiation With Precomputation", CRYPTO '94, pp. 95–107.

24. T. Matsumoto, H. Imai, C.S. Laih and S.M. Yen, "On Verifiable Implicit Asking Protocols for RSA Computation", AUSCRYPT '92, pp. 296–307.

25. T. Matsumoto, K. Kato and H. Imai, "Speeding Up Secret Computations with Insecure Auxiliary Devices", CRYPTO '88, pp. 497–506.

26. National Institute of Standards and Technology (NIST), "FIPS Publication 186-1: Digital Signature Standard", December 15, 1998.

27. P. Nguyen and J. Stern, "The Hardness of the Hidden Subset Sum Problem and its Cryptographic Implications", Crypto '99, pp. 31–46.

28. B. Pfitzmann and M. Waidner, "Attacks on Protocols for Server-Aided RSA Computation", EUROCRYPT '92, pp. 153–162.

29. J.-J. Quisquater and M. De Soete, "Speeding up Smart Card RSA Computation with Insecure Coprocessors", SMART CARD 2000, 1989, pp. 191–197.

30. E.M.Rains and N.J.A. Sloane, "Table of Constant Weight Binary Codes", http://www.research.att.com/~njas/codes/Andw/, 2000.

31. T. Sander, A. Young and M. Yung, "Non-Interactive Crypto Computing for NC^1", FOCS '99, pp. 554–567.

32. C.-P. Schnorr, "Efficient Signature Generation for Smart Cards," Journal of Cryptology, Vol. 4, 1991, pp. 161–174.

33. C.P. Schnorr and M. Euchner, "Lattice Basis Reduction: Improved Practical Algorithms and Solving Subset Sum Problems", Mathematical Programming 66, 1994, pp. 181–199.

34. C.P. Schnorr and H.H. Hörner, "Attacking the Chor-Rivest Cryptosystem by Improved Lattice Reduction", EUROCRYPT '95, pp. 1–12.

35. A.C. Yao, "Protocols for Secure Computations", FOCS '82, pp. 160–164.

A   Privacy Analysis

A scheme is *private* if each set of the queries issued by it is indistinguishable from an equal-sized set of uniformly distributed random queries. We argue that if we choose a sufficient number of blinding factors in our scheme, then our scheme is private.

According to Section 5, an input vector $(k_1, ..., k_n)$ is transformed into the outsourced vector by applying *replication*, introducing *dependencies*, performing *blinding* and applying a permutation. For purposes of privacy analysis it suffices to consider only the permutation as well as the blinding process. The blindings are generated by selecting d of the blinding factors $r_1, ..., r_e$, i.e., $k'_i = k_i + \sum_{j=1}^{e} \gamma_{i,j} r_j$ with $\sum_{j=1}^{e} \gamma_{i,j} = d$ and $\gamma_{i,j} \in \{0, 1\}$. The permutation of the list k'_i is sent to the servers. Let us for sake of an argument assume that an attacker knows the random permutation. Then, the attacker can compute $g^{k_i'}/g^{k_i} = g^{\rho_i}$, where the exponent $\rho_i = \sum_{j=1}^{e} \gamma_{i,j} r_j$ $(1 \leq i \leq n)$ is unknown. Then, following the analyisis in [7], we know that:

Theorem 1. *Assuming that there exists an algorithm that, given g^{ρ_i}, for $\rho_i = \sum_{j=1}^{e} \gamma_{i,j} r_j$, and $1 \leq i \leq n-1$, computes the discrete log of g^{ρ_n} with success rate ϵ, then there is an algorithm to compute the discrete log on arbitrary inputs in expected time $O(1/\epsilon)$ with success rate ϵ.*

However, and just as in [7], there is a further complication in that one component of the signature is a linear function of the secret value k, and the secret key x. This opens up for a host of problems, which we will list and elaborate on in the following. We note, though, that there is no known proof of security, as there are no proofs of the bounds on the complexity of the attacks to be described, and others that are not yet discovered. A reasonable heuristic, though, can be obtained from studying the progress of these attacks.

Attack Type I: Lattice Based Attacks. Since we reuse blinding elements for the different blinding factors, we need to consider the impact of lattice based attacks on our security. In particular, one of these attacks relates to the classical subset sum problem:

Subset Sum Problem: *For given positive integers $w_1, \ldots, w_N$ (the weights) and the sum S, find a subset of the weights, i.e., determine the variables $x_1, \ldots x_N \in \{0, 1\}$ such that $S = \sum_{i=1}^{N} x_i w_i$.*

Transforming the problem into a lattice problem, i.e., reducing it to the problem of finding a shortest vector in a lattice [13] is the most powerful method known to date to attack the classical subset sum problem. In practice, lattice basis reduction methods such as the LLL reduction algorithm or the Blockwise-Korkine-Zolotarev (BKZ) reduction algorithm [13,33,34] provide suitable approximations to the shortest lattice vector. They perform well (in respect to run-time and quality of the approximation) for a small number of weights but break down for $N > 200$. While the LLL algorithm has a binary complexity of $O(N^6 \log^3 B)$ (where B is a bound on the size of the entries of the corresponding lattice basis) there is no polynomial time algorithm known to date for performing a BKZ reduction. On the other hand, BKZ reduction yields better reduction results than the LLL algorithm. For an increasing number of weights the quality of the approximation becomes insufficient for providing a solution to the subset sum problem.

Moreover, since according to the construction of the blinding not only the variables $x_1, \ldots x_N \in \{0, 1\}$ but also the weights $w_1, \ldots, w_N$ are unknown, the attacker is faced with a problem that is even harder to solve:

Hidden Sum Problem: *For a given N and sums $S_1, \ldots, S_l \in \mathbb{Z}_p$, find weights $w_1, \ldots, w_N \in \mathbb{Z}_p$ and determine the variables $x_{1,1}, \ldots x_{N,l} \in \{0, 1\}$ such that $S_j = \sum_{i=1}^{N} x_{i,j} w_i$ for $1 \leq j \leq l$.*

This problem was first introduced in [7]. Apart from exhaustive search, lattice-based methods are once again the most efficient techniques known to date to solve the problem [27]. However, regardless of the density of the subset sum problem neither of these methods is practical for attacking the privacy of our scheme of server-aided signature generation. This is due to efficiency reasons. Both exhaustive search and lattice-based attacks can be performed only for small problem instances with a very few weights. E.g., in [27] the problem could only be solved for up to $N \approx 45$ whereas we consider settings with $N > 80000$.

Attack Type II: Cancellations among Blindings. If an attacker could efficiently select a small number of signatures such that the applied blindings cancel each other, he would be also be able to retrieve the secret key used.

1. *Two identical sets of blinding elements.*
   This case, namely that in which $\{\rho_{1,(\mathcal{G}_3)_i}, \ldots \rho_{4,(\mathcal{G}_3)_i}\} = \{\rho_{1,(\mathcal{G}_3)_j}, \ldots \rho_{4,(\mathcal{G}_3)_j}\}$ for $i \neq j$ is efficiently prevented by the use of enumeration for the selection, which guarantees that no two queries will use the very same set of blinding elements. Thus, for a given input size n, the number of blinding factors has to be chosen such that $\binom{e}{d} \geq n$.
2. *The sums of two blinding sets are equal.*
   This case, namely $\rho_{1,(\mathcal{G}_3)_i} + \ldots + \rho_{4,(\mathcal{G}_3)_i} \bmod q = \rho_{1,(\mathcal{G}_3)_j} + \ldots + \rho_{4,(\mathcal{G}_3)_j} \bmod q$ can be seen to occur only with probability $\frac{1}{q}$, which is negligible.
3. *All blinding elements are selected.*
   We note that it is not possible to cancel the blinding factors by adding all of the resulting queries. This is so even if all the possible enumerations were to be used, since the elements of the linear combination with necessity must have different signs in order for all the blinding elements to cancel.
4. *The attacker identifies more than one but less than all elements.*
   We consider in the following a selection of blinding elements such that any two selections have a Hamming distance of at least 2. In the following, let $B_1, B_2, B_3, \ldots$ be the sets with four blinding factors $b_{i,1}, b_{i,2}, b_{i,3}, b_{i,4}$ ($i = 1, 2, 3, \ldots$). Apparently, an attacker won't succeed by only choosing two sets of blinding factors B_1 and B_2 since the two sets differ in at least one element, and therefore cannot cancel. Thus, in each linear combination of those two sets

$$a_1 \cdot (b_{1,1} + b_{1,2} + b_{1,3} + b_{1,4}) +$$
$$a_2 \cdot (b_{2,1} + b_{2,2} + b_{2,3} + b_{2,4}) \bmod q$$

with $a_1, a_2 \in \mathbb{Z}_q^*$, there will be at least a sum of two elements left. In case of three sets, an attacker is faced with the problem of finding a third set to cancel the sum of the first two. Since the linear combination of the first two will either contain elements with different signs or with different factors, choosing only three sets is not sufficient either. Thus, an attacker will have to choose at least four suitable sets.

There are four cases to be considered; one in which the four chosen sets elements correspond to four different signatures; one in which they correspond to three; then two, with two elements for each; then two, with one element for one and three elements for the other. We will focus on the probability of success for the first of these cases. The probability of success for the others will be smaller, as can be seen from case analysis.

For the first case, the probability of success corresponds to an attack in which the adversary selects three elements (of the outsourced type) at random from all available such elements, and then selects the last one, hoping that the four elements he chose are such that the blinding factors cancel. Then, he selects four signatures to match these four outsourced elements. The probability of the fourth outsourced element having the desired property is $1/(\Delta-3)$, where $\Delta = 3(n+1) < \binom{e}{4}$. The probability of selecting the matching signatures is not better than $1/\binom{n}{4}$. Thus, the success probability of the adversary is smaller than $8/(n-3)^5$. We see that for $n > 99337$ the attacker has a chance less than 2^{-80} to successfully retrieve the private key.

It is left to be shown that for any given three sets of blinding factors B_1, B_2 and B_3, there is at most one fourth set B_4 such that all four are linear dependent, i.e.,

$$\sum_{i=1}^{4} a_i \cdot (b_{i,1} + b_{i,2} + b_{i,3} + b_{i,4}) \bmod q = 0$$

with $a_1, a_2, a_3, a_4 \in \mathbb{Z}_q^*$. Linear dependence of B_1, B_2, B_3 and B_4 can only be achieved if not more than four elements in the linear combination of the given B_1, B_2 and B_3 are left and each element is weighted with the same factor. In the following let the first set of blinding elements be multiplied by factor a_1, the second one with a_2 and the third one with a_3.

(a) If each set contains at least one element that is not contained in any other set, then $a_1 = a_2 = a_3$, since the results in the linear combination will have to have the same factor. But since the sets differ by at least one element, the resulting combination will contain at least 5 elements, thus the cancellation cannot be achieved with only a fourth vector.

(b) In case that only two sets contain elements that are not found in the other sets (where those sets in the linear combination are weighted with a_1 and a_2 respectively), then $a_1 = a_2$. Moreover, there will be at least one element in the sum that is weighted with a_1+a_3 and one with a_1+a_2. Since $a_2 \neq 0$ and $a_3 \neq 0$, the chances that a fourth vector can be found are only in case $a_3 = -a_2 = -a_1$. Thus, the combination of these three vectors consists of only zeros or a_1's. If the number of a_1's is four, there is a fourth vector to achieve cancellation, otherwise there isn't.

(c) In the last case, that only one set (weighted with a_1 in the linear combination) contains elements that are not contained in any of the two other sets, the elements in the linear combination will need to match to zero or a_1. Once again, there is at least one factor $a_1 + a_3$ and at lest one $a_1 + a_2$. With $a_2 \neq 0$ and $a_3 \neq 0$ it follows that in order to keep the chance that a fourth vector can be found, $a_2 = a_3 = -a_1$. If there is a factor $a_1 + a_2 + a_3$ or more than 4 elements left, the fourth vector cannot be found.

This completes the argument. For the smartcard setting, a corresponding argument can be applied for $\Delta = (8 + 1)(n' + 1)$, where n' is the cumulative batch size.

B   Robustness Analysis

A scheme is *robust* if it is not possible for an adversary controlling all the computing servers to produce replies that cause an incorrect output to be generated by the originator. In the following let the vector $\mathcal{G}_3$ (see Section 5) be arranged in a $(n + 1) \times 3$ dimensional matrix, where the elements of the first and second row are the $k_1, \ldots k_{n+1}$ and the third row contains the corresponding checksums. By case analysis over the number of changed columns, we argue that in order to succeed with an attack, it is necessary for an attacker to select a set of computational queries of size at least six from the total $3n + 3$ issued queries, assuming $n \geq 11$. In the following the offsets are described in terms of additions since the results of applying any arbitrarily chosen function can also be achieved by means of performing an addition in Z_q.

1. *One or two altered columns.* Let i be the first column (corresponding to the pre-permutation stage) in which incorrect values are returned. Assume that the non-checksum values and their duplicates are offset by an integer δ. Then, by the recurrence describing how checksums are computed, the checksum in column i needs to be offset by δ, or the resulting checksum verification will fail. Then, turning to the values of column $i + 1$, we see that the difference of the checksum of this column and one of its two non-checksum values has to be offset by -2δ in order for the verification of the checksum of this column to succeed. i.e., If we alter all the values of column $i + 1$, that gives us a total of six values to select. If only the non-checksum value and its duplicate are altered, the sum of the checksum and the non-checksum value of the $i + 2$nd column has to be offset by 2δ, thus at least six values have to be selected. If only the checksum value of the $i + 1$st column is altered, i.e., offset by -2δ, the sum of the non-checksum and checksum values of column $i + 2$ will then in turn have to be offset by 2δ in turn. (By the same argument as above, we would then have to correct the $i + 2$nd column in the same manner as the $i + 1$st.)

2. *More than two, less than n incorrect columns.* Since each original value is duplicated in our scheme, an attacker needs to alter at the very least $2k$ queries in order to corrupt the computation of k values, or the results and their duplicates will not be consistent. (This is so since the original values are not dependent.) For "small" values of k, this amounts to at least six elements, given the restriction $k > 2$. For "large" values of k, the adversary alters all but a few queries, in which case he has to select those which he

will not alter. In order not to affect $n - k$ original values, he needs to select the queries of these values, and the corresponding checksums. Since there remains $3k + 3$ values (where the last portion is due to the added $n + 1$st column) this gives us that at least six values have to be selected, given $k > 0$.

3. *All values incorrect.* Let us consider a few cases: (1) All non-checksum values are *replaced* by the same value. (2) All non-checksum values are *offset* by the same value. (3) All values to be computed (not necessarily including the checksums) are altered.

In the first case, we see from the recurrence equation describing how the checksums are computed (and the fact that all non-checksum values are set to the same value) that the absolute value of all the checksum values will equal the first checksum value, but with alternating signs for each column. Therefore, unless the the non-checksum values are set to zero (which would cause all replies to equal one, and which would therefore not be accepted), it is necessary for the adversary to partition the set of values into at least two sets. As long as $n \geq 11$, this means that the adversary has to select at least select six values from all the values to be computed.

In the second case, by the argument above, all checksums have to be offset by either zero or non-zero. The former would cause no change, and can therefore be ignored; the latter would force the adversary to correctly partition the set, giving us the same result as above.

If all values to be computed are altered then either we need to alter then in the same manner, or we need to partition them into two or more sets, each of which will be altered in a particular manner. Consider the smallest set altered in a particular manner. If it contains six or more elements, we are done. Due to the use of duplication, it cannot contain an odd number. Assume it contains four elements. Given the way the checksums are computed, we know from above that either the two checksums in these two columns have to be altered then, or at least one element in each of the adjacent columns. This again gives us that at least six elements that have to be modified. We are left with the case in which the smallest set contains two elements. If there are two such sets, this gives the same result as if the smallest set were of size four. If there is only one set, it is an identical setting to the argument of "one or two added columns". This concludes the argument.

We argued in Appendix A that each set of query values has a distribution that cannot be distinguished from a uniform at random distribution by the attacker. Therefore, and since a total of $3n + 3$ computational queries will be issued for an input size corresponding to n signature generations, the probability of success for the adversary will be bounded by $1/(3 \cdot \binom{3n+2}{5})$. To obtain a sufficient robustness for the smartcard setting with batch size $n = 20$, the original vector has to be replicated 7 times (making its size eight times that before replication), thus the attacker will have to choose $(8 + 1) \cdot 2$ elements.

C   Efficiency Analysis

The global cost, i.e., the amount of computations to be performed by the external servers, is determined by the size of the delegated vector and amounts to $3n + 3$ exponentiations.

Turning now to the amount of local computation, we can see that for each exponentiation the originator wants to have performed, he will have to perform the following number of multiplications:

$$
\begin{array}{ll}
2 & \text{add'l mult. due to introduced dependencies} \\
+\ 3 \cdot 2 + \frac{1}{n}(200 \cdot 75 + \frac{75(75-1)}{2})) & \text{add'l mult. due to blinding} \\
\hline
\approx\quad 8 & \text{add'l multiplications}
\end{array}
$$

In comparison, addition chain methods for exponentiations require about 10 multiplications per signature for batches of size approximately 100000 signatures [5].

In the smartcard setting, the exponentiation work for generating the blinding factors is performed in a pre-computation step (but the pairing of the blinding factors is still not.) This results in local costs per signature of approximately $2 + 9 \cdot 4 = 38$ multiplications. Since window based methods require about 200 multiplications per signature for batches of size 20, this corresponds to a speed-up of 81%.

Efficient Long-Term Validation
of Digital Signatures

Arne Ansper[1], Ahto Buldas[1], Meelis Roos[2], and Jan Willemson[2]

[1] Cybernetica; Akadeemia 21, Tallinn, Estonia
[2] Cybernetica, Tartu Lab; Lai 36, Tartu, Estonia
{arne,ahtbu,mroos,jan}@cyber.ee

Abstract. Digitally signed documents (e.g. contracts) would quickly lose their validity if the signing keys were revoked or the signature scheme was broken. The conventional validation techniques have been designed just for ephemeral use of signatures and are impractical for long-term validation. We present a new scheme that: (1) provides fast revocation while giving no extra power to on-line service providers; (2) supports long-term validation; (3) is lightweight and scalable.

1 Introduction

Bob lends Alice $100. Alice signs a promissory note stating that she owes Bob $100. It is in Bob's interest that Alice's digital signature is sufficient to convince a judge that she really owes Bob the money. A dispute in court, however, may take place long after the promissory note was signed. Alice's public key certificate may already be revoked. Therefore, it is necessary to ensure that *electronic documents retain provable authenticity long after their creation.*

The evidentiary function is one of the essential properties of handwritten signatures and thereby it may seem natural to assume that digital signatures have this property as well. However, no human being is able to compute digital signatures by heart and it is also hard (if not impossible), with today's technology, to create a signature device which (from the signer's point of view) is absolutely safe to use. On the one hand, it seems unfair to make the owner of a signature device (Alice) liable for everything ever signed with that device. On the other hand, if the burden of proof is completely on the side of the interested party (Bob), no one would trust digital signatures. The best we can do today is to minimize the technological risks and to define some reasonable (as fair as possible) rules for solving disputes on digital signatures, rules that all parties involved in a dispute are aware of. Among many other things, these rules must define what kind of digital information is considered to be admissible evidence in a court of law.

Secure signature devices, fair rules of liability, and up-to-date public key information are the basic problems to be solved before we can seriously speak about the evidentiary function of digital signatures. In this paper, we address

---

[0] All authors were supported by the Estonian SF, grant no. 4150

K. Kim (Ed.): PKC 2001, LNCS 1992, pp. 402–415, 2001.

the last issue, i.e. the problem of efficient distribution and storage of public key information for long-term use. The secure signature devices and the liability problems are not discussed, though, we do not claim they are unimportant or easy to solve.

The first solution in the area of public-key distribution was proposed as early as in 1976. In a pioneering paper [6], the fathers of public-key cryptography – Diffie and Hellman – proposed a modified (on-line) telephone book listing public keys instead of telephone numbers. However, this idea was despised two years later by Loren Kohnfelder [11], the father of public key certificates, due to concern that managing such a telephone book would cause a communication bottleneck. The idea of individually signed certificates seemed far more attractive because the public networks were far from their today's overall availability.

Recently Gassko, Gemmell and MacKenzie [8] took a step towards reviving the modified telephone-book idea proposed by Diffie and Hellman. They showed that for long-term validation it is more efficient to manage public key databases rather than to use individually signed certificates.

In this paper, we will take another step by showing that (using modern cryptographic techniques) we can improve both the efficiency and reliability of on-line validation techniques. We introduce a new *notary service* which confirms the validity of the certificate at the time when the relevant digital signature was created. Instead of indicating the specific time, the *notary confirmation* (signed by the notary) provides a direct (one-way) link between the certificate and the signature. In order to avoid the need to use computationally expensive digital signatures extensively, the notary uses Merkle authentication trees [12,13] to compress answers to questions which clients have submitted during each minute (or some other unit) of time. After each minute, the notary signs the root of the tree. This trick (used already in time-stamping [9,3] and certification [8]) significantly reduces the number of signature creations. We also propose methods how to reduce the role of Trusted Third Parties in long-term validation and thereby improve the reliability of these services.

In Section 2, we describe our model of signature validation scheme including the list of involved parties. We also describe the main goals of this paper. In Section 3, we give a brief overview of the basic principles of public key validation techniques and discuss the main advantages and drawbacks of the on-line validation techniques. In Section 4, we outline a new on-line validation protocol that supports both fast revocation and long-term validation. In Section 5, we discuss how to increase the reliability of on-line validation schemes and present a new scheme with lower trust assumptions.

2   Statement of the Problem

In this section, we give a brief overview of the problems we try to solve and, in order to avoid misunderstandings, also emphasize some problems we *are not* trying to address in this paper. There are five parties involved in our model of signature validation:

- *Certification Authority* (CA) issues public key certificates that bind public keys to identities of their owners.
- *Signer* (Alice, *A*) is a person who, after obtaining a public-key certificate from the CA, creates a digital signature.
- *Prover* (Bob, *B*) or *Interested party* is a party who receives a digital signature from the signer and who is interested in preserving the evidentiary function of this signature.
- *Confirmer* (or *Notary*, *N*) represents a service for obtaining a confirmation that the certificate was valid at the moment the signature was created.
- *Verifier* (or *Judge*) is a party who needs to be convinced (using the signature, the certificate, and the confirmation) about the validity of the signature (possibly, long after the signature was created).

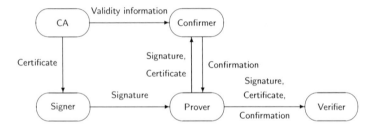

Fig. 1. Our model of signature validation.

We consider that the signature device used by the signer (Alice) is never absolutely secure and may leak the key or be stolen by an adversary. Thereby, the system we use must allow the signer to revoke the certificate immediately when the key or device is suspected of being compromised. Moreover, the Public Key Infrastructure we will develop should guarantee that the revocation notice is (timely) distributed (or made available) to all potential verifiers.

We assume that a signature is considered to be *valid* if it is proved to be created before the corresponding certificate was *revoked*. That is what we call *long-term validation* in this paper. We neither discuss how to develop secure signature devices nor give any hints for the signer how to notice the compromise of these devices. At the same time, we agree that both of these are important practical issues. The problems we are going to address are

1) *how to revoke the certificate timely* if its compromise has been noticed or even suspected; and
2) *how to prove that the certificate was not revoked.*

We *do not* claim that answering to these questions is sufficient to support (or even come close to) *non-repudiation* – the ability to prove (in undeniable manner) to a third party (e.g. a judge) that a document which was received via a public network was, in fact, written and sent by the claimed originator. This property is never assumed to hold even in the case of "true" signatures.

The more specific questions we address in this paper are

1) efficient measures for obtaining and preserving the proofs of validity (compactness of proofs, etc.);
2) computational complexity of obtaining the proofs which has a considerable influence on the prime cost of the validation service;
3) reliability of the service.

3   Existing Solutions and Their Shortcomings

3.1   Traditional Off-Line PKI Solutions

use public directory (that plays the role of the Confirmer) to store the public key information. The directory is updated by the CA in a regular basis (say, daily). The content of the directory is protected with the CA's signature and also with a time stamp in order to guarantee the freshness of the content. The Prover downloads the most recent data from the directory and uses this data later as a part of the validity proof. The verifier checks that the signer's public key certificate is not expired and is not included in the list of revoked certificates. Note that it is necessary to check whether the signature itself was formed at the time the public key information was considered as valid. Therefore, also the signature must be provided with a time stamp in order to prevent back-dating attacks.

The main advantage of this approach is that the Confirmer is a passive intermediary that has no power to modify the validity information. Therefore, only the CA must be assumed to be trusted.

The main shortcoming of this approach, considering the long-term validation, is that if the private key is suspected of being compromised Alice is unable to revoke her certificate immediately, because nobody would know about the revocation until the next update of the directory is issued. On the one hand, it is unfair (from the Alice's point) to consider as *valid* all the signatures given before the next update. Alice should not be liable for events it has no control of. On the other hand, if they are considered as invalid, it would be dangerous (for Bob) to accept any signature before the next update is issued.

Another shortcoming is that if the number of certificates grows, the size of a confirmation (as a linear function of the number of certificates issued by the CA) may become impractically large.

3.2   On-Line Methods

use an intermediary that, having received a request containing the certificate, replies with a *validity confirmation*. The integrity and content of the confirmation is protected with the signature of the Confirmer. As in traditional solutions, the confirmation comprises the date of validity. Generally, a on-line validation protocol runs as follows:

$$
\begin{array}{l}
\text{1. } A \rightarrow B\text{: } \mathsf{Cert}_A, \mathsf{Sig}_A\{X\} \\
\text{2. } B \rightarrow N\text{: } \mathsf{Cert}_A \\
\text{3. } N \rightarrow B\text{: } \underbrace{\mathsf{Valid}(\mathsf{Cert}_A), [t_0, t_1], \mathsf{Sig}_N\{\mathsf{Status}_A\}}_{\mathsf{Status}_A}
\end{array} \tag{1}
$$

where t_0 and t_1 denote the bounds of the validity period of the confirmation (not the certificate), and $\mathsf{Valid}(\cdot)$ denotes the validity statement. For example, the status of the certificate may be confirmed as valid, revoked, not revoked, suspended, etc. Obviously, the validity statement should directly point to the certificate it confirms. The *On-line Certificate Status Protocol* (OCSP) [14] developed by the PKIX working group is a typical example of an on-line validation protocol. The short-lived certificate approach [7] is almost equivalent.

For the persistent use of the validity confirmation we need a time stamp t on $\mathsf{Sig}_A\{X\}$, issued by a trusted *Time-Stamping Authority* (TSA) [2,9,3,5], such that $t_0 \leq t \leq t_1$. Therefore, provided that the public keys of CA, N and TSA are obtained authentically, the verifier should check that:

- $\mathsf{Sig}_A\{X\}$ is properly verifiable using the public key written in Cert_A;
- Cert_A is signed by the CA;
- Status_A confirms the validity of Cert_A at $[t_0, t_1]$;
- Status_A is signed by N;
- the time stamp confirms that $\mathsf{Sig}_A\{X\}$ was created at t, where $t_0 \leq t \leq t_1$;
- the time stamp is signed by the TSA.

The main advantage of this approach over the off-line approach is that the validity information is always up-to-date. We are able to overcome the inconvenient trade-off between the latency of revocation and the service time, because revocation messages can be sent directly to the Confirmer. An example of using secure revocation notes is given by Rivest [15].

However, there are also several shortcomings in this approach. First, the Confirmer must extensively use a digital signature scheme, which is time-consuming and may require special hardware accelerators when the number of requests becomes large. Second, we introduce two additional trusted parties: (1) the Confirmer, and (2) the TSA. Both parties are, in principle, able (without cooperation) to cheat clients.

3.3   Notary Protocols

eliminate the need for a trusted TSA and, therefore, reduce the number of additional third parties to one. Instead of using time stamps, notary protocols give a direct (one-way) link between the signature to be confirmed and the confirmation. Notary protocols are similar to the conventional validation protocols. The main difference is that the notary confirmation comprises the signature the confirmation is about. The protocol itself goes through the following steps:

$$
\begin{array}{l}
1.\ A \rightarrow B:\ \mathsf{Cert}_A,\ \mathsf{Sig}_A\{X\} \\
2.\ B \rightarrow N:\ \mathsf{Cert}_A,\ \mathsf{Sig}_A\{X\} \\
3.\ N \rightarrow B:\ \underbrace{\mathsf{Valid}(\mathsf{Cert}_A),\ \mathsf{Sig}_A\{X\}},\ \mathsf{Sig}_N\{\mathsf{Status}_A\} \\
\qquad\qquad\qquad\qquad \mathsf{Status}_A
\end{array}
\tag{2}
$$

Note that the Notary does not check the validity of users' signatures. A party who verifies the signature would check for the correctness anyway. Thereby, the signature verification by the Notary would give no additional assurance. This fact was noticed by Roos [16].

Provided that the public keys of CA and N are obtained authentically, the verifier should check that:

- $\mathsf{Sig}_A\{X\}$ is properly verifiable using the public key written in Cert_A;
- Cert_A is signed by the CA;
- Status_A confirms the validity of Cert_A and comprises the signature $\mathsf{Sig}_A\{X\}$;
- Status_A is signed by N;

Time stamps are unnecessary because Status_A directly points to the signature $\mathsf{Sig}_A\{X\}$ to be confirmed. Thereby, we have a proof that $\mathsf{Sig}_A\{X\}$ was created before N signed the confirmation.

Most notary protocols proposed to date are computationally expensive. For example, in the Data Validation and Certification Service (DVCS) [1] (PKIX Working Group) the service provider validates users' signatures and checks the full certification path from the certificate's issuer to a trusted point. Thereby, the processing of requests requires large amount of computation. The notary protocol (2) described in this section is much less expensive because request processing does not require extensive computations. However, each request still needs a signed reply. Therefore, we still have the same efficiency concerns as in the case of OCSP.

Our main goal is to develop a signature validation scheme capable of supporting (1) long-term validation, (2) scalability of services and (3) accountability (trust elimination). In the next sections, we discuss some hints that help us to achieve these goals.

4   A New Efficient Notary Protocol

As noticed above, in conventional on-line validation protocols, the server must create one signature per request. Hence, it must be as powerful as all the signers altogether. This can constitute a serious computational bottleneck if the users community grows large. To avoid this problem, we could give one signature to several responses at a time. The server collects all requests obtained during some time interval (referred to as *round*). It then prepares the set S of the corresponding response statements and organizes it as a certain data structure. Instead of signing all the statements independently, the server signs only a short digest $d = D(S)$ of the whole data structure. Note that it is impractical to sign a plain list of all requests because this list must be sent back to all clients, which may cause undesirable communication costs. Merkle authentication tree described in the next subsection turns out to be a suitable data structure for this purpose.

4.1   Merkle Authentication Trees

The Merkle authentication tree [12,13] is one example of a suitable data structure. The Merkle authentication tree for a set S of data items is a labeled tree the leaves of which are labeled with the elements of S and each non-leaf of which is labeled with a hash of the labels of its child-vertices (Figure 2). The digest $d = D(S)$ is defined to be equal to the label of the root vertex.

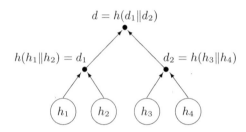

Fig. 2. Merkle tree for $S = \{S_1, S_2, S_3, S_4\}$. Here $h_i = h(S_i)$ for $i = 1...4$.

Each element $S_i \in S$ can be provided with a succinct membership proof $P(S_i, S)$ of the statement $S_i \in S$. Each proof is a formal expression of one variable x. For example (Figure 2), $P(S_2, S)(x) := h(h(h_1, x), d_2)$, where h denotes the hash function used. For verifying the statement $S_i \in S$ one needs to check the equation $P(S_i, S)(h(S_i)) = d = D(S)$. The most important property of Merkle authentication trees is that the size of a proof is $O(\log |S|)$.

4.2   Notary Protocol with Merkle Trees

The notary server works in rounds. Suppose that the duration of these rounds is set to one minute. Instead of answering the requests immediately the server collects the requests submitted during the round. It then organizes the corresponding confirmations as a Merkle tree and signs the root hash of this tree. The protocol with Merkle tree runs as follows:

$$
\begin{array}{l}
\text{1. } A \rightarrow B: \text{Cert}_A, \text{Sig}_A\{X\} \\
\text{2. } B \rightarrow N: \text{Cert}_A, \text{Sig}_A\{X\} \\
\text{3. } N \rightarrow B: \underbrace{\text{Valid}(\text{Cert}_A), \text{Sig}_A\{X\}, P(\text{Status}_A, S), \text{Sig}_N\{D(S)\}}_{\text{Status}_A}
\end{array}
\qquad (3)
$$

Hence, a replay to a request is a triple $(\mathsf{Status}_A, P(\mathsf{Status}_A, S), \mathsf{Sig}\{D(S)\})$. No matter how many requests we have, only one signature per round is required. Such an approach was first used in time-stamping [4,3]. The verification procedure is almost the same as in Protocol (2), except that instead of the final signature verification the verifier

- checks the equation $P(\mathsf{Status}_A, S)(h(\mathsf{Status}_A)) = D(S)$;
- checks that $D(S)$ is signed by N.

Note that this approach has sense only if the request processing itself is computationally much cheaper than signing. This is certainly the case for the PKIX time-stamping and OCSP protocols (though, they do not use this approach!), but is not true for DVCS because each request requires several signature verifications.

4.3 Efficiency Calculations

Let T_h and T_s denote the time needed for hashing and for signing, respectively. Let T_p denote the time which is needed to find an answer to a request. In conventional on-line protocols (OCSP, TSP etc.), serving R requests requires $R \cdot (T_p + T_s)$ time-units (Figure 3). In the hash-tree protocol (Figure 4), if there

Fig. 3. Computations of the Notary in the conventional protocol.

are R requests in one round, we need $R \cdot T_p$ time units to find the corresponding answers, $R \cdot T_h$ time units to compute the hash-tree and find the digest d and proofs $P(\mathsf{Status}_i, S)$, and finally, T_s time units to sign the digest $D(S)$. Assuming

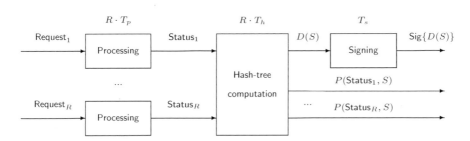

Fig. 4. Computations of the Notary in the protocol with hash-tree.

that hashing is K times faster than signing ($T_s = K \cdot T_h$) and request processing is P times faster than signing ($T_s = P \cdot T_p$), we get that the hash-tree scheme is

$$\lambda = \frac{R \cdot T_p + R \cdot T_s}{R \cdot T_p + R \cdot T_h + T_s} = \frac{1 + \frac{1}{P}}{\frac{1}{P} + \frac{1}{K} + \frac{1}{R}} \qquad (4)$$

times faster. If the processing is much faster than signing (i.e. $T_p \ll T_s$), we have that $\lambda \approx KR/(K + R)$. In OCSP, TSP and the notary protocol, this is indeed the case. Chosen values of λ in that case are shown in Figure 5. For example, if $K = 10,000$ [8] and $R = 1000$, we get that our scheme is nine hundred times faster and if $R = 100$, it is still about one hundred times faster (Fig.5). For example, in OpenSSL (ver 0.94) library 1024-bit RSA with private

λ	$R = 1$	$R = 10$	$R = 100$	$R = 1,000$	$R = 10,000$
$K = 1$	0.5	0.91	0.99	≈ 1	≈ 1
$K = 10$	0.91	5.0	9.1	9.9	≈ 10
$K = 100$	0.99	9.1	50	91	99
$K = 1,000$	≈ 1	9.9	91	500	910
$K = 10,000$	≈ 1	≈ 10	99	910	5000

Fig. 5. Chosen values of λ, provided that $T_p \ll T_s$.

exponent is about 3300 times slower than the hash function SHA-1 with a single 512-bit input block. We see (Figure 5) that the main advantage of our scheme – lower computational cost – is obvious when the number of requests per round becomes large. Therefore, using longer rounds would lower the prime costs of validation services. However, duration of rounds should not exceed the limits of a reasonable service delay.

4.4   Practical Remark: Signatures with Hash Chains

Regardless of the fact that the notary protocol (3) with Merkle trees may increase the efficiency of numerous existing on-line protocols (OCSP, TSP etc.), the standards describing these protocols would be changed in order to use this advantage in practice. A way to overcome such a concern is to define new Object Identifiers (OID) for *signatures with hash chains*. Indeed, in the protocol (3) the proof $P(\mathsf{Status}_A, S)$ and the "ordinary" signature $\mathsf{Sig}_N\{D(S)\}$ may be viewed as a new type of signature on the message Status_A, i.e.

$$\mathsf{Sig}'_N(\mathsf{Status}_A) := (P(\mathsf{Status}_A, S), \mathsf{Sig}_N\{D(S)\}). \qquad (5)$$

If these new signature schemes are supported by the cryptographic libraries, the protocols (2) and (3) are identical from the software engineer's point of view.

4.5   Notary Protocols in Multi-level PKI

Notary protocols (3) with hash-trees and also the signatures with hash-chains (5) allow using on-line validation in the hierarchical multi-level Public Key Infrastructures. The signatures of a Notary service provider (N) on the validity confirmations may be confirmed by a higher level Notary ($\bar{N}$). Such a hierarchical validation scheme allows us to reduce the question of the validity of a certificate to the question of the reliability of a single top-level notary server ("supervised" by a top-level CA). The confirmation protocol runs as follows:

$$
\begin{aligned}
&1.\ A \to B\text{: } \mathsf{Cert}_A, \mathsf{Sig}_A\{X\} \\
&2.\ B \to N\text{: } \mathsf{Cert}_A, \mathsf{Sig}_A\{X\} \\
&3.\ N \text{ finds: } \underbrace{\mathsf{Valid}(\mathsf{Cert}_A), \mathsf{Sig}_A\{X\}}_{\mathsf{Status}_A} \\
&4.\ N \to \bar{N}\text{: } \mathsf{Cert}_N, \mathsf{Sig}_N\{\mathsf{Status}_A\} \\
&5.\ \bar{N} \to N\text{: } \underbrace{\mathsf{Valid}(\mathsf{Cert}_N), \mathsf{Sig}_A\{\mathsf{Status}_A\}}_{\mathsf{Status}_N}, \mathsf{Sig}_{\bar{N}}\{\mathsf{Status}_N\} \\
&6.\ N \to B\text{: } \mathsf{Status}_A, \mathsf{Sig}_N\{\mathsf{Status}_A\} \\
&\qquad\qquad \mathsf{Status}_N, \mathsf{Sig}_{\bar{N}}\{\mathsf{Status}_N\}
\end{aligned}
\tag{6}
$$

Note that using ordinary signature schemes in this protocol would create a communication bottleneck on the top of the hierarchy. The top-level notary server would need as much communication as the leaf-servers altogether. Using hash-chain-signatures (5) in protocol (6) is crucial for preventing such a bottleneck. Indeed, no matter how many requests the notary N obtains from its clients during a round, only one signature is created and needs to be confirmed by the higher-level notary $\bar{N}$. Note also that the total service delay in a hierarchical on-line validation scheme is equal to the sum of delays on a path from the leaf-CA to the top-CA. This fact should be taken into account when developing client-friendly on-line validation services.

5   Reliability Issues

As we mentioned above, one of the main advantages of the traditional (off-line) PKI is that it does not give any extra powers to on-line service providers. In on-line validation protocols, however, we can notice two kinds of reliability concerns:

1) Private key of the Confirmer is used in a device connected to a public network and is therefore a potential target of attacks by network hackers.
2) On-line Confirmers are able to abuse their power to declare a certificate as valid, even if they know it is not. Though, Confirmers can be made accountable for their actions there may exist no effective ways to detect or prove their misbehavior.

On the one hand, we need fast on-line revocation/validation protocols in order to lower the risk of possible abuses of a stolen signature key. On the other hand, on-line services are less secure because of the abovementioned concerns of reliability.

If the value of a digitally signed document is relatively small, a confirmation signed by an on-line service provider may be considered as a sufficient proof. In this case, on-line validation service is a tool that helps to make fast decisions less riskier for the interested party. However, if the value of a signed document is high, for some cases only the CA itself may be reliable enough for confirming the validity of a certificate. But, if the CA updates the validity information once a day (which is a typical practice) the interested party would wait (in the worst case) the whole day before it becomes safe for him/her to accept the signature. Therefore, it seems we have a fundamental trade-off between *reliability* and *service time*.

In the following, we discuss several techniques how to increase the reliability of on-line validation services.

5.1   A Protocol with Short-Lived Certificates

Attacks where the on-line Confirmer (Notary) declares revoked certificates as valid are easily avoidable if the certificates issued by the CA have a short validity period (say one day). Using hash-tree signatures (5) it is relatively easy for the CA to re-issue all the certificates daily [8] and to send these certificates to the Notary. The Notary removes a certificate from its database (of valid certificates) once it has received a suitable revocation note. A verifier of the notary confirmation must check that the certificate confirmed was "fresh" at the moment of confirmation. The message flow in such a protocol would be as follows:

$$
\begin{array}{lll}
(\textit{daily})\ CA \to N\colon & \underbrace{(\mathsf{ID}_A,\ \mathsf{PK}_A,\ \mathsf{date}),\ \mathsf{Sig}_{CA}\{\mathsf{ID}_A,\ \mathsf{PK}_A,\ \mathsf{date}\}}_{\mathsf{Cert}_A(\mathsf{date})} & \\[2ex]
1. & A \to B\colon & \mathsf{Sig}_A\{X\} \\
2. & B \to N\colon & \mathsf{ID}_A,\ \mathsf{Sig}_A\{X\} \\
3. & N \to B\colon & \underbrace{\mathsf{Valid}(\mathsf{Cert}_A(\mathsf{date})),\ \mathsf{Sig}_A\{X\},\ \mathsf{Sig}_N\{\mathsf{Status}_A\}}_{\mathsf{Status}_A}
\end{array} \tag{7}
$$

Suppose that each morning (say 8 am) the CA issues for each client A a new certificate $\mathsf{Cert}_A(\mathsf{date})$ which is valid only for a day (denoted as date). The certificate contains the identity ID_A and the public key PK_A of A. In order to obtain a confirmation for a message $\mathsf{Sig}_A\{X\}$ signed by A, the interested party B sends this signature together with the identity ID_A of A to the Confirmer N. If the certificate of A is in the database of valid certificates, the Confirmer signs a confirmation and sends it back to B. In this protocol, we must assume that the signature $\mathsf{Sig}_A\{X\}$ is also provided with a reliable time stamp t issued by a trusted Time-Stamping Authority (TSA). Each verifier of the signature must always check that the time stamp t belongs to date (i.e. was obtained when date was current). Provided that the public keys of the CA, N and the TSA were authentically obtained, the verifier should check that

- $\mathsf{Sig}_A\{X\}$ is properly verifiable using the public key written in $\mathsf{Cert}_A(\mathsf{date})$;
- $\mathsf{Cert}_A(\mathsf{date})$ is signed by the CA;
- Status_A confirms the validity of $\mathsf{Cert}_A(\mathsf{date})$ and comprises $\mathsf{Sig}_A\{X\}$;
- Status_A is signed by N;
- the time stamp confirms that $\mathsf{Sig}_A\{X\}$ was created at t, where $t \in \mathsf{date}$;
- the time stamp is signed by the TSA.

In such a scheme, the Notary is able to revoke certificates but is unable to declare a certificate as valid if actually the certificate was revoked a day before (or earlier). The most harmful attack the Notary is able to perform is being ignorant to the revocation notes sent by clients. However, using several Notary servers reduces the probability of even this attack.

As we mentioned above, a trusted Time-Stamping Authority is necessary for reliable validity proofs because incorrect time stamps may affect the results of validation. Time-stamping (as the Notary) is an on-line service and suffers thereby from the reliability concerns mentioned at the beginning of this section. Therefore, any advantage of protocol (7) over the previous protocols may seem questionable. In the next paragraph we present a better (though, more complex) solution which does not use trusted on-line parties.

5.2   A Protocol With Off-Line Time Stamps

In order to overcome the need for a trusted on-line Time-Stamping Authority we may use a protocol where the CA itself issues time stamps once a day. Each certificate $\mathsf{Cert}_{A,i}$ (issued by the CA for the i-th day) comprises a certain nonce value d_{-1} which is a digest $D(\Sigma_{i-1})$ of the set Σ_{i-1} of all the signatures submitted during the previous day. This digest is computed using the Merkle authentication tree. If A wants to sign a message X she adds her certificate to the message to be signed. If the i-th day is over, the Notary sends the CA the digest $d_i = D(\Sigma_i)$ of the set of all signatures submitted during the day. The CA then issues a time stamp $\mathsf{Sig}_{CA}\{\mathsf{date}_i, d_i\}$ and sends it back to the Notary. The protocol runs as follows:

$$
\begin{array}{lll}
(day_i) & CA \to N: & \underbrace{(\mathsf{ID}_A, \mathsf{PK}_A, \mathsf{date}_i, d_{i-1})}_{\mathsf{binding}_{A,i}}, \mathsf{Sig}_{CA}\{\mathsf{binding}_{A,i}\} \\
& & \underbrace{\hspace{7cm}}_{\mathsf{Cert}_{A,i}} \\
1. & A \to B: & \sigma_A = \mathsf{Sig}_A\{X, \mathsf{Cert}_{A,i}\} \\
2. & B \to N: & \mathsf{ID}_A, \sigma_A \\
3. & N \to B: & \mathsf{Valid}(\mathsf{Cert}_{A,i}), \sigma_A, \underbrace{\mathsf{Sig}_N\{\mathsf{Status}_A\}}_{\mathsf{Status}_A} \\
& & N \text{ adds } \sigma_A \text{ into } \Sigma_i. \\
(day_{i+1}) & N \to CA: & d_i := D(\Sigma_i) \\
& CA \to N: & \mathsf{Sig}_{CA}\{\mathsf{date}_i, d_i\}
\end{array}
\tag{8}
$$

In this protocol we do not need additional time-stamping services because the one-way links between the time-stamps and the signatures give an undeniable proof that the A's signature was in fact created at the i-th day. Indeed, we have a one-way relationship

$$d_{i-1} \longrightarrow \mathsf{Cert}_{A,i} \longrightarrow \mathsf{Sig}_A\{X, \mathsf{Cert}_{A,i}\} \longrightarrow d_i.$$

Moreover, if we do not want to take risk of accepting the signatures using on-line notary confirmations we can always wait till the next morning and obtain a one-way link

$$\mathsf{Sig}_A\{X\} \longrightarrow d_i \longrightarrow \mathsf{Cert}_{A,i+1}$$

which proves the validity of the signature entirely independent of any on-line validation services.

Thus, a verifier who has authentic copies of the public keys of the CA and N must check that

- $\sigma_A = \mathsf{Sig}_A\{X, \mathsf{Cert}_{A,i}\}$ is properly verifiable with PK_A written in $\mathsf{Cert}_{A,i}$;
- $\mathsf{Cert}_{A,i}$ is signed by the CA;
- Status_A confirms the validity of $\mathsf{Cert}_{A,i}$ and comprises σ_A;
- Status_A is signed by N;
- the equation $P(\sigma_A, \Sigma_i)(h(\sigma_A)) = d_i$ holds;
- $\mathsf{Sig}_{CA}\{\mathsf{date}_i, d_i\}$ is properly verifiable using the public key of the CA.

A verifier who does not trust N completely may also obtain the next certificate $\mathsf{Cert}_{A,i+1} = \mathsf{Sig}_{CA}(\mathsf{ID}_A, \mathsf{PK}_A, \mathsf{date}_{i+1}, d_i)$ and check that

- $\mathsf{Cert}_{A,i+1}$ comprises d_i and PK_A,

which confirms the validity of the signature independent of N because if A's certificate is revoked during date_i the CA does not issue $\mathsf{Cert}_{A,i+1}$.

6   Conclusions

We presented a long-term digital signature validation scheme that does not suffer from the main disadvantages often associated with on-line techniques. Our scheme supports fast revocation while giving no extra power to on-line validation services. Due to the efficient hash-chain-signatures our protocol is efficient and scalable. One advantage over the previous schemes is that our scheme does not require additional trusted parties.

References

1. Adams, Sylvester, Zolotarev, and Zuccherato. Data Validation and Certification Server Protocols. Technical report, PKIX Working Group, October 1999.
2. Carlisle Adams and Robert Zuccherato. Time stamp protocols. Technical report, PKIX Working Group, 1999.
3. Dave Bayer, Stuart Haber, and W. Scott Stornetta. Improving the efficiency and reliability of digital time-stamping. In *Methods in Communication, Security, and Computer Science – Sequences'91*, pages 329–334, 1992.

4. Josh Benaloh and Michael de Mare. Efficient broadcast time-stamping. Technical Report 1, Clarkson University Department of Mathematics and Computer Science, August 1991.

5. Ahto Buldas, Peeter Laud, Helger Lipmaa, and Jan Villemson. Time-stamping with binary linking schemes. In *Advances in Cryptology – CRYPTO'98*, volume 1462 of *LNCS*, pages 486–501, Santa Barbara, 1998. Springer-Verlag.

6. Whitfield Diffie and Martin Hellman. New directions in cryptography. *IEEE Transactions on Information Theory*, 22:644–654, 1976.

7. Barbara Fox and Brian LaMacchia. Online certificate status checking in financial transactions: the case for re-issuance. In *Financial Cryptography – FC'99*, volume 1648 of *LNCS*, pages 104–117, Anguilla, February 1999.

8. Irene Gassko, Peter S. Gemmell, and Philip MacKenzie. Efficient and fresh certification. In *Public Key Cryptography – PKC'2000*, volume 1751 of *LNCS*, pages 342–353, Melbourne, Australia, January 2000. Springer-Verlag.

9. Stuart Haber and W.Scott Stornetta. How to time-stamp a digital document. *Journal of Cryptology*, 3(2):99–111, 1991.

10. Paul C. Kocher. On certificate revocation and validation. In *Financial Cryptography: FC'98*, volume 1465 of *LNCS*, pages 172–177, Anguilla, February 1998. Springer-Verlag.

11. Loren M. Kohnfelder. Toward a practical public-key cryptosystem. 1978.

12. Ralph C. Merkle. Protocols for public key cryptosystems. In *Proceedings of the 1980 IEEE Symposium on Security and Privacy*, pages 122–134, 1980.

13. Ralph C. Merkle. A certified digital signature. In *Advances in Cryptology – CRYPTO'89*, volume 435 of *LNCS*, pages 218–238, Santa Barbara, 1989. Springer-Verlag.

14. Michael Myers, R. Ankney, A. Malpani, S. Galperin, and Carlisle Adams. RFC2560: X.509 Internet Public Key Infrastructure Online Certificate Status Protocol - OCSP. June 1999.

15. Ronald Rivest. Can we eliminate certificate revocation lists? In *Financial Cryptography: FC'98*, volume 1465 of *LNCS*, pages 178–183, Anguilla, February 1998. Springer-Verlag.

16. Meelis Roos. Integrating time-stamping and notarization. MSc Thesis, Tartu University, http://home.cyber.ee/mroos/thesis/. May 1999.

A Novel Systolic Architecture
for an Efficient RSA Implementation

Nikos K. Moshopoulos and K.Z. Pekmestzi

National Technical University of Athens
Iroon Polytechneiou 9
15773 Zographou
Athens, GREECE
{nikos, pekmes}@microlab.ntua.gr

Abstract: A new systolic serial-parallel scheme that implements the Montgomery multiplier is presented. The serial input of this multiplier consists of two sets of data that enter in a bit-interleaved form. The results are also derived in the same form. The design, with minor modifications, can be used for the implementation of the RSA algorithm. The circuit yields low hardware complexity and permits high-speed operation with 100% efficiency.

1 Introduction

The core of an RSA [1] crypto-system is the modular exponentiation, which can be fragmented into a sequence of modular multiplications and squarings. These operations have to be performed in a serial pipelined way, because of the operands length (>512 bits). The most efficient algorithm for modular multiplication was presented by Montgomery [2]. One approach [3], [4] proposes a direct implementation of the Montgomery scheme by using two similar circuits: one for multiplication and one for squaring. However, it suffers from a large combinational delay. Another approach [5], [6] suggests the realization of the modular multiplication and squaring in two discrete stages: the pure product generation and the modular reduction. In this approach, the combinational delay is reduced to half, over doubling the performance.

In this paper, a new implementation of a Montgomery multiplier is presented, which is based on the direct approach achieving higher performance. The circuit is modified in an elegant way in order to realize both the modular multiplication and squaring in a bit-interleaved form. The modular exponentiation takes approximately $2n^2$ clock cycles with the minimum hardware complexity per bit, reported so far.

K. Kim (Ed.): PKC 2001, LNCS 1992, pp. 416–421, 2001
© Springer-Verlag Berlin Heidelberg 2001

2 The Montgomery Multiplier

The Montgomery algorithm is presented below:

(Inputs)

Modulus   : N (n-bits integer)

Multiplier   : B (n bits integer); $B = b_{n-1}, b_{n-2}, ..., b_0$

Multiplicand : A (n bits integer); $A = a_{n-1}, a_{n-2}, ..., a_0$

(Output)

$P := (A \cdot B \cdot 2^{-n})$ mod N; Modular product.

(Algorithm)

```
          P  := 0;

          q₀ := 0;

          for i:= 0 to n do
```

$$P := [(P+q_i \cdot N)/2] + b_i \cdot A; \qquad (1)$$

$$q_{i+1} = P \bmod 2; \qquad (2)$$

```
          End; {For}
```

Given that N is an odd number we define $N' = (N+1)/2$. Thus, (1) can be rewritten as follows:

$$P = [P/2] + q_i N' + b_i A \qquad \textbf{(3)}$$

At the ith step, the term $q_i N' + b_i A$ is computed in the circuit's upper part of Fig. 1b, while the results are shifted and accumulated in the lower part according to (3). The q_i values are derived serially during the first n cycles, while at the next n cycles the modular product P is produced. The systolic operation of this circuit requires the interleaving of the serial data b_i with zeros. Due to the internal pipelining, the feedback of q_i is delayed by two clock cycles. The zero-bit interleaving enables the synchronization of q_i with the next iteration of (3). The Montgomery product P is derived in the same bit-interleaved way. However, the idle time slot can be exploited by computing the modular product of a second number. In this manner, two modular product bits are generated in successive clock cycles without interference of their intermediate results.

In each multiplication cycle, the control line R is fed with two traveling 'ones', which enable the downloading of two interleaved Montgomery products into a register via a multiplexer in each cell.

The carry generated by the upper part of the (n-1)th cell must be added with the carry of the lower part, within an extra Full-Adder as shown in Fig. 1b.

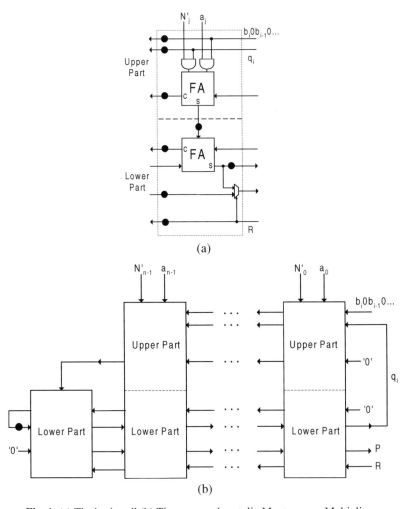

Fig. 1. (a) The basic cell (b) The proposed systolic Montgomery Multiplier

3 The Montgomery Exponentiator

The RSA algorithm can be implemented with the use of the square-and-multiply scheme.

(Inputs)

Message   : M (n-bits integer)

Encryption Key : E $(e_{n-1}, ..., e_0)$

(Output)

Encrypted Message: B

(Algorithm)

A:= M; {A is an intermediate variable}

If e_0 = 0 then

    B := 1;

else

    B := M;

End {If}

For i:= 1 to n-1 do {n is the number of bits}

    A: = $A^2 \cdot 2^{-n}$ mod N; {Mod. squaring}   (4)

    If e_i = 1 then

     B:= $A \cdot B \cdot 2^{-n}$ mod N; {Mod. multiplication} (5)

    End {If}

End; {For}

The previously presented interleaved computation of two Montgomery products in two consecutive time slots, can be of great interest regarding that, the above algorithm requires one multiplication and one squaring per iteration. The first slot can be used for the modular squaring $(A^2 \cdot 2^{-n})modN$ while the second for the modular multiplication $(A \cdot B \cdot 2^{-n})modN$. The squaring result A is produced in both serial and parallel form. The parallel form is latched and used at the next iteration as the parallel input for both operations. The latching is controlled by the R signal. The new cell is shown at Fig. 2a.

The initial value of the latches is the value of M. The P line carrying the a_i, b_i interleaved bits of $A=(A^2 \cdot 2^{-n})modN$ and $B=(A \cdot B \cdot 2^{-n})modN$ respectively, is redirected into the serial input of the multiplier via a multiplexer, for the next iteration. This multiplexer permits the input of the initial value of B. The encrypted message is obtained after $2n^2$ clock cycles as the final value of B.

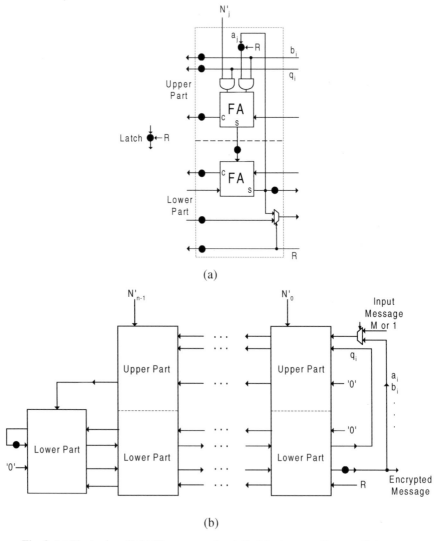

(a)

(b)

Fig. 2. (a) The basic cell (b) The proposed systolic Montgomery Exponentiator

4 Conclusions

The circuit of Fig. 2 is systolic, operates with 100% efficiency, interleaving multiplication and squaring on a bit basis, while the maximum combinational delay is equal to that of a gated Full-Adder (T_c). The utilization of the proposed design for both

squaring and multiplication, permits the application of large numbers, i.e. over 1024 bits. The critical path delay of [4] and [5] comprises two Full-Adders and some controlling logic. Therefore, it is normalized to $2T_c$. Additionally, the architecture of [6], does not include the control circuit for the RSA algorithm realization. An overall comparison in terms of hardware complexity (H), the time required for a full exponentiation (T_{exp}) and performance ($C_p = H \cdot T_{exp}$), is depicted at Table 1.

Table 1. Comparison of RSA systolic arrays

De-sign	H(gates)	T_{EXP}	$C_p = H \cdot T_{EXP}$
[4]	$(4FA+8D+4G)n = 104n$	$4n^2 \cdot T_c$	$\bullet 416n^3 \cdot T_c$
[5]	$(2FA+9D+3G+8SW)n = 117n$	$4n(1.5n+2) \cdot T_c$	$\bullet 702n^3 \cdot T_c$
[6]	$(2FA+10D+4G+4SW)n = 114n$	$2n(n+5) \cdot T_c$	$\bullet 228n^3 \cdot T_c$
Our	$(2FA+9D+2G+1SW)n = 95n$	$2n(n+2) \cdot T_c$	$\bullet 190n^3 \cdot T_c$

FA:Full-Adder, D:Delay Element, G:Gate, SW:Multiplexer;   FA=9G, D=8G, SW=3G

The proposed design is approximately 2 and 3 times more efficient than [4] and [5] respectively. Compared to [6], our circuit's performance is about 20% higher. This is due to the direct implementation of the Montgomery algorithm, which yields a decrease of the circuit's complexity, equal to 19 gates per bit.

References

1. RIVEST, R. L., SHAMIR, A., ADLEMAN, L.: "A method for obtaining digital signature and public-key cryptosystems", Commun. ACM, 1978, VOL. 21, pp. 120-126.
2. MONTGOMERY, P. L.: "Modular multiplication without trial division", Math. Computation, 1985, VOL. 44, pp.519-521.
3. ELDRIDGE, S.E., WALTER, C. D.: "Hardware Implementation of Montgomery's modular multiplication algorithm", IEEE Trans. On Computers, 1993, VOL. 42, NO 6, pp. 693-699.
4. KORNERUP, P.,: "A systolic, linear-array multiplier for a class of right-shift algorithms", IEEE Trans. On Comput., 1994, VOL. 43, NO. 8, pp. 892-898.
5. YANG, C., CHANG, T., JEN, C.: "A new RSA cryptosystem hardware design based on Montgomery algorithm", IEEE Trans. On Circuits and Systems II, 1998, VOL. 45, NO 7, pp. 908-913.
6. C. Y. SU, S. A HWANG, P. S. CHEN, C. W. WU, "An improved Montgomery's algorithm for high-speed RSA Public-Key cryptosystem" IEEE Transactions on VLSI Systems, 1999, VOL. 7, no. 2, pp. 280-284.

Author Index

Lecture Notes in Computer Science

For information about Vols. 1–1910
please contact your bookseller or Springer-Verlag

Vol. 1941: A.K. Chhabra, D. Dori (Eds.), Graphics Recognition. Proceedings, 1999. XI, 346 pages. 2000.

Vol. 1942: H. Yasuda (Ed.), Active Networks. Proceedings, 2000. XI, 424 pages. 2000.

Vol. 1943: F. Koornneef, M. van der Meulen (Eds.), Computer Safety, Reliability and Security. Proceedings, 2000. X, 432 pages. 2000.

Vol. 1944: K.R. Dittrich, G. Guerrini, I. Merlo, M. Oliva, M.E. Rodriguez (Eds.), Objects and Databases. Proceedings, 2000. X, 199 pages. 2001.

Vol. 1945: W. Grieskamp, T. Santen, B. Stoddart (Eds.), Integrated Formal Methods. Proceedings, 2000. X, 441 pages. 2000.

Vol. 1946: P. Palanque, F. Paternò (Eds.), Interactive Systems. Proceedings, 2000. X, 251 pages. 2001.

Vol. 1948: T. Tan, Y. Shi, W. Gao (Eds.), Advances in Multimodal Interfaces – ICMI 2000. Proceedings, 2000. XVI, 678 pages. 2000.

Vol. 1949: R. Connor, A. Mendelzon (Eds.), Research Issues in Structured and Semistructured Database Programming. Proceedings, 1999. XII, 325 pages. 2000.

Vol. 1950: D. van Melkebeek, Randomness and Completeness in Computational Complexity. XV, 196 pages. 2000.

Vol. 1951: F. van der Linden (Ed.), Software Architectures for Product Families. Proceedings, 2000. VIII, 255 pages. 2000.

Vol. 1952: M.C. Monard, J. Simão Sichman (Eds.), Advances in Artificial Intelligence. Proceedings, 2000. XV, 498 pages. 2000. (Subseries LNAI).

Vol. 1953: G. Borgefors, I. Nyström, G. Sanniti di Baja (Eds.), Discrete Geometry for Computer Imagery. Proceedings, 2000. XI, 544 pages. 2000.

Vol. 1954: W.A. Hunt, Jr., S.D. Johnson (Eds.), Formal Methods in Computer-Aided Design. Proceedings, 2000. XI, 539 pages. 2000.

Vol. 1955: M. Parigot, A. Voronkov (Eds.), Logic for Programming and Automated Reasoning. Proceedings, 2000. XIII, 487 pages. 2000. (Subseries LNAI).

Vol. 1956: T. Coquand, P. Dybjer, B. Nordström, J. Smith (Eds.), Types for Proofs and Programs. Proceedings, 1999. VII, 195 pages. 2000.

Vol. 1957: P. Ciancarini, M. Wooldridge (Eds.), Agent-Oriented Software Engineering. Proceedings, 2000. X, 323 pages. 2001.

Vol. 1960: A. Ambler, S.B. Calo, G. Kar (Eds.), Services Management in Intelligent Networks. Proceedings, 2000. X, 259 pages. 2000.

Vol. 1961: J. He, M. Sato (Eds.), Advances in Computing Science – ASIAN 2000. Proceedings, 2000. X, 299 pages. 2000.

Vol. 1963: V. Hlaváč, K.G. Jeffery, J. Wiedermann (Eds.), SOFSEM 2000: Theory and Practice of Informatics. Proceedings, 2000. XI, 460 pages. 2000.

Vol. 1964: J. Malenfant, S. Moisan, A. Moreira (Eds.), Object-Oriented Technology. Proceedings, 2000. XI, 309 pages. 2000.

Vol. 1965: Ç. K. Koç, C. Paar (Eds.), Cryptographic Hardware and Embedded Systems – CHES 2000. Proceedings, 2000. XI, 355 pages. 2000.

Vol. 1966: S. Bhalla (Ed.), Databases in Networked Information Systems. Proceedings, 2000. VIII, 247 pages. 2000.

Vol. 1967: S. Arikawa, S. Morishita (Eds.), Discovery Science. Proceedings, 2000. XII, 332 pages. 2000. (Subseries LNAI).

Vol. 1968: H. Arimura, S. Jain, A. Sharma (Eds.), Algorithmic Learning Theory. Proceedings, 2000. XI, 335 pages. 2000. (Subseries LNAI).

Vol. 1969: D.T. Lee, S.-H. Teng (Eds.), Algorithms and Computation. Proceedings, 2000. XIV, 578 pages. 2000.

Vol. 1970: M. Valero, V.K. Prasanna, S. Vajapeyam (Eds.), High Performance Computing – HiPC 2000. Proceedings, 2000. XVIII, 568 pages. 2000.

Vol. 1971: R. Buyya, M. Baker (Eds.), Grid Computing – GRID 2000. Proceedings, 2000. XIV, 229 pages. 2000.

Vol. 1972: A. Omicini, R. Tolksdorf, F. Zambonelli (Eds.), Engineering Societies in the Agents World. Proceedings, 2000. IX, 143 pages. 2000. (Subseries LNAI).

Vol. 1973: J. Van den Bussche, V. Vianu (Eds.), Database Theory – ICDT 2001. Proceedings, 2001. X, 451 pages. 2001.

Vol. 1974: S. Kapoor, S. Prasad (Eds.), FST TCS 2000: Foundations of Software Technology and Theoretical Computer Science. Proceedings, 2000. XIII, 532 pages. 2000.

Vol. 1975: J. Pieprzyk, E. Okamoto, J. Seberry (Eds.), Information Security. Proceedings, 2000. X, 323 pages. 2000.

Vol. 1976: T. Okamoto (Ed.), Advances in Cryptology – ASIACRYPT 2000. Proceedings, 2000. XII, 630 pages. 2000.

Vol. 1977: B. Roy, E. Okamoto (Eds.), Progress in Cryptology – INDOCRYPT 2000. Proceedings, 2000. X, 295 pages. 2000.

Vol. 1979: S. Moss, P. Davidsson (Eds.), Multi-Agent-Based Simulation. Proceedings, 2000. VIII, 267 pages. 2001. (Subseries LNAI).

Vol. 1983: K.S. Leung, L.-W. Chan, H. Meng (Eds.), Intelligent Data Engineering and Automated Learning – IDEAL 2000. Proceedings, 2000. XVI, 573 pages. 2000.

Vol. 1984: J. Marks (Ed.), Graph Drawing. Proceedings, 2001. XII, 419 pages. 2001.

Vol. 1987: K.-L. Tan, M.J. Franklin, J. C.-S. Lui (Eds.), Mobile Data Management. Proceedings, 2001. XIII, 289 pages. 2001.

Vol. 1989: M. Ajmone Marsan, A. Bianco (Eds.), Quality of Service in Multiservice IP Networks. Proceedings, 2001. XII, 440 pages. 2001.

Vol. 1991: F. Dignum, C. Sierra (Eds.), Agent Mediated Electronic Commerce. VIII, 241 pages. 2001. (Subseries LNAI).

Vol. 1992: K. Kim (Ed.), Public Key Cryptography. Proceedings, 2001. XI, 423 pages. 2001.

Vol. 1995: M. Sloman, J. Lobo, E.C. Lupu (Eds.), Policies for Distributed Systems and Networks. Proceedings, 2001. X, 263 pages. 2001.